This handbook is a real tour de force: It combines cutting-edge insights into substantive aspects of decision-making, policy change and the external dimension of EU justice and home affairs with an unmatched exploration of advances, challenges and promising new avenues of research in this dynamic EU policy domain. It sets a new standard and will be a stimulating companion for anyone working in the field.

Jörg Monar, College of Europe, Belgium

This excellent book provides a major and authoritative review of the main theoretical, sectoral, geographical and institutional aspects of EU Justice and Home Affairs cooperation. With its comprehensive coverage and in-depth analyses, it is an essential resource for both incoming and established scholars working in the field.

Sandra Lavenex, University of Geneva, Switzerland

This Handbook is a success on at least two levels. First, it brings together leading experts to get to grips with the dynamics of cooperation and integration on JHA issues. Second, it provides a wealth of information that makes it essential reading for anyone wanting to understand these important issues.

Andrew Geddes, European University Institute, Italy

THE ROUTLEDGE HANDBOOK OF JUSTICE AND HOME AFFAIRS RESEARCH

Justice and Home Affairs is one of the fastest expanding areas of research in European Studies. The European response to security concerns such as terrorism, organised crime networks, and drug trafficking as well as to the challenge of managing migration flows are salient topics of interest to an increasing number of scholars of all disciplines, the media and general public. This handbook takes stock of policy development and academic research in relation to justice and home affairs and analyses the field in an unprecedented thematic depth.

The book comprehensively investigates the field from the perspective of the three dimensions central to European integration: the sectoral (policies), the horizontal (states, regions) and the vertical (institutions, decision-making) dimensions. It also discusses the most important theoretical approaches used in this research area and provides the reader with a state of the art picture of the field.

By adopting such a comprehensive and broad-based approach, the handbook is uniquely positioned to be an important referent for scholars, practitioners and students interested in the area of justice, home affairs and European politics.

Ariadna Ripoll Servent is Professor of Political Science and European Integration at the University of Bamberg, Germany.

Florian Trauner is Research Professor at the Institute for European Studies and the Department of Political Science of the Vrije Universiteit Brussel, Belgium, and a Visiting Professor at the College of Europe.

THE ROUTLEDGE HANDBOOK OF JUSTICE AND HOME AFFAIRS RESEARCH

Edited by Ariadna Ripoll Servent and Florian Trauner

LONDON AND NEW YORK

First published 2018
by Routledge
2 Park Square, Milton Park, Abingdon, Oxon OX14 4RN

and by Routledge
711 Third Avenue, New York, NY 10017

Routledge is an imprint of the Taylor & Francis Group, an informa business

© 2018 selection and editorial matter, Ariadna Ripoll Servent and Florian Trauner; individual chapters, the contributors

The right of Ariadna Ripoll Servent and Florian Trauner to be identified as the authors of the editorial matter, and of the authors for their individual chapters, has been asserted in accordance with sections 77 and 78 of the Copyright, Designs and Patents Act 1988.

All rights reserved. No part of this book may be reprinted or reproduced or utilised in any form or by any electronic, mechanical, or other means, now known or hereafter invented, including photocopying and recording, or in any information storage or retrieval system, without permission in writing from the publishers.

Trademark notice: Product or corporate names may be trademarks or registered trademarks, and are used only for identification and explanation without intent to infringe.

British Library Cataloguing in Publication Data
A catalogue record for this book is available from the British Library

Library of Congress Cataloging in Publication Data
Names: Ripoll Servent, Ariadna, editor. | Trauner, Florian, editor.
Title: The Routledge handbook of justice and home affairs research / edited by Ariadna Ripoll Servent and Florian Trauner.
Other titles: Handbook of justice and home affairs research
Description: Abingdon, Oxon ; New York, NY : Routledge, 2018. | Includes bibliographical references and index.
Identifiers: LCCN 2017027103| ISBN 9781138183759 (hardback) | ISBN 9781315645629 (ebook)
Subjects: LCSH: European federation. | European Union countries–Politics and government–21st century. | European Union countries–Emigration and immigration–Government policy. | Justice, Administration of–European Union countries.
Classification: LCC JN15 .R69 2018 | DDC 364.94–dc23
LC record available at https://lccn.loc.gov/2017027103

ISBN: 978-1-138-18375-9 (hbk)
ISBN: 978-1-315-64562-9 (ebk)

Typeset in Bembo
by Wearset Ltd, Boldon, Tyne and Wear

Printed in the United Kingdom
by Henry Ling Limited

CONTENTS

List of figures	*xii*
List of tables	*xiii*
Notes on contributors	*xiv*
Acknowledgments	*xxii*

PART I
Introduction   1

1 Justice and home affairs research: introducing the state of the art and
   avenues for further research   3
   Florian Trauner and Ariadna Ripoll Servent

PART II
Theories of justice and home affairs   17

2 The governance of internal security: beyond functionalism and the finality
   of integration?   19
   Raphael Bossong and Hendrik Hegemann

3 Securitization: turning an approach into a framework for research on EU
   justice and home affairs   30
   Christian Kaunert and Ikrom Yakubov

4 Public policy approaches and the study of European Union justice and
   home affairs   41
   Mark Rhinard

PART III
Analyzing justice and home affairs policies (the sectoral dimension)   57

5   Asylum and refugee protection: EU policies in crisis   59
Petra Bendel and Ariadna Ripoll Servent

6   The irregular immigration policy conundrum: problematizing 'effectiveness' as a frame for EU criminalization and expulsion policies   70
Sergio Carrera and Jennifer Allsopp

7   Informalizing EU readmission policy   83
Jean-Pierre Cassarino

8   Border management: the Schengen regime in times of turmoil   99
Ruben Zaiotti

9   EU visa policy: decision-making dynamics and effects on migratory processes   110
Mathias Czaika and Florian Trauner

10   EU labor immigration policy: from silence to salience   124
Georg Menz

11   Organized crime: balancing national sensitivities with global necessities   136
Daniela Irrera

12   Cyber crime as a fragmented policy field in the context of the area of freedom, security and justice   146
Helena Carrapico and Benjamin Farrand

13   EU counter-terrorism: glass half-full or half-empty?   157
Oldrich Bures

14   Data protection policies in EU justice and home affairs : a multi-layered and yet unexplored territory for legal research   169
Paul De Hert and Vagelis Papakonstantinou

15   EU home affairs and technology: how to make sense of information and data processing   180
Julien Jeandesboz

16   EU criminal law: an expanding field for research, with some unchartered territories   192
Anne Weyembergh and Chloé Brière

17 Judicial cooperation in civil matters: coming of age? 203
    Eva Storskrubb and Anna Wallerman

18 Family reunification and migrant integration policies in the EU: dynamics
    of inclusion and exclusion 215
    Saskia Bonjour

PART IV
Justice and home affairs inside and outside Europe (the horizontal dimension) 227

19 Europe's core member states: intended and unintended consequences of
    strong policy-shaping traditions 229
    Andreas Ette

20 Southern Europe: twenty-five years of immigration control on the
    waterfront 240
    Claudia Finotelli

21 Differentiated integration and the Brexit process in EU justice and home
    affairs 253
    Steve Peers

22 Central and Eastern Europe: the EU's struggle for rule of law pre- and
    post-accession 264
    Ramona Coman

23 The Western Balkans: decreasing EU external leverage meets increasing
    domestic reform needs 275
    Florian Trauner and Zoran Nechev

24 Justice and home affairs in EU–Turkey relations: mutual interests but much
    distrust 287
    Alexander Bürgin

25 The Eastern Partnership countries and Russia: a migration-driven
    cooperation agenda with the European Union 298
    Oleg Korneev and Peter Van Elsuwege

26 The Southern Mediterranean: a testing ground and a litmus test for EU
    JHA policies and research? 310
    Sarah Wolff and Patryk Pawlak

27 Africa–EU relations on organized crime: between securitization and fragmentation 323
Judith Vorrath and Verena Zoppei

28 The evolution of transatlantic legal integration: truly, madly, deeply? EU–US justice and home affairs 336
Elaine Fahey

29 EU cooperation in justice and home affairs with Australia and Canada: new ties that bind? 346
Agnieszka Weinar

30 The EU and Latin America: a real security and development nexus or a superficial one? 358
Arantza Gómez Arana

31 The EU–ASEAN relationship: cooperation on non-traditional security threats between discourse and practice 371
Angela Pennisi di Floristella

PART V
EU institutions and decision-making dynamics (the vertical dimension) 383

32 The European Parliament in justice and home affairs: becoming more realistic at the expense of human rights? 385
Ariadna Ripoll Servent

33 The European Court of Justice as a game-changer: fiduciary obligations in the area of freedom, security and justice 396
Ester Herlin-Karnell

34 The European Commission in justice and home affairs: pushing hard to be a motor of integration 409
Natascha Zaun

35 The Council and European Council in EU justice and home affairs politics 421
Christof Roos

36 The role of national parliaments in the Area of Freedom, Security and Justice: high normative expectations, low empirical results 434
Angela Tacea

37 The EU's agencies: ever more important for the governance of the Area of
    Freedom, Security and Justice   445
    Juan Santos Vara

38 NGOs go to Brussels: challenges and opportunities for research and practice
    in the Area of Freedom, Security and Justice   458
    Emek M. Uçarer

39 International organizations and the Area of Freedom, Security and Justice   468
    Claudio Matera

Index   *480*

FIGURES

7.1	Number of bilateral readmission agreements concluded with non-EU countries: from the EU-6 to the EU-28	89
9.1	Internal versus external visa restrictions of EU member states	112
9.2	Visa requirements for the Schengen area (2017)	116

TABLES

6.1	Third-country nationals ordered to leave and enforced returns EU-28 (2008–2015)	74
7.1	EU readmission agreements and arrangements linked to readmission, October 2016	92
9.1	EU visa facilitation and visa liberalization processes	114
23.1	State of play of the Western Balkan countries with regard to the EU accession process (as of February 2017)	279
23.2	Country- and policy-specific dialogues in the Western Balkans (as of February 2017)	280
30.1	Regional cooperation	363
30.2	A sample of the types of programs that are being funded by country in the area of justice	365
30.3	A sample of activities in the area of democratic governance linked to JHA by country	366
30.4	Cooperation programs on drugs between the European Union and Latin America from 2004 to 2015	367
30.5	Cooperation programs on drugs between the European Union and Latin America from 2004 to 2015 at multi-regional level	367
34.1	List of interviewees	418
39.1	Examples of the cooperation of JHA agencies with IOs	471

CONTRIBUTORS

Jennifer Allsopp is a DPhil student at the University of Oxford (UK) funded by the Economic and Social Research Council, and a commissioning editor for openDemocracy 50.50. She has conducted research at the universities of Exeter, Birmingham and Oxford, and with CEPS regarding asylum, gender, poverty and EU migration policy.

Petra Bendel is a Professor of Political Science at the Friedrich-Alexander-Universität Erlangen-Nürnberg (FAU) in Germany. She serves as Academic Director of the Center for Area Studies, Vice President of the Center for Human Rights Erlangen-Nuremberg (CHREN), chairwoman of the Academic Advisory Council of the Federal Office for Migration and Refugees (BAMF), member of the Expert Council of German Foundations on Integration and Migration (SVR), and as a consultant for numerous expert commissions.

Saskia Bonjour is an Assistant Professor of Political Science at the University of Amsterdam. She studies the politics of migration and citizenship in Europe, with a particular interest in family migration, civic integration, gender and intersectionality, law and politics, and Europeanization.

Raphael Bossong is a research associate at the German Institute for International and Security Affairs. His research interests span across the breadth of EU internal security cooperation, with a special emphasis on the governance of counter-terrorism, border security and disaster management. His recent publications include *Theorising EU Internal Security Cooperation* (with Mark Rhinard; Oxford University Press 2016), *EU Borders and Shifting Internal Security* (with Helena Carrapico; Springer International 2016) and *European Civil Security Governance* (with Hendrik Hegemann; Palgrave Macmillan 2015).

Chloé Brière is a post-doctoral researcher at the Vrije Universiteit Brussel (FRC research group) and an affiliated member to the Centre for European Law of the Université libre de Bruxelles. She completed a doctorate in law, delivered in co-sponsorship by the Université libre de Bruxelles and the University of Geneva (2016 – Summa cum Laude). Her doctoral research focused on the European legal framework in relation to the fight against trafficking in human beings, and on its external dimension. She is also interested in other aspects of European criminal law, in EU migration law and in the free movement of persons within the European Union.

Oldrich Bures is Head of the Center for Security Studies at Metropolitan University Prague. His research focuses on the privatization of security and the fight against terrorism, and has been published in *Security Dialogue* and *Terrorism and Political Violence*, among other key journals. He is the author of several monographs, including *EU Counterterrorism Policy: A Paper Tiger?* (Ashgate 2011), and (co-)editor of several edited volumes, including *A Decade of EU Counter-Terrorism and Intelligence: A Critical Assessment* (Routledge 2016).

Alexander Bürgin is an Associate Professor, Jean Monnet Chair and Head of the European Union Research Centre at Izmir University of Economics in Turkey. His research focuses on governance in the EU and EU–Turkey relations. His articles have been published in journals including *Journal of European Integration*, *Journal of European Public Policy*, *South European Society and Politics*, *Turkish Studies*, *German Politics*, *Journal of Balkan and Near Eastern Studies*, and *European Integration Online Papers*.

Helena Carrapico is Senior Lecturer in Politics and International Relations at Aston University. She is Co-Director for the Aston Centre for Europe. Her research focuses on European internal security, in particular EU organized crime policies. She has considerable experience publishing on this topic in journals such as the *Journal of Common Market Studies*, *European Foreign Affairs Review*, *Crime, Law and Social Change*, *European Security*, and *Global Crime*.

Sergio Carrera is a Senior Research Fellow and Head of Justice and Home Affairs Programme at CEPS. He is a Visiting Professor at the Paris School of International Affairs (PSIA) at Sciences Po (France); Associate Professor/Senior Research Fellow at the Faculty of Law at Maastricht University (The Netherlands); and Honorary Industry Professor/Senior Research Fellow at the School of Law at Queen Mary University of London (UK).

Jean-Pierre Cassarino is a Research Fellow at the Institut de Recherche sur le Maghreb Contemporain (IRMC, Tunisia). His research interests focus on patterns of international cooperation, and on the governance of international migration and asylum. Selected recent publications include *Readmission Policy in the European Union* (Brussels: European Parliament Publications Office), and *Unbalanced Reciprocities: Cooperation on Readmission in the Euro-Mediterranean Area* (Washington, DC: Middle-East Institute).

Ramona Coman is an Associate Professor of Political Science and Director of the Institute for European Studies at the Université libre de Bruxelles (ULB). Her research focuses on the rule of law and judicial reforms in Central and Eastern Europe, while her wider current research interest is to understand how EU modes of governance have been reshaped by the eurozone crisis. She recently published 'Strengthening the Rule of Law at the Supranational Level: The Rise and Consolidation of a European Network' in the *Journal of Contemporary European Studies* (2015).

Mathias Czaika is an Associate Professor of Migration and Development and Director of the International Migration Institute (IMI) at the University of Oxford. He is leading an interdisciplinary research group focusing on the drivers and dynamics of international migration processes and their impacts. His wider research interest is to understand the role and relative importance of migration policy in shaping patterns of international migration. He has a PhD in Political Economy from the University of Freiburg in Germany, where he graduated writing a dissertation on 'The Political Economy of Refugee Migration and Foreign Aid', published by Palgrave Macmillan in 2009.

Paul De Hert is a human rights and law and technology scholar working in the area of constitutionalism, criminal law and surveillance law. He is interested both in legal practice and more fundamental reflections about law. At the Vrije Universiteit Brussel (VUB), he holds the Chair of European Criminal Law. He is Director of the Research Group on Fundamental Rights and Constitutionalism (FRC), Director of the Department of Interdisciplinary Studies of Law (Metajuridics) and a Co-Director of the Research Group on Law Science Technology & Society (LSTS). He is an Associate Professor at Tilburg University where he teaches 'Privacy and Data Protection' at the Tilburg Institute of Law, Technology, and Society (TILT).

Andreas Ette is a Senior Research Fellow at the Federal Institute for Population Research in Wiesbaden, where he heads the International Migration Research Group. He obtained his PhD from Bielefeld University while researching the Europeanization of Germany's refugee and migration policy. His research centers on the politics and sociology of migration and mobility, focusing in particular on the effects of institutional changes on migration and integration trajectories.

Elaine Fahey is Reader in Law and Associate Dean (International) at the Institute for the Study of European Law (ISEL), the City Law School, and City University London. She is an Emile Noël Fellow at New York University (NYU) Law School and a Visiting Fellow for the year 2017 at the Centre for European Policy Studies (CEPS) in Brussels. She is co-investigator in the Marie Curie ITN on TTIP led by the University of Birmingham (2017–2021). In 2016, she was awarded a British Academy/Leverhulme Research Grant for the project 'Between Internal Laws and Global Practices: UN Instruments in the EU's Area of Freedom, Security and Justice'.

Benjamin Farrand is an Associate Professor at the University of Warwick. His research centers predominantly on the interaction between law and politics in the regulation of new technologies. His research has focused on issues such as the development of copyright law and policy at the European level, the role of private actors in developing self-regulatory regimes, and agenda setting in the European Commission. Other research interests include contemporary issues in patent policy, cyber crime and cyber security, and law and policy as applied to human enhancement.

Claudia Finotelli is Senior Lecturer at the Universidad Complutense de Madrid. Her research interests include the study of immigration control and integration policies in Southern Europe. Her most recent publications deal with comparative analyses of labor migration governance in Spain, Germany and Canada.

Arantza Gómez Arana is Lecturer in Security and Criminology at Birmingham City University. Her research interests include EU foreign affairs and security, with a focus on the EU's relations with Latin American and North Africa. She has conducted research on European Union–Latin American policies for several years and has recently published *The EU's Policy Towards Latin America: Responsive Not Strategic? An Analysis of EU Relations with Mercosur* (Manchester University Press). She was also part of the FP7 project 'Grasping the Links in the Chain: Understanding the Unintended Consequences of International Counter-Narcotics Measures for the EU'.

Hendrik Hegemann is Senior Lecturer in International Relations & Peace and Conflict Studies at the University Osnabrueck in Germany. He focuses on global and regional security governance, the political response to transnational security risks as well as terrorism and counter-terrorism. His current project examines the forms, conditions and consequences of politicization in security governance. Recent publications include *European Civil Security Governance* (with Raphael Bossong; Palgrave Macmillan 2015), *Putting Security Governance to the Test* (with Hans-Georg Ehrhart and Martin Kahl; Routledge 2015), and *International Counterterrorism Bureaucracies in the United Nations and the European Union* (Nomos 2014).

Ester Herlin-Karnell is Professor of EU Constitutional Law and Justice and a University Research Chair at the Vrije Universiteit Amsterdam. She is also Co-Director and founder of the VU Centre for European Legal Studies at the VU Amsterdam. She holds degrees from Oxford University (DPhil), King's College London (LLM) and Stockholm University (LLM). Her recent publications include a monograph on the constitutional dimension of European criminal law (Hart Publishing, Oxford 2012). She is currently working on a second monograph on justice and home affairs and questions (forthcoming with Hart Publishing, Oxford 2017) regarding the constitutional structure of the area of freedom, security and justice and the right to justification.

Daniela Irrera is an Associate Professor of International Politics and Global Civil Society at the University of Catania. She has been a Visiting Fellow at various universities in Europe, Asia, and the USA. She serves on the Steering Committee of the ECPR Standing Group on International Relations and the ECPR Standing Group on Organised Crime.

Julien Jeandesboz is Professor at the Université libre de Bruxelles (ULB), where he is also a member of REPI and of the Institute for European Studies (IEE). His research interests include security and surveillance, border control, technology, and international political sociology. His recent publications include two co-edited special issues on 'Questioning security devices' in *Security Dialogue* (with Anthony Amicelle and Claudia Aradau), and on 'Politics and "the digital"' in the *European Journal of Social Theory* (with Mareile Kaufmann).

Christian Kaunert is Academic Director of the Institute for European Studies (IES) and Professor of European Politics at the Vrije Universiteit Brussel (VUB). He was previously Professor of International Politics, as well as Director of the European Institute for Security and Justice at the University of Dundee. Christian Kaunert was awarded a Jean Monnet Chair in EU Justice and Home Affairs (2013), a Marie Curie Career Integration Grant (2012–2016), and a Marie Curie IES Fellowship at the European University Institute in Florence. He holds a PhD in International Politics and an MSc in European Politics from the University of Wales in Aberystwyth. His research has a clear focus on the global security role of the EU, especially in the area of EU justice and home affairs, with a particular focus on terrorism and counter-terrorism.

Oleg Korneev is a Research Fellow at the Centre for Research into Local Action Initiatives (CERAL), Faculty of Law, Political and Social Sciences at University Paris 13 and leading Research Fellow at the Laboratory for Social Anthropological Research (LSAR) of Tomsk State University (Russia). His research focuses on international organizations, global migration governance, production and transfer of expert knowledge, migration policies in Eastern Europe and Central Asia, as well as EU–Russia cooperation on migration.

Contributors

Claudio Matera is an Assistant Professor of European Law and Governance at the University of Twente in The Netherlands. Prior to this, he worked as a researcher for the T.M.C. Asser Institute in The Hague. His research and publications focus on EU external relations and the AFSJ; he has recently edited a volume on the AFSJ with Maria Fletcher and Ester Herlin-Karnell for Routledge (2016). He studied law in Milan and Bruges, and obtained his PhD at the University of Twente with a thesis on the external dimension of the AFSJ written within the research activities of CLEER, the Centre for the Law of EU External Relations.

Georg Menz is a Professor of Political Economy at Goldsmiths College, University of London. He served as Visiting Professor at Australian National University, Georgetown University, University of Pittsburgh, LUISS Guido Carli and Vienna University. He has published widely in the fields of labor market, social and migration policy. Two major research monographs include *The Political Economy of Managed Migration* (Oxford University Press 2009) and *Varieties of Capitalism and Europeanization* (Oxford University Press 2005).

Zoran Nechev is Senior Associate Fellow at the European Union Institute for Security Studies. He is an academic guest at the Center for International and Comparative Studies at the ETH Zürich and a Konrad-Adenauer-Stiftung Macedonia Fellow at the Center for EU integration at the Institute for Democracy 'Societas Civilis' Skopje. His research focuses on EU–Western Balkans relations and external dimensions of justice and home affairs.

Vagelis Papakonstantinou is a co-founder of MPlegal Law Firm in Athens, a senior researcher at the Research Group on Law Science Technology & Society (LSTS) at the Vrije Universiteit Brussels as well as the training programs coordinator of the Brussels Privacy Hub. Since 2016 he has served as a member (alternate) of the Hellenic Data Protection Authority.

Patryk Pawlak is a policy analyst at the European Parliamentary Research Service where he deals primarily with European security issues, including terrorism and resilience building in the Middle East and North Africa. Previously, he worked as a senior analyst at the EU Institute for Security Studies in Paris. From 2009 to 2011, he received the Transatlantic Post-Doctoral Fellowship for International Relations and Security (TAPIR). His work on terrorism and the European Union's security policies has appeared in several peer-reviewed journals and edited volumes. He holds a PhD in Political Science from the European University Institute in Florence.

Steve Peers is Professor of Law at the University of Essex. He received a BA (Hons.) in history from McMaster University (Canada) in 1988, an LLB from the University of Western Ontario (Canada) in 1991, an LLM in EU Law from the London School of Economics in 1993, and a PhD from the University of Essex in 2001. His research interests include EU Constitutional and Administrative, Justice and Home Affairs, External Relations, Human Rights, Internal Market and Social Law. He has written over fifty articles on many aspects of EU law in journals, and is the author of *EU Justice and Home Affairs Law*, the co-author of *EU Immigration and Asylum Law: Text and Commentary* and *EU Citizenship Directive*, and the co-editor of *Commentary on the EU Charter of Fundamental Rights*.

Angela Pennisi di Floristella is a Lecturer in International Relations at the University of Malta. Her research is in Asian Pacific security cooperation with a special focus on the Association of Southeast Asian Nations (ASEAN) and on ASEAN–EU interregional relations.

She has authored the book *The ASEAN Regional Security Partnership* published by Palgrave Macmillan in 2015.

Mark Rhinard is Professor of International Relations at Stockholm University and a Senior Research Fellow at the Swedish Institute of International Affairs. His research examines international cooperation on complex threats, with a special interest in the European Union. His recent works include *Theorizing Internal Security Cooperation in the European Union* (with Raphael Bossong; Oxford University Press 2016) and *The European Commission* (with Neill Nugent; Palgrave 2015).

Ariadna Ripoll Servent is a Junior Professor of Political Science and European Integration at the University of Bamberg. Her research interests include European institutional and policy change in the area of EU internal security policies, in particular asylum, irregular immigration, counter-terrorism and data protection. She has published widely on the role of the European Parliament in the area of freedom, security and justice.

Christof Roos is Assistant Professor for European and Global Governance at the University of Flensburg and a Research Associate at the Institute for European Studies at the Vrije Universiteit Brussel. His research focuses on migration and mobility policy at the EU, national, and international level. He contributed to migration and EU studies with research on agenda setting, decision-making, and negotiations in the policy area of legal migration, freedom of movement, and asylum.

Juan Santos Vara is Professor of Public International Law and European Law, Director of the Master's in European Studies and coordinator of the European Joint Master's in Strategic Border Management at the University of Salamanca. His research is mainly focused on the EU's external relations and the area of freedom, security and justice, and he has been involved in several research projects financed by national and international institutions. Currently, he is the main researcher in the project 'EU External Action and Democratic Control (EUDECEXT)', DER2015–70082-P (MINECO/FEDER). He holds a Jean Monnet Chair in EU External Action and is also co-editor of *European Papers – A Journal on Law and Integratio*.

Eva Storskrubb is Associate Professor in Procedural Law and researcher at the University of Uppsala. She also works as a practicing lawyer. Her research focuses on the impact of EU law on civil justice. Her most recent publications include: 'Mutual Recognition as a Governance Strategy for Civil Justice' in Hess, Bergström and Storskrubb (eds) *EU Civil Justice: Current Issues and Future Outlook* (Hart 2016) and 'Civil Justice – Constitutional and Regulatory Issues Revisited' in Fletcher, Herlin-Karnell and Matera (eds) *The EU as an Area of Freedom, Security and Justice* (Routledge 2016).

Angela Tacea is a Postdoctoral Fellow of the FWO at the Institute for European Studies (IES), VUB. Her research and teaching interests are in comparative constitutional law and legislative studies, data protection and border control. She has recently published a book chapter on the use of the Early Warning Mechanism by the French Parliament in *National and Regional Parliaments in the EU-Legislative Procedure Post-Lisbon* (edited by Anna Jonsson Cornell and Marco Goldoni; Hart Publishing) and wrote several chapters for the *Palgrave Handbook on National Parliaments and the European Union*.

Contributors

Florian Trauner is a Research Professor at the Institute for European Studies (IES) of the Vrije Universiteit Brussel. He has published widely on topics relating to EU justice and home affairs, EU rule of law promotion, EU–Western Balkans relations and migration dynamics in West Africa. He had permanent or visiting positions at Renmin University of Beijing, the University of Vienna, Science Po's Centre d'études européenne, and the EU Institute for Security Studies. He also acted as an external expert for the European Commission, the European Parliament, the Norwegian Government and the International Centre for Migration Policy Development.

Emek M. Uçarer is a Professor of International Relations at Bucknell University. Her research interests include governance of immigration and asylum in the European Union, the Europeanization of these issues, and the interaction between non-state actors and intergovernmental organizations. She is the author of 'Tempering the EU? NGO Advocacy in the Area of Freedom, Security, and Justice' in the *Cambridge Review of International Affairs*.

Peter Van Elsuwege is Professor in EU Law and Co-Director of the Ghent European Law Institute (GELI) at Ghent University. He is also Co-Director of Ghent University's Russia Platform. His research activities essentially focus on the law of EU external relations. Specific attention is devoted to the legal framework of the relations between the European Union and its East European neighbors.

Judith Vorrath is a Senior Associate in the International Security Division of the German Institute for International and Security Affairs (SWP). She is currently working on a project dealing with illicit economies in African borderlands as well as on different aspects of organized crime in sub-Saharan Africa more generally. Since 2013, her focus has mainly been on West Africa with field studies in Liberia, Sierra Leone, Guinea and Ghana. Previously she has been a post-doc fellow at SWP, at the U.S. Institute of Peace in Washington, DC and the European Union Institute for Security Studies in Paris. She holds a Doctor of Science from the Swiss Federal Institute of Technology (ETH).

Anna Wallerman is Associate Senior Lecturer at the University of Gothenburg and a Max Weber Fellow at the European University Institute (2017/2018). She conducts research in civil procedure and EU law. Her publications include 'Towards an EU Law Doctrine on the Exercise of Discretion in National Courts?' (*CML Review* 2016), for which she was awarded the Common Market Law Review Prize 2015, and 'Harmonization of Civil Procedure: Can the European Union Learn from Swiss Experiences?' (*ERPL* 2016).

Agnieszka Weinar is a Research Fellow at the Robert Schuman Centre for Advanced Studies at the European University Institute and an Adjunct Research Professor at Carleton University. Her current research interests address internal and external aspects of EU migration policy, as well as global policy learning in the area of JHA.

Anne Weyembergh is a full-time Professor at the Université libre de Bruxelles (Faculty of Law and Institute for European Studies). Her main research activities focus on EU criminal law, namely police cooperation and judicial cooperation in criminal matters. Together with Serge de Biolley, she founded the European Criminal Law Academic Network (ECLAN) in 2004. Since October 2014, she has been President of the Institute for European Studies of the ULB. Since May 2014, she has been Chief Editor of the *New Journal of European Criminal Law* with Paul De

Hert, Valsamis Mitsilegas, Scott Crosby and Holger Matt. She is also General Editor of the *EU Criminal Law* series of Hart Publishing with Valsamis Mitsilegas and Katalin Ligeti, and a member of the Comité de rédaction des Cahiers de droit européen (CDE).

Sarah Wolff is Lecturer in Public Policy at Queen Mary University of London. She is an expert on EU–Mediterranean cooperation on justice and home affairs, migration and border management policies. Her monograph *The Mediterranean Dimension of the European Union's Internal Security* (Palgrave 2012) builds on fieldwork in Europe, Morocco, Egypt and Jordan. Her current research project investigates the role of religion and secularism in EU foreign policy. She holds a PhD in International Relations (LSE 2009), an MSc in European Politics and Governance (LSE 2004) and a BA in Public Administration (Science Po Grenoble 1999).

Ikrom Yakubov received his PhD from the University of Dundee. His research examines intelligence, terrorism and securitization processes in Western societies. He previously received a MLitt in International Politics from the University of Dundee, and has many years of experiences as a security practitioner.

Ruben Zaiotti (PhD Toronto, MA Oxford, BA Bologna) is Director of the Jean Monnet European Union Centre of Excellence and Associate Professor in the Political Science department at Dalhousie University in Canada. His main areas of interest are European Union politics, border control and immigration policy, and transatlantic relations. He is the author of the monograph *Cultures of Border Control: Schengen and the Evolution of European Frontiers* with the University of Chicago Press and editor of books on language and globalization and on migration policy. He has published articles for the *Review of International Studies*, *European Security*, *Journal of European Integration*, *Journal of Borderland Studies*, and *International Journal of Refugee Law*.

Natascha Zaun is Assistant Professor in Migration Studies at the European Institute of the London School of Economics and Political Science. Her research focuses in particular on international and EU decision-making in the areas of asylum and immigration policies. She is the author of *EU Asylum Policies: The Power of Strong Regulating States* (Palgrave Macmillan 2017).

Verena Zoppei is a Research Fellow in the International Security Division of the German Institute for International and Security Affairs (SWP), focusing on anti-money laundering, including organized crime investments in legitimate businesses. She received her PhD from Humboldt University in Berlin and from Milan University. She has an LLM from the University of the Western Cape (Cape Town) on transnational criminal justice and crime prevention with a focus on international anti-corruption and instruments to prevent and combat money laundering.

ACKNOWLEDGMENTS

This handbook has been a rewarding journey into many different research areas of justice and home affairs. Albeit it has taken a perceived 10,000 emails to coordinate fifty authors for thirty-nine chapters, it has been good fun and an experience in which we happened to work with a group of highly dedicated researchers. We would like to thank all the authors who very kindly agreed to participate in this project. The handbook has only been possible thanks to their expertise and willingness to explore the different scholarly discussions in more depth. We would also like to express our gratitude to Amanda Henson, Stella Neelsen and Fanny Baudoin for their editorial support and enthusiasm. A special thanks also to Sophie Iddamalgoda and Andrew Taylor from Routledge for their confidence and support throughout the publication process.

Last but certainly not least, many thanks also to our respective families, who have had to live through many stressful moments but continue to offer their support.

PART I

Introduction

1
JUSTICE AND HOME AFFAIRS RESEARCH

Introducing the state of the art and avenues for further research

Florian Trauner and Ariadna Ripoll Servent

Introduction

The European integration process has become more contested. The resilience of democratic standards in view of populist governments and parties, slow economic growth and inflated public debts, migratory pressure, terrorist attacks and the departure of the United Kingdom from the EU are among the internal challenges facing the Union. Many of these issues are interlinked with developments in the outside world, notably instability or the consolidation of authoritarian rule in a range of third countries. This combination of internal and external forces has led to a process of politicization, which has been defined as 'an increase in polarization of opinions, interests or values and the extent to which they are publicly advanced towards the process of policy formulation within the EU' (Wilde 2011: 560). Indeed, we see how the outcome of national and European elections is increasingly determined by the way in which politicians deal with immigration, border control, counter-terrorism and citizens' and migrants' access to justice and rights. Justice and home affairs (JHA), being a particularly sensitive field of public policy and closely linked to states' sovereignty, has become a playing field for those attempting to politicize EU integration.

Therefore, this handbook comes at a crucial moment in time. The volume takes stock of policy developments and academic research in relation to JHA and aims to analyze this field in unprecedented thematic depth. The volume contains thirty-nine chapters that investigate the research area from the three dimensions central to European integration: the sectoral dimension, looking at specific policies and how they relate to each other; the horizontal dimension, which concentrates on specific states and regions; and the vertical dimension, which examines the role of EU institutions and changes to policy-making processes (Schimmelfennig and Rittberger 2006). However, these different dimensions cannot be understood without looking into the different research perspectives and theories to grasp the fundamental changes and challenges that JHA policies are facing today. Therefore, the chapters provide the reader with an up-to-date picture of what has happened thus far (either in theory or policy development), how we can make sense of these developments and what the likely avenues of future research are.

Academic research in the field of JHA

There is a multiplicity of scholarly terms to refer to the field of internal security, most of them reflecting domestic cultures and institutional evolutions. We have opted to maintain the original term used in the framework of EU integration. Justice and home affairs has been employed since the introduction of the 'third pillar' in the Treaty of Maastricht (1992) as an umbrella concept to grasp the wide range of internal security and migration-related issues that the European Community/European Union has dealt with since the mid-1970s. Therefore, JHA is, by nature, related to the EU and its particular jargon, and may be compared to other, similar wordings like 'homeland security' in US 'home affairs' or 'internal security' more generally. To complicate matters, the Treaty of Amsterdam (1997) established an 'Area of Freedom, Security and Justice' as an EU objective and its abbreviation – AFSJ – is now also commonly used to refer to this policy field. Still, the wording 'justice and home affairs' has remained relevant in political debates and the specialized literature. In the EU institutions, the Council of the EU's formation in charge of internal security is still called the 'Justice and Home Affairs Council', the Commission now has a 'Just' (justice and consumers) and a 'Home' (migration and home affairs) Directorate General, and the European Parliament's specialized committee bears the title 'Committee on Civil Liberties, Justice and Home Affairs' (LIBE). Therefore, JHA continues to be connected with the policy area and is still generally of use, while the AFSJ refers rather to a goal set by the treaties designing the ideal shape that European integration should take.

The academic communities dominating JHA research

There are two kinds of 'academic communities' that participate in or contribute to this research field – one that originates in European studies and takes JHA as a specific field of study, and another that stems from various fields of policy analysis (like migration studies) and uses the EU as an example or case study. Among the first group – that of EU scholars interested in processes of European integration and policy-making – the analysis of JHA has become a burgeoning field of research on its own. This is reflected in the considerable number of recently released books focusing on the Area of Freedom, Security and Justice as a whole (Bossong and Rhinard 2016; Kaunert 2010; Monar 2010; Eckes and Konstadinides 2011; Walker 2004; Kaunert *et al.* 2013; Trauner and Ripoll Servent 2015; Guild and Geyer 2008; Wolff *et al.* 2011; Holzhacker and Luif 2014; Aden 2014; Bendel *et al.* 2011; Peers 2016; Cremona *et al.* 2010; Bigo *et al.* 2010; Fletcher *et al.* 2016).

Scholars from migration studies, criminal law and security studies have also developed the research field. Researchers in these fields have gradually incorporated the EU as an additional arena or factor of influence. Coming from area studies their research has prioritized policy aspects, such as the effect of Europeanization on domestic policies. Over time, some of the sub-fields of JHA have become flourishing research fields in their own right: European migration and asylum policies or EU criminal law are obvious cases. However, other AFSJ sub-fields such as EU civil law receive only limited academic attention (Skorskrubb and Wallerman, Chapter 17, this volume).

Scholars doing research on JHA policies can now rely on a range of specialized journals such as the *European Journal of Migration and Law*, the *Journal of Ethnic and Migration Studies*, *The European Review of Organised Crime* or the *European Criminal Law Review*. They have reached a degree of organization and networking, usually structured along disciplinary boundaries. A case in point is the European Criminal Law Academic Network (ECLAN) created in 2004. This now counts more than 200 specialized scholars (see Weyembergh and Brière, Chapter 16, this volume). The Odysseus Network for Legal Studies on Immigration and Asylum in Europe, founded and coordinated by Philippe de Bruycker, is another example. These kinds of networks have gained relevance by exchanging views and research findings among scholars. They also tend to engage with practitioners in the EU's institutions and member states. A close cooperation with the academic world has become a means and a strategy of the European Commission to strengthen the legitimacy of its policy proposals, for instance, in the field of immigrant integration (Bonjour, Chapter 18, this volume; see also Geddes and Scholten 2015).

In terms of disciplines, the research field – similar to this handbook – is dominated by lawyers and political scientists. Other disciplines such as sociology and anthropology tend to focus on a few AFSJ sub-fields, notably migration and migrant integration policies. Since they are generally situated in area studies, their research often concerns less the dynamics of policy-making or the substance of the adopted laws and regulations and focuses rather on the role, behavior and experience of the 'subject' of such a policy, i.e., the migrant. Therefore, there is some space for furthering interdisciplinarity, even beyond the social sciences. For instance, it could be beneficial to strengthen collaboration with academic communities that have so far been neglected, such as science and technology studies (STS) (Jeandesboz, Chapter 15, this volume).

Not surprisingly, given the geographical focus of JHA policies, most research has been done by academics in Europe looking at Europe. However, there is a growing body of projects applying a comparative focus on different regions, for instance, by investigating the similarities and differences of migration management or counter-terrorism policies in the USA, Australia and Canada (see Weiner, Chapter 29, and Fahey, Chapter 28, this volume). There are notable gaps in this respect, with only very limited research done on cooperation and policy developments in Asia, Africa and Latin America (see Pennisi di Floristella, Chapter 31, Vorrath and Zoppei, Chapter 27, and Gómez Arana, Chapter 30, this volume).

Normative versus non-normative approaches

It has become a distinctive feature of the academic debates in the field whether or not authors argue normatively. Scholars often (implicitly or explicitly) adhere to normative standards; for instance, perceiving the protection of human rights as a 'desirable' objective. Normative arguments are particularly common in the field of law, where scholars often suggest what should be done in order to achieve a specific outcome. This may mean 'a more inclusive, multilayered and multicultural conception of citizenship' (Kostakopoulou 2007: 623), more or less harmonization in EU civil justice (Storskrubb and Wallerman, Chapter 17, this volume), or a better safeguarding of rule of law at EU or member state level (Herlin-Karnell, Chapter 33 and Coman, Chapter 22, this volume).

In addition, the turn made by security studies at the end of the 1990s towards more 'critical' approaches (Bossong and Hegemann, Chapter 2, this volume) served to emphasize alternative understandings of security. As a result, scholars started to problematize (often in normative terms) how governments and societies interact in the creation of security and insecurity (e.g., Bigo *et al.* 2010). The concept of *securitization* that emerged from this 'critical' turn has featured prominently in the field (Kaunert and Yakubov, Chapter 3, this volume). This concept focuses on what 'internal security' means and why some fields like migration have become associated with it. By contrast, governance and institutionalist approaches have concentrated on the dynamics of decision-making, the role of actors and policy outcomes (Rhinard, Chapter 4, and Bossong and Hegemann, Chapter 2, this volume). In these approaches, a stronger emphasis tends to be placed on research design and case selection to 'objectivize' the academic interest.

By assembling a diverse group of academics for this handbook, we can see that the trend towards more politicization is not reserved to the political sphere. Indeed, various chapters indicate that academic research is also getting more polarized along normative discussions. We have given the authors academic freedom to discuss these issues, but have insisted on the need to back claims with empirical evidence. The main normative dimension continues to follow the traditional cleavage of 'security vs. liberty'. For instance, in counter-terrorism, there is a growing divide on whether it is legitimate to curtail fundamental rights and civil liberties in the fight against terrorism, and if yes, to what extent. In the area of migration, the main question continues to be how open or closed 'Europe' should be to migrants, notably asylum-seekers. For instance, when discussing the crisis of the EU's asylum regime, Carrera and Allsopp (Chapter 6, this volume) critically question the focus on 'efficiency' in the EU's 'fight' against irregular migration, while Menz (Chapter 10, this volume) highlights the desirability of an end to liberal migration policies and criticizes Germany's behavior when facing migratory pressures. This shows the multifaceted nature of the field and the challenge to assess it 'objectively'.

The major lines of research

The thirty-nine chapters in this volume provide a fascinating and multifaceted journey through many different research arenas within the JHA field. This introduction refrains from claiming that it summarizes or reflects all of them. It has the more modest ambition of identifying some major lines of research and points, later on, to potential areas of future research.

Dynamics of decision-making and the role of EU institutions

A first area of research concerns the dynamics of European decision-making and the role of EU institutions. Research has investigated both inter-institutional dynamics and individual EU actors and institutions. A particular interest has been to grasp the consequences of treaty changes, notably the introduction of co-decisions and the empowerment of supranational EU institutions. In so doing, scholars have often relied on the rich 'toolbox of public policy analysis' and new institutionalist theories (Rhinard, Chapter 4, this volume).

When studying the impact of institutional change in the JHA field it is important in to consider to what extent it fits within broader patterns of EU integration. European integration in internal security matters has often been regarded as a special – or even unique – case due to the field's intergovernmental origins (Monar 2001) and its reliance on transgovernmental networks of law enforcement officials (Lavenex 2009). However, the field has been progressively *communitarized* and brought in line with the traditional 'regulatory' mode of EU policy-making such as economic governance or the Single Market. This means that the European Commission, the European Parliament and the Court of Justice of the EU have gained a much bigger say in JHA matters.

This handbook demonstrates that some of the expectations raised in the context of the 'normalization' of the field have failed to manifest themselves. Yet the question remains whether these outcomes indicate specificities of JHA or whether they rather reflect wider trends in EU decision-making patterns. The empowerment of the European Parliament is a case in point. Its transformation into a co-decider was seen as a window of opportunity to soften the security-led rationales of many sub-policy areas. However, the EP has rather shifted towards a 'more pragmatic behavior that has brought it closer to the restrictive positions of member states' (Ripoll Servent, Chapter 32, this volume). This shift has been explained by looking at the changes in cost–benefit calculations as well as an evolution of intra- and inter-institutional social practices and norms under co-decision. Similarly, the expectation that a closer inter-parliamentary cooperation between the EP and national parliaments would develop following the Lisbon Treaty has not materialized. As Tacea (Chapter 36, this volume) remarks, this is not surprising given that national parliaments are usually dominated by their governments and may not have any incentives to oppose them. On the contrary, governments have found in national parliaments a new channel to express themselves in the European arena.

Indeed, national governments continue to occupy a central space in JHA policy-making. There are different reasons for this. For one, they have been central in shaping the core of EU policies in the field, and have, therefore, more expertise (Trauner and Ripoll Servent 2016). In addition, since they are responsible for implementing policies, they are more concerned about wide-ranging changes or potential budgetary implications. Their reluctance to introduce major revisions to existing policies has become particularly noticeable since the mid-2010s, which have seen a clear trend towards more politicization of JHA policy-making within the Council. As a result, more decisions are taken directly by the EU ministers of interior and justice instead of lower administrative levels (Roos, Chapter 35, this volume; see also Maricut 2016). With the shift to qualified majority voting and the emergence of more populist political forces, member states seem to place less value on consensus-seeking and deliberation than they have in the past (Aus 2007; Lewis 2005). This is of particular relevance in policy fields with high public salience such as border management. As Zaiotti (Chapter 8, this volume) highlights with regard to border management, 'conflict, and not compromise, has become this policy field's new modus operandi'.

The increasingly important role of national governments, notably EU heads of state and government in the European Council, has been noted by scholars applying 'new intergovernmentalism' (Maricut 2016; Fabbrini and Puetter 2016). While this trend has implications for all EU institutions, it presents a particular challenge for the European Commission, whose right of initiative has been called into question. This has clear implications for policy-making, especially when it comes to proposals that aim to further European integration. Indeed, the Commission has been described as an 'opportunistic actor', particularly in the context of the debate on security vs. liberty (Zaun, Chapter 34, this volume). While it has at times advanced more security-oriented positions and on other occasions worked towards the strengthening of rights, it has continuously pushed for deeper European integration. Under certain circumstances – for instance, when the member states have struggled to find a consensus or when the EU was under pressure to act following some external event like a terrorist attack – the Commission has gained greater importance and contributed to exiting 'decision traps' (Zaun, Chapter 34, and Bürgin, Chapter 24, this volume).

The empowerment of the Court of Justice of the EU (CJEU) has had considerable implications. As Herlin-Karnell puts it, 'the Court of Justice has been a prominent game-changer in the AFSJ and especially in the area of mutual recognition' (Chapter 33, this volume). For instance, the number of cases dealing with EU criminal law has continually increased, making the Court an essential player in shaping this sub-policy area (Weyembergh and Brière, Chapter 16, this volume). The Court has also been essential in settling high-stakes cases involving civil liberties and human rights. Examples thereof are cases determining the conditions for the return of migrants (Bendel and Ripoll Servent, Chapter 5, this volume) or cases dealing with child abduction (Storskrubb and Wallerman, Chapter 17, this volume). The Court has often acted as the last resort in settling highly political questions, which may be seen as political activism on the part of the CJEU or just reflect the inability (or unwillingness) of the legislators to settle political conflicts and controversial matters during the decision-making stage.

Finally, the sensitive character of this policy area may be seen in two trends that remain particular to JHA. On the one hand, the governance of the AFSJ continues to rely on EU agencies which have increased in number and power. Their role in and contribution to policing and border control has become an autonomous research field (Santos Vara, Chapter 37, this volume), which points to the important differences in the willingness of member states to participate and cooperate within them. While Europol continues to suffer from member states' reluctance to share sensitive information in the field of police cooperation, Frontex now has more tools to act in an integrated manner in the area of border management. On the other hand, it is noticeable that civil society organizations remain largely absent from policy-making. Indeed, there seem to be considerable differences in terms of how EU actors interact with NGOs and many struggle to exert influence, as 'the AFSJ is still seen as too sensitive for NGO inclusion' (Uçarer, Chapter 38, this volume). With the increasing politicization of JHA, we need to pay more attention to the role of NGOs and contemplate the possibility that EU institutions are also the object of other forms of lobbying, particularly those related to the security and technological industries.

Policy change, impact and implementation

Another line of research has concentrated on policy-related analyses, which look at questions such as the interactions between EU laws and instruments, the degree of policy change and the dynamics of policy implementation.

As mentioned above, policy analyses have been largely dominated by the wider debate on freedom versus security. Scholars have looked into the contents of policy outputs in order to determine their impact on individual rights, civil liberties and international protection regimes. Put differently, how does the EU affect the daily lives of people living in Europe or seeking to come to the EU? The academic debate is still ongoing: for some, the EU is now acting as a 'liberal constraint' on member states in their pursuit of restrictive migration policies; for others, the EU is achieving quite the opposite policy outcome, namely that of transforming the EU into a 'fortress Europe' (Bendel and Ripoll Servent, Chapter 5, this volume; see also Bonjour et al. 2017). Critical security scholars have also been interested in why certain security instruments proliferate; for instance, why it has become legitimate for security agents to store more personal data. Jeandesboz (Chapter 15, this volume) questions the 'functionalist' hypothesis (we need data-sharing tools because there is a 'security problem'). Instead, he highlights the politics behind these policy developments such as the diffusion, promotion, internalization and adaptation of norms relating to 'good' border security or counter-terrorist instruments.

Another focus of policy-oriented research has been the question of 'effectiveness'; that is, whether EU policies have had any sort of impact on domestic structures and/or international regimes (Herlin-Karnell, Chapter 33, this volume) or how different legal layers and instruments interact, for instance, in the field of data protection (De Hert and Papakonstantinou, Chapter 14, this volume). The effectiveness of EU policies is sometimes difficult to determine. It requires an in-depth examination of policy change. For instance, changes in a EU policy may happen in an incremental manner, which makes it difficult to assess the consequences of recurrent yet minor reforms. This has happened in the field of EU counter-terrorism policy, with the result that 'the current counter-terrorism capacity may already be greater than commonly understood' (Bures, Chapter 13, this volume). This is a departure from the early days of the EU's cooperation on counter-terrorism when the EU was seen as a 'paper tiger' (Bures 2007). Change may also come as a result of feedback loops from previous efforts to Europeanize a policy area, which means that we should adopt a longer term perspective when examining the driving factors of policy change and policy stability (see also Trauner and Ripoll Servent 2015). Indeed, major shifts in policy paradigms may occur at several levels and be influenced by national politics and international norms. For instance, Bonjour (Chapter 18, this volume) shows how national interpretations of EU law have made it easier to shift the understanding of migrant integration policies, which have made access to social, education and employment rights conditional.

In terms of implementation, there is a wide consensus that EU policies make a difference by now. Even in areas in which the EU has few competences such as migrant integration policies, 'the influence of EU law and policies […] is far from negligible' (Bonjour, Chapter 18, this volume). However, EU outputs may affect some member states more than others. Finotelli, for example, shows how 'neither Italy nor Greece, two major countries of arrival, had any asylum legislation until 2007 and 2001, respectively, which stood in clear contrast with the better organized asylum systems in traditional Northern European asylum countries' (Chapter 20, this volume). These countries have been under much higher pressure to adapt and raise their standards to the same level as those of Northern European countries, which helps us to understand their difficulties in dealing with the Dublin regime (Zaun 2017).

This does not imply that all EU instruments are embraced by member states. For instance, it has proved a challenge for the EU to provide 'an added value to member states' modus operandi and practices as applied to readmission' (Cassarino, Chapter 7, this volume). The EU has sought to respond by 'informalizing' its readmission policy. Diverse (often legally non-binding) migration deals should result in a higher rate of returns even in the absence of formal EU readmission agreements. Similarly, other EU instruments have had only limited practical impact. For instance, EU visa facilitation agreements have been strongly promoted by the EU, which has led to high expectations in their partner countries, but they have ultimately failed to provide 'much improvement' for individual applicants (Korneev and Van Elsuwege, Chapter 25, this volume). Therefore, the importance of implementation should not be underestimated. We see a growing gap between policy outputs at the EU level and concrete outcomes on the ground. This implementation gap deserves further attention. It can help to illuminate the behavior and interests of member states and explain the disillusionment that some EU citizens and third countries experience concerning the actual benefits of EU policies in their daily lives. If people cannot see the added value of EU policies in areas like counter-terrorism, it may lead to a further politicization of JHA policies.

The external dimension of JHA

The research on the effectiveness of the EU's external engagement touches upon questions of interest and power. There, the EU is on the demanding side vis-à-vis third countries, given that a closer external cooperation is seen to help with internal problem-solving. As Zaiotti (this volume) shows,

> European policymakers have realized that targeting only individuals appearing at the continent's gates, or already within it, has not been sufficient to properly manage contemporary migratory flows. The answer has been to externalize border management, namely to stop or regulate incoming migrants *before* they reach their final destination.

A first body of literature looks mostly at how the EU has made use of conditionality to change the internal structures of third countries. There, the EU has faced a growing 'paradox' with regard to the respect of rule of law and judicial independence in and beyond Europe: 'while the enlargement process empowered the Commission in its relations with candidate countries […], its prerogatives with regard to member states' commitment to the rule of law after accession remains weak' (Coman, Chapter 22, this volume). This is a problem, as judicial independence and the separation of powers are under attack not only in a range of third countries but also within the European Union. Such concerns have been voiced in relation to Hungary under Victor Orban's government and Poland under the Eurosceptic Law and Justice Party (PiS) (ibid.). Similar concerns are discussed in the context of the EU's enlargement to the western Balkans. Compared to the eastern enlargement, the EU's external leverage has decreased in this southeastern European setting due to its multifaceted internal crises and the inability or unwillingness to make credible a membership promise. Therefore, it has become more difficult to ensure efficiency in the EU's conditionality approach, which is problematic in a region facing 'increasing domestic reform needs', especially in view of rising illiberalism and the threat of 'state capture(s)' (Trauner and Nechev, Chapter 23, this volume). Another dilemma is emerging in EU–Turkish relations; these two partners are characterized by their strong interdependence in JHA-related matters, but they also deeply distrust one another (Bürgin, Chapter 24, this volume).

Outside the enlargement context the EU is increasingly differentiating among the countries of the same region, not only in the Mediterranean region (Wolff and Pawlak, Chapter 26, this volume) but also in Eastern Europe. There, Russia has become essential when it comes to determining the scope and quality of the EU's relations on migration with individual Eastern Partnership countries (Korneev and Van Elsuwege, Chapter 25, this volume). Another question has been whether the EU can raise or has already raised its 'security profile' in more remote regions such as Southeast Asia (Pennisi di Floristella, Chapter 31, this volume) or Africa (Vorrath and Zoppei, Chapter 27, this volume). The EU has sought to become more active in tackling non-traditional security threats, reflected by a changing discourse and more ambitious goals defined by senior EU officials and politicians. The EU is indeed increasingly defining the agenda and financing many activities on issues such as fighting drug trafficking in Africa. Yet, it is still not entirely clear to what extent its (often rhetorical) engagement has already borne fruits. Often, the structures are not easily compatible. The cooperation of ASEANPOL, Asia's regional policing body, with Europol serves to illustrate these difficulties. While both are regional policing bodies, ASEANPOL acts primarily as a 'discussion forum for ASEAN police chiefs', whereas Europol has its own financial and operational resources (Pennisi di Floristella, Chapter 31, this volume).

Avenues of future research

As this handbook shows, research on JHA has reached its maturity. As a result, we have now a more multifaceted and complex debate on the sectoral, horizontal and vertical dimensions of JHA integration. This has led to an increasing specialization, with sub-policy fields becoming independent areas of study. It also raises questions about the future avenues of research. Should JHA research continue to be treated as something unique or should we aim for a 'normalization' of this area and its full integration into other fields of research (e.g., international relations, policy analysis or area studies)?

Dynamics of decision-making and the role of EU institutions

If we want to mainstream JHA research, we need to ask ourselves how our knowledge of internal security policies might contribute to wider debates in EU studies. For instance, what can JHA research tells us about the politicization of EU integration, the dynamics of disintegration or the study of crises?

When it comes to the politicization of EU integration, the question of who drives the 'policy' area is likely to remain salient. With raising populist forces and illiberal trends in both

Western and Eastern European countries, EU internal policies may become even more polarized and contested. We may examine in more depth how domestic politics affect the EU agenda on issues like freedom of movement, migrants' rights or the externalization of refugee protection. Polarization may take various forms; for instance, increasing conflicts between member states (as was the case with the relocation of asylum-seekers) or the unwillingness to offset financially those member states that experience stronger pressure on their domestic systems. To what extent does politicization have an impact on the substance of policies (e.g., a shift towards more restrictive or *securitized* policies) or lead to decision-making deadlock and policy stability?

We can already witness the effects of more polarized positions on issues like the EU's relations with Turkey. The increasing politicization is likely to affect the EU's capacity to act and decide on issues such as border control or visa liberalization (Czaika and Trauner, Chapter 9, this volume). Similarly, the effects of politicization post-migration crisis deserve further attention. It is still an open question whether we will see the emergence of a more permanent alliance of immigration-skeptic member states (Menz, Chapter 10, this volume). To what extent are they able to water down or even prevent the adoption of new EU immigration laws? There is, therefore, space for research looking at how the domestic politics of member states play out and whether it leads to more convergence or divergence on the EU level. Scholars may also investigate the causal mechanisms and the conditions under which particular national governments upload their domestic interests and influence EU policy developments (Ette, Chapter 19, this volume). It would be innovative to include new (quantitative) measurements over longer periods to actually check how member states align and adapt.

The governance concept presented by Bossong and Hegemann (Chapter 2, this volume) may also provide fresh perspectives on the field, notably after Brexit. It is not always necessary to take the EU as a point of departure, but to consider rather the networks of cooperation that have emerged at various levels of 'governance'. In the words of Bossong and Hegemann, 'what could we, as EU scholars, learn from an open-ended security governance perspective that pays equal attention to genuinely "polycentric" arrangements, including many regional or even local cross-border arrangements, for instance, in European policing?'

Indeed, this raises questions about how integration and disintegration play out in European governance. JHA can contribute to the wider literature by using insights from its own experiences with differentiated integration. The various 'opt-outs' have shown how influence can be exerted even under conditions of non-participation. For instance, despite its opt-out, the UK has been a highly influential player in police cooperation, particularly in matters of counter-terrorism. Brexit opens up many new questions (Peers, Chapter 21, this volume): how will it influence the way in which other member states interact? How will it affect the policy-making dynamics within the UK? How do epistemic communities, including policemen, lawyers and judges, position and behave in times of 'critical junctures' such as the Brexit process?

Finally, JHA can contribute to the study of crises and their impact on institutional and policy change. Despite the rapidly emerging research agenda in mainstream EU studies (e.g., Saurugger 2014), JHA scholars can make a contribution to the influence of 'crises' in EU integration, since the area has often been driven by such external events. External events may be used as a trigger for policy changes, but this mechanism is not automatic – it requires entrepreneurs who are willing to use a crisis to instigate change (Kaunert 2010; Trauner and Ripoll Servent 2015). A crisis may seem to create a momentum for change, but urgency may lead only to showing action without any actual effects or real follow-up at the level of the member states. Past examples may help in considering how crises affect the conditions for change, but also in examining the key actors driving these processes. JHA scholars can contribute to studying the role of EU institutions in crisis situations and to what extent they differ from previous patterns of cooperation.

For instance, do we see an increased presence of the European Council following the impact of crises on the EU's asylum system? Have the Commission and the EP been sidelined from major policy decisions? To what extent are member states shifting their responsibility towards third countries or EU regulatory agencies? These questions will shed light on broader processes of EU integration and the changing dynamics between EU institutions and member states.

Policy change, impact and implementation

The literature on policy change, policy impact and implementation is likely to benefit from a more systematic development of research designs and conceptualization. We have often talked in too general terms about 'what is change', 'how are preferences formed' and 'how does power play out' (Bonjour *et al.* 2017). These questions are particularly relevant given that the focus of the EU has moved towards the implementation of past policies.

Academic research can deepen our knowledge of the dynamics of implementation and adaptation. For instance, one can ask how certain member states adapt to pressures deriving from Europeanization processes and their increased responsibility to protect the EU external border. Finotelli (Chapter 20, this volume) shows how 'Southern European countries have balanced JHA imperatives on external controls with "national" internal control strategies to correct the dysfunctionalities arising from their status as external border watchers'. Such strategies include individual and hidden regularization procedures for irregular migrants, contrary to the stated preferences of Northern member states. Therefore, we need more research on how EU policy *outputs* become *outcomes*; that is, whether and how implementation occurs in a practical manner and what implications it has for EU governance. There, JHA research may profit from other areas, such as public administration or political sociology, which examine the role of (street-level) bureaucrats and their impact on how policies play out on a daily basis in the tradition of Lipsky (1980). Indeed, work on implementation is a major gap in JHA research and calls for innovative methods (e.g., ethnography) and more comparative research.

The handbook also shows how individual JHA sub-policies can contribute to illuminating wider developments in world governance. This may include the 'progressing militarization' of integrated border management (Wolff and Pawlak, Chapter 26, this volume) or the consequences of the 'digital revolution' (Carrapico and Farrand, Chapter 12, this volume). Technological developments have considerable implications for current policing. Although the EU is promoting the fight against cyber crime, the field has 'developed as a reactive, self-regulatory and scattered set of disparate policies' (Carrapico and Farrand, Chapter 12, this volume). To what extent are these policies and objectives translated into operational work and successful prosecutions?

Research on sub-policy areas should also consider how EU rules actually interact with the behaviors and strategies of EU citizens and migrants. EU policies may lead to unexpected, and even undesired, effects. Visa restrictions, for instance, 'come with significant economic costs, not only through deterring unwanted migrants, but also desired travelers, trade, investors, scientists and others who can make a positive economic and non-economic contribution to the recipient countries' (Czaika and Trauner, Chapter 9, this volume). It is important, thus, to keep in mind the broader repercussions of EU policies and how they affect other sub-policies that may appear only tangentially connected to the original issue area.

Research on the external dimension of JHA

Recent events such as the election of Donald Trump in the USA and the 2017 Turkish referendum installing an 'executive democracy' for President Erdogan highlight that liberal norms and democratic standards are being challenged in different places. This will influence the way in which the EU interacts with particular partners. How will the EU exert influence on a country such as Turkey given that the EU accession policy has reached stalemate? In which ways do institutions and laws created by the governments of partner countries in response to EU conditionality interact with local realities and informal 'ways-of-doing-things' (Trauner and Nechev, Chapter 23, this volume)? To what extent can national and regional bureaucracies and civil society networks trigger 'Europeanization' and policy adaptation even in the absence of the momentum associated with EU accession? According to Bürgin (Chapter 24, this volume), there may be 'policy learning processes' outside of the formal accession negotiations that represent 'an opportunity to keep the Europeanisation process in Turkey alive'. A new body of literature is developing with regard to the question of 'societal and state resilience', for instance, in the Mediterranean region (Wolff and Pawlak, Chapter 26, this volume). We need, therefore, to examine which norms are being diffused, how this is done and whether these efforts are successful – bearing in mind that these norms may not always be 'liberal' in nature.

Researchers may also look at the dynamics derived from the EU's efforts to externalize migration control, both at the EU and member state level. Countries like Italy and Spain have built a wide web of cooperation agreements; however, 'bilateral cooperation promoted by Southern European countries is part of a "passing-the-buck" strategy in which guaranteeing humanitarian standards seems to play a second fiddle to the EU's commitment to secure its borders more efficiently' (Finotelli, Chapter 20, this volume). What are the implications of such cooperation for migrant rights? How effective is it given the lukewarm support of such initiatives by neighboring states? Korneev and Van Elsuwege (Chapter 25, this volume) suggest that our understanding of the EU's external relations in JHA may be further improved if we 'transcend binary oppositions such as neighbors–non-neighbors, interest–values, conditionality–interdependence in order to better reflect on goals, challenges and prospects of EU internal security and migration policies towards the Eastern Partnership countries and Russia'.

It also underlines the bias towards the EU's neighborhood in this area of research. We need to cast the net wider, looking further afield to regions like Asia, sub-Saharan Africa and Latin America. How are we actually interacting with these regions and what is the nature of cooperation between the EU and countries beyond the immediate neighborhood? Legal scholars may contribute to furthering our knowledge of EU cooperation, for instance, by examining Mutual Legal Assistance agreements with countries like Japan which have not yet been adequately addressed (Weyembergh and Brière, Chapter 16, this volume).

An outlook to the handbook

This chapter has sought to present the basic ideas and some of the key discussions of the handbook. Each chapter provides detailed and fascinating accounts of what scholars have dealt with in their respective areas of research. Some are more theory-oriented while others concentrate on policy issues.

Therefore, the handbook highlights the transformative changes taking place in Europe and their effects on our way of doing research. If Ruben Zaiotti (Chapter 8, this volume) calls for a better theory development with regard to the study of border management, this appeal may be considered to be of relevance for the field of JHA more generally.

> The assumption that European border management is following the path of other policy areas within the European Union, namely that it is steadily becoming more integrated or that it will acquire the features of the more established (read 'national')

political systems, is now under question. Works that rely on integrative analytical frameworks for the study of the EU, and that emphasize concepts such as Europeanization, might therefore have to rethink their approaches in light of the new empirical reality.

(Zaiotti, Chapter 8, this volume)

Bibliography

Aden, H. (ed.) (2014). *Police Cooperation in the European Union under the Treaty of Lisbon – Opportunities and Limitations*. Baden-Baden: Nomos.

Aus, J.P. (2007). EU Governance in an Area of Freedom, Security and Justice: Logics of Decision-making in the Justice and Home Affairs Council. Arena Working Paper No. 15, University of Oslo: Arena Centre for European Studies, October.

Bendel, P., Ette, A. and Parkes, R. (eds) (2011). *The Europeanization of Control. Venues and Outcomes of EU Justice and Home Affairs Cooperation*. Münster: LIT-Verlag.

Bigo, D., Carrera, S., Guild, E. and Walker, R.B.J. (eds) (2010). *Europe's 21st Century Challenge. Delivering Liberty*. Aldershot: Ashgate.

Bonjour, S., Ripoll Servent, A. and Thielemann, E. (2017). Beyond Venue Shopping and Liberal Constraints: A New Research Agenda for EU Migration Policies and Politics. *Journal of European Public Policy*. Available at: http://dx.doi.org/10.1080/13501763.2016.1268640 (early view).

Bossong, R. and Rhinard, M. (eds) (2016). *Theorizing Internal Security in the European Union*. Oxford: Oxford University Press.

Bures, O. (2007). EU Counterterrorism Policy: A Paper Tiger? *Terrorism and Political Violence*, 18(1), pp. 57–78.

Cremona, M., Monar, J. and Poli, S. (eds) (2010). *The External Dimension of the Area of Freedom, Security and Justice*. Brussels: Peter Lang-P.I.E.

Eckes, C. and Konstadinides, T. (eds) (2011). *Crime within the Area of Freedom, Security and Justice*. Cambridge: Cambridge University Press.

Fabbrini, S. and Puetter, U. (2016). Integration without Supranationalisation: Studying the Lead Roles of the European Council and the Council in Post-Lisbon EU Politics. *Journal of European Integration*, 38(5), pp. 481–495.

Fletcher, M., Herlin-Karnell, E. and Matera, C. (eds) (2016). *The European Union as an Area of Freedom, Security and Justice*. Abingdon. Routledge.

Geddes, A. and Scholten, P. (2015). Policy Analysis and Europeanization: An Analysis of EU Migrant Integration Policymaking. *Journal of Comparative Policy Analysis*, 17(1), pp. 41–59.

Guild, E. and Geyer, F. (eds) (2008). *Security versus Justice? Police and Judicial Cooperation in the European Union*. Aldershot: Ashgate.

Holzhacker, R. and Luif, P. (eds) (2014). *Freedom, Security and Justice in the European Union. Internal and External Dimensions of Increased Cooperation after the Lisbon Treaty*. New York: Springer.

Kaunert, C. (2010). *European Internal Security: Towards Supranational Governance?* Manchester: Manchester University Press.

Kaunert, C., Léonard, S. and Pawlak, P. (eds) (2013). *European Homeland Security. A European Strategy in the Making?* London: Routledge.

Kostakopoulou, D. (2007). European Union Citizenship: Writing the Future. *European Law Journal*, 13(5), pp. 623–646.

Lavenex, S. (2009). Transgovernmentalism in the European Area of Freedom, Security and Justice. In Verdun, A. and Tömmel, I. (eds), *Innovative Governance in the European Union: The Politics of Multilevel Policymaking*. Boulder, CO: Lynne Rienner, pp. 255–272.

Lewis, J. (2005). The Janus Face of Brussels: Socialization and Everyday Decision Making in the European Union. *International Organization*, 59(4), pp. 937–971.

Lipsky, M. (1980). *Street-level Bureaucracy: The Dilemmas of Individuals in the Public Service*. New York: Sage.

Maricut, A. (2016). With and Without Supranationalisation: The Post-Lisbon Roles of the European Council and the Council in Justice and Home Affairs Governance. *Journal of European Integration*, 38(5), pp. 541–555.

Monar, J. (2001). The Dynamics of Justice and Home Affairs: Laboratories, Driving Factors and Costs. *Journal of Common Market Studies*, 39(4), pp. 747–764.

Monar, J. (ed.) (2010). *The Institutional Dimension of the European Union's Area of Freedom, Security and Justice*. Brussels: Peter Lang.
Peers, S. (2016). *EU Justice and Home Affairs Law. Fourth Edition*. Oxford: Oxford University Press.
Saurugger, S. (2014). Europeanisation in Times of Crisis. *Political Studies Review*, 12(2), pp. 181–192.
Schimmelfennig, F. and Rittberger, B. (2006). Theories of European Integration: Assumptions and Hypotheses. In Richardson, J. (ed.), *European Union. Power and Policy-making*. London: Routledge, pp. 73–96.
Trauner, F. and Ripoll Servent, A. (eds) (2015). *Policy Change in the Area of Freedom, Security and Justice: How EU Institutions Matter*. London: Routledge.
Trauner, F. and Ripoll Servent, A. (2016). The Communitarization of the Area of Freedom, Security and Justice: Why Institutional Change does not Translate into Policy Change. *Journal of Common Market Studies*, 54(6), pp. 1417–1432.
Walker, N. (ed.) (2004). *Europe's Area of Freedom, Security and Justice*. Oxford: Oxford University Press.
Wilde, P.D. (2011). No Polity for Old Politics? A Framework for Analyzing the Politicization of European Integration. *Journal of European Integration*, 33(5), pp. 559–575.
Wolff, S., Goudappel, F. and de Zwaan, J. (eds) (2011). *Freedom, Security and Justice after the Lisbon Treaty and the Stockholm Programme*. The Hague: TMC Asser Press.
Zaun, N. (2017). *EU Asylum Policies: The Power of Strong Regulating States*. Basingstoke: Palgrave Macmillan.

PART II

Theories of justice and home affairs

2
THE GOVERNANCE OF INTERNAL SECURITY

Beyond functionalism and the finality of integration?

Raphael Bossong and Hendrik Hegemann

Introduction

Governance has risen to prominence as an academic concept and political practice across different fields and disciplines. Despite persisting diversity and disagreements, its various applications basically revolve around the emergence of new forms of coordination, steering and regulation that transcend traditional, state-centered understandings of political rule by hierarchical and formal structures of command-and-control (Rhodes 1996; Stoker 1998). The broader 'governance turn' has identified the European Union (EU) as an ideal case of modern governance (Kohler-Koch and Rittberger 2006) and even extended this argument to the purportedly special field of security provision in and by the EU (Kirchner and Sperling 2007; Schroeder 2011; Christou *et al.* 2010). Research on EU internal security policy, or justice and home affairs (JHA), has been no exception to this trend (Bossong and Lavenex 2016). The varied references to governance in this area, however, do not yet add up to a cumulative research agenda and there is still a need to carve out the value-added by a governance perspective and what it offers to the field. Therefore, this chapter focuses on different foundational perspectives and questions that are highlighted by a governance perspective, rather than seeking to review the growth of empirical studies that employ the term *governance*.

Research needs to address at least three challenges in order to realize the full potential of the governance perspective. First, many studies use governance in a mere metaphorical sense and describe something as a governance practice without further explication. A certain degree of flexibility is probably inevitable in view of the concept's wide-ranging application and may even be considered one of its key strengths. If a governance perspective wants to make a distinct contribution to the field, scholars, however, need to be more specific and clear regarding the key propositions and elements associated with governance. Second, governance often favors a problem-solving approach analyzing how governance systems produce specific solutions to a given problem. A growing critical and reflexive perspective warns us that governance remains a contentious exercise of political rule that is subject to imminent contingencies and uncertainties (Bevir 2010; Davies 2011; Hegemann and Kahl 2016). Hence, one should not simply buy into a technocratic or depoliticized reading of governance Third, uses of governance in the internal security field should not forget the security dimension of it, which becomes evident in the existence of a distinct literature on security governance (Krahmann 2003; Webber *et al.* 2004; Ehrhart *et al.* 2014; Webber 2014). Governance logics fundamentally depend on the underlying security logics, which remain subject to change and contestation (Christou *et al.* 2010). Hence we should view internal security governance within the larger context of evolving concepts and practices of security provision in the post-Cold War and post-9/11 context. After setting out these basic reflections on governance and security governance, the final section of this chapter briefly charts out the trajectory of related research on EU JHA. In particular, we focus on the insights from governance research on (1) the evolution of authority and shape of policy networks in EU JHA; (2) its contested effectiveness and legitimacy, and (3) EU internal security governance as one expression of a larger transformation of security provision.

The governance perspective: family resemblances

Governance seems to be almost ubiquitous in academic discourses on contemporary politics. Debates on governance go back to the search for new ways of political steering in Western welfare states that promise more efficient and flexible ways of managing public affairs beyond established patterns of hierarchical, top-down decision-making by a monolithic state (Rhodes 1996). Later, EU scholars also suggested that new forms of coordination and regulation, including a broader range of actors from different levels, might promise a solution to notorious gridlocks in intergovernmental bargaining and formal implementation (Kohler-Koch and Rittberger 2006). In this sense, governance is not only an academic concept but also a political practice and program, insofar as it tends to 'prescribe an ideal as well as an empirical reality' (van Kersbergen and van Waarden 2004: 152). At the same time, the governance perspective is held together by only a few assumptions that may better be approached as 'family resemblances', i.e., as a set of related similarities in some key dimensions, where no one feature is necessarily common to all manifestations (Bevir and Rhodes 2011: 111; Ehrhart *et al.* 2014: 148).

In a first dimension, applications of governance typically make assumptions about the mode of cooperation. Large parts of governance research started out with the assumption that coordination in contemporary settings cannot work effectively through the top-down exercise of force and coercion, but requires a more informal arrangement that transcends the dichotomy of pure hierarchy versus market (Rhodes 1996). The instruments of choice, hence, are flexible networks and rather 'soft' modes of cooperation, such as negotiation, dialogue, standardization, benchmarking and concertation. However, as governance research evolved, it became increasingly open to empirical investigations of how far elements of hierarchy are mixed into, or required for, different styles of governance, as in the debate on governing 'in the shadow of hierarchy' (Héritier and Lehmkuhl 2008). Moreover, the discussion on the hollowing out of the state in times of globalization has clearly been tempered over the years by much more nuanced observations about the interplay of liberalization and privatization with the extended reach of liberal governments by means of complex forms of cooptation or co-regulation with business and civil society in many areas, which allows the state to steer political developments and exercise rule without having to resort to visible forms of command and control (Leibfried *et al.* 2015).

Regarding a second major dimension, a governance perspective typically builds on the assumption that multiple actors are involved. In this view, public actors and national governments are no longer the sole or even dominant actors in the political process. One of the empirical strengths of governance research has been the corresponding emphasis on private actors in the production of public goods and policy, which share and compete for authority with public actors. Yet, the debate here has also broadened. Governance – in the views of many – neither presumes nor rules out the participation of governments. Governance, then, refers to 'governance without government', but can also encompass elements of 'governance with government' and even 'governance by government' (Zürn 1998: 169–170). Thus, the exact definition of governance is dynamic and context-sensitive, but this does not mean that governance is just what actors make of it. Rather, it is necessary to stipulate why and in what way a specific case should be discussed through the prism of governance and which elements commonly ascribed to governance it displays, or not.

Governance approaches also differentiate themselves with respect to problem-solving versus critical approaches, following Robert Cox's (1981) famous differentiation. Traditional governance research was based on the assumption that governance represents a pragmatic – though not necessarily always ideal – solution to problems that would not fit conventional political decision-making structures. Governance in this sense focuses on the process through which specific solutions for given problems are produced following the overall goal 'to get things done' (Stoker 1998: 24). Such a perspective does not have to translate into pure functionalism, but nevertheless emphasizes the inherent issue dynamics over institutional influences, social contexts and power relations that shape the perception and development of problems in the first place.

A second wave of governance research challenged this orientation. In real policy settings it is extremely difficult to control for multiple causation, to have a clearly defined baseline against which to measure change, to work with clearly defined time frames that condition impact assessments, or to have suitably precise empirical indicators while remaining open to unforeseen policy effects. Working with non-hierarchical networks and voluntary instruments accentuates these hurdles further, so that proponents of the problem-solving capacity of governance tend to resort to indirect indicators, such as stakeholder engagement, or point to failed attempts of hierarchical regulation. However, legitimating governance arrangements by counter-factuals or by mere procedural qualities of policy-making risks obfuscating questions of power, hegemony, contestation and exclusion (Davies 2011). This becomes evident in neoliberal reforms that introduced ideas associated with governance, such as self-regulation, decentralization, public–private partnerships or joined-up government. Whether these become successes or produce 'governance failure' (Jessop 1998) depends largely on specific conditions, while adopting such a governance approach may also erode trust in the ability of state institutions to provide basic goods and services. Moreover, a critical governance perspective raises many concerns about democratic legitimacy and accountability of complex, non-accountable and non-transparent networks (Bevir 2010). In sum, conventional narratives about gains in effectiveness, efficiency and legitimacy of new governance arrangements have been replaced by a more reflexive, critical perspective that underlines contextual factors and inherent tradeoffs.

The governance of internal security and the transformation of security provision

While governance emerged mainly in debates on economic and social policy, it has increasingly been transferred to the security realm as the seemingly last stronghold of Westphalian sovereignty and realist 'high politics'. The growing literature on security governance basically mirrors the 'family resemblances' of governance approaches identified above and highlights trends towards informalization, privatization and internationalization (Krahmann 2003; Webber *et al.* 2004; Webber 2014). This raises the fundamental question of whether governance in the security realm is actually special, or whether we can treat it as a secondary spill-over effect from other governance areas driven by globalization and neoliberalism (Bevir and Hall 2014). For instance, the privatization of telecommunication infrastructures and complexities of 'internet governance' led to related challenges for security policy networks that include a wide variety of public and private actors. Yet security governance may also be considered as a standalone trend which has been driven by the post-Cold War discourse on the widening and deepening of security. This narrative highlighted the emergence of 'new' and 'complex' security risks, such as transnational terrorism and cyber security, which are supposed to require new forms of collaboration and resource mobilization. Flexible networks, like the Proliferation Security Initiative or voluntary compliance mechanisms, such as in the Financial Action Task Force, serve as prominent examples. Overall, new governance initiatives in the area of security are part of broader transformations in the security field and cannot be separated from the underlying security and threat narratives (Christou et al. 2010).

Consequentially, *security* governance has a distinct logic that is more specific than the broad family resemblances of governance approaches outlined above. Here, one is faced with a more pronounced differentiation between assumptions about the non-hierarchical and radically dispersed nature of governance among a wide variety of actors – as exemplified by contributions on 'nodal policing governance' (Shearing and Wood 2003) – and more 'conventional' perspectives that still assign a pre-eminent role to public authorities in the provision of security (Kirchner and Sperling 2007). The traditional absence of private actors in security provision by the modern Westphalian state has led to a particularly strong interest in their resurgence, especially when it comes to private military and security companies. Yet just as in previous debates on economic globalization, privatization in the field of security does not have to lead to a weakening of the state, but can actually widen executives' leeway of action by outsourcing and evading public control and scrutiny (Abrahamsen and Williams 2009).

Moreover, the critique of functionalist readings of governance outlined above is particularly pertinent in the field of security. Claims about 'effective' security measures are often based on problematic counterfactual arguments; for instance, why no terrorist attack occurred in a given time period, while secrecy about some actions or information held by security services limits external scrutiny. In addition, the drivers or facilitating conditions of terrorism and of regular crime remain intensely contested, while interventions to increase security in complex conflicts are prone to unintended consequences and side effects (Daase and Friesendorf 2010). The potential for 'best practices' and 'lessons learned' in the area of (internal) security that should be disseminated via governance networks is therefore considerably constrained. Most importantly, the questions of 'security for whom', 'security by what costs' and 'security with what means' constitute a core area of political contention (Ehrhart et al. 2014) and cannot be avoided through attempts of technocratic depoliticization in the name of efficiency and evidence-based policy (Hegemann and Kahl 2016). This also points to Foucauldian-inspired studies in governmentality, which range across all aspects of modern power but have a particular emphasis on notions of control and discipline (Merlingen 2011). Whether one adopts such radical perspectives or not, analysts of security governance at least need to critically probe arguments whereby criminal or 'dark' networks can only be countered by similar networks among security authorities.

Governance in EU justice and home affairs

Against this background, the application of governance to EU JHA needs to be sensitive to different research agendas and related normative questions. On the one hand, building on the general governance literature, EU 'modes of governance' have been intensively researched and compared across many different policy areas, including JHA. On the other hand, security scholars have focused on the transformation of the state and new security challenges, in relation to which the EU serves as a prominent, but not exclusive, case for the rise of security governance. We now briefly review these perspectives in turn.

The perspective of EU governance applied to the area of JHA focuses mainly on two concerns: namely the evolution of EU authority and the shape of governance arrangements that do not neatly coincide with the boundaries of the EU. EU JHA evolved from weak community competences and largely horizontal or voluntary coordination mechanisms into an increasingly regularized or hierarchical field of 'supranational governance', with a growing role of supranational institutions (Kaunert and Léonard 2012). Typically, governance scholars on EU JHA start out by highlighting the so-called transgovernmental networks that have developed between high-level bureaucrats and security professionals since the 1970s, and which formed the basis for many of the crucial political agreements and institutional innovations, such as the Schengen Convention (especially its later policing and border security dimension) or the creation of the so-called Third Pillar. The resulting proliferation of professional forums has also been labeled as important 'laboratories' for overcoming practical constraints as well as political sovereignty reservations (Monar 2001). These transgovernmental networks in JHA, which are also a prevalent feature in many other areas of global governance (Slaughter 2004), came to inspire an entire mode of EU governance, the so-called 'intensive transgovernmentalism' (Wallace and Lavenex 2005; Lavenex 2009).

The postulated special intensity of European interactions goes hand in hand with a general analytical assumption of transgovernmentalism, namely the supposed partial independence of network participants from political leadership. This partial independence is seen as an ambivalent feature that allows for international cooperation beyond formal political constraints, such as sovereignty concerns, but also raises critical questions of accountability. Thus, early work on EU JHA governance generally welcomed the dynamism of cooperation in a changed post-Cold War environment and increasingly open borders (Anderson and Den Boer 1994), but also highlighted the potential for 'executive empowerment' via transgovernmental networks in contrast to accountable decision-making venues (Guiraudon 2000). In this context, the initially weak legal competences of the Union in JHA accentuated its general preference of 'negative integration', i.e., for mutual recognition and liberalization of standards, which could be considered especially problematic in areas that touch upon fundamental rights and liberties (Lavenex and Wagner 2007). So, rather than seeing integration as an inherent good or self-reinforcing process – as in classic neo-functionalism – JHA governance scholars have generally welcomed the increasing degree of hierarchy, legal codification and institution-building on the grounds that this is likely to generate superior policy-making processes and outcomes.

This gives rise to the question of whether governance – understood in a comparatively narrow sense as largely non-hierarchical transgovernmental networks – remains relevant to analyzing contemporary EU JHA affairs. With the Treaty of Lisbon the 'ordinary legislative procedure' has been extended to almost all aspects of EU JHA cooperation. Moreover, one can also point to a dramatic increase in politicization and the involvement of top politicians, up to the European Council, in JHA policy-making. Yet, this reading glosses over the remaining sovereignty reservations in matters of internal security and police cooperation (mainly Art. 4(2) TEU and Art. 73 TFEU), which continue to fuel a wide range of more flexible and softer governance arrangements. For example, the so-called 'policy cycle' for fighting serious and organized crime constitutes a soft governance framework for synchronizing the crime-fighting priorities of national police forces with the assistance of EUROPOL, even if the EU cannot directly order police measures at the national level (Paoli 2014). At the same time, the notion of internal security, which has gained increasing traction in EU discourses over the past few years, covers a wide range of objectives that are only partially covered by the Area of Freedom, Security and Justice (Title V of the Treaty of the Functioning of the European Union). This applies, for instance, to the field of civil protection and disaster management, which remains a supportive weak competence of the Union and could, until today, be considered a stronghold of conventional 'intensive transgovernmentalism' (Hollis 2010).

Conversely, all areas of EU policy-making have shown that legal communitarization does not lead to an eradication of complex and often informal governance arrangements. A heightened legal and institutional profile for EU actors is quite likely to stimulate the formation of European-wide networks for monitoring, early coordination, policy implementation – or even for sidestepping formal legislation (Christiansen and Neuhold 2012). This line of analysis builds on, and co-evolves with, a larger debate on the EU as a 'regulatory polity' (Genschel and Rittberger 2014), which may have formal powers of legislation but is otherwise highly limited in terms of direct administrative capacity or general authority to induce compliance. Instead, the EU is under constant pressure to legitimate its role by superior expertise or technical efficiency – which crystallizes into standalone agencies that are seen as less costly in terms of sovereignty than the strengthening of EU institutions – while also being open to involve a wide range of stakeholders in more voluntary implementation. The resulting agentification of EU governance has been particularly prominent in JHA (Kaunert *et al.* 2013; see also Chapter 37, this volume), leading to further rich research debates on the tradeoffs between output effectiveness or legitimization and the need for political control and accountability in this sensitive field (Busuioc and Groenleer 2013). In short, rather than ending with the onset of 'supranational governance' for the Area of Freedom, Security and Justice, we need to remain open to a constantly changing empirical field of research.

The second major concern of EU JHA governance research is to analyze continuously shifting policy arrangements and coordination networks that do not respect the formal institutional and legal set-up of the European Union. The literature on external governance covers all EU policy fields, but has gained special relevance in matters of JHA (Lavenex and Wichmann 2009). EU governance has not only become increasingly externalized as a structural side effect of internal integration, as in matters of economic regulation, but governance arrangements for JHA have also, from the very beginning, been intimately connected with notions of 'flexible integration' or 'variable geometry' (Tekin 2012; see also Chapter 22, this volume). The clearest and most important example is the Schengen agreement, which – due to various opt-outs of member states – falls short of as well as reaches beyond the territorial boundaries of the EU, including EFTA member states that seek to enjoy the advantages of freedom of movement and enhanced police cooperation. Furthermore, much of the core EU competences in JHA are inherently tied to transnational relations and coordination processes, from visa policies and the control of irregular migration to the facilitation of information exchanges in the fight against organized crime and terrorism. In these and many other topics of internal security, the EU has woven a dense net of agreements and coordination processes over its neighborhood as well as positioned itself as a central intermediary between, on the one hand, global organization or the USA, and its member states on the other hand. Conversely, it should be remembered that many aspects of European internal security cooperation remain more localized and regional, such as in the case of binational police cooperation centers that have come to play an increasing role for EU police information exchanges (Gruszczak 2016). The analysis of any field of EU JHA cooperation therefore involves paying attention to dense, overlapping and multi-level governance networks, where the EU and its agencies or institutions variously occupy a position of leading driver, central coordination node or simple network participant.

As with the early governance literature on intensive transgovernmentalism, the ambivalent effects of increasing cooperation beyond borders versus questions of accountability, fairness and hidden empowerment drive much of the academic debate on EU external governance in JHA (Balzacq 2009). Scholars generally recognize functional drivers for extending cooperation beyond the EU's borders, but have also strongly criticized the potential for a renewed or even enhanced executive empowerment by this avenue. Thus, while the initial venue-shopping to move 'up' to the EU level has been caught up with in the course of supranationalization, the further step to move 'out' of the Union is harder to oversee for parliaments, courts and civil society (Lavenex 2006). Nevertheless, it remains a matter of rich empirical investigations in how far the EU actually exercises effective external governance, which is not only dependent on highly divergent third countries (Trauner and Wolff 2014), but also on ever-shifting policy priorities, resource mobilization and inherent issue dynamics. For instance, even if the EU's external migration governance has risen to the top of the political agenda since 2015, one can point to more limited effects of comparable efforts over the past decade (Wunderlich 2012; Hampshire 2016). Similarly, the transatlantic governance networks for counter-terrorism cooperation have become politicized and formalized (Pawlak 2009; Kingah and Zwartjes 2015).

Turning to the second major research perspective (i.e., security governance as opposed to EU governance), analysts typically do not concern themselves with comparisons across different EU policy areas, but tend to regard the EU as a 'comprehensive' governance actor that mobilizes a wide and innovative range of incentives and policy instruments to tackle particular security problems (Christou *et al.* 2010; Ehrhart *et al.* 2014; Zwolski 2012). At a systemic level, the European security governance architecture is also of particular interest due to the overlapping activities of a still unrivalled number of international organizations (NATO, OSCE, EU, Council of Europe) or regional forums, among which the EU may often assume significant networking functions (Sperling and Webber 2014). Thus, despite well-known limits in the area of 'hard security', the EU should serve as a leading if not the only venue for the development of security governance, understood as issue-specific, if comprehensive and partly voluntary coordination activities among a wide range of stakeholders. This has been amply illustrated in the fight against terrorism (Monar 2014) and many related security concerns that straddle the boundaries between internal and external security, such as the financing of terrorism. Security governance may also be particularly helpful in charting out the EU's role in emergent transnational security fields, such as disaster management and related regulatory challenges. Elsewhere, we have termed this area which partially intersects with the EU's Area of Freedom, Security and Justice 'civil security governance' (Bossong and Hegemann 2015), which also implies a strong multi-level component from local to global governance. Yet the tension between, on the one hand, increasing organizational complexity in multi-stakeholder settings and increasing functional specialization, as in the case of EU JHA agencies, and on the other hand, the strategic narratives on the EU's 'added value' as a comprehensive security provider has also been critically discussed (Schröder 2011). Thus, despite the general functionalist inclinations of governance approaches outlined in the first part of this chapter, security governance scholars that analyze the EU have, by and large, adopted a skeptical view.

The specific interest of the wider literature on security governance with privatization dynamics provides a similar critical angle on the EU. The EU has a distinct profile as a market-making organization and is comparatively more open to private (business) actors than many nation-states. As such, the propagated need to form new kinds of public–private partnerships and to include business actors, especially in new fields such as cyber security and critical infrastructure protection, should also manifest itself in a prominent manner in the EU. This is a somewhat different, but equally important, issue to the original concern of security governance scholars with the use of private military companies. Recent contributions have, therefore, used the EU as a significant case to analyze wider dynamics – and especially effectiveness and accountability problems – of public–private partnerships for non-traditional security (Bossong and Wagner 2016). This may also be related to a growing body of research on the intersection of business interests with the expansion of EU border security, or 'smart borders', even if many critical security scholars may also use alternative, or more radical and specific, analytical concepts, such as biopolitical governmentality (Tazzioli and Walters 2016) or actor-network theory (Jeandesboz 2016). Finally, however, mainstream governance approaches also remind us to remain alert to the involvement of other non-public and not-for-profit actors. In various national settings civil society organizations have long-standing and formal partnerships with public authorities for a wide range of JHA issues, such as emergency response, migrant integration, privacy protection and countering hate speech. At the level of the EU this is comparatively rare, but also a growing trend. For instance, the EU has sponsored a 'Radicalisation Awareness Network' that unites a wide range of public authorities and civil society organizations for the exchange of best practices in the prevention of terrorism, which, however, remains unable to overcome fundamental uncertainties and conflicts in this area that is as contingent as it is contested (Bossong 2014; Hegemann and Kahl 2016).

Conclusions and outlook

Governance is a multifaceted and rich perspective that, at its most basic, helps to recognize the complexity, diversity and lack of a uniform logic of EU JHA, just as much as it highlights its depth and reach beyond formal legal and institutional competences. Thus, even if the development from transgovernmental networks to the 'Lisbonization' of EU JHA is far from complete – or may partly remain blocked in practice based on the legacy of previous policies (Trauner and Ripoll Servent 2015) – governance research can also alert us to the emergence of new implementation or soft operational coordination networks, the interactions of agencies and the shape of many issue-specific governance arrangements below and beyond the Union.

Against this background, EU scholars have long developed arguments about the need for transnational cooperation as well as critical readings of EU governance in general. The standard functionalist account that highlights the inherent spill-over effects of the freedom of movement, the abolition of border controls within Schengen and the transboundary reach of terrorism, organized crime and irregular migration, to name only the most important ones, remains as pertinent as ever. Therefore, functionalist readings of governance that see it as a necessary complement or alternative to standard policy-making and hierarchical government are equally valid. Yet we have also made the case here that one needs to be conscious of many possible negative side effects of governance, be it the concern with the dominance of negative integration, executive empowerment, lack of accountability or with technocratic legitimation. Thus, scholars should be explicit and reflexive on their underlying normative assumptions when applying notions of governance to EU JHA, even if they opt for a 'mainstream' functionalist perspective that casts the EU as a positive laboratory for cooperation and comprehensive action. Simply assuming such a functionalist orientation of governance arrangements is not adequate when dealing with security and related contentious value choices and becomes even more problematic with a view to current politicization dynamics that – especially surrounding the 'refugee crisis' or the response to recent terrorist attacks – increasingly also affect EU internal security policy.

Correspondingly, the relative emphasis given to comparative governance dynamics versus more issue-specific concerns is important. In this chapter, we could only briefly touch upon the range of existing literature that matches security governance with the study of the EU, but arguably it still remains underdeveloped when compared to the legacy of EU governance research. The issue orientation of this handbook should give an additional impetus to reflect on our analytical priorities. Are we giving too much room to the EU when faced with complex internal security problems, such as the fight against international terrorism and organized crime?

Even critical discussions that highlight the EU's limits tend to result in conclusions on how to improve its governance capacities or related normative framings. Conversely, what could we, as EU scholars, learn from an open-ended security governance perspective that pays equal attention to genuinely 'polycentric' arrangements, including many regional or even local cross-border arrangements, for instance, in European policing? In light of the repeated pressures to repeal Schengen, ever more externalized migration governance, much of it at the bilateral level with EU member states – as well as renewed global pressures for cooperation such as US demands for border security – we should take such a reading of governance without any hidden assumptions about the 'finality' of European integration more seriously than ever.

Bibliography

Abrahamsen, R. and Williams, M.C. (2009). Security beyond the State. Global Security Assemblages in International Politics. *International Political Sociology*, 3(1), pp. 1–17.

Anderson, M. and Den Boer, M. (1994). *Policing Across National Boundaries*. London: Pinter.

Balzacq, T. (2009). *The External Dimension of EU Justice and Home Affairs: Governance, Neighbours, Security*. Basingstoke: Palgrave Macmillan.

Bevir, M. (2010). *Democratic Governance*. Princeton, NJ: Princeton University Press.

Bevir, M. and Hall, I. (2014). The Rise of Security Governance. In M. Bevir, O. Daddow and I. Hall (eds), *Interpreting Global Security*. London: Routledge, pp. 17–34.

Bevir, M. and Rhodes, R.A.W. (2011). The Stateless State. In M. Bevir (ed.), *The SAGE Handbook of Governance*. London: Sage, pp. 203–217.

Bossong, R. (2014). EU Cooperation on Terrorism Prevention and Violent Radicalization: Frustrated Ambitions or New Forms of EU Security Governance? *Cambridge Review of International Affairs*, 27(1), pp. 66–82.

Bossong, R. and Hegemann, H. (eds) (2015). *European Civil Security Governance. Cooperation and Diversity in Crisis and Disaster Management*. Basingstoke: Palgrave.

Bossong, R. and Lavenex, S. (2016). Governance and EU Internal Security. In R. Bossong and M. Rhinard. (eds), *Theorizing Internal Security in the European Union*. Oxford: Oxford University Press, pp. 86–108.

Bossong, R. and Wagner, B. (2016). A Typology of Cybersecurity and Public–Private Partnerships in the Context of the EU. *Crime, Law and Social Change* (OnlineFirst).

Busuioc, M. and Groenleer, M. (2013). Beyond Design: The Evolution of Europol and Eurojust. *Perspectives on European Politics and Society*, 14(3), pp. 285–304.

Christiansen, T. and Neuhold, C. (2012). *International Handbook on Informal Governance*. Cheltenham: Edward Elgar.

Christou, G., Croft, S., Ceccorulli, M. and Lucarelli, S. (2010). European Union Security Governance. Putting the 'Security' Back In. *European Security*, 19(3), pp. 341–359.

Cox, R.W. (1981). Social Forces, States and World Orders: Beyond International Relations Theory. *Millennium – Journal of International Studies*, 10(2), pp. 126–155.

Daase, C. and Friesendorf, C. (eds) (2010). *Rethinking Security Governance. The Problem of Unintended Consequences*. London: Routledge.

Davies, J.S. (2011). *Challenging Governance Theory: From Networks to Hegemony*. Bristol: The Policy Press.

Ehrhart, H-G., Hegemann, H. and Kahl, M. (2014). Towards Security Governance as a Critical Tool. A Conceptual Outline. *European Security*, 23(2), pp. 145–162.

Genschel, P. and Rittberger, V. (eds) (2014). *Beyond the Regulatory Polity? The European Integration of Core State Powers*. Oxford: Oxford University Press.

Gruszczak, A. (2016). Police and Customs Cooperation Centres and Their Role in EU Internal Security Governance. In R. Bossong and H. Carrapico (eds), *EU Borders and Shifting Internal Security. Technology, Externalisation and Accountability*. Heidelberg: Springer, pp. 157–176.

Guiraudon, V. (2000). European Integration and Migration Policy: Vertical Policy-making as Venue Shopping. *JCMS: Journal of Common Market Studies*, 38(2), pp. 251–271.

Hampshire, J. (2016). Speaking With One Voice? The European Union's Global Approach to Migration and Mobility and the Limits of International Migration Cooperation. *Journal of Ethnic and Migration Studies*, 42(4), pp. 571–586.

Hegemann, H. and Kahl, M. (2016). Security Governance and the Limits of Depoliticisation. EU Policies to Protect Critical Infrastructures and Prevent Radicalization. *Journal of International Relations and Development* (OnlineFirst).

Héritier, A. and Lehmkuhl, D. (2008). The Shadow of Hierarchy and New Modes of Governance. *Journal of Public Policy*, 28(1), pp. 1–17.

Hollis, S. (2010). The Necessity of Protection: Transgovernmental Networks and EU Security Governance. *Cooperation and Conflict*, 45(3), pp. 312–330.

Jeandesboz, J. (2016). Smartening Border Security in the European Union: An Associational Inquiry. *Security Dialogue* (OnlineFirst).

Jessop, B. (1998). The Rise of Governance and the Risks of Failure. The Case of Economic Development. *International Social Science Journal*, 50(155), pp. 29–45.

Kaunert, C. and Léonard, S. (2012). Introduction: Supranational Governance and European Union Security after the Lisbon Treaty. Exogenous Shocks, Policy Entrepreneurs and 11 September 2001. *Cooperation and Conflict*, 47(4), pp. 417–432.

Kaunert, C., Léonard, S. and Occhipinti, J. (2013). Agency Governance in the European Union's Area of Freedom, Security and Justice. *Perspectives on European Politics and Society*, 14(3), pp. 273–284.

Kingah, S. and Zwartjes, M. (2015). Regulating Money Laundering for Terrorism Financing: EU–US Transnational Policy Networks and the Financial Action Task Force. *Contemporary Politics*, 21, pp. 341–353.

Kirchner, E. and Sperling, J. (2007). *EU Security Governance*. Manchester: Manchester University Press.

Kohler-Koch, B. and Rittberger, B. (2006). The 'Governance Turn' in EU Studies. *Journal of Common Market Studies*, 44(1), pp. 27–49.

Krahmann, E. (2003). Conceptualizing Security Governance. *Cooperation and Conflict*, 38(1), pp. 5–26.

Lavenex, S. (2006). Shifting Up and Out: The Foreign Policy of European Immigration Control. *West European Politics*, 29(2), pp. 329–350.

Lavenex, S. (2009). Transgovernmentalism in the European Area of Freedom, Security and Justice. In Amy Verdun and Ingeborg Tömmel (eds), *Innovative Governance in the European Union: The Politics of Multilevel Policymaking*. Boulder, CO: Lynne Rienner, pp. 255–272.

Lavenex, S. and Wagner, W. (2007). Which European Public Order? Sources of Imbalance in the European Area of Freedom, Security and Justice. *European Security*, 16(3–4), pp. 225–243.

Lavenex, S. and Wichmann, N. (2009). The External Governance of EU Internal Security. *European Integration*, 31(1), pp. 83–102.

Leibfried, S., Huber, E., Lange, M., Levy, J.D., Nullmeier, F. and Stephens, J.D. (eds) (2015). *The Oxford Handbook of the Transformations of the State*. Oxford: Oxford University Press.

Merlingen, M. (2011). From Governance to Governmentality in CSDP. Towards a Foucauldian Research Agenda. *Journal of Common Market Studies*, 49(1), pp. 149–169.

Monar, J. (2001). The Dynamics of Justice and Home Affairs: Laboratories, Driving Factors and Costs. *Journal of Common Market Studies*, 39(4), pp. 747–764.

Monar, J. (2014). EU Internal Security Governance: The Case of Counter-terrorism. *European Security*, 23(2), pp. 195–209.

Paoli, L. (2014). How to Tackle (Organized) Crime in Europe? The EU Policy Cycle on Serious and Organized Crime and the New Emphasis on Harm. *European Journal of Crime, Criminal Law and Criminal Justice*, 22(1), pp. 1–12.

Pawlak, P. (2009). Network Politics in Transatlantic Homeland Security Cooperation. *Perspectives on European Politics and Society*, 10 (4), pp. 560–581.

Rhodes, R.A.W. (1996). The New Governance. Governing without Government. *Political Studies*, 44(4), pp. 652–667.

Schroeder, U. (2011). *The Organization of European Security Governance. Internal and External Security in Transition*. London: Routledge.

Shearing, C. and Wood, J. (2003). Nodal Governance, Democracy and the New Denizens. *Journal of Law and Society*, 30(3), pp. 400–419.

Slaughter, A-M. (2004). *A New World Order*. Princeton, NJ: Princeton University Press.

Sperling, J. and Webber, M. (2014). Security Governance in Europe. A Return to System. *European Security*, 23(2), pp. 126–144.

Stoker, G. (1998). Governance as Theory. Five Propositions. *International Social Science Journal*, 50(155), pp. 17–28.

Tazzioli, M. and Walters, W. (2016). The Sight of Migration: Governmentality, Visibility and Europe's Contested Borders. *Global Society*, 30(3), pp. 445–464.

Tekin, F. (2012). *Differentiated Integration at Work. The Institutionalisation and Implementation of Opt-outs from European Integration in the Area of Freedom, Security and Justice*. Baden-Baden: Nomos.

Trauner, F. and Ripoll Servent, A. (2015). *Policy Change in the Area of Freedom, Security and Justice: How EU Institutions Matter*. London: Routledge.

Trauner, F. and Wolff, S. (2014). The Negotiation and Contestation of EU Migration Policy Instruments: A Research Framework. *European Journal of Migration and Law*, 16(1), pp. 1–18.

Van Kersbergen, K. and Van Waarden, F. (2004). 'Governance' as a Bridge between Disciplines: Cross-disciplinary Inspiration Regarding Shifts in Governance and Problems of Governability, Accountability and Legitimacy. *European Journal of Political Research*, 43, pp. 143–171.

Wallace, H. and Lavenex, S. (2005). Justice and Home Affairs. In H. Wallace, W. Wallace and M. Pollack (eds), *Policy-making in the European Union*. Oxford: Oxford University Press, pp. 457–482.

Webber, M. (2014). Security Governance. In J. Sperling (ed.), *Handbook of Governance and Security*. Cheltenham: Edward Elgar, pp. 17–40.

Webber, M., Croft, S., Howorth, J., Terriff, T. and Krahmann, E. (2004). The Governance of European Security. *Review of International Studies*, 18(3), pp. 435–478.

Wunderlich, D. (2012). The Limits of External Governance: Implementing EU External Migration Policy. *Journal of European Public Policy*, 19(9), pp. 1414–1433.

Zürn, M. (1998). *Regieren jenseits des Nationalstaates. Globalisierung und Denationalisierung als Chance*. Frankfurt: Suhrkamp.

Zwolski, K. (2012). The EU As an International Security Actor after Lisbon: Finally a Green Light for a Holistic Approach? *Cooperation and Conflict*, 47(1), pp. 68–87.

3

SECURITIZATION

Turning an approach into a framework for research on EU justice and home affairs

Christian Kaunert and Ikrom Yakubov

Introduction

Since its emergence as an alternative approach to traditional security studies, securitization has become an attractive concept for researchers of EU justice and home affairs, and European studies and international relations more broadly. It has helped to more systematically determine, present and explain how mundane occurrences are transformed into security issues (Stefan 2006; Donnelly 2013; Floyd 2008; Trombetta 2008; Balzacq and Léonard 2013; Diez and Squire 2008; Huysmans 2006; Emmers 2003; Loader 2002; Salter 2011; Sjostedt 2008). This approach was first proposed by the so-called Copenhagen School to underpin the 'widening' remit of security studies. Its devisers, Buzan, Waever and Wilde, defined securitization as 'the move that takes politics beyond the established rules of the game and frames the issue either as a special kind of politics or as above politics' (Buzan et al. 1998: 23). In other words, securitization was presented as

> an intersubjective process that is the most extreme or the highest level of politicisation in which the issue is presented as an existential threat to the referent object by a securitising actor through so-called 'speech acts' and requiring emergency measures and justifying actions outside the normal bounds of political procedure.
>
> *(Buzan et al. 1998: 23)*

The Copenhagen School places a premium on 'speech acts', stressing that the very utterance of 'security' is more than just saying or describing something, but also the performing of an action (Kaunert and Léonard 2011; Stritzel 2007; Balzacq 2011; Roe 2008; Waever 1995).

In this chapter, we would like to suggest that securitization is better conceptualized as a strategic or pragmatic practice – rather than just a speech act as proposed by the Copenhagen School – taking place in a specific set of circumstances, including a specific context and the existence of an audience that has a particular 'psycho-cultural disposition' (Balzacq 2005: 172). From this viewpoint, securitization is understood as 'a sustained strategic practice aimed at convincing a target audience to accept, based on what it knows about the world, the claim that a specific development (oral threat or event) is threatening enough to deserve an immediate policy to alleviate it' (Balzacq 2005: 173). This has important consequences for the securitizing actor, as it means that (s)he is more likely to be successful if (s)he can rightly perceive the feelings and needs of the audience and can use a language that will resonate well with that audience (2005: 184). Audiences may also vary according to the political system and the nature of the issue, an aspect that still needs to be probed further. In recent works on securitization theory, the importance of the political context within which securitization takes place has been emphasized (e.g., Léonard 2007, 2009, 2010; Barthwal-Datta 2012; Léonard and Kaunert forthcoming). However, while scholars have become increasingly sensitized to the importance of political contexts, what remains relatively under-explored is which contexts matter and how they matter. This chapter aims to outline the Copenhagen School approach, as well as the important criticism raised towards it. It further aims to outline a framework that helps with the way in which we can use securitization but, while so doing, also outline the challenges in examining EU justice and home affairs issues. While its use can sometimes prove challenging, this framework nonetheless provides an excellent starting point for further analysis of the EU's emerging Area of Freedom, Security and Justice (AFSJ).

Securitization in its original formulation by the Copenhagen School

The end of the Cold War and the emergence of a new security environment in which non-state actors started to play a role almost equal in importance to state actors showed the incoherences and limitations of traditional security studies. The latter concentrated on state actors and their roles, and considered them as rational actors in both domestic and international politics. However, the emergence of terrorist groups with global presence and ideology, international organized crime and money laundering, globalization, cyber threats, societal disputes, and environmental issues called for an alternative perspective that would have higher explanatory value (Phythian 2009: 60–61; Mearsheimer 2006: 234–235).

As a result, the Copenhagen School emerged as an alternative approach that aimed to explore the 'widening' of the security concept. The attempt was to answer the question: 'How could security complex theory be blended with the wider agenda of security studies, which covered not only the traditional military and political sectors but also the economic, societal, and environmental ones?' (Buzan et al. 1998: vii). Therefore, an underlying trait of this approach is that it shifts security from a narrow conceptualization (e.g., military and political) and presents it as a particular type of politics applicable to more fields (Buzan et al. 1998: vii; Waever 1995: 47). The Copenhagen School's 'widening' placed a particular emphasis upon the social aspects of security and built upon three interconnected concepts – security sectors, regional security complexes and securitization (Buzan et al. 1998), the latter being their most salient concept. Indeed, Buzan et al. (1998) considered securitization as a concept that underpinned the 'widening' perspective and helped conceptualize and measure security. It is defined as 'the move that takes politics beyond the established rules of the game and frames the issue either as a special kind of politics or as above politics' (Buzan et al. 1998: 23). They also saw securitization 'as a more extreme version of politicisation'; that is, as an essentially intersubjective process (Buzan et al. 1998: 23; Balzacq 2011: 3), which always occurs 'for the sake' or 'in the name' of security. Therefore, it cannot be studied on its own without scrutinizing the *conditions* or *processes* which have direct implications for security (Buzan et al. 1998: 25).

The most distinguishing feature of securitization is a synthesis of social constructivism and realism. In other words, securitization brings two competing analytical frameworks under one roof. It seeks to complement them by determining and combining their congruent aspects. Furthermore, securitization does not completely negate other schools of thought and methods in international relations and security studies (Buzan et al. 1998: 4; Fierke 2013: 189–196).

It rather embraces a materialist conception of international politics, international relations and security (Flockhart 2012: 82; Waever 1995: 51), while stressing that there are more dimensions and values (e.g., social factors, interactions, belief, language, behavior, ideas, ideologies and identities) in security studies than just material factors (Fierke 2013: 193).

Core tenets of securitization

Securitization presents security as a 'speech act' (Buzan et al. 1998: 26; Waever 1995: 54–55; Roe 2008: 617; Stritzel 2007: 358; Balzacq 2005: 174–179) and is largely defined as a completely intersubjective and socially constructed phenomenon involving four components: (1) A securitizing actor, who sets off securitization through a securitizing move; (2) an issue that is shifted to the level of existential threat via 'speech acts'; (3) a referent object, i.e., an entity that is threatened and requires urgent protection with extraordinary means and measures; and (4) a relevant audience for the 'speech acts' whose assent is sought by a securitizing actor for the implementation of extraordinary measures (Waever 1995: 54–55; Balzacq 2015: 106; Buzan et al. 1998: 40–41; Balzacq et al. 2015: 2; Roe 2008: 618; Stritzel 2007: 362; Kaunert and Léonard 2011: 58; Waever 2008: 581–593). Therefore, it examines a *process* whereby a given actor frames a specific issue as an 'existential threat', which is then presented to a target audience for approval in order to employ extraordinary means and measures (Kaunert and Léonard 2011: 57).

While securitization has become an often-used approach by scholars of international relations, security studies and adjacent disciplines in the post-Cold War era, it has received criticism for being under-theorized. The relationship between the two main agents – a securitizing actor and the audience – and what or who constitute the relevant audience are considered as the most problematic aspects of the approach (Stritzel 2007: 363; Kaunert and Léonard 2011: 57). These criticisms and potential remedies will be examined in more detail in the following section.

From criticisms to improvements

As mentioned, the concept of securitization has been attractive to many disciplines, but several of its assumptions have been criticized. Scholars have maintained that securitization, in its initial formulation by the Copenhagen School, needs improvement. The question of what may be understood as audience and its interactions with a securitizing actor is underdeveloped, lacks precision and is even contradictory (Kaunert and Léonard 2011: 57–65; Stritzel 2007: 363; Eriksson 1999; Balzacq 2011: 1–2; Roe 2008: 617–618). Another point of contestation has been that the process of securitization itself is under-theorized and may need to be reformulated.

The roots of some problematic aspects (e.g., interactions between a securitizing actor and the audience, their constituents and the exact role of the audience) may be found within securitization's basic ontological framework: social constructivism. To be precise, the Copenhagen School took the concepts relating to 'agent' and 'structure' directly from social constructivism and reconceptualized them as a securitizing actor and a relevant audience. This was a fitting theoretical background for the Copenhagen School's new 'widening' perspective and the processes of securitization. However, they failed to engage with the long-standing debate on the relationship between agent and structure (Hay 1995; Hill 2016: 47; Wendt 1999: 58; Carlsnaes 1992, 1994, 2002), which meant that the relationship between a securitizing actor and the audience remained under-theorized. As a result, the academic debate moved on and sought to remedy these shortcomings. A case in point has been Kaunert and Léonard's (2011) reformulation of securitization processes, in which they focus on the original conceptualization of the relationship between a securitizing actor and the audience to better theorize the role of the audience in securitization processes. Their criticism of the original securitization framework is that it 'gave the audience an important role in securitisation processes, as securitisation is presented as a fundamentally intersubjective process' (Kaunert and Léonard 2011: 58). They then argued that 'the Copenhagen School implicitly downplays the role of the audience refuting the idea that the "security-ness" of an issue can be objectively assessed' (2011: 58). Therefore, they showed how two fundamental arguments – on the role of the actor and the audience – are contradictory in the original approach formulated by the Copenhagen School.[1]

This criticism was followed by the proposal to use Kingdon's 'multiple streams framework' to further refine and reconceptualize these aspects (cf. Kingdon 1984). The use of the three streams – problems, politics and policies –

> allows for (1) a clearer operationalisation of key concepts such as securitising actor and audience, (2) an understanding of the audience as actually comprising different audiences, which are characterised by different logics of persuasion, and (3) a more systematic analysis of the linkages between the various audiences and their respective impact on the overall policy-making process.
> (Kaunert and Léonard 2011: 58–64)

While they (2011: 64) seek to develop a more robust and complete securitization framework, they see possibilities for 'convergence and cross-fertilisation' between Kingdon's model and the securitization framework, especially given that the core theoretical assumptions and levels of analysis – based on a constructivist understanding of agenda-setting processes – are almost identical (see also Chapter 4, this volume). The approach bridges Kingdon's 'three-stream model' with a securitization framework and seeks to refine the concepts of securitizing actor, speech acts, the audience and interactions between them.

Other scholars have also contributed to developing and refining the securitization approach. For instance, Eriksson (1999) argued that securitization does not provide a tangible explanation as to why only certain instances of securitization influence the security agenda but not others. Balzac offered a deeper commentary on the concept of securitization, considering that it should be split into philosophical/traditional and social/pragmatic variants. While the former variant reflects the 'speech act'-driven understanding of securitization that reduces security to a conventional procedure, such as marriage or betting, the latter variant is a process-oriented securitization; that is, a strategic process which occurs within and as part of a configuration of circumstances. This includes the context, the psycho-cultural disposition of the audience, and the power that both speaker and listener bring to the interaction (Balzacq 2011: 1–2). The core constituents of the securitization process – speech acts, securitizing actor and the audience – are seen to be equally important for both philosophical and sociological approaches to securitization. Still, their way of operation is fundamentally distinct in each variant. For instance, if the audience is a formal – a given – category for the philosophical view, then the sociological view (Paris School) emphasized the mutual constitution of securitizing actors and their audience (Bigo 1998a, 1998b, 2000, 2001, 2002; Balzacq 2011: 2).

Roe's (2008) contribution went in a similar direction. The multiplicity of audiences requires that a researcher splits securitization into the stage of identification/mobilization and that of implementation. Although the audience is one of the key constituents in securitization processes, its role is marginalized in certain securitization processes, such as in cases of 'institutionalized securitization'. In order to substantiate the claim, the argument has been made that 'most visibly in the military sector, "persistent or recurrent" threats are often institutionalized, with states having "built up standing bureaucracies, procedures and military establishments to deal with those threats"' (Roe 2008: 618; Buzan *et al.* 1998: 27–28). Therefore, in the military sector, a securitizing actor such as the government or military has the ability to securitize an issue without the assent of the audience. He further contended:

> This is particularly so in the case of pre-emptive or covert military strikes – for example, where the need exists for operational details to be kept secret because of the danger of revealing vital information to the enemy. Moreover, a previously successful securitization may legitimize a further series of measures over a given period of time.

As a consequence, the interactions between a securitizing actor and the audience have to be reconceptualized (Roe 2008: 618). Stritzel also sought to better conceptualize the relationship between the core constituents of securitization – securitizing actor, speech acts and audience. The focus is then on the relationships between core constituents in each phase (Stritzel 2007: 360–362).

This scholarly debate suggests that securitization as an approach can still become more mature and refined. Due to its inextricable association with security, securitization will remain as a case-specific approach. Therefore, its usefulness as an analytical framework will depend on the nature of the security issues under research and the researcher's ability to engage with the concept and its operationalization. In the following section, we propose a re-conceptualization of its core tennets – a securitizing actor, the audience and interactions between them – focusing on the case of EU counter-terrorism policies.

Turning an approach into a framework

According to the Copenhagen School and other scholars of securitization, there are two principal constituents in securitization processes – a securitizing actor and the audience – whose interactions, in fact, trigger securitization (Buzan *et al.* 1998: 31–33; Kaunert and Léonard 2011: 61; Vultee 2011: 80; Salter 2011: 117–118; Roe 2008: 620; Stritzel 2007: 368; Balzacq 2011: 13). The literature reveals that political leaders, bureaucracies, governments, lobbyists and pressure groups are mainly seen as a securitizing actor (Buzan *et al.* 1998: 40). However, as mentioned above, what or who constitutes the audience and under what conditions an entity turns into an audience remains unclear.

The Copenhagen School's formulation of a securitizing actor is also contentious, especially since some entities do not fall under the Copenhagen School's definition, but still behave de facto as securitizing actors. An example would be intelligence and security agencies which, due to their *raison d'être* – alerting and warning – act as a securitizing actor (Yakubov 2017). Similarly, supranational organizations like the EU and the UN, which are political, economic and socio-cultural conglomerates, may also actively perform a security actor role in a wide range of security areas, such as counter-terrorism, policing, cyberspace, economic and financial spheres, non-proliferation of WMD, poverty and health issues, as well as space and environmental issues (Zwolski 2013; Rozee 2013). Neither the Copenhagen School nor its critics ever explicitly presented intelligence and security services or supranational organizations as securitizing actors, which may seem contradictory to the 'widening' claim.

This criticism has to be addressed before the securitization approach may be applied to analyze the securitizing role of the EU. Kaunert and Léonard (2012) suggest a reformulation of the securitization approach in order to make the concept of securitization a more flexible analytical tool. For instance, despite not being contemplated in the original approach, a supranational institution like the EU could potentially act as a securitizing actor, given that everything necessary for a securitizing actor to *securitize* (e.g., issue identification, securitizing move, speech acts, interactions, the relevant audience, and crafting and implementing emergency measures) is present. The EU establishes legislation and influences the security agenda of its member states. It comprises all of the necessary conditions for securitization processes; however, due to its convoluted structure, there are multiple actors (the European Council, the Council of the EU, the European Commission) within the EU that could equally participate in securitization processes and constitute a securitizing move. As a result, the relevant audience for the securitizing move may be different depending upon which one of these actors is involved in the process. For instance, if the European Parliament or the EU member states are acting as securitizing actors, EU populations are the most likely audiences. Indeed, the multiplicity of the audience (Roe 2008: 618) and who or what constitutes them depends on the nature of the existential threat as well as the system within which securitization occurs. While reformulating the securitization approach, the multiplicity of its key constituents (e.g., a securitizing actor and the audience) has to be borne in mind; otherwise, securitization may become contradictory to its underpinning claim – 'widening'. In the following section, some of these analytical claims will be tested empirically using the concept of the EU's counter-terrorist policies.

Securitization: avenues for research

In this section, we would like to outline potential avenues for future justice and home affairs research that builds on securitization, notably (1) migration and borders, and (2) terrorism and counter-terrorism. As suggested above, securitization is better conceptualized as a strategic or pragmatic practice rather than a speech act, which makes it more realistic in terms of empirical investigations.

First, the issue of migration has increasingly given rise to intense political debates. It has played a crucial role in several national electoral campaigns over the past few years. In several EU countries, radical right-wing parties campaigning on an anti-immigration platform have achieved electoral successes, including the BNP and UKIP in the UK, the Swedish Democrats, the Freedom Party in Austria under Joerg Haider, and, more recently, Heinz-Christian Strache and Norbert Hofer, Marine Le Pen's National Front in France, the Northern League in Italy, the People's Party in Denmark, the Pim Fortuyn List, as well as the Freedom Party under Geert Wilders in The Netherlands, and the Vlaams Blok (now Vlaams Belang) in Belgium. Nevertheless, the importance of the issue of migration has not been confined to heated electoral debates and rhetoric. It has also become one of the main items on the policy-making agenda in several EU member states. Such developments have prompted numerous observers (including non-governmental organizations (NGOs), journalists and scholars) to claim that migration flows have increasingly been seen as a security threat in Europe and that this interpretation has influenced the development of both EU and domestic policies on asylum and migration. The vast majority of observers have, implicitly or explicitly, drawn upon the Copenhagen School's securitization theory and spoken of the securitization of asylum and migration in the European Union: that is, their social construction as security issues. Indeed, the idea that migration issues have been securitized in the EU – on both domestic and EU levels – has become ubiquitous in the academic literature on the subject. As a result, there has been an active debate on the 'securitization' of the EU asylum and migration policy (Huysmans 2000, 2004, 2006; Bigo 1998a, 1998b, 2001, 2002; Guild 2002, 2003a, 2003b, 2003c, 2004, 2006; Guiraudon 2000, 2003).

Second, the issue of terrorism and counter-terrorism has also given rise to very intense political debates, in particular following the European refugee crisis of 2015. Among scholars of EU counter-terrorism, there are diverging opinions as to what extent EU competences matter in the fight against the global terrorist threat. One the one hand, the EU is characterized as a 'paper tiger' (Bures 2006: 57) and thus is an ineffective counter-terrorism actor. On the other hand, scholars point out that the EU has taken great strides towards increasing integration and encouraging cooperation between member states since 9/11 (Kaunert 2010; see also Chapter 13, this volume). After the 9/11 terrorist attacks, the EU recognized Islamic terrorism conducted by Al-Qaeda and its affiliated organizations as an immediate threat. The European Council declared that 'the fight against terrorism' was a priority objective for the Union (European Council 2001). The event had a very significant impact on how decisions were made in the EU. The US pressured the EU and other international actors to join the war against terrorism.

Thus, even though few scholars have analyzed counter-terrorism from the securitization perspective, it is a very important future avenue for research. There is a misconception that, while migration is clearly not a traditional security issue, terrorism is. This leads scholars, mistakenly, to under-research terrorism from a securitization perspective. However, this is a misunderstanding of the Copenhagen School, as all issues need to be securitized to become a security issue – not just 'soft security issues', but all security issues. In their conceptualization, no policy issue can be a security issue unless it is securitized – their theoretical framework is meant to analyze the process by which this occurs. The following paragraph gives an example of such a securitization process in the EU. After 9/11, a platform for an emerging norm to engage internationally in the 'war on terrorism' was first established with Bush's 'act of war speech' (Kaunert 2010). In this, Bush declared:

> The deliberate and deadly attacks, which were carried out yesterday against our country, were more than acts of terror. They were acts of war. [...] This enemy attacked not just our people but all freedom-loving people everywhere in the world [...] We will rally the world [...] This will be a monumental struggle of good versus evil, but good will prevail.
> *(BBC News, September 12, 2001, cited in Kaunert 2010)*

Bush defined appropriate action in terms of fighting the 'war against terrorism', and made an even stronger case by distinguishing between 'good and evil'. Later, Bush enforced this emerging norm by stating that 'you are either for us or against us'. Thus, the political pressure is such that the appropriate course of action became defined by whether EU governments gave support to US initiatives or not.

While not being involved in the core securitization discourse emanating from Washington, Europe created its own form of securitization by rallying behind the USA. For example, Germany's Chancellor Gerhard Schroeder called on European nations to band together within the framework of the EU to fight global terrorism:

> Only if we put in place common policing and judicial resources can we ensure that there will be no hideouts for terrorists and other criminals in the European Union. [...] We are ready to make Europe into an international player with global influence.

It was now quite clear that the EU would take part in the 'war on terror' (BBC News, October 18, 2001, cited in Kaunert 2010). In the case of the European Arrest Warrant, the Commission followed up this rhetoric politically with a very timely proposal. This proposal for the policy had already been under preparation for about two years before it was launched. Ministers in the AFSJ were under intense pressure to behave appropriately, settle their differences and adopt an ambitious proposal. Therefore, the Commission's strategy was for the arrest warrant to be presented as an anti-terrorist measure and to be amalgamated with other such measures, such as the Framework Decision on the Definition of Terrorism. Since then, the EU has securitized even more related issues. According to Baker-Beall (2009: 189), this includes the legitimization of recourse to war in Afghanistan and Iraq, the creation of the status of enemy combatants, extraordinary rendition and Guantanamo Bay, the strengthening of external border controls, and the introduction of biometric passports and increased surveillance. The important finding in this case is not these counter-terrorism policies and strategies themselves, but rather how and why the EU designed them, and the way in which securitization was used to adopt policies that, hitherto, had been outside the realm of possibility.

Conclusion

This chapter has aimed to turn the securitization approach into a framework through which the role of the constituents of securitization may be outlined. We suggest that securitization is better conceptualized as a strategic or pragmatic practice taking place in a specific set of circumstances, including a specific context. From this viewpoint, securitization is understood as 'a sustained strategic practice aimed at convincing a target audience to accept, based on what it knows about the world, the claim that a specific development (oral threat or event) is threatening enough to deserve an immediate policy to alleviate it' (Balzacq 2005: 173). Audiences of securitizing moves may also vary according to the political system and the nature of the issue. Thus, the role of political contexts needs to be probed further.

However, while difficult to implement, this chapter has argued for the use of a securitization framework as an excellent starting point to further analyze the EU's emerging Area of Freedom, Security and Justice. Kaunert and Léonard (2011) suggested a framework that brings together securitization and Kingdon's policy-making and agenda-setting as a beneficial way forward. They suggested Kingdon's 'three-streams model' (i.e., the problem, policy and politics streams) to further refine securitization. Kingdon's model is also broadly constructivist and analyzes agenda-setting and policy-making. Kaunert and Léonard (2012) contribute to making securitization a more flexible analytical approach by proposing that there can be multiple securitizing actors and audiences, which is particularly relevant in a EU context. The EU is neither a state nor an intergovernmental organization; yet it can securitize, as outlined in some of the empirical paragraphs in this chapter. The EU establishes legislation and influences the security agenda of its member states. This chapter outlined two potential avenues for future research on justice and home affairs using a securitization framework: (1) migration and (2) counter-terrorism. Migration has become a particularly hot topic over the past few years, particularly so in several national electoral campaigns, including Austria, The Netherlands, France and the United States, as well as the Brexit Referendum of 2016. In several EU countries, radical right-wing parties have campaigned on an anti-immigration platform with strong securitization discourses; for example, Norbert Hofer in Austria in 2016, Marine Le Pen's National Front in France in 2017, the Freedom Party under Geert Wilders in The Netherlands in 2017, and UKIP and the Tory Party during the Brexit Referendum of 2016 as well as the General Elections in 2017. Nevertheless, the importance of the issue of migration has not been confined to heated electoral debates and rhetoric; it has also been linked to the issue of terrorism and counter-terrorism, in particular following the European refugee crisis of 2015. Thus, even though fewer scholars have analyzed counter-terrorism from the securitization perspective, it is a very important future avenue for research, especially with the increasingly linked discourse to migration, refugees and borders in Europe after 2015. Baker-Beall (2009) also mentions this issue linkage, including the wars in Afghanistan and Iraq, extraordinary rendition and the strengthening of external border controls.

Yet, what will be most interesting to researchers in the future are not the policies and strategies themselves, but how and why the EU designed them in the first place. This will be the future of scholarship on securitization and the EU's Area of Freedom, Security and Justice.

Note

1 The Copenhagen School argues: 'It is the actor [...] who decides whether something is to be handled as an existential threat'; 'Successful securitisation is not decided by the securitiser but by the audience of the security speech act', and these core arguments are considered as contradictory by other scholars and researchers. For an overview see Buzan et al. (1998: 31).

Bibliography

Baker-Beall, C. (2009). The Discursive Construction of EU Counter-terrorism Policy: Writing the 'Migrant Other', Securitisation and Control. *Journal of Contemporary European Research*, 5(2), pp. 188–206.

Balzacq, T. (2005). The Three Faces of Securitization: Political Agency, Audience and Context. *European Journal of International Relations* (Sage Publications and ECPR-European Consortium for Political Research), 11(2), pp. 171–201.

Balzacq, T. (2011). A Theory of Securitisation: Origins, Core Assumptions, and Variants. In Balzacq, T. (ed.), *Securitization Theory: How Security Problems Emerge and Dissolve*. Abingdon: Routledge, pp. 1–30.

Balzacq, T. (2015). The 'Essence' of Securitisation: Theory, Ideal Type, and a Sociological Science of Security. *International Relations*, 29(1), pp. 103–113.

Balzacq, T. and Léonard, S. (2013). Information-sharing and the EU Counter-terrorism Policy: A 'Securitisation Tool' Approach. In Kaunert, C. and Léonard, S. (eds), *European Security, Terrorism and Intelligence: Tackling New Security Challenges in Europe*. Basingstoke: Palgrave Macmillan, pp. 127–141.

Balzacq, T., Léonard, S. and Ruzicka, J. (2015). 'Securitization Revisited': Theory and Cases. *International Relations Journal* (Sage Publications), 30(4), pp. 494–531.

Barthwal-Datta, M. (2012). *Understanding Security Practices in South Asia: Securitization Theory and the Role of Non-state Actors*. Abingdon: Routledge.

Bigo, D. (1998a). Europe passoire et Europe forteresse: La sécurisation/humanitarisation de l'immigration. In Rea, A. (ed.), *Immigration et racisme en Europe*. Brussels: Complexe, pp. 203–241.

Bigo, D. (1998b). L'Immigration à la Croisée des Chemins Sécuritaires. *Revue Européenne des Migrations Internationales*, 14(1), pp. 25–46.

Bigo, D. (2000). When Two Become One: Internal and External Securitizations in Europe. In Kelstrup, M. and Williams, M.C. (eds), *International Relations Theory and the Politics of European Integration: Power, Security and Community*. London: Routledge, pp. 171–204.

Bigo, D. (2001). Migration and Security. In Guiraudon, V. and Joppke, C. (eds), *Controlling a New Migration World*. London: Routledge, pp. 121–149.

Bigo, D. (2002). Security and Immigration: Toward a Critique of the Governmentality of Unease. *Alternatives*, 27 (Special Issue), pp. 63–92.

Bures, O. (2006) EU Counter-terrorism Policy: A 'Paper Tiger'? *Terrorism and Political Violence*, 18(1), pp. 57–78.

Buzan, B., de Wilde, J. and Waever, O. (1998). *Security: A New Framework for Analysis*. Boulder, CO: Lynne Rienner.

Carlsnaes, W. (1992). The Agency-structure Problem in Foreign Policy Analysis. *International Studies Quarterly*, 36(3), pp. 245–270.

Carlsnaes, W. (1994). In Lieu of a Conclusion: Compatibility and the Agency-structure Issue in Foreign Policy Analysis. In Carlsnaes, W. and Smith, S. (eds), *European Foreign Policy: The EC and Changing Perspectives in Europe*. London: Sage, pp. 274–287.

Carlsnaes, W. (2002). Foreign Policy. In Carlsnaes, W., Risse, T. and Simmons, B.A. (eds), *Handbook of International Relations*. London: Sage, pp. 298–325.

Diez, T. and Squire, V. (2008). Traditions of Citizenship and the Securitisation of Migration in Germany and Britain. *Citizenship Studies*, 12(6), pp. 565–581.

Donnelly, F. (2013). *Securitization and the Iraq War: The Rules of Engagement in World Politics*. Abingdon: Routledge.

Emmers, R. (2003). ASEAN and Securitisation of Transnational Crime in South-east Asia. *The Pacific Review*, 16(3), pp. 419–438.
Eriksson, J. (1999). *Agendas, Threats, and Politics: Securitisation in Sweden*. Paper presented at the ECPR Joint Sessions Mannheim, March 26–31.
European Council (2001). Conclusions and Plan of Action of the Extraordinary Meeting on September 21, 2001. SN140/01.
Fierke, K.M. (2013). Constructivism. In Dunne, T., Kurki, M. and Smith, S. (eds), *International Relations Theories: Discipline and Diversity*. Oxford: Oxford University Press (3rd edn), pp. 189–196.
Flockhart, T. (2012). Constructivism and Foreign Policy. In Smith, S., Hadfield, A. and Dunne, T. (eds), *Foreign Policy: Theories, Actors and Cases*. Oxford: Oxford University Press (2nd edn), pp. 78–93.
Floyd, R. (2008). The Environmental Security Debate and its Significance for Climate Change. *International Spectator*, 43(3), pp. 51–65.
Guild, E. (2002). Between Persecution and Protection – Refugees and the New European Asylum Policy. In *Cambridge Yearbook of European Legal Studies*. Oxford: Hart.
Guild, E. (2003a). International Terrorism and EU Immigration, Asylum and Borders Policy: The Unexpected Victims of 11 September 2001. *European Foreign Affairs Review*, 8(3), pp. 331–346.
Guild, E. (2003b). Immigration, Asylum, Borders and Terrorism: The Unexpected Victims of 11 September 2001. In Gökay, B. and Walkers, R.B.J. (eds), *11 September 2001: War, Terror and Judgement*. London: Frank Cass, pp. 176–194.
Guild, E. (2003c). The Face of Securitas: Redefining the Relationship of Security and Foreigners in Europe. In Craig, P. and Rawlings, R. (eds), *Law and Administration in Europe: Essays in Honour of Carol Harlow*. Oxford: Oxford University Press, pp. 139–153.
Guild, E. (2004). Seeking Asylum: Stormy Clouds between International Commitments and EU Legislative Measures. *European Law Review*, 29(2), pp. 198–218.
Guild, E. (2006). The Europeanisation of Europe's Asylum Policy. *International Journal of Refugee Law*, 18, pp. 630–651.
Guiraudon, V. (2000). European Integration and Migration Policy: Vertical Policy-making as Venue Shopping. *Journal of Common Market Studies*, 38(2), pp. 251–271.
Guiraudon, V. (2003). The Constitution of a European Immigration Policy Domain: A Political Sociology Approach. *Journal of European Public Policy*, 10(2), pp. 263–282.
Hay, C. (1995). Structure and Agency. In Marsh, D. and Stoker, G. (eds), *Theory and Methods in Political Science*. London: Macmillan, pp. 189–206.
Hill, C. (2016). *Foreign Policy in the Twenty-First Century* (2nd edn). London: Palgrave.
Huysmans, J. (2000). The European Union and the Securitization of Migration. *Journal of Common Market Studies*, 38, pp. 751–777.
Huysmans, J. (2004). A Foucaultian View on Spill-over: Freedom and Security in the EU. *Journal of International Relations and Development*, 7(3), pp. 294–318.
Huysmans, J. (2006). *The Politics of Insecurity: Fear, Migration and Asylum in the EU*. London and New York: Routledge.
Kaunert, C. (2010). *European Internal Security: Towards Supranational Governance in the Area of Freedom, Security and Justice*. Manchester: Manchester University Press.
Kaunert, C. and Léonard, S. (2011). Reconceptualising the Audience in Securitisation Theory. In Balzacq, T. (ed.), *Securitization Theory: How Security Problems Emerge and Dissolve*. Abingdon: Routledge, pp. 57–76.
Kaunert, C. and Léonard, S. (2012). Introduction: Supranational Governance and European Union Security after the Lisbon Treaty – Exogenous Shocks, Policy Entrepreneurs and 11 September 2001. *Cooperation and Conflict*, 47(4), pp. 417–432.
Kingdon, J.W. (1984) *Agendas, Alternatives, and Public Policies*. New York: Harper Collins.
Léonard, S. (2007). *The European Union and the 'Securitization' of Asylum and Migration: Beyond the Copenhagen School's Framework*. PhD thesis, Aberystwyth: University of Wales, Aberystwyth.
Léonard, S. (2009). The Creation of FRONTEX and the Politics of Institutionalisation in the EU External Borders Policy. *Journal of Contemporary European Research*, 5(3), pp. 371–388.
Léonard, S. (2010). EU Border Security and Migration into the European Union: FRONTEX and Securitisation through Practices. *European Security*, 19(2), pp. 231–254.
Léonard, S. and Kaunert, C. (forthcoming). *Refugees, Security and the European Union*. Abingdon: Routledge.
Loader, I. (2002). Policing, Securitisation and Democratisation in Europe. *Criminology and Criminal Justice*, 2(2), pp. 125–153.

Mearsheimer, J. (2006). Conversations in International Relations: Interview with John J. Mearsheimer. *International Relations*, 20(2), Part II.

Phythian, M. (2009). Intelligence Theory and Theories of International Relations: Shared World or Separate Worlds? In Gill, P., Marrin, S. and Phythian, M. (eds), *Intelligence Theory: Key Questions and Debates*. Abingdon: Routledge, pp. 54–72.

Roe, P. (2008). Actor, Audience(s) and Emergency Measures: Securitization and the UK's Decision to Invade Iraq. *Security Dialogue* (Sage Publications), 39(6), pp. 615–635.

Rozee, S. (2013). The European Union as a Comprehensive Police Actor. In Kaunert, C. and Léonard, S. (eds), *European Security, Terrorism and Intelligence: Tackling New Security Challenges in Europe*. Basingstoke: Palgrave Macmillan, pp. 40–61.

Salter, M.B. (2011). When Securitisation Fails: The Hard Case of Counter-terrorism Programs. In Balzacq, T. (ed.), *Securitization Theory: How Security Problems Emerge and Dissolve*. Abingdon: Routledge, pp. 116–130.

Sjostedt, R. (2008). Exploring the Construction of Threats: The Securitisation of HIV/AIDS in Russia. *Security Dialogue*, 39(1), pp. 7–29.

Stefan, E. (2006). Should HIV/AIDS be Securitised? The Ethical Dilemmas of Linking HIV/AIDS and Security. *International Studies Quarterly*, 50(1), pp. 119–144.

Stritzel, H. (2007). Towards a Theory of Securitisation: Copenhagen and Beyond. *European Journal of International Relations*, 13(3), pp. 357–383.

Trombetta, M.J. (2008). Environmental Security and Climate Change: Analysing the Discourse. *Cambridge Review of International Affairs*, Special Issue, 21(4), pp. 585–602.

Vultee, F. (2011). Securitisation as a Media Frame. In Balzacq, T. (ed.), *Securitization Theory: How Security Problems Emerge and Dissolve*. New York: Routledge, pp. 77–93.

Waever, O. (1995). Securitization and Desecuritization. In Lipschutz, R.D. (ed.), *On Security*. New York: Columbia University Press, pp. 48–86.

Waever, O. (2008). The Changing Agenda of Societal Security. In Brauch, H.G. *et al.* (eds), *Globalization and Environmental Challenges: Reconceptualising Security in the 21st Century*, ed. Hexagon Series on Human Security and Environmental Security and Peace, Vol. 3. Berlin, Heidelberg, New York: Springer Verlag, pp. 581–593.

Wendt, A. (1999). *Social Theory of International Politics*. Cambridge: Cambridge University Press.

Yakubov, I. (2017). *The Role of Intelligence in Securitization Processes: A Tool or an Agent*. Unpublished PhD dissertation, University of Dundee.

Zwolski, K. (2013). The European Union and International Security: Developing a Comprehensive Approach. In Kaunert, C. and Léonard, S. (eds), *European Security, Terrorism and Intelligence: Tackling New Security Challenges in Europe*. Basingstoke: Palgrave Macmillan, pp. 17–39.

4

PUBLIC POLICY APPROACHES AND THE STUDY OF EUROPEAN UNION JUSTICE AND HOME AFFAIRS

Mark Rhinard

Introduction

Public policy approaches to studying justice and home affairs (JHA) cooperation in the European Union (EU) have proliferated of late, and it is no wonder why. For one, EU policy outputs in this expanding domain have grown. Policy expansion took place against the backdrop of constitutional change in the EU, related mainly to the Maastricht, Amsterdam and Lisbon treaties. The first two treaty changes drew the previously distinct and state-controlled policy domain (Monar 2016) into the EU's supranational legal framework, albeit preserving a degree of intergovernmental control in some areas. The Lisbon Treaty fully incorporated JHA issues into the supranational policy-making framework, complete with the Community Method of decision-making and full participation by EU institutions. Concurrently, JHA policy outputs rose considerably to become one of the more prolific areas of EU policy-making. Recent crises to strike Europe – from mass migration to terrorist attacks – served to further focus both official and scholarly attention in the field and boost outputs. Scholars have been keen to discover the multitude of factors that shape policy outcomes in this vibrant domain, and the toolbox of public policy analysis fits that task appropriately.

This chapter reviews the public policy approach to studying JHA cooperation in the EU and illustrates the kinds of research taking place in line with that approach. A 'public policy approach' is not easy to demarcate from its broader parent discipline of political science, but may be described generally as research concerned with the various factors that shape outcomes in the public policy-making process. This includes the initiation, formulation, adoption and implementation of policy. A focus on policy is not new in EU studies; much research taking place on the EU examines policy-making in some way, shape or form. But it was not always so. For much of the history of the research on the EU – dating back to the late 1950s – international relations approaches dominated the field. As the EU grew into a productive policy-making system not unlike a traditional state, scholars familiar with studying national policy-making turned their attention to European processes. Research agendas shifted from explaining why states cooperate to what the outcomes of cooperation look like. That changed agenda – facilitated and encouraged by EU policy journals and scholarly associations – opened up the intellectual space which many JHA scholars now occupy. Today it is hardly uncommon to read studies that employ public policy concepts such as 'policy entrepreneurs', 'epistemic communities', 'implementation deficits' or 'punctuated equilibrium', to name just a few examples (Zahariadis 2013).

To provide an accessible overview of the public policy approach and to present representative studies in that vein, this chapter first explains how such approaches found their way into EU studies as the broader context within which JHA studies is situated. It then reviews the approach and its traditional emphasis on three sets of factors shaping policy outcomes: actors, institutions and ideas. It illustrates what those factors mean and how they are studied in practice, before offering some cross-cutting concepts that help bring together the study of actors, institutions and ideas in EU policy-making to enhance explanation.

The public policy 'turn' in EU studies and JHA research

The use of public policy approaches to study JHA cooperation in the EU may be traced back to a major debate in the field of EU studies in the early 1990s. The debate, which played out in the pages of journals such as *West European Politics* and *Journal of European Public Policy*, pitted scholars who used the toolkit of international relations (IR) to study the EU against scholars who advocated a move towards approaches drawn from the political science subdiscipline of comparative politics (CP). The former tended to come from the American scholarly community, which was among the first to 'discover' the EU as a fascinating object of study from an IR perspective (Eilstrup-Sangiovanni 2006). American scholars of the EU focused on explaining why and how sovereign states came together to create a dense thicket of rules and obligations to guide cooperation. Indeed, debates between functionalists like Haas (1958) and intergovernmentalists like Hoffmann (1966) structured the field of EU studies from its earliest years, and both are linked to IR-related approaches that continued to dominate theoretical debate (see also Moravcsik 1991).

Comparative politics scholars turned away from questions of interstate relations and explanations of why states integrate and instead took the EU for what it had become: an enclosed, functioning political system that, although not 'traditional' in terms of holding a monopoly of violence within a distinct territory, could be studied using the tools traditionally applied to explaining national political outcomes. Richardson (1996) argued that the EU had 'state-like attributes', thus encouraging a focus on how its institutions work and relate, for instance. Hix critiqued IR scholars for focusing narrowly on 'integration', defined as the sweeping question of system transformation, when they could also, in his opinion, focus on 'politics', understood as policy-making and interaction within a given and authoritative institutional structure (Hix 1994: 11–12; see also Jupille and Caporaso (1999) on this point). Hix argued that the study of EU politics should take precedence over the study of integration and that CP performs better in this area than do approaches based in IR (see also Heritier 1997). Rebuttals came fast and furious (see e.g., Hurrell and Menon 1996) and the debate was launched.

The emergence of CP approaches in the early 1990s – which meant a shift in focus from interstate relations towards state-like politics and policy-making in the EU – created intellectual space and opportunity for various new perspectives, including regulatory politics, executive relations, judicial politics, decision-making models, parliamentary accountability, party systems and public policy-making. In Caporaso's words:

> Understandably perhaps, a newer generation of scholars, uninspired by debates between intergovernmentalism and neo-functionalism, and bemused by all the fuss over abstract terms such as spillover, sovereignty, autonomy, and a non-territorial approach to problem-solving, struck out on their own. Some of them tried the route of policy

analysis (Hix 1994; Heritier 1997). Having grown up with the European Community as a fact of life (rather than a novel experiment), some scholars accept it as a partial polity, within which policy-making can be carried out as if the setting were national.
(Caporaso 1998: 6–7)

These approaches were legitimized and publicized in new journals such as the *Journal of European Public Policy* – started in the early 1990s. Suddenly, various EU policy sectors became the focus of study – including banking, competition, pharmaceuticals, environment, commercial policy, social policy, and eventually, justice and home affairs – on their own merits, using traditional tools of public policy analysis. There was a proliferation of approaches using, for instance, policy networks, advocacy coalitions, agenda-setting, the joint decision trap, framing, process dynamics, punctuated equilibrium, policy streams and policy entrepreneurship in the pages of EU-focused books and articles.

Categorizing these approaches is not an easy task, but for the sake of stocktaking it is useful to identify the central empirical focus of analysis used in various approaches. Those foci are *actors*, mainly in the guise of networks and organizations acting as policy change agents; *institutions*, namely as constraining or enabling structures in which policy-making takes place, and *ideas*, or deep-seated normative and cognitive beliefs about what policy should achieve. Reviewing approaches in this fashion allows us to pinpoint the various analytical tools and methods used to study the main factors which shape JHA policy outcomes. Of course, some approaches span two or more of these categories; these are both noted below and highlighted in the conclusion as important avenues for further analytical development.

Actor-based approaches

A popular way to study EU policy-making is to focus on the actors directly involved in it. In some respects this is obvious. The people crafting, deciding upon, shaping and implementing policies are human beings with histories, mindsets, preferences and strategies that directly affect outcomes. The broader question facing scholars in public policy research on the EU, however, is to show how and why actors shape policies. This section examines several actor-based explanations typically used to do so and illustrates how they have been used by JHA scholars. Actor-based explanations often invoke the concepts of 'policy networks', 'advocacy coalitions' and 'epistemic communities' to help explain JHA outcomes. Studies of 'policy entrepreneurship' also fit into this category, since, whether key motivators of policy change are individuals or organizations, they tend to behave as relatively coherent actors. This section expounds upon these four agendas.

Policy networks

A central public policy approach to studying outcomes is to focus on the various constellations of actors involved in policy-making. Actors do not act alone, nor do they act in strict hierarchies. On the contrary, early work on actor-based approaches to policy-making at national levels countered conventional, formalistic models of policy-making with a more accurate account of the modern policy process. Richardson and Jordan (1979) kick-started research on 'policy networks' in the late 1970s, which initially used the concept as a heuristic device for identifying the many stakeholders, or sets of actors in specific policy domains, as a first step to analyzing the detailed process of policy-making (Thatcher 1998). Stakeholders seeking policy change or defending existing policies appreciate that interests cannot be pursued unilaterally;

they know that 'collaboration may be the best means of extending the Pareto boundary to mutual advantage' (Richardson 1996: 36).

Networks are useful for studying policy-making in the EU because they proliferate in a political system that: lacks a unified center of power, displays significant bureaucratic fragmentation, and has a highly fluid and unpredictable policy process (Rhinard 2010). Indeed, networks are the preferred mode of organization among actors participating in, and seeking influence over, policy-making in the EU (Peterson 1995). For observers of the EU political system, the network concept helps us understand and analyze the 'loose-jointed power play' taking place among actors participating in policy-making (Richardson 1996: 36). For practitioners, networks serve the critical purpose of drawing together key stakeholders and resources essential to protecting turf, preparing policy and promoting change.

Public policy research, however, has differentiated various kinds of networks. The 'Rhodes Model' of network analysis uses the term 'policy network' as an umbrella description of actor-based networks on a continuum, ranging from tightly integrated 'policy communities' at one end to looser, less consensual 'issue networks' at the other. In between these extremes lie different types of networks distinguished by (1) the relative stability (or instability) of network membership, (2) the relative insularity (or permeability) of networks, and (3) the relative strength (or weakness) of resource dependencies (Rhodes 1990, 2008). Various distinctions on the network spectrum, from policy communities to issue networks, can usefully help identify key actors, their durability and their dependencies in various domains of EU policy-making.

The general policy network approach (as opposed to the specific use of epistemic communities or advocacy coalitions) has been used effectively by Den Boer and colleagues (2008) to illustrate how, in European law enforcement circles, counter-terrorism networks tend to be preferred to formal bureaucratic structures because of their flexibility and directness. The authors find that the 'clubbiness' of privileged networks, however, can undermine EU agencies and EU institutions seeking to formalize policy-making.

Epistemic communities

An actor-focused approach with particular relevance for EU policy-making encompasses networks of knowledge-based experts, or 'epistemic communities' (Haas 1992). This approach represents a refinement of the generic policy network model, insofar as Haas and his colleagues explain more precisely coalition formation and durability as well as mechanisms of influence. The term *epistemic community* defines 'a network of professionals with recognized expertise and competence in a particular domain and an authoritative claim to policy-relevant knowledge' within that domain or issue area (Haas 1992: 3; see also Dunlop 2013). The dependent variable in the original epistemic community model is the behavior of states in international policy coordination, but Haas' approach is employed in an array of policy explanations, including EU monetary union (Verdun 1999), EU tax policy (Radaelli 1997), and even security cooperation (Cross 2011).

The approach rests on the premise that policy-making in modern societies is complex and uncertain. Such conditions drive policy-makers towards the use of knowledge-based communities of actors or 'epistemic communities'. These groupings operate on the basis of shared expertise and beliefs – beliefs that influence policy when the community's advice is solicited by policy-makers or when community members gain administrative positions in governments and bureaucracies. Epistemic communities remind us that actor-based networks form not only because actors share common material interests. Actors holding certain beliefs also 'tend to affiliate and identify themselves with groups that likewise reflect and seek to promote those beliefs' (Haas 1992: 19).

A leading proponent of the epistemic community approach in JHA studies is Bossong (2007, 2012), who uses it to illustrate how new networks of counter-terrorism experts converged on the EU JHA policy domain after September 11. These experts, many of whom shared a common professional background as ex-governmental officials or highly specialized academics, worked with Commission officials and national diplomats to craft anti-terror legislation in the EU. Cross (2007) uses the concept to show how transnational experts, promoting and employing certain security technologies to enhance internal security intelligence, may be seen to be building a 'homeland security' supranational order.

Advocacy coalitions

Another kind of actor-based approach used to study EU policy-making is the 'Advocacy Coalition Framework' (ACF). An ACF approach characterizes policy processes by the presence of several coalitions. Like the policy network model, advocacy coalition analysis directs our attention to the domain level of policy-making. Sabatier and his collaborators tell us to look broadly when identifying advocacy coalition members. His basic premise challenges the conventional notion that an actor's organizational affiliation is primordial – that 'interest group leaders and legislators are politically active in seeking to influence public policy, while agency officials, researchers, and journalists tend to be perceived as more passive and/or policy indifferent' (Sabatier 1998: 107; see also Sabatier and Jenkins-Smith 1993). Advocacy coalitions may include elected and agency officials, researchers, journalists and interest group leaders who may not share similar roles in the policy process but do share a particular belief system and show a non-trivial degree of coordinated activity over time. Coalitions, bound by shared beliefs, will seek to alter policies and institutions over a period of a decade or more, incrementally if necessary, in their effort to provoke change.

Of all the actor-based, network-oriented explanations of EU policy outcomes, perhaps advocacy coalitions are most prevalent in theory and practice. This is consistent with findings that multiple advocacy coalitions characterize most EU policy domains (Dudley and Richardson 1998), and makes sense intuitively: the relatively open policy-making process of the EU attracts a wide array of actors, and collective action demands the organization of such actors into cohesive and durable coalitions. Drawn together by shared beliefs, advocacy coalition members bring a wide, diverse array of participants and resources to bear upon policy outcomes. This makes them particularly well suited for influencing policy change, in that membership includes 'insiders' and 'outsiders' from the policy-making process (Rhinard 2010). Indeed, this is the kind of coalition frequently noted by Bossong (2007; Bossong and Rhinard 2013) as highly active in the JHA domain, and helps explain policy change in areas such as Passenger Name Recognition (PNR) and counter-terrorism. However, it should be noted that research shows little evidence of tightly bound, lasting advocacy coalitions in the field of JHA – partly because the field is still developing a stable, equilibrium set of dominant actors (Bossong and Rhinard 2013; Ripoll Servent and Trauner 2014).

Policy entrepreneurship

Another public policy approach with an actor-focused orientation centers on organizational entrepreneurship. These kinds of studies are popular within the domain of JHA studies: they emphasize how organizations like the European Parliament or European Commission have either carved out a role for themselves in shaping JHA outcomes or in taking the lead in policy development (the fact that these studies focus on EU 'institutions' should not distract from the fact that they are actor-focused analyses examining the 'actorness' of different organizations). The notion of EU institutions as policy entrepreneurs dates back several decades, although early use of the concept focused mainly on the European Commission (Cram 1994; Fligstein and Mara-Drita 1996; Nugent 1995; Wendon 1998). The European Commission continues to be the main focus of analysts as a policy entrepreneur (Rhinard 2010), and within the JHA domain has been studied by authors like Kaunert (2010) and Caviedes (2016), who both adopt a sweeping perspective on the role of the Commission in helping to build the Area of Freedom, Security and Justice (AFSJ) over several decades and via several treaty revisions, as well as Bossong (2012), who demonstrates the cultivating role played by the Commission in forging new, supportive policy coalitions. The policy entrepreneur perspective, however, has been broadened to include other EU institutions' roles in JHA policy-making. Thus, Kaunert and Della Giovanna (2010) examine the Council Secretariat's role in building consensus on terrorism financing regulations. Groundbreaking studies have been written on the entrepreneurship qualities of the European Parliament by Ripoll Servent (2015) and Trauner (2012), who examine the critical oversight and influence role won (and exploited) by the EP over JHA policy in recent treaty revisions. Another institution with growing influence over JHA policy outcomes is the Court of Justice of the EU (CJEU), examined by Mitsilegas in terms of how the Court has established a critical presence in shaping policy (2016) and by Kaunert and Léonard in terms of how actors have used the CJEU as a new 'venue' for policy competition (2012). The concept of policy entrepreneurship is closely related to approaches using the 'multiple streams framework', in which problems, policies and politics flow through different streams but are occasionally drawn together by entrepreneurs to produce change (Kingdon 1995; Argomaniz 2009; Bossong 2012). Since multiple streams approaches attempt to bridge actor-based, institution-based and idea-based concepts, further discussion is found in the conclusion of this chapter.

Institutional-focused approaches

During the 1990s, the 'institutionalist turn' across the social sciences took hold in EU studies. Some scholars turned away from actor-focused approaches towards perspectives that prioritized the rules, norms and scripts that shape actor behavior (Hall and Taylor 1996). Institutions, at their most basic, may be described as the 'rules of the game' or, more formally, 'as the humanly devised constraints that shape human interactions' (North 1990: 3). Not all approaches to studying institutional effects on policy outcomes agree on the fundamental relationship between actors and institutions (whether actors shape structures or whether structures shape actors). That debate explains the wide variety of approaches captured by the 'new institutionalism' moniker from the 1990s. New institutionalism suggests that the institutional context in which policy-making occurs constrains, refracts and shapes behavior.

What was 'new', at the time, about the approach was two-fold. First, the interpretation of what constitutes an institution was broadened. There was a shift away from formal constitutional-legal approaches to government, with their tendency to be configurative (Bulmer 1998: 369). A new institutionalist focus encompassed the less formalized arenas of policy-making and the less explicit routines and patterns of behavior which structure those arenas. Second, the new institutionalism highlights the 'beliefs, paradigms, codes, cultures, and knowledge' embedded within institutions (March and Olsen 1989: 26). The approach recognizes that institutional values are important, since 'the machinery of government is steeped in norms and codes of conduct', and it is difficult to separate formal institutional rules from their normative context (Bulmer 1998: 369).

Thus, the fountainhead of new institutionalism gave way to many small streams of research which are difficult to easily categorize. One way to do so is to use the popular heuristic of the three branches of new institutionalism which each emphasize different aspects and effects of institutions (for a full review, see Hall and Taylor 1996; Peters 1999).

Historical institutionalism

The historical variant of new institutionalism was one of the first to emerge within political science, and is most concerned with the constraining and 'path-dependent' impact of institutional structures (Krasner 1984; Pierson 1998). Here, the legacy of the past is considered crucial: choices made when an institution is being formed, or when a policy is initiated, will have a continuing and even deterministic influence over behavior and policy outcomes. Initial patterns will persist unless there is some force sufficient to overcome them. A historical institutional approach has been used to explain how varying 'historical capacities' and 'policy legacies' result in different policy trajectories in different countries over time (Weir and Skocpol 1985; Thelen and Steinmo 1992). In the EU setting, historical institutionalism has proved useful in studying how EU policy-making can often appear bound by past decisions: situations of 'lock in' and 'path dependency' (Pollack 2009).

In the area of JHA studies, historical institutionalism has been employed less than other institutionalist variants, arguably because the policy field has a relatively recent history. When it has been used, historical institutionalism reveals the critical importance of critical junctures – usually terror attacks – which shift policy-making in new directions. That is the orientation of Wolff (2009), for instance, in exploring how terrorism served to speed up the institutionalization of counter-terrorism as a mainstream EU policy area (see also Argomaniz (2009) for research that shares a similar historical perspective on the development of institutions for counter-terrorism policy in the EU). The findings of a comparative project by Boin and colleagues (2008), which measured levels of the institutionalization of different JHA policy sub-sectors, also falls into the historical institutionalism category because it examines the key factors that shaped institutional development in multiple sectors over time. Ekelund (2014) demonstrates the advantages of using historical institutionalism over rational choice institutionalism to explain the evolution of Frontex, not only because it is sensitive to key moments in time but also because it can draw in contextual factors to exchange change. In this case, the enlargement of the EU to include Malta and Cyprus – two island nations in the Mediterranean with high migration exposure – helped fuel the rise of Frontex. Argomaniz (2009) applies a historical institutionalist perspective to explain path dependence in the evolution of EU counter-terrorism cooperation, focusing on how major terrorist attacks served to shift, incrementally, the direction of policy – in line with the 'punctuated equilibrium' concept associated with historical institutionalism (Baumgartner and Jones 1993).

Sociological institutionalism

A more sociologically oriented approach to institutions developed within the field of organizational theory. Here, scholars emphasize the 'thicker' end of the institutional spectrum by studying the normative and cultural dimensions that shape behaviors in modern organizations (Powell and DiMaggio 1991). According to sociological institutionalists, these forms should be seen not as the result of a rational search for ever-more efficient structures, but rather as culturally specific practices. In the words of McNamara (2002: 59), 'the choice of organizational form is linked to social processes that legitimate certain types of institutional choices as superior to others'.

According to this approach, even the most seemingly bureaucratic of practices in the lowest administrative arenas must be understood in light of cultural values, symbols and scripts that guide action (March and Olsen 1989: 39–52). Individuals turn to these broader values in order to interpret not only what 'should' be done, but what 'can' be done (Powell and DiMaggio 1991). Eventually, established routines and familiar patterns of behavior emerge to guide political action in a domain. In this sense, domain-level routines are linked to broader cultural norms and values. Actors 'embrace specific routines and patterns of behavior because the latter are widely valued within a broader cultural environment' (Hall and Taylor 1996: 949). Certain behaviors are thus legitimized as 'socially appropriate' and appear to 'make sense' to policy-making actors. Sociological institutional approaches differ in the degree to which they attribute causal effect to the social elements of institutions. To simplify the point, some authors argue that socially constructed norms drive human behavior, while others argue that such norms can be strategically constructed.

Since sociological institutionalist approaches resemble the ideational approaches discussed below, this section highlights JHA research which uses sociological institutionalism in comparison to historical and rational choice variants. Testing the logics of decision-making in a comprehensive study of the JHA Council, for instance, Aus (2008) finds that the 'logic of appropriateness', with its social determinants, rather than the 'logic of consequentiality', can dominate intergovernmental decision-making under certain conditions (a similar, more generic argument may be found in Lewis (2000); while a counter-argument may be found in Cortinovis (2015)). Ripoll Servent (2012) compared the relative explanatory power of institutionalisms when analyzing the emergence of security norms in the European Parliament. She finds that rational choice institutionalism cannot explain that emergence, and argues that scholars must look at the broader, social process of change linked to the EP's desire to become more 'responsible' under co-decision. Kostakopoulou (2005) explains changing norms on European citizenship using a sociological institutionalist logic, although she qualifies her findings. She includes actors' creative capacities to produce, construct, change and transform discursive landscapes, which inform and shape, but do not determine their identities. This is emblematic of a growing effort in recent years to bridge the institutionalisms (see, e.g., Jupille *et al.* 2003).

Rational choice institutionalism

A third variant of new institutionalism may be described as being at the 'thin' end of institutionalism. Rational choice institutionalism builds upon an essentially rational choice model of politics, in which policy-making is characteristically viewed as a series of collective action dilemmas and in which the ontology is focused on individual action. Institutions assist actors in solving such dilemmas by providing a means of avoiding risk, reducing transaction costs and ensuring compliance (Ostrom 1991). In this way, the rational choice institutionalism approach integrates a prominent model of the individual with a role for structural variables like institutions. Peters points out two important elements of this version of new institutionalism (1999). On the one hand, it assumes that individuals will act rationally within the constraints imposed upon them by the layers of rules which structure a decision arena. On the other hand, the actors making decisions within such institutions are not as atomistic as they may appear in 'pure' rational choice models. Institutions in this approach are conceptualized as 'permitting a range of behaviors, as well as prescribing and proscribing other behaviors' (Peters 1999: 175).

Rational choice approaches enjoy a long history of use in JHA analysis, as Ripoll Servent and Kostakopoulou (2016) show elsewhere. Some of these analyses investigate how key actors exploit existing institutionally provided opportunities for policy influence. Such a focus underpins analysis of 'venue-shopping' – when sufficiently strategic actors shift policy competition to different venues in order to enhance their chances of shaping outcomes. Guiraudon (2000) was the first to illuminate how national governments, for instance, expanded JHA cooperation in the EU partly as a strategy to bypass domestic institutional constraints (e.g., 'prying' parliaments and 'inconvenient' courts). Lavenex (2006) undertook research in the same vein, noting how national governments sought to avoid the institutional constraints that came with supranational policy-making (e.g., participation by the Commission and CJEU) by placing some internal security issues like counter-terrorism in the external policy realm of the EU, where member states have more control.

Other kinds of studies follow a similar track in showing how actors use existing institutions to enhance their influence. One such approach focuses on 'principal–agent' dynamics. These studies explore why and how principals (typically member states) choose to delegate authority to a particular agent (typically EU institutions) in order to enhance efficiency in policy-making. Under some conditions, agents can move beyond their initial remits to affect policy outcomes in unintended ways (Pollack 1994). Thus, Stetter (2000) shows that JHA questions were moved to the Community Method of decision-making (the 'first pillar') under the Amsterdam Treaty only because member state principals added special controls on supranational agents like the Commission. Other authors expand the principal–agent assumptions to examine how institutions like the European Parliament act as principals in trying to control EU agencies such as Frontex or Europol, which are increasingly active in JHA policy-making (Kaunert *et al.* 2013; Trauner 2012; but see Ekelund 2014) or examine how the European Parliament attempts to shape international negotiators when internal security agreements are being made with third countries (Ripoll Servent 2014). In a similar vein, but focusing mainly on the actions of national governments, Adler-Nissen (2009) shows how member states with formal 'opt-outs' in JHA policy-making manage to circumvent formal rules to influence policy outcomes.

Other studies do not assume static institutions but instead reveal how they can be strategically changed to enhance the policy preferences of certain actors. The present author set out these kinds of approaches in a book on the subject (Rhinard 2010) and within the JHA field specifically, similiar studies have emerged. Thus, Balzacq and Hadfield (2012) have examined the emergence and strategic design of institutional arrangements associated with the Prüm Treaty, noting that these 'differentiated' arrangements do not actually lead to integration progress. Because they are filled with concerns regarding the protection of power and interests, they can lead to suboptimal policy outcomes. Cortinovis (2015) shows how member states manipulated institutions structuring Frontex's mandate and operating guidelines, keeping some of the soft law elements that characterized previous cooperation in order to maximize their own control. As may be noted here, too, fewer scholars of late take an 'either-or' approach to applying institutionalisms, with most seeking theoretical complementarity.

Ideas-based approaches

The last of three categories of public policy research examined in this chapter, namely ideas-based approaches, examines the constitutive effects of cognitive and normative factors on policy outcomes. Studies in this category argue that interests and institutions cannot explain everything about why policy looks the way it does. As Hall famously argued, policy-making takes place within an 'interpretive' or 'ideational' framework that must be accounted for in analysis (Hall 1989: 383; see also Hall 1993; Schmidt 2008). What is called the 'ideas-based' literature within political science consists of analyses within comparative politics, political economy, foreign policy and historical analysis that bring ideas, culture and other cognitive factors back into the analysis of politics (for reviews, see Yee 1996; Béland and Cox 2011). Scholars employ cognitive factors to explain how policy processes are shaped, and how national deviations in policy adoption can be explained by the transmission or rejection of certain ideas (Hall 1989, 1993; Kingdon 1995; Radaelli 1997; Sabatier and Jenkins-Smith 1999). Scholars working within the field of international relations have argued that economic and rational choice explanations of decision-making cannot explain certain policy outcomes adequately; the solution, they maintain, is to include cognitive factors in the causal equations that explain outcomes (Goldstein and Keohane 1993).

Where scholars in this category differ from sociological institutionalists is in the degree to which they attribute causation to the 'power of ideas'. As Ripoll Servent and Kostakopoulou (2016) show, sociological institutionalists working in the field of JHA studies generally take a 'thin' approach to social structures, arguing that such structures can be manipulated and exploited (e.g., 'lesson-learning') by public policy officials. The ontology of ideas-based approaches, in contrast, is oriented towards much more deeply rooted structures which shape behavior in subconscious ways. JHA studies in this vein include the work by Bigo (2016) and Huysmans (2006) who, although working with empirical material highlighting professional actors and social networks, note how deep-seated behaviors in the actions of policy-makers change because of who they engage with, the rationales which are (subconsciously) assumed, and the way in which problems are conceived and acted upon. Studies focused on the lack of cohering concepts in the field of JHA studies also fall into this category. For instance, scholars like Allum and Den Boer (2013) reveal conceptual (in)coherence in organized crime cooperation in the EU and note how it inhibits effective approaches, while Bossong and Rhinard (2013) look at the failure of the EU's Internal Security Strategy to guide action in any deep-seated, meaningful way owing to conceptual fuzziness and fragmentation. A related use of ideas-based approaches to studying JHA outcomes is the work done on 'narratives' as powerful shapers of behavior – and thus as important factors necessary for understanding policy outcomes (Boswell et al. 2011).

The securitization literature, which has been used to a considerable extent in studying JHA cooperation in the EU, studies the evolution of threat discourses which shape security policy in critical ways. These discourses may be partly strategic, but even the public officials making the 'utterances' in question are not fully aware of how the pre-existing ideational environment influences how discourses are constructed (Balzacq 2010, 2016). 'Securitization practices' have been the focus of Léonard (2010), who examines how the daily practices of Frontex and Commission officials have led, intentionally or not, to the securitization of border control in the EU. A slightly different empirical perspective was used by Neil (2009), who found that member states' securitizing activities played little role in shaping the rules and structures establishing Frontex.

Conclusion: cross-cutting approaches and next steps in research

The public policy approach to studying JHA cooperation in the EU sheds much light on what is emerging from this increasingly active and vibrant policy domain. It asks what factors shape policy outcomes and, as seen above, tends to group factors into key *actors* (usually working in networks or defined as organizations), structuring *institutions* and constitutive *ideas*. The focus is not just on actors, institutions and ideas alone it is also on the processes by which these key determinants of policy outcomes emerge, develop and intermingle. The public policy approach may not speak to the big questions of 'where Europe is going' or 'what drives integration' but it answers equally critical questions about the main forces shaping policies that constitute the EU and directly affect citizens' lives. If anything, the public policy approach seems to be gaining speed as a preferred way of studying the JHA domain – even if the EU as a whole, at the time of writing, is undergoing an unprecedented critique from national levels. Nevertheless, several aspects of the public policy approach to studying JHA in the EU deserve to be further developed.

The final part of this chapter thus looks at three aspects that have been cast into sharp relief by recent empirical developments and the need to engage in bridge-building across public policy approaches.

The first aspect concerns how increasing Euroskepticism across the EU may influence policy outcomes in Brussels. Euroskepticism could potentially influence policy-making from different angles. One is a slowing interest at national levels in 'uploading' policy ideas for collective consideration in Brussels. Another, more immediate, question is how Euroskepticism may be shaping domestic administrations and how they handle European policies. Will political resistance (in some quarters, and among some parties) trickle down into administrations and slow the machinery of everyday policy cooperation? The assumption of a 'slow-down' in JHA policy-making should be carefully assessed, however, since a paradox is present in this domain. Growing Euroskepticism exists side by side with political enthusiasm for JHA cooperation in the wake of terror attacks in several European countries. How will this paradox be reconciled? Trauner (2016) has embarked upon studying this intriguing set of policy-related questions, and the general study of implementation problems in JHA has generated some thought-provoking initial findings (Block 2011; Argomaniz 2010), but more research needs to be done.

The second aspect concerns the Lisbon Treaty's *communautarization* of the JHA field. As is well known, the application of the Community Method to JHA decision-making via its move to the first pillar has been slow but steady, with some safeguards put in place to ensure member state control. But for the most part a new mode and pattern of policy-making has been identified. A number of studies of individual EU institutions' roles in policy-making post-Lisbon have emerged, as described above, but few researchers systematically measure the nature of the current mode of governance now underway (cf. Trauner and Ripoll Servent 2015). The question beckoning is whether it is truly *communautarized* or whether some sort of modified 'intergovernmental-plus' arrangement (akin to the classic definition of 'intensive transgovernmentalism' by Wallace 2000) is now operating. Some studies have touched upon this question, and Caviedes (2016) has made some important inroads, but more work is needed to systematically assess the extent of what is also called the 'normalization' of JHA policy-making.

The third aspect that deserves to be further explored relates not to real-life events but to theoretical orientations. As exemplified by this chapter, public policy approaches – both in general and when they are applied to JHA cooperation – fall into the three categories previously described. More work must be done in bridging these categories to show, for instance: how actors manipulate institutions; precisely how and when ideas shape policy-makers' actions; and, when institutions change in ways that undermine both actor networks and ideas. To an extent, the new institutionalisms are accomplishing some of this bridge-building, with work on 'opportunity structures' and 'venue-shopping', as discussed earlier, revealing how strategic actors interact with existing institutions. Incisive research using Kingdon's 'multiple streams' approach (1995) also succeeds in drawing together previously isolated analytical categories, as demonstrated by Bossong (2012). More work should be done, however, on how actors manipulate institutions and ideas when recrafting (e.g., helping to institutionalize or reinstitutionalize) policy domains within JHA. A great deal of research has alluded to the strategic intent of actors, not only in shaping outcomes but also in shaping institutions to lock in long-term advantages for particular interests and ideas. But few studies systematically specify how, when and with what effect actors strategically shape institutions, a gap also identified by Saurugger (2013).

Two exceptions to this gap stand out which could be developed further. One is Ripoll Servent and Kostakopoulou's work on constructivist institutionalism, which not only melds rational choice and sociological institutionalism, but more importantly specifies the key variables that contribute to an actor-based theory of non-linear, incremental and transformative institutional change in JHA matters. Specifically, they show how actors 'produce, construct, change, and transform discursive landscapes' (Ripoll Servent and Kostakopoulou 2016: 153; see also Ripoll Servent and Busby 2013). Another is the present author's work on 'strategic framing', by which actors package culturally and socially attractive narratives, mobilize supportive networks around them, and use those networks to embed institutions with new values. The approach theorizes across the three categories and applies to newer policy domains and more mature policy domains alike (Rhinard 2010).

With additional attention devoted to these three research gaps, the use of public policy approaches to studying JHA cooperation in the EU is bound to not only continue its upward trajectory but – more importantly – to improve our understanding of JHA policy outcomes well into the future.

Acknowledgment

This chapter benefited from research assistance and editorial help provided by Sarah Backman (Stockholm University) and Costan Barzanje (Swedish Institute of International Affairs).

Bibliography

Adler-Nissen, R. (2009). Behind the Scenes of Differentiated Integration: Circumventing National Opt-outs in Justice and Home Affairs. *Journal of European Public Policy*, 16(1), pp. 62–80.
Allum, F. and Den Boer, M. (2013). United We Stand? Conceptual Diversity in the EU Strategy against Organized Crime. *Journal of European Integration*, 35(2), pp. 135–150.
Argomaniz, J. (2009). Post-9/11 Institutionalisation of European Union Counter-terrorism: Emergence, Acceleration and Inertia. *European Security*, 18(2), pp. 151–172.
Argomaniz, J. (2010). Before and After Lisbon: Legal Implementation as the "Achilles Heel" in EU Counter-terrorism? *European Security*, 19(2), pp. 297–316.
Aus, J. (2008). *EU Governance in an Area of Freedom, Security and Justice: Logics of Decision making in the Justice and Home Affairs Council*. University of Oslo.
Balzacq, T. (2010). *Securitization Theory: How Security Problems Emerge and Dissolve*. London: Routledge.
Balzacq, T. (2016). Securitization: Understanding the Analytics of Government. In R. Bossong and M. Rhinard (eds), *Theorizing Internal Security Cooperation in the European Union*. Oxford: Oxford University Press.
Balzacq, T. and Hadfield, A. (2012). Differentiation and Trust: Prüm and the Institutional Design of EU Internal Security. *Cooperation and Conflict*, 47(4), pp. 539–561.
Baumgartner, F.R. and Jones, B.D. (1993). *Agendas and Instability in American Politics*. Chicago, IL: Chicago University Press.
Béland, D. and Cox, R.H. (2011). *Ideas and Politics in Social Science Research*. Oxford: Oxford University Press.
Bigo, D. (2016). International Political Sociology: Internal Security as Transnational Power Fields. In R. Bossong and M. Rhinard (eds), *Theorizing Internal Security Cooperation in the European Union*. Oxford: Oxford University Press.
Block, L. (2011). *From Politics to Policing: The Rationality Gap in EU Council Policy-making*. The Hague: Eleven International Publishing.
Boer, M. Den, Hillebrand, C. and Nölke, A. (2008). Legitimacy under Pressure: The European Web of Counter-terrorism Networks. *Journal of Common Market Studies*, 46(1), pp. 101–124.
Boin, A., Ekengren, M. and Rhinard, M. (2008). *Security in Transition: Towards a New Paradigm for the European Union ACTA Series*. Stockholm: Swedish Defence College.
Bossong, R. (2007). The Action Plan on Combating Terrorism: A Flawed Instrument of EU Security Governance. *JCMS: Journal of Common Market Studies*, 46(1), pp. 27–48.
Bossong, R. (2012). *The Evolution of EU Counter-terrorism: European Security Policy After 9/11*. London: Routledge.

Bossong, R. and Rhinard, M. (2013). The EU Internal Security Strategy: Towards a More Coherent Approach to EU Security? *Studia Diplomatica*, 66(2), pp. 45–58.

Boswell, C., Geddes, A. and Scholten, P. (2011). The Role of Narratives in Migration Policy Making: A Research Framework. *The British Journal of Politics & International Relations*, 13(1), pp. 1–11.

Bulmer, S.J. (1998). New Institutionalism and the Governance of the Single European Market. *Journal of European Public Policy*, 5(3), pp. 365–386.

Caporaso, J. (1998). Regional Integration Theory: Understanding Our Past and Anticipating Our Future. *Journal of European Public Policy*, 5(1), pp. 1–16.

Caviedes, A. (2016). European Integration and the Governance of Migration. *Journal of Contemporary European Research*, 12(1), pp. 552–U202.

Cortinovis, R. (2015). The Evolution of Frontex Governance: Shifting from Soft to Hard Law?. *Journal of Contemporary European Research*, 11(3), pp. 252–267.

Cram, L. (1994). The European Commission as a Multi-organization: Social Policy and IT Policy in the EU. *Journal of European Public Policy*, 1(2), pp. 195–217.

Cross, M.K.D. (2007). An EU Homeland Security? Sovereignty vs. Supranational Order. *European Security*, 16(1), pp. 79–97.

Cross, M.K.D. (2011). *Security Integration in Europe*. Ann Arbor, MI: University of Michigan Press.

Dudley, G. and Richardson, J. (1998). Arenas without Rules and the Policy Change Process: Outsider Groups and British Roads Policy. *Political Studies*, 19, pp. 727–747.

Dunlop, C.A. (2013). Epistemic Communities. In E. Araral et al. (eds), *Routledge Handbook of Public Policy*. London: Routledge, pp. 229–243.

Eilstrup-Sangiovanni, M. (2006). *Debates on European Integration: A Reader*. Basingstoke: Palgrave Macmillan.

Ekelund, H. (2014). The Establishment of FRONTEX: A New Institutionalist Approach. *Journal of European Integration*, 36(2), pp. 99–116.

Fligstein, N. and Mara-Drita, I. (1996). How to Make a Market: Reflections on the Attempt to Create a Single Market in the European Union. *American Journal of Sociology*, 102(1), pp. 1–33.

Goldstein, J. and Keohane, R.O. (1993). *Ideas and Foreign Policy: Beliefs, Institutions, and Political Change*. Ithaca, NY: Cornell University Press.

Guiraudon, V. (2000). European Integration and Migration Policy: Vertical Policy-making as Venue Shopping. *Journal of Common Market Studies*, 38(2), pp. 251–271.

Haas, E.B. (1958). *The Uniting of Europe: Political, Social, and Economic Forces, 1950–1957*. Stanford, CA: Stanford University Press.

Haas, P. (1992). Introduction: Epistemic Communities and International Policy Coordination. *International Organization*, 46(1), pp. 1–35.

Hall, P.A. (1989). *The Political Power of Economic Ideas*. Princeton, NJ: Princeton University Press.

Hall, P.A. (1993). Policy Paradigms, Social Learning, and the State: The Case of Economic Policymaking in Britain. *Comparative Politics*, 25(3), pp. 275–296.

Hall, P.A. and Taylor, R.C.R. (1996). Political Science and the Three New Institutionalisms. *Political Studies*, 44(5), pp. 936–957.

Heritier, A. (1997). Policy-making by Subterfuge: Interest Accommodation, Innovation and Substitute Democratic Legitimation in Europe – Perspectives from Distinctive Policy Areas. *Journal of European Public Policy*, 4(2), pp. 171–189.

Hix, S. (1994). The Study of the European Community: The Challenge to Comparative Politics. *West European Politics*, 17(1), pp. 1–30.

Hoffmann, S. (1966). Obstinate or Obsolete? The Fate of the Nation-state and the Case of Western Europe. *Daedalus*, 95(3), pp. 862–915.

Hurrell, A. and Menon, A. (1996). Politics Like Any Other? Comparative Politics, International Relations and the Study of the EU. *West European Politics*, 19(2), pp. 386–402.

Huysmans, J. (2006). Agency and the Politics of Protection: Implications for Security Studies. In J. Huysmans, A. Dobson and R. Prokhovnik, eds, *The Politics of Protection: Sites of Insecurity and Political Agency*. London: Routledge.

Jupille, J. and Caporaso, J.A. (1999). Institutionalism and the European Union: Beyond International Relations and Comparative Politics. *Annual Review of Political Science*, 2(1), pp. 429–444.

Jupille, J., Caporaso, J.A. and Checkel, J.T. (2003). Integrating Institutions: Rationalism, Constructivism, and the Study of the European Union. *Comparative Political Studies*, 36(1/2), pp. 7–41.

Kaunert, C. (2010). The Area of Freedom, Security and Justice in the Lisbon Treaty: Commission Policy Entrepreneurship? *European Security*, 19(2), pp. 169–189.

Kaunert, C. and Della Giovanna, M. (2010). Post-9/11 EU Counter-terrorist Financing Cooperation: Differentiating Supranational Policy Entrepreneurship by the Commission and the Council Secretariat. *European Security*, 19(2), pp. 275–295.

Kaunert, C. and Léonard, S. (2012). The Development of the EU Asylum Policy: Venue-shopping in Perspective. *Journal of European Public Policy*, 19(9), pp. 1396–1413.

Kaunert, C., Léonard, S. and Occhipinti, J.D. (2013). Agency Governance in the European Union's Area of Freedom, Security and Justice. *Perspectives on European Politics and Society*, 14(3), pp. 273–284.

Kingdon, J.W. (1995). *Agendas, Alternatives, and Public Policies*. New York: Longman.

Kostakopoulou, D. (2005). Ideas, Norms and European Citizenship: Explaining Institutional Change. *The Modern Law Review*, 68(2), pp. 233–267.

Krasner, S. (1984). Approaches to the State: Alternative Conceptions and Historical Dynamics. *Comparative Politics*, 16(2), pp. 223–246.

Lavenex, S. (2006). Shifting Up and Out: The Foreign Policy of European Immigration Control. *West European Politics*, 29(2), pp. 329–350.

Léonard, S. (2010). EU Border Security and Migration into the European Union: FRONTEX and Securitisation through Practices. *European Security*, 19(2), pp. 231–254.

Lewis, J. (2000). The Methods of Community in EU Decision-making and Administrative Rivalry in the Council's Infrastructure. *Journal of European Public Policy*, 7(2), pp. 261–289.

March, J.G. and Olsen, J.P. (1989). *Rediscovering Institutions: The Organizational Basis of Politics*. New York: The Free Press.

McNamara, K.R. (2002). Rational Fictions: Central Bank Independence and the Social Logic of Delegation. *West European Politics*, 25(1), pp. 47–76.

Mitsilegas, V. (2016). Rule of Law: Theorizing EU Internal Security Cooperation from a Legal Perspective. In R. Bossong and M. Rhinard (eds), *Theorizing Internal Security Cooperation in the European Union*. Oxford: Oxford University Press.

Monar, J. (2016). EU Internal Security Cooperation after Four Decades: Observations and Reflections. In R. Bossong and M. Rhinard (eds), *Theorizing Internal Security Cooperation in the European Union*. Oxford: Oxford University Press.

Moravcsik, A. (1991). Negotiating the Single European Act. *International Organization*, 45(1), pp. 651–688.

Neil, A.W. (2009). Securitization and Risk at the EU Border: The Origins of FRONTEX. *JCMS: Journal of Common Market Studies*, 47(2), pp. 333–356.

North, D.C. (1990). *Institutions, Institutional Change and Economic Performance*. Cambridge: Cambridge University Press.

Nugent, N. (1995). The Leadership Capacity of the European Commission. *Journal of European Public Policy*, 2 (February 2015), pp. 603–623.

Ostrom, E. (1991). *Governing the Commons*. Newbury Park, CA: Sage.

Peters, B.G. (1999). *Institutional Theory in Political Science: The New Institutionalism*. London: Pinter.

Peterson, J. (1995). Decision-making in the European Union: Towards a Framework for Analysis. *Journal of European Public Policy*, 2(1), pp. 69–93.

Pierson, P. (1998). The Path to European Integration: A Historical-institutionalist Approach. In W. Sandholtz and A. Stone Sweet (eds), *European Integration and Supranational Governance*. Oxford: Oxford University Press, pp. 27–58.

Pollack, M.A. (1994). Creeping Competence: The Expanding Agenda of the European Community. *Journal of Public Policy*, 14(2), pp. 95–145.

Pollack, M.A. (2009). The New Institutionalisms and European Integration. In A. Wiener and T. Diez (eds), *European Integration Theory*. Oxford: Oxford University Press, pp. 125–144.

Powell, W.M. and DiMaggio, P.J. (1991). *The New Institutionalism in Organizational Analysis*. Chicago, IL: Chicago University Press.

Radaelli, C.M. (1997). *The Politics of Corporate Taxation in the European Union: Knowledge and International Policy Agendas*. London: Routledge.

Rhinard, M. (2010). *Framing Europe: The Policy Shaping Strategies of the European Commission*. Boston, MA: Martinus Nijhoff.

Rhodes, R.A.W. (1990). Policy Networks: A British Perspective. *Journal of Theoretical Politics*, 2(3), pp. 292–316.

Rhodes, R.A.W. (2008). Policy Network Analysis. In R.E. Goodin, M. Moran and M. Rein (eds), *The Oxford Handbook of Public Policy*. Oxford: Oxford University Press, pp. 425–443.

Richardson, J. (1996). *European Union: Power and Policy Making*. London: Routledge.

Richardson, J. and Jordan, G. (1979). *Governing Under Pressure: The Policy Process in a Post Parliamentary Democracy*. Oxford: Martin Robertson.

Ripoll Servent, A. (2012). Playing the Co-decision Game? Rules' Changes and Institutional Adaptation at the LIBE Committee. *Journal of European Integration*, 34(1), pp. 55–73.

Ripoll Servent, A. (2014). The Role of the European Parliament in International Negotiations after Lisbon. *Journal of European Public Policy*, 21(4), pp. 568–586.

Ripoll Servent, A. (2015). *Institutional and Policy Change in the European Parliament: Deciding on Freedom, Security and Justice*. Basingstoke: Palgrave Macmillan.

Ripoll Servent, A. and Busby, A. (2013). Introduction: Agency and Influence inside the EU Institutions. *European Integration online Papers (EIoP)*.

Ripoll Servent, A. and Kostakopoulou, D. (2016). Institutionalism: Shaping Internal Security Cooperation in the EU. In R. Bossong and M. Rhinard (eds), *Theorizing Internal Security Cooperation in the European Union*. Oxford: Oxford University Press, pp. 153–175.

Ripoll Servent, A. and Trauner, F. (2014). Do Supranational EU Institutions Make a Difference? EU Asylum Law before and after 'Communitarization'. *Journal of European Public Policy*, 21(8), pp. 1142–1162.

Sabatier, P.A. (1998). The Advocacy Coalition Framework: Revisions and Relevance for Europe. *Journal of European Public Policy*, 5(1), pp. 98–130.

Sabatier, P.A. and Jenkins-Smith, H.C. (1999). The Advocacy Coalition Framework: An Assessment. In P.A. Sabatier (ed.), *Theories of the Policy Process*. Boulder, CO: Westview Press.

Sabatier, P.A. and Jenkins-Smith, H.C. (1993). *Policy Change and Learning: An Advocacy Coalition Approach*. Boulder, CO: Westview Press.

Saurugger, S. (2013). Constructivism and Public Policy Approaches in the EU: From Ideas to Power Games. *Journal of European Public Policy*, 20(6), pp. 888–906.

Schmidt, V.A. (2008). Discursive Institutionalism: The Explanatory Power of Ideas and Discourse. *Annual Review of Political Science*, 11(1), pp. 303–326.

Stetter, S. (2000). Regulating Migration: Authority Delegation in Justice and Home Affairs. *Journal of European Public Policy*, 7(1), pp. 80–103.

Thatcher, M. (1998). The Development of Policy Network Analyses: From Modest Origins to Overarching Frameworks. *Journal of Theoretical Politics*, 10(4), pp. 389–416.

Thelen, K. and Steinmo, S. (1992). Historical Institutionalism in Comparative Politics. In K. Thelen, S. Steinmo and F. Longstreth (eds), *Structuring Politics: Historical Institutionalism in Comparative Analysis*. Cambridge: Cambridge University Press, pp. 1–32.

Trauner, F. (2012). The European Parliament and Agency Control in the Area of Freedom, Security and Justice. *West European Politics*, 35(4), pp. 784–802.

Trauner, F. (2016). Asylum Policy: The EU's 'Crises' and the Looming Policy Regime Failure. *Journal of European Integration*, 38(3), pp. 311–325.

Trauner, F. and Ripoll Servent, A. (2015). *Policy Change in the Area of Freedom, Security and Justice: How EU Institutions Matter*. Abingdon: Routledge.

Verdun, A. (1999). The Role of the Delors Committee in the Creation of EMU: An Epistemic Community? *Journal of European Public Policy*, 6(4), pp. 308–328.

Wallace, H. (2000). The Policy Process: A Moving Pendulum. In H. Wallace and W. Wallace (eds), *Policy-making in the European Union*. Oxford: Oxford University Press, pp. 39–64.

Weir, M. and Skocpol, T. (1985). State Structures and the Possibilities for Keynesian Responses to the Great Depression in Sweden, Britain and the United States. In P.B. Evans, D. Rueschemeyer and T. Skocpol (eds), *Bringing the State Back In*. Cambridge: Cambridge University Press, pp. 107–164.

Wendon, B. (1998). The Commission as Image-venue Entrepreneur in EU Social Policy. *Journal of European Public Policy*, 5, pp. 339–353.

Wolff, S. (2009). The Mediterranean Dimension of EU Counter-terrorism. *Journal of European Integration*, 31(1), pp. 137–156.

Yee, A. (1996). The Causal Effects of Ideas on Policies. *International Organization*, 50(1), pp. 69–108.

Zahariadis, N. (2013). Building Better Theoretical Frameworks of the European Union's Policy Process. *Journal of European Public Policy*, 20(6), pp. 807–816.

PART III

Analyzing justice and home affairs policies (the sectoral dimension)

5
ASYLUM AND REFUGEE PROTECTION
EU policies in crisis

Petra Bendel and Ariadna Ripoll Servent

Introduction

Asylum has become a key subject of debate in national and European politics, especially since what has been named the 'refugee crisis' of 2015 and 2016. The countries of the European Union (EU) have always been normatively attached to the international regime that emerged following the 1951 Geneva Refugee Convention. After all, the need for international norms on refugee protection came as a response to the post-war situation in Europe. However, it was not until the 1990s that the policy area was regarded as a matter of common interests. Its origins relate to the 'compensatory measures' of the Schengen project. EU cooperation has, therefore, been characterized by the difficult efforts of member states to find ways to share the responsibility of asylum-seekers. On the one hand, they work to guarantee international norms and rights, and on the other, there is an unwillingness to show solidarity towards those in need or fellow member states. This chapter reviews the evolution of EU asylum policies by outlining the main rationales behind its construction and its failures to deal with recent increases in the number of asylum-seekers. It then considers the main debates that have accompanied the construction of this policy field, focusing on four aspects: burden-sharing, securitization, institutional change and externalization. In view of the current political and institutional development, the conclusion provides some gaps that can serve as a starting point for future research.

Evolution of EU asylum policies

EU asylum policies have been at the avant-garde of EU action in the field of justice and home affairs. The need to find a solution at the European level emerged as a spill-over of the Schengen project and has tested the willingness of member states to cooperate and share their responsibility for asylum-seekers. The history of EU asylum policies may be divided into three main periods: the first dates back to 1957, when member states started to coordinate their asylum policies within the framework of the European Economic Community (EEC). Although the EEC did not have genuine competences in this area, its member states did recognize the need to cooperate in internal security matters, especially after the signature of the 1985 Schengen Agreement. The second period started in 1990 with the signature of the Dublin Convention and is characterized by its intergovernmental nature. Given that Schengen planned to abolish the internal borders between participating member states, there were growing concerns that this might lead to increased "asylum-hopping" or "asylum-shopping" (as it was named pejoratively) – that is, asylum-seekers profiting from the open borders and trying their luck in several member states. On the other hand, human rights activists feared that Schengen would end up creating refugees 'on orbit'; that is, unable to ascertain which country was responsible for guaranteeing them the international protection they were seeking. These fears were accentuated by the rapid influx of refugees during the wars in the former Yugoslavia, which saw a peak in the number of asylum claims, especially in Germany. Member states recognized that Schengen required a new form of cooperation at the European level, since they needed to find a form to determine who was responsible for taking care of those seeking asylum (Guild 2006; Lavenex 2001). Despite attempts by the German government to introduce a distribution key that would share the number of applications proportionally to the size of each member state, the idea was rejected in favor of a 'responsibility system'. This principle determined that responsibility should be allocated to the member state that let asylum-seekers into the Schengen territory and naturally led to the 'first country of entry' logic that still constitutes the core of the Dublin logic and the whole EU asylum system (Thielemann and Armstrong 2013).

Since this principle does not allow asylum-seekers to choose a specific country to submit their claim for protection, it became evident that the EU should also try to harmonize national asylum systems so that people would have, at least approximately, the same chances and enjoy the same standards wherever they were asked to lodge their application. To this effect, the Treaty of Maastricht (1992) determined that asylum policy would from then on be regarded as a matter of common interest (i.e., be Community-regulated), but incorporated it as part of the third pillar, which gave national governments control over policy outputs. Recurrent deadlocks in the Council led to a major institutional shift in the Treaty of Amsterdam (1997), which inaugurated the third phase in the development of this policy field. The Treaty shifted asylum policies to the first pillar, which meant a 'communitarisation' of the field. Unwilling to let go of their control, member states introduced a transitional period, in which decision-making remained intergovernmental. It was, thus, not until 2005 that asylum policies came to be decided under qualified majority voting (QMV) in the Council and co-decision with the European Parliament (changed into the 'ordinary legislative procedure' by the Treaty of Lisbon).

This third phase also saw the emergence of multi-annual working programs decided by the European Council that set out the main policy directions for justice and home affairs. The first of these programs, agreed in Tampere in 1999, set out an ambitious, liberal plan that aimed to create a pro-active and coherent Common European Asylum System (CEAS). The Commission followed up on the program with various proposals for directives and regulations that set up the basic standards of the CEAS. These core legislative texts aimed to determine who could claim to be a refugee (the so-called Qualification Directive 2003/9/EC), how asylum-seekers should be received in the member states (Reception Directive 2005/85/EC) and which procedural rights they enjoyed during the asylum process (Asylum Procedures Directive 2004/83/EC). The Commission also proposed to integrate the Dublin Convention as a regulation into EU legislation and to help its implementation with a new database that collected the fingerprints of asylum-seekers (Dublin and EURODAC Regulation 2000/2725/EC, 2003/343/EC). These efforts were supported by a new European Refugee Fund, established initially for the period from 2000 to 2004 (2000/596/EC) and in existence until 2013, when it was incorporated into the Asylum, Migration and Integration Fund (AMIF). In addition, two directives were agreed upon in order to regulate the rights of long-term residents (2003/109/EC) and establish the standards for giving temporary protection in the event of a mass influx of displaced persons (2001/55/EC), although the latter has never been activated. Although the initial proposals by the Commission followed the liberal spirit instituted by Tampere, the change in direction of asylum policies was short-lived, especially after the adoption of the Hague Programme in 2004, which was far less ambitious and more security-oriented. The return to a more restrictive stance on asylum policies was a response to the rise in security concerns that followed the terrorist attacks of 11 September 2001 and 11 March 2004 in Madrid, which changed the perception of migration, and also reflected a new political constellation in the Council (Guild 2006; Ripoll Servent and Trauner 2014).

The Stockholm Programme, following in 2009, was decided upon under changed political circumstances: Member states were more sceptical with regard to supranational decisions and reluctant to further harmonize asylum policies. Consequently, the proposals made by the Swedish presidency to introduce the mutual recognition of asylum decisions and to create a strong asylum office (which eventually became the European Asylum Support Office, EASO) were watered down. In this context, the reform of the CEAS between 2005 and 2013 proved slow and difficult. The recast of the main legal texts showed the unwillingness of member states to create a properly harmonized CEAS and did not introduce major changes that would effectively avoid the inconsistent implementation of EU asylum policy at the national level (Ripoll Servent and Trauner 2014). Consequently, recognition rates, reception conditions and asylum procedures continued to vary strongly across member states – what has become known as the 'asylum lottery' (ECRE 2008; see also Toshkov and Haan 2013). The 2014 Strategic Guidelines for the area of freedom, security and justice were criticized, once again, for being strongly driven by the interests of national ministries of the interior, who promoted a return to intergovernmentalism (Carrera and Guild 2014). Therefore, it is not surprising, that the Commission saw the necessity to propose a new revision of the CEAS legislation in the aftermath of the 2015 'refugee' crisis. Cooperation in the field of asylum has not been restricted to internal policy-making. Indeed, refugee protection is closely linked to border management as well as to immigration and visa policies; it is also becoming increasingly dependent on cooperation with third countries (see Chapters 6, 9 and 10). As a result, the focus of EU asylum policies has gradually moved towards external issues, which means an increasing overlap with foreign, security and defense policy. Cooperation with countries of origin and of transit has been present since 2005, particularly since the Global Approach for Migration and its 2011 successor, the Global Approach for Migration and Mobility (see also Lavenex 2006). The influx of asylum-seekers to Europe in 2015 and 2016, often named a 'refugee crisis' (although it was rather a crisis of refugee policies), emphasized the use of policies designed to tackle the root causes of migration and reduce the drivers for onward migration after asylum-seekers have arrived to transit destinations like Turkey or northern Africa. This has led to new concerns about the trend towards an externalization or extra-territorialization of EU asylum policies.

The main scholarly debates

Research on EU asylum policy has followed its rapid Europeanization and placed a special emphasis on its institutional development (cf. Bendel 2007; Guild 2006; Ripoll Servent and Trauner 2014; Thielemann and Armstrong 2013). Indeed, they have often been analyzed critically both in law and political science, which shows how inter- or rather multi-disciplinarity has thus far remained one of the key features of academic debates on EU asylum and refugee policies (e.g., Carlier and De Bruycker 2005; Hailbronner 1998). Indeed, asylum is a policy area which raises particular challenges because it is tightly embedded in international law (Lavenex 2001; Roos and Zaun 2014), which has led legal and political science scholars to emphasize normative issues based on human rights – with some adopting a pro-active and even activist orientation

(Baldaccini *et al.* 2007; Bendel 2016; Huysmans 2006). This trend results from the interaction between academics and non-academics coming from think-tanks (for instance, the European Policy Center, the Migration Policy Institute, the Center for European Policy Studies), INGOs (notably UNHCR), European agencies like the Fundamental Rights Agency, Frontex and EASO as well as NGOs (especially the European Consortium for Refugees and Exiles (ECRE)), who have together built a rights-based policy agenda and sought actively to give policy advice, lobbying for refugee and migrant rights (Thiel and Uçarer 2014; see also Chapters 38 and 39, this volume). Although many of these contributions show numerous overlaps, we distinguish between four main debates: the nature of European integration, the content of EU asylum policies, the impact of institutional change on policy change and the trend towards externalization and extra-territorialization.

The nature of European integration: burden-sharing and the principle of responsibility

The question of why member states agreed to cooperate in this policy area has been at the core of academic debates from the start. Thus, research has concentrated on understanding the nature of the problem and why it has been so difficult to implement proper 'burden-sharing' solutions. Indeed, in view of the inequalities that have emerged in the aftermath of the Dublin Convention, it is still difficult to understand why member states at the border accepted this solution. One potential answer comes from 'public goods' theories, which have shown how the emphasis on external borders is due to Schengen being based on a 'weakest link': internal security can only be ensured as long as the weakest member state protects the external border as well as the strongest. This logic led to a very particular distribution of costs and benefits, and may explain why member states at the border accepted the Dublin Convention – taking responsibility for the borders was seen as a tradeoff for the benefits they would enjoy as members of the Schengen area. Dublin was, therefore, the entry price they had to pay to get into the Schengen club (Thielemann 2003; Thielemann and Armstrong 2013). Dublin certainly led to unexpected consequences: not only did it shift the number of applications towards countries at the EU's external borders, but it also helped entrench and even amplify a cleavage between 'strong regulators' like Germany, the United Kingdom, The Netherlands, France and Sweden, which had well-functioning domestic asylum systems and 'weak regulators' like Greece, Italy and Portugal, whose administrations were less effective and could not cope with extensive reforms to their asylum systems (Zaun 2017). Despite efforts to offset these weaknesses by providing 'in-kind' assistance, most notably in the shape of financial contributions through the European Refugee Fund (ERF) (Thielemann 2005) and operational support through EASO, the need to improve 'burden-sharing' and to find a more balanced form of cooperation among member states remains a major debate in academic and non-academic spheres (e.g., Angenendt *et al.* 2013; Thielemann 2010).

Securitization

The literature on burden-sharing served also to show how asylum policies had acquired a negative overtone in EU policy-making. The term 'burden' already pointed to the negative light in which refugees and asylum-seekers were frequently perceived by the member states. In addition, the link between Schengen and Dublin reinforced the potential for 'securitizing' asylum policies, since they were treated primarily as an after-effect of external border management. As a result, many researchers paid increasing attention to the content of EU asylum policies, pointing in particular to the aspects of securitization and control that had also been highlighted in border studies (Bendel *et al.* 2011; Huysmans 2006; Lavenex 2001). This strand of the literature used critical security studies to show how further stressing security aspects in asylum policies might jeopardize a vision centered on the protection needs of asylum-seekers and refugees. On the other hand, others pointed to the fact that minimum common rules agreed at the EU level had prevented a 'race to the bottom' and provided asylum-seekers with a minimum level of protection (El-Enany and Thielemann 2011; Kaunert and Léonard 2012). This debate was largely influenced by normative stances and led to a lively debate between research and activism, but it also served to highlight the importance of looking beyond policy outputs and examining the actual impact of EU policies upon member states' practices. Indeed, the first efforts to create a CEAS showed that minimum standards left the member states too much room for maneuver and thus thwarted a real 'common' asylum system. Ever since, lack of coherence has been an important claim; member states have tended to 'cherry-pick' only certain standards while leaving out others in the transposition and implementation of commonly agreed norms (El-Enany 2013; Zaun 2017). These debates have continued following the 2013 reform of the CEAS and the so-called 'refugee crisis' in 2015. They have underlined the need to distinguish between two policy dimensions: substantive content and procedural disagreements over the level of EU integration. In the first case, the extent to which asylum policies have been securitized continues to be disputed – the reform of the CEAS in 2013 did show some improvements, but did not manage to put a rights-based approach at the core of policy debates (Chetail *et al.* 2016; Ripoll Servent and Trauner 2014). As for the level of integration, scholars have also questioned whether the EU proposals corresponded to the aims proclaimed in the Tampere and the Hague work programs, underlining that the need for more common European actions should be reinforced (Berger and Heinemann 2016).

Institutional and procedural aspects

The observation on the nature of this policy area and its level of integration has opened up questions regarding the role of supranational EU institutions and their capacity to influence policy outputs. This line of research has concentrated on the process of institutional change this policy area has witnessed since the early 1990s and whether the shift in decision-making rules has contributed to substantial policy changes. We can appreciate two waves of scholarly debate (see also Bonjour *et al.* 2017). The first one was largely influenced by the institutional architecture provided by the Schengen Agreement and the Treaty of Maastricht. The predominance of intergovernmentalism led to the observation that national governments were using the EU as an alternative policy-making 'venue', which made it easier for them to upload more restrictive views on migration and circumvent potential critical voices at the domestic level, a phenomenon known as 'venue-shopping' (Guiraudon 2000). In the area of asylum, this particularly benefited 'strong regulators', which were able to upload their national standards to the EU level (Zaun 2017).

The second wave emerged alongside the formal institutional changes introduced in the Treaty of Amsterdam, which led to a normalization of policy-making in the area of asylum as of 2005 and the subsequent empowerment of the EU's supranational institutions (the Commission, the EP and the CJEU). Their shifting roles in legislation were important research topics for scholars of 'classical' EU and comparative politics (Boswell 2008; Uçarer 2001). This line of research started to question the validity of the 'venue-shopping' thesis, considering that, with their growing role in decision-making, supranational EU institutions now had the power to 'constrain' member states and force a more liberal view on migration policies (Bendel *et al.*

2011; El-Enany and Thielemann 2011). In the area of asylum, Kaunert and Léonard (2012) noted the need to evaluate asylum policies as more liberal than other contiguous areas, notably border policies. They also assumed that the EP, the CJEU and the Commission would contribute to rebalancing EU policy outputs towards a rights-based approach. Some scholars noticed that the liberal character of the EU institutions was taken as a *fait accompli* that needed to be tested in real life (Maurer and Parkes 2007). The process that led to the recasting of the CEAS in 2013 showed that, in general, the Commission and the EP were largely willing to accommodate the wishes of member states in the area of asylum: this means that legislative reforms served to introduce only secondary changes in non-controversial areas, but still left wide room for manoeuvre to national administrations that did not encourage efforts to close the existing gaps in implementation (Bendel 2013; Ripoll Servent and Trauner 2014).

These empirical findings have opened up new lines of research and brought to our attention the need to merge institutional and policy studies: in order to understand policy-making in the area of asylum, developments such as the increasing importance of consensus in co-decision negotiations or the political role of the European courts in migration matters have to be taken into account (Costello 2012; see also Chapters 32 and 33, this volume). Since the late 2000s, several decisions were taken by the European Court of Human Rights (ECtHR) on the national asylum systems as well as on the CEAS, particularly regarding the Dublin system. It is indeed due to the intervention of the Courts that member states stopped sending people back to countries like Greece or Bulgaria, which were considered to provide insufficient standards of protection (Mitsilegas 2014). In addition, these continued failures in the implementation stage have underlined the importance of practical operational cooperation and the networking potential of Frontex and the EASO. Indeed, these two agencies have been strengthened and further supranationalized after 2015: both agencies are to receive stronger powers of monitoring and coordination. This means that, in cases where member states may not be able to cope with border control or asylum procedures, the agencies may intervene in that member state, whether or not it wishes to receive their support. The aim would then be to gradually eliminate the differences in acceptance rates and thus end the asylum 'lottery' that continues to exist in Europe.

External dimensions of migration and extra-territorialization of protection responsibilities

Besides developing a CEAS, from 2000 onward the European Commission began to stress the idea of a 'coherent global approach to migration' or the need to develop the 'external dimension' of migration (Boswell 2003; Papagianni 2013). This trend led to the development of a Global Approach for Migration (2005), replaced by the Global Approach for Migration and Mobility in 2011, which included both a strategy for asylum and for legal migration and development. Here, the scholarly debate has focused again on procedural and substantive dimensions of the 'external dimension'. When it comes to procedural matters, Lavenex (2006) remarked how the gradual communitarization of migration policies led to shifting the 'venue-shopping' strategy from the internal to the external domain, since foreign policy remains under the control of member states. Indeed, others have remarked upon the possibilities of 'cross-pillarization', which means that instruments of foreign policy become increasingly used in justice and home affairs policies (Pawlak 2009). On the substantive side, some have raised concerns about the loose framework developed by the European Commission, which made intensive use of instruments such as returns and readmission agreements for those who are not able to secure some sort of international protection in a EU member state (den Heijer 2012; Giuffré 2013; see also Chapter 7, this volume). However, asylum policies have been particularly affected by the trend towards 'outsourcing' or 'extra-territorializing' protection responsibilities to third countries, for instance, by expanding the use of 'safe third countries' of origin and transit, using development and trade to force countries at the border to enhance the control of their borders or launching initiatives for extraterritorial processing of asylum applications (Gammeltoft-Hansen 2012; Garlick 2006; Levy 2010; Sterkx 2008).

The 2015 crisis of EU refugee policies

This previous overview of EU legislation and the main academic debates it has raised in the last couple of decades should help in understanding why we are now witnessing what many have come to call an 'asylum' or 'refugee crisis'. This crisis reached its peak in late 2015/early 2016, but several incidents, like the repeated drownings on the shores of Lampedusa in 2013, had already served as warning signs. Indeed, only a month after the reform of the CEAS was concluded in June 2013, there were voices claiming that there was a need to reform the EU's asylum policies (Bendel 2013; Ripoll Servent and Trauner 2014). The crisis has, therefore, showed mostly the failure to harmonize refugee protection at the EU level, and the lack of solidarity, shared responsibility and trust among member states. The efforts to find a common solution to the problem have revealed the lack of political will to reach a consensus on a reform of the common asylum policy and has led to 'Council-mania' (Bertoncini and Pascouau 2016: 2) that has put the European Council at the core of decision-making and emphasized national instead of European solutions. Even the reform of the CEAS, which was started in 2016 with the aim of speeding up the asylum process and harmonizing standards across the EU, has been confronted with serious deadlocks. The rapid growth in numbers of asylum-seekers during these years has led to an unprecedented political polarization among the member states and within the EU institutions. This manifested itself especially in disputes about the (mandatory) distribution of refugees. Underlying these conflicts remains a deep disagreement about both the question of EU competences and the substantive direction that asylum policies should take in the future (cf. Trauner 2016).

These cleavages appeared with particular sharpness during negotiation on the relocation of asylum-seekers who had been able to cross the external borders of Schengen. The proposed system, designed to relieve the so-called 'hotspots' in Italy and Greece by relocating asylum-seekers to other member states through a fixed distribution key, demonstrated a reluctance to agree to any compulsory mechanism. It also showed the reluctance of new EU member states to welcome people in need of international protection to their territory. The relocation system is supported by Migration Management Support Teams and in cooperation with EU agencies, but it has proved to be of limited success: member states have proved reluctant to accept their share, which means that countries at the external borders have not been able to overcome their backlog and have even been accused of not doing justice to the asylum-seekers' protection needs. In view of these difficulties, in 2016, the Commission suggested a new reform to the Dublin III Regulation (2016/0133/COD), which essentially retained the principle that the countries of first arrival in the EU are responsible for admitting asylum-seekers. It has, however, introduced a 'fairness mechanism' similar to that proposed in the relocation system to be managed by an upgraded version of the EASO. The proposal has been seen as highly controversial: for some, it fails to introduce any substantial changes that could contribute to going beyond the 'first-country-of-entry' principle, while for others it is a step too far in the direction of more EU integration.

We have seen, therefore, the Commission struggling to produce significant changes to the content and structure of the CEAS. That is why some of the more innovative proposals have come instead from the external dimension of asylum policies. Although still without a concrete proposal from the Commission, extraterritorial processing of asylum claims has been a much debated possibility since Tony Blair's 2003 'New Vision for Refugees', which proposed the creation of 'Regional Protection Zones' and 'Transit Processing Centres' (Garlick 2006; Levy 2010). The attractiveness of such proposals evidently lies in the fact that refugees and asylum-seekers with some prospect of being accepted could come to Europe via secure and legal routes. This would at the same time lower the number of those who come without any prospects and reduce the need to return failed asylum-seekers. However, the debate gives rise to concerns in terms of human and refugee rights, particularly the extent to which the European Union and its member states outsource part of their responsibility to protect and transfer the responsibility for reception and protection to third parties. One should not forget that the principle of *non-refoulement* applies also outside one's own national territory, whether in international waters, border areas or on the territory of another state, as long as states exercise effective control over individuals. This also includes the need for compliance with procedural protection measures such as access to a hearing, legal aid, interpreters, information and access to legal remedies. Alternative policy recommendations thus far focus on the necessity of access to the territory via legal routes, for instance, by providing humanitarian visas (Collett *et al.* 2016; Fundamental Rights Agency 2015; Jensen 2014). In July 2016, the Commission proposed a coordinated resettlement approach (2016/0225/COD) as an alternative avenue to allow third-country nationals to enter the EU legally and safely.

The influx of asylum-seekers in 2015 and 2016 also underlined the importance of cooperating with third countries. Indeed, the much-contested EU–Turkey statement may become a blueprint for negotiations with other northern African states (Carrera *et al.* 2016; see also Chapters 24 and 26, this volume), which is certainly problematic, given the criticisms raised regarding the lack of human and refugee rights guarantees in Turkey itself as well as the steps backward that the country has taken in the area of rule of law, human rights and protection for minorities. Human rights organizations claim that asylum-seekers' right to non-refoulement is often not considered, they often have no way to access a fair and efficient asylum process and they have no prompt access to a lasting solution, such as return, integration or resettlement (Pro Asyl 2016). Therefore, the problematic legal basis at the core of the EU–Turkey deal and its consequences for asylum-seekers raise important questions when considering similar agreements with countries like Libya or Egypt that, given their poor human rights performances, would be problematic to consider as 'safe third countries'.

Conclusion and agenda for research

As a particularly active policy field, EU asylum has attracted scholars right from the start. Academic research has focused on policy shifts, discourses and practices as well as on institutional developments, thereby linking concepts derived from political science and law. The nature of EU asylum and refugee policies has emphasized its normative dimension and strengthened its links with non-academic organizations and political activism. Although this is important in a policy area that is intimately linked to the protection of human beings, it has often led to emphasizing the empirical side of the field and disregarding theoretical concepts. Therefore, working towards a stronger link between the theoretical and methodological aspects of political science is recommendable. We propose here some avenues for further research and new interdisciplinary work.

First, the institutional changes that have taken place in this policy area have emphasized the importance of a more diverse group of actors for policy-making, slowly achieving more sophisticated understandings of the role of member states and the European Parliament in this field while largely neglecting the Commission and the Court of Justice. It is, therefore, important to pay more attention to these EU institutions in the future. The role of external actors like NGOs and private companies (especially when dealing with databases or border management) could do with more systematic analyses. Finally, the new role of the European Council and the cleavages that have emerged among member states will need to be further explored in the years to come. Given the rise in populist politics and the trend towards renationalization, whether member states manage to overcome their distrust may become a breaking point for the future of the CEAS.

Second, more attention needs to be paid to concepts and how to operationalize them. Many of the academic debates we have raised show that misunderstandings often correspond to a lack of common and transparent definitions. For instance, there have been very diverse methods to measure policy change or to define 'liberal' and 'restrictive'. We need to be more careful in how we create categories, what we compare and how we do it. The EU is an extremely complex system of governance; therefore, we need to be transparent about our levels and objects of analysis (see also Bonjour et al. 2017). In addition, we still have a large gap to fill when it comes to comparative analysis, especially at the member state level. We need to further our understanding of how recent changes in refugee protection and asylum laws have impacted the different member states. That may require the use of mixed methods to inquire into domestic implementation, in order to capture patterns across the countries participating in asylum policies as well as investigating more in-depth, informal practices and shifting norms among street-level bureaucrats.

Finally, the latter point reveals the need to open up to further disciplines like ethnography, area studies, developmental studies, transition studies and conflict analysis if we want to understand phenomena like root causes of migration, the situation in countries of origin and transit or the way asylum-seekers and refugees adapt to EU policies. The fact that recent political decisions on asylum and refugees have shifted more and more towards cooperation with third countries means that we need to better understand the effects of EU policies on these third countries and on the fundamental rights of refugees and asylum-seekers as well as the growing importance of foreign (or even defense) policy tools for the management of migration. To this effect, alternative methods like risk analysis and scenario-building may prove beneficial to the field.

Bibliography

Angenendt, S., Engler, M. and Schneider, J. (2013). *Europäische Flüchtlingspolitik: Wege zu einer fairen Lastenteilung*. Available at www.swp-berlin.org/fileadmin/contents/products/aktuell/2013A65_adt_engler_schneider.pdf (accessed April 2017).

Baldaccini, A., Guild, E. and Toner, H. (2007). *Whose Freedom, Security and Justice? EU Immigration and Asylum Law and Policy*. Portland: Hart Publishing.

Bendel, P. (2007). Everything under Control? The European Union's Policies and Politics of Immigration. In T. Faist and A. Ette (eds), *The Europeanization of National Policies and Politics of Immigration*. Basingstoke: Palgrave Macmillan, pp. 32–48.

Bendel, P. (2013). Nach Lampedusa – das Neue Gemeinsame Europäische Asylsystem auf dem Prüfstand. *Studie im Auftrag der Abteilung Wirtschafts- und Sozialpolitik der Friedrich-Ebert-Stiftung; WISO-Diskurs*. Available at http://library.fes.de/pdf-files/wiso/10415.pdf (accessed November 2014).

Bendel, P. (2016). *Refugee Policy in the European Union: Protect Human Rights!* Bonn: Friedrich-Ebert-Stiftung. Available at http://library.fes.de/pdf-files/wiso/12405.pdf (accessed January 2017).

Bendel, P. (2017). *EU refugee policy in crisis. Blockades, decisions, solutions*, Bonn. Available at http://library.fes.de/pdf-files/wiso/13536.pdf (accessed September 2017).

Bendel, P., Ette, A. and Parkes, R. (eds) (2011). *The Europeanization of Control: Venues and Outcomes of EU Justice and Home Affairs Cooperation*. Münster: LIT Verlag.

Berger, M. and Heinemann, F. (2016). *Why and How There Should Be More Europe in Asylum Policies*. Available at http://ftp.zew.de/pub/zew-docs/policybrief/pb01-16.pdf (accessed April 2017).

Bertoncini, Y. and Pascouau, Y. (2016). *What Migration Strategy for the EU?* Jacques Delors Institute. Available at www.delorsinstitute.eu/media/eumigrationstrategy-bertoncinipascouau-jdi-mar16.pdf (accessed April 2017).

Bonjour, S., Ripoll Servent, A. and Thielemann, E. (2017). Beyond Venue Shopping and Liberal Constraint: A New Research Agenda for EU Migration Policies and Politics. *Journal of European Public Policy*. doi: 10.1080/13501763.2016.1268640.

Boswell, C. (2003). The 'External Dimension' of EU Immigration and Asylum Policy. *International Affairs*, 79(3), pp. 619–638.

Boswell, C. (2008). Evasion, Reinterpretation and Decoupling: European Commission Responses to the 'External Dimension' of Immigration and Asylum. *West European Politics*, 31(3), pp. 491–512.

Carlier, J-Y. and De Bruycker, P. (2005). *Immigration and Asylum Law of the EU: Current Debates*. Brussels: Bruylant.

Carrera, S., Cassarino, J-P., El Qadim, N., Lahlou, M. and den Hertog, L. (2016). *EU–Morocco Cooperation on Readmission, Borders and Protection: A Model to Follow?* Available at www.ceps.eu/publications/eu-morocco-cooperation-readmission-borders-and-protection-model-follow (accessed April 2017).

Carrera, S. and Guild, E. (2014). The European Council's Guidelines for the Area of Freedom, Security and Justice 2020: Subverting the "Lisbonisation" of Justice and Home Affairs? *CEPS Essay*, (13). Available at www.ceps.eu/publications/european-council%E2%80%99s-guidelines-area-freedom-security-and-justice-2020-subverting- (accessed April 2017).

Chetail, V., Bruycker, P.D. and Maiani, F. (2016). *Reforming the Common European Asylum System: The New European Refugee Law*. Boston, MA: Brill Nijhoff.

Collett, E., Clewett, P. and Fratzke, S. (2016). *No Way Out? Making Additional Migration Channels Work for Refugees*. Available at www.migrationpolicy.org/sites/default/files/publications/MPIEurope_UNHCR-Resettlement-FINAL.pdf (accessed April 2017).

Costello, C. (2012). Courting Access to Asylum in Europe: Recent Supranational Jurisprudence Explored. *Human Rights Law Review*, 12(2), pp. 287–339.

den Heijer, M. (2012). *Europe and Extraterritorial Asylum*. Portland: Hart Publishing.

ECRE (2008). *Ending the Asylum Lottery – Guaranteeing Refugee Protection in Europe*.

El-Enany, N. (2013). The EU Asylum, Immigration and Border Control Regimes: Including and Excluding the 'Deserving Migrant'. *European Journal of Social Security*, 15(2), pp. 171–186.

El-Enany, N. and Thielemann, E. (2011). The Impact of EU Asylum Policy on National Asylum Regimes. In S. Wolff, F. Goudappel and J.W. De Zwaan (eds), *Freedom, Security and Justice after Lisbon and Stockholm*. The Hague: TMC Asser, pp. 97–117.

Fundamental Rights Agency (2015). *Legal Entry Channels to the EU for Persons in Need of International Protection: A Toolbox*. Available at http://fra.europa.eu/sites/default/files/fra-focus_02-2015_legal-entry-to-the-eu.pdf (accessed April 2017).

Gammeltoft-Hansen, T. (2012). The Externalisation Of European Migration Control And The Reach Of International Refugee Law. In E. Guild and P. Minderhoud (eds), *The First Decade of EU Migration and Asylum Law*. Leiden: Martinus Nijhoff Publishers, pp. 273–298.

Garlick, M. (2006). The EU Discussions on Extraterritorial Processing: Solution or Conundrum? *International Journal of Refugee Law*, 18(3–4), pp. 601–629.

Giuffré, M. (2013). Readmission Agreements and Refugee Rights: From a Critique to a Proposal. *Refugee Survey Quarterly*, 32(3), pp. 79–111.

Guild, E. (2006). The Europeanisation of Europe's Asylum Policy. *International Journal of Refugee Law*, 18(3/4), pp. 630–651.

Guiraudon, V. (2000). European Integration and Migration Policy: Vertical Policy-making as Venue Shopping. *Journal of Common Market Studies*, 38(2), pp. 251–271.

Hailbronner, K. (1998). European Immigration and Asylum Law under the Amsterdam Treaty. *Common Market Law Review*, 35(5), pp. 1047–1067.

Huysmans, J. (2006). *The Politics of Insecurity: Fear, Migration and Asylum in the EU*. London: Routledge.

Jensen, U.I. (2014). *Humanitarian Visas: Option or Obligation?* Available at www.europarl.europa.eu/RegData/etudes/STUD/2014/509986/IPOL_STU(2014)509986_EN.pdf (accessed June 2015).

Kaunert, C. and Léonard, S. (2012). The Development of the EU Asylum Policy: Venue-shopping in Perspective. *Journal of European Public Policy*, 19(9), pp. 1396–1413.

Lavenex, S. (2001). The Europeanization of Refugee Policies: Normative Challenges and Institutional Legacies. *Journal of Common Market Studies*, 39(5), pp. 851–874.

Lavenex, S. (2006). Shifting Up and Out: The Foreign Policy of European Immigration Control. *West European Politics*, 29(2), pp. 329–350.

Levy, C. (2010). Refugees, Europe, Camps/State of Exception: 'Into The Zone', the European Union and Extraterritorial Processing of Migrants, Refugees, and Asylum-seekers (Theories and Practice). *Refugee Survey Quarterly*, 29(2), pp. 92–119.

Maurer, A. and Parkes, R. (2007). The Prospects for Policy-change in EU Asylum Policy: Venue and Image at the European Level. *European Journal of Migration and Law*, 9, pp. 173–205.

Mitsilegas, V. (2014). Solidarity and Trust in the Common European Asylum System. *Comparative Migration Studies*, 2(2), pp. 181–202.

Papagianni, G. (2013). Forging an External EU Migration Policy: From Externalisation of Border Management to a Comprehensive Policy? *European Journal of Migration and Law*, 15(3), pp. 283–299.

Pawlak, P. (2009). The External Dimension of the Area of Freedom, Security and Justice: Hijacker or Hostage of Cross-pillarization? *Journal of European Integration*, 31(1), pp. 25–44.

Pro Asyl (2016). *Observations on the EU–Turkey Deal: Is There Really Effective Access to Asylum in Turkey?* May 13, 2016. Available at www.proasyl.de/en/news/observations-on-the-eu-turkey-deal-is-there-really-effective-access-to-asylum-in-turkey/ (accessed April 2017).

Ripoll Servent, A. and Trauner, F. (2014). Do Supranational EU Institutions Make a Difference? EU Asylum Law before and after 'Communitarization'. *Journal of European Public Policy*, 21(8), pp. 1142–1162.

Roos, C. and Zaun, N. (2014). Norms Matter! The Role of International Norms in EU Policies on Asylum and Immigration. *European Journal of Migration & Law*, 16(1), pp. 45–68.

Sterkx, S. (2008). The External Dimension of EU Asylum and Migration Policy: Expanding Fortress Europe? In J. Orbie (ed.), *Europe's Global Role: External Policies of the European Union*. Farnham: Ashgate, pp. 117–138.

Thiel, M. and Uçarer, E.M. (2014). Access and Agenda-setting in the European Union: Advocacy NGOs in Comparative Perspective. *Interest Groups & Advocacy*, 3(1), pp. 99–116.

Thielemann, E. (2003). Between Interests and Norms: Explaining Burden-sharing in the European Union. *Journal of Refugee Studies*, 16(3), pp. 253–273.

Thielemann, E.R. (2005). Symbolic Politics or Effective Burden-sharing? Redistribution, Side-payments and the European Refugee Fund. *Journal of Common Market Studies*, 43(4), pp. 807–824.

Thielemann, E.R. (2010). The Common European Asylum System: In Need of a More Comprehensive Burden-sharing Approach. In A. Luedtke (ed.), *Migrants and Minorities: The European Response*. Newcastle-upon-Tyne: Cambridge Scholars Publishing, pp. 82–97.

Thielemann, E. and Armstrong, C. (2013). Understanding European Asylum Cooperation under the Schengen/Dublin System: A Public Goods Framework. *European Security*, 22(2), pp. 148–164.

Toshkov, D. and Haan, L. de (2013). The Europeanization of Asylum Policy: An Assessment of the EU Impact on Asylum Applications and Recognitions Rates. *Journal of European Public Policy*, 20(5), pp. 661–683.

Trauner, F. (2016). Asylum Policy: The EU's 'Crises' and the Looming Policy Regime Failure. *Journal of European Integration*, 38(3), pp. 311–325.

Uçarer, E.M. (2001). From the Sidelines to Center Stage: Sidekick No More? The European Commission in Justice and Home Affairs. *European Integration online Papers (EIoP)*, 5(5). Available at http://eiop.or.at/eiop/pdf/2001-005.pdf (accessed July 2011).

Zaun, N. (2017). *EU Asylum Policies: The Power of Strong Regulating States*. Basingstoke: Palgrave Macmillan.

6

THE IRREGULAR IMMIGRATION POLICY CONUNDRUM

Problematizing 'effectiveness' as a frame for EU criminalization and expulsion policies

Sergio Carrera and Jennifer Allsopp

Introduction

One of the priorities identified by EU policies in response to the 2015/2016 'refugee crisis' was the need to increase the effectiveness of EU irregular immigration policies, in particular increasing the enforcement rate of expulsions of irregular immigrants. The anti-smuggling and expulsion-driven rationale that guides current policies is symptomatic of a deeper dilemma which has characterized 'Europeanization' dynamics over the past three decades (Guiraudon 2000; Block and Bonjour 2013; Bonjour and Vink 2014). Since the first steps, European integration processes have displayed an ambivalent relationship with the mobility of non-EU nationals. This has been particularly the case in relation to those who are not deemed 'useful' to the labor market or in need of international protection, and thus fall within the elusive label of irregular immigrants (Guild 2004). The materialization of freedom of movement for EU citizens and the abolition of internal border controls under the Schengen system have been key drivers of the increasing involvement of the EU in migration management and in the co-creation of 'irregularity'. Schengen has developed multi-functional frontiers (Anderson 1996) between those individuals who can travel lawfully and those who cannot.

This chapter draws upon the preliminary findings of the research project 'Anti-smuggling Policies and their Intersection with Humanitarian Assistance and Social Trust', funded by the ESRC/AHRC. It addresses one of the most contested challenges facing irregular immigration policies: their effectiveness. It is argued that how effective or ineffective migration control policies are deemed to be is determined by the actor who asks the question – whose effectiveness, and whether an assessment is made in terms of the effects of these policies in the short, medium or long term. Where effectiveness is found lacking as an appropriate lens, we ask what alternative criteria might be employed to gain a better understanding of the challenges at stake.

It is argued that the ineffectiveness of norms and practices propagated by member states and by the multiple EU institutional actors and agencies involved in anti-smuggling and expulsion policies are the product of their interests and struggles over specific forms of 'capital' in relation to competences (legal mandates) and resources. Moreover, they have often been the result of strategies to escape or evade legal, democratic and judicial accountability in pursuing these policies. Ineffectiveness claims aimed at justifying the enactment of security policies have profound repercussions for social trust, humanitarian assistance and fundamental rights. An increasingly securitized and non-transparent role for the EU and its multiple actors working on irregular immigration, we conclude, will relocate mistrust on irregular immigration policies from domestic actors and venues towards those of the Union, which will in turn undermine the EU's legitimacy. The chapter concludes with some reflections on possible avenues for future research in light of gaps in the scholarly literature.

'Expulsion' is employed in this chapter to denote the removal of an irregular migrant from a EU member state, which sometimes occurs against the will of the individual; 'return migration', meanwhile, encompasses a broader range of subjects and situations from participation in 'voluntary' return programs to forced removals. A critical theorization of return migration and its associated terms ('deportation', 'expulsion' and 'return'), while crucial to understanding EU policy dynamics (Cassarino 2004), falls beyond the scope of this chapter.

Irregular immigration and the EU: background and state of play

Pursuant to a period of *rapprochement* between EU member states' Ministries of Interior on questions of policing irregular migration, expulsion and repatriation (Bigo 1996, 2005), the European Community formally acquired shared legal competence to legislate on matters related to migration and asylum in May 1999 under the Amsterdam Treaty. Freedom of movement within the Schengen area was artificially linked to potential insecurities such as irregular immigration and crime. The lifting of internal border controls on persons was thus coupled with a set of 'compensatory' or 'flanking' policing measures addressed to 'non-admissible or unwanted third country nationals' who have come to be controversially known as 'illegal immigrants' in the EU Treaties. The 2009 Lisbon Treaty consolidated the previous migration-related EU competences, including those concerning deportation and expulsion (Peers *et al.* 2012; Cassarino, Chapter 7, this volume).

Since 2005, the EU has created an evolving toolkit of migration management comprising a matrix of laws, institutions/agencies and technologies focused on strengthened external borders and visa policies (Guild 2006). These tools include, among others: (1) a common list of countries whose nationals are exempted or required to have visas to enter the Schengen territory for short stays (visits of up to three months), a common format and rules on short-stay visas and a Community Code on Visas (Regulation No. EC/810/2009; Regulation No. EC/539/2001); (2) common rules on external border controls under the Schengen Borders Code (Regulation No. EC/339/2016); (3) large-scale databases like the Visa Information System (VIS) and the Schengen Information System (SIS) allowing for exchange of information between law enforcement authorities and the holding of biometric data respectively on visa holders and irregular migrants (Regulation No. EC/767/2008 and Regulation No. EC/1987/2006); and (4) the creation of Frontex, the European Agency for the Management of Operational Cooperation at the External Borders, which has now become the European Border and Coast Guard (Regulation No. EC/2007/2004; Regulation (EU) 2016/1624).

This toolkit has ushered in a phenomenon described by the literature as the 'criminalization of migration': the progressive merging of criminal and migration law (Guild 2010; Provera 2015; Parkin 2013). Mitsilegas (2015) has understood the 'criminalization of migration' as comprising a three-fold process through which migration management takes place via (1) the adoption of substantive criminal law; (2) recourse to traditional criminal law enforcement mechanisms including surveillance and detention; and (3) the development of mechanisms of prevention and pre-emption. The 'criminalization' approach has more visibly taken place through the adoption of the following set of EU Directives.

First, the 'Facilitators Package' adopted in November 2002 (Council Directive 2002/90/EC and Council Framework Decision 2002/946/JHA) applies criminal penalties to the facilitation of entry and residence of irregular immigrants. Second, the 2001 Directive allowed for the mutual recognition of expulsion decisions (Council Directive 2001/40/EC). Third, the 2001 Directive on carrier sanctions requires member states to stipulate penalties to carriers transporting third-country nationals without proper documents to enter the EU's territory and to return those who have been refused entry (Council Directive 2001/51). The EU's intervention in this field took another far-reaching step with the adoption of the so-called 'Returns Directive' setting common minimum standards on expulsion in 2008 (Directive 2008/115/EC), and with the 'Employers Sanctions Directive' providing sanctions against employers of irregular immigrants in 2009 (Directive 2009/52).

Expulsion and smuggling policies: Europeanization dynamics in a multi-actor field

The role played by member states' Ministries of Interior in the Europeanization of immigration policy has been particularly central since the 1990s. Guiraudon (2000) has argued that the Europeanization or 'vertical' policy-making on migration control has led to a process which has served various interests by shifting policy elaboration away from national democratic and judicial controls. Moving outside of these domestic sites of resistance and checks and balances may have been helpful for actors trying to escape the legal, democratic and judicial 'obstacles' – or rather 'guarantees' and 'frameworks of rights' – which are often deemed by Ministries of Interior and related actors to be a step towards effectiveness for the purposes of expulsion and immigration control.

This dynamic has been equally important for understanding the priorities and demands from member states so that the EU can help render 'effective' the expulsion of irregularly entering/staying third-country nationals. Well before the formal adoption of the EU Returns Directive, a key challenge between member states and the Commission in this policy area related to the domain of 'readmission'; that is, cooperation with third countries on questions related to expulsion through the conclusion of international agreements (Cassarino, Chapter 7, this volume; Cassarino 2010; Carrera 2016). The EU Returns Directive grants the EU clear legal competence over expulsion standards and procedures, and the buck has now ended up in the hands of the EU Frontex External Borders Agency (see Santos Vara, Chapter 37, this volume).

The recent adoption of the European Border and Coast Guard Regulation (EU/2016/1624) has led to the creation of a EU Returns Office within the agency, entrusted with enhancing EU expulsion policy. It is granted powers to coordinate and organize joint return operations and to be involved in national return procedures, including cooperation with third countries. A key goal is to better match the number of return decisions to the number of enforced expulsion orders.

In addition to Frontex, other actors are newly involved in anti-smuggling policies in the Mediterranean. These include EU agencies such as Europol, and more controversially, the military. In May 2015 the European Commission published a 2015 to 2020 EU Action Plan against Migrant Smuggling, which proposed concrete policy actions to counter and prevent migrant smuggling. These included increased tasks for EU agencies to support member states in the investigation and prosecution of migrant smuggling networks and a 'multi-agency approach'. The effects were three-fold: (1) the establishment of a European Migrant Smuggling Centre inside Europol (Europol 2016a, 2016b); (2) Europol's involvement in the Hotspots established in Greece and Italy in supplying joint mobile teams to provide operational and information support to these states (COM(2015) 510); and (3) the continuation of its Joint Operational Team (JOT) MARE in the Mediterranean Sea. The latter has aimed at the exchange of information 'in real time to disrupt smuggling networks operating from Turkey, as well as from Libya and other North African countries' (Europol 2015). The increasing role of EU policing agencies further fosters the criminalization of cross-border mobility. Accountability and legal scrutiny challenges also characterize the operational activities and practices of EU justice and home affairs' agencies such as Frontex and Europol. These become even more legally and ethically sensitive in the context of the expulsion and criminalization of asylum-seekers and irregular immigrants (Carrera *et al.* 2013).

In addition to 'EU efforts', the Action Plan underlines that its proposed actions 'should also be seen in connection with on-going work to establish a Common Security and Defense Policy (CSDP)' to tackle migrant smuggling. Indeed, the EUNAVFOR-MED Operation ('Operation Sophia') launched in May 2015 was granted an international legal mandate to intercept, inspect, seize and destroy vessels on the high seas off the coast of Libya for a period of one year in cases where there were 'reasonable grounds to believe' that these vessels, inflatable boats, rafts and dinghies were being used for smuggling and human trafficking (UN Resolution 2240 (2015)). In June 2016, Operation Sophia's mandate was extended for another year and two new tasks were added: training Libyan coastguards and contributing to the implementation of the UN arms embargo in the high seas (UN Resolution 2291 (2016)). The effectiveness and proportionality of Operation Sophia has been questioned, not least by the UK House of Lords (2015), which concluded that there remain significant gaps in the operation's understanding of smuggling networks and their *modus operandi* in Libya. According to an internal report released by Wikileaks, the operation's intentions and objectives exceed what could be realistically achieved (European External Action Service (EEAS) 2016)).

The resulting picture is one where 'anti-smuggling' and 'maritime surveillance' seem to have become policy domains in which an increasing set of EU actors and agencies are interested, and in which they struggle for authority and resources. Concerns abound regarding the scope and effects of these developments. Having outlined the background, state of play and normative context of EU irregular migration policies, this chapter will now consider how effectiveness/ineffectiveness creates a challenge in policy justification and evaluation.

'Measuring' effectiveness: deceptive statistics

Statistics are not neutral. They play an important role in politically shaping the migration debate in the EU and justifying EU policy formulation and evaluation. Numbers, like other measures, can be employed to demonstrate effectiveness or ineffectiveness depending on the point of analysis or interest(s) at stake (Czaika and Haas 2013a). Much of the aforementioned policy developments have been justified by suggestions to either increase the number of returns of irregular migrants or decrease the number of arrivals.

The Commission's May 2015 European Agenda on Migration (COM(2015)240) stated that 'one of the incentives for irregular migration is the knowledge that the EU's system to return irregular migrants is not sufficiently effective'. A similar logic was put forward in the 2015 Commission's Action Plan on Return (COM(2015)453), which signaled that during 2014 'less than 40% of the irregular migrants that were ordered to leave the EU departed effectively' and therefore called for the 'systematic return, either voluntary or forced, of those who do not or no longer have the right to remain in Europe'.

The 2015 Council Conclusions, which followed on 'Increasing the effectiveness of the EU system to return irregular migrants' (10170/15), also underlined that both 'the EU and its Member States must do more in terms of return' (paragraph 5). Member states' representatives equally highlighted in these conclusions the long-standing priority regarding readmission agreements.

A strong emphasis in EU policy documents has thus been placed on increasing the 'enforcement rate' of expulsions and a quantitative understanding of 'effectiveness' with regard to matching the number of removal orders issued with those actually being implemented by member states. This is in addition to ensuring 'swift' returns, including through the conclusion of more readmission agreements. What do the statistics tell us about this 'ineffectiveness' picture? In 2015, according to the latest statistics on enforcement of immigration legislation by Eurostat, which includes data extracted in June 2016, 530,000 third-country nationals were issued an order to leave EU territory. Thirty-six percent of those were returned to their country of origin, which amounts to a total of 193,565 persons (Eurostat 2016).

Since 2008 there has been a progressive decrease in the number of removal orders issued by EU member states; from 603,000 in 2008 to 533,000 in 2015. Table 6.1 shows how the total number of removal orders and returns have remained in a stable decreasing trend since 2008, with a slight increase in 2015. From the 533,000 registered in 2015, the main countries of issuance were Greece, France, the United Kingdom and Germany. Previous research has shown that a similar decreasing trend in the number of expulsions may be found in respect of third countries with which the EU has concluded a Readmission Agreement, for example, Pakistan, Georgia, Armenia, Cape Verde and Azerbaijan (Carrera 2016). This not only questions the effectiveness, but also the main purpose and motive behind EU Readmission Agreements in easing or facilitating expulsions of third-country nationals to countries of origin and/or transit.

It is inadvisable to draw conclusive findings from this statistical coverage due to limitations on the data presented and the fuzziness of some of the concepts used by Eurostat when presenting them. The data available on the kinds of returns constitute a key limitation to such evaluation. This not only relates to the limited and fragmented numbers which have been gathered regarding 'voluntary returns': significantly, they do not clarify whether the counted individuals are third-country nationals who have received a negative decision on asylum applications or migrants who have entered irregularly and not sought asylum. There is also a complete lack of detail regarding the legal framework within which these expulsions have taken place (e.g., within the scope of bilateral or informal readmission arrangements).

Most importantly, these statistics tell us nothing about five key issues. First, the extent to which EU member states may be issuing too many or a disproportionate number of removal orders for people who are clearly non-returnable or for people who the relevant authorities know to be non-removable. Second, the extent to which those removal orders which are not enforced are in fact due to ongoing appeal processes foreseen by the EU Returns Directive (in line with Article 14 of the EU Charter of Fundamental Rights on 'effective remedies'). Third, whether the persons concerned may be non-removable, in line with Article 14 of the EU Returns Directive, which foresees 'safeguards pending return' owing to wider fundamental human rights obligations. Fourth, what of the practical and political obstacles to expulsion,

Table 6.1 Third-country nationals ordered to leave and enforced returns EU-28 (2008–2015)

	2008	2009	2010	2011	2012	2013	2014	2015
Third-country nationals returned	211,350	211,785	198,910	167,150	178,500	184,765	168,925	193,565
Third-country nationals ordered to leave	603,360	594,600	540,080	491,310	483,650	430,450	470,080	533,000

Source: Eurostat (2016a).

which fall inside and outside the scope of EU Readmission Agreements? These mainly relate to what has been referred to as an 'identity determination dilemma'; hiding profound disagreement between EU member states' competent authorities on enforcing return and those of third countries concerned regarding who is a national of which country. These sovereignty-related challenges very often translate into a failure to issue the identification and travel documents necessary for effective repatriation or expulsion (European Migration Network 2014). A fifth argument relates to cost and resource constraints.

'Effective' management of arrivals?

Beyond numbers, there exist important gaps in qualitative and comparative social sciences research, which raises key empirical gaps in the ineffectiveness/effectiveness debate at the point of policy formulation and evaluation. The bolstering of the common European frontier through Frontex-led operations echoed a trend long documented in migration studies, for example, in literature on the US–Mexico border (Andreas 2012): often closing one route leads to another. In recent months, following the closing of the West Balkan migrant route and the initiation of a deal between the EU and Turkey to return irregular migrants to Turkey, research suggests that increasing numbers have turned to smugglers to facilitate travel through alternative and more dangerous routes, including journeying across the Mediterranean from the North African coast to Italy (Crawley *et al.* 2016). Therefore, it is difficult to assess which of these trends constitutes displaced movements or independent flows. Again, statistics can be misleading.

Accounting for migrant deaths along such shifting routes has come to be used by some as a stark measure of the ineffectiveness of policies that seek to manage the arrivals of irregular migrants to Europe. Reflecting a broader trend in critical migration scholarship, it places individual migrant experiences at the center of analysis, in contrast with the securitization discourse identified commonly with state practices (Huysmans 2006). This humanitarian focus has nevertheless penetrated political discourse. Indeed, human dignity was the lens through which the European Commission President spoke on April 29, 2015 when he admitted that 'it was a serious mistake to bring the Mare Nostrum operation to an end' because 'it cost human lives' (Juncker 2015). The 'discursive gap' between rhetoric and policy is one of the challenges of assessing the effectiveness of immigration policies (Czaika and Haas 2013a, 2013b; Massey *et al.* 1998).

The causal relationship between EU policy and migrant deaths continues to be debated by scholars, policy-makers and practitioners. Recently, researchers have argued that the 22,000 documented deaths at sea over the past twenty-five years have been the structural product of EU migration policies that have denied legal access to EU territory to the impoverished citizens of the Global South since the end of the 1980s (Forensic Oceanography/Watch the Med 2016). The militarization of border surveillance and its externalization to North African states, they argue, has forced migrants wishing to reach EU territory to turn to smugglers and to take longer and ever more dangerous routes.

Other research has suggested that the cutting of state-supported humanitarian actors at sea prompted a 'search-and-rescue' deficit in which ill-equipped private actors and civil society organizations were forced to fill the gaps (Carrera *et al.* 2015). Researchers calculate that the 2015 scrapping of the Italian-led Mare Nostrum search-and-rescue operation and its replacement by the Frontex Operation Triton rendered crossing the Mediterranean thirty times more dangerous compared to the previous year (Forensic Oceanography/Watch the Med 2016). It was this, they contend, that led to disastrous consequences; including several well-documented shipwrecks, such as that of April 18, 2015 in which a boat carrying over 800 people sank upon collision with the cargo ship seeking to rescue them. Only twenty-eight people survived.

To try to understand the measures of effectiveness employed collectively and individually by EU member states in determining policy towards irregular migrants, some look to how states respond to such dramatic events. The launch of the EU military operation EUNAVFOR MED against smugglers in the wake of such events has been accompanied by a tripling of Frontex's budget; this may be interpreted as an explicit refocusing – from stopping the migrants to stopping the smugglers – yet the actual 'effectiveness' of such a strategy remains by and large unclear.

Meanwhile, the policy focus on stopping migrants continues in the background. The strict liability enshrined in the Carriers Sanctions EU Directive has been said to lead to the 'privatization' of controls, in turn leading asylum-seekers to rely increasingly on smugglers and to pursue more life-threatening routes of entry overland as well as at sea (Peers et al. 2012: 348). Similarly, the Employers Sanctions Directive has been said to transform employers into 'watchdogs of the EU': they are now forced to control access to employment by third-country nationals without ensuring efficient complaint mechanisms for employees' rights violations (Carrera and Guild 2007).

Cholewinski (2012: 201) is among scholars who have argued in this context that the EU's approach to irregular immigration has 'lacked balance because of a failure to devote sufficient attention to the protection of the rights of migrants in an irregular situation'. Interestingly, while the EU Returns Directive has been amply criticized by academics due to its restrictive and security-driven approach (Acosta 2012; Baldaccini 2009), this directive now sets a supranational framework of standards, procedural guarantees and rights subject to judicial scrutiny by the Luxembourg Court. This has brought positive consequences regarding the rights of irregular immigrants in relation to procedural remedies and time limits concerning detention (Peers 2015). Furthermore, Recital 4 of the directive sets as one of its core objectives 'clear, transparent and fair rules' so as to ensure 'effective return policy'. Perhaps unsurprisingly, several EU actors are increasingly conceiving 'rights' as 'pull factors' and key ingredients undermining the 'effectiveness' of EU expulsion policies.

Expulsions: a myopic view

While the question of how to most effectively manage the arrival of irregular migrants to Europe remains a battlefield between actors engaged in international relations, security and humanitarianism, expulsion policies pose a number of quandaries of their own. We know little either numerically or qualitatively of the experiences of expelled migrants due to poor tracing. Beyond a concern for individual dignity or human rights, these individual experiences fuel future trends, which have a direct impact upon the sending states; for example, through 'remigration'.

EU law does not oblige member states to complete any follow-up activities with returned irregular migrants (Cherti and Szilard 2013). Instead, international organizations, including the International Organization for Migration (IOM), complete or implement the limited work in this area. This 'out of sight out of mind' approach means that the effectiveness of return is measured almost solely from the point of removal with no long-term view. Scholarship suggests that the sustainability of returns of irregular migrants depends on at least three factors: (1) livelihood options for the returned migrants (e.g., Peutz 2010; (2) the ability of the country of return to reintegrate migrants (e.g., Schuster and Majidi 2013); and (3) the viability of expulsion as a long-term policy solution for liberal, democratic sending countries (e.g., Gibney 2008). Cassarino, meanwhile, has identified patterns of resource mobilization and preparedness as crucial to a theorization of 'return migration', which recognizes both the diversity of returnees and how subjective and structural factors converge in a continuum of agency and coercion (Cassarino 2004).

Although the research on 'returned migrants' is scant, it suggests that expulsions often fail to provide effective durable solutions for the individual migrant, the country of return or the sending country.

A fourth key dimension of 'effective' expulsions policy, which has become especially acute in the context of the 'European refugee crisis', concerns the proper resourcing of screening and asylum determination procedures upon arrival. While EU-funded 'hotspots' were framed as effective solutions to the under-resourced and overburdened southern coastlines in Italy and Greece, human rights organizations such as Amnesty International (2016) have argued that the new system has served to further stretch frontline resources, resulting in human rights violations and *refoulement*.

Afghanistan is among the countries that have seen increased EU returns in recent years and it has received some – albeit limited – academic attention. While Afghanistan remains one of the main origin countries for asylum-seekers, with over 85,000 claiming asylum in the EU in the first half of 2016 and 178,000 in 2015 (second only to Syria: Eurostat 2016), it is also one of the main countries for refusals. Refusal decisions commonly accept risk of persecution in a particular region, but counsel relocation to Kabul. Thus, post-arrival in the EU, many Afghans transit from the regular status of asylum-seekers into 'irregular migrants'. Policy on returns to Afghanistan is inconsistent across the EU, despite efforts in recent months to foster a common regional return agreement (EU and Government 2016). Such differences may be accounted for with reference to different interpretations of international human rights instruments in addition to resource constraints (Guild 2016); as well as inter-state sovereignty challenges (Carrera 2016).

Countries, including the UK and Sweden, regularly charter flights to send refused asylum-seekers back to Afghanistan (Reuters 2016); yet 'return' in this context is an ambiguous outcome. Some of these migrants have never known the city or country of removal, having spent their lives as IDPs and refugees in neighboring countries. Others have spent their formative years abroad and feel they belong there (Allsopp *et al.* 2015).

In this unfamiliar context, academic research suggests that the majority of 'returnees' fail to establish livelihoods post-return, and consequently remigrate, to Europe and in some cases to the very cities from which they have been returned (Schuster and Majidi 2013). For the receiving countries too, 'return migration' can be hard to manage effectively. In 2015, the Minister for Refugees and Repatriation asked the EU to halt returns until they could develop effective reintegration strategies (Schuster and Majidi 2013). While each return country is characterized by a unique set of circumstances, there is evidence to suggest that problems of reintegration and of remigration are widespread. Research on returns to Nigeria has stressed the need for more resources to ensure long-term reintegration (Pennington and Balaram 2013); meanwhile the stigma of expulsion has been shown to cause additional reintegration difficulties for Somali returnees (Peutz 2010).

Measuring the effectiveness or ineffectiveness of expulsions is thus far from a zero-sum game: it is ambiguous from the perspective of the individual, the sending and the receiving countries, and in terms of short-term or long-term effects.

Criminalization measures 'in country': unintended consequences?

Evidence from Ghana and Bangladesh suggests that pre-return policies, which serve to criminalize migrants, such as detention, can also actively impede reintegration (Garner 2014). However, from the point of view of host states, detention may, in the short term, serve to increase migrants' willingness to return. Although causality is complex and under-explored in this area, it is worth noting that of the 4,257 individuals who took part in the UK's Assisted Voluntary Returns Programme from April 2013 to March 2014, over 50 percent were detained at the point of application (Garner 2014).

Like detention, the practice of enforced destitution is widespread among member states. Scholars have long claimed that experiences of poverty, or 'enforced destitution' (Allsopp et al. 2014) among asylum-seekers, and among refused asylum-seekers in particular, may be a planned outcome of public policy aimed to 'disincentivize' their stay (Cholewinski 1998; Crawley et al. 2011) and deter future arrivals (Block 2000). Once again, the access which irregular migrants have to the rights and the level of welfare support offered to asylum-seekers and refused asylum-seekers differs according to the state (Guild 2016). There is some evidence to suggest that prospective migrants and asylum-seekers may take social and economic rights into account as part of a raft of factors when making migratory decisions. Similarly, some evidence suggests that – as referenced above in relation to detention – an absence of rights may encourage irregular migrants already present to opt for voluntary removal (Allsopp et al. 2014). Yet there is also evidence that an absence of rights serves to further marginalize irregular migrants (who may become regular) and increase social insecurity and risk. In other words, the effects are multi-fold and poorly evidenced (Allsopp et al. 2014).

Scholars appear to agree that 'enforced destitution' policies are specifically 'ineffective' as a policy response for certain national groups of asylum-seekers who are refused protection but are unable to return home. This was the case for thousands of Zimbabweans left in limbo in the UK in the 2000s (Crawley et al. 2011). Return is blocked for other refused asylum-seekers owing to challenges in accessing travel documents or in being recognized by their countries of origin (Allsopp et al. 2014). The financial costs of keeping such individuals outside of the labor market, on benefits or in immigration detention have been articulated as an argument against the effectiveness of such policies. Where irregular immigration policy interacts with social policy and labor market policy, measuring effectiveness once again becomes a difficult – and somewhat different – game.

Social trust

Beyond economic factors, criminalization tactics affect social trust among the polity as a whole (Allsopp 2016). Some have argued that these effects are deliberate, serving to reify the 'boundaries of belonging' to the national community (Anderson et al. 2011). Stumpf (2006), referencing Garland (2001: 34–35), argues that 'imposing increasingly harsh sentences and using deportation as a means of expressing moral outrage is attractive from a political standpoint, regardless of its efficacy in controlling crime or unauthorized immigration'. Yet such policies have a direct as well as discursive impact upon communities. Many individuals who are detained are eventually released back into the community; they may suffer ongoing traumas exacerbated or sparked by their incarceration, which effect their prospects of (re)integration (Garner 2014). Individuals who have experienced poverty as a result of their irregular migrant status and who go on to become regularized, in turn, may face specific challenges entering the labor market and, as a consequence, require access to costly psycho-social support (Allsopp et al. 2014; Du Preez 2014).

Where criminalization policies induce vulnerabilities for irregular migrants, it is often civil society that responds. Concerns have been expressed regarding the implications of the EU Facilitators Package, specifically in relation to its effects on the provision of humanitarian assistance by civil society. Article 1.2 of the Facilitation Directive gives member states the option to apply an exception to the criminalization envisaged when the aim of the assistance is humanitarian. Because of the article's discretionary nature, there are nevertheless member states where humanitarian actors may face or have faced sanctions when assisting irregular immigrants. Research has brought to light evidence that civil society organizations fear sanctions and experience intimidation, a potential deterrent effect on their work (Carrera *et al.* 2015).

As policy-making powers and operational control over irregular migration have become progressively centralized by the process of Europeanization, communities and grass-roots actors report that their experiences – and voice – are increasingly overlooked in this sphere (Carrera *et al.* 2015). This perceived eclipsing of the everyday experiences of migrants and their service providers is being challenged directly from below. NGOs have argued that their fear of criminalization is a bar to effective service delivery to irregular migrants in need. Meanwhile, the European Ship Owners Association has reiterated its members' concern that they are ill-qualified to serve the search-and-rescue mandate imposed upon them and fear criminalization under new EU rules and regulations (Carrera *et al.* 2015). The increasing role and politicization of irregular migration management in the EU thus appears to be shifting public distrust from the national actors towards EU venues and agencies.

Conclusions and avenues for future research

This chapter has sought to demonstrate that how effective or ineffective migration control policies are deemed to be is largely determined by the point of analysis of the actor concerned: actors from the host state, those in the receiving state in the context of return migration, as well as the individual migrant and the society as a whole. Most frequently, however, the fragmented EU actors' apparatus employs its own self-propagating criteria and notions for setting and evaluating effectiveness and ineffectiveness in this policy area, leaving us with what we might term an irregular immigration policy conundrum. In the current EU context, domestic and EU actors mandated or practically engaged in return and anti-smuggling policies and practices appear to primarily view ineffectiveness from the perspective of numbers, control, their own mandates and resources, rather than other factors such as human dignity, long-term legitimacy outcomes and trust, which are important components of liberal democratic regimes.

This chapter has suggested that the increasing involvement of the EU and its actors in irregular immigration is likely to displace mistrust on the effectiveness of irregular immigration policies from domestic actors towards the EU. It is therefore central for the Union's legitimacy that its migration policies and priorities shift towards a more liberal agenda. The 2016 UN New York Declaration on Migration and Refugees has recently highlighted the need to develop legal pathways for access to international protection and economic migration (at all skill levels). This constitutes a central challenge for EU policies which, as this chapter has illustrated, are still too focused on prevention, expulsion and criminalization practices that are often non-transparent and, as such, unaccountable to the European polity and those affected.

Finally, this chapter has highlighted some of the under-researched dimensions of policy ineffectiveness to pose a counter-perspective to the securitization *zeitgeist*. More research is needed into the ways in which public policies (and the actors behind them) aimed at addressing smuggling can be designed and evaluated in ways compatible with humanitarian assistance and with the fundamental rights of asylum-seekers and migrants without undermining social trust. There is also a 'knowledge gap' regarding the effects that European laws and the activities of EU agencies on irregular immigration are having on the ground, as well as the ways in which the rights of individuals are guaranteed throughout the various phases comprising expulsion processes and procedures.

Bibliography

Acosta, D. (2012). The Good, the Bad and the Ugly in EU Migration Law: Is the European Parliament Becoming Bad and Ugly? (The adoption of the Directive 2008/115: The returns Directive). In Guild, E. and Minderhoud, P. (eds), *The First Decade of EU Migration and Asylum Law*. Leiden: Martinus Nijhoff, pp. 179–205.

Allsopp, J. (2016). The European Facilitation Directive and the Criminalization of Humanitarian Assistance to Irregular Migrants: Measuring the Impact on the Whole Community. In Carrera, S. and Guild, E. (eds), *Irregular Migration, Trafficking and Smuggling in Human Beings*. Brussels: CESP Paperback, pp. 47–57.

Allsopp, J., Chase, E. and Mitchell, M. (2015). The Tactics of Time and Status: Young People's Experiences of Constructing Futures while Subject to Immigration Control. *Journal of Refugee Studies*, 28(2), pp. 163–182.

Allsopp, J., Sigona, N. and Phillimore, J. (2014). *Poverty among Refugees and Asylum Seekers in the UK: An Evidence and Policy Review*. Birmingham: IRIS.

Amnesty International (2016). *Hotspot Italy: How EU's Flagship Approach Leads to Violations of Refugee and Migrant Rights*. London: Amnesty International.

Anderson, B., Gibney, M.J. and Paoletti, E. (2011). Citizenship, Deportation and the Boundaries of Belonging. *Citizenship Studies*, 15(5), pp. 547–563.

Anderson, M. (1996). *Frontiers, Territory and State Formation in the Modern World*. Cambridge: Polity Press.

Andreas, P. (2012). *Border Games: Policing the US–Mexico Divide*. New York: Cornell University Press.

Baldaccini, A. (2009). The Return and Removal of Irregular Migrants under EU Law: An Analysis of the Returns Directive. *European Journal of Migration and Law*, 11(1), pp. 1–71.

Bigo, D. (1996). *Polices en réseaux: l'expérience européenne*. Paris: Presse de Sciences Po.

Bigo, D. (2005). Frontier Controls in the European Union: Who is in Control? In Bigo, D. and Guild, E. (eds), *Controlling Frontiers: Free Movement into and within Europe*. Aldershot: Ashgate Publishing, pp. 49–99.

Bloch, A. (2000). A New Era or More of the Same? Asylum Policy in the UK. *Journal of Refugee Studies*, 13(1), pp. 29–42.

Block, L. and Bonjour, S. (2013). Fortress Europe or Europe of Rights? The Europeanisation of Family Migration Policies in France, Germany and the Netherlands. *European Journal of Migration and Law*, 15(2), pp. 203–224.

Bonjour, S. and Vink, M. (2014). When Europeanisation Backfires: The Normalisation of European Migration Politics. *Acta Política*, 48(4), pp. 389–407.

Carrera, S. (2016). *Implementation of EU Readmission Agreements: Identity Determination Dilemmas and the Blurring of Rights*. Springer Briefs in Law, Springer International Publishers.

Carrera, S. and Guild, E. (2007). *An EU Framework on Sanctions against Employers of Irregular Immigrants: Some Reflections on Scope, Features and Added Value*. CEPS Policy Brief No. 140, Brussels.

Carrera, S., Hertog, L. den and Parkin, J. (2013) The Peculiar Nature of EU Home Affairs Agencies in Migration Control: Beyond Accountability versus Autonomy? *European Journal of Migration and Law*, 15(4), pp. 337–358.

Carrera, S., Guild, E., Aliverti, A., Allsopp, J., Manieri, M-G. and Levoy, M. (2015). *Fit for Purpose? The Facilitation Directive and the Criminalisation of Humanitarian Assistance to Irregular Migrants*. Brussels: European Parliament. Available at www.ceps.eu/publications/fit-purposethe-facilitation-directive-and-criminalisation-humanitarian-assistance (accessed September 12, 2016).

Cassarino, J.P. (2004). Theorising Return Migration: The Conceptual Approach to Return Migrants Revisited. *International Journal on Multicultural Societies*, UNESCO, 6(2), pp. 253–279.

Cassarino, J.P. (2010). *Readmission Policy in the European Union*. Study for the European Parliament, Brussels.

Cherti, M. and Szilard, M. (2013). *Returning Irregular Migrants: How Effective is the EU Response*. London: IPPR. Available at www.ippr.org/files/images/media/files/publication/2013/02/returning-migrants-EU-130220_10371.pdf?noredirect=1 (accessed September 12, 2016).

Cholewinski, R. (1998). Enforced Destitution of Asylum Seekers in the United Kingdom: The Denial of Fundamental Human Rights. *International Journal of Refugee Law*, 10(3), pp. 462–498.

Cholewinski, R. (2012). The EU Acquis on Irregular Migration Ten Years On. In Guild, E. and Minderhoud, P. (eds), *The First Decade of EU Migration and Asylum Law*. Leiden: Martinus Nijhoff, pp. 127–178.

Crawley, H., Hemmings, J. and Price, N. (2011). *Coping with Destitution: Survival and Livelihood Strategies of Refused Asylum Seekers Living in the UK*. Swansea: Centre for Migration Policy Research (CMPR).

Crawley, H., Düvell, F., Jones, K., McMahon, S. and Sigona, N. (2016). *Destination Europe? Understanding the Dynamics and Drivers of Mediterranean Migration in 2015, MEDMIG Final Report*. Available at www.medmig.info/research-brief-destination-europe.pdf (accessed January 7, 2017).

Czaika, M. and Haas, H. de (2013a). The Effectiveness of Immigration Policies. *Population and Development Review*, 39(3), pp. 488–508.

Czaika, M. and Haas, H. de (2013b). Measuring Migration Policies: Some Conceptual and Methodological Reflections. *Migration and Citizenship*, 1(2), pp. 40–47.

Du Preez, B. (2014). No End to the Horrors of Detention. openDemocracy, December 1. Available at www.opendemocracy.net/author/ben-du-preez (accessed September 12, 2016).

European External Action Service (EEAS) (2016). UNAVFOR MED Op Sophia – Six Monthly Report, June 22 to December 31, 2015. Published by Wikileaks, February 17, 2016. Available at https://wikileaks.org/eu-military-refugees/EEAS/page-1.html (accessed January 7, 2017).

European Migration Network (EMN) (2014). *Good Practices in the Return and Reintegration of Irregular Migrants: Member States' Entry Bans Policies and Use of Readmission Agreements between Member States and Third Countries*. Brussels: European Commission.

Europol (2015). Joint Operational Team Launched to Combat Irregular Migration in the Mediterranean, Press Release, issued March 17, 2015. Available at www.europol.europa.eu/newsroom/news/joint-operational-team-launched-to-combat-irregular-migration-in-mediterranean (accessed January 7, 2017).

Europol (2016a). European Migrant Smuggling Centre Infographic. Available at www.europol.europa.eu/sites/default/files/publications/emsc_infographic_final.pdf (accessed January 7, 2017).

Europol (2016b). Migrant Smuggling in the EU, the Hague. Available at www.europol.europa.eu/content/joint-operational-team-launched-combat-irregular-migration-mediterranean (accessed January 7, 2017).

Eurostat (2016). Statistics on Enforcement of Immigration Legislation, data extracted June 2016. Available at http://ec.europa.eu/eurostat/statistics-explained/index.php/Statistics_on_enforcement_of_immigration_legislation (accessed January 7, 2017).

EU and Government (2016). *Joint Way Forward on Migration Issues between the EU and Afghanistan*. Kabul, October 2, 2016. Available at https://eeas.europa.eu/sites/eeas/files/eu_afghanistan_joint_way_forward_on_migration_issues.pdf (accessed January 7, 2017).

Forensic Oceanography/Watch the Med (2016). Death by Rescue. Available at hhtp://deathbyrescue.org/report (accessed September 12, 2016).

Garland, D. (2001). *The Culture of Control: Crime and Social Order in Contemporary Society*. Chicago, IL: University of Chicago Press, pp. 34–35.

Garner, S. (2014). Life after Detention. openDemocracy, December 1. Available at www.opendemocracy.net/5050/saskia-garner/life-after-detention (accessed November 14, 2016).

Gibney, M.J. (2008). Asylum and the Expansion of Deportation in the United Kingdom 1. *Government and Opposition*, 43(2), pp. 146–167.

Guild, E. (2004). Who is an Irregular Migrant? In Bogusz, B. et al., *Irregular Migration and Human Rights: Theoretical, European and International Perspectives*. Leiden: Martinus Nijhoff, pp. 3–17.

Guild, E. (2006). Danger – Borders under Construction: Assessing the First Five Years of Border Policy in an Area of Freedom, Security and Justice. In De Zwaan, J. and Goudappel, F.A.N.G. (eds), *Freedom, Security and Justice in the European Union: Implementation of the Hague Programme*. The Hague: T.M.C. Asser Press, pp. 62–67.

Guild, E. (2010). *The Criminalisation of Migration in Europe: Human Rights Implications*, Council of Europe, Strasbourg. Available at https://wcd.coe.int/ViewDoc.jsp?id=1579605 (accessed January 7, 2017).

Guild, E. (2016). The Complex Relationship of Asylum and Border Controls in the European Union. In Chetail, V., De Bruycker, P. and Maiani, F. (eds), *Reforming the Common European Asylum System: The New European Refugee Law*. Boston, MA: Brill Nijhoff, pp. 39–54.

Guiraudon, V. (2000). European Integration and Migration Policy: Vertical Policy Making as Venue Shopping. *Journal of Common Market Studies*, 38, pp. 227–251.

Huysmans, J. (2006). *The Politics of Insecurity: Fear, Migration and Asylum in the EU*. Abingdon: Routledge.

Juncker, J.C. (2015). Speech at the Debate in the European Parliament on the Conclusions of the Special European Council on 23 April: 'Tackling the Migration Crisis'. Available at http://europa.eu/rapid/press-release_SPEECH-15-4896_en.htm (accessed January 23, 2017).

Massey, D.S., Arango, J., Hugo, G., Kouaouci, A. and Pellegrino, A. (1998). *Worlds in Motion: Understanding International Migration at the End of the Millennium*. Oxford: Clarendon Press.

Mitsilegas, V. (2015). *The Criminalisation of Migration in Europe: Challenges for Human Rights and the Rule of Law*, Springer Briefs in Law. London: Springer.

Parkin, J. (2013). *The Criminalisation of Migration in Europe: A State of the Art of the Academic Literature and Research*, CEPS Papers in Liberty and Security in Europe, No. 61. CEPS, Brussels.

Peers, S. (2015). Irregular Migrants: Can Humane Treatment Be Balanced against Efficient Removal? *European Journal of Migration Law*, 17(4), pp. 289–304.

Peers, S., Guild, E., Acosta, D., Groenendijk, K. and Moreno Lax, V. (2012). EU Immigration and Asylum Law (Text and Commentary), *Volume 2: EU Immigration Law*. Leiden: Martinus Nijhoff, pp. 18–19.

Pennington, J. and Balaram, B. (2013). *Homecoming: Return and Reintegration of Irregular Migrants from Nigeria*. London: IPPR. Available at www.ippr.org/publications/homecoming-return-and-reintegration-of-irregular-migrants-from-nigeria (accessed September 12, 2016).

Peutz, N. (2010). 'Criminal Alien' Deportees in Somaliland. In De Genova, N. and Peutz, N. (eds), *The Deportation Regime: Sovereignty, Space, and the Freedom of Movement*. Durham, NC: Duke University Press, pp. 371–409.

Provera, M. (2015). *The Criminalisation of Irregular Migration in the European Union*, CEPS Papers on Liberty and Security in Europe, No. 80. CEPS, Brussels.

UK House of Lords (2015). Operation Sophia, the EU's Naval Mission in the Mediterranean: An Impossible Challenge. European Union Committee, Fourteenth Report of Session 2015–2016, published May 13, 2016. Available at www.publications.parliament.uk/pa/ld201516/ldselect/ldeucom/144/144.pdf (accessed January 7, 2017).

Reuters (2016). As Sweden Tightens Borders, an Afghan Faces Return to Home he Doesn't Know, published October 20, 2016 by Scrutton, A. and Dickson, D. Available at www.reuters.com/article/us-europe-migrants-sweden-insight-idUSKCN12K10D (accessed January 7, 2017).

Schuster, L. and Majidi, N. (2013). What Happens Post-deportation? The Experience of Deported Afghans. *Migration Studies*, 1(2), pp. 221–240.

Stumpf, J. (2006). The Crimmigration Crisis: Immigrants, Crime and Sovereign Power. *American University Law Review*, 56(2), pp. 367–419.

7

INFORMALIZING EU READMISSION POLICY

Jean-Pierre Cassarino

Introduction

In 2002, when the General Secretariat of the Council (GSC) listed the various key criteria that needed to be taken into consideration in order to identify non-EU (or third) countries with which to negotiate EU readmission agreements, it underlined that EU readmission agreements 'should involve added value for member states in bilateral negotiations' (European Council 2002: 3) with a given third country (Cassarino 2010: 12; Carrera 2016: 37).

Since the 1999 entry into force of the Treaty of Amsterdam (ToA), which empowered the European Commission to negotiate and conclude EU readmission agreements with third countries, adding value has not only been a key criterion, as stated by the GSC; it has also been a growing concern for the EU.

Externally, negotiations with some third countries, especially with those located in the southern Mediterranean, have either been deferred (Algeria), extremely lengthy (Turkey) or thorny (Morocco). Internally, the European Commission has been confronted with growing criticisms on the part of those who mandated it to negotiate readmission agreements, namely EU member states. Of course, such criticisms are not new considering the history of EU institution-building. Invariably, since 1999, they have accompanied the creation and development of the Common European Asylum System, including the need to adopt common rules and procedures aimed at protecting the fundamental rights of asylum-seekers and people in need of protection. Member states' criticisms have been symptomatic of the resilient and unresolved tensions between bilateralism, intergovernmentalism and supranationalism.

Such tensions have ritually emerged following the arrival of large numbers of migrants in Europe, together with recurrent official calls for enhanced cooperation with third countries of origin and of transit in the 'fight against illegal migration'. Recently, the governments of the Visegrad Group (V4)[1] delivered a joint statement in September 2016 urging the EU institutions to 'restore common trust in the European project and its institutions and empower the voice of member states'. They also stated that 'migration policy should be based on the principles of "flexible solidarity" [...] [to] enable member states to decide on specific forms of contribution taking into account their experience and potential'.[2] In late August 2016, the Weimar Triangle[3] also delivered a joint statement where representatives of France, Germany and Poland expressed, among others, their desire to 'show that Europe is of use to its citizens' and to revitalize the European project in a post-Brexit context.

Arguably, the European Commission has been aware that providing an added value to member states' *modus operandi* and practices as applied to readmission constitutes a daunting challenge. This is all the more so in the realization that, since 1999, its action was already embedded in a context marked by the predominance of bilateral patterns of cooperation on readmission (Cassarino 2010). This study sets out to analyze the conditions under which the European Union has addressed this challenge. Having highlighted the *contingency gap*, which markedly distinguishes the drivers shaping the EU's approach to cooperation on readmission from those shaping member states' priorities in the field of readmission, this chapter examines the reasons why flexibility and informality have gradually gained momentum in the EU's readmission policy and in its external relations, especially since 2005. The various implications of this perceptible informalization process at EU level are detailed.

Unmet preconditions

Whereas the ToA established Union competence, the Treaty of Lisbon (TL) introduced several amendments that, to some extent, reaffirmed in a more explicit and unquestionable manner the shared competence of the Union in the field of readmission. Articles 3 and 4 of the Treaty on the Functioning of the European Union (TFEU) respectively list the areas of exclusive and shared competences. 'Freedom, Security and Justice' (FSJ) constitutes an area of shared competence in Article 4 (TFEU) and readmission belongs logically to this area.

Admittedly, the clear existence of a Union competence in the above areas is congruent with the reinforced integration of migration issues in the EU's external relations with third countries. In theory, the existence of a shared competence between the Union and the member states in the field of readmission should not be problematic. It is worth recalling that, in the scope of a EU readmission agreement concluded with a third country, member states have to comply with the general principles of EU law (legal certainty, legitimate expectations, effective remedies, proportionality and fundamental rights). In practice, however, this presupposes three preconditions which, to date, continue to be unmet.

First, member states would need to regularly notify the Commission, the Council and the European Parliament of their planned negotiations or talks on readmission with third countries. They would also have to notify them of their existing bilateral agreements linked to readmission. The notification procedure would necessarily address the variety of cooperative patterns linked to readmission (e.g., cfccfcf standard readmission agreements, exchanges of letters, intergovernmental arrangements, memoranda of understanding, framework agreements) that several member states have concluded over approximately the last three decades to ensure the operability of their cooperation with third countries.

Second, another precondition lies in establishing monitoring mechanisms aimed at understanding whether and how member states comply with their international obligations and the EU treaties when implementing EU readmission agreements. To be clear, each EU readmission agreement foresees the creation of a Joint Readmission Committee (JRC) comprising representatives of the European Commission (EC), assisted by experts from the member states and representatives of the third country. Actually, a JRC is in charge of promoting regular exchanges among the individual member states and the third country on issues regarding the application and interpretation of the EU agreement. Member states may conclude bilateral implementing protocols by listing the competent authorities that should receive and process readmission applications in accordance with the time limits set out in the agreement, the border crossing points, the role of escorting officers and the means of identification.

However, experience has shown that member states may implement the concluded EU readmission agreements with some third countries without necessarily having a bilateral implementing protocol. Adding value to the action of the member states would logically require the knowledge and understanding of existing bilateral patterns of cooperation on readmission.

Undoubtedly, monitoring mechanisms are essential to understanding how the terms of a EU readmission agreement have been concretely translated, if not reinterpreted, in the course of the implementation. This refers not only to procedures per se, but also to the respect of the fundamental rights of the persons to be readmitted with which each member state must comply, especially since the Charter of Fundamental Rights of the European Union has become part of the core legislation of the EU following the entry into force of the Treaty of Lisbon. Moreover, monitoring mechanisms are necessary to ensure the full and independent exercise of the European Parliament's legislative and budgetary functions, which logically and invariably depend on the extent to which the European Parliament will have access to information relating to the implementing phase of EU readmission agreements and to their compatibility with the treaties.

To date, the need for regular notification procedures and the establishment of monitoring mechanisms constitute two unmet preconditions. This becomes clear if one realizes member states' poor level of communication on their various patterns of cooperation on readmission with third countries, including their reluctance to disclose their scope and content.

The contingency gap

There exists, however, a third precondition. It refers to the convergence of contingencies and priorities between member states on the one hand, and the Union on the other. Contingencies pertain to the factors and conditions shaping patterns of cooperation on readmission (namely, how the cooperation on readmission has developed), whereas priorities refer to the drivers of cooperation (namely, which factors motivated the contracting parties). When convergence is optimal, member states would entrust or be fully supportive of the Union in the field of readmission while recognizing the added value and effectiveness of its action.

However, in practice, this optimal degree of convergence has never been reached, leading to a contingency gap. Convergence of contingencies and priorities is essential to capturing the difficulty with which the European Commission tackled the added-value criterion since it was mandated to negotiate and conclude EU readmission agreements. When this occurred, various EU member states had already concluded a substantial number of bilateral agreements linked to readmission, be they standard or non-standard,[4] with third countries worldwide. Moreover, the conclusion of bilateral agreements does not necessarily mean that the contracting parties implement them consistently and fully. Readmission inevitably implies unequal costs and benefits for the contracting parties, as well as unbalanced reciprocities (Cassarino 2010), even if the terms of the agreement are framed in a reciprocal context. These aspects have been amply addressed elsewhere (Cassarino 2007; Roig and Huddleston 2007; Trauner and Kruse 2008; El Qadim 2015). As a result of their long and varied experiences in the field, various EU member states have learned that exerting pressure on uncooperative third countries needs to be cautiously evaluated lest other issues of high politics be jeopardized. As already shown in previous works (Cassarino 2010), readmission cannot be isolated from a broader framework of interactions, including other strategic if not more crucial issue areas such as police cooperation in the fight against international terrorism, energy security, border control, and other diplomatic and geopolitical concerns. Exerting pressure on uncooperative third countries may even turn out to be a risky or counterproductive endeavor, especially when the latter can capitalize on their empowered position in other strategic issue areas (Cassarino 2005; El Qadim 2015). Nor can bilateral cooperation on readmission be viewed as an end in and of itself, since it has often been grafted onto the aforementioned broader framework of interactions.

Taking into consideration these past lessons is important in understanding the complex reasons for which the existence of an agreement does not automatically lead to its full implementation. This is because the latter is contingent upon an array of factors that codify the bilateral interactions between two contracting parties. Using an oxymoron, it is possible to argue that, over the past decades, various EU member states have learned that bilateral cooperation on readmission constitutes a central priority in their external relations, which at the same time remains peripheral to other strategic issue areas.

This paradox has characterized the contingencies faced by various member states. In a similar vein, factors motivating the conclusion of various bilateral agreements linked to readmission have been informed by the above-mentioned contingencies.

How has the EU tackled such contingencies, including the above-mentioned paradox, in its attempt to add value to member states' bilateral negotiations? As of 2000, when the European Commission received its first mandates to negotiate EU readmission agreements, more than 100 bilateral agreements had already been concluded by the member states with non-EU countries (see Figure 7.1). Bilateralism was strongly and deeply rooted in their external relations. Three key aspects played in favor of a harmonized approach to readmission at the EU level. The first was that speaking with one voice at the EU level would strengthen the leverage of individual member states in their negotiations with non-EU countries. The second pertained to the need for common procedures aimed at removing irregular migrants, in line with the EU treaties and in accordance with international law. The third aspect, closely linked with the second, referred to the respect of human rights standards and international obligations on removal, especially those contained in the 1950 European Convention for the Protection of Human Rights and Fundamental Freedoms (ECHR) and the Charter of Fundamental Rights of the European Union, which were both proclaimed in December 2000.

1999 to 2005: the drive for normative readmission

When the Area of Justice Freedom and Security was established following the 1999 Treaty of Amsterdam, the European Commission adopted a strictly technical-legal approach to readmission based on the oft-cited reference to states' obligations 'under customary international law'[5] to take back their own nationals (Hailbronner 1997; Roig and Huddleston 2007; Coleman 2009). This reference was clearly mentioned in the Conclusions of the European Council in Tampere in October 1999.

The 1999 European Council of Tampere is remembered as an event that marked a watershed in the intensification of the cooperation of JHA and migration management with third countries. It is also remembered because it conferred powers upon the Commission to negotiate and conclude EU readmission agreements with third countries.

Logically, these policy developments underlined the importance of collecting and analyzing systematic data and information as well as the need to have a commonly agreed statistical framework with a view to monitoring the impact and implementation of EU legislation and policy (European Commission 2003). However, attempts to collect data on member states' bilateral patterns of cooperation on readmission and on their concrete effects proved extremely difficult. This was not only because of the existence of significant statistical mismatches, but also because data remained either incomplete or reinterpreted locally or was simply not communicated by the member states. The establishment of an Area of Freedom, Security and Justice implied the recognition of shared principles and common standards at EU level without, however, 'challenging the legal and judicial traditions of the member states' (European Commission 2004: 10).

Readmission became a pivotal element of the joint management of migration flows, especially with reference to the 'fight against illegal migration', as well as a major cross-over issue in various internal and external policy domains. Their detailed analysis would go beyond the scope of this study. It is, however, important to stress that such developments, driven by an extraordinary sense of normative and bureaucratic rationality, contributed to the growing visibility of readmission in migration talks, especially in the external relations of the EU and its member states. Readmission became a key component of the action plans that the EU negotiated with third countries located in its eastern and southern regions, in the framework of the European Neighborhood Policy. These developments were also conducive to stronger expectations on the part of some EU member states who, on various occasions, criticized the slow progress in the negotiations undertaken by the European Commission in the field of readmission. The European Commission was called to deliver promptly and the European Council proposed to nominate a 'special representative on a common readmission policy'[6] (Papagiani 2006: 157; Coleman 2009: 194).

The years 2005 to 2009: prelude to the EU drive for flexibility

Member states have demonstrated their concerns in numerous ways regarding the capacity of the EU institutions to deal effectively with irregular migration, including readmission. Groups of EU member states proliferated. Officially, they were presented as intergovernmental fora aimed at opening and sustaining state-to-state informal consultations on border controls, asylum, human trafficking, border surveillance and the 'fight against illegal migration'. However, these groupings went much further than the mere promotion of intergovernmental consultations and dialogues while acquiring a certain degree of authoritativeness. Indeed, some of them were explicitly meant to influence EU policy-making at a time when the management of the post-2004 eastward enlargement of the EU and the rejection of Europe's Constitutional Treaty were stirring populist and protectionist discourses in Europe. For example, the May 2005 Prüm Convention[7] and the Group of 6 (or G6) epitomized the desire of some EU member states to collectively exert their leverage on the EU institutions, especially the European Commission, in the field of justice and home affairs. In September 2006, an open letter was sent to the then Finnish Presidency of the Council of the European Union calling for reinforced common concrete actions to counter 'mass arrivals of migrants' in Southern Europe. The letter came from the heads of state of Cyprus, France, Greece, Italy, Malta, Portugal, Slovenia and Spain. Later, a document was sent to the then Czech Presidency of the Council of the European Union pressing for the conclusion and effective implementation of EU readmission agreements. This document, dated January 13, 2009, came from Cyprus, Greece, Italy and Malta. These four countries formed the *Quadro Group* during the French EU Presidency (July to December 2008) to keep illegal immigration on the EU agenda.

These internal policy challenges, including the proliferation of informal regional groups within the EU, shed a clear light on the tricky conditions under which the European Commission was operating. In an attempt to respond to such internal challenges and to safeguard its credibility in dealing with irregular migration, the Commission expressed its intention to 'broker a deal'[8] with a view to facilitating the conclusion of EU readmission agreements with third countries while learning from the bilateral experiences of the EU member states. This statement did mark a watershed in the EU approach to negotiations on readmission, as it revealed the growing awareness on the part of the European Commission that its role as leader in the establishment of a EU-wide readmission policy could be jeopardized lest no new compromise be found.

This new compromise found its expression in the Global Approach to Migration (GAM), which was described as 'a comprehensive approach [combining] measures aimed at facilitating legal migration opportunities with those reducing illegal migration' (European Council 2007: 3). Key mechanisms for strategic cooperation with selected third countries were introduced within the framework of the GAM, including mobility partnerships (Parkes 2009; Reslow 2012). Mobility partnerships and their rationale form an integral part of the GAM. They are 'not designed to create legal rights or obligations under international law'. They encompass a broad range of issues ranging from development aid to temporary entry visa facilitation, circular (or temporary) migration schemes and the fight against illegal migration, including cooperation on readmission. They are also selective in that they are addressed to those third countries meeting certain conditions, such as cooperation in the fight against irregular migration and the existence of 'effective mechanisms for readmission'.[9]

The EU's attempt to conditionally link MPs with cooperation on readmission reflects how this issue has become a central component of its migration management policy. However, despite its official claim to draw upon bilateral experiences, the conditionality enshrined in MPs was at variance with the rationale for the EU member states' patterns of cooperation on readmission.

Actually, EU member states have often used material and non-material incentives, not conditionalities, in order to ensure the cooperation of third countries on migration management issues, including reinforced border controls and readmission. Material incentives include the conclusion of financial protocols to support foreign direct investments and job-creating activities in third countries' labor markets. In addition, technical equipment and capacity-building programs aimed at upgrading their law enforcement bodies were part of the incentives. Non-material incentives refer to strategic alliances aimed at reinforcing the international recognition of the political leadership of a cooperative third country or at defending its voice in the international community.

Moreover, the use of incentives (not coercive conditionalities) has been motivated by the perceptible empowerment of some third countries as a result of their pro-active involvement in the reinforced control of the EU external borders. For example, some member states have experienced in their bilateral interactions with third countries located in the Mediterranean that the latter were prone to capitalize upon crucial issue areas (fight against international terrorism, intelligence cooperation, energy security, border controls, to name but a few) to defend their own views and priorities. In other words, not only have some Mediterranean third countries been empowered, but they also have a capacity to exert a form of reverse leverage on their European counterparts (Cassarino 2007; Paoletti 2011; El Qadim 2015). As mentioned earlier, bilateral cooperation on readmission cannot be viewed as an end in itself, especially when dealing with strategic and empowered third countries. Moreover, member states know that the costs and benefits of bilateral cooperation on readmission are too asymmetric to ensure its durable implementation in the long run, just as they learned that readmission cannot be isolated from other geopolitical questions of high politics that no EU member state can afford to place in jeopardy.

Arguably, the above considerations may account for the reasons why MPs have been introduced with a view to *enabling* a non-legally binding framework of informal interactions on an array of joint actions ranging from visa facilitation to readmission, the promotion of assisted voluntary return (AVR) programs, migration and asylum, economic development, and border controls, among many others.[10] More importantly, the main issue at stake is not only about laying the groundwork for cooperation on migration and border management issues. Rather, through repetition and regular exchanges among stakeholders, MPs also contribute to consolidating a *system* whereby the cooperation on readmission, be it based on standard EU readmission agreements or on atypical arrangements, would become more predictable and unproblematic.

The year 2010 to the present: the EU drive for flexibility

It is worth recognizing that when the Treaty of Lisbon entered into force in December 2009, the above-mentioned system was already well developed. On the one hand, the EU member states had concluded more than 240 bilateral agreements linked to readmission with non-EU countries. On the other hand, around thirty bilateral implementing protocols were signed by the member states following the entry into force of eleven EU readmission agreements (see Figure 7.1). To date, this European readmission system has been in full expansion across all continents while encompassing highly diverse countries: rich, poor, aid-dependent, signatories of the 1951 Refugee Convention, conflict-ridden, peaceful, safe, unsafe, democratically organized and authoritarian. There is no question that the European readmission system has become powerfully inclusive.

The historical predominance of bilateralism (see Figure 7.1) has never been contested or challenged by the Union, above all when considering its shared competence in the field of readmission with the member states and as long as the latter's bilateral agreements are not incompatible with the obligations and international standards contained in a EURA. As explained earlier, this aspect is contingent upon notification procedures and effective monitoring mechanisms. True, the Union has been adamant about protecting its exclusive mandate once it was granted by the Council. It is also true that it has called upon member states to make sure that the terms of the EURAs be respected in their implementation phase and in line with the procedural guarantees enshrined in the 'return directive'.[11]

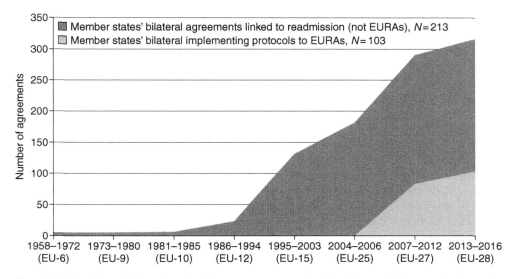

Figure 7.1 Number of bilateral readmission agreements concluded with non-EU countries: from the EU-6 to the EU-28

However, one is entitled to wonder how the above-mentioned monitoring mechanisms and notification procedures can be effective when the inflow of data and information allowing infringements to be detected exclusively comes from the member states or when the latter turn out to be reluctant to disclose to their European counterparts, let alone the public, the terms and rationale for the numerous bilateral agreements and secret arrangements they have concluded with third countries. If readmission is rhetorically presented by the member states as a priority in domestic policy-making, they know it cannot be presented as *the* compelling priority in their bilateral interactions with third countries, especially when the latter are strategic and empowered partners capable of defending their own vested interests and views. Some member states have acquired long experience in dealing with the centrality/periphery paradox (see Part I, this volume), which often characterizes their cooperation on readmission. Many have learned that laying too much emphasis on readmission in their external relations may turn out to be counterproductive as applied to other strategic issue areas. Arguably, this consideration is important in understanding why the negotiations of EURAs have been extremely lengthy and difficult.[12] Incidentally, more than ten years following its mandate to negotiate EURAs, the European Commission called on the member states to 'support its readmission negotiating efforts more wholeheartedly and not lose sight of the overall interest that a concluded EURA represents for the entire EU' (European Commission 2011: 8).

In an attempt to 'avoid the risk that concrete delivery is held up by technical negotiations for a fully-fledged formal [readmission] agreement' (European Commission 2016a: 3), the EU started to design a new Partnership Framework which would foster 'mutual understanding' on migration management issues as well as their operationalization into 'compacts'. Similar to mobility partnerships (MPs), compacts are tailor-made informal arrangements. However, unlike MPs, 'effective mechanisms on readmission' are not conditionally linked with the implementation of the new Partnership Framework. Nonetheless, they are highly prioritized. Arguably, the new Partnership Framework introduced in 2015 took stock of the misconception of MPs. It is aimed at moving progressively towards the attainment of specific 'migration management' objectives, which 'reconcile the interests and priorities of the parties' with reference to 'shared and common principles'. Dialogues, mutual understandings and informal arrangements are at the heart of the Partnership Framework. The latter cannot be coined 'readmission agreements'. However, whether these arrangements take the form of a 'joint declaration', 'statement', 'common agenda' or 'joint way forward', they are no less EU-wide deals based on reciprocal commitments between the EU and its member states on the one hand, and a third country on the other. More importantly, patterns of cooperation stemming from a partnership framework are aimed at dealing with, among others, readmission and readmission-related issues in the short to long term.

The new Partnership Framework draws upon the political declaration of the Valletta Summit (November 11–12, 2015) which identified in its action plan five priority domains on migration management with African countries including, among others, the need for 'mutually agreed arrangements on return and readmission'. Since then, various types of arrangements have been agreed upon or are being negotiated under the umbrella Partnership Framework (PF) with third countries (see Table 7.1). In 2016, the EU started to negotiate two EU-wide Standard Operating Procedures (SOPs) with Mali and Bangladesh for the identification and return of persons without an authorization to stay. SOPs are aimed at swiftly improving cooperation between national consulates in order to accelerate procedures for identification, redocumentation and readmission.

Two Joint Migration Declarations (JMDs) on migration management, including the issue of readmission, have been signed with Niger and Ghana. JMDs deal with, among others, readmission and enhanced cooperation on the 'timely delivery of travel documents'.

Three Common Agendas on Migration and Mobility (CAMMs) have been signed with India, Nigeria and Ethiopia. CAMMs existed before the adoption of Partnership Frameworks. They are described as non-exhaustive flexible frameworks for cooperation of mutual interest based on the principle of voluntary participation of the EU member states.

One Joint Way Forward (JWF) has been concluded with Afghanistan. JWFs are not legally binding in the sense that, formally, they do not create legal rights or obligations for the contracting parties which cooperate on migration issues, especially on readmission. In practice, however, they define mutual commitments whose application and potential readjustments are closely monitored by a joint working group.

The new PF and its various compacts have been presented as a 'new comprehensive cooperation with third countries on migration' (European Commission 2016b: 5) where effective cooperation on readmission and the 'sustainability of return' remain key priorities.

For various member states, however, this type of informal broad arrangement or atypical agreement is far from being new. Over the past two decades, various EU member states (e.g., the United Kingdom, France, Italy and Spain) have excelled in these informal deals based on memoranda of understanding, administrative arrangements and bilateral police cooperation agreements, including a detailed clause on readmission (Cassarino 2007). For member states, grafting readmission onto a broader framework of interactions is not uncommon. However, as already underlined, readmission has been viewed by the latter as one of the many means of consolidating a bilateral cooperative framework, but not as an end in itself, depending on how they codified their bilateral relations with a given third country. By contrast, for the European Commission and the European External Action Service (EEAS), readmission continues to be presented as *the* compelling priority, which progressively determines a whole framework of cooperation with a given third country. Admittedly, the same contingency gap between the EU and some member states continues to exist.

Member states' bilateral arrangements on readmission on the one hand, and the new compacts resulting from the new EU-wide Partnership Framework on the other, share three common denominators. First, they both reify the capacity of law enforcement authorities and decision-makers to control legal and irregular migration while showing constituencies that policy measures aimed at stemming irregular migration are or may be taken. Second, their rationale lies in making cooperation upon readmission more flexible while avoiding lengthy ratification procedures and, consequently, parliamentary oversight. Third, they tend to respond to emergencies and external shocks (e.g., arrivals of large numbers of irregular migrants and asylum-seekers), whether or not their response is adequate.

These common attributes are useful in capturing the urgency with which the aforementioned bilateral PF arrangements have been agreed. Apart from the resilient criticisms coming from some European political leaders regarding the ability of the EU to deal with irregular migration and inflows of asylum-seekers, especially since social unrest which took place in various Arab countries in 2011, unprecedented disputes on internal border controls and the reintroduction of intra-Schengen controls emerged among various EU member states (Moreno-Lax 2015), putting the Common European Asylum System under stress. Rising populism and Euroskepticism, added to the ascent of anti-immigrant political parties in the West by way of growing economic insecurity as a result of a resilient financial crisis, created a sense of emergency to which both the EU and its member states had to respond.

While these unprecedented events may call for urgent provisions and policy action – in accordance with the fundamental rights principles that the Union seeks to advance in its external action – the adoption of EU-wide flexible, swift and atypical arrangements on migration issues with third countries of origin and of transit raises a host of challenges and serious concerns.

Table 7.1 EU readmission agreements and arrangements linked to readmission, October 2016

Country	Formal EU readmission agreements (EURAs)		Non-standard non-legally binding EU-wide deals linked to readmission					
	EURA entered into force	Negotiating mandate	MP	CAMM	JWF	JS	SOP	JMD
Afghanistan						October 2, 2016		
Albania	May 1, 2006	November 2002						
Algeria		November 2002						
Armenia	January 1, 2014	December 2011	October 27, 2011					
Azerbaijan	September 1, 2014	December 2011	December 5, 2013					
Bangladesh							N/A	
Belarus		March 2011						
Bosnia Herzegovina	January 1, 2008	November 2006	October 13, 2016					
Cape Verde	December 1, 2014	June 2009	June 5, 2008					
China		November 2002						
Ethiopia				November 11, 2015				
FYROM	January 1, 2008	November 2006						
Ghana								June 6, 2016
Georgia	March 1, 2011	November 2008	November 30, 2009					

Hong Kong	March 1, 2004	April 2001	
India			March 29, 2016
Jordan	June 1, 2004	March 2016	October 9, 2014
Macao		April 2001	
Mali			N
Moldova	January 1, 2008	December 2006	June 5, 2008
Mongolia	January 1, 2008	November 2006	
Montenegro		September 2000	June 7, 2013
Morocco			
Niger		September 2016	
Nigeria		September 2000	March 12, 2015
Pakistan	December 1, 2010	September 2000	
Russia	June 1, 2007	November 2006	
Serbia	January 1, 2008	September 2000	
Sri Lanka	May 1, 2005		
Tunisia		December 2014	March 3, 2014
Turkey	October 1, 2014	November 2002	
Ukraine	January 1, 2008	June 2002	May 3, 2016

Source: EU documentation. Author's own elaboration. MP = Mobility Partnership; CAMM = Common Agenda on Migration and Mobility; JWF = Joint Way Forward; JS = Joint Statement; SOP = Standard Operating Procedure; JMD = Joint Migration Declaration; N = Negotiations.

First, 'the paramount priority set by the EU to achieve fast and operational returns, and not necessarily formal readmission agreements' (European Commission 2016b: 7) starkly reflects a reconsideration of the EU's approach to a 'common readmission policy' which has veered from a normative to a flexible approach. As Sergio Carrera (2016: 47) rightly noted, while the EU claims to build common and harmonized procedures, such a reconsideration may 'increase the inconsistencies and, arguably, further undermine the credibility of the EU's readmission policy'. Moreover, when realizing that the drive for flexibility turns the EU into a facilitator (not a supervisor) who lays the groundwork for reinforced and variegated bilateral cooperative patterns (Favilli 2016: 422), especially when it comes to dealing with rules of identification and redocumentation of migrants, interagency cooperation, the effective protection of personal data, exchange of information between each member state and a cooperative third country, and, last but not least, with fair and legal remedy procedures. Perhaps never before has bilateralism been so intertwined with supranationalism.

The issue at stake is to understand whether the various types of non-legally binding arrangements, beyond their official designation, constitute mere international arrangements or turn out to have a binding force on the contracting parties once their implementation takes place. Recently, as a result of the controversial EU–Turkey statement on refugees concluded on March 7, 2016,[13] the French Independent Constitutional Authority for the Defense of Rights, a kind of ombudsman, submitted a report to the Senate in July 2016 stressing that the case law of the Court of Justice of the European Union (CJEU) does not limit itself to the form of bilateral undertakings, but also considers the intentions[14] of the contracting parties and the legal effects of their acts. The same considerations apply to the numerous deals that have been concluded to date as part of the new Partnership Framework.

To date, beyond the growing controversy and contradictory academic debates on whether or not these arrangements constitute international agreements, there seems to be concordance between EU lawyers and scholars that such EU-wide 'arrangements' tend to avoid parliamentary oversight at EU and national levels (Carrera 2016; Favilli 2016; Gatti 2016). Technically, they do not fall within the scope of Article 218 of the TFEU, which regulates the adoption of international agreements in accordance with the ordinary legislative procedure (or co-decision procedure shared between the European Parliament and the Council), and which allows the European Parliament to 'obtain the opinion of the Court of Justice as to whether an agreement envisaged is compatible with the Treaties'. Practically, however, it seems that the commitments and intentions of the contracting parties explicitly mentioned in the various texts of these EU-wide arrangements call for a fair and honest assessment of their concrete implications for migrants' fundamental rights and for states' international obligations.

Conclusion

The drive for flexibility was already a *fait accompli* at a bilateral level long before the entry into force of the 1999 Treaty of Amsterdam, which empowered the Union to negotiate and conclude formal EU readmission agreements with third countries (Cassarino 2007). This study has set out to demonstrate that the drive for flexibility has also become a *fait accompli* at the EU level, seven years after the 2009 entry into force of the Treaty of Lisbon.

Yet today, making an inventory based exclusively on the number of formal EURAs the Union has concluded with third countries would never suffice to illustrate the scope and rationale for its 'common readmission policy'. An array of informal arrangements need to be taken into consideration to capture the emergence of new patterns of cooperation on readmission driven by the prioritization of operable means of implementation and flexibility (see Table 7.1).

However, this perceptible prioritization process, including its wide acceptance at EU level, may dilute international norms and standards that had been viewed as being sound and secure (Hathaway 2016). This is because it rests on a subtle denial whereby the enforceability of universal norms and standards on human rights is weakened or 'disregarded' (Basilien-Gainche 2016: 339–344) without necessarily ignoring or denying their existence.

A clear illustration of this subtle denial lies in the way in which the 'more for more' principle gradually veered from a conditionality based on effective political and democratic reforms in third countries to a conditionality based on enhanced cooperation on border and migration controls, including readmission. As a result of the Arab Spring, the 'more for more' principle was initially aimed at promoting human rights observance as well as democratic and political reforms in third countries (European Commission and European External Action Service 2012: 3–4).

As of February 2014, the 'more for more' principle became equated with a conditionality (Carrera *et al.* 2016) aimed at incentivizing the cooperation of third countries on migration-related issues, including readmission. Today, the Commission is intent upon using 'trade policy and development aid to gain more leverage in the area of readmission, building on the "more for more" principle which was applied in relation with countries in the EU's neighborhood' (Avramopoulos 2015: 8). This intention was made explicit in the June 2015 European Council's conclusions calling for wider efforts to 'contain the growing flows of illegal migration' (2015: 1).

Making trade policy and development aid conditional upon the cooperation on border surveillance and readmission (including the swift delivery of travel documents) may be at variance with Article 208 of the TFEU, and with the mutual commitments taken in the various dialogues, declarations and ministerial conferences on migration and development organized since 2004 between the EU and non-EU countries. Incidentally, it is worth recalling that during the oft-cited July 2004 Rabat Process – which has been presented as a template for subsequent dialogues and exchanges on migration matters between European and African representatives – some strategic third countries explicitly relayed their claims to France and Spain (Wolff 2012: 140) in order to place at the center of discussions the need for economic development, conflict prevention and poverty eradication in countries of origin and of transit when dealing with the management of international migration. Such claims were clearly reiterated by African leaders at the November 2015 Valletta meeting on migration. The extent to which the Commission will reconcile its altered vision of the 'more for more' principle with the above-mentioned mutual commitments remains unclear.

How can these recent political developments, including the EU drive for flexible cooperation upon readmission, be addressed? When considering that the drive for flexibility at the EU level has been responsive to internal and external factors, one is entitled to wonder whether the recurrent reference to the securitization of migration policies in the West continues to adequately address the scope of these policy developments. Moreover, don't their policy and societal implications call for a much-needed reflection on the ways in which the relationships between European states and their own constituencies have been reconfigured over the past decades? For now, these questions constitute further avenues for research across disciplines.

Notes

1 Research for this chapter was carried out within the framework of the research project 'BORDERLANDS: Boundaries, Governance and Power in the European Union's Relations with North Africa and the Middle East', funded by the European Research Council (ERC) under Grant Agreement Number 263277. The project is hosted at the European University Institute, Robert Schuman Centre

for Advanced Studies, and directed by Raffaella Del Sarto. The usual disclaimers apply, including the Czech Republic, Hungary, Poland and Slovakia. See www.visegradgroup.eu.

2 See Joint Statement of the Heads of Government of the V4 Countries, 16 September 2016. Available at www.visegradgroup.eu/calendar/2016/joint-statement-of-the-160919.
3 A trilateral group of EU member states, including France, Germany and Poland.
4 Standard bilateral agreements refer to fully fledged readmission agreements defining the reciprocal obligations of the contracting parties. Under certain circumstances, however, two states may agree to conclude a bilateral agreement without necessarily formalizing their cooperation upon readmission. Governments may decide to graft readmission onto a broader framework of bilateral cooperation (e.g., police cooperation agreements with a clause on readmission, administrative arrangements and partnership agreements) or through other channels (e.g., by using exchanges of letters and memoranda of understanding). This dual approach explains why it is important to talk about agreements *linked* to readmission (Cassarino 2007), since it encompasses agreements that may be standard and non-standard.
5 Sergio Carrera notes, however, that there is no 'consensus as regards the actual scope of that obligation, and the extent to which it relates to the right to leave and return by individuals of these same states as enshrined in international human rights instruments' (Carrera 2016: 48); see also Giuffré 2015.
6 On October 24, 2005, the Commission appointed Karel Kovanda, Deputy Director-General of DG External Relations, as Special Representative for a common readmission policy.
7 The Prüm Treaty or Convention was initially signed by seven EU member states: Austria, Belgium, France, Germany, Luxembourg, The Netherlands and Spain. The Convention is aimed at stepping up cross-border police cooperation and exchanges between members' law enforcement agencies with a view to combating organized crime, terrorism and illegal migration more effectively. Provisions of the Prüm Treaty dealing with police cooperation and information exchange on DNA-profiles and fingerprints were transposed in the legal framework of the European Union following a Council Decision dated June 23, 2008.
8   Experiences have demonstrated that to broker a deal the EU needs to offer something in return. In their bilateral readmission negotiations member states are increasingly offering other forms of support and assistance to third countries to facilitate the conclusion of such agreements, and the possibilities of applying this wider approach at EU level should be explored.

(European Commission 2006: 9)

9 Mobility partnerships 'would be agreed with those third countries committed to fighting illegal immigration and that have effective mechanisms for readmission' (European Commission 2007: 19).
10 Since their introduction in 2006, nine MPs have been concluded with non-EU countries, namely with Armenia (2011), Azerbaijan (2013), Belarus (2016), Cape Verde (2008), Georgia (2009), Jordan (2014), Moldova (2008), Morocco (2013) and Tunisia (2014).
11 The 'Return Directive' (Directive 2008/115/EC of the European Parliament and of the Council of December 16, 2008 on common standards and procedures in member states for returning illegally staying third-country nationals) was adopted in December 2008 with a transposition deadline into national law on December 24, 2010. It establishes common rules for the removal of third-country nationals who do not, or no longer, fulfil the conditions for entry, stay or residence in a member state, and in accordance with the principle of *non-refoulement* which applies to all illegally staying third-country nationals, be they asylum-seekers or not. Among many others, the Directive deals with the issuance of return decisions, effective remedy to appeal and review return decisions as well as with conditions of detention.
12 As of October 2016, seventeen EURAs entered into force with Albania (2006), Armenia (2014), Azerbaijan (2014), Bosnia and Herzegovina (2008), Cape Verde (2014), FYROM (2008), Georgia (2011), Hong Kong (2004), Macao (2004), Moldova (2008), Montenegro (2008), Pakistan (2010), Russia (2007), Serbia (2008), Sri Lanka (2005), Turkey (2014) and Ukraine (2008). Put together, the total time elapsing between the negotiating mandates conferred upon the European Commission and the entry into force of all the seventeen EURAs amounts to 67.2 years: an average of 3.9 years per EURA.
13 The March 2016 Joint Statement (JS) between Turkey and the EU delimits the framework of a broad cooperation aimed, among others, at 'returning all migrants not in need of international protection'

from Greece to Turkey. This JS facilitates the bilateral cooperation between Greece and Turkey on the removal of irregular migrants.
14 Original text: 'Notons que la jurisprudence de la CJUE ne s'arrête pas à l'aspect formel de l'acte mais s'intéresse à l'intention des parties et aux actions concrètes mises en œuvre pour parvenir aux objectifs' (Défenseur des Droits 2016: 4).

Bibliography

Avramopoulos, D. (2015). *Letter from Commissioner Dimitris Avramopoulos to Ministers.* Brussels, June 1, Ares (2015) 2397724.

Basilien-Gainche, M.L. (2016). Leave and Let Die: The EU Banopticon Approach to Migrants at Sea. In Moreno-Lax, V. and Papastavridis, E. (eds), *'Boat Refugees' and Migrants at Sea: A Comprehensive Approach: Integrating Maritime Security with Human Rights.* Leiden: Martinus Nijhoff, pp. 327–350.

Carrera, S. (2016). *Implementation of EU Readmission Agreements: Identity Determination Dilemmas and the Blurring of Rights.* London: Springer Open.

Carrera, S., Cassarino, J-P., El Qadim, N., Lahlou, M. and den Hertog, L. (2016). EU–Morocco Cooperation on Readmission, Borders and Protection: A Model to Follow? Brussels: *CEPS Paper in Liberty and Security in Europe,* No. 87.

Cassarino, J-P. (2005). Migration and Border Management in the Euro-Mediterranean Area: Heading towards New Forms of Interconnectedness. In *Mediterranean Yearbook.* Barcelona: IEMed, pp. 227–231.

Cassarino, J-P. (2007). Informalising Readmission in the EU Neighbourhood. *The International Spectator,* 42(2), pp. 179–196.

Cassarino, J-P. (2010). *Readmission Policy in the European Union.* Brussels: European Parliament.

Coleman, N. (2009). *European Readmission Policy: Third Country Interests and Refugee Rights.* Leiden: Martinus Nijhoff.

Défenseurs des Droits (2016). *Avis du Défenseur des Droits n°16–18, 8 juillet 2016.* Paris: Défenseur des Droits.

El Qadim, N. (2015). *Le gouvernement asymétrique des migrations. Maroc/Union européenne.* Paris: Dalloz.

European Commission (2002). *Action Plan for the Collection and Analysis of Community Statistics in the Field of Migration.* COM(2003) 179 final.

European Commission (2004). *Area of Freedom, Security and Justice: Assessment of the Tampere Programme and Future Orientations.* COM(2004) 4002 final.

European Commission (2006). *The Global Approach to Migration One Year On: Towards a Comprehensive European Migration Policy.* COM(2006) 735 final.

European Commission (2011). *Evaluation of the EU Readmission Agreements.* COM(2011) 76 final.

European Commission (2016a). *First Progress Report on the Partnership Framework with Third Countries under the European Agenda on Migration.* COM(2016) 700 final.

European Commission (2016b). *Establishing a New Partnership Framework with Third Countries under the European Agenda on Migration.* COM(2016) 385 final.

European Commission and European External Action Service (2012). *Delivering on a New European Neighbourhood Policy.* JOIN 2012(14) final.

European Council (2002). *Criteria for the Identification of Third Countries with which New Readmission Agreements Need to be Negotiated.* 7990/02, April 16, Brussels.

European Council (2007). *Council Conclusions on the Global Approach to Migration 2807th Justice and Home Affairs Council Meeting.* Luxembourg, June 12 and 13.

European Council (2015). *Conclusions.* EUCO 22/15, June 26, Brussels.

Favilli, C. (2016). La cooperazione UE–Turchia per contenere il flusso dei migranti e dei richiedenti asilo: Obiettivo riuscito? *Diritti umani e diritti internazionali,* 10(2), pp. 405–426.

Gatti, M. (2016). The EU–Turkey Statement: A Treaty That Violates Democracy. *EJIL: Talk!: Blog of the European Journal of International Law.* Available at www.ejiltalk.org/the-eu-turkey-statement-a-treaty-that-violates-democracy-part-1-of-2/ (accessed December 15, 2016).

Giuffré, M. (2015). Obligation to Readmit? The Relationship between Interstate and EU Readmission Agreements. In Ippolito, F. and Trevisanut, S. (eds), *Migration in the Mediterranean: Mechanisms of International Cooperation.* Cambridge: Cambridge University Press, pp. 263–287.

Hailbronner, K. (1997). Readmission Agreements and the Obligation of States under Public International Law to Readmit their Own and Foreign Nationals. *Zeitschrift für ausländisches öffentliches Recht und Völkerrecht,* No. 57.

Hathaway, J.C. (2016). A Global Solution to a Global Refugee Crisis. *European Papers*, 1(1), pp. 93–99.
Moreno-Lax, V. (2015). *Europe in Crisis: Facilitating Access to Protection, (Discarding) Offshore Processing and Mapping Alternatives for the Way Forward*. Brussels: Red Cross EU Office.
Paoletti, E. (2011). *The Migration of Power and North–South Inequalities: The Case of Italy and Libya*. New York: Palgrave Macmillan.
Papagiani, G. (2006). *Institutional and Policy Dynamics of EU Migration Law*. Leiden: Martinus Nijhoff.
Parkes, R. (2009). EU Mobility Partnerships: A Model for Policy Coordination? *European Journal of Migration and Law*, 11(4), pp. 327–345.
Reslow, N. (2012). The Role of Third Countries in EU Migration Policy: The Mobility Partnerships. *European Journal of Migration and Law*, 14(4), pp. 393–415.
Roig, A. and Huddleston, T. (2007). EC Readmission Agreements: A Reevaluation of the Political Impasse. *European Journal of Migration and Law*, 9, pp. 363–387.
Trauner, F. and Kruse, I. (2008). EC Visa Facilitation and Readmission Agreements: Implementing a New EU Security Approach in the Neighbourhood. Brussels: *CEPS Working Document* No. 290.
Wolff, S. (2012). *The Mediterranean Dimension of the European Union's Internal Security*. New York: Palgrave Macmillan.

8
BORDER MANAGEMENT
The Schengen regime in times of turmoil

Ruben Zaiotti

Introduction

Contemporary Europe represents a unique laboratory for the conduct of political experiments involving territoriality (Green 2013). The most far-reaching of these experiments is the unbundling of what has traditionally been a national prerogative – the management of a country's borders – and the 'pooling' of this task among multiple national and regional political entities. Today, border practices in Europe are no longer limited to the territorial edges separating sovereign states, nor are they managed by a single, hierarchically defined authority; they are instead geographically diffused both within and beyond the continent and their governance is polycentric and network-like (Delanty 2006; Axford 2006; Parker and Adler-Nissen 2012). In this post-national territorial arrangement, the fortified lines that once separated European countries have become 'internal' crossing points monitored only in exceptional circumstances. In turn, some borders are now both national *and* European, since they are situated along the continent's external perimeter. Although they have not disappeared, borders have also become more 'ephemeral and impalpable' (Vaughan-Williams 2009: 583) thanks to sophisticated new techniques such as surveillance and data mining.

The institutional arrangement that has made these transformations possible is the Schengen border regime. Created in the mid-1980s as an intergovernmental arrangement outside the European Union (EU), Schengen has become one of the pillars of the EU's architecture and has been hailed as a success story of European integration (Walters 2002; Zaiotti 2011).[1] Thanks to this arrangement, the old continent has witnessed an unprecedented process of regionalization of border policies. The ultimate goal of creating truly 'integrated border management' as envisioned by EU officials (European Commission 2002),[2] however, is far from accomplished. The sheer complexity of such an endeavor, coupled with lingering misgivings about the loss of national sovereign control over a sensitive policy area, have limited the pace, coherence and depth of the Europeanization of border policies. External shocks, such as the sudden increase in migratory pressures on Europe's borders due to the Syrian conflict, have highlighted the regime's shortcomings (Vaughan-Williams 2015a). This state of turmoil has led to the further strengthening of existing external border controls, and more problematically, it has also stimulated the reimposition of controls at various European 'internal' borders. The politics of building barriers, or what Rosières and Reece (2012) call *teichopolitics*, has thus taken center stage in Europe.

This re-bordering process has caused growing internal tensions in the Schengen regime, raising the specter of its ultimate demise (Cornelisse 2014; Brouwer et al. 2015; Zaiotti 2013).

With this background in mind, this chapter offers an overview of the main features of border management in the European Union and the main challenges it faces today.[3] Two main areas that constitute this policy field are explored here: its governance – who manages borders and how key policy decisions are taken – and policies – how borders are regulated on the ground. In doing so, this chapter presents some of the key debates surrounding the Schengen regime and tries to make sense of the transformations that characterize European borders in the current turbulent times. The chapter concludes by exploring some of the possible scenarios for border management in the European Union over the coming years.

Managing teichopolitics: border governance in the European Union

In order to properly understand the dynamics that characterize the management of European borders, it is necessary to analyze the policy-making structures, processes and actors that sustain them; in other words, their governance. The premise for this argument is that borders should be considered not as natural and static entities, but as continually being made (Newman 2006). From this perspective, borders are social and political constructions created 'by someone, for some purpose and managed to serve particular interests' (Newman 2006: 35). As a result of the increasing migratory pressures and the heightened state of security that have followed the terrorist attacks in the United States and Europe since 2001, the governance of borders, especially in Western countries, has experienced substantial restructuring. The European continent has been at the forefront of these transformations. As has been the case for other policy fields, the ongoing process of European integration has provided the background and impetus for the developments characterizing the management of Europe's frontiers.

Since the start of the millennium the stated objective followed by European policy-makers has been that of achieving integrated border management. In this context, 'integrated' does not necessarily mean greater *communitarization* (i.e., transfer of powers to the EU), although for its proponents this is undoubtedly an important aspect of their strategy. The term is used here in its literal sense of 'combining or coordinating separate elements so as to provide a harmonious, interrelated whole'.[4] The efforts to render this policy field more coherent and coordinated started in the 1990s, and have involved both a widening and deepening of European border governance. On the one hand, countries on the continent's periphery have joined the Schengen regime and have become actively involved in the management of Europe's external borders. On the other, cooperation among EU member states has increased, as has the involvement of EU institutions. These achievements are particularly notable given the sheer complexity of coordinating the actions of a large group of sovereign states and of accommodating their often clashing interests (Thielemann and Armstrong 2013; Gaisbauer 2013). EU institutions have been a crucial engine of this integrative process, taking on the role of 'supranational policy entrepreneurs' (Kaunert 2010; Huber 2015). This is the case not just for policy-making units (e.g., the European Commission and its Directorates General), but also for operational agencies such as Frontex (Reid-Henry 2013). Since its creation in 2005, Frontex has been an active player in the management of the EU's external frontiers. The EU border agency, for instance, has coordinated joint patrols of European maritime forces along the Mediterranean and West African coasts and, in some cases, has adopted a more operational role (e.g., Joint Operation Triton). This activism is likely to increase given the new powers and personnel Frontex has acquired with its relaunch as the 'European Border and Coast Guard Agency' in October 2016.

In parallel with the redistribution of some responsibilities to the regional level, the governance of EU borders has also been characterized by the progressive delegation of important operational tasks to non-governmental actors. This is the case for visas (Zaiotti 2016: 14–16). If not granted on arrival, these documents are typically issued through a prior application at a country's embassy or consulate. More and more, however, visas are processed by private for-profit companies that are granted the authority by foreign governments to issue international travel documents. In the European context, some of these applications have been pooled among EU member states. Airline carriers and other transport companies have also been compelled, under threat of penalties, to take up more and more border control duties by making decisions on the possession and authenticity of relevant documents on behalf of governments. For some commentators, these trends represent a neoliberal turn in border management (Prokkola 2013). The outsourcing of border services that this approach fosters, while allowing governments to increase efficiency and reduce costs, has also reduced public accountability and possibilities for legal recourse (Taylor 2011: 5).

Another important development characterizing the governance of EU borders has been its progressive 'internationalization' (Wolff et al. 2013). Since the millennium, EU institutions and member states have established a thick network of cooperative arrangements with sending and transit countries of migration around the world. These moves are a reflection of the contribution these countries make to the management of international migration. The EU has tried to strengthen the capacity of local authorities in refugee-producing or transit regions through a mix of financial incentives and operational support. The European Union has, for instance, introduced Regional Protection Programs, which are elaborated in collaboration with EU member states and the targeted countries with the purpose of building local capacities to manage migratory flows an to promote durable solutions for asylum-seekers in transit countries (European Commission 2005). The first programs of this type were implemented in the mid-2000s in Eastern Europe and the African Great Lakes region, and then extended to the Horn of Africa and North Africa. In 2015 the EU signed an agreement with Turkey to stem the flow of migrants crossing into Europe. In order to deal with failed asylum-seekers and, more generally, undocumented migrants already present in their territory, and to dissuade potential new claimants, individual EU member states have negotiated readmission agreements with sending and receiving countries (Wolff 2016; Panizzon 2012). These agreements oblige countries to accept not only their own nationals, but also third-country nationals in exchange for compensatory measures like visa facilitation programs or financial support. Spain and Morocco signed such an agreement in 2003; and in December 2013 the EU finalized a similar arrangement with Turkey. The EU has also spearheaded regional political dialogues aimed at finding jointly agreed solutions to manage migratory flows. One example of these initiatives is the *EU–Horn of Africa Migration* Route Initiative (known as the Khartoum Process).

Besides sending and transit countries, EU institutions and member states have actively involved international organizations in the management of European borders (Geiger and Pécoud 2014). The EU and the International Organization for Migration (IOM), for instance, have collaborated in the context of the Border Assistance Mission to Moldova and Ukraine (EUBAM).[5] The European Union has also provided funds to the IOM to support detention efforts in Ukraine, and has supported the creation and management of detention facilities within the framework of 'twinning programs' – initiatives in which EU states partner with governments in Europe's neighborhood to strengthen local administrative and bureaucratic capacity.

These trends indicate that power in the governance of European borders has been diffused both vertically (to the European Union) and horizontally (within and beyond Europe). These dynamics have not always been visible, but their effects have been substantial in terms of degree of coherence of the policy-making process and resources necessary to manage a complex policy field such as border control. For some commentators, the result has been the transformation of EU border governance into a particular technology of power that regulates certain populations and sustains the legitimacy of the institutions that manage it (Vaughan-Williams 2009).

Yet the progressive integration of border governance in the EU is far from being complete and unchallenged (Müller 2014), and concerns over sovereignty and national security remain, even in an allegedly post-national Europe (Parker and Adler-Nissen 2012). Even more than for the EU integration project as a whole, the tension between the national and post-national dimension of the governance of EU borders is a key feature of this policy field. This state of affairs is reflected in the fragmented nature of the border management institutional architecture (Cornelisse 2014). While over the years the EU has acquired more responsibilities in this field, some relevant competences (e.g., the everyday management of borders) are still under national control. National actors therefore play a central role in this field, whether they are ministries of interior (Ripoll Servent and Trauner 2014) or operational agencies such as national coast guards (Bigo 2014). Even among EU institutions there are conflicting interests and competition (Huber 2015). It is not surprising, therefore, that the approach to border management has largely taken the form of 'enhanced cooperation', rather than the more communitarized approach defining other EU policy areas. The Syrian refugee crisis has heightened these already existing tensions. Exemplary in this regard is the saga of the EU-sponsored refugee redistribution scheme, which the European Commission has tried to impose upon member states, but member states have either vocally opposed it or dragged their feet in its implementation.

The result of these dynamics has been the politicization of the border policy field. Traditionally, decisions within this field have been taken by stealth and with limited democratic input. Today, migration and border issues have reached the top of the EU political agenda. The new scrutiny that has come with this development has put pressure on EU institutions and member states to deliver on their commitments and to assume more accountability for their actions. At the same time, the politicization of migration and border issues has seriously challenged the technocratic, solution-oriented philosophy behind the idea of integrated border governance, and arguably the EU as a whole (Walters 2004). Conflict, and not compromise, has become this policy field's new *modus operandi*.

Teichopolitics in action: EU border policies

Over the years, the European Union has built a large set of formal rules and procedures to govern the movement of people across European borders. These provisions, outlined in the *Schengen Borders Code*, deal with short-term visas, asylum requests and border checks. Their existence is a prerequisite for the functioning of the regime. In practice, however, their application has not been uniform. Differences among Schengen members in terms of capacity and political commitment have affected the Code's implementation. Despite these limitations, the degree of harmonization that characterizes EU border policies is nonetheless impressive (Takle 2012). Spurred by the Syrian refugee crisis, the regime's member states have also progressively upgraded the policy toolkit at their disposal with a view to increasing the reliability and efficiency of control measures both at and beyond Europe's external borders.

The introduction of 'smart borders' initiatives goes in this direction (Carrera and Hernanz 2015). Since the start of the millennium, Schengen members have deployed a greater number of technological devices, often borrowed from the intelligence and military realms, for the purpose of collecting and sharing travelers' information (e.g., large databases), verifying identity (e.g., biometric scanners) and detecting suspicious movements (e.g., drones, sensors and satellite tracking systems; Kenk *et al.* 2013; Ajana 2013). In 2013 the European Commission tabled the Smart Borders Package, which includes the proposal for an Entry–Exit System and a Registered Traveller Program to track cross-border travelers (European Commission 2013). The EU has spearheaded the European Border Surveillance System (EUROSUR), a program that since 2013 has supported EU member states' authorities in carrying out border surveillance. Technologically advanced procedures have also been deployed extensively in visa and asylum processing. European countries have spearheaded the establishment of electronic visas, whereby travel documents are stored in a computer and are electronically tied to passport numbers. The processing of electronic visas has been reinforced with the requirement to include biometric technology. Biometrics are the cornerstone of the Visa Information System (VIS), a common system of communication which facilitates the exchange of information about visas among EU member states and their consular services around the world. To monitor asylum applications, a fingerprint database (EURODAC) was established in 2003. As evidence of the ongoing securitization of migration policy, the mandate of EURODAC has recently been expanded to allow national police forces and Europol to compare fingerprints linked to criminal investigations.

The use of new technologies, and in particular information technology, to manage borders raises thorny ethical and legal questions (Donohue 2013; Rosière and Reece 2012). The 'social sorting' (Dijstelbloem and Broeders 2015) of migrants engendered by these technologies creates categories of people deemed inadmissible based on their background, economic status and location. Rules governing the storing and sharing of information about migrants are also often opaque, inconsistent and weakly enforced, particularly when exchanges between foreign governments are involved. More generally, although the proponents of these technologies have presented them as a way to de-securitize border control, they seem to have had the opposite effect (Carrera and Hernanz 2015; Neal 2009; Léonard 2015; see more on this point below).

The introduction of smart technologies has reinforced the protection of European borders. At the same time, European policy-makers have realized that targeting only individuals appearing at the continent's gates, or already within it, has not been sufficient to manage contemporary migratory flows efficiently. The answer has been to externalize border management, namely to stop or regulate incoming migrants *before* they reach their final destination (Zaiotti 2016). Although not a new phenomenon, since the start of the millennium this practice has been upgraded and expanded. Visa applications, which allow receiving countries to screen potential travelers in advance, have become stricter. European countries have expanded the interview requirements at consulates and introduced additional security checks on visa applicants, new special registration programs and biometric identifiers (Taylor 2011: 5). The extraterritorial presence of government agencies for the purpose of combatting illegal immigration has expanded. Since 2001, the EU has established a network of Immigration Liaison Officers (ILOs), civil servants posted abroad whose task is to gather information, support and train airline companies, and cooperate with local authorities. In some circumstances, these officers have been given the power to screen incoming travelers before departure. Belgium, France and the United Kingdom, for instance, have introduced so-called 'juxtaposed controls' in each other's jurisdiction allowing immigration pre-checks on selected routes across the English Channel (Clayton 2010). One of the side effects of the surge in the phenomenon of 'boat people' risking their lives to reach European shores has been the parallel expansion of interdiction practices in the Mediterranean. Spain and Italy have been among the most active in maritime interdiction. Spain's *Sistema Integrado de Vigilancia Exterior* (SIVE), one of the first of this kind in Europe (it became operational in 2002), employs radar and surveillance cameras to detect incoming vessels and to intercept them if they are suspected of carrying irregular migrants (Lutterbeck 2006: 2).

As for migration more generally, European governments have tried to externalize their asylum policy to circumvent their legal obligations (See Chapter 5, this volume). One of the centerpieces of this approach is the so-called 'safe country of asylum' policy (Kneebone 2008). The concept of 'safe country of asylum' is the key component of the *Dublin Convention*.[6] In parallel with, and as a corollary measure to the safe country of asylum arrangement, European governments have pushed, so far unsuccessfully, for the establishment of asylum-processing facilities outside the continent. The intent is to compel migrants to submit asylum claims before they reach their final destination (Flynn 2014: 23). The idea of establishing external processing centers was mooted again in 2015 as the number of boat people crossing the Mediterranean reached new record levels. Logistical, legal and political problems have prevented this project from materializing. Meanwhile, processing centers ('hotspots') have been set up *within the EU* in areas directly affected by the migration crisis, namely Greece and Italy.[7] The EU and its member states have also delegated to transit countries the responsibility of building and managing centers for irregular migrants. In 2002, for instance, the Mauritanian government, with the financial support of its Spanish counterpart, created a detention center on its soil for irregular migrants (Dünnwald 2016). Similar facilities have sprung up in other locations (e.g., Ukraine, Belarus).

These developments are part of a larger trend, namely the politicization of hitherto mostly technical and lightly scrutinized border practices. This is especially the case for visas. Although the original purpose of visas is to manage mobility in general, European countries have resorted to using this instrument as a means to prevent, or at least limit, unwanted migration. Evidence of this phenomenon is represented by the fact that the number of countries to which European states have applied visa restrictions since the 1990s closely reflects rising concerns over asylum (Hobolth 2014). Visas are also more frequently used as foreign policy tools. European countries have used the promise of lifting entry requirements into the European Union as bargaining chips with their neighbors, especially those who wish to join the EU or seek closer relations with the Union (e.g., Ukraine). Visas have also been employed as 'weapons' alongside more traditional tools of coercive diplomacy such as sanctions (Zaiotti 2016: 15). Exemplary in this regard is the EU's imposition of visa bans upon Russian officials believed to be involved in the conflict in eastern Ukraine, which has been brewing since 2014. Not surprisingly, the politicization of visas has been a source of tension. Officials of countries whose citizens still require visas to access Europe have complained about the creation of 'paper walls', and, more generally, the bullying attitude of Western governments on the issue of cross-border mobility. Bilateral relations have been put under strain as a result. This is not just the case for relations between sending and receiving countries, but also between sending and transit countries (e.g., EU vs. Turkey), and even between allies (e.g., EU vs. United States).

The strengthening of checks at European borders and beyond has been justified as increasing the continent's security and maintaining the Schengen regime's stability. Some of these practices, such as sea patrols, have also been presented as a way to help migrants in their perilous journeys. While officials acknowledge the existence of human rights violations, these breaches have been explained in terms of either a lack of proper implementation of existing policies or the ineffectiveness of these policies (Pedersen 2015). The ineffectiveness of traditional border policies, for instance, has been used as justification for the introduction of smart borders policies (Carrera and Hernanz 2015; see above). At the same time, a growing number of commentators have highlighted these policies' exclusionary and discriminatory features (Vaughan-Williams 2015b; Van Houtum and Boedeltje 2009). The main target has been 'illegal' migrants, although other citizens from developing countries have been caught in the net, creating categories of 'privileged border-crossers' (Rosière and Reece 2012). In recent times, even EU nationals have been affected. The extension of 'systematic' checks at external borders in the aftermath of the

Syrian refugee crisis was intended to target travelers carrying a EU passport (previously, EU citizens were only the object of 'targeted' checks). This trend has affected Schengen's internal borders as well. As noted earlier, cases of temporary reintroductions of controls within Europe have spiked since 2015 (Casella-Colombeau 2015).

The discourse supporting EU border policies is also often dehumanizing, as evidenced by the zoological tropes that often appear in official narratives about migration in Europe (Vaughan-Williams 2015b). Authors inspired by a Foucauldian approach to the study of security have argued that the apparent tension with the proclaimed humanitarian spirit driving EU-led policies is not as inconsistent as it might appear. As Vaughan-Williams (2015b: 1) points out: 'While bordering practices are designed to play a defensive role, they contain the potential for excessive security mechanisms that threaten the very values and lives they purport to protect.' Far from being contradictory, these narratives actually feed on each other, contributing to their perpetuation.

Conclusion: towards a Schengen redux?

Scholars from various disciplines and theoretical orientations have been fascinated by the scope and pace of the policy experiments involving European borders since the 1990s. The ongoing 'EU border crisis' (Vaughan-Williams 2015a), and, more generally, the state of turmoil that currently afflicts the European integration project, have increased public attention over migration and other border-related matters and offered fresh intellectual impetus to scrutinize how borders are managed in Europe. This state of affairs has stimulated academic and public debates about the limits of the Schengen regime and the courses of action the European Union and its member states might take to address the challenges the old continent is facing (Fijnaut 2015; Peers 2013; Barker and Wagstyl 2015). Thus far, these discussions have had a mainly empirical and practical focus, as their main purpose has been to capture the rapidly evolving developments in Europe's border policy field and to assess the Schengen regime's short- and long-term viability. More analytically oriented reflections that attempt to make sense of the events occurring in Europe are still rare (Vaughan-Williams 2015a). If past 'crises' in the European integration project are any indication, works that rely on state-centric assumptions about politics and that are skeptical of further regional integration (e.g., works inspired by intergovernmentalism), are likely to take a prominent role in the literature on European borders. The same could be said of works inspired by sociological approaches to the study of European integration, since they are better equipped to address themes of change, conflict and contestation (Favell and Guiraudon 2011; Saurugger 2016). The assumption that European border management is following the path of other policy areas within the European Union, namely that it is steadily becoming more integrated or that it will acquire the features of the more established (read 'national') political systems, is now under question. Works that rely on integrative analytical frameworks for the study of the EU, and that emphasize concepts such as Europeanization, may therefore have to rethink their approaches in light of the new empirical reality (Saurugger 2014).[8] No matter their theoretical orientation, one of the common features of current works on border management in Europe is a general skepticism regarding the future of the Schengen regime, and more generally, of the EU's post-national territorial experiment.

If we were to believe in symbolism, the fate of Schengen might already be sealed. On May 10, 2016, the museum created to celebrate the Schengen regime – evocatively located in the eponymous Luxemburg town by the river Moselle – was damaged by the collapse of one of its ceilings. Happening in the midst of the Syrian refugee crisis, it was an eerie omen of the regime's current predicament (*Luxemburger Wort* 2016). Indeed, an increasing number of cracks have begun to appear in what is still considered a central pillar of European integration. The breakdown of the Dublin Convention arrangement brought about by the sudden flow of Europe-bound migrants and the ensuing squabbles over the EU-led redistribution of asylum-seekers across the continent, together with the reintroduction of internal controls, have rattled the regime's foundations. A rising populist backlash against the idea of a 'border-free Europe' has also brought into question the regime's *raison d'être* and challenged its legitimacy. In this context, it is not surprising that references to 'the end of Schengen' have become ubiquitous (Fijnaut 2015; Zaiotti 2013).

Yet, the situation is not as dire as it appears. After all, it is not the first time the Schengen regime has experienced periods of turmoil. In the early 1990s, for instance, the French government's recalcitrance to fully lift internal controls at its borders stalled the regime's launch (Pauly 1994). While the possibility exists that the reinstatement of internal border controls within the Schengen area may become permanent, the European Commission and all member states have confirmed their commitment to lift these checks once the emergency period is over. Moreover, there are signs that the current crisis may actually lead to the regime's further integration, as the recent upgrading of the EU border agency Frontex suggests.

The strongest argument in support of the Schengen regime, however, is that even if it were to collapse, the need for European governments to address migratory pressures on Europe would not disappear. Unilateral actions such as the permanent reinstatement of national border controls might replicate the phenomenon of The Jungle, the notorious makeshift camp erected – and disbanded in October 2016 – in the northern French city of Calais. A Europe-wide 'Jungle effect' would be politically untenable. It is therefore difficult to foresee a solution that does not involve at least a modicum of cooperation among European governments and some level of coordination among EU institutions. In other words, the most likely scenario in the case of the regime's collapse is a *Schengen redux*. Such an arrangement would resemble the current regime, but with its priorities reversed. The strengthening of external borders, hitherto considered a compensatory measure to balance the lifting of internal ones, would become the primary objective. A border-free Europe would remain a desirable outcome worth pursuing, but not if this meant compromising security. This shift of priorities is already apparent in the current post-crisis context; yet it is, at least on paper, only temporary and ad hoc. In the Schengen redux scenario outlined here, it would be become official and permanent. This new arrangement would also be less institutionalized, with more emphasis on enhanced cooperation. One of this scenario's downsides is that, since the lifting of internal borders is dependent on the strengthening of external ones, Schengen would compromise its primary source of legitimacy, namely its close connection with the European integration project. By diluting this historical tie, the political will to keep Schengen alive, even in the form of 'Schengen-light', would be seriously reduced.

The damage to the Schengen museum turned out to be minor. The building was quickly restored and patrons were once again able to marvel at the regime's accomplishments. European policy-makers would certainly welcome a similar outcome for the real-life entity the museum celebrates. They would also be pleased if the 'renovations' they are currently considering work out well, and that they do not turn out to be mere temporary patches. If the latter turns out to be the case, another serious incident affecting the Schengen regime may offer them no choice but to demolish its entire structure.

Notes

1 As of 2017, the Schengen regime comprises twenty-six members. Non-EU countries participating in the regime are Iceland, Norway, Lichtenstein and Switzerland. Some EU countries remain excluded by choice (the United Kingdom and Ireland) or because they do not yet meet the criteria for membership (Romania, Bulgaria, Cyprus, Croatia).
2 'Towards an integrated management of the external borders of the Member States of the European Union.' *Commission Communication to the Council and the European Parliament*, Brussels COM(2002) 233 final.
3 Some clarification is in order regarding the choice of terminology in this chapter. The term *border management* is often used interchangeably with *border control*. Control, however, has the narrower meaning of verifying or checking a particular activity. Management refers instead to the 'direct handling and manipulating or manoeuvring toward a desired result' (Merriam–Webster Dictionary). Managing a particular policy area therefore involves both issues of governance (the structures and processes defining that policy area) and policy (the outcomes of the policy-making process).
4 Merriam–Webster Dictionaries, *s.v.* 'integration', accessed December 11, 2016, www.merriam-webster.com/dictionary/integration.
5 In this project, launched in 2005, European border control officials are posted in the two Eastern European countries with the purposes of training local border officials.
6 The central tenet of the Convention *determining the state responsible for examining applications for asylum lodged in one of the member states of the European Communities* (Dublin Convention) is that if an alien applies for asylum after traveling through another European country that is considered safe, he or she will be sent back to that country to file his or her application. This arrangement became operational in 1997.
7 As of November 2016, nine of these hotspots were operational; five in Greece and four in Italy.
8 Examples of how this theoretical adaptation might look are provided by works that rely on concepts such as *punctuated equilibrium* taken from the policy studies literature (Capoccia and Kelemen 2007; Zaiotti 2013).

Bibliography

Ajana, B. (2013). Asylum, identity management and biometric control. *Journal of Refugee Studies*, 26(4), pp. 576–595.
Axford, B. (2006). The dialectic of borders and networks in Europe: reviewing 'topological presuppositions'. *Comparative European Politics*, 4(2), pp. 160–182.
Barker, A. and Wagstyl, S. (2015). If Schengen fails: four scenarios threatening passport-free zone. *The Financial Times*.
Bigo, D. (2014). The (in)securitization practices of the three universes of EU border control: military/navy–border guards/police–database analysts. *Security Dialogue*, 45(3), pp. 209–225.
Brouwer, E.R., Guild, E., Groenendijk, C.A. and Carrera, S. (2015). What is happening to the Schengen borders? *CEPS Policy Briefs*, 86.
Capoccia, G. and Kelemen, R.D. (2007). The study of critical junctures: theory, narrative, and counterfactuals in historical institutionalism. *World Politics*, 59, pp. 341–369.
Carrera, S. and Hernanz, N. (2015). Re-framing mobility and identity controls: the next generation of the EU migration management Toolkit. *Journal of Borderlands Studies*, 30(1), pp. 69–84.
Casella-Colombeau, S. (2015). Policing the internal Schengen borders – managing the double bind between free movement and migration control. *Policing and Society*, 1–14.
Clayton, G. (2010). The UK and extraterritorial immigration control: entry clearance and juxtaposed control. In Ryan, B. and Mitsilegas, V. (eds), *Extraterritorial Immigration Control*. Leiden: Martinus Nijhoff, pp. 391–423.
Cornelisse, G. (2014). What's wrong with Schengen? Border disputes and the nature of integration in the area without internal borders. *Common Market Law Review*, 51(3), pp. 741–770.
Delanty, G. (2006). Borders in a changing Europe: dynamics of openness and closure. *Comparative European Politics*, 4(2–3), pp. 183–202.
Dijstelbloem, H. and Broeders, D. (2015). Border surveillance, mobility management and the shaping of non-publics in Europe. *European Journal of Social Theory*, 18(1), pp. 21–38.
Donohue, L.K. (2013). Technological leap, statutory gap, and constitutional abyss: remote biometric identification comes of age. *Minnesota Law Review*, 97, pp. 407–559.

Dünnwald, S. (2016). Europe's global approach to migration management: doing border in Mali and Mauritania. In Zaiotti, R. (ed.), *Externalizing Migration Management: Europe, North America and the Spread of 'Remote Control' Practices*. London: Routledge, pp. 113–133.
European Commission (2002). Towards an integrated management of the external borders of the Member States of the European Union. *Commission Communication to the Council and the European Parliament*. Brussels, COM(2002) 233 final.
European Commission (2005). On regional protection programmes. *Communication from The Commission to The Council And The European Parliament*. Brussels, 1.9.2005 COM(2005) 388 final.
European Commission (2013). Proposal for a regulation of the European Parliament and of The Council establishing an Entry/Exit System (EES) to register entry and exit data of third country nationals crossing the external borders of the Member States of the European Union. Brussels, 28.2.2013 COM(2013) 95 final.
Favell, A. and Guiraudon, V. (eds) (2011). *Sociology of the European Union*. Basingstoke: Palgrave Macmillan.
Fijnaut, C. (2015). The refugee crisis: the end of Schengen? *European Journal of Crime, Criminal Law and Criminal Justice*, 23(4), pp. 313–332.
Flynn, M. (2014). How and why immigration detention crossed the globe. *Global Detention Project Working Paper No. 8*, April.
Gaisbauer, H. (2013). Evolving patterns of internal security cooperation: lessons from the Schengen and Prüm laboratories. *European Security*, 22(2), pp. 185–201.
Geiger, M. and Pécoud, A. (2014). International organisations and the politics of migration. *Journal of Ethnic and Migration Studies*, 40(6), pp. 865–887.
Green, S. (2013). Borders and the relocation of Europe. *Annual Review of Anthropology*, 42, pp. 345–361.
Hobolth, M. (2014). Researching mobility barriers: the European Visa Database. *Journal of Ethnic and Migration Studies*, 40(3), pp. 424–435.
Huber, K. (2015). The European Parliament as an actor in EU border policies: its role, relations with other EU institutions, and impact. *European Security*, 24(3), pp. 420–437.
Kaunert, C. (2010). *European Internal Security: Towards Supranational Governance?* Manchester: Manchester University Press.
Kenk, V.S., Križaj, J., Štruc, J. and Dobrišek, S. (2013). Smart surveillance technologies in border control. *European Journal of Law and Technology*, 4(2). Available at http://ejlt.org/article/view/230 (accessed July 21, 2017).
Kneebone, S. (2008). The legal and ethical implications of extraterritorial processing of asylum seekers: the 'safe third country' concept. In McAdam, J. (ed.), *Forced Migration, Human Rights and Security*. Oxford and Portland, OH: Hart Publishing, pp. 129–154.
Léonard, S. (2015). Border controls as a dimension of the European Union's counter-terrorism policy: a critical assessment. *Intelligence and National Security*, 30(2–3), pp. 306–332.
Lutterbeck, D. (2006). Policing migration in the Mediterranean. *Mediterranean Politics*, 11(1), pp. 58–82.
Luxemburger Wort (2016). Mayor Ben Homan speaks out Schengen European museum ceiling collapse, May 11. Available at www.wort.lu/en/luxembourg/mayor-ben-homan-speaks-out-schengen-european-museum-ceiling-collapse-an-eu-omen-573424edac730ff4e7f60493 (accessed November 27, 2016).
Müller, A. (2014). *Governing Mobility Beyond the State: Centre, Periphery and the EU's External Borders*. London: Palgrave Macmillan.
Neal, A.W. (2009). Securitization and risk at the EU border: the origins of FRONTEX. *JCMS: Journal of Common Market Studies*, 47(2), pp. 333–356.
Newman, D. (2006). Borders and bordering towards an interdisciplinary dialogue. *European Journal of Social Theory*, 9(2), pp. 171–186.
Panizzon, M. (2012). Readmission agreements of EU member states: a case for EU subsidiarity or dualism? *Refugee Survey Quarterly*, 31(4), pp. 101–133.
Parker, N. and Adler-Nissen, R. (2012). Picking and choosing the 'sovereign' border: a theory of changing state bordering practices. *Geopolitics*, 7(4), pp. 773–796.
Pauly, A. (ed.) (1994). *Schengen en panne*. European Institute of Public Administration.
Pedersen, M.J. (2015).The intimate relationship between security, effectiveness, and legitimacy: a new look at the Schengen compensatory measures. *European Security*, 24(4), pp. 541–559.
Peers, S. (2013). *The Future of the Schengen System*. Sieps.
Prokkola, E.K. (2013). Neoliberalizing border management in Finland and Schengen. *Antipode*, 45(5), pp. 1318–1336.

Reid-Henry, S.M. (2013). An incorporating geopolitics: Frontex and the geopolitical rationalities of the European border. *Geopolitics*, 18(1), pp. 198–224.

Ripoll Servent, A. and Trauner, F. (2014). Do supranational EU institutions make a difference? EU asylum law before and after 'communitarization'. *Journal of European Public Policy*, 21(8), pp. 1142–1162.

Rosière, S. and Reece, J. (2012). Teichopolitics: re-considering globalization through the role of walls and fences. *Geopolitics*, 17(1), pp. 217–234.

Saurugger, S. (2014). Europeanisation in times of crisis. *Political Studies Review*, 12(2), pp. 181–192.

Saurugger, S. (2016). Sociological approaches to the European Union in times of turmoil. *Journal of Common Market Studies*, 54(1), pp. 70–86.

Takle, M. (2012). The Treaty of Lisbon and the European border control regime. *Journal of Contemporary European Research*, 8(3), pp. 280–299.

Taylor, N.E. (2011). Cutting off the flow: extraterritorial controls to prevent migration. Paper presented at *Cutting off the Flow: Extraterritorial Controls to Prevent Migration* Conference, Berkeley Law, April 22.

Thielemann, E. and Armstrong, C. (2013). Understanding European asylum cooperation under the Schengen/Dublin system: a public goods framework. *European Security*, 22(2), pp. 148–164.

Van Houtum, H. and Boedeltje, F. (2009). Europe's shame: death at the borders of the EU. *Antipode*, 41(2), pp. 226–230.

Vaughan-Williams, N. (2009). *Border Politics: The Limits of Sovereign Power*. Edinburgh: Edinburgh University Press.

Vaughan-Williams, N. (2015a). *Europe's Border Crisis: Biopolitical Security and Beyond*. Oxford: Oxford University Press.

Vaughan-Williams, N. (2015b). 'We are not animals!' Humanitarian border security and zoopolitical spaces in Europe. *Political Geography*, 45, pp. 1–10.

Walters, W. (2002). Mapping Schengenland: denaturalizing the border. *Environment and Planning D: Society and Space*, 20(5), pp. 561–580.

Walters, W. (2004). Some critical notes on 'governance'. *Studies in Political Economy*, 73(1), pp. 25–42.

Wolff, S. (2016). The politics of negotiating EU readmission agreements: insights from Morocco and Turkey. In Zaiotti, R. (ed.), *Externalizing Migration Management: Europe, North America and the Spread of 'Remote Control' Practices*. London: Routledge, pp. 89–112.

Wolff, S., Wichmann, N. and Mounier, G. (eds) (2013). *The External Dimension of Justice and Home Affairs: A Different Security Agenda for the European Union?* London: Routledge.

Zaiotti, R. (2011). *Cultures of Border Control: Schengen and the Evolution of Europe's Frontiers*. Chicago, IL: University of Chicago Press.

Zaiotti, R. (2013). The Franco-Italian row over Schengen, critical junctures, and the future of Europe's border regime. *Journal of Borderland Studies*, 28(3), pp. 337–354.

Zaiotti, R. (2016). Mapping remote control: the externalization of migration management in the 21st century. In Zaiotti, R. (ed.), *Externalizing Migration Management: Europe, North America and the Spread of 'Remote Control' Practices*. London: Routledge, pp. 3–30.

9
EU VISA POLICY
Decision-making dynamics and effects on migratory processes

Mathias Czaika and Florian Trauner

Introduction

In today's public and political discourses, European and other Western destinations are often described as being 'flooded' and 'invaded' by 'bogus' asylum-seekers and irregular migrants (Huysmans 2006; Massey and Pren 2012). As a consequence, policies have become more restrictive in many parts of Europe in an attempt to manage, and de facto to reduce the present and future inflow of unwanted migrants. Political and administrative actions focus increasingly on extra-territorial measures such as visa restrictions, carrier sanctions, readmission agreements and safe third-country regulations aiming to limit the ability of migrants to arrive in destination states and claim asylum or stay irregularly (Gammeltoft-Hansen 2011).

Visa regulations are an important instrument in the policy toolbox that governments have at their disposal to monitor, control and limit the cross-border flow of people. Visa restrictions are often seen as the 'first line of defence' (Torpey 1998: 252) against the entry of unwanted people as they allow the visa-issuing country to pre-screen applicants before they start their journey and arrive at the border or even enter their territory. Other than revenues generated by the visa fee, the main benefit to a visa-requiring country is the screening procedure. Its aim is to either deter or filter out potential irregular immigrants, potential terrorists and criminals as well as other *persona non grata* who may potentially pose a risk to the security, wealth and identity of a country (Torpey 2000; Mau *et al.* 2015).

This chapter will analyze academic research dealing with the political dynamics and migratory effects of the visa policy of the EU. The focus is on the EU's Schengen visas given that the EU controls only the issuance of short-stay (for a three-month trip) travel visas. Long-stay visas have remained within the jurisdiction of EU member states and are not an element of common EU policy. The chapter is split into two main sections. Whereas the first section deals with the politics of EU visa harmonization and liberalization, the second looks in more detail at the ways in which visa policies interact with migratory processes and trajectories.

The politics of EU visa harmonization and liberalization

Developing a common EU visa policy

Following up on the intergovernmental Schengen 'laboratory' (Monar 2001), the Amsterdam Treaty (1999) provided the EU with the legal wherewithal to develop a common EU visa policy (with opt-out possibilities for the United Kingdom, Ireland and Denmark). In March 2001, the Justice and Home Affairs Council adopted a key visa law, Council Regulation 539/2001. It set out two lists: a 'negative' list of countries, implying that their citizens require a visa to enter the EU; and a 'positive' list, providing visa-free entry for the citizens of these countries. Besides a common visa list, the EU has also introduced a uniform format for a visa sticker and a common 'Visa Code' (EC Regulation 810/2009). The code clarifies the procedures and conditions for issuing visas and has been accompanied by operational manuals and handbooks on how to implement the instructions on a day-to-day basis.

While EU citizens tend to be socialized towards visa-free travel and do not attach much importance to this seemingly trivial administrative procedure, EU visa policies are often of keen interest to those countries whose citizens need a Schengen visa. By reviewing visa policies of over 150 countries as of 1969, Mau *et al.* (2015) have been able to demonstrate a growing 'global mobility divide'. Many citizens of OECD countries seem to enjoy more mobility rights, while citizens from poorer regions, notably from Africa, face increasingly constrained travel opportunities. However, by drawing on the new DEMIG VISA database covering global bilateral travel restrictions from 1973 to 2013, Czaika *et al.* (2017) challenge the idea of a growing global mobility divide between 'North' and 'South' by suggesting a more complex image of the global visa regime which instead reflects a rather multi-polar and multi-layered configuration of international visa regimes. While predominantly European and North American OECD countries maintain high levels of entry visa restrictiveness for regions like Africa and Asia, the latter regions have the highest overall levels of entry restrictions themselves. Although citizens of wealthy countries generally enjoy the greatest visa-free travel opportunities, this primarily reflects their freedom to travel to other OECD countries. Evidence shows that visa-free travel is mostly realized between geographically neighboring countries of regionally integrated blocs such as the EU (Czaika *et al.* 2017). Over the past four decades, visa policies of EU member states have remained relatively stable against mostly non-European countries, with visa restrictions in place for more than 70 percent of non-European nationalities (Figure 9.1). At the same time, visa restrictions of the then EU/EC members for today's EU-28 nationalities have been continuously relaxed, in particular of course since the implementation of the Schengen agreement in 1995.

One strand of research has concerned the drivers of visa policies, for instance, in comparison with other regional integration projects (Gülzau *et al.* 2016; Neumayer 2006). Another has been to look at the functioning of the EU's policy tools and instruments such as the European visa database (Hobolth 2014) or to investigate the 'European' impact of the visa issuance practices of member states. These practices still seem to diverge, regardless of the EU's harmonization efforts (e.g., Boratynski *et al.* 2006; Jileva 2002). By comparing the consulates of Belgium, France and Italy in Morocco, Infantino (2016) finds substantial cross-national differences in the implementation of EU visa policies. Her explanation points to a continued relevance of 'state-bound logics' such as 'bilateral relations, historical pasts, and contemporary foreign affairs concerns' (Infantino 2016: 14). Fernández (2008: 21) also sees many differences, but she emphasizes that the EU visa policy has been a 'catalyst for change in the working of consular services' of member states, and that while this process is 'state-controlled' it is slowly paving the way for a 'European administrative sphere'.

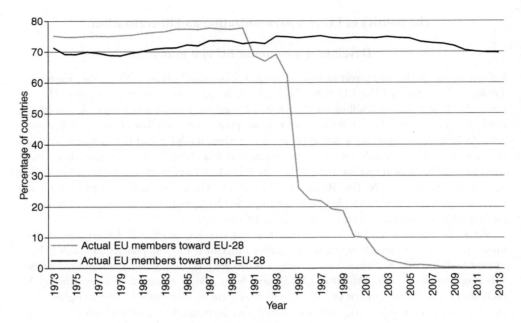

Figure 9.1 Internal versus external visa restrictions of EU member states (percentage of countries)
Source: Czaika et al. (2017).

The development of EU visa policies has not been devoid of political conflict. A contested question has been how to ensure visa reciprocity with key partner states such as the USA or Canada. When the number of Czech asylum-seekers rose, Canada reimposed visas upon Czech citizens in 2009. The visas had previously been waived as an element of the Canada–EU visa waiver program. In the following 'visa war' (Salter and Mutlu 2010), the Czech government asked for EU support yet the Commission did not manage to make Canada reverse its decision. In response, the EU amended its reciprocity mechanism in 2013 to be able to reimpose visas more easily in such situations (Peers 2012). The conflict was settled in 2013 after Canada introduced a status that declared the EU's member states as safe (Weinar, Chapter 29, this volume).

Another question that has drawn scholarly attention has been whether Schengen visas are compatible with the EU's obligation to adhere to international refugee protection norms (Moreno-Lax 2008). It has become almost impossible to physically enter the EU in a legal way if you are a potential asylum-seeker. Should the Schengen visa regime allow more openness for refugees? Moreno-Lax (2008: 315) suggests that the question is 'ambiguously dealt with within EU law', recommending that EU rules be developed and clarified. While policy-makers have not yet taken up such a call, the courts are increasingly compelled to find an answer. According to Advocate General Mengozzi of the Court of Justice of the EU (CJEU), member states have to issue a Schengen visa on humanitarian grounds if a refusal may place an applicant at risk of torture or inhumane or degrading treatment (Court of Justice of the European Union 2017). His opinion concerned the case of a Syrian couple and their three children living in Aleppo, Syria. They applied for a visa in the Belgium embassy in Beirut and returned to Syria, whereupon the Belgian authorities refused the application. The Belgian Ministry of Interior also refused to adhere to the judgment of a Belgium court recommending the family be let in. The final judgment of the CJEU did not follow the Advocate General's advice, but maintained that the issuance of humanitarian visas is the preserve of individual member states (C638/16). Still, the case highlights the tensions between the humanitarian obligations of member states and their ever more pronounced desire to seal the EU's external borders and thus reduce the numbers of asylum-seekers in Europe.

Visa facilitation and liberalization

When the EU decided on Council Regulation 539/2001, it put all its neighboring countries to the east, south and southeast onto the negative EU visa list; the two exceptions being Croatia and Israel. This decision was bound to have major implications. Indeed, the call for EU visa facilitation and visa liberalization quickly arose in many third countries. The quest for an alternative visa regime was particularly salient in Eastern and Southeastern Europe. The (then) candidate countries of Central and Eastern Europe had a liberal migration regime with their eastern neighbors. The imposition of a stricter visa regime (for instance, between Poland and Ukraine) was seen to jeopardize their close socio-economic and political ties (Jileva 2002; Grabbe 2002). In view of Bulgaria and Romania's accession to the EU, the citizens of the Western Balkans felt particularly isolated given that they had become surrounded by EU member and Schengen-participating states (ICG 2005).

In view of this situation, the EU started to implement visa facilitation regimes (see Table 9.1). For some of the neighboring states, the process was then extended to the installation of a full visa-free regime. Visa facilitation was intended to fulfill a double objective for the EU. First, it should soften the 'sharp edges of Europe' (Grabbe 2000) following the EU's eastern enlargement vis-à-vis the Eastern Partnership countries and the Western Balkans. Second, it should also allow the EU to incentivize third countries to accept EU readmission agreements – a prized EU tool to curb irregular migration (Trauner and Kruse 2008). The visa facilitation–readmission nexus became firmly established, notably in Eastern Europe (Hernández i Sagrera 2010).

In the regional setting of the Western Balkans the EU developed its policy approach on visa liberalization. In addition to the conclusion of a readmission agreement, the 'visa incentive' was used by the EU to force the Western Balkans to adhere to a long list of justice and home affairs-related conditions such as the introduction of biometric passports, reinforced border controls, the reform of public administration, the fight against organized crime and the protection of minorities. This 'policy conditionality' allowed the EU to compensate for a lack of external leverage in the context of its accession policy caused by a rather vague and questionable promise of membership for the countries of the Western Balkans (Trauner 2009).

Serbia and Montenegro were granted visa-free travel in 2009, and Albania and Bosnia and Herzegovina in 2010. Their citizens praised the end of visa requirements as a first visible sign of the countries' integration into the EU. Yet, the EU's experience with this region also triggered the establishment of a 'visa suspension mechanism' and a monitoring regime, which followed visa liberalization in 2013. In the first year after visa liberalization, asylum applications from Serbian citizens increased by 76 percent and those of Macedonian nationals seven-fold (for a detailed breakdown see Trauner and Manigrassi 2014). To reduce this flow of migration, the governments of the Western Balkans introduced stricter exit controls, effectively amounting to a kind of 'ethnic profiling' for specific minorities, notably Roma. These policies therefore created concerns that already marginalized groups would be further marginalized (Kacarska 2012). The issue of 'Balkan asylum-seekers' in the EU eventually lost political salience and the EU visa suspension mechanism – tailor-made for these countries – was not triggered.

The EU Visa-Free Dialogues for Eastern Partnership countries and Russia have been advancing at a slower pace. The exception was Moldova, which received visa-free travel in April 2014. Moldova may be seen as a special case, since many of its citizens could apply for a Romanian

Table 9.1 EU visa facilitation and visa liberalization processes (as of March 2017)

Third country	Negotiating mandate		Agreements signed	Start of visa-free dialogue	Visa-free travel
	Readmission	Visa facilitation			
Albania	November 2002	November 2006	November 2007	January 2008	December 2010
Bosnia and Herzegovina	November 2006	November 2006	November 2007	January 2008	December 2010
Serbia	November 2006	November 2006	November 2007	January 2008	December 2009
Montenegro	November 2006	November 2006	November 2007	January 2008	December 2009
Macedonia	November 2006	November 2006	November 2007	January 2008	December 2009
Kosovo	February 2011	February 2011		January 2012	2017**
Belarus	February 2002	November 2005			
Ukraine	December 2006	December 2006	June 2007	October 2008	2017**
Moldova	November 2008	November 2008	October 2007	June 2010	April 2014
Georgia	December 2011	December 2011	November 2010	June 2012	May 2017**
Armenia	December 2011	December 2011	December 2012/April 2013		
Azerbaijan	September 2000	July 2004	November 2013/February 2014		
Russia	November 2002	February 2011	May 2006	April 2007	
Turkey	June 2009	October 2012	December 2013*	June 2012	2017**
Cape Verde	September 2000	December 2013	October 2013		
Morocco					

Notes
* Only the readmission agreement was signed.
** Scheduled.

passport (Dura 2006). Visa-free travel was therefore seen to reduce the incentives for Moldovan citizens to apply for Romanian (and hence EU) passports. In February 2017, the European Council agreed on visa liberalization for Georgia as the second of the Eastern Partnership countries. Russia has also been interested in visa-free travel with the EU, but dialogue between the two parties was frozen as part of the sanctions imposed in the wake of the annexation of Crimea in 2014. More generally, the intensifying EU–Russian competition in the Eastern European neighborhood has had an impact on the EU's capabilities to influence Eastern European states on migration issues (Ademmer and Börzel 2013; Ademmer and Delcour 2016). Russia has sought to prevent the EU's eastern neighbors from integrating into Euro-Atlantic institutions. To do so, it has also relied on migration-related instruments, such as enforcing more restrictive access to the Russian labor market or (threatened) deportations for citizens of neighbors unwilling to cooperate (Ademmer and Delcour 2016: 90).

At the time of writing (Spring 2017), the countries still pursuing visa-free travel were Ukraine, Kosovo and Turkey. All three have made considerable progress towards meeting the benchmarks set by the EU in their respective visa liberalization roadmaps. In December 2015 and May 2016, the Commission (2015a, 2015b, 2016) considered that Ukraine and Kosovo would meet all of the benchmarks of their respective visa roadmaps and thus qualify for visa-free travel. In March 2016, the EU and Turkey also agreed on an accelerated visa liberalization process as one of the incentives for Turkey to take back all the migrants leaving its shores irregularly for Greece (European Council 2016). The question as to how to link Turkey's objective of visa liberalization with the EU's interests in having closer cooperation on return and readmission is a long-standing one (Icduygu and Aksel 2014; Wolff 2014; Bürgin 2013), pre-dating the events of the 2015 'EU migration crisis'. In late 2016, the EU–Turkey visa liberalization process stalled again due to a disagreement over the application and reform of Turkey's anti-terror laws, which the EU defined as a precondition for visa-free travel. The Turkish government has repeatedly emphasized that only a visa waiver will guarantee a continuation of its efforts to curb the flow of irregular migrants in the Aegean Sea. While Turkey has not (yet) stopped fulfilling the commitments it made under the EU–Turkey deal of March 2016, the EU tried to adjust its internal visa arrangements in light of the altered context. In December 2016, the EU reformed its visa suspension mechanism so that it is now able to reintroduce visa requirements in an easier and quicker way than before (Trauner 2017).

In brief, visa facilitation and liberalization have primarily concerned the EU's eastern and southeastern neighbors. The visa policy has remained 'remarkably rigid across the Mediterranean' (Finotelli and Scirotino 2013) and beyond, where the EU and its member states have been reluctant to envisage more relaxed visa policies (Figure 9.2). Visa liberalization has become a more politicized issue in recent years. The current political climate in Europe is not conducive to more liberal admission and migration policies. The EU discussion on visa liberalization with (and about) Ukraine, a populous country of forty-five million, and Turkey, a problematic partner, reveal deep cleavages among member states and within the EU institutions. While proponents tend to emphasize that the abolition of visa requirements will foster good neighborly relations and improve the EU's 'soft power' abroad, opponents highlight that a softer visa regime may open up new pathways for irregular migration. The next section will investigate how visa policies actually affect international migration and mobility processes.

The effects of visa policies

Although visa restrictions are primarily targeting temporary visitors and travelers, visa policies play a central role in controlling and ultimately preventing potential migrants from certain

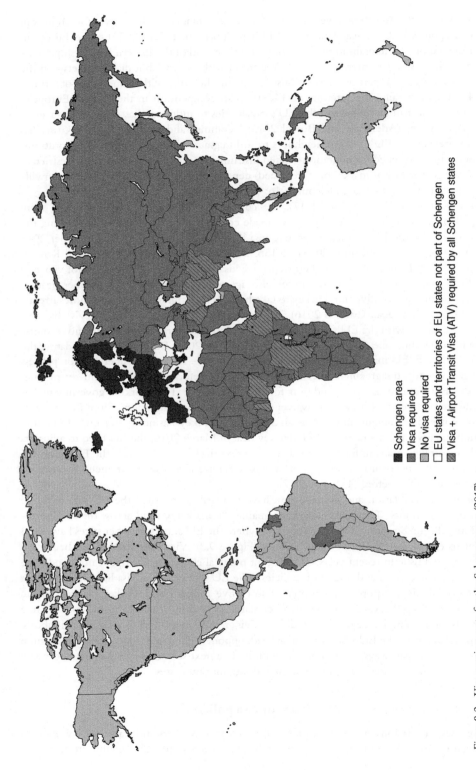

Figure 9.2 Visa requirements for the Schengen area (2017)

Source: https://ec.europa.eu/home-affairs/what-we-do/policies/borders-and-visas/visa-policy_en.

countries of origin from entering Europe, and in particular national territories. The majority of migrants without residence documents enter regularly, often on a short-term tourist visa (cf. Schoorl *et al.* 2000; Düvell 2005). For instance, many former 'guestworkers' entered legally as tourists before obtaining work and, consequently, residence permits. This is generally not permitted on a tourist visa. Once migrants stay longer than their tourist visa allows, their stay becomes unauthorized. However, in the long term, many unauthorized migrants may eventually obtain residency documents and thereby 'regularize' their legal status (cf. Fakiolas 2003; Zincone 2006).

The visa policy's influence on migratory processes

The impact of migration policy on international migration and mobility processes is a well-established and long-standing subject of political and academic debate. Yet only recent conceptual and empirical progress has shed new light on the role of state policies in international migration and mobility processes. For instance, scholarship has long ignored the unintended consequences of entry (i.e., immigration) policies on reverse flows and overall circulation in addition to other potential 'substitution effects' (Czaika and Haas 2015). These are, for instance, a deflection of migration and travelers to other, more liberal destinations, or the deflection of potentially legal migrants into irregular entry or stay routes. Furthermore, Czaika and De Haas (2016) investigate potential asymmetries in visa policy effects, which is the possibility that the introduction and removal of restrictions may have different (i.e., 'asymmetric') effects on migratory processes and do not necessarily mirror each other. By drawing from unique new datasets on bilateral migration flow data (DEMIG C2C) and bilateral visa data (DEMIG VISA) covering thirty-eight European and non-European countries between 1973 and 2012, they analyze to what extent introductions and removals of short-stay visa requirements affect the levels and timings of immigration and emigration flows and how these effects interfere with economic migration determinants. First of all, and unsurprisingly, they identify a significant deterrence effect of visa restrictions, which leads in turn to a decrease in immigration flows. However, this immigration-reducing effect is found to be partly counterbalanced by a concomitant reduction in emigration (including return) flows. Immigration restrictions, therefore, not only reduce the inflow of people, but also the overall circulation of people across borders. This supports the hypothesis that immigration and travel restrictions can push (temporary) migrants into permanent settlement.

Besides decreasing overall circulation intensity, they also find that visa restrictions reduce to virtually zero intended responsiveness of human mobility and migration to economic fluctuations. This implies that visa restrictions disconnect migration and mobility processes from temporal pushes and pulls of economic growth cycles in both countries of origin and destination. Business cycles are generally a key driver of migration and mobility flows in visa-free corridors, yet these labor market mechanisms are largely neutralized when visas partly interrupt the free flow of labour. Visa policy effects are also asymmetrical. The introduction of restrictive mobility measures translates into lower levels of migration inflows only very gradually. It may take more than a decade for immigration levels to reach the lower average levels of visa-constrained corridors. This path-dependency and resilience of migration corridors is often facilitated and self-perpetuated by well-established migrant networks. A policy change in the opposite direction, however, has an almost immediate effect: removal of travel visas increases immigration within one to three years to that of the average levels of visa-free migration corridors. Migration flows may even temporarily 'overshoot' these long-term average levels for several years (Czaika and De Haas 2016). Thus, visa liberalization seems to ignite in the short term a 'now-or-never' response of a 'latent' migration potential in the short-term before immigration (and partly also emigration) numbers converge to long-term levels.

Extra-territorial refusal of visa applications also seems to contribute to heightened numbers of irregular migrants. In combination with restrictive migration policies, extra-territorial processing and potential refusal of travel visa applications seems to increase the numbers of irregular border crossings. Travel and migration restrictions often compel migrants to travel by unorthodox routes and means. Recent empirical research has provided some nuanced evidence for such spatial and categorical *deflection* effects. For instance, although stricter entry regimes may deter some asylum-seekers, such policies also tend to have the effect of forcing asylum-seekers into an irregular status (Massey and Pren 2012; Czaika and Hobolth 2016). As access to refugee protection becomes more circumscribed, some potential or rejected asylum-seekers may instead choose to go 'underground'. Czaika and Hobolth (2016) find evidence of such a 'deflection into irregularity'. This unintended consequence has considerable bearing on our understanding of migration policy effects in general, and visa policy in particular. Based on data on irregular migration, proxied by border and on-territory apprehensions, Czaika and Hobolth (2016) look at twenty-nine European countries from 2008 to 2012. Their findings suggest a significant increase in irregular border crossings (border apprehensions) as a consequence of more restrictive visa practices. An increase in visa refusals by 10 percent, *ceteris paribus*, results in a 5 to 7 percent increase in apprehensions at the border. While visa refusal seems to increase the arrival of irregular migrants at the border, visas as a condition *sine qua non* for legal entry of most third-country nationals has a relatively strong overall deterrence effect upon irregular entries.

Thus, visa restrictions tend to do both: they deter irregular entries, but more restrictive visa practices in terms of higher visa refusal rates also increase irregular entry and attempted irregular entry. This implies that restrictive visa policies and practices may deter potential migrants altogether, but also deflect those migrants who are not deterred into clandestine entry routes and irregular status. This implies that some policy-makers may have overstated the overall deterring impact of restrictive migration and visa policies upon inflows of unwelcome migrants. More restrictive entry regulations and practices may partly deflect arrivals into more 'invisible' types of immigration, which are harder to detect and measure.

Given that for most non-Europeans legal entry into the EU is largely impossible without a valid travel visa or other type of entry visa, most asylum claims are likely filed after irregularly entering a EU country of destination or transit. Based on existing evidence about deterrence effects of restrictive asylum policy on asylum applications (e.g., Hatton 2011; Toshkov 2014), a visa requirement may additionally deter potential asylum-seekers from migrating. But some of those who are – after all – applying for a subsequently rejected visa are deflected into irregular entry routes and access a European destination by irregular means before claiming asylum or establishing irregular residence. This mechanism seems to be a major force in the context of the EU's 'refugee crisis'. To some extent, this is the consequence of highly restrictive entry policies that generate a 'market' for an industry that facilitates irregular migration (Andersson 2014).

Economic implications of visa restrictions

Selective visa policies allow countries to discriminate against different nationalities. Some nationalities do not require a visa and are *prima facie* regarded as 'low-risk' visitors. Those who need a visa and have been given one are regarded as welcome upon closer screening. However, those who need a visa and have been denied one are considered to be 'high-risk' visitors and potential overstayers, and are thus unwelcome. Consequently, visa restrictions not only – according to the policy's intention – deter unwanted visitors and migrants; they also deter visitors such as tourists and businesspeople who would be welcome, but who are simply not willing to undergo a visa issuance procedure. Thus, there is a likely negative economic impact in the form of reduced numbers of travelers, traders and foreign investors (Czaika and Neumayer 2017).

In the current era of globalization we have seen an unprecedented growth in cross-border flows of people, goods and services, and capital. International tourism flows have increased from twenty-five million globally in 1950, 278 million in 1980, 674 million in 2000, to over 1.1 billion in 2015. Inbound traveling to European destinations makes up about half of these global numbers (UNWTO 2015). International travel and tourism has developed into the world's fourth largest industry, contributing 9.8 percent of global GDP, 4.3 percent of total investments, 5.7 percent of world exports and more than 250 million jobs, i.e., 9.4 percent of total global employment (WTTC 2015).

As a consequence, travel barriers such as visa restrictions come with significant economic costs of forfeited bilateral tourist arrivals, trade and foreign direct investment (FDI). Hu (2013), for instance, estimates that the US Visa Waiver Program (VWP) has saved between US$1.9 billion and US$3.2 billion in administrative costs and has contributed a further US$6.9 billion to US$10 billion in direct tourist spending per year. Neiman and Swagel (2009) find that changes in visa policy have contributed relatively little to the decrease in travel to the USA after 9/11, since the largest decline was among travelers under the visa waiver program, i.e., those who were not required to obtain a visa (see also Bangwayo-Skeete and Skeete 2016). For China, Song et al. (2012) and Li and Song (2013) report detrimental impacts from visa restrictions upon the tourism sector and the wider economy.

The negative repercussions of visa restrictions are expected to be strongest among tourism sectors, as 'freedom of travel *is* freedom to trade' (O'Byrne 2001). Tourists and travelers usually visit for a short period of time and typically have alternative travel options and 'substitute destinations'. Visa restrictions, although burdensome in many cases, deter only some tourists. Overall, visa restrictions may not only reduce the volume, but also change the spatial direction of international travel and other international flows (Czaika and Neumayer 2017).

Neumayer (2010, 2011) provides evidence that visa restrictions decrease bilateral trade (by about 21 percent) and FDI (by about 32 percent). It is estimated that visa restrictions decrease international travel by about 52 to 63 percent, although Lawson and Roychoudhury (2016) believe the respective visa effect to be even higher, at 70 percent. However, due to the cross-sectional character of these studies, they cannot control for many unobserved factors that impact tourist arrivals, trade and FDI, and that may be correlated with visa restrictions, which is likely to cause an omitted variable bias.

Czaika and Neumayer (2017) have addressed this potential bias to the greatest possible extent by using the aforementioned bilateral visa policy database (DEMIG VISA), which covers 194 destination and 214 origin countries from 1995 to 2013. They estimate that bilateral travel increases on average by about 24.6 percent as a consequence of visa removal and declines by around 19.7 percent after visa introduction. Foreign suppliers and investors usually have a significant economic interest in the country to which they wish to export their goods and services or in which to invest their capital. However, much of international exchange in trade, FDI, but also scientific knowledge transfer (see below), requires personal or face-to-face contacts with trading and investment partners (Storper and Venables 2004; Hovhannisyan and Keller 2015), not least because of the importance of tacit knowledge (Gertler 2003). But Czaika and Neumayer (2017) find the deterrence effects of visa restrictions to be smaller for trade and FDI than for tourist flows, with an estimated visa effect upon trade of 4.6 percent. The respective visa effect on bilateral FDI is somewhere in between the effects on tourism and trade. Visa restrictions also reduce international tourism, trade and FDI, but some of the deterred flows in tourists and goods and services are redirected to other (visa-free) destinations (Czaika and Neumayer 2017). This deterrence-cum-deflection effect of travel restrictions implies significant economic costs for both visa-issuing and visa-targeted countries, but it also creates some positive externalities for more liberal countries that benefit from additional flows of tourists, trade and investment.

Mobility barriers in terms of visa restrictions also seem to play a role in processes of international knowledge transfer and diffusion. Although Czaika and Orazbayev (2017) find that visa restrictions are much less of a barrier for mobile scientists than other (lower skilled) international migrants, visa restrictions nevertheless establish a strong effect on the intensity of international research collaborations. Visas, even if granted, constitute a barrier for internationally mobile scientists in terms of conference attendance, research stay, face-to-face meetings, etc. As a consequence, the intensity of international research collaborations, as measured by the number of internationally co-authored research articles, is significantly lower in visa-restricted corridors compared to free mobility spaces. This has a far-reaching bearing on the international diffusion of scientific knowledge and Europe's integration into and standing within the global science system (Czaika and di Lillo 2017).

Conclusions

This chapter has investigated the political dynamics and migratory effects of the EU's visa policy. The harmonization of the EU's visa policy has aimed at providing third-country nationals with the same entry rules for the Schengen area, irrespective of which member state consulate they contact. Research has shown that these visa issuance practices still tend to differ in respect of target third-country nationalities. Certain 'state-bound logics' (Infantino 2016) such as a colonial past and bilateral ties influence the visa practices. A key issue in the politics of EU visa policy has been to define the balance between the Schengen zone's openness and restrictiveness vis-à-vis short-term travelers. While third countries, in particular those neighboring the EU, have lobbied for quick visa liberalization schemes, the EU has only reluctantly used visa relaxations due to concerns over irregular migration. Thus far, EU visa policies have been relaxed for western Balkan states (except Kosovo) as well as for Georgia and Moldova in Eastern Europe. The visa liberalization process has lately become more politicized, notably with respect to Ukraine and Turkey.

The effects of visas on migration and mobility processes are manifold and rather ambiguous. Empirical evidence suggests a significant deterrence effect of visa restrictions on cross-border flows of people (migrants and travelers), trade in goods and services, FDI, and also knowledge. The size of respective deterrence effects can vary widely by type of flow and depends largely on the alternative options in redirecting flows to other destinations or categories of entry (including irregular entry). By and large, visa restrictions come with significant economic costs, not only through deterring unwanted migrants but also desired travelers, trade, investors, scientists and others who can make a positive economic and non-economic contribution to the recipient countries. A more comprehensive assessment of visa restrictions requires that not only the direct tradeoffs between (negative) economic impacts and (possibly positive) implications for security are taken into account, but also the less visible effects of retrenchments on people's freedom of mobility which unintentionally create undesirable situations in which people, faced with no alternative, choose irregular routes of entry and informality of stay.

Bibliography

Ademmer, E. and Börzel, T. (2013). Migration, Energy and Good Governance in the EU's Eastern Neighbourhood. *Europe-Asia Studies*, 65, pp. 581–608.

Ademmer, E. and Delcour, L. (2016). With a Little Help from Russia? The European Union and Visa Liberalization with Post-Soviet States. *Eurasian Geography and Economics*, 57(1), pp. 89–112.

Andersson, R. (2014). *Illegality, Inc.: Clandestine Migration and the Business of Bordering Europe*, Vol. 28. Berkeley: University of California Press.

Bangwayo-Skeete, P.F. and Skeete, R.W. (2016). Who Travels Visa-free? Insights into Tourist Hassle-free Travel. *Journal of Travel Research*. doi: 0047287516643410.

Boratynski, J., Chajewski, L., Hermelinski, P., Szymborska, A. and Tokarz, B. (2006). *Visa Policies of European Union Member States. Monitoring Report*. Warsaw, June. The Stefan Batory Foundation.

Bürgin, A. (2013). Salience, Path Dependency and the Coalition between the European Commission and the Danish Council Presidency: Why the EU Opened a Visa Liberalisation Process with Turkey. *European Integration online Papers*, 17(9). Available at http://eiop.or.at/eiop/index.php/eiop (accessed April 11, 2017).

Court of Justice of the European Union (2017). *Advocate General's Opinion in Case C-638/16 PPU. X and X v État Belge*. Luxembourg, February 7.

Czaika, M. and de Haas, H. (2015). Evaluating Migration Policy Effectiveness. In A. Triandafyllidou (ed.), *Routledge Handbook of Immigrant and Refugee Studies*. Abingdon: Routledge, pp. 34–40.

Czaika, M. and de Haas, H. (2016). The Effect of Visas on Migration Processes. *International Migration Review*. doi: 10.1111/imre.12261.

Czaika, M. and Hobolth, M. (2016). Do Restrictive Asylum and Visa Policies Increase Irregular Migration into Europe? *European Union Politics*, 17(3), pp. 345–365.

Czaika, M. and di Lillo, A. (2017). Visa Restrictions and International Research Collaborations. IMI working paper, University of Oxford, forthcoming.

Czaika, M. and Neumayer, E. (2017). Visa Restrictions and Economic Globalisation. *Applied Geography*, forthcoming.

Czaika, M. and Orazbayev, S. (2017). The Globalisation of Scientific Mobility, 1970–2014. IMI working paper, University of Oxford, forthcoming.

Czaika, M., de Haas, H. and Villares-Varela, M. (2017). The Evolution of Global Visa Regimes: Patterns and Trends of Multi-polar Power Asymmetries Based on the DEMIG VISA Database. IMI working paper No 134, University of Oxford.

Dura, G. (2006). A Tale of Two Visa Regimes – Repercessions of Romania's Accession to the EU on the Freedom of Movement of Moldavan Citizens. *EuroJournal.org – Journal of Foreign Policy of Moldova*, 1.

Düvell, F. (ed.) (2005). *Illegal Immigration in Europe. Beyond Control?* Basingstoke: Palgrave Macmillan.

European Commission (2015a). *Fourth Progress Report on Georgia's Implementation of the Action Plan on Visa Liberalisation*. COM(2015) 684 final, December 18.

European Commission (2015b). *Sixth Progress Report on the Implementation by Ukraine of the Action Plan on Visa Liberalisation*. COM(2015) 905, December 18.

European Commission (2016). *European Commission Proposes Visa-free Travel for the People of Kosovo*. Brussels. Press Release IP/16/1626.

European Council (2016). *EU–Turkey Statement*, March 18.

Fakiolas, R. (2003). Regularising Undocumented Immigrants in Greece: Procedures and Effects. *Journal of Ethnic and Migration Studies*, 29(3), pp. 535–561.

Fernández, A.M. (2008). Consular Affairs in the EU: Visa Policies as a Catalyst for Integration? *The Hague Journal of Diplomacy*, 3(1), pp. 21–35.

Finotelli, C. and Scirotino, G. (2013). Through the Gates of the Fortress: European Visa Policies and the Limits of Immigration Control. *Perspectives on European Poltiics and Society*, 14(1), pp. 80–101.

Gammeltoft-Hansen, T. (2011). *Access to Asylum: International Refugee Law and the Globalisation of Migration Control*. Cambridge: Cambridge University Press.

Gertler, M.S. (2003). Tacit Knowledge and the Economic Geography of Context, or the Undefinable Tacitness of Being (There). *Journal of Economic Geography*, 3(1), pp. 75–99.

Grabbe, H. (2000). *The Sharp Edges of Europe: Security Implications of Extending EU Border Policies Eastwards*. Occasional Paper 13, March. Paris: Institute for Security Studies.

Grabbe, H. (2002). Stabilising the East While Keeping Out the Easterners: Internal and External Security Logics in Conflict. In S. Lavenex and E.M. Uçarer (eds), *Migration and the Externalities of European Integration*. Lanham, MD: Lexington Books, pp. 91–104.

Gülzau, F., Mau, S. and Zaun, N. (2016). Regional Mobility Spaces? Visa Waiver Policies and Regional Integration. *International Migration*, 54(6), pp. 164–180.

Hatton, T. (2011). *Seeking Asylum. Trends and Policies in the OECD*. London: Centre for Economic Policy Research (CEPR).

Hernández i Sagrera, R. (2010). The EU–Russia Readmission–Visa Facilitation Nexus: An Exportable Migration Model for Eastern Europe? *European Security*, 19(4), pp. 569–584.

Hobolth, M. (2014). Researching Mobility Barriers: The European Visa Database. *Journal of Ethnic and Migration Studies*, 40(3), pp. 424–435.

Hovhannisyan, N. and Keller, W. (2015). International Business Travel: An Engine of Innovation? *Journal of Economic Growth*, 20(1), pp. 75–104.

Hu, X. (2013). Economic Benefits Associated with the Visa Waiver Program – A Difference-in-difference Approach. *Global Journal of Business Research*, 7(1), pp. 81–89.

Huysmans, J. (2006). *The Politics of Insecurity: Fear, Migration and Asylum in the EU*. Routledge.

Icduygu, A. and Aksel, D.B. (2014). Two-to-tango in Migration Diplomacy: Negotiating Readmission Agreement between the EU and Turkey. *European Journal of Migration and Law*, 16(3), pp. 337–363.

ICG (2005). *EU Visas and the Western Balkans*. Europe Report No. 168, November 29. Brussels: International Crisis Group.

Infantino, F. (2016). State-bound Visa Policies and Europeanized Practices. Comparing EU Visa Policy Implementation in Morocco. *Journal of Borderlands Studies*, 31(2), pp. 171–186.

Jileva, E. (2002). Visa and Free Movement of Labour: The Uneven Imposition of EU Acquis on the Accession States. *Journal of Ethnic and Migration Studies*, 28(4), pp. 683–700.

Kacarska, S. (2012). *Europeanisation through Mobility: Visa Liberalisation and Citizenship Regimes in the Western Balkans*. CITSEE Working Paper Series 2012/21. Edinburgh.

Lawson, R.A. and Roychoudhury, S. (2016). Do Travel Visa Requirements Impede Tourist Travel? *Journal of Economics and Finance*, 40(4), pp. 817–828.

Li, S. and Song, H. (2013). Economic Impacts of Visa Restrictions on Tourism: A Case of Two Events in China. *Annals of Tourism Research*, 43, pp. 251–271.

Massey, D.S. and Pren, K.A. (2012). Unintended Consequences of US Immigration Policy: Explaining the Post-1965 Surge from Latin America. *Population and Development Review*, 38(1), pp. 1–29.

Mau, S., Gülzau, F., Laube, L. and Zaun, N. (2015). The Global Mobility Divide: How Visa Policies Have Evolved Over Time. *Journal of Ethnic and Migration Studies*, 41(8), pp. 1192–1213.

Monar, J. (2001). The Dynamics of Justice and Home Affairs: Laboratories, Driving Factors and Costs. *Journal of Common Market Studies*, 39(4), pp. 747–764.

Moreno-Lax, V. (2008). Must EU Borders have Doors for Refugees? On the Compatibility of Schengen Visas and Carriers' Sanctions with EU Member States' Obligations to Provide International Protection to Refugees. *European Journal of Migration and Law*, 10(3), pp. 315–364.

Neiman, B. and Swagel, P. (2009). The Impact of Post-9/11 Visa Policies on Travel to the United States. *Journal of International Economics*, 78(1), pp. 86–99.

Neumayer, E. (2006). Unequal Access to Foreign Spaces: How States Use Visa Restrictions to Regulate Mobility in a Globalized World. *Transactions of the Institute of British Geographers*, 31(1), pp. 72–84.

Neumayer, E. (2010). Visa Restrictions and Bilateral Travel. *The Professional Geographer*, 62(2), pp. 1–11.

Neumayer, E. (2011). On the Detrimental Impact of Visa Restrictions on Bilateral Trade and Foreign Direct Investment. *Applied Geography*, 31(3), pp. 901–907.

O'Byrne, D.J. (2001). On Passports and Border Controls. *Annals of Tourism Research*, 28, pp. 399–416.

Peers, S. (2012). *Amending the EU's Visa List Legislation*. Statewatch analysis, London.

Salter, M.B. and Mutlu, C.E. (2010). *Asymmetric Borders: The Canada–Czech Republic 'Visa War' and the Question of Rights*. CEPS Liberty and Security Series. Brussels: Centre for European Policy Reforms.

Schoorl, J., Heering, L., Esveldt, I., Groenewold, G., van der Erf, R., Bosch, A., de Valk, H. and de Bruijn, B. (2000). *Push and Pull Factors of International Migration: A Comparative Report*. Luxembourg: Eurostat, European Communities.

Song, H., Gartner, W.C. and Tasci, A.D. (2012). Visa Restrictions and Their Adverse Economic and Marketing Implications – Evidence from China. *Tourism Management*, 33(2): pp. 397–412.

Storper, M. and Venables, A.J. (2004). Buzz: Face-to-face Contact and the Urban Economy. *Journal of Economic Geography*, 4(4), pp. 351–370.

Torpey, J. (1998). Coming and Going: On the State Monopolization of the Legitimate 'Means of Movement'. *Sociological Theory*, 16, pp. 239–259.

Torpey, J. (2000). *The Invention of the Passport: Surveillance, Citizenship and the State.* Cambridge: Cambridge University Press.

Toshkov, D. (2014). The Dynamic Relationship between Asylum Applications and Recognition Rates in Europe (1987–2010). *European Union Politics*, 15(2), pp. 192–214.

Trauner, F. (2009). From Membership Conditionality to Policy Conditionality: EU External Governance in South Eastern Europe. *Journal of European Public Policy*, 16(5), pp. 774–790.

Trauner, F. (2017). *The EU Visa Suspension Mechanism.* Alert No. 2. Paris: EU Institute for Security Studies.

Trauner, F. and Kruse, I. (2008). EC Visa Facilitation and Readmission Agreements: A New Standard EU Foreign Policy Tool? *European Journal of Migration and Law*, 10(4), pp. 411–438.

Trauner, F. and Manigrassi, E. (2014). When Visa-free Travel Becomes Difficult to Achieve and Easy to Lose: The EU Visa Free Dialogues after the EU's Experience with the Western Balkans. *European Journal of Migration and Law*, 16(1), pp. 125–145.

UNWTO (2015). *Statistical Information on CD-Rom.* Madrid: World Tourism Organization.

Wolff, S. (2014). The Politics of Negotiating EU Readmission Agreements: Insights from Morocco and Turkey. *European Journal of Migration and Law*, 16(1), pp. 69–95.

WTTC (World Travel and Tourism Council) Tourism and Travel (2015). Economic Impact 2015. Available at www.wttc.org/-/media/files/reports/economic%20impact%20research/regional%202015/world2015.pdf (accessed on April 11, 2017).

Zincone, G. (2006). The Making of Policies: Immigration and Immigrants in Italy. *Journal of Ethnic and Migration Studies*, 32(3), pp. 347–375.

10
EU LABOR IMMIGRATION POLICY
From silence to salience

Georg Menz

Introduction

European Union (EU) migration policy is of relatively recent provenance. Correspondingly, scholarly interest in the matter emerged only in the late 1990s. The aim of this chapter is to trace the genesis of European-level labor migration policy and chart the scholarly debate analyzing it. I will also point to lacunae and gaps in the existing scholarly literature. The central focus will rest on labor migration as opposed to other channels of legal or illegal immigration. We will proceed chronologically by juxtaposing both policy development and the concurrent treatment in the scholarly literature in the first major section, followed by a thorough exploration of key research questions. In the final section I put forward several possible future trajectories that will in time pose significant policy challenges and theoretical research questions for scholars.

As we will see, EU labor immigration policy is of very recent provenance. It was created as one of the many offshoots of the 1993 Treaty on European Union. In many ways, the policy field came to maturity as member states agreed to Europeanization. Concerns over national sovereignty meant that early attempts by the European Commission to create a policy framework were unsuccessful. Similarly, though the freedom of labor mobility was one of the core four freedoms enshrined in the Treaty of Rome, relatively modest wage gaps among the founding members of the European Community meant that there was little incentive to take advantage of any such right for the first few decades of the existence of the EU. However, there was a flurry of activity in the early 2000s. Since then, a fairly comprehensive set of policies has been created, though this process has been heavily contested politically. Although, in the regulation of other immigration policy matters there has been a pattern of bottom-up Europeanization, in labor migration policy, most of the dynamics are more accurately described as being instances of top-down Europeanization (Menz 2009). We will explore some of the political conflicts in this chapter. Finally, the muddled response to the enormous increase in illegal immigration in 2014/2015 may jeopardize any further progress in labor migration policy-making, as the sheer volume of illegal immigration and the problems it engenders has led to a degree of salience that renders further liberalization increasingly unlikely.

The genesis of EU migration policy

Legally and analytically, it is customary to distinguish between internal (intra) EU migration and immigration by non-EU nationals. There are significant legal distinctions between the two categories of immigrants, even though the two are often conflated in public debates. The freedom of labor mobility is one of the four freedoms enshrined in the 1957 Treaty of Rome, though it was not phased in until 1968. By contrast, during the early decades of European integration, no tangible measures were taken regarding a common immigration policy. Early attempts by the European Commission to motion such an initiative came to naught (Geddes 2000). Accordingly, both scholars of EU integration in general and of immigration more specifically paid little attention to the EU level, preferring instead to focus their attention on developments at the national level. The scholarly literature of the 1970s and 1980s certainly did so. The thrust of the neo-Marxist literature of the 1970s and 1980s (Castles and Kosack 1973; Cohen 1987) focused on the (ab)use of labor migrants as a tool to place downward pressure on wages and working conditions by enlarging the overall size of the workforce or, in Marxist terms, by means of creating a reserve army of workers. Meanwhile, the tempestuous political and economic climate during that decade had helped convince policy-makers throughout Europe to end or at least radically scale back the size of active labor recruitment programs. In 1971, British legislation curtailed access to citizenship and reined in immigration rights by those without ethnic ties to the British Isles. In 1973, West Germany ended its active labor recruitment programs. France and The Netherlands followed suit in 1974. For the next twenty-five years or so, legal labor immigration to Europe was reduced to a trickle, consisting mainly of limited temporary labor schemes, for example, in France in the 1980s (Hollifield 1992), and in the German construction sector in the 1990s (Menz 2001).

In fact, the possibility of active labor recruitment via immigration experiencing a renaissance seemed so remote that in 1990 one prominent analyst of European migration policies (Messina 1990) predicted that immigration from outside of the EU would never be revived. He identified three key reasons: the emergence of the anti-immigration Far Right family of parties throughout Europe, the politicization of the migration issue in general, and the abandonment of advocacy for immigrant rights by the political Left. This analysis may have been correct at the time of writing, but did not prove very prescient. Yet there were serious grounds on which to doubt that any such liberal labor immigration policy would be revisited. Messina did not mention residential ghettoization, ethnic and racial tensions, including race riots, serious problems with meaningful integration into European societies or the role of structural mass unemployment, but all of these factors obviously also weighed on the minds of decision-makers in the national capitals of Europe. Somewhat surprisingly, given the decidedly mixed track record of the first wave of labor migration and the attendant integration problems, by the tail end of the 1990s, labor migration policy targeted at non-Europeans was being liberalized across Europe (Geddes 2003; Menz 2009). European governments either dusted off or redesigned sectoral labor migration schemes, targeting specific sectors of the economy, especially agriculture, tourism and gastronomy, and, in countries such as the United Kingdom, healthcare and highly skilled professions in finance and information technology (Caviedes 2010).

This policy u-turn seems surprising for a number of reasons. Much of the post-war wave of labor migrants consisted of unskilled or low-skilled workers that fed into Western Europe's manufacturing sectors and heavy industries. The contribution of the labor migrants to economic recovery was only marginal, given that they were directed towards entry-level positions. Many of these jobs were starting to disappear in the wake of deindustrialization either concurrently with labor recruitment or shortly thereafter. It seems odd to repeat similar mistakes in current policy design by once again recruiting labor immigrants to fill positions that are poised to disappear due to automation, rationalization, and the onset of the knowledge economy (Borjas 2016). In addition, labor immigration proved unpopular at the polls, as reflected not only in the rise of xenophobic right-wing political parties, but also in the perennial skepticism towards immigration expressed in the opinion polls. According to the 2015 Eurobarometer Survey (Eurobarometer 2015: 151–157), across the EU-28 56 percent of all respondents held negative sentiments towards non-European immigrants, with some countries recording scores of up to 81 percent. With the past track record of labor migration recruitment from source countries outside of Europe looking decidedly mixed, why was this policy reinvented?

Part of the answer may lie in the crucial fact that other forms of legal immigration proved so challenging to regulate or indeed limit. With the sensitivity of the migration issue duly recognized, European governments did devise a plethora of multilateral fora for policy discussion and deliberation, as immigration pressures and numbers began to mount during the 1980s and skyrocket after the fall of the Iron Curtain. Most of those focused on combatting illegal immigration and seeking to reduce the number of asylum-seekers. The 1993 Treaty on European Union committed the member states to the construction of a third pillar on justice and home affairs (Geddes 2000). During the first decade of the twenty-first century rapid and tangible progress was made in terms of formulating and implementing EU-level migration policy, since the Amsterdam Treaty was a *communitarized* policy. Following the 1999 Tampere Council meeting, key framework directives were passed regarding family reunion, asylum qualification and procedures, as well as sectoral aspects of labor migration, pertaining to students, researchers, interns, and, eventually, to highly skilled labor migrants (for a summary of the conclusions, see European Parliament 1999). The European Commission failed in its attempts to deliver a single comprehensive labor migration directive in 2001. While much of the pushback from national governments, especially the German, Austrian and French representatives, was presented on technical grounds, questioning the legal competence of the Commission in this matter, it is safe to assume that the real source of motivation was political in nature (Menz 2009).

At the same time, as suggested earlier, member states started liberalizing their national policies regarding labor migration, implementing provisions for both temporary and permanent immigration for employment purposes. This trend commenced in the United Kingdom, but governments across continental Europe and Ireland followed suit in rapid succession. In many ways, this reflected a paradigmatic shift towards the embrace of 'managed migration'. A number of European governments were rediscovering the alleged benefits of calibrated labor immigration programs. As the European Commission was soon to discover, however, this entailed a focus on skilled immigrants. Consequently, the Commission and core member states could agree on the need for legal channels for skilled labor immigrants, but the Commission's enthusiasm for liberalization of migration provisions towards other groups was not shared outside the Brussels Beltway (Menz 2009). Even governments that perceived a need for unskilled labor immigration, such as the British and the Irish, did not strongly support unskilled immigration programs for non-Europeans set at the EU level, given the option of recruiting both domestically and from the EU newcomer countries in central and eastern Europe.

With the early attempt at creating a single labor directive frustrated, the Commission changed tactics slightly, presenting sectoral directives instead, including notably the directive on highly skilled employees (Cerna 2014), the single permit (Roos 2015) and third-country seasonal workers. In 2004, the right to initiative for policy proposals which had hitherto been shared between the Commission and the member states reverted to being exercised exclusively by the former. Alongside the introduction of the ordinary legislative procedure and the involvement of the Court of the European Union in immigration policy, this points to significant

Europeanization in the decision-making mode. As the Parliament is also subject to considerable lobbying by pressure groups, this development may in time lead to a shift in policy outcome. Bonjour and Vink (2013) correctly criticize the fact that this shift in policy-making mode has not as of yet attracted significant scholarly interest.

About a quarter of a century after the end of the guestworker programs of the post-war decades, European governments reintroduced similar schemes. This seems somewhat peculiar in light of the mixed track record of earlier recruitment efforts, the poor integration record of the second and third European-born generation, and the attendant problems with crime, social deviancy, political violence, and cultural and religious tensions (Koopmans 2010; Caldwell 2010). Across Western Europe, labor market participation rates are lower for non-EU nationals than for nationals: 63.43 versus 78.25 percent in France, 68.17 versus 82.80 in Germany and 73.12 versus 78.61 percent in the UK (EU Labor Force Survey data, in Kahanec et al. 2010: 29–31). The data are even more troubling for foreign-born (first-generation) immigrants.

The arguments advanced by supporters of such liberalization critically hinged on two related claims. The first claim put forward pertained to the low total fertility rates of European women, hovering around 1.5 children per woman and thus well below the replacement level of fertility at 2.1. There are ready alternatives to immigration for demographic reasons, such as improving childcare provision, facilitating the work–life balance for employed women and proffering tax breaks for parents. A modest improvement of childcare facilities combined with changes to the tax code in Germany has already delivered a slight increase in the total fertility rate, from 1.38 to 1.63 between 2000 and 2010 (OECD data in Hansen and Gordon 2014: 1207). The second argument often submitted in political discussions is equally flawed: presumably there are worker shortages, especially in skilled niche labor markets. Such claims are commonly advanced by employers with a clear agenda of liberalization (Menz 2009). The European Commission submits a similar claim in the preamble to the Blue Card Directive 2009/50/EC (European Commission 2009). Here, too, there would be ready alternatives to immigrant recruitment, including automation, raising wages, more pro-active domestic recruitment efforts, and efforts to ramp up apposite domestic training schemes (Menz 2015a; Borjas 2016). In fact, the timing seems peculiar, not least in light of persistently high unemployment in some of the countries rolling out labor migration recruitment and given the lasting legacy of the Great Recession commencing in 2008. A 2008 report by the UK House of Lords found no evidence that immigration was having any discernible positive economic effect on the British population (House of Lords 2008). The authors argued (2008: 5):

> We do not support the general claims that net immigration is indispensable to fill labor and skills shortages. Such claims are analytically weak and provide insufficient reason for promoting net immigration. Vacancies are, to a certain extent, a sign of a healthy economy. Immigration increases the size of the economy and overall labor demand, thus creating new vacancies. As a result, immigration is unlikely to be an effective tool for reducing vacancies other than in the short term.

Scholarly debates regarding EU labor migration policy-making

With the progress made in constructing a European-level immigration policy scheme, scholarly interest experienced a renaissance. Andrew Geddes (2000, 2003) chronicled both national-level and EU-level immigration policy-making in considerable detail. The key research question in the rapidly burgeoning literature became to identify the key causal driver that would explain the Europeanization of immigration policy. Was a neofunctionalist emphasis on the spill-over effects of completing the Single Market truly sufficient? Early work usually implicitly assumed that this was indeed the single most important factor. Most recently, Alex Caviedes (2016) has argued that no major theory of European integration accounts for developments in justice and home affairs particularly well, at least not for the entire period of its existence. Roos' (2013) account of immigration policy-making emphasizes that both member state interest and the Commission's policy entrepreneurship matter, with final directives usually constituting a messy compromise solution. Christian Kaunert (2010) and Arne Niemann (2006) both argued that the renaissance in EU immigration policy-making could be ascribed to the functional pressures exerted by the advancing unfolding of the Single Market, in line with early neofunctionalist predictions. By contrast, in an influential contribution, Virginie Guiraudon (2000) argued that national decision-makers preferred the more secretive and opaque European level to national venues in designing immigration policy. Far from Europeanization constituting the inevitable result of functional pressures, she argued that national decision-makers simply preferred to 'escape to Brussels' for a more amiable and secluded decision-making venue.

The problem with the venue-shopping argument was two-fold. First, its temporal applicability was always going to be limited. From 2004 onward, the right to initiate policy passed from being jointly held by the Commission and the member states to the Commission only. Second, the claim implicitly insinuated that national politicians preferred the European venue to hatch plans for a more restrictive policy. But in many instances, EU-level policy, for example, on asylum, is, in fact, more liberal and generous than anything likely to have seen the light of day at the national level (Kaunert and Léonard 2012; for a dissenting view see Ripoll Servent and Trauner 2014). Georg Menz (2009) demonstrated how national governments were playing two level games both at home and in Europe. Using a comparative political economy approach, he demonstrated that employer organizations wield considerable influence regarding labor migration policy design, whereas non-governmental organizations exert a proportionally less significant degree of influence on asylum policies. Depending on the respective variety of capitalism in which they are embedded, employers prefer either only skilled labor migrants, as is true in coordinated market economies, or both skilled and unskilled migrants, as is the case in liberal market economies. Devitt (2011) similarly points out that the perceived need for certain groups of immigrants, especially unskilled ones, varies enormously across Europe and is most pronounced in liberal market economies.

Rather than applying one of the major theories of European integration, it may be more fruitful to look to the principal agent approach for shedding light on the dynamics of European-level policy-making. According to this concept, member states delegate the task of finding mutually acceptable compromise solutions to the 'agent', i.e., the European Commission. As tends to be the case, shirking and mission creep are real-life problems, with the Commission taking advantage of often somewhat lax oversight, conflicting interests among the member states and the fairly generously defined mission brief. In an early but seemingly overlooked contribution, Stetter (2000) argued that this concept goes a long way towards accounting for the uneven and at times even conflictual growth trajectory of policy in this domain. Menz (2015b) makes a similar argument regarding the ways in which the member states use the Commission to help them manage migration control on the southern border of the European Union.

As has been shown, the exact nature of the drivers of Europeanizing immigration policy has been contested. Are member states propelling the process forward or is it the Commission? Menz (2009) argued that member states can attempt to upload their own policy regulations as blueprints for future EU-level regulation. Roos (2015) suggests that given the involvement of the European Parliament, national room for fine-tuning of EU directives is being curtailed, contrasting the much more loosely constructed Blue Card Directive with the more tightly calibrated Single Permit Directive. Geddes and Guiraudon (2004) present an argument along somewhat similar lines, demonstrating how the momentum for an anti-discrimination directive built at the national level eventually leads to the EU-wide implementation of such a policy instrument. They also analyzed and chronicled how member states will attempt to dilute and thwart top-down Europeanization. This has been particularly true for EU labor migration policy. The Commission failed spectacularly in 2001 in its attempt to propose a single comprehensive labor migration directive, owing both to member states' concerns over sovereignty and the perceived excessively liberal bias of its content. Not one to capitulate readily, the Commission continued in its quest from 2002 onward, changing tactics by focusing on select groups of labor migrants, including students, interns and highly skilled immigrants. In so doing, it was able to avoid the backlash it encountered over alleged mission creep. By accepting that certain operational details, including the politically important matter of annual quotas, was to be set at the member state level, the directive for highly skilled workers was much easier to find acceptance for among member states (Cerna 2014).

With this matter largely settled, another major point of contestation concerns the very nature of labor migration policy regulation. At the heart of it is what Hollifield (1992) more than twenty years ago referred to as the control paradox, namely the difficulty liberal Western states have in controlling immigration flows effectively. Practical experience in Europe suggests that solicited labor migration in the long-term migration flows is considered less desirable, for example, family reunion, illegal immigration and asylum-seekers from the same countries or regions (Joppke 1998; Messina 2007). Given the obvious problems with the integration of the second and third generation of descendants of immigrants and given the general lack of popularity of liberal immigration policy as reflected in public opinion polls, such as the ones recorded by Eurobarometer, why is labor immigration to Europe permitted at all? The question is not as naïve as it may seem. Persistently high unemployment throughout the early 2000s, further exacerbated by the 2008 global economic recession, has left Europe with a real and persistent unemployment problem, affecting both young and senior citizens with particular vengeance in southern Europe (Hansen and Gordon 2014). Mediterranean Europe records youth unemployment in excess of 30 percent, while the EU-28 average stood at 20.4 percent in 2016 (OECD 2016). Looming automation and future technological breakthroughs in digitization will dramatically reduce the need for low-skill employees (Kaplan 2015; Schwab 2016). In the future, policy-makers will grapple with the challenge of identifying employment opportunities for unskilled members of the domestic labor force (Standing 2014).

This paradox has largely been accounted for by pointing to political lobbying. Gary Freeman (1996, 2006) argued that interest groups play a central if often under-appreciated role in shaping (liberal) immigration policies, not only in the United States but also in Europe. With diffused costs but concentrated benefits, employers benefit from a flexible and motivated addition to the domestic labor pool. Hollifield (2004) took this argument even further, claiming that the early twenty-first-century 'migration state' perceived liberal migration policies as an added element to its arsenal of business-friendly policies to enhance competitiveness. In light of the liberal approach which major Western governments adopted towards labor migration, this conclusion certainly seemed tempting. Employer organizations did indeed play a central role in advocating for the liberalization of labor policy (Menz 2009), although they did so at the national level, not in Brussels. Curiously, trade unions simply played along (Menz and Caviedes 2010), having abandoned the more skeptical stance of yore (Watts 2002). Cerna (2009) also points out that unions and employers may form alliances, as highly skilled employees may actually perceive liberalized migration provisions not as a potential source of unwanted competition, but rather as a source of complementary employees. Caviedes (2010) concurs to a certain degree, pointing to his detailed empirical research on different dynamics across various sectors of the economy. Highly skilled sector employees generally regard the notion of liberalized labor migration favorably, while the opposite is true for those employees in unskilled sectors.

However, it is very clear that employer organizations and business lobbyists need to tread carefully. Not only is the systemic need for a large-scale, low-skill labor pool a feature that may well disappear by the mid-twenty-first century (Kaplan 2015), but what Piore (1979) described as the bottom tier of a dual labor market may well shrink dramatically in size and thus no longer constitute a compelling claim for liberal immigration policy. Immigration policy may also become politicized, as high-issue salience will (Givens and Luedtke 2004) significantly complicate any policy-making process in this domain. It is thus conceivable that the liberalization of labor migration policy may be scaled back, not least in light of the rising backlash visible across Europe as the long-term consequences of the financial crisis and the crisis of the single currency begin to bite.

Future policy and research challenges in labor migration studies

This helps us segueway to the final section of this chapter, in which the focus will be on avenues for future research. I will identify four key causes of considerable political upheaval in Europe that may in time lead to a recalibration of labor migration policy at the EU level.

First, following the referendum on the exit of the United Kingdom from European Union membership (Brexit) in June 2016, all eyes will be on negotiations of the exact terms. The issue of immigration from the rest of the EU proved both politically highly important and hugely unpopular in the run-up to the referendum, with opinion polls suggesting that more than 50 percent of the electorate considered immigration to be a key issue (*The Guardian* 2016a). The United Kingdom received more than 150,000 EU migrants annually between 2006 and 2016 (ONS 2016), with the total permanent resident Polish population being estimated to stand at 550,000, though media reports suggest the real number may be closer to a million (*The Guardian* 2016b), with in excess of 1.3 million national insurance numbers having been issued to East Europeans. Following the decision in 2004 to open up the British labor market to all new EU citizens unconditionally, labor migration to the UK reached unprecedented levels. If British negotiators were to obtain continued privileged access to the Single Market without conceding unlimited access to the British labor market for other EU citizens, exit from the EU might appeal much more to voters in other countries with sizable Euroskeptic parties or movements. A likely outcome may involve a tightly monitored annual quota for EU citizens wishing to work in the UK. While the current (2017) German government refuses to concede any ground on the principle of freedom of labor mobility, the rising backlash in Germany may in time lead to a softening of the German position on intra-EU migration. Momentum for the pushback against open borders is building in three countries with national elections in 2017, namely The Netherlands, the Czech Republic and France. Given the likely shift to the center-right in all three countries in the medium-term future, it is not inconceivable for the freedom of labor mobility to be restrained considerably or indeed abandoned altogether as its political ramifications prove to be not just controversial, but explosive. It is worth remembering that the original provision pertained in the European Community of the 1950s, in which socio-economic heterogeneity was minimal, with the notable exception of southern Italy. With wage gaps of the magnitude of 1:30 across the EU-27 (Höpner and Schäfer 2012), it is possible that this particular element of the Single Market will fall by the wayside or at least be heavily regulated. Future scholarship should find ample nourishment arising from the possible renegotiations surrounding the freedom of labor mobility. The enormous wage gaps in the EU-27 and the discontent that massive East to West migration has triggered may well turn out to be decisive.

Second, popular discontent over immigration levels may affect labor migration. While pro-migration advocates, including business lobbies and employers, attempt to justify the continued maintenance of liberal migration channels, from a historical point of view, the fact that the 2008 crisis has not yet had a decisive impact on reducing immigration levels is surprising. Recall how, in the early 1970s, every West European government one after another abandoned active labor migration recruitment in light of concerns over rising unemployment and rapid slowdowns in economic growth. Similar restrictions may at last be implemented again, especially given that the recovery from 2008 has been both uneven and very slow in the making. Such restrictions may or may not be the result of political pressure exercised by the Far Right. Pragmatic policy-makers may simply decide that after a decade and a half of extremely liberal (labor) immigration policies, it is time to put citizens first and avoid exacerbating the problems related to chronic and structural unemployment alluded to earlier. Consider that EU labor migration directives leave the fine-tuning and setting of annual quotas to member states. In light of economic concerns, national governments may settle for minimal annual quotas, thus de facto ending all momentum for future EU labor migration policy-making. Such development would placate a conservative electorate, but would require considerable political force to pushback against the status quo of the past two decades, during which employers and pro-migration lobbies have been very successful in shaping migration policy design. There are signs that in this respect also the United Kingdom may be the first out of the box. Just as it was the first to liberalize labor migration in 1999, so the sea change on immigration that was discernible in the aftermath of the Brexit referendum may prove contentious and serve as a harbinger of more restrictive policy amendments elsewhere in continental Europe. There is plenty of material here for enterprising scholars who can chart the articulation of political pressure both through traditional channels and new and unconventional forms of political activity. For example, the US presidential elections in 2016 highlighted the importance of social media and raised questions about the impact that more traditional media outlets and conventional party machines manage to exercise.

Third, past empirical work (Geddes 2003; Menz 2009; Roos 2013) has recorded a fairly docile stance on the part of the 2004 and 2007 newcomers from central and eastern Europe. There is no reason to presume that this stance will continue unchanged. Over time, new coalitions may emerge with Central European countries' members playing a lead role in favor of a more restrictive stance regarding immigration from outside of the EU. The resistance by member states from the region to the current German government's unilateral open-door policy for illegal immigrants may be the harbinger of changes to come. In the past, central European governments have been skeptical of liberal EU-level immigration policy because their own citizens had still been subject to migration controls (Menz 2009). However, in the future, the chief concern may be more related to immigration in general, given that central European governments are well aware of the manifold social, economic, cultural, political and religious problems that mass immigration has brought to countries such as France, Germany and the United Kingdom (Caldwell 2010). While decision-making in the Council of Ministers relies on qualified majority voting, a steady bloc of immigration skeptics, comprising Poland, Hungary, Slovakia, and possibly the Czech Republic, may well prove highly influential in impeding ambitious future policy-making on all matters related to immigration. Note also that countries from this region, whose governments are concerned with maintaining intra-EU labor mobility rights, may value the preservation of such a pan-European labor market much more than constructing new access channels for non-Europeans. Future scholarship could thus forensically explore the decision-making process inside the Council of Ministers, which promises to be more contentious in years to come.

Fourth and finally, the de facto suspension of the Dublin Convention in 2015 in the wake of record levels of illegal immigrants pushing their way into Europe, and the EU's muddled and slow response to the catastrophic situation in Greece, Cyprus, Malta and Italy, may in time kill off all political appetite for the further Europeanization of immigration policy. There are two reasons for this. First, the Merkel government tried to sell its unilateral decision to waive through 1.5 million immigrants in 2015 by claiming that it would address labor market shortages. Major German businesses joined this campaign. In the autumn of 2015, CEOs of both Daimler Benz and VW made lofty declarations of support for Merkel's open-door policy. Daimler Benz CEO Zetsche claimed that 'refugees [...] [would provide the] [...] basis for the next German economic miracle'. By the summer of 2016, it emerged that neither company had hired a single refugee. Germany's top-thirty stock market-listed companies had employed fifty-four of the 1.3 million immigrants. Fifty of those were hired by partially state-owned Deutsche Post (FAZ, July 4, 2016). German economic research institute IFW estimates that future annual expenditure for the unwanted newcomers will cost between twenty-five and fifty-five billion euro annually, depending on the volume of future asylum-seekers and the success rate of deportations (IFW 2016). Second, though asylum and labor migration are legally separate channels, in the eyes of the general public this distinction is often lost. Pakistanis, Albanians, Russians and Nigerians, three nationalities prominently represented among the asylum-seekers in Germany, are clearly largely not fleeing political persecution. Their low recognition rates as asylum-seekers reflect the large-scale abuse: 7.3 percent for Pakistan, 0.4 for Albania, 5.1 for Russia and 9.5 for Nigeria (Statista 2016). Between 2014 and 2015, the number of apprehended criminal foreign nationals in Germany rose from 617,392 to 911,864, or 38.49 percent of the total (BMI 2015: 44). Extrapolating from local German media coverage, 2016 has seen high levels of crime being reached, especially regarding rape and sexual abuse. An estimated 300,000 to 500,000 immigrants have absconded altogether from their hostels. The fact that the Islamist terrorist attacks in Paris, Brussels, Nice, Ansbach, Reutlingen and Berlin in 2016 were all carried out by immigrants who had entered Europe as refugees purporting to be Syrian is not lost on members of the general public.

Despite the German and even the Swedish governments slowly waking up to reality, much of the damage has been done. The immigration crisis is far from over. Cash-strapped Greek and Italian authorities are unwilling or unable to defend their national borders and refuse to turn around shipments organized by crime syndicates ferrying illegal immigrants to European shores (Manrique Gil et al. 2014). The fair-weather construct that is Schengen has collapsed under pressure and will probably have to be abandoned permanently. There are serious dark clouds on the horizon. Consider that, in 2012, the United Nations had to revise their assessment of total fertility rates (TFR) for much of sub-Saharan Africa upward. With the exception of South Africa, the entire region has TFR projections for 2015 to 2020 in excess of four. In some countries, such as Niger, a woman will have an average number of 7.5 children. Following a lull in the early 2000s, annual population growth for all of Africa is forecast to be 2.55 percent for 2015 to 2020 (UN 2015). This will theoretically lead to the continent's population reaching 3.95 billion inhabitants by 2100. African policy-makers will struggle to find space, jobs and food for even a fraction of those people. European policy-makers would be well advised to protect their borders sooner rather than later. In this political climate, it is hard to see how EU labor migration policy will evolve further, though future scholarship could examine the exact impact of the handling of the immigration crisis.

The field of justice and home affairs in general and labor migration in particular has been characterized by a recent growth in scholarly activity, coinciding with the rediscovery of labor migration in late 1999 and the emergence of a tangible EU-level regime of migration policies.

Over the course of the past two decades, scholarly contributions have focused on identifying the key drivers, namely identifying regular patterns, linking immigration policy to mainstream debates about European integration, and making sense of the rapidly changing rules of the game. The European Parliament is now a co-legislator following the implementation of the Lisbon Treaty. The Council of Ministers relinquished its sole right to provide policy proposals in 2004. Much of the groundwork in terms of EU legislative activity has been laid, but labor migration has proven highly politically contentious, which is why much of the operational detail remains within the regulatory confines of the member states. As we have seen, there are a number of avenues for future research, as the dramatic events of 2015/2016 appear likely to have permanent ramifications for migration governance. Brexit is likely to act as a stimulus for debate – if perhaps nothing else – regarding the intra-EU freedom of labor mobility. Meanwhile, the inability of the EU to respond swiftly and robustly to the illegal mass migration of the summer of 2015 has driven home the need for national governments to remain vigilant regarding border control. The lessons learned from the dramatic events of that summer and the fall-out of the unilateral decision by the German government to open its doors to millions of unvetted young men of military age may well be that leaving border control to other member states is simply too risky. The extremist policies of ultra-liberal countries such as Sweden and Germany create serious knock-on effects for countries at the outer fringes of the Schengen zone. The ultimate outcome may therefore be the abandonment of Schengen. Future scholars of EU (labor) migration policy are unlikely to be bored or to run out of material.

Bibliography

BMI – Bundesministerium des Inneren (2015). *Polizeiliche Kriminalstatistik 2015*. Berlin: BMI.

Bonjour, S. and Vink, M. (2013). When Europeanization Backfires: The Normalization of European Migration Politics. *Acta Politica*, 48(4), pp. 389–407.

Borjas, G. (2016). *We Wanted Workers: Unravelling the Immigration Narrative*. New York, London: W.W. Norton.

Caldwell, C. (2010). *Reflections on the Revolution in Europe: Immigration, Islam and the West*. London: Penguin.

Castles, S. and Kosack, G. (1973). *Immigrant Workers and Class Structures in Western Europe*. London: Oxford University Press.

Caviedes, A. (2010). *Prying Open Fortress Europe: The Turn to Sectoral Labor Immigration*. Lanham, MD: Lexington Books.

Caviedes, A. (2016). European Integration and the Governance of Migration. *Journal of Contemporary European Research*, 12(1), pp. 552–565.

Cerna, L. (2009). The Varieties of High-skilled Immigration Policies: Coalition and Policy Outputs in Advanced Industrial Countries. *Journal of European Public Policy*, 16(1), pp. 144–161.

Cerna, L. (2014). The EU Blue Card: Preferences, Policies, and Negotiations between Member States. *Migration Studies*, 2(1), pp. 73–96.

Cohen, R. (1987). *The New Helots: Migrants in the International Division of Labor*. Aldershot: Avebury.

Devitt, C. (2011). Varieties of Capitalism, Variation in Labor Immigration. *Journal of Ethnic and Migration Studies*, 37(4), pp. 579–596.

Eurobarometer (2015). *Public Opinion in the European Union*. Standard Eurobarometer, spring. Brussels: DG for Communication.

European Commission (2009). Council Directive 2009/50/EC of 25 May 2009 on the Conditions of Entry and Residence of Third-country Nationals for the Purposes of Highly Qualified Employment.

European Parliament (1999). Tampere European Council: 15 and 16 October 1999 Presidency Conclusions. Available at www.europarl.europa.eu/summits/tam_en.htm, internet (accessed December 17, 2016).

FAZ (2016). Dax-Konzerne stellen nur 54 Flüchtlinge ein. July 4.

Freeman, G. (1996). Modes of Immigration Politics in Liberal Democratic States. *International Migration Review*, 38(3), pp. 881–902.

Freeman, G. (2006). National Models, Policy Types, and the Politics of Immigration in Liberal Democracies. *West European Politics*, 29(2), pp. 227–247.
Geddes, A. (2000). *Immigration and European Integration: Towards Fortress Europe?* Manchester: Manchester University Press.
Geddes, A. (2003). *The Politics of Migration and Immigration in Europe*. London: Sage.
Geddes, A. and Guiraudon, V. (2004). Britain, France, and EU Anti-discrimination Policy: The Emergence of an EU Policy Paradigm. *West European Politics*, 27(2), pp. 334–353.
Givens, T. and Luedtke, A. (2004). The Politics of European Union Immigration Policy: Institutions, Saliency, and Harmonization. *Policy Studies Journal*, 32(1), pp. 145–165.
The Guardian (2016a). Britain and Europe: The Survey Results. March 20.
The Guardian (2016b). Britain's Poles: Hard Work, Yorkshire Accents, and Life Post-Brexit Vote. October 25.
Guiraudon, V. (2000). European Migration and Migration Policy: Vertical Policy as Venue-shopping. *Journal of Common Market Studies*, 10(2), pp. 251–271.
Hansen, R. and Gordon, J. (2014). Deficits, Democracy and Demographics: Europe's Three Crises. *West European Politics*, 37(6), pp. 1199–1222.
Hollifield, J. (1992). *Immigrants, Markets, and States: The Political Economy of Postwar Europe*. Cambridge, MA: Harvard University Press.
Hollifield, J. (2004). The Emerging Migration State. *International Migration Review*, 38(3), pp. 885–912.
Höpner, M. and Schäfer, A. (2012). Integration Among Unequals: How the Heterogeneity of European Varieties of Capitalism Shapes the Social and Democratic Potential of the EU. MPI Discussion Paper 12/5. Cologne: MPI.
House of Lords (2008). *The Economic Impact of Immigration. Volume I: Report*. London: Stationery Office.
IFW (2015). Simulation von Flüchtlingskosten bis 2022: Langfristig bis zu 55 Mrd Euro jährlich. Available at www.ifw-kiel.de/medien/medieninformationen/2015/simulation-von-fluchtlingskosten-bis-2022-langfristig-bis-zu-55-mrd-20ac-jahrlich (accessed December 17, 2016).
Joppke, C. (1998) Why Liberal States Accept Unwanted Immigration. *World Politics*, 50(2), pp. 266–293.
Kahanec, M., Zaiceva, A. and Zimmermann, K. (2010). Ethnic Minorities in the European Union: An Overview. IZA Discussion Paper No. 5397. Bonn: IZA.
Kaplan, J. (2015). *Humans Need Not Apply: A Guide to Wealth and Work in the Age of Artificial Intelligence*. New Haven, CT: Yale University Press.
Kaunert, C. (2010). *European Internal Security: Towards Supranational Governance in the Area of Freedom, Security and Justice?* Manchester: Manchester University Press.
Kaunert, C. and Léonard, S. (2012). The Development of the EU Asylum Policy: Venue Shopping in Perspective. *Journal of European Public Policy*, 19(9), pp. 1396–1413.
Koopmans, R. (2010). Trade-offs Between Equality and Difference: Immigrant Integration, Multiculturalism, and the Welfare State in Comparative Perspective. *Journal of Ethnic and Migration Studies*, 36(1), pp. 1–26.
Manrique Gil, M., Barna, J., Hakala, P., Rey, B. and Claros, E. (2014). Mediterranean Flows into Europe: Migration and the EU's Foreign Policy, Brussels: Directorate General for Foreign Relations. Available at www.europarl.europa.eu/RegData/etudes/briefing_note/join/2014/522330/EXPO-JOIN_SP(2014) 522330_EN.pdf (accessed October 5, 2016).
Menz, G. (2001). Beyond the *Anwerbestopp*? The German–Polish Bilateral Labor Treaty. *Journal of European Social Policy*, 11(3), pp. 253–269.
Menz, G. (2009). *The Political Economy of Managed Migration: Nonstate Actors, Europeanization and the Politics of Designing Migration Policies*. Oxford: Oxford University Press.
Menz, G. (2015a). Framing the Matter Differently: The Political Dynamics of European Union Labor Migration Policymaking. *Cambridge Review of International Affairs*, 28(4), pp. 554–570.
Menz, G. (2015b). The Promise of the Principal–Agent Approach for Studying EU Migration Policy: The Case of External Migration Control. *Comparative European Politics*, 13(3), pp. 307–324.
Menz, G. and Caviedes, A. (2010). Introduction; Pattern, Trends, and (Ir)Regularities in the Politics and Economics of Labor Migration in Europe. In Menz, G. and Caviedes, A. (eds), *Labor Migration in Europe*. Basingstoke: Palgrave, pp. 1–24.
Messina, A. (1990). Political Impediments to the Resumption of Labor Migration to Western Europe. *West European Politics*, 13(1), pp. 31–46.
Messina, A. (2007). *The Logics and Politics of Post-WWII Migration to Western Europe*. New York: Cambridge University Press.

Niemann, A. (2006). *Explaining Decisions in the European Union*. Cambridge: Cambridge University Press.

OECD (2016). Youth Unemployment Rate. Available at https://data.oecd.org/unemp/youth-unemployment-rate.htm (accessed December 20, 2016).

ONS (Office for National Statistics) (2016). Provisional Long-term International Migration Estimates. Available at www.ons.gov.uk/peoplepopulationandcommunity/populationandmigration/internationalmigration/datasets/migrationstatisticsquarterlyreportprovisionallongterminternationalmigrationltimestimates (accessed December 20, 2016).

Piore, M. (1979). *Birds of Passage: Migrant Labor and Industrial Societies*. Cambridge: Cambridge University Press.

Ripoll Servent, A. and Trauner, F. (2014). Do Supranational EU Institutions Make a Difference? EU Asylum Law Before and After 'Communitarization'. *Journal of European Public Policy*, 21(8), pp. 1142–1162.

Roos, C. (2013). *The EU and Immigration Policies: Cracks in the Frontiers of Fortress Europe?* Basingstoke: Palgrave.

Roos, C. (2015). EU Politics on Labor Migration: Inclusion versus Admission. *Cambridge Review of International Affairs*, 28(4), pp. 536–553.

Schwab, K. (2016). *The Fourth Industrial Revolution*. Geneva: World Economic Forum.

Standing, G. (2014). *A Precariat Charter: From Denizens to Citizens*. London: Bloomsbury Academic.

Statista (2016). Gesamtschutzquote der Asylbewerber aus den Hauptherkunftsländern in Deutschland im Jahr 2016. Available at http://de.statista.com/statistik/daten/studie/451967/umfrage/anerkennungsquote-der-asylbewerber-aus-den-hauptherkunftslaendern/ (accessed December 17, 2016).

Stetter, S. (2000). Regulating Migration: Authority Delegation in Justice and Home Affairs. *Journal of European Public Policy*, 1, pp. 80–103.

UN (2015). UN Department of Economic and Social Affairs, Population Division. *World Population Prospects, the 2015 Revision*. Available at https://esa.un.org/unpd/wpp/ (accessed December 17, 2016).

Watts, J. (2002). *Immigration Policy and the Challenge of Globalization: Union and Employers in Unlikely Alliance*. Ithaca, NY: Cornell University Press.

11
ORGANIZED CRIME
Balancing national sensitivities with global necessities

Daniela Irrera

Introduction

The fight against organized crime (OC) constitutes an important field of research and is exemplary of the EU's performance in JHA. In contrast with other threats, like terrorism, EU member states have made a case for EU action against OC on several occasions. Yet there has also been opposition, which has had a negative impact upon the harmonization of policing practices and the development of a common policy. As a result, the intersections and connections of organized crime groups with other actors, above all terrorists, have not been adequately considered.

This chapter offers an overview of the EU policies towards OC in the framework of JHA. It provides a set of theoretical reflections and investigates the key political developments. It is divided into three sections. In the first section the origins and evolution of OC policies are examined through a literature review, discussing what scholars see as the main achievements and failures regarding EU governance. The analysis of JHA in this specific policy field of organized crime offers a chance to reflect more broadly on the EU's abilities to tackle security issues related to terrorism and political violence, both outside and inside the borders of the EU. The second section describes the major theoretical debates, stressing the internal and external dimension of JHA. It proposes to understand OC as the centerpiece of a collection of related policies. Despite the fact that they have emerged in an ad hoc fashion, they have contributed to shaping the performance of the EU at a global level and its relations with other international actors. The third section underlines the relevance of political developments and investigates the remaining gaps (particularly for harmonizing the definition of OC and the main forms of cooperation). The main conclusion is that the field requires further scholarly attention, as well as the use of new and more comprehensive concepts.

The origins and evolution of OC

An analysis of JHA in this policy field offers a chance to discuss OC from a broader security perspective. It reflects the abilities of the EU to tackle this threat in connection with other security issues, including terrorism, irregular migration and political violence, both outside and inside the borders of the EU.

The European Council of Santa Maria de Feira (European Council 2000) provided JHA with a list of priorities, which included, next to migration and terrorism, the fight against specific forms of crime, drug trafficking and development along with consolidation of the rule of law in countries on the path to democracy. Since the beginning, it has been clear that the approach established during that Council meeting was meant to be comprehensive. The set of objectives was ambitious and included threats inside and outside the borders. More importantly, the approach required constant and frequent interactions and a coordination mechanism between the Council and the Commission. In order to guarantee the necessary coordination, JHA has developed into a complex framework in which distinctive instruments are used. Given its controversial nature (and practical implications), OC has offered policy-makers a rewarding field for experimentation and innovation. Academics have followed these developments with interest.

The operationalization of OC is not an easy task, since it has been difficult to reach a jointly agreed definition. This is part of a broader discussion dealing with OC as a serious threat, capable not only of endangering national security, but also of impacting regional and global systems. International relations literature has copiously contributed to this debate, including OC networks in the list of those subversive non-state actors that challenge the state and its institutions (Strange 1996). Such non-state actors are usually based within the territory of a state, but national borders do not pose any real constraint for their action. They are often well-organized and, even if they defend interests that are often illegal or subversive, they are autonomous and may exert influence on the global system (Irrera 2011). Therefore, fragmented political and economic contexts, with neither cohesion nor autonomy, represent the best ground for OC groups to intermingle and challenge state structures. The retreat of the state and the rise of these actors have clear detrimental effects on the state and, subsequently, on the overall international system. Their activities can cause a lot of harm, especially since these types of non-state actors generally need to function within national institutions; as a result, they challenge national legal systems and rules. That is why most state actors have tried to fight OC through their national legislation and/or international conventions. In particular, those states with a long-standing problem of criminal activity have developed counter-strategies: laws and regulations, police officer codes, and specialized agencies (Rosenau 1990; Jackson 1990; Grossman 1999; Williams 2001).

The internationalization of policing primarily reflects the efforts made by Western powers to export their own definitions and understanding of *crime* (Andreas and Nadelmann 2006). Any process that attempts to internationalize the definition of crime and attempts to establish how it could be best controlled generally reflects an effort to export domestic perceptions and definitions. These are, in turn, the reflection of specific relations among (national) political powers. This process takes place through the production of formal definitions, norms and documents, which are based on governments' different understandings of threats (Irrera 2016). Within this process, the EU – as a whole and through its member states – has developed its own model and nested it in the wider JHA framework.

Therefore, we need to understand how OC has affected the institutional development and dynamics of JHA over the past decades. Studies on the internal dimension of JHA have focused on the distribution of competences and resources among different actors and levels of governance. These studies produced some significant debates on the performance of EU institutions and the ability of member states to promote and sustain efficient cooperation (Fijnaut 1992; Calderoni 2010; Longo 2012). Debates on OC may also be relevant for the literature on EU external governance, especially in issues where the EU has been granted responsibilities and has the competence to act outside the borders of the EU. Other debates stress the effects of globalization on the emergence of a new security agenda, which has raised the need for more cooperation and turned JHA into a more important external policy than the CSDP (Attinà 2000).

Given the national sensitivities prevailing in the JHA area, the balance between a supranational and intergovernmental dimension has been difficult to achieve. At the start, external developments pushed the need to cooperate in OC. In the mid-1970s, member states had to face the challenges posed by ideological and radicalized terrorism, which led them to establish the first type of intergovernmental cooperation in the form of the TREVI network. In the 1980s, the collapse of the Soviet Union opened up a huge new black market, which was exploited for illegal activities. In the 1990s, the Balkan wars jeopardized regional stability and favored the penetration of the legal economy by OC all over Europe. These external challenges emphasized the links between OC and the implementation of the Single Market. The need to prevent organized groups from profiting from a border-free market for their criminal activities facilitated the introduction of measures in police and judicial cooperation, including the compensatory measures contemplated in the Schengen Agreement as well as the German proposal to create a central European Criminal Investigation Office (Fijnaut 1992).

Indeed, the creation and progressive strengthening of Europol and the adoption of a set of measures against money laundering and corruption were considered to be relevant steps in the fight against OC. Therefore, the establishment of a third JHA pillar in the Maastricht Treaty formalized cooperation in this area and incorporated its security logic, based on the potential negative externalities for the internal market, into the EU institutional structure.

The first Action Plan to Combat OC, in 1997 (Council of the European Union 1997), was perceived as a first move towards a more supranational dimension. The establishment of agencies like Europol and Eurojust, and the formal definition of OC as a priority of the Area of Freedom, Security and Justice (AFSJ) in the Treaty of Amsterdam, contributed to the deepening of cooperation among member states. As a result, national legislation dealing with the fight against organized crime became subject to a harmonization process (Calderoni 2010). This was a crucial phase for the enhancement of anti-OC policies at the EU level (Longo 2012; Balzacq and Carrera 2006). On the one hand, OC instruments became more sophisticated and were included as an integral part of the JHA five-year programs – Tampere (1999–2004), The Hague (2004–2009) and Stockholm (2009–2014). National definitions on specific types of OC, such as trafficking of drugs, financial crimes and trafficking of human beings, were progressively harmonized at the EU level. On the other hand, more and more actors entered the fight against OC. Besides member states' governments, this included national law enforcement agencies, European institutions and agencies as well as third countries.

However, the regulatory impulses of the EU were not the only factor to significantly shape national authorities in charge of investigations and prosecution. However, as Den Boer (2001) maintains, despite efforts to harmonize, decentralized criminal investigation tasks were maintained in nearly all member states.

In brief, OC became an early and independent policy that preceded the full development of the AFSJ. This development was event-driven and characterized by a struggle to balance member states' national sensitivities with supranational needs.

Theoretical debates

Scholars who have examined the development of OC as a sub-policy of the AFSJ stem from various subdisciplines – from international relations to European studies, including security studies. Such contributions have provided rich descriptions and explained how the EU's fight against OC originated within the JHA pillar, but produced additional effects on the EU's external dimension, especially in the framework of its Security Strategy and the Common Security and Defence Policy (CSDP) (Paoli and Fijnaut 2006; Mitsilegas 2007; Wolff and Mounier 2012;

Trauner and Carrapico 2012; Allum and Den Boer 2013; Longo 2013; Trauner and Ripoll Servent 2015). This overview intends to offer the most important insights and the most controversial puzzles exposed by this growing literature.

The first problem in operationalizing OC as a concept derives from the lack of a widely agreed definition, which may shape common policies and cooperation. Article 3 of the United Nations Convention Against Transnational Organized Crime – thus far the only universal legal tool – defines OC groups as (1) a collaboration of at least three people; (2) gathered for a prolonged or indefinite period; (3) suspected or convicted of committing serious criminal offenses, and (4) pursuing profit and/or power (United Nations 2000). Within the EU, establishing a common view has remained an intricate and imprecise exercise (Allum and Den Boer 2013; Carrapico 2013). Apart from the need to tackle OC as a serious threat – able to produce implications for national and regional security – discussions are still far from achieving consensus on key issues. On the one hand, OC is characterized by its nature, organizational structure, ability to make alliances with other subversive actors, and to make use of corruption; on the other, there are other relevant features, like the nature of the activities, the influence on the markets and the offenses committed (Den Boer 2001; Von Lampe 2009; Paoli and Fijnaut 2006). Basing a common definition on certain features may have practical consequences, since it may call for specific policies with very different implications for member states. The first consequence is, according to Carrapico (2013), the total disconnection between rhetoric and practice, which means that the field becomes fragmented and sub-policies develop autonomously. The second consequence is the failure to produce more harmonization, particularly in the field of criminal law. Effective cooperation against OC requires an extensive harmonization of criminal legislation, which would mean that member states; particularly those with more experience and more advanced legislations in the field such as Italy, Spain and the UK, would be pushed to make additional efforts.

The second general problem underlined by the literature is related to the ongoing debate about the distinction between an internal and an external dimension to EU security. The academic community has recently started to analyze this linkage explicitly and, by doing so, has left behind the artificial separation of these two dimensions (Monar 2001, 2004a; Mitsilegas 2007).

Works on the external dimension generally concentrated on certain specific issue areas, particularly migration and terrorism (Freyburg 2012; Argomaniz 2010). By contrast, in the case of organized crime, the literature was more focused on OC's role as a key driver for developing the internal dimension of EU security (Allum et al. 2010; Allum and Den Boer 2013; Paoli and Fijnaut 2006). Indeed, OC policies were analyzed as a tool for improving police and judicial cooperation among member states, rather than as a set of norms that could be exported outside of the EU's borders or that may potentially affect the EU's international role.

Some authors, however, already anticipated the need to analytically combine these two dimensions (Scherrer 2009; Longo 2013). Not only does the differentiation appear irrelevant but it is also counterproductive for EU security. Critical security scholars, for example, started to become more interested in the analysis of JHA cooperation, maintaining that security is a multifaceted and busy policy space in which numerous actors compete for power and influence and attempt to gain support for their threat perceptions (Bigo 1996). This is compatible with the theoretical developments in the field of security studies among IR scholars, who also started to develop more comprehensive definitions and policy-oriented approaches.

Similarly, JHA cooperation has also come to be viewed as a 'policy universe', made up of a wide range of issues and institutional arrangements. Asylum policy, terrorism and OC have an 'internal dimension', involving coordination and policy-making, which principally relates to the EU's borders, and an 'external dimension', which deals with the incorporation of JHA issues in the relations of the EU with countries outside its borders (Smith 2009).

Analyses of OC in connection with other security threats (e.g., terrorism, political violence, instability) imply the EU's capacity to act as a security provider, not only towards neighbors and third countries but also on a wider multilateral level, other than the need to consider the changes occurring to security on a global level as well as the necessity to coordinate tools and policies dealing with OC beyond the JHA – particularly those developed within the context of CSDP (Trauner and Carrapico 2012).

The inclusion of a new JHA pillar in the Maastricht Treaty did not bring with it any provisions for the cooperation of the EU with third countries. Therefore, JHA action in crucial areas, such as police cooperation, the fight against OC and immigration, was constrained and dependent on the efforts made by the Presidency to ensure better coordination. Multilateral cooperation with the USA and Canada increased in 1993 due to the implementation of anti-drugs policies, while contacts with Central and Eastern Europe became more important following the collapse of the Soviet Union. The Treaty of Amsterdam in 1999 attempted to provide the EU with a formal capacity to act internationally, facilitated by the creation of an Area of Freedom, Security and Justice, as well as more competences to improve cooperation with third states.

The role of OC policies profited from this general institutional change, but also contributed to shape the external dimension of JHA. Its understanding as a very serious security threat has also been confirmed in the Strategy for the External Dimension, issued in 2005 by the Commission, which placed OC as the EU's second-highest priority (European Commission 2005). In the document, OC is defined as one of the root causes of security instability (together with poverty, deprivation and corruption) with the ability to profit from vulnerabilities at the EU's external borders. Therefore, the perception of OC as a potential threat that may profit from insecurity outside the EU has been highly instrumental in justifying the need to develop and expand the external dimension of JHA (Wolff *et al.* 2010; Balzacq 2008).

However, others sustain that even the creation of a general strategy for this area did not bring further coherence to the field of OC, which continued to produce fragmented forms of governance tailored to specific geographical regions and activities (Carrapico 2013). As a result, OC has remained a separate policy that has evolved autonomously from other related fields, notably the EU anti-drugs external agenda (Trauner and Carrapico 2012; Longo 2013).

Policy debates

As seen above, OC was perceived since the beginning as a very sensitive issue, which made it difficult for member states and EU institutions to translate general threat perceptions into specific policy measures. In the first place, there were concerns linked to the necessity of identifying and formally prosecuting those activities defined as 'criminal'. This process opened up not only problems in the harmonization of legal procedures, but also raised issues in the relations among different actors and the problem of interoperability. On the one hand, it was not always straightforward how to define which authorities should be responsible for police and judicial cooperation and how this would be coordinated at the national and European level, particularly in regard to agencies like Europol. On the other hand, the functioning of mechanisms like the interoperability of agencies or the coordination of competences was often delimited by political dynamics, notably the need to find a balance between member states' behavior and the functional pressures for common action at the EU level. This is certainly a common problem in all JHA policy areas, but is particularly true for OC due to the lack of common definitions and understandings. Therefore, we need to consider both the legal and political implications of OC policies; although they are both inextricably connected, isolating the main features should make it easier to understand why – in the end – OC policies are so difficult to plan and implement.

Among these problems, criminal and judicial cooperation has been underlined as particularly challenging, especially when it comes to the real commitment of member states to harmonize their norms and practices. For instance, copious amounts of literature on Europol and Eurojust have focused on whether these two agencies, which were expected to promote and strengthen judicial and criminal cooperation, have managed to fulfill these tasks (Scherrer *et al.* 2010; Carrapico 2013). Improved cooperation has been achieved by pushing member states to harmonize their norms and to develop further collaboration within the agencies in an incremental manner. On the legislative level, several important decisions have underpinned this development. The adoption by the Council on July 22, 2003 of the framework decision (2003/577/JHA) on the execution of orders for freezing property or evidence in the framework of criminal proceedings provided more clarity in legal procedures, pushing the requesting judicial authority of another member state to execute the order immediately and with no further formality. The framework decision was also essential in the fight against terrorism, since it represented a further important application of the mutual recognition principle to the criminal justice domain. Indeed, it was an example of the extent to which mutual recognition can be taken, since it asked for the automatic execution of judicial decisions in another member state (Scherrer *et al.* 2010). Also in 2003, with the adoption of the protocol amending the Europol Convention (Council of the European Union 2003), the Commission contributed strongly to the enhancement of measures that had already been agreed upon at the EU level – such as those related to the fight against money laundering and terrorism. Most of these measures sought to extend Europol's advisory and research functions to training, equipment and crime prevention. Additional decisions attempted to strengthen the common use of liaison officers posted abroad in order to promote more solidarity between member states (2003/170/JHA) and to combat corruption in the private sector by providing a common definition of corrupt business practices (2003/568/JHA). This last measure was a rare example of real harmonization in the fight against crime.

Beyond formal achievements, both judicial and police cooperation have suffered a set of functional problems since the beginning. Europol and Eurojust failed to produce the expected interoperability (important in OC, but also in the fight against terrorism). The collaboration between the two agencies was characterized by growing competition (Monar 2004b; Calderoni 2008; Scherrer *et al.* 2010). Others sustain that the European organized crime policy also suffered a wider lack of knowledge, and as a result failed to produce outputs of sufficient quality. This is visible in the documents and reports produced by Europol, the Organized Crime Threat Assessments (OCTAs), which instead of being verifiable sources of information and following a shared methodology that could be distributed among national police forces, appear as mere lists of information and a collection of data (van Duyne and Vander Beken 2009).

In sum, there is a further puzzle that is destined to remain an area of research within the JHA agenda to be monitored and deepened by academics and practitioners. On the one hand, the success of such policies and the achievement of common goals depends on the efficiency of judicial, police and law enforcement measures, which are, in turn, an essential part of how states have traditionally managed their security. On the other hand, given the changes at the regional and global level, this success depends on the ability – and the willingness – to integrate and coordinate such measures at the European level. Finally, success also depends on the ability of the EU and its member states to understand OC as a complex security threat, which inevitably requires it to be closely associated with other policy areas, notably the CSDP.

Indeed, as is seen for the external dimension, one of the main challenges to the JHA agenda originates from the internal developments of security and the capacity of OC to intersect with other subversive actors, such as terrorists. It is true that the two actors are provided with different natures (entrepreneurial for criminals and political for terrorists). Indeed, the intensification of the transnational dimension of organized crime activities in the 1990s and the changing nature of terrorism have blurred the boundaries between the two. This requires an adjustment of practices and a better coordination of policies. The academic debate has only recently developed the concept of the 'crime–terror nexus', notably Tamara Makarenko (2004, 2009), who was the first to describe the environment in which such threats emerge and to use the term *nexus*. She sustained that the immediate post-Cold War environment provided actors with better access to technological advancements and to financial and global market structures. These factors have led to the renewal of existing operational and organizational similarities. She has depicted the phenomenon as distinct phases that can be placed along a *continuum*: the first step starts with the mutual adoption of tactics with the aim of achieving mutual benefits; this can lead to a deepening of alliances that merge criminal and terror groups and result in the transformation of one entity into the other. The objective is to understand the conditions and causes that explain this evolutionary *continuum* or its different phases (Makarenko 2004).

This nexus is apparent mostly at the operational level, since it is generally constituted by terrorist groups that engage in criminal activities in order to fund their activities. Although this may appear at first sight to be only a minor extension of the problems engendered by terrorism, the presence of this network engenders a larger unpredictability and creates new security threats. Some trends have already been observed and analyzed, such as short-term alliances between OC groups and terrorists along Europe's border regions. Alliances are basically functional, since criminal networks have the capacity and infrastructures to provide transactional assistance to terrorist groups who seek access to European markets in order to finance terrorist operations in their home countries. In addition, terrorist groups are becoming better at exploiting criminal markets and using criminal tactics to acquire funds to sustain terror operations. These types of linkages between OC and terrorism are relatively straightforward to identify but more difficult to tackle (Makarenko and Mesquita 2014).

The EU has started to show concern about these growing intersections, particularly regarding the lack of reliable and systematic empirical data on the nexus. In October 2012, the European Parliament asked a panel of experts to produce a report for a detailed study of the problem (European Parliament 2012). The report attempted to understand the phenomenon and to collect data about the potential impact upon EU security, but there was no real follow-up. A more recent phenomenon (at least in its visibility), which contributes to exacerbating these concerns, is represented by the linkages between OC and militant Islamist cells in Europe and its periphery looking for logistical support (Bakker 2011).

Despite the skepticism and controversies that surround these 'new' phenomena and the fact that it is often difficult to identify how existing tools may be used and adapted, these trends will definitively require further and deeper analysis and additional work on the JHA agenda.

Conclusions: a new research agenda on organized crime

Given this theoretical and policy overview, it should be easier to understand what has been achieved and what is still on the table for OC policies. It should also be clear why the development of such policies has been so complicated and continues to be somewhat vague, despite the improvements and compromises already made.

As anticipated in the introduction, this chapter has aimed to offer a broader perspective of EU perceptions of OC and a critical discussion of its main unsolved problems, stressing how this essential security threat has been at the core of ad hoc policies and contributed to the shaping of EU performance on a global level towards other relevant international actors.

The topic is broad and involves the interests of a wide variety of practitioners, apart from academics of various backgrounds. Therefore, it can only be concluded with a long-term look at the current research agenda, which considers the future development within OC and its practical implications. Four main points are still open and require further work.

First, the debate on the nature and definitions of OC is still ongoing. Normative and political definitions and meanings are still important for the functioning of JHA. They are relevant not only for continuing to strengthen the harmonization process among member states, but also for improving functional judicial and police cooperation, avoiding concurrence among agencies and possibly enlarging their competences.

Second, OC is strictly related to our perception of security. As stressed above, understanding OC as both an internal and external threat reflects a holistic approach to security, which needs to be translated into a new course of action. The internal and external dimensions of JHA should continue to parallel each other, producing norms and practices that are the outcome of a real understanding of problems. This means that the 'knowledge-based' character of OC policymaking should be enhanced.

Third, the internal dimension of JHA is far from being completed. OC has definitively been at the core of the development of various ad hoc policies. Significant improvements have been put in place, especially since 2003. However, judicial and police cooperation still suffer from two main challenges; first, the resistance of member states to develop a genuine trust in cooperation at EU level; and second, the scarce interoperability of agencies, which continue to function in conflict with each other rather than in collaboration. In addition, a process of harmonization that goes beyond the legal terms and involves real political will is still necessary. Fourth, this also includes the external dimension of JHA, since it affects the role of the EU in the world and how the EU applies its governance model to external relations. In this respect, there is a need to make the JHA mechanisms linked to OC more clear and functional outside the EU borders and to work on the growing intersections with other security threats, particularly terrorism. Despite the skepticism and uncertainty about labels and definitions – for example, the 'crime–terror nexus' – terrorists make use of criminal activities as a source of funding and this should affect the JHA agenda. It will inevitably be conducive to further overlap with the CSDP and will imply more coordination among law enforcement, intelligence, police and judicial operators – another sign that the internal and external dimensions of JHA cannot be separated.

Obviously, this is not a complete list. The JHA agenda is too large and controversial, and OC policies still harbor many critical problems. However, these four points assure a wide and comprehensive overview of the main challenges JHA may face in the short and long term if it wants to reach a real and functioning cooperation in OC policies. This requires combined efforts originating from different actors and means that academics and practitioners should continue to work together.

Bibliography

Action Plan to Combat Organised Crime (1997). OJEU, C 251, August 15.

Allum, F. and Den Boer, M. (2013). United we stand? Conceptual diversity in the EU strategy against organized crime. *Journal of European Integration*, 35(2), pp. 135–150.

Allum, F., Longo, F., Irrera, D. and Kostakos, P. (2010). *Defining and Defying Organised Crime: Discourse, Perceptions and Reality*. London: Routledge.

Andreas, P. and Nadelmann, E. (2006). *Policing the Globe. Criminalisation and Crime Control in International Relations*. Oxford: Oxford University Press.

Argomaniz, J. (2010). Before and after Lisbon: legal implementation as the 'Achilles Heel' in EU counter-terrorism? *European Security*, 19(2), pp. 297–316.

Attinà, F. (2000). The European Union and the global system: international and internal security. In L. Aggestam and A. Hyde-Price (eds), *Security and Identity in Europe. Exploring the New Agenda*. London: Macmillan, pp. 111–133.

Attinà, F. (2011). CSDP operations and the participation of the old and new member countries. In A. Tahir Naveed (ed.), *East and Central Europe: The Impact of EU Membership on Foreign Policy, Domestic Politics and Economy*. Karachi: Area Study Centre for Europe, University of Karachi, pp. 51–68.

Attinà, F. and Irrera, D. (eds) (2010). *Multilateral Security and ESDP Operations*. Farnham: Ashgate.

Bakker, E. (2011). Characteristics of Jihadi terrorists in Europe (2001–2009). In R. Coolsaet (ed.), *Jihadi Terrorism and the Radicalisation Challenge: European and American Experiences*. Farnham: Ashgate, pp. 131–144.

Balzacq, T. (2008). *The External Dimension of EU Justice and Home Affairs: Tools, Processes, Outcomes*. CASE Network Studies and Analyses No. 377.

Balzacq, T. and Carrera, S. (2006). *Security versus Freedom. A Challenge for Europe's Future*. Aldershot: Ashgate.

Bigo, D. (1996). *Polices en réseaux. L'expérience européenne*. Paris: Presses de Sciences Po.

Calderoni, F. (2008). A definition that could not work: the EU framework decision on the fight against organized crime. *European Journal of Crime, Criminal Law and Criminal Justice*, 16, pp. 265–282.

Calderoni, F. (2010). *Organized Crime Legislation in the European Union*. Heidelberg: Springer.

Carrapico, H. (2013). The external dimension of the EU's fight against organized crime: the search for coherence between rhetoric and practice. *Journal of Contemporary European Research*, 9(3), pp. 460–476.

Council of the European Union (1997). Action plan to combat organized crime (97/C 251/01). OJ C 251, 15.8.1997. Available at http://eur-lex.europa.eu/legal-content/EN/TXT/?uri=CELEX%3A51997 XG0815 (accessed March 31, 2017).

Council of the European Union (2003). Council Act 13650/03. Europol 53. Council Act drawing up, on the basis of Article 43(1) of the Convention on the Establishment of a European Police Office (Europol Convention), a Protocol amending that Convention. Available at www.statewatch.org/news/2007/jan/europol-third-protocol-2003.pdf (accessed March 31, 2017).

Den Boer, M. (2001). The fight against organised crime in Europe: a comparative perspective. *European Journal on Criminal Policy and Research*, 9, pp. 259–272.

Duchêne, F. (1973). The European Community and the uncertainties of interdependence. In M. Kohnstamm and W. Hager (eds), *A Nation Writ Large? 'Foreign-policy Problems before the European Community'*. London: Macmillan, pp. 1–21.

EU Parliament (2012). *Study on Europe's Crime–Terror Nexus: Links between Terrorist and Organised Crime Groups in the European Union*. PE 462.503.

EU Commission (2005). *A Strategy on the External Dimension of the Area of Freedom, Security and Justice*. COM(2005) 491 final.

EU Council (2000). *Conclusions of the Presidency*. Santa Maria de Feira.

Fijnaut, C. (1992). Policing Western Europe: Interpol, TREVI and Europol. *Police Studies*, 15(3), pp. 101–106.

Freyburg, T. (2012). The Janus face of EU migration governance: impairing democratic governance at home – Improving it abroad? *European Foreign Affairs Review*, 17(2), pp. 289–230.

Grossman, H.I. (1999). Rival kleptocrats: the mafia versus the state. In G. Fiorentini and S. Zamagni (eds), *The Economics of Corruption and Illegal Markets*. Cambridge: Cambridge University Press, pp. 143–155.

Irrera, D. (2011). The EU strategy in tackling organized crime in the framework of multilateralism. *Perspectives in European Politics and Society*, 12(4), pp. 407–419.

Irrera, D. (2016). The crime–terror–insurgency 'nexus'. Implications on multilateral cooperation. In S. Romaniuk and S. Webb (eds), *Insurgency and Counterinsurgency in Modern War*. New York: CRC Press, pp. 39–52.

Jackson, R.H. (1990). *Quasi-states: Sovereignty, International Relations and the Third World*. Cambridge: Cambridge University Press.

Lavenex, S. (2004). EU external governance in wider Europe. *Journal of European Public Policy*, 11(4), pp. 680–700.

Longo, F. (2012). Justice and home affairs as a new tool of European policy: The case of Mediterranean countries. In F. Bindi and I. Angelesca (eds), *The Foreign Policy of the European Union: Assessing Europe's Role in the World*. Washington, DC: Brookings Institution Press, pp. 85–96.

Longo, F. (2013). Justice and home affairs as a new dimension of the European security concept. *European Foreign Affairs Review*, 18(1), pp. 29–46.

Makarenko, T. (2004). The crime–terror continuum: tracing the interplay between transnational organized crime and terrorism. *Global Crime*, 6(1), pp. 129–145.

Makarenko, T. (2009). Terrorist use of organized crime: operational tool or exacerbating the threat? In F. Allum, F. Longo, D. Irrera and P. Kostakos (eds), *Defining and Defying Organized Crime: Discourse, Perceptions, and Reality*. London: Routledge.

Makarenko, T. and Mesquita, M. (2014). Categorizing the crime–terror nexus in the European Union. *Global Crime*, 15(3–4), pp. 259–274.

Mitsilegas, V. (2007). The external dimension of EU action in criminal matters. *European Foreign Affairs Review*, 12, pp. 457–497.

Monar, J. (2001). The dynamics of justice and home affairs: laboratories, driving factors and costs. *Journal of Common Market Studies*, 39(4), pp. 747–764.

Monar, J. (2004a). Justice and home affairs. *Journal of Common Market Studies*, 42 (Annual Review), pp. 117–133.

Monar, J. (2004b). The EU as an international actor in the domain of justice and home affairs. *European Foreign Affairs Review*, 9, pp. 395–415.

Paoli, L. and Fijnaut, C. (2006). Organised crime and its control policies in Europe. *European Journal of Crime, Criminal Law and Criminal Justice*, 14(3), pp. 307–327.

Rijpma, J. and Cremona, M. (2007). *The Extra-territorialisation of EU Migration Policies and the Rule of Law*. EUI Working Paper LAW 01/2007.

Rosenau, J.N. (1990). *Turbulence in World Politics. A Theory of Change and Continuity*. New York: Harvester Wheatsheaf.

Scherrer, A. (2009). *The International Fight against Organized Crime: The G8 against Transnational Organized Crime*. Farnham; Burlington, VT: Ashgate.

Scherrer, A., Megie, A. and Mitsilegas, V. (2010). La stratégie de l'Union européenne contre la criminalité organisée: entre lacunes etinquiétudes, Cultures et Conflits. *Sécurité et protection des données*, 74, pp. 91–110.

Smith, K.E. (2009). The justice and home affairs policy universe: some directions for further research. *Journal of European Integration*, 31(1), pp. 1–7.

Strange, S. (1996). *The Retreat of the State: The Diffusion of Power in the World Economy*. Cambridge: Cambridge University Press.

Trauner, F. and Carrapico, H. (2012). The external dimension of EU justice and home affairs after the Lisbon Treaty: analyzing the dynamics of expansion and diversification. *European Foreign Affairs Review*, 17 (Special Issue), pp. 1–18.

Trauner, F. and Ripoll Servent, A. (2015). *Policy Change in the Area of Freedom, Security and Justice: How EU Institutions Matter*. London: Routledge.

United Nations (2000). *United Nations Convention against Transnational Organized Crime*. Available at www.unodc.org/documents/treaties/UNTOC/Publications/TOC%20Convention/TOCebook-e.pdf (accessed March 31, 2017).

van Duyne, P.C. and Vander Beken, T. (2009). The incantations of the EU organized crime policy making. *Journal of Crime Law and Social Change*, 51, pp. 261–281.

Von Lampe, K. (2009). The study of organised crime: an assessment of the state of affairs. In K. Ingvaldsen and V. Lundgren Sorli (eds), *Organised Crime: Norms, Markets, Regulation and Research*. Oslo: Unipub, pp. 165–211.

Waltz, K. (1979). *Theory of International Politics*. Reading, MA: Addison Wesley.

Williams, P. (2001). 'Transnational crime and corruption', in: B. White, R. Little and M. Smith (eds), *Issues in World Politics*. New York: Palgrave.

Wolff, S. and Mounier, G. (2012). 'A kaleidoscopic view on the external dimension of justice and home affairs'. *European Foreign Affairs Review*, 2(1), pp. 143–162.

Wolff, S., Wichmann, N. and Mounier, G. (eds) (2010). *The External Dimension of Justice and Home Affairs: A Different Security Agenda for the European Union?* London: Routledge.

Zielonka, J. (1998). *Paradoxes of European Foreign Policy*. The Hague; London; and Boston, MA: Kluwer Law International.

12
CYBER CRIME AS A FRAGMENTED POLICY FIELD IN THE CONTEXT OF THE AREA OF FREEDOM, SECURITY AND JUSTICE

Helena Carrapico and Benjamin Farrand

Introduction

Cyber crime has recently become one of the most important internal security priorities for the European Union (EU), second only to the disruption of international organized crime networks and the prevention of terrorism (European Commission 2010). It is considered as an ever-growing threat to the lives of citizens, the political systems and economic infrastructures in the EU (European Commission 2015c): 'The threat is very much a real one. The number of cyber attacks in the world is on the rise and the cost of cybercrime is skyrocketing' (Malmström 2011: 1). The understanding of this phenomenon as having become exacerbated has been the result not only of the perceived risks associated with the increased technological dependency of Europe, and indeed the proliferation of new technologies such as smartphones, which create new vulnerabilities and opportunities for criminal activity, but also of a societal pressure to take swift action in this field. After all, as the saying goes, 'something must be done'. In recent years, the number of objects and processes that have incorporated advanced computerized elements has grown exponentially, to include not only laptops, tablets and smartphones, but also cars, fridges, toys, classrooms and musical instruments. In 2012 there were 8.7 billion devices connected to the Internet, a figure that had grown by 2014 to 10 billion (Europol 2014a), and is projected to increase to 50 billion by 2020 (Europol 2014b). The 'digital revolution' has led to dramatic changes in the way we live our personal lives, interact with others, conduct business and learn in school. Although predominantly portrayed in a very positive light through having brought significant economic development and improved quality of life, these technologies are also understood as vulnerable, insecure and easily taken advantage of by criminals (European Commission 2015c). The idea that technology, and more specifically cyberspace-related activities, are susceptible to attacks has also become widespread among the European population, which has expressed concern over the frequency and severity of cyber crime risks and the existence of insufficient measures. According to the 2015 security Eurobarometer, 63 percent of the population believes that cyber crime will continue to increase, with 20 percent of the population believing that it is the most important security threat the EU currently faces (European Commission 2015b). In addition, only 28 percent of the global population feels that law enforcement has the adequate tools to respond to this problem (PWC Global 2016). Such societal pressure has contributed considerably to the development of a range of 'anti-cyber crime' measures as part of the EU's cyber security strategy. Although the field of cyber crime is a fairly recent policy development,[1] the EU has already invested heavily in preventive programs, enhancing law enforcement capabilities, fostering awareness and developing institutional coordination mechanisms.

Despite an increasing interest in the field among political actors and the general public, cyber crime attracts limited attention from international relations and European studies scholars. This chapter aims to contribute towards the expansion of this narrow literature by: (1) reviewing the current academic approaches to cyber crime beyond international relations and European integration, and understanding why the conceptualization of this phenomenon remains problematic; (2) exploring the emergence and evolution of cyber crime in the EU from an economic issue to a security threat; and (3) analyzing the challenges contributing to cyber crime remaining a fragmented policy area. The chapter concludes with a reflection on how the EU's cyber crime measures relate and contribute to the wider context of the Area of Freedom, Security and Justice (AFSJ).

Conceptualizing cyber crime

As mentioned in the introduction, cyber crime is understood to be one of the most urgent security problems that governments, industry and citizens currently have to face (Yar 2013). Industry evaluates the total annual bill for cyber crime as being situated between $375 billion and $575 billion per year (McAfee 2014), with 594 million annual victims (Symantec 2016). In the EU, the losses are also estimated in the billions of euro per year, with a million victims a day, as a result of the 150,000 viruses currently in circulation in addition to other forms of malicious attacks (European Commission 2015a). Unlike other areas of criminality, which are considered to be high profit but also high risk (such as drug trafficking or human smuggling), cyber crime is seen as allowing for very high gains with a minimum of risk. This low-risk character has enabled the field to grow at a fast rate and move in the direction of more professional and structured criminal activity (Europol 2014b). In fact, the idea of cyber crime as being committed by young hackers looking for a challenge has long been replaced by the insight that it is based on a profit-driven business model, which continually adapts to the existing demand, as well as to technological change more effectively than law enforcement, which is seen as largely reactive rather than pro-active. According to Europol (2015), cyber criminals are becoming more aggressive in their approaches, which include the continued recourse to malware[2] (and the more recent and pernicious ransomware[3]), the growing use of off-the-shelf tools (also known as crime-as-a-service),[4] and the increased focus on more challenging but also more profitable targets, such as companies (rather than individual citizens).

Although the analysis of these trends constitutes an important element of the EU's counter-cyber crime governance, it is also relevant to point out that any statistics evaluating the dimension of the problem need to be treated with considerable caution. This is particularly the case due to significant variation in figures recorded by national institutions, rendering cross-country comparisons quite difficult. There are a number of reasons for this discrepancy, namely (1) a lack of consistent methodology across studies and surveys (Wall 2007); (2) the under-reporting of cyber attacks on the side of companies to avoid loss of customer confidence or legal liability (Yar 2013); and (3) the under-reporting of attacks by citizens due to a minimization of their importance (how many of us really report every piece of spam that appears in our inboxes?) combined with a lack of knowledge hindering the identification of such attacks (Barrinha and Carrapico 2016).

Although cyber crime is clearly included among the policy areas under the umbrella of the Area of Freedom, Security and Justice, it has rarely featured as an explicit object of study for international relations and, more specifically, for European studies. With the exception of a few authors such as Christou (2015), Kshetri (2010), Giacomello (2010) and Mendez (2005), it has mainly remained a research interest of neighboring disciplines such as law (Clough 2015; Fahey 2014; Summers *et al.* 2014) and criminology (Smith *et al.* 2011; Savona 2010; Wall 2007). These works, which have been central to the development of our reflection on cyber crime and the awareness of its relevance, have focused on definitional debates, the causes behind criminal behavior in cyberspace, the organized character of those committing these forms of offenses, the efficiency of legal instruments and the regulation of cyber crime. As a result of how this topic has been addressed in the academic literature, issues of cooperation, sovereignty, the role of international and supranational organizations, actors' interests, and policy coherence in the governance of cyber crime have received limited attention. This chapter does not propose to touch upon all these topics, but rather to draw the reader's attention to selected issues.

Problematic definitions

A specific area where the absence of international relations approaches is particularly apparent is the definitional debate on cyber crime and its consequences for the governance of this policy field. The use of the prefix 'cyber' refers to a set of activities related to the use of computers and electronic networks (Fafinski *et al.* 2010). As we will see in greater detail in the second section of this chapter, the EU has historically used a number of different terms to refer to cyber crime, ranging from high-tech crime to computer crime, although none of the early documents containing these terms fully explained what this phenomenon was (European Commission and Bangemann Group 1994). In fact, the first EU document that included a deeper reflection on the concept of cyber crime and which proposed a fully fledged definition emerged only in 2007, following the 2001 Council of Europe Convention on Cyber Crime: 'cybercrime is understood as criminal acts committed using electronic communications networks and information systems or against networks and systems' (European Commission 2007: 2). As may be seen from the wording of the definition, the dual use of technology implies that computers and information systems can constitute both a means of attack and a target. In practice, the focus on technology duality resulted in the development of a broad definition, which covers three types of criminal activities: traditional forms of crime committed through electronic means (such as the exchange of child abuse images), the publication of illegal content (copyright-related offenses) and crimes against electronic networks (including, for instance, the use of viruses or distributed denial of service attacks[5]). On the basis of the EU's policy definition, cyber crime seems to include a very large and disparate number of phenomena ranging from online data and identity theft to cyber terrorism and cyber espionage.

The problem with having such a wide definition is that, although cyber crime has gradually become more relevant in EU internal security policy-making, its conceptualization has also remained problematic because of its vague and controversial character, rendering cyber crime a clear example of an essentially contested concept (Gallie 1956). Academics and policy-makers have not only failed to agree on a more narrow meaning of cyber crime, but they have also been unable to adequately transpose it into the legal order: 'there are no universally accepted definitions of computer crime [and] high technology crime. Each of these terms have different meanings to criminal justice professionals around the world' (Goodman 2011). In fact, the current concept of cyber crime goes so far as to include elements for which, for the moment, we have no legal basis, as is the case of cyber rape[6] (Fafinski *et al.* 2010). The concept of cyber crime reveals a degree of policy entrepreneurship whereby those responsible for policy-making have an interest in pushing for the creation of this category of crime, and indeed its constituent activities and elements.

The evolution of cyber crime as a EU policy field

Although its rapidly expanding capacity for disruption is regarded as having achieved previously unthinkable levels, cyber crime itself is not presented as a new phenomenon (Newman 2009). In fact, among the different EU cyber security policy elements, which also include Critical Information Infrastructure protection (CIIP)[7] and Cyber defense,[8] cyber crime features as the oldest element. Whereas CIIP only emerged as a priority with the 2004 and 2005 terrorist attacks on the Madrid and London transport systems, and cyber defense only started to become a reality with the 2007 Estonia attacks, cyber crime, or computer crime as it was then called, was already a general concern back in the late 1980s (Porcedda 2011).

The first national attempts to regulate illegal activities in cyberspace may be found in the United States' Comprehensive Crime Control Act of 1984, which would later on lead to the enactment of separate legislation such as the Computer Fraud and Abuse Act of 1986 (Computer Crime and Intellectual Property Section Criminal Division 2007). This security concern was also visible at the international level, with the Council of Europe's proposal to create the category of computer crime in the early 1980s, as well as the Organization for Economic Cooperation and Development (OECD) and the Group of Eight (G8)'s initiatives in the area of harmonization of European computer crime legislation in the mid-1980s (Deflem and Shutt 2006).

The European Economic Community, on the other hand, was not so quick to follow this trend, given its limited mandate in the area of security. This security agenda absence, however, should not be interpreted as a lack of interest in this topic. In fact, the protection of information and communication technologies featured clearly in documents such as the 1985 White Paper on Completing the Internal Market, the 1993 White Paper on Growth, Competitiveness and Employment, and the 1994 Bangemann Report, based on the idea that this sector was an essential element in the development of the Single Market (European Commission 1985, 1993; European Commission and Bangemann Group 1994). This link points to the idea that although cyber crime was not framed as a security concern at the time, it certainly constituted an economic one, akin to espionage and the stealing of commercial or trade secrets.

The transition from an economic to a security rationale took place at the end of the 1990s as a result of two distinct but interrelated processes: (1) the perception of cyber crime as an increasing problem; and (2) the creation of the third pillar and the emergence of EU security-related policies.

In 1996, the European Telecommunication and Culture Ministers of the member states pointed out that illegal content and activities on the Internet, such as the facilitation of anonymous sales of illegal drugs to end-users, were having an increasing detrimental impact on the efficient functioning of the Internal Market and should be considered an urgent priority (European Council 1996).[9] Such concerns led the European Commission to call for more systematic studies regarding the impact of cyber crime upon the economic activities of the European Union. One of the earlier studies, entitled COMCRIME, quickly revealed, however, that this impact went far beyond the economic one:

> computer crime has developed into a major threat for today's information society. The spreading of computer technology into almost all areas of life as well as the

interconnection of computers by international computer networks has made computer crime more diverse, more dangerous, and internationally present.

(Sieber 1998: 3)

The shift of cyber crime from an economic to a security concern was reflected not only in a number of operational documents, such as the Action Plan to Combat Organised Crime (Council of the European Union 1997) and the Safer Internet Action Plan (European Parliament and Council of the European Union 1999), but also in the proliferation of political documents such as Council Conclusions (European Council 1998, 1999). Since the mainstreaming of cyber crime as a security threat within EU discourse and policy-making, the evolution of this field has been pushed by two main elements: (1) reactive policy-making in relation to external events; and (2) the internal dynamics of the AFSJ and the influence of other more developed internal security policies.

Where the first is concerned, and as mentioned above, the perception that cyber crime is increasing and becoming more dangerous to society has driven policy-makers to engage with this area:

The threat is very much a real one. The number of cyber attacks in the world is on the rise and the cost of cybercrime is skyrocketing. You can seldom open a paper these days without reading about a new major cyber attack.

(Malmström 2011: 1)

This general perception was not only based on the multiplication of attacks, but also on the fact that the increasingly networked nature of critical institutions meant that they were now susceptible to attacks, including national security facilities, governmental websites holding citizens' data and the websites of European institutions (Schjolberg 2014).

The development of the field also benefitted from the political momentum behind the combatting of other security threats such as terrorism and the sexual abuse/exploitation of children. As a response to the 9/11 attacks, the EU proposed the Framework Decision on Attacks Against Information Systems (European Commission 2002), which focused on the effects of large-scale cyber attacks on member states' infrastructures and the coordination of their protection. The perception that there was a boom in the sexual exploitation of children and that the Internet played an important role in that increase by providing a means of ostensibly anonymous dissemination also enabled the EU to push cyber crime policy further: as the European Parliament stated prior to the revision and updating of key legislation in this field, 'the link between widespread Internet coverage and the dramatic growth of child sexual abuse is unquestionable' (2015: 39). The result was the Framework Decision on Combatting the Sexual Exploitation of Children and Child Pornography (Council of the European Union 2004).

Regarding the second element, the expansion of the AFSJ and the influence of more developed internal security policies also played an important role in the development of EU cyber crime policy. In the early 2000s, the EU prioritized combatting cyber crime through the development of a coordinated approach based on the harmonization of national definitions, the approximation of member states' legislations, the setting of minimum policy standards and the development of joint instruments (Mendez 2005).

Such an approach, however, was not an original, tailor-made strategy for this specific phenomenon. In fact, the idea underlying this approach was very much the same used for most justice and home affairs policies. It was based on the understanding that cyber crime was a growing threat of a transnational nature, in the face of which member states' border controls and legislations were either irrelevant or poorly equipped. In order to prevent further damage to the Single Market and to the third pillar, the Commission and the Council successfully advocated that an adequate response implied a EU-level cooperative approach (European Council 1999).

In practice, we can observe this policy field being constructed through, first, its inclusion in legal and policy texts of more established policies, allowing it then to develop into a self-standing policy with its own dedicated instruments. This is clear, for instance, in the case of the inclusion of cyber crime elements in the organized crime policy (Council of the European Union 1997). If initially most cyber crime instruments did not focus on this phenomenon exclusively, as in the case of the 2001 Framework Decision on Combatting Fraud and Counterfeiting, and the 2002 ePrivacy Directive,[10] from the mid-2000s, the EU started to produce specific cyber crime instruments in an attempt to create greater policy coherence. Among these instruments it is important to highlight the Communication towards a General Policy on the Fight against Cyber Crime (European Commission 2007) and the creation of EC3, the EU Cyber Crime Centre.

Cyber crime polic(y/ies) challenges and their impact upon the area of freedom, security and justice

Throughout the years, the EU has portrayed its growing cyber crime policy as being necessary, coherent and comprehensive (European Commission and High Representative of the European Union for Foreign Affairs and Security Policy 2013). In this final section, however, we argue that it has been developed as a reactive, self-regulatory and scattered set of disparate policies, which constitutes an important challenge to its development.

The second section of this chapter mentioned that cyber crime policy had partly evolved as a response to perceived external problems. Although a reactive approach is not unusual among AFSJ policies – organized crime and terrorism would be clear examples, as mentioned by Monar (2007) – it can still be considered problematic. Having a reactive approach has meant that law enforcement and policy-makers have remained one step behind cyber criminals: 'criminals are ahead of us when it comes to imagination and cooperation' (Malmström 2013: 1). As Europol argues, reactive law enforcement has always been the norm, although this has often been seen as incompatible with the EU's focus on crime prevention, in particular in an area such as cyber crime, where technology evolves quickly and new malware is developed daily (2011). Reactive policy-making experiences similar problems to reactive law enforcement in the sense that it is also emergency driven, thus setting priorities in response to perceived problems that may be unrelated or even blown out of proportion.

Such an approach has led to cyber crime policies being developed in an ad hoc or piecemeal fashion, resulting in a disjointed policy universe rather than in a well-thought-out, long-term strategy (Van de Heyning 2016; European Commission 2006). The disjointed character of the field may be observed at different levels, despite the recurrent rhetorical emphasis on the need to develop a coherent policy (Fahey 2014; European Commission 2007). The lack of consistency may be analyzed in terms of horizontal coherence (inter-actor relations at different national and supranational levels), as well as vertical coherence (between the national and supranational level).

Where the first is concerned, there is evidence of cyber crime being a fragmented policy field in terms of (1) coordination among member states; (2) cooperation between the state sector and private actors; and (3) differing EU institutional approaches to cyber crime. Regarding member state coordination (1), not all EU countries have the same operational capabilities for the collection and analysis of cyber crime data, or the institutional framework necessary for information exchange (European Commission and High Representative of the European Union for Foreign Affairs and Security Policy 2013). As a specific example, the EU Cyber Security Strategy required all member states to implement national cyber crime units to enable cooperation. By 2015, however, the platform comprising the heads of the cyber crime units of member states (Joint Cyber Crime Action Task Force – J-CAT) was still limited to Austria, France, Germany, Italy, Spain, The Netherlands and the United Kingdom (Reitano et al. 2015).

Regarding the fragmentation between the state and the private sector (2), it has frequently been underlined how the success of cyber crime policy is dependent on effective cooperation between the two (European Commission and High Representative of the European Union for Foreign Affairs and Security Policy 2013). Given that cyberspace has largely become the domain of private companies, namely due to the privatization of telecommunications operations in the EU and most critical information infrastructures being owned by the private sector, the EU considers that the latter needs to share similar security priorities and risk awareness (European Commission 2016). This view is very much related to the understanding that cyber crime policy needs to be comprehensive, in the sense that all members of society need to play an active role (including the state, the private sector, NGOs and individual citizens) (Avramopoulos 2015).

There are, however, considerable differences between the protective logic of the EU and the commercial rationale of companies, which consider, for instance, that the reporting of cyber attacks could put them at a disadvantage in relation to their competitors (interview with official of the European Parliament, 2016; Christou 2015). Companies are under a legal obligation to report cyber attacks (European Parliament and the Council of the European Union 2016). However, as may be seen from attacks, such as the one on Yahoo! (which saw the personal data of 500 million of its accounts stolen) or on Ashley Madison (an online dating site that was unable to protect the data of 11 million customers), companies often try to hide the fact that they have been targeted in order to prevent loss of customer confidence, loss of profits and negative brand projection.

Still in regard to the lack of horizontal coherence, we also find differing EU institutional approaches to cyber crime (3). For example, whereas the Parliament has asked for more measures to be taken in this area, and for an increase in the transfer of powers to the EU level, the Council has been reluctant to do so, underlining that the EU should just maintain a coordination role in this area (interview with official of the Computer Emmergency Response Team EU, 2016). Another example related to the existence of different approaches at the EU level concerns the sidestepping of EU bodies, in particular the European Cyber Crime Centre (EC3), in the recent Network and Information Systems Directive. Whereas the Commission and the Parliament supported a mandatory exchange of information between national competent authorities and EC3, the Council voted to make that exchange voluntary, or alternatively in the form of a summary, as a way to protect member state sovereignty. The result of this decision is seen by the Parliament as diminishing the knowledge base, and subsequently, the capacity for insight which EU bodies possess regarding cyber crime, thus leading to the potential for fragmentation in terms of decision-making (Van der Meulen et al. 2015).

Finally, where vertical coherence is concerned, the main issue is related to the existence of differences among national cyber crime legislation, which have been indicated as causing difficulty in conducting cross-border European investigations and prosecutions. Although this may appear to be a national issue alone, it actually relates to the EU level, insofar as it is the result of the incomplete transposition of EU legislation into domestic law (Europol and Eurojust 2016). This has led to differences not only in the criminalization of cyber crime, but also in the investigation techniques and capacities for legal cooperation, resulting in the lack of a commonly agreed mechanism for cyber crime data collection, failing to establish principles of jurisdiction in cyberspace, limiting the ability to conduct cross-border investigations, failing to ensure mutual legal assistance, and hindering initiatives to improve capacity building and the level of expert knowledge in member states (Council of the European Union 2016). A specific example of problematic transposition may be found in the 2005 Framework Decision on Attacks against Information Systems which, according to the Commission, has been implemented in many different ways in different member states (or in some instances has failed to be implemented), leading to wide gaps between national legal concepts and approaches.

Conclusion

This chapter has aimed to provide a reflection on the evolution of the EU's cyber crime policy by exploring how the concept has been constructed and used throughout the years, how the concern with this phenomenon shifted from an economic issue to a security one, and how particular challenges continue to significantly hinder the coherent development of this policy. In particular, this chapter has underlined that, despite not being a new policy area, cyber crime remains deeply fragmented and better described as a policy universe, rather than as a coherent JHA policy. Although the final section has pointed out what the consequences for this specific field are, we would like to conclude the chapter by widening this reflection to the remainder of the AFSJ, by highlighting possible avenues for research. In other words, are there any consequences of cyber crime policy fragmentation for the development of the AFSJ?

As mentioned previously in the second and third sections, the evolution of cyber crime policy has been very much shaped by law enforcement areas with a higher priority profile. Nevertheless, this situation may change in the near future. Given that cyber crime is now the EU's third internal security priority and the production of measures has considerably accelerated over the past few years, we may soon see it become a policy exporter for emerging policy areas. We can identify at least two problems with this potential development in terms of its consequences for the AFSJ, which we hope will attract further academic attention in the future.

The first problem relates to the definition discussion presented in the first section, which explored the link between the broad concept of cyber crime and the emergence of legal uncertainty. As mentioned, the existing ambiguity at the heart of the concept of cyber crime, whose use has varied between its narrow understanding (offenses *against* computer and information networks) and its larger one (committing 'traditionally offline' offenses *using* computers and information networks), has significantly hindered the development of a coherent EU cyber crime policy, its translation into an operational legal framework and its implementation resulting in successful prosecutions. This ambiguity and lack of coherence can only be detrimental to the AFSJ, and in particular to the growing field of EU criminal law and policies, which rely on legal certainty to operate and further expand.

The second problem relates to that of coordination and information exchange between state institutions and private companies. As stated previously, the private sector has increasingly become responsible for network and information infrastructures all over Europe. Such development has not led, however, to increased information exchange, despite it being crucial to the process of policy-making. Although this problem is more prominent in cyber security than in other fields of the AFSJ, there is a clear tendency to move in the direction of integrating private companies into security governance (Carrapico and Farrand 2016). As such, there is a considerable risk that if this issue is not addressed properly it could spread to other policy areas, thus undermining their development.

Notes

1 The European Security Strategy of 2003, for instance, made no reference to this area (Council of the European Union 2003).
2 Malware constitutes a form of malicious software, which can be used to disrupt the normal functioning of information networks or individual computers. There are different forms of malware, namely viruses, worms, Trojan horses and spyware, which affect devices in different ways, including giving access to data such as credit card information that may have been stored locally.
3 Ransomware consists in malicious software developed with the intention of blocking the user's access to his or her computer or information system. The software will grant access once the user has agreed to pay a given sum of money.
4 Crime-as-a-service is a business model based on the supply of ready-made malicious software, which enables a part of the population, that would otherwise lack the technical skills, to take part in cyber criminal activities. The demand for ready-made products, such as viruses, has led an important part of the sector to shift from carrying out cyber attacks to producing the tools enabling the attacks.
5 A distributed denial of service is an attack on an online server with the aim to render it inaccessible to regular users by bombarding it with access requests. The server usually overloads and shuts down.
6 An example of a highly mediatized and sensationalized form of misconduct, in which a malicious script or text may be used to simulate the 'rape' of a character avatar in a online game such as Second Life. The use of this term, and whether it should be treated as a serious and reprehensible offense akin to the criminal act of rape, is disputed.
7 Critical information infrastructures constitute physical and digital services and facilities that are essential to the efficient functioning of a society. If taken away or compromised, they would seriously affect the quality of life and even the survival of a given population. Such infrastructures include not only the hospital and communications systems, but also banking (Dunn and Kristensen 2014).
8 Cyber defense covers the protection of the communication and information systems at the basis of national defense apparatus (European Commission and High Representative of the European Union for Foreign Affairs and Security Policy 2013).
9 The internal market development implied the abolishing of national physical borders. Given that illegal online products and activities were considered as transnational, their potential free circulation around a borderless Europe was considered a threat to the Single Market project.
10 The Framework Decision on Combatting Fraud and Counterfeiting assists member states' fight against electronic payment fraud and counterfeiting, and the ePrivacy Directive regulates how electronic communication providers must secure clients' data.

Bibliography

Avramopoulos, D. (2015). Commissioner Avramopoulos Presents European Agenda on Security at European Parliament. SPEECH/15/4885.
Barrinha, A. and Carrapico, H. (2016). The Internal, the External and the Virtual: The EU and the Security of Cyberspace. In *The EU, Strategy and Security Policy: Regional and Strategic Challenges*, edited by L. Chappell, J. Mawdsley and P. Petrov. Abingdon: Routledge, pp. 104–118.
Carrapico, H. and Farrand, B. (2016). 'Dialogue, Partnership and Empowerment for Network and Information Security': The Changing Role of the Private Sector from Objects of Regulation to Regulation Shapers. *Crime, Law and Social Change*, 67(3), pp. 245–263.
Christou, G. (2015). *Cybersecurity in the European Union: Resilience and Adaptability in Governance Policy* (1st edn). Basingstoke; New York: AIAA.
Clough, J. (2015). *Principles of Cybercrime* (2nd edn). Cambridge: Cambridge University Press.
Computer Crime and Intellectual Property Section Criminal Division (2007). *Prosecuting Computer Crimes*. Office of Legal Education Executive Office for United States Attorneys.
Council of the European Union (1997). Action Plan to Combat Organised Crime, No. C251/1–15.8.97. Official Journal of the European Communities, Brussels.
Council of the European Union (2003). *European Security Strategy – A Secure Europe in a Better World*. Brussels.
Council of the European Union (2004). Council Framework Decision on Combatting the Sexual Exploitation of Children and Child Pornography. 2004/68/JHA. Brussels.

Council of the European Union (2016). Presidency Conference 'Crossing Borders: Jurisdiction in Cyberspace'. 7323/16. Brussels.
Deflem, M. and Shutt, E. (2006). Law Enforcement and Computer Security Threats and Measures. In *Handbook of Information Security, Information Warfare, Social, Legal, and International Issues, and Security Foundations*, edited by H. Bidgodi, Vol. 2. New York: John Wiley & Sons, pp. 200–209.
Dunn, M.A. and Kristensen, K.S. (2014). *Securing 'the Homeland': Critical Infrastructure, Risk and (In)security*. Abingdon: Routledge.
European Commission (1985). *White Paper: Completing the Internal Market*. COM(85) 310 final. Brussels: European Commission.
European Commission (1993). *Growth, Competitiveness, Employment: The Challenges and Ways Forward into the 21st Century – White Paper*. COM(93)700 final.
European Commission (2002). *Proposal for a Council Framework Decision on Attacks against Information Systems*. COM(2002)173 final.
European Commission (2005). *Report Based on Article 12 of the Framework Decision of 24 February 2005 on Attacks against Information Systems*. COM(2008)448.
European Commission (2006). *Commission Staff Working Document – Accompanying Document to the Communication from the Commission to the European Parliament, the Council and the Committee of the Regions – Towards a General Policy on the Fight against Cyber Crime – Summary of the Impact Assessment*. COM(2006)267 final.
European Commission (2007). *Towards a General Policy on the Fights against Cyber Crime*. COM(2007)267.
European Commission (2010). *Communication from the Commission to the European Parliament and the Council – The EU Internal Security Strategy in Action: Five Steps towards a More Secure Europe*. COM(2010)673 final. Brussels.
European Commission (2015a). Cyber Security – Special Eurobarometer 423.
European Commission (2015b). Special Eurobarometer 432 – European's Attitudes Towards Security. Wave EB83.2.
European Commission (2015c). *Communication from the Commission to the European Parliament, the Council, the European Economic and Social Committee and the Committee of the Regions – The European Agenda on Security*. COM(2015)185 final. Strasbourg.
European Commission (2016). *Communication from the Commission to the European Parliament, the Council, the European Economic and Social Committee and the Committee of the Regions*. COM(2016)41 final. Brussels.
European Commission, and Bangemann Group (1994). Europe and the Global Information Society: Recommendations of the High-level Group on the Information Society to the Corfu European Council. S.2/94. Brussels.
European Commission, and High Representative of the European Union for Foreign Affairs and Security Policy (2013). Cybersecurity Strategy of the European Union: An Open, Safe and Secure Cyberspace. JOIN(2013) 1. Brussels.
European Council (1996). Council Conclusions. Bologna.
European Council (1998). Council Conclusions. Vienna.
European Council (1999). Council Conclusions. Tampere.
European Parliament (2015). Combatting Child Sexual Abuse Online-study. PE 536.481. Directorate General for Internal Policies, Policy Department C: Citizens' Rights and Constitutional Affairs. Brussels.
European Parliament and Council of the European Union (1999). Decision No. 276/1999/EC of the European Parliament and of the Council of 25 January 1999 Adopting a Multiannual Community Action Plan on Promoting Safer Use of the Internet by Combating Illegal and Harmful Content on Global Networks.
European Parliament and the Council of the European Union (2016). Directive (EU) 2016/1148 of the European Parliament and of the Council Concerning Measures for a High Common Level of Security of Network and Information Systems across the Union. 19.7.2016 L194/1. Official Journal of the European Union. Brussels.
Europol (2011). The Future of Organised Crime – Challenges and Recommended Actions. European Police Chiefs Convention.
Europol (2014a). *EC3 First Annual Report*. The Hague.
Europol (2014b). *iOCTA – The Internet Organised Crime Threat Assessment*. The Hague.
Europol (2015). *The Internet Organised Crime Threat Assessment (iOCTA)*. The Hague.

Europol and Eurojust (2016). *Common Challenges in Combatting Cyber Crime*. EDOC 802918. The Hague.

Fafinski, S., Dutton, W. and Margetts, H. (2010). Mapping and Measuring Cybercrime. Forum Discussion Paper No. 18. Oxford Internet Institute.

Fahey, E. (2014). The EU's Cybercrime and Cyber-security Rulemaking: Mapping the Internal and External Dimensions of EU Security. *European Journal of Risk Regulation (EJRR)*, 5, p. 46.

Gallie, W.B. (1956). Essentially Contested Concepts. *Proceedings of the Aristotelian Society*, 56, pp. 167–198.

Giacomello, G. (2010). *International Relations and Security in the Digital Age*, edited by J. Eriksson (1st edn). London; New York: Routledge.

Goodman, M. (2011). International Dimensions of Cybercrime. In *Cybercrimes: A Multidisciplinary Analysis*, edited by S. Ghosh and E. Turrini. Berlin; Heidelberg: Springer, pp. 311–339.

Kshetri, N. (2010). *The Global Cybercrime Industry: Economic, Institutional and Strategic Perspectives*. Berlin; Heidelberg: Springer.

Malmström, C. (2011). It's Time to Take Cyber Criminals Offline. SPEECH/11/260.

Malmström, C. (2013). Speech: EC3, a European Response to Cybercrime. The Hague.

McAfee (2014). Net Losses: Estimating the Global Cost of Cybercrime – Economic Impact of Cybercrime II. Center for Strategic and International Studies.

Mendez, F. (2005). The European Union and Cybercrime: Insights from Comparative Federalism. *Journal of European Public Policy*, 12(3), pp. 509–527.

Monar, J. (2007). The EU's Approach Post-September 11: Global Terrorism as a Multidimensional Law Enforcement Challenge. *Cambridge Review of International Affairs*, 20(2), pp. 267–283. doi: 10.1080/09557570701414633.

Newman, G.R. (2009). Cybercrime. In *Handbook on Crime and Deviance*, edited by M. Krohn, A.J. Lizotte and G. Penly Hall. Heidelberg; London; New York: Springer.

Porcedda, M.G. (2011). Translantic Approaches to Cybersecurity and Cybercrime. In *The EU-US Security and Justice Agenda in Action*, edited by Patryk Pawlak. Chaillot Papers.

PWC Global (2016). Global Economic Crime Survey. Available at www.pwc.com/gx/en/services/advisory/consulting/forensics/economic-crimesurvey/cybercrime.html.

Reitano, T., Oerting, T. and Hunter, M. (2015). Innovations in International Cooperation to Counter Cybercrime: The Joint Cybercrime Action Taskforce. *The European Review of Organised Crime*, 2(2), pp. 142–154.

Savona, E.U. (ed.) (2010). *Crime and Technology: New Frontiers For Regulation, Law Enforcement And Research*. Softcover reprint of hardcover 1st edn (2004). New York: Springer.

Schjolberg, S. (2014). *The History of Cybercrime*. Norderstedt: Books on Demand.

Sieber, U. (1998). *Legal Aspects of Computer-related Crime in the Information Society*. University of Würzburg.

Smith, R.G., Grabosky, P. and Urbas, G. (2011). *Cyber Criminals on Trial*. Cambridge: Cambridge University Press.

Summers, S., Schwarzenegger, C., Ege, G. and Young, F. (2014). *The Emergence of EU Criminal Law: Cyber Crime and the Regulation of the Information Society*. Oxford; Portland, OR: Hart Publishing.

Symantec (2016). *Norton Cybersecurity Insights Report*.

Van de Heyning, C. (2016). The Boundaries of Jurisdiction in Cybercrime and Constitutional Protection. In *The Internet and Constitutional Law – The Protection of Fundamental Rights and Constitutional Adjudication in Europe*, edited by O. Pollicino and G. Romeo. London; New York: Routledge.

Van der Meulen, N., Jo, E.A. and Soesanto, S. (2015). *Cybersecurity in the European Union and Beyond: Exploring the Threats and Policy Responses*. PE 536.470. Study for the LIBE Committee. Brussels: European Parliament, Directorate General for Internal Policies.

Wall, D.S. (2007). *Cybercrime: The Transformation of Crime in the Information Age*. Cambridge: Polity Press.

Yar, M. (2013). *Cybercrime and Society* (2nd revised edn). Los Angeles, CA: Sage.

13
EU COUNTER-TERRORISM
Glass half-full or half-empty?

Oldrich Bures

Introduction

Following the tragic events of September 11, 2001 (9/11), terrorism has become one of the major security threats. The fight against terrorism has, correspondingly, become a key priority for national governments and national security agencies, as well as an important part of the agenda of various international organizations, including the European Union (EU). As a consequence, there has been a proliferation of the academic literature analyzing various aspects of EU counter-terrorism efforts that already span across all of the EU's former three pillars. In this chapter, only the key debates and findings that go beyond the academic ivory tower are presented.

The chapter comprises three main sections. The first offers a succinct overview of the historical evolution and introduces the key actors and dimensions of EU counter-terrorism. The second section offers a comprehensive literature review, structured along the important theoretical debates. The third section summarizes two key interlinked debates regarding the difficult tradeoff between security, accountability and justice, and the effectiveness of EU counter-terrorism measures, respectively. The chapter concludes with a few notes on the current state of the art in EU counter-terrorism.

Historical evolution and key actors and aspects of EU counter-terrorism

The origins of a genuine EU counter-terrorism policy pre-date it and may be traced to the early 1970s, when a span of terrorist incidents perpetrated by autochthonous Western European (e.g., IRA, ETA, Red Brigades) as well as Middle Eastern organizations (e.g., Popular Front for the Liberation of Palestine) and a growing dissatisfaction with the existing international counter-terrorism policies (Wilkinson 1986: 292) prompted the member states (MSs) of the then European Communities (EC) to develop what may be termed an EC counter-terrorism policy at two key levels: legal and operational. The former consisted of efforts to overcome the substantial differences in national criminal codes when it comes to defining and punishing the crime of terrorism, which all EC MSs perceived as being of predominantly political nature, thus significantly complicating cross-border counter-terrorism cooperation. Albeit a number of both EU (e.g., the 1995 Convention on Simplified Extradition Procedure between the MSs of the EU) and non-EU (e.g., the 1977 Council of Europe's European Convention on the Suppression of Terrorism) conventions have been adopted, and the Maastricht Treaty on European Union specifically referred to terrorism as a serious form of crime to be combatted via the approximation of MSs' rules on criminal matters, overall the EU made only slow progress in constructing a true area of 'freedom, security and justice' prior to 9/11 (Bures 2011).

At the operational level, the Terrorism, Radicalism, Extremism and political Violence (TREVI) group was formed in 1975 by European police officials to exchange information and provide mutual assistance on terrorism. While TREVI's work was considered useful by EC MSs, its legal basis and its relationship to other EC institutions remained unclear (Lodge 1989: 42). As a consequence, it was ultimately replaced with Europol, which started limited operations in 1994 in the form of a drugs unit. Counter-terrorism was added to its remit in 1999 following the formal ratification of the Europol Convention by all EU MSs.

Overall, it is possible to argue that when the United States were hit on September 11, 2001, the EU did not possess a coherent counter-terrorism policy. While the representatives of all EU MSs had consistently condemned terrorism and several MSs had a long history of fighting terrorism at the national level since the 1960s, prior to 9/11 the EU's position towards terrorism has been limited to a strictly political level (Tsoukala 2004: 29). To some extent, this was a consequence of substantial differences in the perceptions of both the salience and nature of the threats posed by contemporary terrorism within EU MSs. Regarding the former, databases on terrorist incidents[1] indicate that only six EU MSs – Spain, France, Greece, Germany, Italy and the United Kingdom – account for almost 90 percent of all terrorist attacks perpetrated on the territory of the EU since 1968. Regarding the latter, the available data suggest that a vast majority of terrorist attacks in Europe were attributed to ethno-separatist terrorist groups rather than to Islamist terrorist groups that have received the bulk of attention among both scholars and practitioners of counter-terrorism since 9/11 due to several spectacular and mass-casualty terrorist attacks on European soil (Madrid 2004, London 2005, Paris 2015, Brussels 2016).

The counter-terrorism dynamics prevalent in the aftermath of 9/11 were seized on by the EU as both opportunity and proof of the necessity to further reinforce its internal coherence in the fight against a new type of transnational terrorist threat in a 'borderless' Europe. Already in November 2001, the European Council adopted an Action Plan on Combatting Terrorism (SN/140/01), and a EU Counterterrorism Strategy (14469/4/05 REV 4) was agreed in December 2005 following the terrorist attacks in Madrid and London. The former plan called for action in five areas: (1) enhancing police and judicial cooperation; (2) developing international legal instruments; (3) putting an end to the funding of terrorism; (4) strengthening air security; and (5) coordinating the European Union's global action. The latter strategy set out the following four key objectives of EU counter-terrorism: (1) to prevent new recruits to terrorism; (2) to protect potential targets; (3) to pursue members of existing terrorist networks; and (4) to respond to the consequences of terrorist attacks. For each of these objectives there is a list of key priorities, and the updated EU Action Plan on combatting terrorism now contains more than 200 specific measures. Moreover, these general documents were soon complemented by specific strategies on radicalization and recruitment into terrorism in 2005 (14781/1/05, revised in 2008 as 15175/08 and in 2014 as 5643/5/14), terrorist financing in 2004 (16089/04, revised in 2008 as 11778/1/08), and most recently, on the Daesh threat and foreign fighters in 2015 (7267/15). In December 2003, the European Council also adopted a European Security Strategy, where terrorism heads the list of threats facing the member states and which proclaims that concerted European action against terrorism is 'indispensable', a call that was renewed in its 2008 update. The fight against terrorism is also a key element in the 2010 Internal Security Strategy and in the 2015 European Agenda on Security.

While there is no space here to go into details of all specific legal measures adopted since 9/11, it is worth highlighting at least the key measures. Since 2002 the EU has possessed a common minimum definition of terrorism, thus eliminating a crucial shortcoming of the global counter-terrorism efforts that are still hampered by bitter 'one man's terrorist is another man's freedom fighter' debates. This has allowed for the introduction of several additional legal instruments, such as the European Arrest Warrant (2002/584/JHA) which is based on the principle of mutual recognition of judicial decisions among the EU MSs and which made the EU legal process of extradition more efficient and transparent than the previous myriad extradition conventions and bilateral agreements. Also noteworthy is a series of legal measures designed to disrupt terrorist financing, track operatives, chart relationships and deter individuals from supporting terrorist organizations. Additional legal instruments have been adopted in the aftermath of the recent attacks in Paris and Brussels in response to 'foreign fighters' (individuals from EU countries who engaged in the conflicts in Syria and Iraq), including the EU Passenger Name Record Directive (7829/16), which requires airlines to transfer passenger data from all EU third-country flights to national authorities, while also allowing EU MSs to voluntarily apply it to flights within the EU.

Similarly, there has been a dramatic growth in the past decade of the number of EU bodies engaged in counter-terrorism at different levels. Most notably, Europol and Eurojust competences and resources in the area of counter-terrorism have gradually risen along with the increases of both the quantity and quality of their terrorism cases workload. But the list of EU-level actors involved in counter-terrorism is much longer, including the EU Clearing House which channels the EU's fight against terrorism financing; SitCen/IntCen in the area of intelligence analysis; several expert networks in the area of (counter)radicalization (e.g., the European Network of Experts on Radicalisation or the Radicalisation Awareness Network); and, most recently, the new European Border and Coast Guard (formally Frontex) when it comes to foreign fighters' travel from/to the EU. In addition, there has been a proliferation of Council committees working on various dimensions of the terrorist threat, and the relevant Directorate-Generals (DG) of the European Commission (as of 2016 primarily DG Migration and Home Affairs and DG Justice and Consumers) have used the momentum generated by major terrorist attacks in Europe to promote specific steps leading towards a more full-fledged EU counter-terrorism policy. Moreover, in response to the spate of terrorist attacks in EU MSs in the summer of 2016 and the Brexit referendum results in June 2016, a new British commissioner was nominated for the newly created post of Commissioner for Security Union, with a specific emphasis on EU counter-terrorism. The European Parliament's (EP) role has been elevated from consultation to co-decision with the Treaty of Lisbon in 2009, thus making it a new and important player in EU counter-terrorism. Finally, in order to ensure coordination of all EU bodies involved in the fight against terrorism, the post of EU Counterterrorism Coordinator has been created in the aftermath of the Madrid terrorist attacks (3/11), albeit the critics have pointed out that he still lacks both formal powers and resources (Bures 2011: 138–139).

Literature review and theoretical explanations of EU counter-terrorism

In spite of its political relevance and decade-long history, the topic of EC/EU counter-terrorism has received due attention in the academic community only relatively recently. Although a handful of relevant studies were published shortly after 9/11 (Den Boer and Monar 2002; Bensahel 2003; Müller-Wille 2004; Occhipinti 2003; Wouters and Naert 2004), most have been published over the past decade (Argomaniz 2009a; Bossong 2013; Bures 2006; Kaunert 2010b; Keohane 2005; Léonard 2010; Müller-Wille 2008; Wolff 2009; Zimmermann 2006). Similarly, while the first edited volumes (Fijnaut *et al.* 2004; Spence 2007) were published shortly after the Madrid and London terrorist attacks, the special journal issues that have focused on specific aspects of the EU counter-terrorism efforts (Argomaniz *et al.* 2015; Edwards and Meyer 2008; Ferreira-Pereira and Martins 2012) and the four comprehensive monographs on the subject (Argomaniz 2011; Bossong 2012; Bures 2011; Kaunert 2010a) were only published after 2008.

As a general rule, much of the available academic literature has attempted to determine the extent to which the EU has put into practice its own counter-terrorism policy plans and to discuss the political and institutional factors behind successes and failures. To complement these efforts, several contributions have also followed a thematic approach towards matters such as the evolving importance of institutional actors for EU counter-terrorism, the impact of EU policies upon national systems or the centrality accorded to intelligence efforts in the European response. However, although the general goal has been to provide explanations of either the evolution of EU counter-terrorism over time and/or the contributions the EU has (not) made in the fight against terrorism, the conceptual and theoretical approaches adopted by different authors have varied substantially. In addition to the usual epistemological and ontological preferences of individual scholars, this is primarily due to the fact that EU counter-terrorism is not a clearly delimitated policy area – as discussed above, it consists of numerous actors and a growing number of legal measures in different areas of justice and home affairs (and beyond) and, as discussed below, a series of internal and external factors may be singled out as either enablers or inhibitors of EU-level efforts to tackle terrorism.

Counter-terrorism as a process of gradual European integration

When it comes to the evolution of EU counter-terrorism over time, three major theoretical arguments have been advanced. First, building on public policy-making literature, several authors have put special emphasis on the importance of supranational policy entrepreneurs for the growing role of the EU in counter-terrorism. Kaunert (2010b) and Occhipinti (2015), for example, have stressed the Commission and the Council Secretariat's influence as interest shapers that have invested resources into a specific counter-terrorism proposals (e.g., the European Arrest Warrant or the rules against terrorist financing) and successfully lobbied for their acceptance, thus weakening MSs' attachment to national sovereignty in counter-terrorism. Similarly, Bossong (2012) has argued that during the windows of opportunity in the aftermath of the 9/11 and 3/11 attacks, the Commission and the Council Secretariat played a significant entrepreneurial role, whereas their agenda-setting role is usually delimited or formally non-existent in EU security policy. This was mainly due to exceptional time pressures and expectations of joint problem-solving, which MSs states had difficulty in meeting without such 'external' agenda-setters.

Second, some authors have preferred a historical institutionalist perspective, emphasizing the importance of path dependency, the institutional setting of the EU and critical junctures as the decisive, intertwined factors when it comes to reconstructing the stages by which counter-terrorism became an area of European governance. Argomaniz (2011) has contended that the intergovernmental form of counter-terrorism cooperation in the 1970s to 1980s and prior political decisions made in the 1990s have constrained institutional actors' reaction to 9/11 – the sunk costs derived from switching from one alternative (complete new policies tailored to the terrorist threat) to the pre-existing one (the rapid adoption of previously tabled instruments for criminal matters cooperation) were simply too high and the political pressure to 'do something' obliged MSs to an immediate policy reaction. In Argomaniz's view, path dependency also helps explain the transformation of Europol into a full-fledged European agency and stronger competences for the Commission, European Parliament and the Court of Justice in the European fight against terrorism, as these could all be seen as examples of reconfiguration and the reuse of 'old' EU structures to perform new counter-terrorism functions. Similarly, Bossong (2012) argued that due to the importance of historically contextual factors, large parts of the EU's counter-terrorism agenda were only loosely attached to the threat of terrorism in a process that approximates the garbage-can model of policy-making. This meant that the contingent availability of pre-existing policy proposals was more important than their relevance to the fight against terrorism. Alternatively, Wolff's (2009) account of the evolution of the EU's counter-terrorism policy in the Mediterranean emphasized the importance of cultural frames in addition to the weight of history and critical junctures.

Third, several other authors have attributed much of the drive for the EU's growing involvement in counter-terrorism to the impact of the shocks produced by major terrorist attacks in Europe after 9/11. Most importantly in this social constructivist account, these attacks led to a change in the perception of terrorism across Europe and, consequentially, also of the instruments that the EU MSs should put in place to fight this security threat (Bakker 2006; Edwards and Meyer 2008; Meyer 2009; Monar 2007). Since the threat was publicly framed as transnational, national governments rapidly agreed on the need for coordinated European action. Thus, although there are still diverging views among scholars about whether this threat perception is truly European, due to the fact that only some European countries have suffered from sustained terrorist campaigns within their borders, there is a general agreement on the view that, at least in the EU discourse, terrorism has been internalized as a 'European threat'. This has allowed the EU to present a common discourse that has sustained political consensus and, to a degree, unity of action, despite this action being often concocted by only a small group of countries within the Union. It is important to note, however, that some other authors have emphasized the importance of major terrorist attacks as the key explanation for the incident-driven formulation of EU counter-terrorism, which tended to produce a highly inconsistent (over-) reaction in the aftermath of major attacks and a counter-terrorism fatigue in periods between major attacks (Bossong 2012; Bures 2011).

Future accounts of EU counter-terrorism could also draw upon the concept of Europeanization, which has already been successfully used for the analysis of other EU policies (Featherstone and Radaelli 2003). Specifically, from the many existing strands in the Europeanization literature (see Graziano and Vink 2008), the minimalist concept focused on the two-way process of adaptation of the policy and policy processes appears the most promising for the analysis of EU counter-terrorism. The bottom-up dimension ('uploading') would entail the analyses of the influence of EU MSs' counter-terrorism policies on the construction of EU counter-terrorism, while the top-down dimension ('downloading') would focus on the impact of EU counter-terrorism on EU MSs.

Alternatively, the more recent differentiated integration theory may offer new insights into the study of EU counter-terrorism. It starts with the assumption that there is no uniformly integrated EU – while some EU policy fields are integrated, others, including counter-terrorism, are still based mainly on intergovernmental cooperation. Differentiated integration theory therefore conceptualizes the EU as a system in which the level of centralization and territorial extension varies by function (Leuffen et al. 2012). The EU counter-terrorism policy may therefore be described as both vertically and horizontally differentiated because almost all competences remain at the level of EU MSs, which often do not genuinely participate in/contribute to all its aspects. Moreover, to explain the occurrence of differentiated integration, the theory proposes to look at both the demand and supply side of integration. The demand side describes both the needs and preferences of MSs' governments on integration, which are shaped by policy problems, interdependences, as well as by interests and ideas. The supply side looks at the constellation of these preferences, the institutional context, sphere of negotiations (intergovernmental versus supranational), and MSs' constraints (Leuffen et al. 2012: 34–36). The key constraint of preference convergence among EU MSs is operationalized as the concept of 'politicization', which consists of three parts: (1) the salience of an issue; and (2) the polarization of opinion and the engagement of audiences in the EU (De Wilde et al. 2016: 5). It may therefore be hypothesized that differentiated integration in EU counter-terrorism is the result of little preference convergence among European MSs, high and asymmetric politicization across MSs, asymmetrical interdependence and relatively weak supranational actors.

Policy outputs in EU counter-terrorism

When it comes to assessments of the contributions the EU has (not) made in the fight against terrorism, Argomaniz (2011) has used Simon Nuttall's institutionalist model of consistency in European decision-making to analyze the coherence of EU counter-terrorism by separating the notion into three differentiated manifestations: (1) institutional (processes of cooperation and communication between European and national actors); (2) horizontal (whether the separate measures adopted by the EU in the area of counter-terrorism are congruent); and (3) vertical (the extent to which the constituent elements of the EU's bureaucratic apparatus in this field operate in a coordinated manner). He argued that there are significant flaws in all of these consistency dimensions of the EU counter-terrorism system and this has undermined its overall effectiveness.

Bures (2011) attempted to evaluate the value-added of the EU's legal counter-terrorism instruments by drawing upon studies of sanctions implementation, which suggest the need to differentiate between three aspects of policy implementation of EU initiatives: (1) key provisions of the EU's counter-terrorism measures; (2) their transposition into national legal frameworks; and (3) their actual utilization by relevant national authorities. When it comes to evaluating the value-added of the EU agencies involved in the fight against terrorism, Bures drew upon the intelligence studies literature, according to which a supranational agency adds value if: (1) it produces something that can, is or will not be produced at the national level; (2) the responsibility for a certain form of intelligence product is transferred to the European level, i.e., if the European unit can relieve national authorities. After applying these two criteria to the first decade of EU counter-terrorism, he concluded that it has at times been more of a paper tiger than an effective counter-terrorism device.

Bossong (2013) has offered an analysis of EU counter-terrorism from the perspective of public goods theory. He argued that while the EU has been comparatively effective in responding to 'weaker' link vulnerabilities, it could not effectively aggregate resources and act jointly in the international fight against terrorism due to the non-excludable nature of benefits (as in the case of foreign policy) and partial rivalry of consumption (as in the case of sensitive information). Overall, therefore, concerns about free-riding and overcrowding are outweighing the weakest-link stimulus for cooperation.

Building on analyses of the role of international bureaucracies in international relations theory, Hegemann (2014) has examined how and to what degree international counter-terrorism bureaucracies such as the EU exercise autonomy and perform distinct functions. He argued that the EU needs to reconcile calls for effective counter-terrorism with the need to maintain an impression of technical impartiality in a particularly contested policy field and suggested that similar to the UN, the EU responded to this challenge with different strategies of politicization and depoliticization.

Finally, in addition to the aforementioned accounts of EU counter-terrorism linked to specific theories, there has also been a difference of opinion regarding the importance of internal versus external factors. On the one hand, some scholars have argued that the transformation of the initial external crisis (the 9/11 attacks in the USA) into sustained European action has been facilitated by internal and EU-specific enabling factors, such as the Lisbon Treaty reforms that have empowered the Union in terms of competences and instruments (Monar 2015). Alternatively, from a more functionalist perspective, others have highlighted that some internal enabling factors are a by-product of the Single Market (Bures 2011; Occhipinti 2015). While freedom of movement of capital, goods, services and labor are welcome features of the common European market, free movement of criminals and terrorists is clearly an unwanted corollary. Thus, already since the late 1980s, a key argument for a EU counter-terrorism role has been the need to prevent borderless terrorist networks from taking advantage of differences in national counter-terrorism laws and existing gaps in international police and judicial cooperation across Europe. As a consequence, most EU counter-terrorism has been conducted within the borders of Europe and most experts have been generally rather skeptical about the EU's external efforts, albeit some of the more recent literature suggests that over time, the EU has become increasingly accepted as a potential counter-terror partner in its own right by third countries due to the use of political dialogues, counter-terrorism clauses, capacity-building, economic assistance and other external relations instruments (Ferreira-Pereira and Martins 2012; MacKenzie et al. 2015).

The impact of external actors upon EU counter-terrorism

On the other hand, some of literature has indicated that the encouragement of a more proactive EU role in counter-terrorism has also come from external actors. Bures (2010), for instance, showed how the smart sanctions and the anti-money-laundering approaches to counter-terrorist financing adopted by the EU were in fact standards originally drafted by other international bodies, such as the UN Security Council and the Financial Action Task Force. Likewise, Argomaniz (2015a, 2015b) has stressed the importance of the International Civil Aviation Organization and International Maritime Organization guidelines for the EU transport security policies, and argued that external actors are likely to drive further developments in new areas of recent EU activity, such as cyber security. Finally, several authors have pointed out the importance of external pressure by the United States on the EU and argued that EU–US collaboration in counter-terrorism has been very substantial, sometimes even controversially so (e.g., data protection concerns regarding EU–US passenger name records; see Argomaniz 2009b; Kaunert et al. 2015; Ripoll Servent and MacKenzie 2012).

Major debates: security, accountability, justice, effectiveness

When it comes to counter-terrorism, two interlinked debates have generated the most heated discussions among both scholars and practitioners: (1) the debate about how to assess the effectiveness of existing counter-terrorism policies, and (2) the debate about tradeoffs between liberty, transparency, accountability, justice and security. Neither of these debates is new, nor specific to the EU, but the post-9/11 EU counter-terrorism policy has been criticized for failing on both fronts, i.e., 'for being ineffective, slow and incoherent as well as for taking disproportionate, self-serving and partly illegal measures that undermine democratic and judicial oversight as well as civil liberties' (Edwards and Meyer 2008: 15). This section does not and cannot provide a comprehensive account of all issues and questions involved (see Balzacq and Carrera 2006; Guild and Geyer 2008), but the key points of contention concern the following issues.

How effective is the EU in the field of counter-terrorism?

First, there is little doubt that the ever-richer tapestry of legal instruments and institutional bodies with competences in fighting terrorism at the European level has significant ramifications, especially for the democratic oversight of European counter-terrorism efforts. Arguably the most important issue in this regard is the oversight of EU counter-terrorism intelligence exchange, which is hampered by a rather considerable list of challenges, including the networked character of the intelligence, the duplication that comes from parallel bilateral exchange processes, the increasing implication of barely regulated private actors and the growing exchange of data with third countries with lower protection standards (Den Boer 2015). If we turn the spotlight onto the democratic accountability of the institutional actors, lightly anchored agencies (SitCen/IntCen) and European-scale intelligence networks (Police Working Group on Terrorism) have little or no accountability at all and, in addition to this, voids and gaps still exist when it concerns the specific responsibilities of official EU agencies, as in Europol's work within the Terrorist Financing Tracking Programme (TFTP).

A tradeoff between security and liberty?

Second, several aspects of EU counter-terrorism have highlighted the importance of the security versus/and/or justice/liberty question(s). Many of these have been raised by the European Parliament Committee on Civil Liberties (2011), whose reports track how 'mass surveillance has become a key feature of counter-terrorism policies' and how 'the large-scale collection of personal data, detection and identification technologies, tracking and tracing, data mining and profiling, risk assessment and behavioral analysis are all used for the purpose of preventing terrorism'. The concern is that these policies shift the burden of proof to the citizen while it is an open question whether all these measures would pass a proportionality test. Many scholars (including this author) therefore believe that the EU legitimacy as a counter-terror actor is dependent not only on the delivery of policies that are broadly seen as effective, but also proportional to the threat and respectful of European democratic values.

This in turns suggests that an important assumption in the aforementioned security/liberty debates is that we actually know how to assess the effectiveness of existing counter-terrorism policies. Unfortunately this assumption is not warranted, as there is a remarkable lack of analyses of the impact of adopted counter-terrorism measures at all levels (Chasdi 2010; Lum and Kennedy 2012). As a consequence, not just at the EU level, 'it remains largely a matter of faith that anti-crime and anti-terror efforts have some impact beyond the immediate operational outcomes' (Levi 2007: 264). To some extent, this is due to the methodological difficulties regarding the quality and quantity of data, as well as finding the right proxy indicators that would complement the readily available yet inherently limited quantitative criteria (such as the number of arrests, requests for assistance or amounts of frozen terrorist money) that do not shed much light on the actual effects of counter-terrorism measures on specific cultures, groups and individuals.

An additional EU-specific obstacle is the multi-level system of governance involving national, subnational and supranational actors, which complicates attempts at tracing back the origin of specific outcomes to certain policies and/or actors. The high density of factors affecting the incidence of terrorist violence and the difficulty in isolating the short- and long-term impact of individual variables undermine the capacity of national and supranational actors to deliver evidence-based policies sustained by meaningful cost-effectiveness analyses, whose overall impact and implications can be measured in a thorough and credible manner. The repercussions deriving from these limitations are evident in 'real-life' counter-terrorism – note, for example, the prevailing skepticism on the value of both European governments' and EU counter-radicalization efforts (Bakker 2015).

Finally, it is also important to note that with the exception of the EU's Counterterrorism Coordinator, none of the EU agencies and institutions has a counter-terrorism-only mandate. Similarly, many of the EU-level legal instruments used in the fight against terrorism are general anti-crime measures. Thus, it is important to keep in mind that there are actually three levels of abstraction of the EU's counter-terrorism capacities: (1) capacities explicitly engineered towards the fight against terrorism; (2) capacities directed towards managing complex threats and natural disasters in general; and (3) capacities found in EU institutions that may help national agencies, of any type, to respond to adverse events. This further complicates attempts to evaluate the effectiveness of EU counter-terrorism policies:

> It is hard to predict how the EU can and will employ the tools explicitly designed for counter-terrorism purposes, it is impossible to foresee if and how the Union will employ its generic tools that were originally designed for other purposes.
> *(Rhinard et al. 2007: 99)*

At the same time, it is important to note that the standard of comparison clearly matters when it comes to evaluating the effectiveness of any type of policy. Some experts have therefore argued that the critics of counter-terrorist efforts should remain realistic and bear in mind that '[g]overnments have to be lucky all the time and the terrorist needs to be lucky only once' (Neuhold 2006: 42).

Concluding remarks

Even from the brief account of EU counter-terrorism presented in this chapter, it is clear that the European Union has accomplished a surprising amount in the past fifteen years. From a position of almost total irrelevance at the time of the 9/11 attacks, and, as a reaction to a series of mass-casualty attacks on European soil, the EU has become increasingly active in the field of counter-terrorism. Using a set of policy programs, strategy documents and a list of priorities as foundations, the EU has aimed to coordinate member states' policies, to harmonize national legislation and even to support some operational work conducted by national authorities. As importantly, several opportunities have emerged recently to redress the initial post-9/11 emphasis on security with more attention being paid to the consequences of these policies for European citizens' liberties. These include the increased importance of fundamental rights in the Lisbon Treaty and the new powers it bestows upon the European Court of Justice to protect these rights and upon the European Parliament as a co-legislator in JHA and overseer of EU agencies' activities in this area. Thus, taking into account the tentative evidence of incrementally growing EU officials' reputation and national security actors' operational use of EU counter-terrorism agencies and instruments, it may be argued that the current EU counter-terrorism capacity may already be greater than is commonly understood. This general lack of awareness of an enhanced EU counter-terrorism role is due to several reasons, including its incremental development, its often technical nature, and the well-known fact that many EU MSs' politicians prefer to present to the general public the failures of EU policies rather than their successes.

At the same time, however, the proliferation of legal measures and relevant actors at the European level should not be assumed uncritically as having in principle a direct and substantial contribution to a stronger counter-terror response in practice. This is not only because new counter-terrorism initiatives keep mushrooming while the existing arrangements continue to flourish, albeit many of the formal EU agencies suffer from an output deficit. The recent terrorist attacks in Belgium and France have once again highlighted the contradiction between the seemingly free movement of terrorists across Europe and the lack of EU-wide police cooperation and intelligence-sharing, where long-standing bilateral and/or non-EU multilateral arrangements are still preferred by national agencies tasked with counter-terrorism. Similarly, in terms of prevention, despite the proclamations following all major terrorist attacks in Europe, the EU has still done relatively little to tackle the root causes of terrorism and radicalization, both abroad and in Europe itself. Moreover, despite the fact that up to 5000 European of Daesh's foreign fighters have come from Europe and 20 to 30 percent had already returned, the EU's role in this key area of counter-terrorism is bound to remain relatively limited due to the lack of relevant competences and tools. Outside of Europe, institutional complexity and cross-policy coordination problems (between the external JHA dimension, the CFSP and external economic relations) continue to act as powerful constraints upon the EU's nascent external counter-terrorism role.

Taken together, these shortcomings represent an important reminder that the EU is ultimately its member states, without whose wholehearted support even the most elaborate and innovative counter-terrorism structures and mechanisms remain useless. But they also suggest that as long as it is uncertain whether extra layers of communication systems, databases and practitioners' meetings at the European level are really the recipe for superior results, a more crowded map of EU counter-terrorism arrangements may not always represent the best way forward when it comes to addressing the contemporary terrorist threats in Europe. The reader is therefore encouraged to further explore the field of EU counter-terrorism in order to judge whether the glass is half-full or half-empty.

Note

1 The RAND–St. Andrews' Chronology of International Terrorism, the US Department of State's Patterns of Global Terrorism, and the National Consortium for the Study of Terrorism and Responses to Terror's Global Terrorism Database.

Bibliography

Argomaniz, J. (2009a). Post-9/11 Institutionalization of European Union Counterterrorism: Emergence, Acceleration and Inertia. *European Security*, 18(2), pp. 151–172.

Argomaniz, J. (2009b). When the EU is the 'Norm-Taker': The Passenger Name Records Agreement and the EU's Internalization of US Border Security Norms. *Journal of European Integration*, 31(1), pp. 119–136.

Argomaniz, J. (2011). *The EU and Counter-terrorism: Politics, Polity and Policies After 9/11*. London: Routledge.

Argomaniz, J. (2015a). The European Policies on the Protection of Infrastructure from Terrorist Attacks: A Critical Assessment. *Intelligence and National Security*, 30(2–3), pp. 259–280.

Argomaniz, J. (2015b). European Union Responses to Terrorist Use of Internet. *Cooperation and Conflict*, 50(2), pp. 250–268.

Argomaniz, J., Bures, O. and Kaunert, C. (2015). A Decade of EU Counter-terrorism and Intelligence: A Critical Assessment. *Intelligence and National Security*, 30(2–3), pp. 191–206.

Bakker, E. (2006). Difference in Terrorist Threat Perceptions in Europe. In D. Mahncke and J. Monar (eds), *International Terrorism. A European Response to a Global Threat?* Brussels: Peter Lang, pp. 47–62.

Bakker, E. (2015). EU Counter-radicalization Policies: A Comprehensive and Consistent Approach. *Intelligence and National Security*, 30(2–3), pp. 281–305.

Balzacq, T. and Carrera, S. (2006). *Security Versus Freedom? A Challenge for Europe's Future*. Aldershot: Ashgate.

Bensahel, N. (2003). The Counterterror Coalitions: Cooperation with Europe, NATO, and the European Union. Available at www.rand.org/publications/MR/MR1746/MR1746.pdf (MR-1746-AF, RAND) (accessed October 1, 2005).

Bossong, R. (2012). *The Evolution of EU Counter-terrorism Policy: European Security Policy After 9/11.* London: Routledge.

Bossong, R. (2013). Bossong Public Good Theory and the 'Added Value' of the EU's Anti-terrorism Policy. *European Security*, 22(2), pp. 165–184.

Bures, O. (2006). EU Counterterrorism Policy: A Paper Tiger? *Terrorism & Political Violence*, 18(1), pp. 57–78.

Bures, O. (2010). EU's Fight against Terrorist Finances: Internal Shortcomings and Unsuitable External Models. *Terrorism & Political Violence*, 22(3), pp. 419–438.

Bures, O. (2011). *EU Counterterrorism Policy: A Paper Tiger?* Burlington, VA: Ashgate.

Chasdi, R.J. (2010). *Counterterror Offensives for the Ghost War World: The Rudiments of Counterterrorism Policy.* Plymouth: Lexington Books.

Den Boer, M. (2015). Counter-terrorism, Security and Intelligence in the EU: Governance Challenges for Collection, Exchange and Analysis. *Intelligence and National Security*, 30(2–3), pp. 402–419.

Den Boer, M. and Monar, J. (2002). Keynote Article: 11 September and the Challenge of Global Terrorism to the EU as a Security Actor. In G. Edwards and G. Wiessala (eds), *The European Union: Annual Review of the EU 2001/2002*. Oxford: Blackwell, pp. 11–28.

De Wilde, P., Leupold, A. and Schmidtke, H. (2016). Introduction: The Differentiated Politicisation of European Governance. *West European Politics*, 39(1), pp. 3–22.

Edwards, G. and Meyer, C.O. (2008). Introduction: Charting a Contested Transformation. *Journal of Common Market Studies*, 46(1), pp. 1–25.

European Parliament Committee on Civil Liberties (2011). *Report on the EU Counter-terrorism Policy: Main Achievements and Future Challenges 2010/2311 (INI)*. A7–0286/2011. Available at www.europarl.europa.eu/sides/getDoc.do?pubRef=-//EP//NONSGML+REPORT+A7-2011-0286+0+DOC+PDF+V0//EN (accessed February 22, 2015).

Featherstone, K. and Radaelli, C.M. (2003). *The Politics of Europeanization*. Oxford: Oxford University Press.

Ferreira-Pereira, L.C. and Martins, B.O. (2012). The External Dimension of the European Union's Counter-terrorism: An Introduction to Empirical and Theoretical Developments. *European Security*, 21(4), pp. 459–473.

Fijnaut, C., Wouters, J. and Naert, F. (2004). *Legal Instruments in the Fight against International Terrorism: A Transatlantic Dialogue.* Leiden: Martinus Nijhoff.

Graziano, P. and Vink, M. (eds) (2008). *Europeanization New Research Agendas*. London: Palgrave Macmillan.

Guild, E. and Geyer, F. (2008). *Security versus Justice: Police and Judicial Cooperation in the European Union.* Aldershot: Ashgate.

Hegemann, H. (2014). *International Counterterrorism Bureaucracies in the United Nations and the European Union*. Baden-Baden: Nomos.

Kaunert, C. (2010a). *European Internal Security: Towards Supranational Governance in the Area of Freedom, Security and Justice?* Manchester: Manchester University Press.

Kaunert, C. (2010b). Towards Supranational Governance in EU Counter-Terrorism? – The Role of the Commission and the Council Secretariat. *Central European Journal of International and Security Studies*, 4(1), pp. 8–31.

Kaunert, C., Léonard, S. and MacKenzie, A. (2015). The European Parliament in the External Dimension of EU Counter-terrorism: More Actorness, Accountability and Oversight 10 Years On? *Intelligence and National Security*, 30(2–3), pp. 327–376.

Keohane, D. (2005). *The EU and Counter-terrorism*. Center for European Reform.

Léonard, S. (2010). The Use and Effectiveness of Migration Controls as a Counter-terrorism Instrument in the European Union. *Central European Journal of International and Security Studies*, 4(1), pp. 33–50.

Leuffen, D., Rittberger, B. and Schimmelfennig, F. (2012). *Differentiated Integration: Explaining Variation in the European Union*. London: Palgrave Macmillan.

Levi, M. (2007). Lessons for Countering Terrorist Financing from the War on Serious and Organized Crime. In T.J. Biersteker and S.E. Eckert (eds), *Countering the Financing of Terrorism*. London: Routledge, pp. 260–288.

Lodge, J. (1989). Terrorism and the European Community: Towards 1992. *Terrorism & Political Violence*, 1(1), pp. 28–47.

Lum, C. and Kennedy, L.W. (2012). *Evidence-based Counter-terrorism Policy*. Heidelberg: Springer.

MacKenzie, A., Kaunert, C. and Léonard, S. (2015). *The EU as a Global Counter-terrorism Actor: Spillovers, Integration, and Institutions*. Cheltenham: Edward Elgar.

Meyer, C.O. (2009). International Terrorism as a Force of Homogenization? A Constructivist Approach to Understanding Cross-national Threat Perceptions and Responses. *Cambridge Review of International Affairs*, 22(4), pp. 647–666.

Monar, J. (2007). Common Threat and Common Response? The European Union's Counter-terrorism Strategy and its Problems. *Government and Opposition*, 42(3), pp. 292–313.

Monar, J. (2015). The EU as an International Counter-terrorism Actor: Progress and Constraints. *Intelligence and National Security*, 30(2–3), pp. 333–356.

Müller-Wille, B. (2004). *For Our Eyes Only? Shaping an Intelligence Community within the EU*. Occasional Papers No. 50. Paris: Institute for Security Studies.

Müller-Wille, B. (2008). The Effect of International Terrorism on EU Intelligence Co-operation. *Journal of Common Market Studies*, 46(1), pp. 49–73.

Neuhold, H. (2006). International Terrorism: Definitions, Challenges and Responses. In D. Mahncke and J. Monar (eds), *International Terrorism. A European Response to a Global Threat?* Brussels: Peter Lang, pp. 23–46.

Occhipinti, J.D. (2003). *The Politics of EU Police Cooperation: Toward a European FBI?* Boulder, CO: Lynne Rienner.

Occhipinti, J.D. (2015). Still Moving Toward a European FBI? Re-examining the Politics of EU Police Cooperation. *Intelligence and National Security*, 30(2–3), pp. 234–258.

Rhinard, M., Boin, A. and Ekengren, M. (2007). Managing Terrorism: Institutional Capacities and Counter-terrorism Policy in the EU. In D. Spence (ed.), *The European Union and Terrorism*. London: John Harper, pp. 88–104.

Ripoll Servent, A. and MacKenzie, A. (2012). The European Parliament as a 'Norm Taker'? EU–US Relations after the SWIFT Agreement. *European Foreign Affairs Review*, 17(2/1), pp. 71–86.

Spence, D. (2007). Introduction. International Terrorism – The Quest for a Coherent EU Response. In D. Spence (ed.), *The European Union and Terrorism*. London: John Harper, pp. 1–29.

Tsoukala, A. (2004). Democracy against Security: The Debates about Counter-terrorism in the European Parliament, September 2001–June 2003. *Alternatives: Global, Local, Political*, 29(4), pp. 417–440.

Wilkinson, P. (1986). *Terrorism and the Liberal State*. London: Macmillan.

Wolff, S. (2009). The Mediterranean Dimension of EU Counter-terrorism. *Journal of European Integration*, 31(1), pp. 137–156.

Wouters, J. and Naert, F. (2004). Of Arrest Warrants, Terrorist Offences and Extradition Deals: An Appraisal of the EU's Main Criminal Law Measures against Terrorism after '11 September'. *Common Market Law Review*, 41(1), pp. 909–935.

Zimmermann, D. (2006). The European Union and Post-9/11 Counterterrorism: A Reappraisal. *Studies in Conflict & Terrorism*, 29(2), pp. 123–145.

14

DATA PROTECTION POLICIES IN EU JUSTICE AND HOME AFFAIRS

A multi-layered and yet unexplored territory for legal research

Paul De Hert and Vagelis Papakonstantinou

Introduction

Data protection is a EU law field that has undergone substantial if not groundbreaking change over the past few years. In April 2016, a five-year law-making process finally came to an end with the formal adoption of the General Data Protection Regulation (Regulation 679/2016/EU) and the Police and Criminal Justice Data Protection Directive (Directive 680/2016/EU). Each one is aimed at replacing the legal instruments already in effect in their respective fields. In particular, the General Data Protection Regulation (the 'GDPR') is intended to replace Directive 95/46/EC; it will find immediate application across the EU on May 25, 2018. On the other hand, the Police and Criminal Justice Data Protection Directive (the 'Directive') is intended to replace Framework Decision 977/2008/JHA; it was also released on the same day as the GDPR, on April 27, 2016, but, being a Directive, it gives member states unti May 6, 2018 to harmonize their national laws with its provisions.

This chapter will focus on the Directive, its subject matter being directly related to the EU justice and home affairs field. The Directive is an ambitious text, aiming at assuming the data protection standard-setting role within this field: all and any personal data processing in the law enforcement field undertaken by member states should observe its provisions. Nevertheless, space for exemptions is provided for. Most significantly, personal data processing performed by EU law enforcement agencies and bodies (Europol, Eurojust, OLAF, the European Border and Coast Guard Agency – Frontex, SIS II, VIS, CIS, Eurodac), is set to follow its own rules and not those of the Directive. At this EU level, the role of the standard-setting text is to be assumed by Regulation 45/2001/EC. Early in 2017, the Commission released its draft proposal for a Regulation replacing it (COM(2017) 8 final). Currently, virtually every EU agency or body active in this field profits from its own particular data protection provisions. In early 2017 these were found at various levels of completion: for example, while Europol and Eurojust are having their respective legal frameworks updated, and the European Public Prosecutor Office (EPPO) is in the process of being newly established, other EU agencies and bodies follow data protection developments in a more passive manner.

It is exactly the interplay of the above legal instruments (the Directive, Regulation 45/2001 or its successor, and agency-specific data protection provisions) that poses the main data protection policy challenge in the EU field of justice and home affairs today. The legal architecture in the field matters in terms of policy-setting, legal clarity, straightforwardness, and ultimately, accountability and adequate protection of the individual right to data protection (De Hert and Papakonstantinou 2014). In particular, the basic question here is whether the cumulative effect of the provisions of all the above instruments that are applicable each time is sufficient in protecting individuals and their right to data protection.

Because the field is currently undergoing substantial legal change, for the time being this is still an open, ongoing discussion. Attention should be given both to the applicable legal framework, meaning the interplay of the above instruments in each particular case, and also to application practices by the actors themselves (member state and EU law enforcement bodies) and data protection supervisors: Data Protection Authorities (DPAs) at the member state level and the European Data Protection Supervisor (the EDPS) at the EU level.

This chapter will first attempt to map the data protection field within the EU justice and home affairs region (sections 1 to 4). This is a not a straightforward task given the multitude of legal documents currently in various stages of the lawmaking process, as well as the multitude of legal layers with agency-specific legal provisions that frequently apply in parallel with general-scope texts (under a *lex specialis/lex generalis* relationship). The first section will discuss EU primary law (the Treaty of Lisbon) and the two basic data protection instruments regulating data processing by police and criminal justice actors in member states before and after Lisbon, the 2008 Framework Decision and the 2016 Police and Criminal Justice Data Protection Directive. The second section looks at some loose ends in this area that co-exist with the Framework Decision and the Directive. Examples that come to mind are bilateral PNR data exchange agreements with the USA, Australia and Canada, each containing specific data protection measures.

In the third section we discuss Regulation 45/2001, a document with general standards for data processing done at the level of the EU, but with remarkably little attention focused on what is happening at the EU level in the justice and home affairs field. In a subsequent section we will highlight instruments aimed at regulating agencies working at the EU level. We will then discuss briefly the (new) 2016 Europol Regulation and the proposed regulations for Eurojust and the European Public Prosecutor's Office.

These descriptions are followed by an analysis of the lack of research in this area and possible main legal and non-legal research issues in order to provide readers with some guidance as to research avenues that are currently open or are likely to be opened in the near future. Finally, some speculation on possible future scenarios with regard to the protection of individuals, which is ultimately the reason why data protection applies in the field, will be attempted in the concluding section.

The general regulatory instruments within the EU justice and home affairs field: from a decision to a Directive after Lisbon (layer 1)

The ratification of the Treaty of Lisbon back in 2009, Article 16 in particular, constitutes a turning point in the relationship between data protection and the EU justice and home affairs field (Hijmans and Scirocco 2009). Up until that time the field was largely fragmented, lacking coherence. Directive 95/46/EC expressly excused itself from undertaking the role of the common text of reference. Article 3 excluded from the scope of the Directive all processing of personal data in areas related to justice and home affairs, public security, defense and state security. Framework Decision 977/2008/JHA, which saw the light of day many years later, was a first attempt to regulate data protection in the EU justice and home affairs field, but only with modest outcomes. One could hardly speak of a common reference text for the field in view of the many exceptions and the limited scope of the instrument (De Hert and Papakonstantinou 2009). Some of the regulative work was done through several sector-specific legal instruments (for example, the Data Retention Directive on electronic communications data or the Passenger Name Records agreements with the USA, Australia and Canada on travel data) introduced particularly in the aftermath of terrorist attacks in the USA (9/11) and Europe. Some of these instruments were proven to be short-lived, as was the case with the EU Data Retention Directive (Directive 24/2006/EC) which was annulled by the CJEU in April 2014 (Joined Cases C-293/12 and C-594/12). Member states were therefore largely left alone to implement their own personal data processing practices at national level. They did so at multiple paces: some experimented enthusiastically in the field through the introduction of specialized legislation at the national level; others were more or less indifferent to it, as perhaps evidenced by their choice to apply their general data protection legislation (as affected by Directive 95/46) also to related personal data processing.

The ratification of the Treaty of Lisbon in November 2009 brought change. Article 16 states:

> [E]veryone has the right to the protection of personal data concerning them. The European Parliament and the Council, acting in accordance with the ordinary legislative procedure, shall lay down the rules relating to the protection of individuals with regard to the processing of personal data by Union institutions, bodies, offices and agencies, and by the Member States when carrying out activities which fall within the scope of Union law, and the rules relating to the free movement of such data. Compliance with these rules shall be subject to the control of independent authorities.

The precise consequences of this important provision remain unclear (De Hert 2015), but the wordings imposed change in the field and seemingly better mandate the EU to regulate data protection more thoroughly in less traditional areas. Nevertheless, Article 16 should be read together with Declaration 21 of the TFEU:

> [T]he Conference acknowledges that specific rules on the protection of personal data and the free movement of such data in the fields of judicial cooperation in criminal matters and police cooperation based on Article 16 of the Treaty on the Functioning of the European Union may prove necessary because of the specific nature of these fields.

In other words, the individual right to data protection is not unreservedly protected within the law enforcement field, or, at least, not in the same unrestricted manner as is the case with all other personal data processing. The Treaty of Lisbon, through Declaration 21, ensured that explicit differentiation is made between the two categories of personal data processing (general purpose, as opposed to that carried out by law enforcement agencies) so as to accommodate the special needs of the law enforcement sector.

As a consequence of the ratification of the Lisbon Treaty, the Police and Criminal Justice Data Protection Directive was introduced on April 27, 2016. Perhaps most importantly, the Directive addresses the main shortcoming of the Framework Decision it replaces, meaning its scope of self-limitation to cross-border processing, by declaring itself applicable to all processing undertaken at member state level (in Article 2). It also strengthens individual rights and adapts novelties introduced by the GDPR into the law enforcement field whenever and wherever applicable (see, for example, the cases of data protection impact assessments or data protection by design and by default). Supervision is granted to member state DPAs. Overall, it constitutes a text moving in the right direction, meaning that of providing adequate protection to individuals while striking a correct balance with law enforcement's personal data processing needs. On the other hand, the Directive leaves outside of its scope the processing performed by EU law enforcement actors (in Article 60), an inevitable choice given that a Directive cannot regulate EU agencies.

The introduction of the Police and Criminal Justice Data Protection Directive concludes an almost ten-year effort by the Commission (work on the Framework Decision began in 2006) to regulate the personal data processing of law enforcement agencies at the member state level according to common data protection standards. However, while harmonization at the member state level is indeed expected to be achieved through the Directive, at the EU level this remains an open issue.

The specific regulatory state within the EU justice and home affairs field: loose ends and umbrellas (layer 2)

In addition to the foregoing, a multitude of texts and initiatives exist in the field with more specific aims. Examples that come to mind are EU texts on Passenger Name Records collection (EU PNR) and EU bilateral agreements with third countries. Because an examination of each one of these cases largely exceeds the purposes of this chapter, this section will mention them only briefly. Directive 681/2016 (the so-called 'EU PNR Directive') was introduced on May 4, 2016 obliging airlines to hand over their passengers' data in order to help the authorities fight terrorism and serious crime. The EU PNR Directive organizes the more systematic collection, use and retention of PNR data (data collected during reservation and check-in procedures) on air passengers, thus affecting their right to data protection. This Directive came after years of elaboration that included a long period, during which it was assumed it was abandoned, as a reply to recent terrorist attacks across Europe – the recent attacks in Paris weighing heavy in this regard. Its introduction, despite its best intentions to comply with the proportionality principle and to apply adequate data protection safeguards, raised a number of data protection concerns; for example, concerning expansive passenger blacklisting or profiling (De Hert and Papakonstantinou 2015).

Long before the EU PNR Directive was introduced, the EU entered bilateral PNR data exchange agreements with the USA, Australia and Canada. Each of these agreements has a long history of multiple versions, court disputes, and long and complex negotiations (Argomaniz 2009; Hornung and Boehm 2012). Attention should therefore be given to each case separately; here it will only be noted that, by early 2017, the EU had effective bilateral PNR Agreements with the United States (since 2012), Canada (since 2006) and Australia (since 2012). In the same context, the EU has also entered bilateral agreements with the USA, namely the Terrorist Finance Tracking Programme (TFTP) in 2010 regulating the transfer of financial messaging data as well as the so-called 'EU–US Umbrella Agreement' which, once formally adopted, will supposedly provide a comprehensive high-level data protection framework for EU–US law enforcement cooperation.

The regulatory state at the high, standard-setting EU level: Regulation 45/2001 (layer 3)

At the EU level, personal data processing is regulated through a two-step process: Regulation 45/2001, or its successor, sets general standards. At the same time each actor in the field also benefits from its own, ad hoc data protection legal regime that should be read in combination with the provisions of Regulation 45/2001. Supervision tasks are awarded to the European Data Protection Supervisor (EDPS).

A number of problems are caused by this policy option. Those originating from Regulation 45/2001 itself are of an interim nature. The Regulation was introduced back in 2001 in order to apply, for the first time, data protection standards upon processing performed at the EU level. It also established the EDPS to supervise the application of these standards across EU institutions. However, Regulation 45/2001 kept away from the processing performed in the justice and home affairs sector, being applicable only to the processing of EU personnel files (through Article 46), but not to their case files. Despite this self-restrained approach, over the years several law enforcement EU actors voluntarily submitted themselves to the supervision powers of the EDPS. In effect, at the time of drafting this text, this has been the case with all EU actors in the field apart from Eurojust and Europol (a situation that, at least for Europol, is about to change). However, these actors were permitted an inexplicable, and unjustifiable, selective submission: while they accepted EDPS supervision, they did not resign from the substantive data protection law and submit themselves only to the provisions of Regulation 45/2001, which after all provide the terms of reference for the EDPS. Instead, each one was allowed to keep its ad hoc data protection regime, and only vest supervision upon the EDPS. The EDPS is therefore entrusted with the nearly impossible legal task of applying different substantive data protection rules to each actor it supervises.

A further problem connected to Regulation 45/2001 is the vagueness of its provisions. They were simply not written to regulate law enforcement personal data processing. Because the Regulation was released as a general-purpose (then first pillar) instrument to regulate all types of personal data processing, it does not cater specifically to the needs of processing undertaken by law enforcement actors. Nevertheless, substantial differences exist between these two types of personal data processing that justified the release of two different instruments to accommodate each one: the GDPR and the Directive. In the previous section we discussed the policy decision reached by the EU and member states about one legal instrument being unable to regulate all personal data processing; hence the co-existence of a general text (GDPR) and a specific text for justice and home affairs (the Police and Criminal Justice Data Protection Directive). What is self-evident at the member state level should also be reflected at the EU level; however, this has not been the case until today, with Regulation 45/2001 striving to hold a catch-all role.

In early 2017, the Commission made available its proposal for a new regulation, replacing Regulation 45/2001. The new regulation will supposedly address shortcomings of the past, taking into account 'the results of enquiries and stakeholder consultations, and the evaluation study on its application over the last 15 years'. While it is too early to assess its provisions, it should be noted that the above two problems are not addressed in its text. Again, a single text is expected to cover both general and law enforcement personal data processing at the EU level, maintaining an inexplicable differentiation between EU and member state personal data processing. Moreover, as far as substantive law is concerned, legal confusion is expected to continue because the Commission proposal prefers to leave the ad hoc data protection regime of each actor intact, merely asking for 'consistency' with the Directive's provisions (in par. 9 of the Preamble).

While the above developments with regard to Regulation 45/2001 and its successor describe change at a high, standard-setting EU level, developments have also been noted at the agency level over the past few years.

The regulatory state at the EU agency level (layer 4)

A multitude of EU actors (agencies, bodies and IT systems) are active in the justice and law enforcement field today. For the time being, each one benefits from its own ad hoc data protection regime as far as substantive data protection law is concerned. On the other hand, data protection supervision tasks are now almost unanimously granted to the EDPS.

With regard to Europol, a new Europol regulation, Regulation 794/2016, was published on May 11, 2016. As far as its substantive data protection regime is concerned, the Regulation includes an ad hoc one that is influenced by Regulation 45/2001, but is also carefully worded so as not to submit itself to its provisions (see, e.g., Recital 40). Accordingly, the Europol ad hoc data protection legal framework is laid down in Articles 17 to 50. On the other hand, as far as data protection supervision is concerned, the EDPS will replace the Europol Joint Supervisory Body (JSB) previously entrusted with this task.

Eurojust is awaiting an amendment to its legal framework. The Commission released its proposal for a regulation for Eurojust on July 17, 2013 (COM 0535 final), together with a proposal for a Council regulation on the establishment of the European Public Prosecutor's Office (COM 0534/final). Both regulations have yet to be finalized. The Commission's approach with regard to their substantive data protection law is to refer directly to Regulation 45/2001 and to its provisions as applicable to all processing operations at Eurojust and the EPPO. As far as supervision is concerned, it is suggested that the EDPS be made responsible for supervision of all personal data processing, thus replacing Eurojust's Joint Supervisory Body (JSB) currently carrying out these tasks.

All other actors in the field benefit from ad hoc, substantive data protection provisions that complement and particularize the provisions found in Regulation 45/2001. While each needs to be examined separately, it is briefly noted here that this is the case for Frontex or the European Border and Coast Guard (through Regulation 1168/2011), Eurodac (through Regulation 603/2013), the EU Visa Information System (through Regulation 767/2008), the EU Customs Information System (through Regulation 515/1997) and the Schengen Information System (through Regulation 1987/2006).

An important point for clarification refers to EU and member state cooperation. Because EU law enforcement actors most likely do not themselves collect the data found in their databases, but instead rely on member states for this task, data protection cooperation and coordination is of crucial importance. However, in practice this distinction between datasets increases regulatory complexity. Essentially, two different sets of data protection rules apply on the same individual file when processed at the member state and EU level. When processed at the member state level, local rules apply; once transmitted to a EU agency, EU rules apply. Cooperation between the two agencies is warranted through 'coordinated supervision' between the two data protection supervisory authorities involved, namely national data protection authorities at the respective member state level and the EDPS for processing at the EU level.

Why so little academic attention in the past?

Although research interest in the broader data protection field has witnessed an unprecedented, exponential growth over the past few years, attention has mostly focused either on general-purpose personal data processing governed by the 1995 Directive (now) or the 2016 GDPR (upcoming), in particular to such issues as internet social networks, cloud computing, the Internet of things, biometric data, drones and other technologies dominating the field, or to novelties in the text of the GDPR (e.g., the right to be forgotten or data protection impact assessments).

In relation to its glamorous sibling, the 2016 Police and Criminal Justice Data Protection Directive has mostly remained in the shadows of legal research, despite its very important subject matter. The same has been the case both with regard to its predecessor, the 2008 Framework Decision, and agency-specific data protection regimes. At least three reasons may have caused this neglect.

First, the lawmakers' approach itself: even during the long negotiations leading to the adoption of the EU data protection reform package, attention was disproportionately awarded to the GDPR. The Directive has always been under the assumption that it would be easier to adopt once the GDPR was concluded and that, in any event, its provisions would have to follow those of its sibling wherever possible. This phenomenon is after all also demonstrable in the Commission's recent proposal for a regulation replacing Regulation 45/2001: while the GDPR is repeatedly acknowledged and referred to, the Police and Criminal Justice Data Protection Directive only receives passing mention in its provisions.

Another reason for the limited interest of legal research in the field may be explained by its subject matter. The processing of personal data for law enforcement purposes gained in importance only relatively recently, after terrorist attacks across the world brought forward this type of personal data processing as an indispensable tool in the 'war against terror'. The majority of relevant legal initiatives have a history of no more than ten years – admittedly, a relatively short period for new legal research to emerge. In addition, the legal framework is in constant flux: at the time of the drafting of this text, the Eurojust and the EPPO draft regulations, as well as the successor to Regulation 45/2001, await finalization. On the other hand, political scientists have approached the field from a different angle, focusing mainly on institutional dynamics in the adoption of data protection laws (Argomaniz 2009; Bellanova and Duez 2012; Ripoll Servent and MacKenzie 2012; Ripoll Servent 2013).

Finally, the inherent difficulty of keeping up with the field should not be overlooked. The complex legal architecture described in the previous chapter affects legal research as well: anyone interested in the field would have to keep up both with general and intra-agency data protection developments. In addition, these would have to be complemented by member state law that, given the lack of the requirement for harmonization until at least May 2018, is at best multi-speed across the EU. As stated by the EDPS as early as 2008 in the context of EU frontier databases, 'the sheer number of these proposals and the seemingly piecemeal way in which they are put forward make it extremely difficult for the stakeholders (European and national Parliaments, data protection authorities including EDPS, civil society) to have a full overview' (EDPS 2008). His views were shared by O'Neill two years later (O'Neill 2010). Consequently, the formulation of a complete picture would have to be performed on an agency-specific level. In addition, the limited information that the agencies themselves (or the EDPS, for the same purposes) make available to the public further hinders legal research in the field.

Main scholarly debates and future research avenues (first series of questions)

Notwithstanding the difficulties mentioned above, or perhaps precisely because of them, the field is currently faced with some very interesting legal questions. First and foremost, the relationship between its basic legal instruments, namely the Directive and Regulation 45/2001 or its successor, is an issue of crucial importance. Disappointingly, the current Commission's draft updating Regulation 45/2001 leaves the issue unaddressed through mere indirect and brief mention in its preamble.

This may well change in the Regulation's final text. The main question here is whether the alignment of two essentially different texts (the Directive being aimed at law enforcement and

Regulation 45/2001 at general processing), which somehow need to co-exist, is at all possible. Once this issue is addressed, their relationship with each agency-specific data protection legal regime will have to be clarified – a far from straightforward issue. For example, with regard to Europol, Cocq (2016) has already noted the difficulties of attempting to align the data protection provisions of its new regulation with those of the Directive in terms of definitions or scope and objectives. Taking into account that supervision will be undertaken by the EDPS, regulated by Regulation 45/2001, the importance of consistency becomes obvious.

At the same high level, the relationship between the GDPR itself and the Directive may also give rise to interesting legal questions. The line separating processing under the GDPR or under the Directive may at times become extremely thin. For example, a police station anywhere in the EU may soon discover that it has to apply both legal instruments: the GDPR while processing personnel or non-law enforcement-related files, and the Directive for the detection, prevention and combatting of crime. In the past, this distinction line, which corresponded broadly to the then first and third pillars respectively, remained blurred. González and Paepe (2008) characterized their relationship as 'conflictive'. In the cases of the first-generation EU PNR bilateral agreement and in the ultimately annulled Data Retention Directive, the Court was called upon to make the necessary adjustments (in joining cases C-317/04 and C-318/04, and Case C-301–06 respectively). In the future, given the intertwining of these two legal instruments, disputes and cases of conflict are expected to increase and will need to be addressed by sound theoretical analysis.

If viewed from a non-*stricto sensu* legal research point of view, the field of EU justice and home affairs is evidently faced with the fundamental contemporary question of reconciling privacy and security (Van Lieshout et al. 2013). Terrorist attacks across EU capitals have increased lawmaking efforts towards warranting security to EU citizens. These initiatives unavoidably conflict with the protection of fundamental rights and the right to data protection is found at the epicenter of this debate. As noted by McGinley and Parkes (2007), as early as 2007, 'the international exchange of information (both raw data and intelligence) has become a cornerstone of efforts to combat internal security threats faced by EU Member States'. The validity, however, of the relevant underlying assumption need not remain unchallenged: legal research could focus on evidencing whether data protection indeed constitutes a constraint upon effective security (combatting crime and counter-terrorism) policy or not. In any event, as given in Article 16 TFEU, the balance between adequate data protection and security needs to be struck carefully. This task is often far from straightforward. González (2012) notes that security has played different roles in EU personal data protection law, functioning both as a limit of its scope of application, whereby data processing concerning 'national security' is expressly excluded, and as a means to justify legitimate restrictions or modulations of otherwise basic data protection law. In the same context, the use of surveillance technologies for crime prevention and investigation purposes may lead to a 'perilous double shift' effect. As noted by Cocq and Galli (2013), surveillance technologies introduced in relation to 'serious crime' are increasingly used for the purpose of preventing and investigating 'minor' offenses, while at the same time surveillance technologies originally used for public order purposes in relation to 'minor' offenses are increasingly guided in the context of prevention and investigation of serious crime.

Main scholarly debates and future research avenues (second series of questions)

Agency-specific research in the field is always welcome – and should be considered interesting at all times, especially if placing all actors in the field under a common axis of analysis, as performed by Gutierrez Zarza (2015). In particular Europol and Eurojust already have a rich data protection history; important changes are under way and critical questions may arise with regard, for example, to supervision by the EDPS or their new substantive data protection regime. While other EU actors in the field may attract less attention, also given their sector-specific type of processing, the question of the adequacy of their data protection regime when compared to the Directive should provide an interesting field for legal research. Research findings in the recent past have not been encouraging in this regard. Boehm (2012: 256, 318) has duly noted the existence of a 'fragmented' and 'stagnating' data protection framework in the field versus increasing 'powers of the AFSJ agencies and OLAF and functionalities of the EU Information Systems'. This led her to highlight the need for a 'central supervisory authority' (Boehm 2012: 394). However, while external supervision is of course important, it would be equally important for legal research to focus on internal supervision as well: what, if anything, will replace the Europol and Eurojust internal Joint Supervisory Bodies when the new regime abolishes them?

In the same context, Article 16 TFEU requires that not only the ad hoc substantive data protection legal regime for each actor in the field be formulated and assessed, but also that this be done from the perspective of data subjects. The means of recourse in the event that one of the EU actors in the field infringes the right to data protection of individuals must become visible and accessible. When the law does not provide such clarity, as is the case today in the field, legal research should take over.

At member state level, it will evidently be interesting for legal researchers to examine how the Directive is implemented in their respective jurisdictions. As is the case also with the GDPR, the Directive allows for significant space for member state differentiation. Although inadvisable because it would ultimately contradict the Directive's own purpose to achieve harmonization across the EU, data protection history has shown that different approaches across the EU are in fact possible and attributable to different legal systems and cultures. However, legal research and the Commission should keep an open mind, so as to identify differences that go beyond the permitted level of local differentiation.

Finally, the specific data protection legal topics within the EU justice and home affairs field frequently provide fruitful areas of legal research. This is the case both with subject-specific new legal instruments, such as the EU PNR Directive, or, in the past, the Data Retention Directive, and with the EU's bilateral agreements with third countries in the field. Special topics such as profiling for law enforcement purposes (Custers *et al.* 2013) or the accessing of private sector data by law enforcement agencies (Goemans-Dorny 2012) also come to mind in this regard. The cooperation between the EU and the USA that spans several modalities in the EU justice and home affairs field in particular should provide a continuous and interesting topic for further research by data protection scholars. Despite the frequent lack of materials that may be characterized as restricted and therefore not be accessible to the public, there is always a lively interest in any new insight in a field that affects a great number of individuals, but which up until today remains largely undocumented.

While possible research topics of immediate use and concern are described above, the field will reach its research maturity once the legal framework has been firmly established and should be considered as settled, at least for the foreseeable future. Only then will researchers be able to finally focus on its actual application. Today, in essence, legal research struggles to formulate a clear and coherent picture with regard to the legal framework applicable each time; it is only reasonable that much less interest is vested in how exactly this legal framework is to be applied in practice. Once these issues have been resolved, legal researchers in the field may finally embark upon the perhaps more interesting questions that their colleagues focusing on the GDPR are already dealing with, meaning the use of new technologies in the field. The same new technologies referred to above with regard to the GDPR (Internet social networks, cloud computing, drones, the Internet of things) are also being used in the law enforcement context. However, up until today they have attracted very limited legal research interest. It is the authors' belief that once issues of the applicable legal framework have been addressed, legal research will be free to indulge itself in these, and, perhaps more relevant (from the data subjects' perspective), future research avenues.

Concluding remarks: data protection in the EU justice and home affairs field as a yet unexplored territory for legal research

The main understanding one derives after closer examination of the EU data protection policies in EU justice and home affairs is that this is a field in constant flux. It gained exponentially in importance following terrorist attacks across Europe. For more than fifteen years it never ceased to develop and change, either centrally or in its constituting parts. At the central level, the need for a standard-setting text was identified as early as 2008, but is hopefully only now on course to be achieved through the interplay of the Police and Criminal Justice Data Protection Directive and the successor of Regulation 45/2001. The relationship between these two instruments is expected to give rise to interesting research and perhaps even disputes and case law. As regards the constituting parts of the EU justice and home affairs field, a basic distinction needs to be made between EU and member state personal data processing. The former is faced with an incomprehensible, unjustifiably complex architecture whereby each single EU agency and body active in the field profits from its own data protection substantive law. Some harmonization is expected to be achieved at the member state level after May 2018, as per the Directive's requirements.

While what is mentioned above may illustrate a complex and fragmented legal environment that actively discourages legal research or even mere interest in the field, the authors wish to see the glass half-full: to their mind, the past fifteen years have been a fast-track process, from the birth of a new type of personal data processing at the national level towards, admittedly, a reluctant EU harmonization. Personal data processing for law enforcement purposes, at least as it is known today, was conceived following 9/11. Member states experimented with it, each at its own pace and with its own idiosyncrasies. Once it was established that this new type of processing was here to stay, the EU intervened and attempted to assume the central monitoring and rule-setting role. The legal ambiguity that we are perhaps still living in today is the hopefully short-term result of this worthy – at least to our mind – effort.

Bibliography

Argomaniz, J. (2009). When the EU is the 'Norm-taker': The Passenger Name Records Agreement and the EU's Internalization of US Border Security Norms. *Journal of European Integration*, 31(1), pp. 119–136.

Bellanova, R. and Duez, D. (2012). A Different View on the 'Making' of European Security: The EU Passenger Name Record System as a Socio-technical Assemblage. *European Foreign Affairs Review*, 17 (Special Issue), pp. 273–288.

Boehm, F. (2012). *Information Sharing and Data Protection in the Area of Freedom, Security and Justice*. New York: Springer.

Cocq, C. (2016). EU Data Protection Rules Applying to Law Enforcement Activities: Towards a Harmonised Legal Framework? *New Journal of European Criminal Law*, 7(3), pp. 263–276.

Cocq, C. and Galli, F. (2016). The Catalysing Effect of Serious Crime on the Use of Surveillance Technologies for Prevention and Investigation Purposes. *New Journal of European Criminal Law*, 4(3).

COM (2013a). 0534: Proposal for a Council Regulation on the Establishment of the European Public Prosecutor's Office.

COM (2013b). 0535: Proposal for a Regulation of the European Parliament and of the Council on the European Union Agency for Criminal Justice Cooperation (Eurojust).

Custers, B., Calders, T., Schermer, B. and Zarsky, T. (eds) (2013). *Discrimination and Privacy in the Information Society Data Mining and Profiling in Large Databases*. New York: Springer.

De Hert, P. (2015). The Right to Protection of Personal Data. Incapable of Autonomous Standing in the Basic EU Constituting Documents? *Utrecht Journal of International and European Law*, 31(80), pp. 1–4.

De Hert, P. and Papakonstantinou, V. (2009). The Data Protection Framework Decision of 27 November 2008 Regarding Police and Judicial Cooperation in Criminal Matters – Modest but not the Data Protection Text Everybody Expected. *The Computer Law & Security Review*, Vol. 25. Elsevier.

De Hert, P. and Papakonstantinou, V. (2014). The Data Protection Regime Applying to the Inter-agency Cooperation and Future Architecture of the EU Criminal Justice and Law Enforcement Area. European Parliament, Committee on Civil Liberties, Justice and Home Affairs.

De Hert, P. and Papakonstantinou, V. (2015). Repeating the Mistakes of the Past will do little Good for Air Passengers in the EU – The Comeback of the EU PNR Directive and a Lawyer's Duty to Regulate Profiling. *New Journal of European Criminal Law*, 6(2), pp. 160–165.

EDPS (2008). Preliminary Comments on COM(2008) 69 final, COM(2008) 68 final, COM(2008) 67 final.

Goemans-Dorny, C. (2012). Accessing Private-sector Data: The Need for Common Regulations for the Police. Data Protection in the Area of European Criminal Justice Today, ERA, Trier.

González Fuster, G. (2012). Security and the Future of Personal Data Protection in the European Union. *Security and Human Rights*, 4, pp. 331–342.

González Fuster, G. and Paepe, P. (2008). Reflexive Governance and the EU Third Pillar: Analysis of Data Protection and Criminal Law Aspects, in Guild, E. and Geyer, F., *Security versus Justice? Police and Judicial Cooperation in the European Union*. Farnham: Ashgate.

Gutierrez Zarza, A. (2015*). Exchange of Information and Data Protection in Cross-border Criminal Proceedings in Europe*. New York: Springer.

Hijmans, H. and Scirocco, A. (2009). Shortcomings in EU Data Protection in the Third and the Second Pillars, Can the Lisbon Treaty Be Expected to Help? *Common Market Law Review*, 46, 1485–1525.

Hornung, G. and Boehm, F. (2012). Comparative Study on the 2011 Draft Agreement between the United States of America and the European Union on the Use and Transfer of Passenger Name Records (PNR) to the United States Department of Homeland Security. Passau/Luxemburg, March 14.

McGinley, M. and Parkes, R. (2007). *Data Protection in the EU's International Security Cooperation: Fundamental Rights vs. Effective Cooperation?* SWP Research Paper No. 5. Berlin: Stiftung Wissenschaft und Politik.

O'Neill, M. (2010). The Issue of Data Protection and Data Security in the (Pre-Lisbon) EU Third Pillar. *Journal of Contemporary European Research*, 6(2), pp. 211–235.

Ripoll Servent, A. (2013). Holding the European Parlament Responsible: Policy Shift in the Data Retention Directive from Consulation to Codecision, *Journal of European Public Policy*, 20(7), pp. 972–987.

Ripoll Servent, A. and MacKenzie, A. (2012). The European Parliament as a 'Norm Taker'? EU–US Relations after the SWIFT Agreement. *European Foreign Affairs Review*, 17 (Special Issue), pp. 71–86.

Van Lieshout, M., Friedewald, M., Wright, D. and Gutwirth, S. (2013). Reconciling Privacy and Security. *Innovation: The European Journal of Social Science Research*, 26, pp.1–2.

15
EU HOME AFFAIRS AND TECHNOLOGY
How to make sense of information and data processing

Julien Jeandesboz

Introduction

The establishment and use of computerized systems for the collection, generation, exchange and analysis of information and personal data are a key part of how European Union (EU) home affairs are conducted today. The first of these networks, the Schengen Information System (SIS), was rolled out in 1995. Since then, the number and scope of home affairs computerized systems in operation and under consideration by the EU institutions has increased dramatically. A 2008 study found fourteen home affairs databases and information systems in operation, under development (the second-generation SIS and the Visa Information System, VIS), under consideration or adopted as a legislative proposal (Geyer 2008). In its first and to this day only overview of home affairs information management, the European Commission (2010) identified seventeen arrangements for collecting, generating, exchanging and analyzing information and personal data in operation, under implementation or consideration in the Area of Freedom, Security and Justice (AFSJ). The document identified four additional arrangements involving the exchange of information and personal data between the EU and third countries: three agreements on Passenger Name Record data (PNR) with Australia, Canada and the USA, and the EU–US agreement on the US Terrorist Finance Tracking Program (TFTP). The same document, finally, announced that the European Commission was planning legislative proposals on three additional information systems, and considering three more, for a grand total of twenty-seven measures. A 2012 study, using a slightly different methodology, came up with a more conservative total of twenty measures in operation, under implementation or consideration (Bigo *et al.* 2012).

The collection, generation, exchange and analysis of information and personal data is thus argued to have become an imperative in EU home affairs (Davidshofer *et al.* 2016). It has certainly become a key site of home affairs *politics* in the EU. A key stake in these politics is that the reliance on such systems involves an exponential growth in the volume of information on and personal data of EU- and non-EU citizens. As previous research has shown with regard to measures related to EU external border control, the SIS has over the past ten years contained around 900,000 individual records per year on persons stored for motives related to external border control, while the Entry/Exit System (EES) that is currently being examined as part of the revised 'smart borders package' would hold 167 million individual records after one year and 269 million after five years (Jeandesboz 2016; Jeandesboz *et al.* 2016). The EU PNR system that was adopted in April 2016 would generate more than 500 million such records a year (European Commission 2010: 17). Accordingly, concerns with data protection rights as well as the right to privacy, to effective remedies and human rights more broadly (Brouwer 2008), have become a key dimension of the home affairs politics of information and data processing, as shown in high-profile cases such as the adoption (and ultimate demise at the hands of the European Court of Justice) of the Data Retention Directive or the successive EU–US PNR and SWIFT agreements (e.g., Argomaniz 2009; De Goede 2012; De Hert and Papakonstantinou 2010; Ripoll Servent 2015).

The previous observations suggest that a basic, and central, research problem and task that students of EU home affairs have to deal with is to explain the proliferation of information and data processing schemes. How and why do such schemes multiply? Asking this question already implies that a straightforward explanation, namely that information and data processing measures constitute a functional response to a pre-existing 'security problem', is not necessarily the most convincing. Accordingly, this chapter explores how various strands of literature have dealt with the 'functionalist hypothesis'.

To what extent, furthermore, can we rely on generalist conceptual frameworks designed to account for a wide range of European integration outcomes, to provide explanations for the proliferation of home affairs information and data processing schemes? The chapter argues that while conventional explanations, focused in particular on the interplay between norms and interests, provide useful insights, they overlook the specific characteristics of these home affairs measures. As such, the survey of the literature developed in the following pages moves from conventional explanations to research that pays specific attention to the particulars of information and data processing as a way to 'make' and perform EU home affairs (e.g., Bellanova and Duez 2012). In particular, the chapter looks to research in the field of political sociology and science and technology studies (STS) for alternative and more tailored frameworks of analysis.

Finally, how does the proliferation of EU home affairs information and data processing schemes affect the people they target? Certainly, the aforementioned controversies over the rights of EU and non-EU citizens in the face of widespread and intensifying information and data processing speak to a broader concern, namely that these measures 'are giving rise to new sites of social power within, between and beyond Europe's nation states' (Loader 2002: 293). As Leese (2016) remarks, for instance, with regard to the 'smart borders' legislative package, information and data processing is part of broader attempts to govern individuals and populations in particular ways, especially as 'pre-emptive governance' (Broeders and Hampshire 2013). The chapter argues in this regard that most of the literature is focused on the production of policy and of specific measures, but does not really consider effects. The conclusion of the chapter suggests that this issue should be at the heart of further research on EU home affairs technology so that it can contribute to the study of the anchoring and effects of European integration in European societies (Favell and Guiraudon 2009; Fligstein 2008; Kauppi and Madsen 2008).

Before proceeding with the remainder of the discussion, a word should be said about terminology. In this chapter I refer to a variety of arrangements for the collection, exchange and analysis of electronic records between the authorities of EU member states and EU agencies (chiefly Europol and Frontex) as information and data processing schemes. There are three reasons for this choice. First, these arrangements are not necessarily all centralized databases as we would commonly imagine them, hence the qualification of 'schemes'. The most 'centralized' schemes such as the SIS and VIS comprise both a central unit (physically located in Strasbourg for both systems) and national systems. Others, such as the 'Swedish initiative' (Council of the EU 2006), are rather measures that regulate information and data exchanges between national authorities, or that organize the interoperability between separate computer networks. Second, the reference to processing is derived from data protection law, where processing refers to any operation or set of operations performed on personal electronic data, including collection, storage, transfer, analysis and so on. Third, the terminology used in this chapter includes the processing of personal data and 'information', insofar as not all the records involved in EU home affairs measures exclusively consist of the former. For instance, the European border surveillance system (Eurosur) established in 2013 carries a wide range of records, including geospatial data, information on vessels at sea or crew manifestos (Jeandesboz 2011; Bellanova and Duez 2016).

The chapter first discusses conventional approaches that focus on explaining EU home affairs information and data processing through mechanisms of norm incorporation and adaptation. It argues that such accounts are limited by a thin concept of actorness and norms, and are too generic to account for the substantial material-technical dimension of information and data processing. It then successively outlines alternative frameworks of analysis that rely on the notions of disposition and practice on the one hand, and of 'actant' on the other, to address these limitations.

Information and data processing as a security norm

The first set of explanations for the proliferation of information and data processing schemes adapts general conceptual frameworks used to account for European integration outcomes to the specific domain of home affairs. This concerns explanations that contrast between interests and norms. Information and data processing here constitutes a particular 'security norm', as Argomaniz (2009) argues in his rendering of the EU–US PNR agreement controversy. Following his and a subset of other studies that consider cases such as the EU–US agreement on SWIFT data (e.g., Ripoll Servent and MacKenzie 2012; Suda 2013), the proliferation of information and data processing schemes in EU home affairs is explained by mechanisms of norm internalization. EU policy-makers and lawmakers agree to and adopt measures such as EU–US agreements on PNR data and the transfer of financial data because they are subjected to norm promotion activities by the US authorities. The EU authorities are found to be 'norm-takers' and likely to be persuaded to adopt US norms with very few changes to their core characteristics under certain conditions: internal norm socialization within the EU institutions (particularly within the executive branch – Commission and Council – presented as closer to the US position), as well as a low degree of 'misfit' between the norm being promoted and wider EU 'meta-norms' (Ripoll Servent and MacKenzie 2012). The studies by Argomaniz as well as Ripoll Servent and MacKenzie find that EU norm-taking to US norm-making and promoting extends to norm 'mirroring' (Argomaniz 2009: 129–132) and 'incorporation' (Ripoll Servent and MacKenzie 2012: 75), insofar as the EU authorities have simultaneously sought to establish EU versions of such schemes: the EU PNR system adopted in April 2016, the EU Terrorist Finance Tracking System (TFTS) considered and eventually put to rest by the European Commission (2013). Suda (2013), on the other hand, finds that the internalization of information and data processing as a security norm is matched by EU norm assertiveness insofar as the EU authorities were able to amend US norms by inserting stronger data protection clauses into PNR and SWIFT agreements.

Explanations of information and data processing proliferation through norms (diffusion, promotion, internalization, adaptation) certainly challenge the functionalist hypothesis insofar as they show that the adoption of EU home affairs measures are mediated through the activation of formal and informal rules and expectations of appropriateness rather than constituting direct responses to pre-defined challenges and threats. Controversies over information and data processing schemes are then ultimately struggles over situated understandings of what constitutes a 'good' border security or counter-terrorism measure. Ripoll Servent and MacKenzie's study, and by extension Ripoll Servent's (2015) stand-alone work on these matters, further show that internalization depends on the availability of legitimization resources ('meta-norms') and the differential capacity of various EU actors to mobilize such resources. In other words, information and data processing has to be made legitimate.

This argument applies to occurrences of international (rather, transatlantic) norm diffusion, but also to measures that are 'domestic' to the EU. The adoption of the Data Retention Directive (DRD) in 2005 and in particular the European Parliament's endorsement of the measure, for instance, was a somewhat unexpected outcome given how much of an encroachment on the right to privacy and data protection it constituted and how wide a margin for maneuver it gave to member state authorities. The outcome can however be explained in terms of the European Parliament's conforming to a new set of procedural 'meta-norms', in this case the injunction for this institution to act in a more 'responsible' fashion in a context of it being granted more extensive co-decision powers in EU home affairs (Ripoll Servent 2015: 69–86). The DRD example also serves as a reminder that the adoption of contentious, 'bulk' information and data collection measures in the EU need not be assigned to the activities of external actors such as the US authorities. EU norm assertiveness is not exclusively tied to the promotion of liberal norms such as respect for the right to privacy or data protection, and does not necessarily constitute a counter-hegemonic move in the face of predominant US security norms (contra Suda 2013). In fact evidence shows that in many instances, information and data processing measures are adopted at the own initiative of EU actors (De Goede 2012) and have been a long-standing feature of EU home affairs (Bigo 1996). The DRD is one example, as are measures related to the surveillance of financial transactions (Amicelle 2011; De Goede 2012), or border security (e.g., Amoore and De Goede 2005; Broeders 2007; Broeders and Hampshire 2013; Brouwer 2008; Jeandesboz 2016).

Norms-focused explanations of information and data processing proliferation, in the meantime, are limited in two ways. First, a general claim leveraged at such explanations, in particular by the political sociology of European integration literature (e.g., Favell and Guiraudon 2009; Georgakakis and Weisbein 2010; Kauppi and Madsen 2008), is that they operate with a thin concept of both actorness, which is mostly bestowed on institutions rather than on individuals (Commission, Council, Parliament, even 'the EU'), and of norms, which are systematically opposed to interests (as in the separation of the logic of appropriateness and consequence). The claim is not always entirely warranted, but the point is that norms-focused explanations do not take the persons who 'embody' EU institutions, their (socially contextual) preferences and their (socially acquired) dispositions as a starting point for their analysis, and grant them explanatory power. The above-mentioned studies on the PNR and SWIFT cases see 'security norms' circulating from one EU institution to the other, but do not tell us why Commission or Council officials (rather, why some specific Commission or Council officials) are more disposed than other people speaking and acting on behalf of the EU to adopt and adapt norms coming from the USA. In these cases, it is also clear that normative and interest-based interactions are not separate. It can fit the 'specific interest' – that is, the contextual, localized rationality of a given actor or group of actors (Martin-Mazé 2015) – to act according to specific norms (even if those norms come from outside the EU), and changes in relative social positions can lead to reconsiderations of normative commitments (as in the change of 'meta-norms' surveyed by Ripoll Servent 2015). What a political sociology perspective adds to analyses of information and data processing in EU home affairs politics, as discussed in the following section, is therefore an explanation in terms of dispositions (to act, think, argue, speak in a specific way) and practices.

Second, norms-focused explanations may well be too generic to account for the specificities of information and data processing measures, which involve a substantial material-technical dimension. Norms-focused explanations take this material-technical dimension for granted: schemes such as the SIS, PNR or SWIFT data are there to be used by EU home affairs actors; they can be questioned and analyzed in relation to their normative fit or misfit, but they are not the focus of inquiry. This constitutes at the very least an empirical problem, given how much attention and time EU home affairs actors dedicate to debating and developing what may seem to be mere technicalities. This issue is discussed in the final section of this chapter before the conclusions.

Information and data processing as disposition and practice

A first alternative framework for understanding and explaining the proliferation of information and data processing in EU home affairs draws upon political sociology contributions to the study of security within critical approaches to security in Europe (c.a.s.e. collective 2006). The focus of these studies is on the routines and daily activities of actors and groups of actors involved in conducting security policies (Balzacq *et al.* 2010) and EU home affairs, rather than on the key decisions and decisive moments such as the adoption of the EU-US PNR or SWIFT agreements, or of the DRD. This approach is less about a 'return' to the individual (and in this sense not a return to classical behaviorism) than about understanding

> social phenomena as the product of an encounter (rarely conscious but played out in practice) between, on the one hand, (individual and collective) dispositions to act (*habitus*), which may be inherited, acquired through social and professional paths or offered by the position [held by a specific individual], and on the other hand, so-called relational contexts, which may be analysed under various forms, in organizations, institutions and fields.
>
> *(Georgakakis and Weisbein 2010: 95; emphasis in original)*

In other words, and in contradistinction with the views of sociological institutionalism, for instance, this approach holds that institutions are the *explanandum* rather than the *explanans*, what has to be explained by looking at the social sources of institutionalization rather than the explanation of social phenomena. To phrase this perspective in ways that are closer to the concerns of this chapter and volume, the consideration, adoption, development and use of information and data processing measures is considered as a practice, as a more or less routinized way of doing EU home affairs, which can be explained as an encounter between dispositions to act and specific contexts of action.

In his analysis of EU border control measures, Bigo (2014) sums up this approach by arguing that practices of control may be analyzed in terms of the 'patrimony of dispositions' of the actors positioned in the various 'social universes' that contribute to the shaping of EU home affairs. The notion of patrimony enables Bigo to adjust the concept of *habitus* (or system of dispositions) found in the sociology of Pierre Bourdieu by removing the assumption that dispositions are fixed and unchanging over time:

> On the contrary, the patrimony of dispositions insists on the strength and time of the actors' socialization by distinguishing between weak and strong systems of dispositions

and competences and by discussing their transposability in each case and context. Some dispositions are activated, others are inhibited, depending on the context or field in which they occur.

(Bigo 2014: 210)

In this perspective, information and data processing is not just proliferating because it is a norm, but because it is rooted in a set of professional habits and ways (including material ways) of doing security: these dispositions 'are activated – or not, as the case may be – by the use of specific technologies, and they determine the capacity to restrain the deployment of these technologies, to modulate them' (Bigo 2014: 210).

This approach to EU home affairs information and data processing draws attention to questions, sites and situations that are not usually investigated in the literature on EU home affairs. The pursuit of US-inspired security measures in EU home affairs, for instance, may be explained as emerging from interactions among officials embedded in transnational and transatlantic interpersonal networks, that are outside the control of a single institution, and actually reach out across institutional and geopolitical boundaries (Pawlak 2009). The persistence, against all odds, of measures such as the 'second-generation' SIS and the VIS, both systems that have been years in the making and have been heavily contested as their development was under way, may be explained by the continued relations between groups of policy-makers in the Council and the Commission that have their roots in the 'old days', legacy and ways of working and thinking about EU home affairs of the Schengen and third pillar cooperation (Parkins 2011). Part of the reason why so many information and data processing measures are produced by the European Commission today may be assigned to the long-standing existence, within the services of DG home affairs, of caretaker units dealing with the management of the Eurodac, SIS and later VIS systems, which were at some point the largest operational units within the European Commission, and whose work has now been largely outsourced to the eu-LISA agency (Jeandesboz 2016). Professional dispositions can also account for why, beyond the Brussels context, information and data processing intensive measures do not necessarily travel very well, as they encounter local ways of doing counter-terrorism, for instance (Bonelli and Ragazzi 2014).

Looking at the proliferation of information and data processing in EU home affairs politics in terms of dispositions and practices, then, allows for the reintroduction of a degree of socio-historical depth beyond the apparent novelty of each new policy outcome. It may explain why some actors are more disposed to accept the normative influence of US authorities, since this has been a major puzzle in the EU home affairs literature. It also recasts information and data processing measures not as a functional response to external stimulus, but as the result of entrenched ways of thinking about, doing and justifying home affairs policy. At the same time, this perspective considers the instruments of information and data processing themselves as part of the context and as a resource, without considering how they actively contribute to shaping policy. In this sense, they share a limitation with norms-focused approaches, which can be addressed by introducing analytical frameworks looking at information and data processing as instrument and actant.

Information and data processing as instrument and actant

There is a second alternative framework for understanding and explaining the proliferation of information and data processing in EU home affairs that ambitions to develop more precise accounts of the material-technical aspects of these measures, by mobilizing findings from the science and technology studies literature, and in particular those coming from actor-network and material-semiotic approaches.

The general rationale for such a focus is that scholarship tends to take the instruments of public policy for granted, as functional and pragmatic consequences of stated policy decisions, aims and goals. Of course, an instrument may be deemed 'flawed', as Bossong argues, for instance, about the EU Action Plan on Combatting Terrorism because 'it fostered rather than contained policy conflict' (Bossong 2008: 43), or ineffective, but the notion that policy instruments may generate their own effects has only recently started to be considered in EU studies, and even less so in studies of EU home affairs (for exceptions see Balzacq 2008; Wolff and Trauner 2014). Findings from the 'public policy instrumentation literature' (e.g., Kassim and Le Galès 2010; Lascoumes and Le Galès 2007) however suggest that such a perspective can add to our understanding of the 'tools' of EU policy, including information and data processing. The instrumentation literature holds two key arguments: that instrumentation 'reveals a (fairly explicit) theorization of the relationship between the governing and the governed' as 'every instrument constitutes a condensed form of knowledge about social control and ways of exercising it' and that 'instruments at work are not neutral devices: they produce specific effects, independently of the objective pursued (the aims ascribed to them), which structure public policy according to their own logic' (Lascoumes and Le Galès 2007: 3). Policy, in this sense, is as much a socio-technical as a socio-political space and the study of instrumentation involves looking at

> the set of problems posed by the choice and use of instruments [...] that allow government policy to be made material and operational [...] not only understanding the reasons that drive towards retaining one instrument rather than another, but also envisaging the effects produced by these choices.
>
> *(Lascoumes and Le Galès 2007: 4)*

Instrumentation approaches are uncommon in EU studies, but have experienced something of a development (e.g., Halpern (2010), Kassim and Le Galès (2010), and Barry and Walters (2003) offer a more pronouncedly Foucauldian take).

In relation to EU home affairs, Wolff and Trauner (2014) have advocated taking a dynamic look at EU migration policy instruments as 'living instruments' by outlining, for instance, how the framing of migration as a threat has contributed to the shaping of the EU readmission agreement instrument, but that the actual use of the instrument, especially by third-country authorities, may be hypothesized to feed back into and change the outlook of the policy (ibid.: 14). Balzacq (2008) examines information and data processing measures across the internal and external dimensions of EU home affairs, and argues that such instruments have 'securitizing effects'. PNR data processing, for example, may be seen as the concretization of a 'security norm', but it does have the practical effect of widening the scope of counter-terrorism measures by expanding suspicion to the entire category of travelers on EU-inbound or -outbound international flights. Approaching EU home affairs information and data processing through instrumentation, then, relates research in this field to studies of security and surveillance which find that such measures are not only about countering threats, but also embody and shape practices of governance and social control (e.g., Aradau and van Munster 2007; Bigo 2002; De Goede 2012; Huysmans 2006, 2011; Leese 2016).

A variant on the instrumentation approach that may be found in the literature draws upon science and technology studies, and in particular on actor-network/material-semiotics approaches (for a brief overview see Law 2008; Bellanova and Duez 2012: 110), for example, borrow from actor-network theory (A-NT) and argue that a key contribution of this approach is the notion of 'actant', which redefines agency as the ability to make a difference in a given situation or context (Akrich and Latour 1992: 259; Latour 2005). The notion proposes to study in the same fashion human agency and the agential effects of devices, instruments and technical systems broadly defined, insofar as they potentially all contribute to mediate action in a given context. Bellanova and Duez (2012) use the notion to study EU-US PNR controversies, and demonstrate that the 'norm-taker' dimension of the outcome is not the only relevant angle. In many ways, PNR as a security measure also operates on the back of a pre-existing 'actant' where PNR is mobilized for economic purposes by airline companies (conspicuously absent in norms-focused accounts), and therefore requires to be substantially modified before it can be translated into a 'security norm'. Investigating border control in Mauritania, Frowd (2014) similarly makes use of the notion of actant to query the way in which prescriptions about border control travel between the EU and sub-Saharan African countries. His focus on the material side of border control enables him to demonstrate how EU norms of integrated border management are repackaged with IOM technical specifications and devices, which are in turn filtered and mediated both by the local dispositions of Mauritanian border officers and the existing infrastructure of border checkpoints in the region. Bourne and colleagues (2015) look at scientific work supported by EU security research and development funding, and demonstrate that 'the laboratory' is an essential link in understanding how ideas about social control in EU home affairs measures are built into specific devices even before they are deployed as part of the implementation of a given policy measure.

Analyzing information and data processing as instrument and actant, then, supports the identification of important yet understudied or obfuscated sites where EU home affairs policies and politics play out. This framework shares with the political sociology perspectives discussed earlier an interest in daily activities and routines that contribute to shape, and to a large extent enable, the so-called 'commanding heights' and rarefied exchanges between élite political and bureaucratic actors in the Brussels context. Thinking of information and data processing as instrument and actant also contributes to challenging the functionalist hypothesis on EU home affairs, by showing that the 'tools' of this policy area embody and shape, before they are even deployed, assumptions about challenges and threats, as well as about power and social control.

Conclusion: the need to study the societal effects of home affairs information and data processing

In providing an overview of the key research problems, questions and contributions that tackle the relation between EU home affairs and technology, this chapter has moved from generic, arguably conventional explanations, to more tailored, alternative and more reflexive, conceptual frameworks. In passing, it has made the case for 'nudging' (Lapid 2001) research on EU home affairs in more epistemologically diverse directions. 'Thinking tools' (Leander 2008) such as dispositions, practices, instrumentation and actants enable research to ask a broader variety of questions from information and data processing measures beyond issues of appropriateness and consequence.

This kind of nudging is more than a matter of epistemology, however It also concerns the scope of the inquiries that are currently being conducted on EU home affairs. A majority of the research reviewed in this chapter examines and reflects the concerns, dispositions and practices of a select group of actors and institutions involved in the production of information and data processing measures. Even in dealing with the production of policy, this literature leaves some blind spots, which concern in particular interactions between the public and private sector, which as some show play a fundamental role in shaping regulatory measures (see Amicelle

(2011) on terrorist finance) and even in making up new markets (see Hoijtink (2014) on the European civil security market). In addition, the aforementioned research has very little to say about how these measures are used by law enforcement and security actors in their daily activities, and even less about their effects on European and other societies. In other words, there remains a vast field of inquiry that is left mostly untouched by studies on EU home affairs (a situation which in this regard is reflective of EU studies more generally). What happens to information and data processing measures when they travel outside of Brussels, are used by what the Commission and other agencies call 'end-users', and how they impact the lives of persons in Europe and elsewhere, then, remains largely out of sight.

On 'end-users', some suggest that EU agencies and professional networks operate as 'socialization platforms' (e.g., Carrapiço and Trauner (2013) on Europol, Horii (2016) on Frontex). In the meantime, we also know from students of European policing, for instance, that measures adopted in Brussels may travel uneasily and become focal points of contestation and adaptation in local circumstances, both in the EU and outside of it. Andersson (2014) highlights, for instance, how efforts by the EU and the member states to support the policing of the borders of sub-Saharan states, including by transferring technological means, are repurposed, made ambivalent and used by border control actors to leverage local social power. Pallister-Wilkins (2015) shows how the entanglement of humanitarian work and classical policing concerns at the Evros border between Greece and Turkey gets reinterpreted, formalized, and adopted as 'best practice' by Frontex officials in order to bring humanitarian activities in line with the agency's mandate. These contributions outline how the 'imperative' of adopting information and data processing that dominates discussions in the Brussels context may well not be reflective of either the making or the state of EU home affairs when they circulate to and from the European Quarter.

Research on the social effects of EU information and data processing measures is even thinner, and should be a key priority area. We know from legal studies that such measures have a significant effect on rights (including, but not limited to, the right to privacy), especially when they concern third-country nationals living in, traveling or planning to travel to the EU (Brouwer 2008). Recent court decisions such as Digital Rights Ireland and the DRD ruling (Guild and Carrera 2014) show that there is a degree of societal mobilization around the issue of mass data processing, namely of 'bulk' electronic surveillance. Studies of visa deliveries at Schengen consulates also show that the experiences of third-country nationals applying to travel to the EU are fundamentally affected by requirements such as the introduction of biometrics (e.g., Infantino 2016; Scheel 2013). These insights, however, remain fragmentary. This situation is a significant knowledge gap, ultimately, because with information and data processing, EU home affairs measures may well have the most measurable and significant impact upon the lives of both EU and non-EU citizens.

Bibliography

Akrich, M. and Latour, B. (1992). A Summary of a Convenient Vocabulary for Semiotics of Human and Nonhuman Assemblies. In Bijker, W. and Law, J. (eds) *Shaping Technology/Building Society: Studies in Sociotechnical Change*. Cambridge, MA: MIT Press.

Amicelle, A. (2011). Towards a 'New' Political Anatomy of Financial Surveillance. *Security Dialogue*, 42(2), pp. 161–178.

Amoore, L. and De Goede, M. (2005). Governance, Risk and Dataveillance in the War on Terror. *Crime, Law and Social Change*, 43(2–3), pp. 149–173.

Andersson, R. (2014). Hunter and Prey: Patrolling Clandestine Migration in the Euro-African Borderlands. *Anthropological Quarterly*, 87(1), pp. 119–150.

Aradau, C. and van Munster, R. (2007). Governing Terrorism through Risk: Taking Precautions, (un)Knowing the Future. *European Journal of International Relations*, 13(1), pp. 89–115.

Argomaniz, J. (2009). When the EU is the 'Norm-taker': The Passenger Name Records Agreement and the EU's Internalization of US Border Security Norms. *Journal of European Integration*, 31(1), pp. 119–136.
Balzacq, T. (2008). The Policy Tools of Securitization: Information Exchange, EU Foreign and Interior Policies. *JCMS: Journal of Common Market Studies*, 46(1), pp. 75–100.
Balzacq, T., Basaran, T., Bigo, D., Guittet, E-P. and Olsson, C. (2010). Security Practices. In Denmark, R.A. *International Studies Encyclopedia Online*. doi: 10.1111/b.9781444336597.2010.x.
Barry, A. and Walters, W. (2003). From EURATOM to 'Complex Systems': Technology and European Government. *Alternatives*, 28(3), pp. 305–329.
Bellanova, R. and Duez, D. (2012). A Different View on the 'Making' of European Security: The EU Passenger Name Record System as a Socio-technical Assemblage. *European Foreign Affairs Review*, 17(2), pp. 109–124.
Bellanova, R. and Duez, D. (2016). The Making (Sense) of EUROSUR: How to Control the Sea Borders? In Bossong, R. and Carrapiço, H. (eds) *EU Borders and Shifting Internal Security*. New York: Springer.
Bigo, D. (1996). *Polices en réseaux: l'expérience européenne*. Paris: Presses de Sciences Po.
Bigo, D. (2002). Security and Immigration: Toward a Critique of the Governmentality of Unease. *Alternatives*, 27 (Special Issue), pp. 63–92.
Bigo, D. (2014). The (In)securitization Practices of the Three Universes of EU Border Control: Military/Navy–Border Guards/Police–Database Analysts. *Security Dialogue*, 45(3), pp. 209–225.
Bigo, D., Carrera, S., Hayes, B., Hernanz, N. and Jeandesboz, J. (2012). *Evaluating Current and Forthcoming Proposals on JHA Databases and a Smart Borders System at EU External Borders*. Brussels: European Parliament (PE 462.513).
Bonelli, L. and Ragazzi, F. (2014). Low-tech Security: Files, Notes, and Memos as Technologies of Anticipation. *Security Dialogue*, 45(5), pp. 476–493.
Bossong, R. (2008). The Action Plan on Combating Terrorism: A Flawed Instrument of EU Security Governance. *JCMS: Journal of Common Market Studies*, 46(1), pp. 27–48.
Bourne, M., Johnson, H. and Lisle, D. (2015). Laboratizing the Border: The Production, Translation and Anticipation of Security Technologies. *Security Dialogue*, 46(4), pp. 307–325.
Broeders, D. (2007). The New Digital Borders of Europe: EU Databases and the Surveillance of Irregular Migrants. *International Sociology*, 22(1), pp. 71–92.
Broeders, D. and Hampshire, J. (2013). Dreaming of Seamless Borders: ICTs and the Pre-emptive Governance of Mobility in Europe. *Journal of Ethnic and Migration Studies*, 39(8), pp. 1201–1218.
Brouwer, D. (2008). *Digital Borders and Real Rights*. Leiden: Martinus Nijhoff.
Carrapiço, H. and Trauner, F. (2013). Europol and the EU's Fight against Organized Crime: Exploring the Potential of Experimentalist Governance. *Perspectives on European Politics and Societies*, 14(3), pp. 357–371.
c.a.s.e. collective (2006). Critical Approaches to Security in Europe: A Networked Manifesto. *Security Dialogue*, 37(4), pp. 443–487.
Council of the EU (2006). *Framework Decision 2006/960/JHA of 18 December 2006 on Simplifying the Exchange of Information and Intelligence between Law-enforcement Authorities of the Member States of the European Union*. OJ L386/89, 29.12.2006.
Davidshofer, S., Jeandesboz, J. and Ragazzi, F. (2016). Technology and Security Practices: Situating the Technological Imperative. In Basaran, T., Bigo, D., Guittet, E-P. and Walker, R.B.J. (eds) *International Political Sociology: Transversal Lines*. London: Routledge.
De Goede, M. (2012). The SWIFT Affair and the Global Politics of European Security: The SWIFT affair and European security. *JCMS: Journal of Common Market Studies*, 50 (2), pp. 214–230.
De Hert, P. and Papakonstantinou, V. (2010). The EU PNR Framework Decision Proposal: Towards Completion of the PNR Processing Scene in Europe. *Computer Law & Security Review*, 26, pp. 368–376.
European Commission (2010). *Overview of Information Management in the Area of Freedom, Security and Justice*. Brussels, COM(2010) 385 final.
European Commission (2011). *Impact Assessment Accompanying the Proposal for a European Parliament and Council Directive on the Use of Passenger Name Record Data for the Prevention, Detection, Investigation and Prosecution of Terrorist Offences and Serious Crime*.
European Commission (2013). *A European Terrorist Finance Tracking System (EU TFTS)*. Brussels, SEC(2011) 132 final.
Favell, A. and Guiraudon, V. (2009). The Sociology of the European Union. *European Union Politics*, 10(4), pp. 550–576.

Fligstein, N. (2008). *Euroclash: The EU, European Identity and the Future of Europe*. Oxford: Oxford University Press.
Frowd, P.M. (2014). The Field of Border Control in Mauritania. *Security Dialogue*, 45(3), pp. 226–241.
Georgakakis, D. and Weisbein, J. (2010). From Above and from Below: A Political Sociology of European Actors. *Comparative European Politics*, 8(1), pp. 93–109.
Geyer, F. (2008). *Taking Stock: Databases and Systems of Information Exchange in the Area of Freedom, Security and Justice*. Brussels: CEPS.
Guild, E. and Carrera, S. (2014). *The Political and Judicial Life of Metadata: Digital Rights Ireland and the Trail of the Data Retention Directive*. Brussels: CEPS.
Halpern, C. (2010). Governing Despite its Instruments? Instrumentation in EU Environmental Policy. *West European Politics*, 33(1), pp. 39–57.
Hoijtink, M. (2014). Capitalizing on Emergence: The 'New' Civil Security Market in Europe. *Security Dialogue*, 45(5), pp. 458–475.
Horii, S. (2016). The Effect of Frontex's Risk Analysis on the European Border Controls. *European Politics and Society*, 17(2), pp. 242–258.
Huysmans, J. (2006). *The Politics of Insecurity: Fear, Migration and Asylum in the EU*. London: Routledge.
Huysmans, J. (2011). What's in an Act? On Security Speech Acts and Little Security Nothings. *Security Dialogue*, 42(4–5), pp. 371–383.
Infantino, F. (2016). State-bound Visa Policies and Europeanized Practices: Comparing EU Visa Policy Implementation in Morocco. *Journal of Borderland Studies*, 31(2), pp. 171–186.
Jeandesboz, J. (2011). Beyond the Tartar Steppe: EUROSUR and the Ethics of European Border Control Practices. In Burgess, J.P. and Gutwirth, S. (eds) *A Threat Against Europe? Security, Migration and Integration*. Brussels: VUB Press.
Jeandesboz, J. (2016). Smartening Border Security in the European Union: An Associational Inquiry. *Security Dialogue*, 47(4), pp. 292–309.
Jeandesboz, J., Rijpma, J. and Bigo, D. (2016). *Smart Borders Revisited: An Assessment of the Commission's Revised Smart Borders Proposal*. Brussels: European Parliament (PE 571.381).
Kassim, H. and Le Galès, P. (2010). Exploring Governance in a Multi-level Polity: A Policy Instruments Approach. *West European Politics*, 33(1), pp. 1–21.
Kauppi, N. and Rask Madsen, M. (2008). Institutions et acteurs: rationalité, réflexivité et analyse de l'UE. *Politique européenne*, 25, pp. 87–113.
Lapid, Y. (2001). Identities, Borders, Orders: Nudging International Relations Theory in a New Direction. In Albert, M., Jacobson, D. and Lapid, Y. (eds) *Identities, Borders, Orders: Rethinking International Relations Theory*. Minneapolis: University of Minnesota Press.
Lascoumes, P. and Le Galès, P. (2007). Introduction: Understanding Public Policy through its Instruments – From the Nature of Instruments to the Sociology of Public Policy Instrumentation. *Governance*, 20(1), pp. 1–21.
Latour, B. (2005). *Reassembling the Social: An Introduction to Actor-network Theory*. Oxford: Oxford University Press.
Law, J. (2008). Actor Network Theory and Material Semiotics. In Turner, B. (ed.) *The New Blackwell Companion to Social Theory*. Oxford: Wiley-Blackwell. doi: 10.1002/9781444304992.ch7.
Leander, A. (2008). Thinking Tools. In Klotz, A. and Prakash, D. (eds) *Qualitative Methods in International Relations: A Pluralist Guide*. London: Routledge.
Leese, M. (2016). Exploring the Security/Facilitation Nexus: Foucault at the 'Smart' Border. *Global Society*, 30(3), pp. 412–429.
Loader, I. (2002). Governing European Policing: Some Problems and Prospects. *Policing and Society*, 12(4), pp. 291–305.
Martin-Mazé, M. (2015). Unpacking Interests in Normative Power Europe. *JCMS: Journal of Common Market Studies*, 53(6), pp. 1285–1300.
Pallister-Wilkins, P. (2015). The Humanitarian Politics of European Border Policing: Frontex and Border Police in Evros. *International Political Sociology*, 9(1), pp. 53–69.
Parkins, J. (2011). *The Difficult Road to the Schengen Information System II: The Legacy of 'Laboratories' and the Cost for Fundamental Rights and the Rule of Law*. Brussels: CEPS.
Pawlak, P. (2009). Network Politics in Transatlantic Homeland Security Cooperation. *Perspectives on European Politics and Society*, 10(4), pp. 560–581.
Ripoll Servent, A. (2015). *Institution and Policy Change in the European Parliament: Deciding on Freedom, Security and Justice*. Basingstoke: Palgrave Macmillan.

Ripoll Servent, A. and MacKenzie, A. (2012). The European Parliament as a 'Norm Taker'? EU–US Relations after the SWIFT Agreement. *European Foreign Affairs Review*, 17 (Special Issue), pp. 71–86.

Scheel, S. (2013). Autonomy of Migration Despite Its Securitisation? Facing the Terms and Conditions of Biometric Rebordering. *Millennium: Journal of International Studies*, 41(3), pp. 575–600.

Suda, Y. (2013). Transatlantic Politics of Data Transfer: Extraterritoriality, Counter-extraterritoriality and Counter-terrorism. *JCMS: Journal of Common Market Studies*, 51(4), pp. 772–788.

Wolff, S. and Trauner, F. (2014). The Negotiation and Contestation of EU Migration Policy Instruments: A Research Framework. *European Journal of Migration and Law*, 16(1), pp. 1–18.

16

EU CRIMINAL LAW

An expanding field for research, with some unchartered territories

Anne Weyembergh and Chloé Brière

Introduction

Contrary to other fields of EU law that were subject to European integration and initiatives since the very beginning of this enterprise, the field of criminal law was left relatively untouched by EU action for a long time. Thus, the field of EU criminal law has a 'recent existence' in research, emerging in the 1990s. It has since been the object of a booming development. In legal terms, the field of EU criminal law has been a privileged topic to analyze the numerous institutional evolutions that marked the EU treaty revisions between 1992 and 2009. In terms of substance, the content of EU actions in this field has also evolved substantially, and the European legislator has demonstrated its activism and dynamism in this field.

These developments are reflected in legal research and, to a lesser extent, in other disciplines such as political science. An ever-increasing number of scholars have described, analyzed, commented on and evaluated these evolutions, leading to numerous publications.

Two factors have fostered discussions and research synergies in EU criminal law. First, the European Criminal Law Academic Network[1] was created in 2004. It gathers experienced and junior academics and researchers who specialize in EU criminal law. Its missions include the promotion of research as well as the facilitation of collaboration and synergies between universities in this field. After ten years of existence, the network counts no fewer than 200 members and has contact points in all EU member states as well as in four non-EU countries (Switzerland, Norway, Iceland and Bosnia Herzegovina). The network organizes a high-level academic conference, a PhD seminar and a summer school every year. These events have contributed to creating a transnational community of junior and experienced researchers in the field of EU criminal law. The second factor resides in the increasing numbers of publications in this field in different EU languages (English, French, Spanish, German, Italian, etc.). More and more attention has been given to EU criminal law in journals specializing in EU law, such as the *Cahiers du droit européen* or the *Common Market Law Review*, or in national criminal law journals like the *Revue de Droit Pénal et de Criminologie* (Belgium). Specialized academic journals have also appeared over past decades, such as the *European Criminal Law Review*, the *New Journal of European Criminal Law* and *EuCrim*.

This chapter will present the main fields of research in EU criminal law and contains a review of the relevant literature. Before entering into more precise debates, it is worth mentioning that general textbooks covering both the institutional and substantial developments of EU criminal law have been published (Flore 2014; Kostoris 2015; Klip 2016; Mitsilegas 2016b). Other textbooks have addressed the issue in connection with justice and home affairs in general (Peers 2016) or international criminal law (Satzger 2012; Ambos 2014). This chapter will provide some examples of scholarly debates and research puzzles. The first section will examine the discussions in the institutional field and the second section will focus on specific substantive research on EU measures.

Evolution of the EU's competence and institutional framework

Since the emergence of EU activity in the field of criminal law, a large number of studies have focused on the evolution of its institutional framework, i.e., the distribution of competences between the EU institutions and the member states. This focus is logical, considering the evolving nature of this field, which has undergone no less than four main stages. Cooperation in criminal matters began as purely intergovernmental cooperation taking place outside of the EC institutional framework. The Maastricht Treaty integrated cooperation in criminal matters into the EU's institutional framework, more precisely into the third pillar, where it kept a predominant intergovernmental nature. The Amsterdam Treaty then introduced a revised third pillar, moving it closer to EC features but remaining intergovernmental in nature. Finally, the Treaty of Lisbon abolished the third pillar and communitarized police and judicial cooperation in criminal matters (albeit with the persistence of some intergovernmental features). Each of these stages and constitutional reforms has given rise to specific studies focusing on the added value of the reforms and the new institutional balances introduced, and evaluating these developments (e.g., for the Lisbon Treaty – Acosta Arcarazo and Murphy 2014; Peers 2008; Mitsilegas 2016a).

The allocation of competences among the member states and their national authorities on the one hand, and the EU and its institutions or bodies on the other hand, has also been the subject of numerous analyses and reflections. Due to the close links between criminal justice and national sovereignty, some fundamental principles of EU law have been of particular importance and interest. This is the case, for instance, with the principle of subsidiarity, which has a special regime in the field of EU criminal law due to the enhanced role granted to national parliaments in its control. Many researchers have used this principle as a lens to examine the opportunity and legitimacy of EU action in criminal matters (e.g., Miettinen 2015; Öberg 2015; De Hert and Wieczoreck 2012; Herlin-Karnell 2012).

The institutional developments mentioned above have also had an impact on the instruments at the disposal of the EU legislator for enacting criminal rules. The legislator has had the possibility of relying on instruments of increasing effectiveness (Lazowski and Kurcz 2006). Third-generation instruments (i.e., directives and regulations) have a binding character and a degree of detail which cannot be compared with that of previous generations' instruments, such as joint actions and conventions (first generation) or framework decisions, decisions and conventions (second generation). The availability of more integrated instruments has substantially changed the relationship between EU criminal law and national criminal law, reinforcing the impact of EU criminal law upon national legislation.

Furthermore, the institutional developments have gone hand in hand with the evolution of the Court of Justice's jurisdiction over EU criminal law (i.e., Weyembergh and Braum 2009; Giudicelli-Delage and Manacorda 2010). As a consequence, the number of cases relating to EU criminal law has constantly increased and the Court has become an essential player in this field. Its case law covers almost all aspects of EU criminal law, such as the interpretation of secondary instruments or the delicate question of the legal basis. This latter aspect is of particular importance for the institutional dimension of EU criminal law, and its relevance is reflected in academic literature through regular columns (e.g., de Biolley and Weyembergh in *Cahiers de Droit européen*) and numerous case notes/analyses.

Many of these case notes have addressed the first case (Case C-176/03) in which the Court was called to solve a conflict of legal basis between the first and third pillar (e.g., White 2006; Vervaele 2006). In that case, the Commission sought (and obtained) the annulment of a Framework Decision on the protection of the environment through criminal law, adopted on the basis of a third pillar provision. The Court ruled that when the application of effective, proportionate and dissuasive criminal penalties by national authorities is an essential measure for combatting serious environmental offenses, the Community may take measures which relate to the criminal laws of the member states to ensure that the rules it lays down on environmental protection are fully effective (par. 48). The measures envisaged should thus have been adopted on the basis of the Community's competence in environmental matters and thus on a provision of the first pillar. The entry into force of the Lisbon Treaty has led to new types of conflicts on a legal basis, and once again the first judgment of the ECJ in this area (C-43/12) has been discussed by both EU criminal lawyers (Vavoula 2016) and EU constitutional lawyers (Szwarc 2015). The case concerned the adoption of a directive aimed at facilitating the cross-border exchange of information on road safety-related traffic offenses. While the Commission proposed its adoption on the basis of the provision on transport policy (Art. 91 (1) TFEU), the Council considered that its adoption should be based on the provision on police cooperation (Art. 87 TFEU). The Court gave reason to the Commission's request for annulment, considering that in respect of both its aims and content, the Directive was a measure to improve transport safety and should have thus been adopted on the basis of Article 91 (1) (c) TFEU. More generally, the abolition of the optional jurisdiction of the ECJ gave a new impetus to the role of the Court, for instance, via the interpretation of EU secondary instruments such as the European Arrest Warrant (EAW).

Concurrent with the progressive communautarization, two other trends have attracted scholars' attention. First, researchers have focused on the increase in participation 'à la carte' and the growing variable geometry in the area of EU criminal justice. This is particularly true with regard to the specific status of three member states, i.e., Ireland, the United Kingdom, and Denmark (e.g., Hinarejos *et al.* 2012; Labayle 2013; Spencer 2016), but attention has also been devoted to the possibility of resorting to enhanced cooperation with regard to specific EU criminal law instruments, especially the EPPO (Schutte, in Erkelens *et al.* 2015). Second, the attribution of increasing competences to the EU in the field of EU criminal law, including those introduced by the Lisbon Treaty, has also had an impact on EU external relations (Cremona 2011; Monar 2012; Brière 2016; Konstadinides 2016). Scholars have discussed the use of the specific legal basis contained in the former third pillar for the conclusion of Mutual Legal Assistance agreements with third countries (e.g., Mitsilegas 2003; Brodowski 2011) and the external actions carried out by EU agencies (e.g., Surano 2012). Others have compared the work of the EU and the Council of Europe in criminal law and have addressed their mutual influences (e.g., Politi and Galli 2013).

These institutional issues and evolutions are not without links to the substance of EU criminal law. Several examples may be provided to illustrate their impact.

The successive Treaty amendments have led to an increasing Europeanization of the field of criminal law, which has in turn impacted the content of national criminal law and the fundamental principles of modern criminal law. For example, some authors have noted the influence of the ECJ's case law on the interpretation of the *ne bis in idem* principle (e.g., Weyembergh 2013b; Lelieur-Fischer 2005; Vervaele 2013), a principle – also known as double jeopardy – that forbids prosecuting or convicting a person twice for the same crime, including in transnational situations. Other authors have proposed new theoretical frameworks for grasping the content of these fundamental principles in EU criminal law (e.g., on the principle of legality see Peristeridou 2015). The issues of coherence and legitimacy are also regularly addressed (Manifesto on European Criminal Policy 2011; Manifesto on European Criminal Procedural Law 2013; Wieczoreck 2016).

The institutional evolution also impacted the content of EU criminal law, particularly due to the role of the European Parliament, which with the introduction of the Lisbon Treaty became co-legislator in the field. Although limited legal research has addressed its influence in a comprehensive manner, legal scholars have highlighted on occasion its influence on the research of specific fields of EU criminal law: the influence of the EP has been noticed, for instance, in the increased level of sanctions foreseen for perpetrators of human trafficking (Weyembergh and Brière 2013), in the insertion of a ground for refusal based on fundamental rights in the EIO Directive (Armada 2015), and during the negotiations on the Directive on the presumption of innocence and the right to be present at trial (Cras and Erbežnik 2016).

One could consider that there is room for improvement in this field of research, i.e., analyzing the interactions between the evolution of the institutional framework of EU criminal law and its content. Although the link is often made, its analysis remains fragmentary and there is a lack of transversal and systematic reflection on this crucial issue. Taking again the example of the evolution of the EP's role in criminal matters, to our knowledge there is no systematic in-depth legal research on the changes brought to the content of EU criminal law, which is attributable to the new role of the Parliament as co-legislator (but see Mitsilegas and Vavoula 2015).

Substance of EU criminal law

The content of EU criminal law has been the object of abundant literature. For clarification purposes, we will try to classify them by different research topics. As a consequence of the evolution of the institutional framework and the dynamism of the EU legislator in this field, many researchers have highlighted the clear evolution in the content of EU law in this field. Their comments have stressed the evolution towards mechanisms of cooperation representative of a higher degree of legal integration. These mechanisms have indeed become increasingly distant from 'classic' mechanisms of cooperation such as those developed in the field of international cooperation or under the auspices of the Council of Europe (e.g., Vermeulen et al. 2012; Vernimmen-Van Tiggelen et al. 2009). The instruments implementing the principle of mutual recognition or the joint investigation teams, for instance, aim at considerably simplifying and accelerating cooperation procedures. They substantially affect the classic principle of the national territoriality of criminal law and impact the exercise of national sovereignty by national authorities. This evolution and other prospects such as the establishment of a European Public Prosecutor's Office have led some authors to compare the developments in EU criminal law with federal systems, for example the USA (e.g., Willems 2016; Gómez-Jara Díez 2015). Others have addressed the existence and/or desirability of a EU criminal policy, i.e., the use of criminal law legislation to prevent and respond to crime (e.g., De Bondt 2012; Miettinen 2013).

The vast majority of studies carried out in the field of EU criminal law have focused on specific aspects of the construction of a EU area of criminal justice.

Some studies have analyzed the principle of mutual recognition, which was launched in 1998 (Suominen 2011). Certain transversal issues have attracted particular attention, such as mutual trust (De Kerchove and Weyembergh 2005; Vermeulen 2014; Mitsilegas 2016b) and all the questions it raises both at the EU and national level (Guild 2006) in terms of its fundaments, legitimacy and potential conflict with fundamental rights. Other studies have focused on secondary instruments implementing the Mutual Recognition principle, such as the European Arrest Warrant (Bot 2009; Klimek 2015; Cartier 2005), probation (Flore et al. 2012) or the European Investigation Order (EIO) (Bachmaier Winter 2010, 2015; Gless 2015; Ruggeri 2014). Conflicts of jurisdiction have also attracted scholars' attention (Vermeulen et al. 2012; Caiero 2010; Böse et al. 2013; see also the research project led by Ligeti et al. (2014)). Concerning EU agencies/bodies such as the EJN or Eurojust, which have been set up to support cross-border judicial cooperation, only a few studies have been conducted (e.g., Suominen 2008; Weyembergh 2011, 2013a; Luchtman and Vervaele 2014). By contrast, a lot more has been written on the European Public Prosecutor's Office (EPPO). This is, in a way, logical, considering that the EPPO was initially a scientific proposal presented by academics in the famous '*corpus juris*' (e.g., Delmas-Marty 1997; Delmas-Marty and Vervaele 2000; Cour de Cassation 2010; Zwiers 2011; Erkelens et al. 2015; Manacorda 2015). Another factor explaining its success relates to the changes its establishment brought about in terms of national sovereignty, i.e., the move from horizontal to vertical cooperation. It has been an important source of inspiration for researchers, since it created many hopes but also disillusionment. Furthermore, although reflections on EU criminal law have often been based on comparative analyses of national criminal laws and systems, such comparisons have multiplied in the context of the reflections on the EPPO (see Delmas-Marty and Vervaele (2000) among others, as well as the research project 'Eurojustice, Rethinking European Criminal Justice': Ligeti 2012, forthcoming; Perrodet 2001).

Concerning the approximation of criminal legislation, many publications have addressed transversal issues such as their functions (for an example of the link between MR and approximation, see Thunberg Schunke (2013), and for a discussion on the importance of approximation for the success of MR, see Weyembergh (2004) and Weyembergh and Galli (2013)). Other studies are more specific and focus on the approximation of either substantive or procedural criminal law. They address these issues in a general way (their evolution, gaps and imbalances) (e.g., Asp 2012, 2016), or on specific issues (Blomsma (2012) on mens rea, i.e., the mental element of crime, the intention and/or knowledge of wrongdoing) or instruments (Spronken (2010) on the letter of rights; Ruggeri (2015) on procedural guarantees in EU criminal law; Caiero (2015) on procedural safeguards).

Police cooperation has been relatively neglected in legal literature. When compared to other aspects of EU criminal law, publications on police cooperation are quite scarce (e.g., Bergström and Cornell 2014; Aden 2015), and many focus on Europol (Darnanville 2002; De Moor 2012). Academics from other scientific backgrounds (e.g., political science) have published more about police cooperation (Bigo 1996; Occhipinti 2003). The reasons for such an imbalance are unclear. One may consider that this form of cooperation presents fewer theoretical questions, since it relies on more traditional forms of exchange of information, and that this field, which is not as developed as the field of judicial cooperation, is less diversified. However, there has been a growing interest in the exchange of information and data protection over the past ten years (e.g., Gutwirth and De Hert 2012; De Busser 2009).

Finally, some studies have gone beyond a focus on either judicial or police cooperation in criminal matters and have addressed the developments in EU criminal law in specific criminal fields such as money laundering (Stessens 2008), cyber crime (Summers et al. 2014), or terrorism (O'Neill: 2012; Murphy 2015; Auvret-Finck 2010; Galli and Weyembergh 2012).

Regardless of the specific aspect addressed, researchers have often stressed the importance of ensuring balanced EU criminal law. This was the focus of the European Criminal Law Academic Network's tenth Anniversary Conference, held in Brussels on April 25 and 26, 2016. This event was an opportunity to reflect on the different balances to be struck, such as the balance between diversity and unity, security and freedom (sword and shield functions of criminal law) or police and justice. In the legal literature, the need to ensure the adequate protection of fundamental rights has received particular attention. In this respect, the limits of mutual recognition and mutual trust have been extensively discussed. An important trigger for this strand of literature was the ECJ's ruling in *Melloni*, in which the Court excluded the application of national constitutional standards of fundamental rights protection concerning judgments *in absentia* because of the existence of commonly agreed EU standards contained in a Framework Decision. Comments on this case have been somewhat contradictory: they have either supported the Court's ruling, relying on the importance of the primacy of EU law, or criticized it for lowering the level of fundamental rights protection granted by other sources of law, such as national constitutional law.

Finally, the links, similarities and/or divergences of EU criminal law with other fields of EU law have been examined. Many studies have, for instance, focused on the comparison between EU criminal law and migration and asylum law. This can be explained by the fact that both fields belong to the Area of Freedom, Security and Justice and are often interconnected, as is illustrated by the following examples. In both fields, the issue of mutual trust among EU member states is crucial, and some of the solutions elaborated in one field may be transposed to the other. This was the case, for instance, with the rebuttable presumption of respect for fundamental rights in the field of asylum introduced by the *NS* judgment, which was later 'transposed' in the *Caldararu and Aryanosi* case with regard to the possibility of refusing the execution of a EAW owing to bad detention conditions (Meijers Committee 2011; Bribosia and Weyembergh 2016). Some criminal areas which have been subject to EU instruments aiming at approximating national criminal law are linked to migration issues. For instance, this is the case in the smuggling of migrants, and to a lesser extent the trafficking of human beings (Guild and Minderhoud 2006). Other studies are also paying attention to the issue of border controls, as these controls are considered essential for fighting crime and especially terrorism (Mitsilegas 2011).

In addition, the comparison between EU criminal law and other aspects of EU law extend to domains that are not part of the AFSJ. This is the case for studies comparing EU criminal law with internal market law: the principle of mutual recognition is indeed present in both domains, albeit with potentially different content (e.g., Ouwerkerk 2011; Janssens 2013). Authors have, for instance, compared the understanding/content of the principle in these two fields, notably to highlight their similarities and differences. Other academics have conducted research on the criminal law dimension of competition law (Bailleux, in Galli and Weyembergh 2014), addressing how this field that has long been regarded as pertaining to the domain of administrative law, but now integrates elements of criminal law, such as the severity of penalties imposed for breaches of competition law.

Conclusions

When analyzing the legal literature on the development of EU integration in the field of criminal law, one witnesses important diversity. Whereas some scholars follow a descriptive approach and pursue the objective of untangling the mechanisms/factors leading to the evolution of EU criminal law, others follow a more normative approach, seeking to promote certain solutions or norms to the EU institutions and member states. Diversity is also present, for instance, regarding the added value of the developments in EU criminal law (the opinions expressed have been either positive, critical or mixed). Finally, a distinction may be drawn from the methodology followed: some legal scholars conduct fundamental research focusing on principles and/or abstract reasoning, while others conduct more empirical research, including interviews with practitioners in order to grasp the challenges they face in negotiating, adopting or implementing EU criminal law, and to address recommendations to the EU institutions. The very diverse positions and approaches among legal scholars may be partially explained by the growing interest in the field of EU criminal law. In that regard, one may regret that this growing interest concerns mostly legal scholars, since there is a lack of multidisciplinary studies through which other scientific disciplines would complement legal research. This would be particularly interesting for analyzing the increasing influence of the EP in criminal matters, since political scientists would undoubtedly help in unveiling dynamics of influence that are less detectable through legal analysis.

However, there remain topics or fields that require further investigation and constitute avenues for future research, such as police cooperation, the cooperation between EU agencies and bodies (Eurojust, Europol and OLAF) or the areas described below.

Although the external dimension of the EU criminal area has become increasingly necessary for addressing today's security challenges, legal research remains limited in this field. The changes introduced by the Lisbon Treaty have not yet been comprehensively analyzed. EU relations with third countries, including those with which the EU has concluded MLA agreements (such as Japan), have been relatively neglected. The same is true for EU relations with other organizations active at the international, regional or subregional levels. Research on the cooperation between the EU and the CoE in criminal matters, for instance, remains quite fragmentary, as does the research on the relationship between the case law of the ECJ and the ECHR. Similarly, the role played by the EU on the international scene (e.g., its capacity to influence the content of international criminal law instruments) is not covered. In this domain, there is a lack of studies addressing comparative regionalism in criminal matters, as both EU and non-EU scholars have failed to compare the different integration processes in this field in Europe, Asia or South America.

More research should be conducted in order to highlight all the delicate and complex legal questions raised by the blurring boundaries among legal disciplines, especially between administrative and criminal law. Another research gap lies in the links and comparisons between judicial cooperation in criminal matters and civil matters. These last two domains would be particularly interesting to analyze, since EU criminal law is often considered a very specific field of EU law. Comparative analysis with other fields of EU law offers an opportunity to measure the specificity of EU criminal law. Such comparison may eventually help determine whether this specificity has not been somehow over-estimated, as this field may present more similariaties with other fields of EU law than was initially envisaged.

Finally, more practical issues should be addressed in order to further enhance research in the field of EU criminal law. Initially, and in the framework of the third pillar, access to sources was particularly problematic. A clear and progressive improvement may be witnessed. This is partially due to the evolution of the institutional framework and the adoption of general rules concerning access to EU documents, as well as to the conduct of private initiatives such as the Statewatch's JHA Archive (1976–2000).[2] Nevertheless, improvements are still required in certain fields. There is, for instance, no database where researchers can consult national case law linked to EU criminal law, which limits the conducting of comparative research. Another gap concerns the lack of reliable criminal statistics on issues such as the number of investigations, prosecutions, convictions, or the recourse to MR instruments. For the collection of these statistics, national rules (and methodologies) are of crucial importance. There is no harmonization in this field, which prevents reliable comparison among countries. Furthermore, when the collection of data is carried out at the EU level, it is often done on an occasional basis, such as through the exercise of mutual evaluations or the assessment of the implementation of an instrument or agreement. There is no continuity in the collection of information. This renders scientific research particularly difficult, but also particularly interesting, since scholars may discover unexplored territories.

Notes

1 Available at www.eclan.eu (accessed April 14, 2017).
2 Available at www.statewatch.org/semdoc/jha-archive.html (accessed April 14, 2017).

Bibliography

Acosta Arcarazo, D. and Murphy, C.C. (2014). *EU Security and Justice after Lisbon and Stockholm*. Oxford: Hart Publishing.
Aden, H. (2015). *Police Cooperation in the European Union under the Treaty of Lisbon: Opportunities and Limitations*. Baden-Baden: Nomos.
Ambos, K. (2014). *Internationales Strafrecht: Strafanwendungsrecht, Völkerstrafrecht, Europäisches Strafrecht, Rechtshilfe; ein Studienbuch*. Munich: Beck.
Armada, I. (2015). The European Investigation Order and the Lack of European Standards for Gathering Evidence: Is a Fundamental Rights-based Ground for Refusal the Solution? *New Journal of European Criminal Law*, 8.
Asp, P. (2012). *The Substantive Criminal Law Competence of the EU*. Juridiska Fakultetens Skriftserie No. 79.
Asp, P. (2016). *The Procedural Criminal Law Competence of the EU*. Juridiska Fakultetens Skriftserie No. 84.
Auvret-Finck, J. (2010). *L'Union européenne et la lutte contre le terrorisme*. Brussels: Larcier.
Bachmaier Winter, L. (2010). *European Investigation Order for Obtaining Evidence in the Criminal Proceedings* (ZIS 9).
Bachmaier Winter, L. (2015). Transnational Evidence: Towards the Transposition of the Directive 2014/41 Regarding the European Investigation Order in Criminal Matters. *EuCrim*, 2, pp. 47–59.
Bergström, M. and Cornell, A.J. (2014). *European Police and Criminal Law Cooperation*. Oxford: Hart Publishing.
Bigo, D. (1996). *Polices en réseaux: l'expérience européenne*. Paris: Presses de Sciences Po.
Blomsma, J. (2012). *Mens rea and defences in European criminal law*. Cambridge: Intersentia.
Böse, M., Meyer, F. and Schneider, A. (2013). *Conflicts of Jurisdiction in Criminal Matters in the European Union*, Vols I–II. Baden-Baden: Nomos.
Bot, S. (2009). *Le mandat d'arrêt européen*. Brussels: Larcier.
Bribosia, E. and Weyembergh, A. (2016). Confiance mutuelle et droits fondamentaux: 'Back to the future'. *Cahiers de droit européen*, 52(II), pp. 469–521.
Brière, C. (2016). *EU's Policy in the Fight against Trafficking in Human Beings, A Representative Example of the Challenges Caused by the Externalisation of the AFSJ*. Doctoral thesis, ULB-UNIGE.
Brodowski, D. (2011). Judicial Cooperation between the EU and Non-member States. *New Journal of European Criminal Law*, 2(2), pp. 21–44.
Caiero, P. (2010). Jurisdiction in Criminal Matters in the EU: Negative and Positive Conflicts, and Beyond. *Kritische Vierteljahresschrift für Gesetzgebung und Rechtswissenschaft*, 93(4), pp. 366–379.
Caiero, P. (2015). *The European Union Agenda on Procedural Safeguards for Suspects or Accused Persons: The 'Second Wave' and its Predictable Impact on Portuguese Law*. Universidade de Coimbra: Instituto Jurídico.
Cartier, M.E. (2005). *Le mandat d'arrêt européen*. Brussels: Bruylant.
Cour de Cassation (2010). *Quelles perspectives pour un ministère public européen?* Paris: Dalloz.
Cras, S. and Erbežnik, A. (2016). The Directive on the Presumption of Innocence and the Right to Be Present at Trial. *EuCrim*, 1, pp. 25–34.
Cremona, M. (2011). The EU External Action in the JHA Domain, A Legal Perspective. In Cremona, M., Monar, J. and Poli, S. (eds), *The External Dimension of the EU's AFSJ*. Brussels: P.I.E. Peter Lang.
Darnanville, H.M. (2002). *Europol*. Presses universitaires du Septentrion.
Delmas-Marty, M. (1997). *Corpus Juris Introducing Penal Provisions for the Purpose of the Financial Interests of the European Union*. Paris: Economica.
Delmas-Marty, M. and Vervaele, J. (2000). *The Implementation of the Corpus Juris in the Member States*, 4 vols. Antwerp: Intersentia.

De Bondt, W. (2012). *Need for and Feasibility of an EU Offence Policy*. Antwerp-Apeldoorn: Maklu.
De Busser, E. (2009). *Data Protection in EU and US Criminal Cooperation: A Substantive Law Approach to the EU Internal and Transatlantic Cooperation in Criminal Matters between Judicial and Law Enforcement Authorities*. Antwerp-Apeldoorn: Maklu.
De Hert, P. and Wieczoreck, I. (2012). Testing the Principle of Subsidiarity in EU Criminal Policy – The Omitted Exercise in the Recent EU Documents on Principles for Substantive European Criminal Law. *New Journal of European Criminal Law*, 3(3), pp. 394–411.
De Kerchove, M. and Weyembergh, A. (2005) *La confiance mutuelle dans l'espace pénal européen*. Ed. de l'Université de Bruxelles.
De Moor, A. (2012). *Europol, Quo Vadis? Critical Analysis and Evolution of the Development of the European Police Office*. Antwerp-Apeldoorn: Maklu.
Erkelens, L.H., Meij, A.W.H. and Pawlik, M. (2015). *The European Public Prosecutor's Office: An Extended Arm or a Two-headed Dragon?* The Hague: T.M.C. Asser Press.
Eurojustice, Rethinking European Criminal Justice (2006). Research Project funded by OLAF and coordinated for the year 2006–2007 by the Max-Planck-Institut für ausländisches und internationales Strafrecht, Freiburg.
Flore, D., Honhon, A. and Maggio, J. (2012). *Probation Measures and Alternative Sanctions in the European Union*. Cambridge: Intersentia.
Flore, D. (with the collaboration of Stéphanie Bosly) (2014). *Droit pénal européen* (2nd edn). Brussels: Larcier.
Galli, F. and Weyembergh, A. (2012). *EU Counter-terrorism Offences*. Ed. de l'Université de Bruxelles.
Galli, F. and Weyembergh, A. (2014). *Do Labels Still Matter? Blurring Boundaries between Administrative and Criminal Law*. Ed. de l'Université de Bruxelles.
Giudicelli-Delage, G. and Manacorda, S. (2010). *Cour de justice et justice pénale en Europe*. Paris: LGDJ.
Gless, S. (2015). Grenzenlos fischen? – Die Europäische Ermittlungsanordnung. In Grafl, C., Klob, B., Reindl-Krauskopf, S. and Winter, C. (eds), *Globalisierte Kriminalität – globalisierte Strafverfolgung?* Frankfurt: Verlag für Polizeiwissenschaft.
Gómez-Jara Díez, C. (2015). *European Federal Criminal Law*. Cambridge: Intersentia.
Guild, E. (2006). *Constitutional Challenges to the European Arrest Warrant*. Nijmegen: Wolf Legal Publishers.
Guild, E. and Minderhoud, P. (2006). *Immigration and Criminal Law in the EU*. Leiden: Martinus Nijhoff.
Gutwirth, S. and De Hert, P. (2012). *European Data Protection: In Good Health?* Amsterdam: Springer.
Herlin-Karnell, E. (2012). *The Constitutional Dimension of European Criminal Law*. Oxford: Hart Publishing.
Hinarejos, A., Spencer, J.R. and Peers, S. (2012). *Opting Out of EU Criminal Law: What is Actually Involved?* University of Cambridge, Faculty of Law, CELS.
Janssens, C. (2013). *The Principle of Mutual Recognition in EU Law*. Oxford: Oxford University Press.
Klimek, L. (2015). *European Arrest Warrant*. Geneva: Springer.
Klip, A. (2016). *European Criminal Law: An Integrative Approach* (3rd edn). Cambridge: Intersentia.
Konstadinides, T. (2016). EU Law and International Cooperation in Criminal Matters: A Tale of Legal Competence and Political Competency. In Mitsilegas, V., Bergström, M. and Konstadinides, T. (eds), *Research Handbook on EU Criminal Law*. Cheltenham: Edward Elgar.
Kostoris, R.E. (2015). *Manuale di procedura penale europea*. Guiffrè.
Labayle, H. (2013). 'Within You, Without You': 'l'opt-out' britannique en matière d'entraide repressive. *Europe*, 23(2), pp. 6–11.
Lazowski, A. and Kurcz, B. (2006). Two Sides of the Same Coin? Framework Decisions and Directives Compared. In Eeckhout, P. and Tridimas, T. (eds), *Yearbook of European Law*. Oxford: Oxford University Press.
Lelieur-Fischer, J. (2005). *La règle ne bis in idem, Du principe de l'autorité de la chose jugée au principe d'unicité d'action repressive* (thesis defended in 2005). Thèse pour le Doctorat en Droit (nouveau régime). Université Panthéon-Sorbonne, Paris.
Ligeti, K. (2012). *Towards a Prosecutor for the European Union – Volume 1: A Comparative Analysis*. Oxford: Hart Publishing.
Ligeti, K. (forthcoming). *Towards a Prosecutor for the European Union – Volume 2: Draft Rules of Procedure*. Oxford: Hart Publishing.
Ligeti, K., Klip, A. and Vervaele, J.A.E. (2014). *Prevention and Settlement of Conflicts of Exercise of Jurisdiction in Criminal Law*. Research project funded by the European Law Institute (November 2014 to February 2017).
Luchtman, M. and Vervaele, J. (2014). European Agencies for Criminal Justice and Shared Enforcement (Eurojust and the EPPO). *Utrecht Law Review*, 10(5), pp. 132–150.

Manacorda, S. (2015). *Le contrôle judiciaire du Parquet européen: Nécessité, Modèles, Enjeux*. Paris: Société de Législation Comparée.
Manifesto on European Criminal Policy (2011). First published in *ZIS*, pp. 697–747, updated in *European Criminal Law Review* (2011), pp. 86–103.
Manifesto on European Criminal Procedure Law (2013). First published in *ZIS*, pp. 412–446.
Meijers Committee (2011). *The Principle of Mutual Trust in European, Asylum, Migration and Criminal Law: Reconciling Trust and Fundamental Rights*. Utrecht: FORUM, Institute for Multicultural affairs.
Miettinen, S. (2013). *Criminal Law and Policy in the European Union*. Abingdon: Routledge.
Miettinen, S. (2015). *The Europeanization of Criminal Law: Competence and its Control in the Lisbon Era*. University of Helsinki, Faculty of Law.
Mitsilegas, V. (2003). The New EU–USA Cooperation on Extradition, Mutual Legal Assistance and the Exchange of Police Data. *European Foreign Affairs Review*, 8: pp. 515–536.
Mitsilegas, V. (2011). Human Rights, Terrorism and the Quest for 'Border Security'. In Pedrazzi, M., Viarengo, I. and Langs, A. (eds), *Individual Guarantees in the European Judicial Area in Criminal Matters*. Brussels: Bruylant.
Mitsilegas, V. (2016a). *European Criminal Law after Lisbon*. Oxford: Hart Publishing.
Mitsilegas, V. (2016b). *EU Criminal Law* (2nd edn). Oxford: Hart Publishing.
Mitsilegas, V. and Vavoula, N. (2015). Criminal Law: Institutional Rebalancing and Judicialization as Drivers of Policy Change. In Trauner, F. and Ripoll Servent, A. (eds), *Policy Change in the Area of Freedom, Security and Justice: How EU Institutions Matter*. London: Routledge.
Monar, J. (2012). *The External Dimension of the EU's Area of Freedom, Security and Justice, Progress, Potential and Limitations after the Treaty of Lisbon*. Stockholm: SIEPS (2012: 1).
Murphy, C.C. (2015). *EU Counter-terrorism Law*. Oxford: Hart Publishing.
Öberg, J. (2015). Subsidiarity and EU Procedural Criminal Law. *European Criminal Law Review*, 5(1), pp. 19–45.
Occhipinti, J.D. (2003). *The Politics of EU Police Cooperation, Toward a European FBI?* Boulder, CO: Lynne Rienner.
O'Neill, M. (2012). *The Evolving EU Counter-terrorism Legal Framework*. Abingdon: Routledge.
Ouwerkerk, J. (2011). *Quid Pro Quo: A Comparative Law Perspective on the Mutual Recognition of Judicial Decisions in Criminal Matters*. Cambridge: Intersentia.
Peers, S. (2008). EU Criminal Law and the Treaty of Lisbon. *European Law Review*, 33(4), pp. 507–529.
Peers, S. (2016). *EU Justice and Home Affairs Law, Volume II*. Oxford: Oxford University Press.
Peristeridou, C. (2015). *The Principle of Legality in EU Criminal Law*. Antwerp: Intersentia.
Perrodet, A. (2001). *Etude pour un ministère public européen*. Paris: LGDJ.
Politi, E. and Galli, F. (2013). Union européenne et Conseil de l'Europe: enrichissement mutuel ou coexistence conflictuelle? In Flaesch-Mougin, C. and Rossi, L.S. (eds), *La dimension extérieure de l'espace de Liberté de Sécurité et de Justice de l'Union Européenne après le Traité de Lisbonne*. Brussels: Bruylant.
Ruggeri, S. (2014). *Transnational Evidence and Multicultural Inquiries in Europe*. New York: Springer International.
Ruggeri, S. (2015). *Human Rights in EU Criminal Law*. New York: Springer International.
Satzger, H. (2012). *International and European Criminal Law*. Oxford: Hart Publishing.
Spencer, J.R. (2016). The UK and EU Criminal Law: Should We Be Leading, Following or Abstaining? In Mitsilegas, V., Alldridge, P. and Cheliotis, L. (eds), *Globalisation, Criminal Law and Criminal Justice*. Oxford: Hart Publishing.
Spronken, T. (2010). *An EU-wide Letter of Rights*. Antwerp: Intersentia.
Stessens, G. (2008). *Money Laundering, A New International Law Enforcement Model*. Cambridge: Cambridge University Press.
Summers, S., Schwarzenegger, C., Ege, G. and Young, F. (2014). *The Emergence of EU Criminal Law, Cybercrime and the Regulation of the Information Society*. Oxford: Hart Publishing.
Suominen, A. (2008). The Past, Present and Future of Eurojust. *Maastricht Journal of European and Comparative Law*, 15(2), pp. 217–234.
Suominen, A. (2011). *The Principle of Mutual Recognition in Cooperation in Criminal Matters*. Universitas Bergensis.
Surano, L. (2012). L'action extérieure d'Eurojust. In Dony, M. (ed.), *La dimension externe de l'espace de liberté, de sécurité et de justice au lendemain de Lisbonne et de Stockholm: un bilan à mi-parcours*. Ed. de l'Université de Bruxelles.
Szwarc, M. (2015). Do the Pillars of the European Union Still Exist? *ECons.LR*, 11, pp. 357–372.

Thunberg Schunke, M. (2013). *Whose Responsibility? A Study of Transnational Defence Rights and Mutual Recognition of Judicial Decisions within the EU*. Antwerp: Intersentia.

Vavoula, N. (2016). Exchanging Information on Road Traffic Offences: A Measure of Police Cooperation or Transport Policy? Case Note on C-43/12 Commission v Parliament and Council. *New Journal of European Criminal Law*, pp. 113–122.

Vermeulen, G. (2014). De mythe van wederzijds vertrouwen en wederzijdse erkenning in de EU. In Pauwels, L. and Vermeulen, G. (eds), *Update in de criminologie VII*. Antwerp-Apeldoorn: Maklu.

Vermeulen, G., de Bondt, W. and Ryckman, C. (2012). *Rethinking International Cooperation in Criminal Matters in the EU*. Antwerp-Apeldoorn: Maklu.

Vernimmen-Van Tiggelen, G., Surano, L. and Weyembergh, A. (2009). *L'avenir de la reconnaissance mutuelle en matière pénale dans l'Union européenne*. Ed. de l'Université de Bruxelles.

Vervaele, J.A.E. (2006). The European Community and Harmonization of the Criminal Law Enforcement of Community Policy. *Eucrim*, 3–4, pp. 87–92.

Vervaele, J.A.E. (2013). Ne Bis In Idem: Towards a Transnational Constitutional Principle in the EU? *Utrecht Law Review*, 9(4), pp. 211–229.

Weyembergh, A. (2004). *L'harmonisation des législations: condition de l'espace pénal européen et révélateur de ses tensions*. Ed. de l'Université de Bruxelles.

Weyembergh, A. (2011). The Development of Eurojust: Potential and Limitations of Art. 85 TFEU. *New Journal of European Criminal Law*, 2, pp. 75–99.

Weyembergh, A. (2013a). An Overall Analysis of the Proposal for a Regulation on Eurojust. *EUCrim*, 4, pp. 75–99.

Weyembergh, A. (2013b). Le principe *non bis in idem*: une contribution essentielle de la CJUE. In *The Court of Justice and the Construction of Europe: Analyses and Perspectives on Sixty Years of Case-law*. The Hague: TMC Asser Press.

Weyembergh, A. and Braum, S. (2009). *Quel contrôle juridictionnel pour l'espace pénal européen?* Ed. de l'Université Libre de Bruxelles.

Weyembergh, A. and Brière, C. (2013). L'Union européenne et la traite des êtres humains. In Bernard, D., Cartuyvels, Y., Guillain, C., Scalia, D. and van de Kerchove, M. (eds), *Fondements et objectifs des incriminations et des peines en droit européen et international*. Limal: Anthémis.

Weyembergh, A. and Galli, F. (2013). *Approximation of Substantive Criminal Law in the EU*. Ed. de l'Université de Bruxelles.

White, S. (2006). Harmonisation of Criminal Law under the First Pillar. *European Law Review*, 31(1), pp. 81–92.

Wieczoreck, I. (2016). *The Legitimacy of EU Criminal Law*. Doctoral thesis, ULB-VUB.

Willems, A. (2016). Extradition on the Two Sides of the Atlantic: The U.S. Model as Blueprint for the European Arrest Warrant? *Criminal Law Forum*, 27(4), pp. 443–493.

Zwiers, M. (2011). *The European Public Prosecutor's Office, Analysis of a Multilevel Criminal Justice System*. Antwerp: Intersentia.

17
JUDICIAL COOPERATION IN CIVIL MATTERS
Coming of age?

Eva Storskrubb and Anna Wallerman

Introduction

Transnational trade and employment often lead to cross-border disputes in civil matters. The actors in such disputes are consumers, small and medium-sized entrepreneurs and businesses, employees, large multinational corporations as well as family members. These disputes may concern faulty consumer goods, large-scale sale of goods contracts, employment relationships, debt collection and family relationships such as divorce. The common element is the cross-border setting, implying that the parties are from separate member states. Alternatively, other factors may entail that the dispute has a cross-border element. The establishment of the EU policy and corresponding competence on judicial cooperation in civil matters may thus be viewed as a consequence of, or necessity for, the success of the Union's internal market. The Union's measures taken under this legal basis, today Article 81 TFEU, have collectively become so significant that some commentators, partly normatively and partly performatively, talk about the establishment of a 'fifth freedom' – the free movement of judgments (see, e.g., Crifò 2009). This chapter will explore the limits to and development of that freedom.

The chapter is divided into four sections. First, a brief overview of the development of the policy area is conducted. The central debates that have arisen in the context of the policy area are presented in the second section. The third section consists of a literature review linking the main paradigms to debates in the scholarly writing. The concluding section looks to the future, reflecting upon avenues for further research and highlighting some developments that are yet to be analyzed.

Historical evolution and key instruments

The importance of cooperation in civil justice matters was, to some extent, foreseen already in the original Treaty of Rome in 1957. That treaty, however, only referred limited matters to the realm of intergovernmental cooperation and did not create any supranational competence. This led to a limiting of legislative progress. Two important cross-border conventions are the exception: the Brussels Convention of 1968 on international jurisdiction and the recognition and enforcement of judgments and the Rome Convention of 1980 on the applicable law for contractual disputes. At the same time, the civil procedural rules of member states remained unharmonized but on a case-by-case basis subject to requirements of equality and effectiveness introduced in the case law of the CJEU.

Although the Maastricht Treaty in 1992 introduced justice and home affairs, including cooperation in civil matters, within the third pillar of its new pillar structure, the cooperation remained intergovernmental and developed only gradually. Significant change came with the 1999 Treaty of Amsterdam, which introduced a competence for judicial cooperation in civil matters into the first pillar (then Article 65 TEC). The competence was conditioned by any measures having to be necessary for the proper functioning of the internal market and have cross-border implications. Furthermore, the competence was to be exercised under a special legislative procedure, echoing the field's intergovernmental past by providing that the Council adopt legislation by unanimity, the Parliament merely having the right to be consulted and the Commission sharing its right of initiative with the member states. In addition, the jurisdiction of the European Court of Justice (CJEU) was circumscribed. These institutional irregularities have been gradually removed by the Treaties of Nice (as regards the legislative procedure) and Lisbon (as regards the jurisdiction of the CJEU), although the unanimity requirement in the Council and the consultation role of the Parliament still applies in family matters. The Treaty of Lisbon also marginally widened the scope of the Union competence by changing the condition of necessity for the proper functioning of the Common Market to an impetus for Union measures under such circumstances. Since the entry into force of the Treaty of Lisbon, the civil justice legal basis is found in Article 81 TFEU.

In the literature, the legislative measures enacted under Article 81 TFEU have been divided into two categories or generations (Hess 2009; Kramer 2011) or three strands (Storskrubb 2008). The first-generation measures include private international law measures in the classical sense, i.e., measures aiming to address the particular problems of coordination occurring in international litigation, rather than aiming to introduce common or harmonized procedural rules. In this first generation of measures, the Brussels I Regulation (44/2001 now 1512/2012) on jurisdiction and on the recognition and enforcement of judgments, which replaced the above-mentioned Convention, is often considered the flagship. Indeed, it is essential for the creation of the free movement of judgments. Other measures include the Rome I and II Regulations (864/2007 and 593/2008) on applicable law in contractual respectively non-contractual disputes, the Service Regulation (1393/2007) on the service of documents and the Evidence Regulation (1206/2001) on cooperation between courts for the purposes of the taking of evidence. In addition, several measures have been specifically enacted for various types of cross-border family law disputes: the Brussels IIa Regulation (2201/2003) dealing with matters of divorce and parental responsibility, the Maintenance Regulation (4/2009), the Succession Regulation (650/2012), the Rome III Regulation dealing with the law applicable to divorce as well as the Property Regulations (1103/2016 and 1104/2016, not yet applicable at the time of writing) on property disputes for marriages and registered partnerships respectively.

The second-generation measures are those that go beyond private international law as it is traditionally and narrowly construed. These measures create common, free-standing procedures applicable throughout the Union in cross-border matters and existing in parallel to the domestic procedures of the member states. The measures of this generation include the Payment Order Procedure and in particular the more elaborate Small Claims Procedure (1896/2006 and 861/2007 respectively, both now amended by 2015/2421), which were greeted as a 'major step' in the harmonization of civil justice within the Union (Kramer 2008). That step appears, however, to have been one of principled rather than practical importance. Use of the regulations remains modest, although there are variations among the member states (Hess 2016a; Crifò 2016). The latest second-generation measure applies from January 2017, namely the European

Account Preservation Order (655/2014). The family law measures cannot be considered to fall fully in the second generation and create specific European procedures. However, some include such elements and show a deepening of cooperation beyond traditional private international law, for example by creating a European-wide certificate of succession.

In addition to the two identified generations of measures, a third category or strand of measures has been identified – so-called 'overarching measures' (Hartnell 2002; Storskrubb 2008). These measures, which are often (but not exclusively) of a soft-law character, seek to promote the smooth functioning of the other measures by facilitating cooperation, encouraging dialogue and mutual learning, supporting research and exchanges, as well as creating practical tools. The EU institutions have hoped and aimed for the development of a mutual judicial culture (The Stockholm Programme – An open and secure Europe serving and protecting citizens [2010] OJ C 115/1). These overarching measures include the European Judicial Network (Decision 470/2001 amended by 568/2009), as well as the online information site the European Judicial Atlas and Handbooks on how the measures work that will all, in the future, be available on the European e-Justice portal that is currently under development (the Multiannual European e-Justice Action Plan 2014–2018 [2014] OJ C 182/2). In addition, the EU has financially supported research and exchanges via specific funding programs – the current one being the Justice Programme for 2014–2020 (Regulation 1382/2013 based on which the Commission adopts annual implementing decisions). Further, the EU supports, encourages and coordinates judicial training (see, e.g., Council Conclusions [2014] OJ C 443/7, European Parliament Resolution [2013] OJ C 251E/42 as well as annual reports of the Commission).

In sum, it is fair to say that the policy area has picked up speed and is becoming increasingly important in the Union judicial landscape. It has also expanded beyond the traditional concepts of transborder civil justice cooperation. However, success cannot be measured solely in legislative activity, and some of the instruments enacted in the policy field have yet to reach their hoped-for uptake and effectiveness. Furthermore, formidable challenges still lie ahead in this area which is considered to be closely connected to member state sovereignty, given that the judicial system belongs traditionally to the core structure of a state (Andersson 2006). These pressing challenges are explored below.

Effective enforcement or judicial protection?

The major debates in the civil justice field of the EU may all be understood in the context of a balance of interests between, on the one hand, the effectiveness of the internal market and the real possibilities of free movement according to the treaties, and, on the other hand, concerns for the level and quality of civil justice and the rights of individuals. This distinguishes the field from many other areas of Union law where individual rights and free movement tend to go hand in hand and the EU institutions are most often perceived as protectors of individual rights (Zetterquist 2008). It is no coincidence that the breaking point between these positions occurs in relation to the policy areas that fall within the political program of creating an Area of Freedom, Security and Justice (AFSJ). The debate may also be interpreted as a sign of the increased completeness and maturity of the Union legal system. As more issues are included in the Union *aquis*, it is natural that the balancing of interests increasingly becomes an internal matter arising within Union law and policy rather than as a vertical tug of war between Union and member states.

The debate has centered around two possible means of integration and of ensuring effective free movement of judgments: (1) the principle of mutual recognition predicated on mutual trust between the member states' courts and legal systems; and (2) the possibility of harmonization of civil procedure. Notably, the means of integration are not mutually exclusive, albeit that in the civil justice field the first means of integration has been the main tool used by the EU institutions thus far.

The complex nature of mutual recognition and mutual trust

In its pure form, mutual recognition entails that a judgment delivered in one member state may be enforced directly in another member state without an interim control procedure or a possibility of refusal. The goal of full mutual recognition lies at the heart of the civil justice policy area and is key to the creation of an area of free movement of judgments (see the Mutual Recognition Programme [2001] OJ C 12/1). The question of mutual trust becomes crucial in order to make mutual recognition successful; mutual trust is a prerequisite for the realization of mutual recognition and free movement of judgments. In the latest recast of the Brussels I Regulation, the Commission attempted to realize the ambition of full mutual recognition by completely abolishing interim procedures and refusal grounds (COM(2010) 748 final). This proved to be politically impossible and the end result was a compromise according to which the interim control procedure was removed, but the member state of enforcement is still allowed to refuse enforcement on the same grounds of refusal as before, including grounds of public policy, if a party brings such a claim and is successful. This may be considered a sign of the continued lack of trust between the judicial systems in the Union or of an understanding that safeguards are still needed in individual cases (*inter alia* Kramer 2013; Storskrubb 2015, 2016a).

The concept of mutual trust has been imported to the AFSJ from the internal market context, but its transplantation has not been seamless. Critics have questioned the appropriateness of the method, as there is clearly a difference between commercial goods and services and a judicial decision. It is uncertain if the member states are really prepared to substitute their own standards for that of another member state in the field of justice (Lavenex 2007). Furthermore, the transplantation appears to have included only the aim of full realization of the principle of mutual recognition, but not many of the safeguards that accompany that principle in the area of free movement of goods. In the latter field, mutual trust is facilitated by harmonization and common minimum requirements, as well as structural features such as cooperation mechanisms that decrease the risk of one member state issuing or approving of standards that are likely to be unacceptable to the other member states. In addition, member states have, under certain circumstances, the opportunity to not recognize and accept goods from other member states (*inter alia* Storskrubb 2016a).

When it comes to judicial decisions, however, the principles of mutual recognition and trust have not been coupled with any significant minimum harmonization of member state domestic procedures. The measures adopted on the basis of Article 81 have been limited to matters with cross-border elements. Even though the Commission, following the Stockholm program, acknowledged that mutual trust requires mutual minimum standards and an understanding of the different legal (procedural) traditions in Europe, there have been few attempts made towards mutual standards or harmonization (Storskrubb 2016b). This means that the requirement of mutual trust is arguably more far-reaching in the AFSJ than in the context of the internal market – even though member states' desire to exert control over procedural matters may be assumed to be greater in the former field than in the latter.

In addition, the CJEU has gone so far as to state that member states are obliged to trust each other and to assume that procedures in other member states fulfill fundamental rights. Checks are permitted only in exceptional cases. The first difficult cases heard by the CJEU in the AFSJ context on mutual recognition show that mutual trust and the upholding of fundamental rights are often presumed (Kramer 2013; Mitsilegas 2012; Requejo Isidro 2016). Upholding a presumption of trust, however, means that mutual trust becomes a fiction rather than an expression of real trust, often referred to as blind trust rather than binding trust (Nicolaïdis 2007). Arguably, this presumption should be rebuttable and mutual trust should instead be linked to the actual and true protection of fundamental rights in the singular case; otherwise the system can quickly serve to feed distrust instead of trust (Mitsilegas 2012). It has further been argued that mutual trust should not simply be presumed in the EU and cannot be a panacea that solves the difficult questions in the AFSJ. Mutual trust cannot be imposed in a top-down manner, nor can it be created by force (Storskrubb 2016b; Weller 2015). The imposition of such requirements may instead contribute to a legitimacy crisis (Requejo Isidro 2016; Storskrubb 2017).

Underlying this debate are several competing and legitimate interests. The creditor's right to collect the judgment debt and to access justice in the case of the debtor's unwillingness or inability to pay weighs in the balance on the same side as the Union interest of free movement. These interests are facilitated by a broad recognition and enforcement of judgments. However, the judgment debtor's right to access to justice and a fair trial, specifically the right not to have a judgment enforced against it which does not respect its right to be heard, weighs on the other side of the scale. Neither of these rights can be wholly discarded. Hence any system of mutual trust must ensure that both interests are furthered by balancing them in an appropriate manner (Storskrubb 2017). Furthermore, the member state of enforcement has an interest in upholding its own *ordre public* and not contributing to the enforcement within its jurisdiction of judgments incompatible to that order. Indeed, if it does so it may be in breach of the European Convention on Human Rights (ECHR) and the EU Charter of Fundamental Rights (EUCFR). However, following the case law of the CJEU, which permits deviations from the principle of mutual trust only in exceptional circumstances, member states may be bound to presume that other member states respect those rights. Thereby the principle of mutual trust may, unless the trust is real and warranted, place member states between the 'Scylla of distrust and the Charybdis of procedural unfairness' (Kohler 2016).

The broad critique of the presumption of mutual trust in the context of all the fields of the AFSJ has recently seen a potentially more nuanced approach in the case of C-404/15 PPU *Pál Aranyosi and Robert Căldăraru* (EU:C:2016:198) concerning the field of criminal cooperation. In the civil justice field, difficult cases have arisen in the family law field, in particular in cases related to child abduction. The rules in the Brussels IIa Regulation related to the return of child enforcement have most direct enforcement rules for valid reasons of wanting to deter abduction. However, these cases of direct enforcement have shown that it may be difficult for the member state courts to actually trust one another. Many of the other civil justice measures include certain limited safeguards against direct enforcement. In particular, the case law of the CJEU with regard to the second-generation measures that create harmonized procedures suggests a greater need for such safeguards. In contrast to the cases in which the CJEU has required a presumption of trust, in these cases the CJEU has emphasized that the safeguards in the Regulations are intended to protect the judgment debtor and its fundamental right to be heard (see joined cases C-119/13 *eco cosmetics* and C-120/13 *Raiffeisenbank* EU:C:2014:2144; C-300/14 *Imtech Marine* EU:C:2015:825; and C-511/14 *Pebros Servizi* EU:C:2016:448). This emphasis has led to the refusal of enforcements. Thus, in the civil justice field there is also some nuance in the approach that gives priority to the fundamental procedural right to be heard over mutual recognition and mutual trust (Storskrubb 2017). To retain some safeguards is arguably necessary to foster trust and is also important in protecting the fundamental rights of the individual litigants.

Is harmonization a viable solution?

Another strategy to support and complement mutual trust is further harmonization. Article 6 ECHR and Article 47 EUCFR, providing for a right of access to justice and a fair trial, may be held to form a basic level of common understanding in relation to procedural rights. A greater degree of harmonization may, according to some scholars, facilitate or enhance mutual trust by ensuring that procedural safeguards apply throughout the Union (Dougan 2004; Commission 2013). It should, however, be noted that procedural rules must be considered in their institutional context. The underlying assumption often appears to be that it is differences in *procedures*, rather than in *judicial cultures, resources or knowledge*, that are the root of distrust. However, this may not be the case.

The harmonization debate is divided into two parts: one concerning the constitutional viability of the project, and the other concerning its political or legal desirability. The first debate, which has occupied both legislative and academic communities, concerns the scope of EU competence provided by Article 81 and in particular its 'cross-border' criterion. Arguments for a broad or narrow construction of the cross-border criterion have been abundant in literature, and have also been the subject of disagreement among the institutions of the Union (Storskrubb 2015, 2016b). Some commentators argue that a broad interpretation is not excluded. It has been pointed out that discrepancies in the member states' civil justice systems may in themselves constitute obstacles to free movement, which would mean that any harmonizing measure would have cross-border implications, at least indirectly (Dougan 2004; van Rhee 2012). However, both in scholarly writing and in legislative practice, a narrower and more literal interpretation of the cross-border criterion has prevailed. This debate also points to the politically sensitive nature of matters related to justice and the fact that the cross-border definition has become the forum for a power struggle between the Commission, whose mandate would be broadened by a more extensive interpretation, and the member states in the Council that resist such an inroad in a field commonly considered to be close to state sovereignty. The precise remit of 'cross-border' has also been reasoned differently in two reports prepared for the European Parliament. One report argues that a 'limited cross-border element' is enough to trigger the Article 81 competence (Radev 2015). The other report notes that only situations where the parties are domiciled in different member states qualify as cross-border within the meaning of that article (Hess 2016b: 5). The latter view appears to be closer to legislative reality.

The debate about if, how and to what extent the harmonization of civil procedure within the Union is desirable is older than the competence in Article 81. The first more ambitious attempt at a common European code of civil procedure was made by the so-called Storme Commission, which produced a set of model rules of civil procedure intended to be enacted as a EU directive (Storme 1994). Today, a large-scale project to develop a model for European Rules of Civil Procedure is being conducted as a joint venture of the European Law Institute (ELI) and the UNIDROIT. This project is interesting because it provides a new platform for in-depth comparative analysis with a broad group of academics from all European procedural traditions. The results may come to show the procedural areas in which the domestic systems are closer to each other than they are in other areas. At best, it may also provide useful and modern model rules that can be an inspiration for both domestic and transnational legislators. However, it is important to note that the project does not, as the Storme report did, adopt any position as to the constitutional viability of harmonization in the EU or at which level any approximation of procedural law should be made.

Any full-scale harmonization of civil procedure at the EU level is likely to encounter obstacles of both constitutional and political nature. Constitutionally, the cross-border limitation of

Article 81 seems to exclude it as the legal basis for harmonization reaching into member state domestic procedures. A harmonization project would thus necessitate either a reinterpretation of Article 81, or reliance on an alternative legal basis. An analysis conducted at the European Parliamentary Research Service argues that Article 114 TFEU, preferably in conjunction with Article 81, would provide such a legal basis and thereby overcome the constitutional obstacle to harmonization (Manko 2015). However, it has also been held that Article 81 TFEU should be viewed as *lex specialis*, and that reliance on Article 114 in a situation where the Article 81 criteria are not fulfilled would constitute a circumvention of the latter article (Peers 2016: 353; Storskrubb 2016b).

Regardless, the political hurdle will also be significant. The Council (i.e., the member state governments) has so far steadfastly held its ground in matters of civil procedure, resisting Commission attempts at extending harmonization into domestic issues (Storskrubb 2016b). Furthermore, the type of harmonization sought has not been clarified. Minimum standards and/or non-binding measures appear to have some advantage in the debate, whereas unreserved proponents of full unification are few and far between. Several documents communicated by the European Parliament advocate minimum standards as the preferable form of harmonization (Manko 2015; Radev 2015). It is not entirely clear what kind of harmonization such minimum standards would entail (Hess 2016b), and the use of minimum standards in procedural matters has recently been shown to be problematic in the CJEU case law (see, e.g., cases C-399/11 *Melloni* EU:C:2013:107, and C-554/14 *Ognyanov*, EU:C:2016:835). Optional instruments have also been held to be preferable over binding legal acts such as directives or regulations (Andrews 2012; Cadiet 2014). This may, however, be considered a compromise solution, since it is doubted how much actual harmonization would be achieved through such an instrument, at least in the short and medium term. Arguably, the largest obstacle to true harmonization lies not in the legal but in the cultural aspects; as long as the judicial cultures among the member states differ, any attempt at harmonization, regardless of its shape, is likely to remain a paper tiger.

The harmonization debate should also be viewed against the backdrop of the increasing constitutionalization and approximation of procedural law being created in the case law of the CJEU, relying in part on constitutional traditions and statutes such as the ECHR and the EUCFR, and in part on implied competences based on the effectiveness or the *effet utile* of substantive Union law (Leible 2014), as well as of the sectoral harmonization of procedural law being brought forward in legislation on substantive competences in fields such as consumer protection, environmental law and intellectual property rights (*inter alia* Tulibacka 2009; Storskrubb 2016b). This could well prove to be a more viable way to achieve approximation of domestic laws of civil procedure within the Union, perhaps at the expense of further harmonization based on Article 81 (Hess 2009, 2016b: 6). However, this development has been criticized for being piecemeal, haphazard and lacking an understanding of the overarching principles and functions of civil procedure, and, at its extreme, liable to deteriorate rather than strengthen the level of judicial protection within the Union (Tulibacka 2009; Wagner 2012; Vernadaki 2013; Hess 2016a; Storskrubb 2016b).

The key scholarly debates

The civil justice field has largely failed to attract the interest of scholars outside of the legal discipline. Empirical and statistical studies of the success or importance of the regulatory work carried out under Article 81 TFEU are scarce, apart from the reports ordered by the Commission in the context of its mandated review of the measures. Much of the literature in the field therefore has a distinctively legal focus, discussing the various measures often in isolation or even section by section and paragraph by paragraph, with the aim of clarifying their legal content. Such literature, of which particularly the German-language literature abounds, is clearly of great practical value for legal practitioners and courts. Typically it does not, however, aim to contribute to a holistic understanding of the development of EU civil justice or its significance for the creation of the AFSJ.

The literature that focuses more generally on the development of civil justice may be divided into two categories: focus on (1) civil procedure and the possibility of its harmonization; or (2) private international law and the problems of mutual recognition and trust. Reflecting the current status of the policy area, literature belonging to the first category tends to be more visionary and holistically oriented, whereas literature falling into the second category includes both overarching arguments and more detailed studies. In the former category, important works include Storme (1994, 2003), Schwartze (2000), Weatherill (2004), Kramer and van Rhee (2012), Vernadaki (2013), Pfeiffer (2014), Hess (2014), the Special Issue of *Uniform Law Review* 19(2) (2014), and Wallerman (2016). In the latter, mention should be made of Storskrubb (2008, 2016a), Hess (2012), Kieninger and Remien (2012), Kramer (2013), Willer (2014), Weller (2015), Rühl and von Hein (2015), Kohler (2016), and two forthcoming contributions: Hazelhorst and Ortalani. Furthermore, mention should be made of some works, a third category, containing both perspectives, including Tulibacka (2009), Hess (2010), Leible (2014), Krans (2015), Storskrubb (2016b), and the contributions in Hess *et al.* (2016) as well as Nylund and Krans (2016).

Because of the mostly legal perspective, the main focus has been on evaluating legislative and judicial developments. There are, however, substantial variations on the perspective and points of departure for such evaluation. In the literature focusing on civil procedure harmonization, one major dividing line is drawn between those advocating harmonization and those warning against it. The most famous advocate for procedural harmonization is, without doubt, Marcel Storme, who was the driving force behind the above-mentioned Storme Committee (Storme 1994). This work immediately sparked the first significant debate on the possibility and desirability of procedural harmonization in the EU. It is to be hoped that the current joint project of the ELI and the UNIDROIT, aiming to present model Rules of Civil Procedure for Europe, will spark a second debate based on current precepts. On the same side in the debate, Schwartze (2000) and Vernadaki (2013) defend the need for harmonization from a mainly economic position, since the differences in procedures create costs for cross-border movements and ultimately weaken the four freedoms.

However, many other commentators were more skeptical (an example from the first debate is Lindblom 1997). Weatherill (2004) identifies three categories of arguments against harmonization: constitutional, cultural and economic. Looking to more recent literature one may perhaps add a fourth category: procedural. Krans (2015) is cautious in his conclusions, but points to problems of uncertainty and fragmentation associated at least with the current form of harmonization. Wallerman (2016) warns that the compromises required to achieve full harmonization may result in an overall decrease in the quality of civil justice, to the detriment of individuals, rather than contributing to more effective judicial protection. One thing is common to virtually all recent contributions in the field, regardless of the commentator's normative views on the development; all call for a more holistic and coherent approach to future developments. This may signify that the area has reached a new stage of maturity, which warrants a shift in policy considerations (Cadiet 2015). Perhaps the time has come for reflection.

Concluding remarks

Civil justice in the member states is currently subject to limited harmonization both under the Article 81 TFEU competence and under sector-specific rules based on the wider Article 114 TFEU competence in fields as diverse as environmental, competition and consumer law. Furthermore, the CJEU contributes to procedural approximation through its case law on the principles of effectiveness and equivalence and Article 47 EUCFR. While such measures may contribute to a nascent harmonization within the Union, they simultaneously create divisions within member state civil justice systems by introducing special regimes for certain types of cross-border or sector-specific disputes and they do not contribute to making the law accessible to individuals. It is an urgent task for future research to continue to adopt a more holistic perspective on the development of EU civil justice and to make renewed efforts to address the central normative questions: What problems should be addressed and who is to gain from civil cooperation in judicial matters? What are the main goals and ambitions of EU civil justice? How should we strike the balance between the effectiveness and protection of procedural rights?

In the future, we may expect to see an increased reliance on soft law measures (Hess 2016b). Several elements of such a development are already present, such as the ELI/UNIDROIT project on a procedural model code and the EU Commission's recommendation on collective redress adopted in June 2015. Another measure of the Commission is the so-called Justice Scoreboard, published annually since 2013. In this publication the justice systems of the member states and their efficiency is monitored on an annual basis by the Commission in the context of the economic cycle of the Union (Dori 2015). The annual scoreboard is a governance tool, providing information about the performance of the national justice systems in terms of efficiency that includes such parameters as length of proceedings, public spending on courts, availability of technology in courts, training of judges and independence of judges. If the scoreboard reveals shortcomings in a member state on a particular aspect, a more thorough analysis is carried out and recommendations for procedural reform may be issued. The member states may also receive financial support from the Union for such reforms.

A welcome feature of the justice scoreboards is that they permit a wider focus on not only procedural rules but also on the institutional factors concerning structural aspects of the member state courts, which are essential to the functioning of the justice system as well as to the trust between member states (Hess 2014; Storskrubb 2017). Compared to many of the other measures discussed in this chapter, the scoreboard can also represent a more subsidiarity-oriented approach to harmonization and the creation of mutual trust. This type of 'very soft law' is probably the only politically viable way for the Union to exercise any influence over national judicial systems, over which it currently appears unlikely that the member states are willing to give up any competences to the Union (Wallerman 2016). However, it is regrettable that the scoreboards tend to reduce the question of quality of a legal system to a rather superficial, statistical comparison of time logs and caseloads. If dialogue and mutual trust are to be achieved, the justice scoreboards seem to be a somewhat failed tool. What is really missing in the discussion about judicial cooperation in civil matters, both in scholarship and among the Union institutions, is an in-depth, analytical discussion of what kind of justice system we strive for, and how we wish to handle the balance between effective free movement with efficient procedures and legal certainty and fundamental rights.

Bibliography

Andersson, T. (2006). Harmonization and Mutual Recognition: How to Handle Mutual Distrust? *European Business Law Review*, 16(3), pp. 747–752.

Andrews, N. (2012). Fundamental Principles of Civil Procedure: Order Out of Chaos. In X. Kramer and C.H. van Rhee (eds) *Civil Litigation in a Globalising World*. The Hague: T.M.C. Asser Press, pp. 19–38.

Cadiet, L. (2014). The ALI–UNIDROIT Project: From Transnational Principles to European Rules of Civil Procedure. *Uniform Law Review*, 19(2), pp. 292–294.

Cadiet, L. (2015). Towards a New Model of Judicial Cooperation in the European Union. In L. Cadiet, B. Hess and M. Requejo Isidro (eds) *Procedural Science at the Crossroads of Different Generations*. Baden-Baden: Nomos, pp. 13–30.

Commission (2013). Assises de la Justice: Discussion Paper 1: EU Civil Law. Available at http://ec.europa.eu/justice/events/assises-justice-2013/files/civil_law_en.pdf (accessed December 14, 2016).

Crifò, C. (2009). *Cross-border Enforcement of Debts in the Eurpean Union: Default Judgments, Summary Judgments and Orders for Payment*. The Hague: Kluwer Law International.

Crifò, C. (2016). 'Trusted with a Muzzle and Enfranchised with a Clog': The British Approach to European Civil Procedure. In B. Hess, M. Bergström and E. Storskrubb (eds) *EU Civil Justice: Current Issues and Future Outlook*. Oxford: Hart, pp. 81–96.

Dori, A. (2015). The EU Justice Scoreboard – Judicial Evaluation as a New Governance Tool. *MPILux Working Paper*, Series 2.

Dougan, M. (2004). *National Remedies before the Court of Justice: Issues of Harmonisation and Differentiation*. Oxford: Hart.

Hartnell, H. (2002). EUstitia: Institutionalizing Justice in the European Union. *Northwestern Journal of International Law & Business*, 23(1), pp. 65–138.

Hazelhorst, M. (2017). *Free Movement of Civil Judgments in the European Union and the Right to a Fair Trial*. The Hague: Asser Press.

Hess, B. (2009). Aktuelle Tendenzen der Prozessrechtsentwicklung in Europa. In M. Casper, A. Janssen, P. Pohlmann and R. Schultze (eds) *Auf dem Weg zu einer europäischen Sammelklage?* Munich: Sellier, pp. 135–148.

Hess, B. (2010). *Europäisches Zivilprozessrecht*. Heidelberg: C.F. Müller.

Hess, B. (2012). Mutual Recognition in the European Law of Civil Procedure. *Zeitschrift für Vergleichende Rechtswissenschaft*, 111(1), pp. 21–37.

Hess, B. (2014). Unionsrechtliche Synthese: Mindeststandards und Verfahrensgrundsätze im aquis communautaire/Schlussfolgerungen für European Principles of Civil Procedure. In M. Weller and C. Althammer, *Mindeststandards im europäischen Zivilprozessrecht*. Tübingen: Mohr Siebeck, pp. 221–235.

Hess, B. (2016a). The State of the Civil Justice Union. In B. Hess, M. Bergström and E. Storskrubb (eds) *EU Civil Justice – Current Issues and Future Outlook*. Oxford: Hart, pp. 1–19.

Hess, B. (2016b). Harmonized Rules and Minimum Standards in the European Law of Civil Procedure, In-depth Analysis for the Juri Committee, European Parliament, Committee on Legal Affairs, Policy Department for Citizens' Rights and Constitutional Affairs. Available at www.europarl.europa.eu/RegData/etudes/IDAN/2016/556971/IPOL_IDA(2016)556971_EN.pdf (accessed December 14, 2016).

Hess, B., Bergström, M. and Storskrubb, E. (eds) (2016). *EU Civil Justice: Current Issues and Future Outlook*. Oxford: Hart.

Kieninger, E-M. and Remien, O. (eds) (2012). *Europäische Kollisionsrechtsvereinheitlichung*. Baden-Baden: Nomos.

Kohler, C. (2016). Vertrauen und Kontrolle im europäischen Justizraum für Zivilsachen. *Zeitschrift für Europarechtliche Studien*, 19(2), pp. 135–152.

Kramer, X. (2008). A Major Step in the Harmonization of Procedural Law in Europe: The European Small Claims Procedure. Accomplishments, New Features and some Fundamental Questions of European Harmonization. In A.W. Jongbloed (ed.) *The XIIIth World Congress of Procedural Law*. Antwerp: Intersentia, pp. 253–283.

Kramer, X. (2011). Cross-border Enforcement in the EU: Mutual Trust Versus Fair Trial? Towards Principles of European Civil Procedure. *International Journal of Procedural Law*, 1(2), pp. 202–230.

Kramer, X. (2013). Cross-border Enforcement and the Brussels I-bis Regulation: Towards a New Balance between Mutual Trust and National Control over Fundamental Rights. *Netherlands International Law Review*, 60(3), pp. 343–373.

Kramer, X. (2016). European Procedures on Debt Collection: Nothing or Noting? In B. Hess, M. Bergström and E. Storskrubb (eds) *EU Civil Justice: Current Issues and Future Outlook*. Oxford: Hart, pp. 97–122.

Kramer, X. and van Rhee, C.H. (eds) (2012). *Civil Litigation in a Globalising World*. The Hague: T.M.C. Asser Press.

Krans, B. (2015). EU Law and National Civil Procedure Law: An Invisible Pillar. *European Review of Private Law*, 23(4), pp. 567–588.

Lavenex, S. (2007). Mutual Recognition and the Monopoly of Force: Limits of the Single Market Analogy, *Journal of European Public Policy*, 14(5), pp. 762–779.

Leible, S. (2014). Strukturen und Perspektiven der justiziellen Zusammenarbeit in Zivilsachen. In S. Leible and J.P. Terhechte (eds) *Europäisches Rechtsschutz- und Verfahrensrecht: Band 3 Enzyklopädie Europarecht*. Baden-Baden: Nomos, pp. 433–481.

Lindblom, P.H. (1997). Harmony of the Legal Spheres. *European Review of Private Law*, 5(1), pp. 11–46.

Manko, R. (2015). Europeanisation of Civil Procedure: Towards Common Minimum Standards? European Parliamentary Research Service. Available at www.europarl.europa.eu/RegData/etudes/IDAN/2015/559499/EPRS_IDA(2015)559499_EN.pdf (accessed December 15, 2016).

Mitsilegas, V. (2012). The Limits of Mutual Trust in Europe's Area of Freedom, Security and Justice: From Automatic Inter-state Cooperation to the Slow Emergence of the Individual. *Yearbook of European Law*, 31, pp. 337–363.

Nicolaïdis, K. (2007). Trusting the Poles? Constructing Europe through Mutual Recognition. *Journal of European Public Policy*, 14(5), pp. 682–698.

Ortalani, P. (forthcoming) The Two Faces of Mutual Trust.

Nylund, A. and Krans, B. (2016). *The European Union and National Civil Procedure*. Intersentia.

Peers, S. (2016). *EU Justice and Home Affairs Law: Volume II, EU Criminal Law, Policing, and Civil Law*, 4th edn. Oxford: Oxford University Press.

Pfeiffer, T. (2014). Transnationale Synthese: ALI/UNIDROIT Principles of Civil Procedure und rechtsvergleichende Lehren. In M. Weller and C. Althammer (eds) *Mindeststandards im europäischen Zivilprozessrecht*. Tübingen: Mohr Siebeck, pp. 115–131.

Radev, E. (2015). Working Document on Establishing Common Minimum Standards for Civil Procedure in the European Union – The Legal Basis. European Parliament, Committee on Legal Affairs. Available at www.europarl.europa.eu/sides/getDoc.do?pubRef=-//EP//NONSGML+COMPARL+PE-572.853+01+DOC+PDF+V0//EN&language=EN (accessed December 14, 2016).

Requejo Isidro, M. (2016). On the Abolition of *Exequatur*. In B. Hess, M. Bergström and E. Storskrubb (eds) *EU Civil Justice: Current Issues and Future Outlook*. Oxford: Hart, pp. 283–298.

van Rhee, C.H. (2012). Harmonisation of Civil Procedure: An Historical and Comparative Perspective. In X. Kramer and C.H. van Rhee (eds) *Civil Litigation in a Globalising World*. The Hague: T.M.C. Asser Press, pp. 39–63.

Rühl, G. and von Hein, J. (2015). Towards a European Code on Private International Law? *Rabels Zeitschrift für ausländisches und internationales Privatrecht*, 79(4), pp. 701–751.

Schwartze, A. (2000). Enforcement of Private Law: The Missing Link in the Process of European Harmonisation. *European Review of Private Law*, 8(1), pp. 135–146.

Storme, M. (ed.) (1994). *Rapprochement du droit judiciaire de l'Union européenne*. Dordrecht: Nijhoff.

Storme, M. (ed.) (2003). *Procedural Laws in Europe – Towards Harmonisation*. Antwerp/Apeldoorn: Maklu.

Storme, M. (2005). A Single Civil Procedure for Europe: A Cathedral Builders' [sic] Dream. *Ritsumeikan Law Review*, 22, pp. 87–100.

Storskrubb, E. (2008). *Civil Procedure and EU Law: A Policy Area Uncovered*. Oxford: Oxford University Press.

Storskrubb, E. (2015). Civil Justice: The Contested Nature of the Scope of EU Legislation. In F. Trauner and A. Ripoll (eds) *Policy Change in the Area of Freedom Security and Justice: How EU Institutions Matter*. London: Routledge, pp. 197–216.

Storskrubb, E. (2016a). Mutual Recognition as a Governance Strategy for Civil Justice. In B. Hess, M. Bergström and E. Storskrubb (eds) *EU Civil Justice: Current Issues and Future Outlook*. Oxford: Hart, pp. 299–318.

Storskrubb, E. (2016b). Civil Justice – Constitutional and Regulatory Issues Revisited. In M. Fletcher, E. Herlin-Karnell and C. Matera (eds) *The EU as an Area of Freedom, Security and Justice*. London: Routledge, pp. 303–336.

Storskrubb, E. (2017). Tillit mellan rättssystemen i EU? Det civilrättsliga perspektivet. In A. Bakardjieva Engelbrekt, A. Michalski and L. Oxelheim (eds) *Tilliten i EU vid ett vägskäl*. Falun: Santérus, pp. 185–210.

Tulibacka, M. (2009). Europeanization of Civil Procedures: In Search of a Coherent Approach. *Common Market Law Review*, 46(5), pp. 1527–1565.

Vernadaki, Z. (2013). Civil Procedure Harmonization in the EU: Unravelling the Policy Considerations. *Journal of Contemporary European Research*, 9(2), pp. 297–312.

Wagner, G. (2012). Harmonisation of Civil Procedure: Policy Perspectives. In X. Kramer and C.H. van Rhee (eds) *Civil Litigation in a Globalising World*. The Hague: T.M.C. Asser Press, pp. 93–119.

Wallerman, A. (2016). Harmonization of Civil Procedure: Can the EU Learn from Swiss Experiences? *European Review of Private Law*, 24(5), pp. 855–876.

Weatherill, S. (2004). Why Object to the Harmonization of Private Law by the EC? *European Review of Private Law*, 12(5), pp. 633–660.

Weller, M. (2015). Mutual Trust: In Search of the Future of European Union Private International Law. *Journal of Private International Law*, 11(1), pp. 64–102.

Willer, R. (2014). Gegenseitiges Vertrauen in die Rechtspflege der Mitgliedstaaten als hinreichende Bedingung für die Anerkennung von Entscheidungen nach der EuGVVO? *Zeitschrift für Zivilprozess*, 127(1), pp. 99–124.

Zetterquist, O. (2008). The Judicial Deficit in the EC – Knocking on Heaven's Door? In U. Bernitz, J. Nergelius and C. Cardner (eds) *General Principles of EC Law in a Process of Development*. Alphen aan den Rijn: Wolters Kluwer, pp. 115–137.

18
FAMILY REUNIFICATION AND MIGRANT INTEGRATION POLICIES IN THE EU

Dynamics of inclusion and exclusion

Saskia Bonjour

Introduction

This chapter surveys the scholarly debate on EU policies pertaining to the integration of third-country nationals (TCNs) in member states' societies. This is not at all self-evident, since the European Union has no competence to regulate migrant integration. In the classic distinction proposed by Thomas Hammar (1985: 7–9), 'immigration regulation' refers to the control of entry and stay of foreigners, while 'immigrant policy' refers to 'the conditions provided for resident immigrants'. With regard to immigration regulation, the European Union has been attributed competence to legislate by the Treaty of Amsterdam (1999), and the 2000s witnessed the development of a European Asylum and Migration Policy. However, immigrant policy – generally labeled 'migrant integration policy' or 'integration policy' in the EU context – has been carefully excluded from harmonization. This is not surprising, considering how closely related migrant integration is to other policy areas where member states have been reticent to relinquish national sovereignty, such as social security, labor market regulation, housing and education. In the Lisbon Treaty (2007), member states explicitly excluded 'any harmonization of the laws and regulations of the Member States' pertaining to the integration of third-country nationals (Article 79.4).

However, notwithstanding these sovereignty concerns and lack of competence, the influence of EU law and policies on the integration of third-country nationals is far from negligible. Carrera (2009) points out that EU-level activity in this policy area has assumed two shapes. First, a series of soft governance measures have been elaborated to 'provide incentives and support for the action of member states with a view to promoting the integration of third-country nationals', as the Lisbon Treaty states in its Article 79.4. Such non-binding forms of cooperation and coordination include exchange of best practices within the European Migration Network, the formulation of Common Basic Principles on Migrant Integration, and the establishment of a European Integration Fund and a European Website on Integration. Second, two directives have been adopted that, while formulating conditions for entry and stay, also affect integration. The Family Reunification Directive and Long-term Residence Directive regulate third-country nationals' access to family reunion and secure residence and mobility rights, respectively. Access to these rights may in itself be considered a crucial aspect of promoting the integration process of third-country nationals. Furthermore, both directives touch upon third-country nationals' access to employment and education, and include provisions for 'integration measures' which may condition access to rights.

The overarching question driving most scholarly analyses of EU migrant integration policies has been whether EU involvement in migrant integration policies has led to the improvement or deterioration of the position of third-country nationals living in the European Union. The development of EU migrant integration policies was kicked off by the European Council in Tampere in 1999 which called for 'a more vigorous integration policy [that] should aim at granting [third-country nationals] rights and obligations comparable to those of EU citizens' (European Council 1999). This set high hopes for academic observers such as Dora Kostakopoulou (2002: 454), who observed that 'a rights-based approach [...] has begun to emerge', which was 'likely to lower barriers to more inclusive policies' (2002: 445). However, academics have also argued that EU citizenship and European identity have been built on the legal and symbolic exclusion of third-country nationals (e.g., Hansen and Hager 2010: 14–15; Rea et al. 2011: 9–11). Scholars remain divided as to whether EU engagement with the integration of third-country nationals is dominated by dynamics of inclusion or exclusion.

This chapter begins by summarizing the content of migrant integration policy in the EU: the Long-term Residence Directive, the Family Reunification Directive and non-binding EU migrant integration policy respectively, pointing out particular issues of scholarly interest for each of these three policy subfields. The second section surveys the literature on the negotiation and implementation of the two directives, exploring in particular the question whether Europeanization should be considered a 'liberal constraint' upon restriction-minded member states. The third and final section reviews the scholarly debate on the role of the EU in the emergence of a new policy paradigm in which integration and migration are fused.

EU migrant integration policies

The Long-term Residence Directive

Following up on the Tampere European Council's call for (near) equal treatment of resident migrants, the Commission first tabled a proposal for a 'Council Directive concerning the status of third-country nationals who are long-term residents' in March 2001. After lengthy negotiations, Directive 2003/109 was adopted in November 2003.

The Directive stipulates that non-EU nationals are entitled to long-term resident status if they have resided for more than five years in a member state and are financially independent. Member states may require TCNs to fulfill integration requirements before granting this status. Initially, refugees were not covered by the Directive, but they were included in its scope in 2011. The Directive states that long-term residents must be treated equally to nationals in areas such as employment, education, social security, taxation and freedom of association; however, it allows member states to restrict equal access in certain circumstances. Long-term residents may move to live, work or study in another EU member state, provided they fulfill certain conditions, most notably sufficient resources. Member states may also subject TCNs' mobility rights to integration conditions.

A focal point in the academic literature about the Long-term Residence Directive is the question of how it relates to EU citizenship. This is a highly normative debate dominated by scholars of law and philosophy of law. Maas (2008: 588) has argued that in parallel with the strengthening of EU citizenship rights, the rights of third-country nationals were 'frozen or reduced'. Maas acknowledges the added value of the Long-term Residence Directive in guaranteeing a set of minimum rights throughout the Union, but emphasizes that these rights fall far short of equal treatment with citizens. A long-standing advocate of granting third-country nationals access to EU citizenship based on residency is Dora Kostakopoulou (2007: 623), who sees the development of EU citizenship as an opportunity to work towards 'a more inclusive, multi-layered and multicultural conception of citizenship'. In her view, this would logically entail freeing EU citizenship from its 'quasi-nationalist trappings' by rooting it in domicile rather than in nationality (2007: 644). Kochenov (2013: 106–107) states that 'it is more or less accepted in the literature that EU citizenship is incomplete unless it takes third-country nationals onboard in some form' and promotes full inclusion of TCNs in EU citizenship as the only sensible way to 'diminish the harshness of *apartheid européen*' (italics in original). Overall, however, scholars are pessimistic about the likelihood of member states accepting the decoupling of access to EU citizenship from access to their own nationality in the foreseeable future.

Given this political reality, some scholars see substantial inclusionary potential in the rights guaranteed by the Long-term Residence Directive and especially in its implementation by the EU Court of Justice. For instance, Wiesbrock (2012) has argued that the Court has shown a tendency to interpret the rights granted to TCNs by the Long-term Residence Directive and other EU law expansively, according to principles governing its jurisprudence on EU citizenship such as the principles of proportionality and non-discrimination on grounds of nationality. If this trend were to persist, it would represent 'a viable alternative to the full extension of Union citizenship' to third-country nationals (Wiesbrock 2012: 91). According to Acosta Arcarazo (2015: 200), 'the Long-term residence directive has created a status that can be considered as a subsidiary form of EU citizenship'. Like Wiesbrock, Acosta Arcarazo attributes a crucial role to EU Court jurisprudence which has turned the Directive into a solid guarantee of a set of rights for TCNs. Notably, the Court has ruled that, if a third-country national fulfills the conditions, member states are obliged to grant long-term residence status. This is fundamentally different from the attribution of nationality, which is at member states' discretion. Acosta Arcarazo (2015: 217) argues that through this and similar jurisprudence, the Court has turned long-term residence into a 'post-national form of membership'.

The Family Reunification Directive

The Commission tabled its first 'Proposal for a Council Directive on the right to family reunification' in December 1999. After intensive discussions among member states led to a deadlock in the Council, the Commission was forced to revise its original proposal twice: in 2000 and 2002. Directive 2003/86 was eventually adopted by the Council in September 2003.

The Directive applies to third-country nationals with a permanent residence permit living in the EU and wishing to bring over non-EU family members. It stipulates that spouses and minor children will be admitted if the applicant has health insurance, appropriate accommodation, and stable and sufficient resources. Member states may also admit parents, adult children and unmarried partners. Foreign family members who pose a threat to public order may be refused admission. Member states may require family members to comply with integration measures, and may set a minimum age for both partners of no more than 21 and a minimum residence period for the applicant of no more than two years. The Directive also contains guarantees for the procedure – such as examination of the application within nine months – and for the rights granted to family members following admission, notably with regard to security of residence and access to employment and education. All norms set by the Directive are minimum norms; member states are free to set less stringent conditions.

A recurring theme in the literature on the Family Reunification Directive is the 'stratification' (i.e., unequal distribution) of family migration rights in Europe. Groenendijk (2006:

215–217) emphasized that three sets of EU rules apply to family reunification. First, EU citizens who live or have lived in another EU country can bring over foreign family members under free movement law. Second, family reunification by Turkish citizens is governed by the Association Agreement between Turkey and the EU. Third, all other third-country nationals can bring over foreign family members according to the conditions set by the Family Reunification Directive (2006: 215–217). Strik and colleagues (2013: 107) add a fourth category, namely highly skilled workers who can bring along family members on very generous terms under the Blue Card Directive. The only category of people whose family reunification rights are not governed by EU law are nationals, i.e., EU citizens who have not moved to another EU country.

This 'fragmentation of the family reunification rights in the European Union' (Strik *et al.* 2013: 108) is generally deplored in the literature. Most notably, scholars criticize the disfavoring of both TCNs and nationals compared to mobile EU citizens (e.g., Kostakopoulou and Ripoll Servent 2016; Strik *et al.* 2013). Free movement law stipulates that this latter category may reunite with foreign family members under very favorable conditions: EU citizens can bring over not only spouses and children under the age of 21 but also older children, (grand)parents or grandchildren if they are dependants. Integration or language conditions may not be imposed. The family reunification rights granted to TCNs under the Family Reunification Directive are much less generous. Moreover, Strik and colleagues (2013: 107–108) point out that the family reunification rights of 'first country nationals' (i.e., EU citizens who have not moved to another country) are left entirely without protection by EU law and that several member states now apply more stringent conditions to their own nationals than to other EU citizens (cf. Block 2015: 1441; Bonjour and Block 2016: 790). This stratification has led to new migratory moves, with EU citizens moving to another EU country in order for the generous conditions of free movement law to apply and to allow them to reunite with their foreign family members (Wagner 2015).

Non-binding EU migrant integration policy

While the EU has no formal competence to harmonize national migrant integration policies, a series of 'soft governance' initiatives have been deployed since the 2000s (Rosenow 2008; Carrera 2009). In 2005, the Commission launched its first 'Common Framework for the Integration of Third-country Nationals', which entailed a series of measures coordinated by the Commission aimed at exchanging policy experiences and the dissemination of best practices. This initiative was guided by the 'Common Basic Principles' on migrant integration adopted by the Council in 2004 and reaffirmed in 2014. A network of National Contact Points on Integration was set up in 2002 with the aim of exchanging information and experiences. A European Integration Fund was introduced which spent 825 million euro between 2007 and 2013 to support migrant integration initiatives. As of 2014, the European Integration Fund was replaced by the Asylum Migration and Integration Fund. In 2009, a European Integration Forum was established, which brought together civil society organizations and EU institutions twice a year. It was reformed into the European Migration Forum in 2015. In addition, the Commission has seen to the publication of a European Website on Integration, a series of Handbooks on Integration, as well as European Integration Modules. Finally, the Commission has developed common 'Indicators for Migrant Integration' to allow for consistent monitoring of migrant integration and cross-country comparisons.

An aspect of EU migrant integration policies that has attracted scholarly attention is the interaction among researchers and policy-makers in the development of these policies. Pratt (2015) explores the involvement of researchers in the elaboration of the Commission 2000 Communication on migrant integration and the Council's Common Basic Principles of 2004. She argues that researchers exerted substantial influence on policy elaboration in these early days, as EU institutions and member states actively sought the input of academic researchers to help shape this new policy field. Geddes and Achtnich (2015) zoom in on the European Migration Network of National Contact Points as an important venue where knowledge about migrant integration is produced at the EU level and conclude that, rather than producing new insights, the Network tends to 'be used as an arena for the substantiation of existing policy choices' (2015: 311). Geddes and Scholten (2015: 42) argue that 'the development of institutional relations between research and policy appears to be a key element of [the EU's] "soft governance" strategy'. They show that, in the absence of formal competences, promoting the exchange and production of knowledge was a way for the Commission to carve out a legitimate role for itself, and to stimulate Europeanization based on the reframing of migrant integration as a 'European' problem that required a 'European' response.

Negotiating and implementing the directives: race to the bottom or safety net for migrants' rights?

A core question in analyses of EU migrant integration policies has been whether Europeanization has been beneficial or detrimental to the level of rights protection enjoyed by third-country nationals. This debate has focused mainly on the two binding directives, since the non-binding policy instruments do not touch upon legal rights. A broadly shared observation is that, while the Commission and Court have tended to adopt pro-rights positions, member state preferences have overall been more restrictive (Luedtke 2009; Acosta Arcarazo 2011; Menz 2011; Strik 2011; Bonjour and Vink 2013; Block and Bonjour 2013; Roos 2013; Schweitzer 2015). The question is then, whether Europeanization has either enabled member states to push their restrictive policy agenda or, to the contrary, limited member states' room for maneuver to restrict migrants' rights.

The Long-term Residence Directive and the Family Reunification Directive were negotiated in parallel. In both cases, the Commission initially tabled proposals that set very high standards of protection for migrants' rights. According to Groenendijk (2007), Roos (2013) and Strik (2011), NGOs significantly influenced the positions adopted by the Commission in this early stage. The Commission strove for harmonization and for the inclusion of TCNs in free movement within the internal market (Roos 2013). While member states' positions diverged, they all strove to minimize adaptation costs, i.e., to ensure that new EU law would require as little modification of national policies as possible (Luedtke 2009; Strik 2011; Roos 2013). The Commission's pro-rights stance was supported by Sweden, France and Belgium. Most member states, however, proved very reticent to cede sovereignty over migrant policies and sought to condition TCNs' rights in different ways. Overall, scholars agree that restriction-minded member states, in particular Germany, Austria and The Netherlands, were most influential in the negotiation process (Leudtke 2009; Acosta Arcarazo 2011; Menz 2011; Strik 2011; Roos 2013). For instance, while the Commission proposed granting long-term residents virtually the same social and mobility rights as EU citizens, member states limited these rights by stipulating that long-term residents could be required to fulfill integration conditions before moving to live or work in another member state, and that access to social security could be restricted to core benefits. Similarly, member states successfully negotiated a series of restrictive adaptations of the Commission's Family Reunification proposal, such as raising the minimum age for spouses from 18 to 21, excluding nationals from the scope of the Directive, and allowing member states to require family migrants to comply with integration measures (Strik 2011; Roos 2013; Bonjour and Vink 2013).

Thus, scholarly assessments of the outcome of the negotiations in terms of migrants' rights protection are generally negative. Scholars who compare this outcome either to normative standards derived from fundamental rights law (Cholewinski 2002; Benarieh Ruffer 2011) or to the goals set by the Tampere Council Conclusions (i.e., equal treatment of TCNs and EU citizens) (Halleskov 2005; Foblets 2016) are especially critical. However, assessments are more mixed if the outcomes of the negotiations are compared to pre-existing national provisions, since the level of rights guaranteed by the Directive is argued to be below the level previously accorded by some member states, but above the level granted by other or even most member states. For instance, the Directive obliged Greece to grant permanent residence after five rather than fifteen years, while it made Luxembourg and Austria open up TCNs' access to social security (Luedtke 2009; Roos 2013; Groenendijk 2007).

Evaluations are more ambivalent still when scholars assess the *implementation* of the Directive in terms of its impact on migrants' rights protection. Different scholars have argued that national governments have strategically used Europeanization to implement restrictive reforms in two distinct ways. First, whereas the directives were intended to establish a minimum level of rights that member states were free to go beyond, member states have 'presented convergence towards that minimum level of rights as a desirable form of harmonization', thus 'building legitimacy for a [...], 'race to the bottom' (Block and Bonjour 2013: 215; cf. Barbou des Places and Oger 2005). For instance, the French government used the Long-Term Residence Directive to defend the extension of the minimum duration of residence before a permanent residence permit was granted (Barbou des Places and Oger 2005: 362–363). Second, the implementation of the directives is observed to have resulted in processes of policy transfer among member states, as it has increased both the availability of and the demand for information about policy practices in other member states (Block and Bonjour 2013). Both directives contain various optional clauses that leave substantial room for interpretation, and many national governments have observed closely how other member states have implemented these provisions. Government representatives in different member states, including The Netherlands, Germany, France, Austria and Belgium, have defended their restrictive reform proposals by pointing out that other member states were implementing similar policies (Block and Bonjour 2013; Bonjour 2014; Strik et al. 2013; Adam and Jacobs 2012). Thus, the introduction of EU law on family reunification and long-term residence is seen to have created new opportunities for member states to legitimize and exchange restrictive policy practices.

However, scholars have also argued that EU legislation has substantially limited the room for maneuver for member states to introduce restrictive reforms. First, the directives have created a 'minimum safety net' as Roos (2013: 108) calls it: a guaranteed level of rights protection that member states are bound to provide. Bonjour and Vink (2013) note that while Dutch negotiators were successful in shaping the Family Reunification Directive, they did not foresee that later governments' preferences would shift ever further towards restriction. The Dutch government already made almost full use of the room for restriction allowed by the Directive at the moment of its transposition. As a result, succeeding Dutch governments have not been able to implement the restrictive policy reforms they favored, including education requirements and a minimum age limit of 24 for sponsors and foreign spouses, because these reforms would be in breach of the Directive.

Furthermore, the introduction of EU law has empowered the European Commission and the EU Court of Justice to assess member states' respect for migrant rights. Different scholars have observed that these supranational institutions have positioned themselves as active protectors of migrants' rights (Groenendijk 2004; Luedtke 2009; Acosta Arcarazo 2015; Block and Bonjour 2013). The Court, supported by the Commission, has expansively interpreted the vaguely worded provisions of the directives. Jurisprudence is still limited at this point, but the EU Court has already established that the two directives are to be interpreted as guaranteeing subjective rights: if an applicant for long-term residence status or family reunification fulfills the conditions set by the directives, member states are no longer at liberty to reject the application. Moreover, the Court has emphasized that both directives aim to further the process of integration of third-country nationals and that member state policies must be effective and proportionate in relation to that goal. As a result, member states have already been obliged to lower income requirements and fees, and their room for restriction may be further reduced in the future as Court jurisprudence develops.

Thus, the picture that emerges from the literature is nuanced: Europeanization of migrant integration is neither purely beneficial nor entirely detrimental to the protection of the rights of third-country nationals. Instead, multiple and various Europeanization processes work in parallel, with often contradictory effects.

Shifting policy paradigms: integration as condition for rights

A final point that has attracted wide scholarly attention is the relative weight of different paradigms of migrant integration in EU policies, and the impact of Europeanization upon the paradigms that shape national integration policies. Community law on the freedom of movement is based on the notion that strong rights in terms of secure residence, family reunification and equal treatment are a condition for migrant integration. The assumption here is that newcomers can only build a life for themselves and participate fully in their host society if they do not fear expulsion, are not separated from their families, and have full access to employment, education, and social rights. This paradigm has remained dominant from the early development of freedom of movement for workers in the 1960s to current EU citizenship law. However, different scholars have noted that with the development of EU integration policies for third-country nationals, a different perspective on integration has been introduced at the EU level, namely the notion that integration is a condition for rights: only if migrants have achieved a certain measure of integration in the host society are they granted access to permanent residence rights, family reunification and mobility rights (Groenendijk 2004; Carrera 2009). Thus, migration and integration policies are fused, as integration becomes a condition for migration. The ways in which migrants are to prove sufficient integration vary, from doing voluntary work to participating in a course or passing a test. The premise here is that migrants will be encouraged to integrate if they are rewarded for their efforts and that the preservation of the cohesion and identity of European societies requires that only those migrants who are able to integrate be allowed to enter and stay. The two competing paradigms thus hold opposite views on the relation between integration and rights: in the first, rights are a condition for integration; while in the second, integration is a condition for rights. Most scholars studying this topic adopt a normative perspective and deplore the introduction of the second paradigm, which they criticize as exclusionary and illiberal (Groenendijk 2004; Carrera 2009; Guild et al. 2009; Kostakopoulou et al. 2009; Kostakopoulou and Ripoll Servent 2016).

Many scholars argue that the Europeanization of migrant integration policies has played a crucial role in the dissemination of the new migrant integration policy paradigm at both the EU and the national level, often referred to as the 'civic integration' turn in Europe. It is generally acknowledged that the new paradigm has its roots in domestic politics, and was introduced at the EU level by The Netherlands, Austria and Germany. It is due to their successful lobbying during negotiations on the Long-term Residence and Family Reunification Directives that member states are now allowed to require third-country nationals to fulfill integration conditions at different moments: before allowing them to immigrate as family members; before granting them permanent resident status; and before allowing them to immigrate from another EU country once they have permanent resident status (Groenendijk 2004; Carrera 2009; Acosta Arcarazo 2011; Roos 2013; Geddes and Scholten 2015). 'Uploading' these policy practices to the European level not only helped entrench integration conditions in Dutch, Austrian and German policies (Roos 2013); it also contributed to their transfer to other countries, including France, Spain, Denmark and the United Kingdom (Carrera 2009; Carrera and Wiesbrock 2009; Bonjour 2014).

The 'integration as a condition for rights' paradigm is argued to have been further reinforced by the non-binding migrant integration policies adopted at the EU level. Thus the Common Basic Principles, adopted by the Council in 2004, include the statements that 'integration implies respect for the basic values of the European Union' and that 'basic knowledge of the host society's language, history, and institutions is indispensable to integration' (Council 2004). The Commission is argued to have endorsed integration courses for migrants in different policy communications and agendas as well as through practical support for civic integration courses via the Handbooks on Integration, the European Modules on Migrant Integration and the European Integration Fund. Finally, exchange of information and 'best practices' via the network of National Contact Points is said to have contributed significantly to the dissemination of integration courses and tests among member states (Carrera 2009; Carrera and Wiesbrock 2009).

However, in contrast to these accounts, which argue that Europeanization has contributed to the dissemination of integration conditions, there are also scholars who emphasize that the European Commission and the EU Court have sought to counter the introduction of such policies. In its original proposals for the Long-term Residence Directive and Family Reunification Directive, the Commission followed the original integration policy paradigm, i.e., the notion that strong rights are a prerequisite for integration (Acosta Arcarazo 2011; Roos 2013). Elements of this paradigm are still present in the provisions of the directives (Schweitzer 2015). For instance, the fourth recital of the Family Reunification Directive states that 'family reunification [...] helps to create sociocultural stability facilitating the integration of third-country nationals in the Member State'.

More recently, the Commission has been very critical especially of pre-departure integration requirements. It launched an infringement procedure against Germany for allowing entry to family migrants only if they passed a language test and argued explicitly before the EU Court that pre-entry tests were not compatible with the Family Reunification Directive (Block and Bonjour 2013). It has been the long-standing hope of legal scholars that the Court would adopt the same position (Groenendijk 2006, 2011; Jesse 2011). In recent jurisprudence, however, the Court has ruled that integration requirements are admissible both before and after migration to the EU, provided that they represent effective and proportionate means to further the integration of migrants – rather than being used to select migrants. Law scholars take opposite views on whether this implies that the Court has endorsed (Thym 2016) or rejected (Acosta Arcarazo 2015) the 'integration as a condition for rights' paradigm favored by many member states. All legal analyses agree, however, that the EU Court has set limits to what member states can do when implementing integration conditions: for instance, they cannot impose excessive administrative fees (Acosta Arcarazo 2015; Jesse 2016; Thym 2016). The Commission for its part appears to have given up its outright resistance to pre-departure integration measures: in its 2016 Action Plan on the Integration of Third-Country Nationals, such measures are listed as a first policy priority. However, the Commission refers to 'pre-departure/pre-arrival measures', which are to be implemented not only in countries of origin but also in member states to prepare local communities for the arrival of newcomers. Moreover, the Commission emphasizes the need for cooperation with countries of origin in elaborating pre-departure measures and focuses on the ways in which such measures may be included in resettlement programs for refugees (European Commission 2016: 5–6). Thus, the Commission implicitly continues its resistance to member states' use of pre-departure integration measures as selection mechanisms, by reframing such measures as part of a pro-active migrant integration policy.

Conclusion

Notwithstanding its limited competences, the European Union's policies and institutions have come to shape the field of migrant integration in significant ways. Scholars have explored EU involvement mostly from a normative perspective, inquiring to what extent it enhances or undermines the protection of the rights of third-country nationals. Their findings are mixed: processes of Europeanization appear to be complex and multiple, with contradictory effects. Scholarship broadly agrees that member states have predominantly used binding and non-binding forms of Europeanization to push restrictive policy agendas. The European Commission and Court appear to have overall adopted pro-rights positions, although they are also argued to have contributed to the propagation of the 'integration as a condition for rights' paradigm in Europe. Furthermore, the assessment of the impact of Europeanization varies depending on the benchmark adopted: a comparison with pre-existing national policies yields a more positive evaluation than a comparison with the equal treatment promised at Tampere, or with a normative standard derived from human rights law.

The prevalence of normative perspectives is not surprising considering the extent to which this field has been dominated by law scholars. With some exceptions, including Roos (2013), Geddes and Scholten (2015), Luedtke (2009) and Bonjour (2014), political scientists and political sociologists have neglected the Europeanization of migrant integration policies – in contrast to fields like asylum or border control policies where political science analyses have been much more forthcoming. As a result, a number of typical political science questions remain understudied. For instance, we know relatively little about the power relations among member states and EU institutions: how relative power is shaped by institutional structures, political context and strategic agency, and how power relations vary over time and in different subfields. Another black-box that begs opening is the preference formation of EU institutions, most notably the European Commission and Court: all too often their preferences are taken as given, rather than as shaped by internal and external circumstances and changing over time (cf. Bonjour *et al.* 2017). Finally, with the exception of well-studied countries such as The Netherlands and Germany, we know relatively little about the impact of Europeanization upon national and local migrant integration policies in different member states.

EU migrant integration policies remain a field in flux. The substance and scope of the impact of the European Union are continuously (re)shaped by Court jurisprudence, policy entrepreneurship of the Commission and political circumstances in member states. In the wake of the asylum crisis of recent years, both the family reunification rights of refugees and their integration are high on policy agendas in Brussels and in many European capitals. Now and in the foreseeable future, no student of inclusion and exclusion of third-country nationals in Europe can afford to neglect the role of the European Union in migrant integration policy.

Bibliography

Acosta Arcarazo, D. (2011). *The Long-term Residence Directive as a Subsidiary Form of EU Citizenship. An Analysis of Directive 2003/109*. Leiden: Martinus Nijhoff.

Acosta Arcarazo, D. (2015). Civic Citizenship Reintroduced? The Long-term Residence Directive as a Post-national Form of Membership. *European Law Journal*, 21(2), pp. 200–219.

Adam, I. and Jacobs, D. (2012). Bridging the Divide. How European Integration Shapes Belgian Immigrant Politics. Paper presented at the ECPR EU Conference, Tampere, September.

Barbou des Places, S. and Oger, H. (2005). Making the European Migration Regime: Decoding Member States' Legal Strategies. *European Journal of Migration and Law*, 6(4), pp. 353–380.

Benarieh Ruffer, G. (2011). Pushed beyond Recognition? The Liberality of Family Reunification Policies in the EU. *Journal of Ethnic and Migration Studies*, 37(6), pp. 935–951.

Block, L. (2015). Regulating Membership. Explaining Restriction and Stratification of Family Migration in Europe. *Journal of Family Issues*, 36(11), pp. 1433–1452.

Block, L. and Bonjour, S. (2013). Fortress Europe or Europe of Rights? The Europeanisation of Family Migration Policies in France, Germany and the Netherlands. *European Journal of Migration and Law*, 15(2), pp. 203–224.

Bonjour, S. (2014). The Transfer of Pre-departure Integration Requirements for Family Migrants among Member States of the European Union. *Comparative Migration Studies*, 2(2), pp. 203–226.

Bonjour, S. and Block, L. (2016). Ethnicizing Citizenship, Questioning Membership. Explaining the Decreasing Family Migration Rights of Citizens in Europe. *Citizenship Studies*, 20(6–7), pp. 779–794.

Bonjour, S. and Vink, M. (2013). When Europeanization Backfires: The Normalization of European Migration Politics. *Acta Politica*, 48(4), pp. 389–407.

Bonjour, S., Ripoll Servent, A. and Thielemann, E. (2017). Beyond Venue Shopping and Liberal Constraint: A New Research Agenda for EU Migration Policies and Politics. *Journal of European Public Policy*. doi: 10.1080/13501763.2016.1268640.

Carrera, S. (2009). *In Search of the Perfect Citizen. The Intersection between Immigration, Integration and Nationality in the EU*. Leiden; Boston, MA: Martinus Nijhoff.

Carrera, S. and Wiesbrock, A. (2009). *Civic Integration of Third-country Nationals. Nationalism versus Europeanisation in the Common EU Immigration Policy*. Brussels: Center for European Policy Studies.

Cholewinski, R. (2002). Family Reunification and Conditions Placed on Family Members: Dismantling a Fundamental Human Right. *European Journal of Migration and Law*, 4(3), pp. 271–290.

Council of the European Union (2004). Press Release on 2618th Council Meeting, Justice and Home Affairs, Brussels, November 19 (14615/04).

European Commission (2016). Action Plan on the Integration of Third Country Nationals. COM(2016) 377 final.

European Council (1999). Tampere Presidency Conclusions, October 15–16.

European Council (2008). European Pact on Immigration and Asylum, Brussels, September 24 (13440/08).

Foblets, M. (2016). Migration and Integration of Third-country Nationals in Europe: The Need for the Development of an Efficient, Effective, and Legitimate System of Governance. In F. von Benda-Beckmann, K. von Benda-Beckmann and J. Eckert (eds), *Rules of Law and Laws of Ruling. On the Governance of Law*. London/New York: Routledge, pp. 191–216.

Geddes, A. and Achtnich, M. (2015). Research–Policy Dialogues in the European Union. In P. Scholten, H.B. Entzinger, R. Penninx and S. Verbeek (eds), *Integrating Immigrants in Europe: Research–Policy Dialogues* (pp. 339–362). New York: Springer Open, pp. 339–362.

Geddes, A. and Scholten, P. (2015). Policy Analysis and Europeanization: An Analysis of EU Migrant Integration Policymaking. *Journal of Comparative Policy Analysis*, 17(1), pp. 41–59.

Groenendijk, K. (2004). Legal Concepts of Integration in EU Migration Law. *European Journal of Migration and Law*, 6(2), pp. 111–126.

Groenendijk, K. (2006). Family Reunification as a Right under Community Law. *European Journal of Migration and Law*, 8, pp. 215–230.

Groenendijk, K. (2007). The Long-term Residents Directive, Denizenship and Integration. In A. Baldaccini, E. Guild and H. Toner (eds), *Whose Freedom Security and Justice*. Oxford and Portland, OR: Hart, pp. 429–450.

Groenendijk, K. (2011). Pre-departure Integration Strategies in the European Union: Integration or Immigration Policy? *European Journal of Migration and Law*, 13(1), pp. 1–30.

Guild, E., Groenendijk, K. and Carrera, S. (2009). Understanding the Contest of Community: Illiberal Practices in the EU? In E. Guild, K. Groenendijk and S. Carrera (eds), *Illiberal Liberal States. Immigration, Citizenship and Integration in the EU*. London: Ashgate, pp. 1–25.

Halleskov, L. (2005). The Long-term Residents Directive: A Fulfilment of the Tampere Objective of Near-equality? *European Journal of Migration and Law*, 7, pp. 181–201.

Hammar, T. (1985). Introduction. In T. Hammar (ed.), *European Immigration Policy: A Comparative Study*. Cambridge: Cambridge University Press, pp. 1–13.

Hansen, P. and Hager, S.B. (2010). *The Politics of European Citizenship. Deepening Contradictions in Social Rights & Migration Policy*. New York; Oxford: Berghahn Books.

Jesse, M. (2011). The Value of 'Integration' in European Law – The Implications of the Förster Case on Legal Assessment of Integration Conditions for Third-country Nationals. *European Law Journal*, 17(2), pp. 172–189.

Jesse, M. (2016). The Unlawfulness of Existing Pre-departure Integration Conditions Applied in Family Reunification Scenarios – Urgent Need to Change National Laws in the European Union. *International Journal of Migration and Border Studies*, 2(3), pp. 274–288.

Kochenov, D. (2013). The Essence of European Citizenship Emerging from the Last Ten Years of Academic Debate: Beyond the Cherry Blossoms and the Moon? *International & Comparative Law Quarterly*, 62(1), pp. 97–136.

Kostakopoulou, T. (2002). Long-term Resident Third-country Nationals in the European Union: Normative Expectations and Institutional Openings. *Journal of Ethnic and Migration Studies*, 28(3), pp. 443–462.

Kostakopoulou, T. (2007). European Union Citizenship: Writing the Future. *European Law Journal*, 13(5), pp. 623–646.

Kostakopoulou, T. and Ripoll Servent, A. (2016). The Rule of Life. Family Reunification in EU Mobility and Migration Laws. In M. Fletcher, E. Herlin-Karnell and C. Matera (eds), *The European Union as an Area of Freedom, Security and Justice*. London and New York: Routledge, pp. 246–262.

Kostakopoulou, T., Carrera, S. and Jesse, M. (2009). Doing and Deserving: Competing Frames of Integration in the EU. In E. Guild, K. Groenendijk and S. Carrera (eds), *Illiberal Liberal States: Immigration, Citizenship and Integration in the EU*. Farnham: Ashgate, pp. 167–186.

Luedtke, A. (2009). Uncovering European Union Immigration Legislation: Policy Dynamics and Outcomes. *International Migration*, 49(2), pp. 1–27.

Maas, W. (2008). Migrants, States, and EU Citizenship's Unfulfilled Promise. *Citizenship Studies*, 12(6), pp. 583–596.

Menz, G. (2011). Stopping, Shaping and Moulding Europe: Two-level Games, Non-state Actors and the Europeanization of Migration Policies. *Journal of Common Market Studies*, 49(2), pp. 437–462.

Pratt, S. (2015). EU Policymaking and Research: Case Studies of the Communication on a Community Immigration Policy and the Common Basic Principles for Integration. In P. Scholten, H.B. Entzinger, R. Penninx and S. Verbeek (eds), *Integrating Immigrants in Europe: Research–Policy Dialogues*. New York: Springer Open, pp. 117–129.

Rea, A., Bonjour, S. and Jacobs, D. (2011). Introduction. In S. Bonjour, A. Rea and D. Jacobs (eds), *The Others in Europe: Legal and Social Categorization in Context*. Brussels: Les Editions de l'Université de Bruxelles, pp. 7–20.

Roos, C. (2013). *The EU and Immigration Policies. Cracks in the Walls of Fortress Europe?* Basingstoke and New York: Palgrave Macmillan.

Rosenow, K. (2008). Die Entstehung einer integrationspolitischen Agenda auf der Ebene der europäischen Union. In U. Hunger, C.M. Aybek, A. Ette and I. Michalowski (eds), *Migrations- und integrationsprozesse in Europa. Vergemeinschaftung oder nationalstaatliche Lösungswege*. Wiesbaden: VS Verlag für Sozialwissenschaften, pp. 123–142.

Schweitzer, R. (2015). A Stratified Right to Family Life? On the Logic(s) and Legitimacy of Granting Differential Access to Family Reunification for Third-country Nationals Living within the EU. *Journal of Ethnic and Migration Studies*, 41(13), pp. 2130–2148.

Strik, T. (2011). *Besluitvorming over asiel- en migratierichtlijnen. De wisselwerking tussen nationaal en Europees niveau*. Den Haag: Boom Juridische Uitgevers.

Strik, T., Hart, B.D. and Nissen, E. (2013). *Family Reunification: A Barrier or Facilitator of Integration? A Comparative Study*. Brussels/Dublin: European Integration Fund/Immigrant Council of Ireland. Available at https://emnbelgium.be/sites/default/files/publications/familyreunification-web.pdf (accessed January 26, 2017).

Thym, D. (2016). Towards a Contextual Conception of Social Integration in EU Immigration Law. Comments on P & S and K & A. *European Journal of Migration and Law*, 18, pp. 89–111.

Wagner, R. (2015). Family Life across Borders: Strategies and Obstacles to Integration. *Journal of Family Issues*, 36(11), pp. 1509–1528.

Wiesbrock, A. (2012). Granting Citizenship-related Rights to Third-country Nationals: An Alternative to the Full Extension of European Union Citizenship? *European Journal of Migration and Law*, 14(1), pp. 63–94.

PART IV

Justice and home affairs inside and outside Europe (the horizontal dimension)

19
EUROPE'S CORE MEMBER STATES
Intended and unintended consequences of strong policy-shaping traditions

Andreas Ette

Introduction

The historical developments of European justice and home affairs (JHA) are inextricably linked with the activities of Europe's core member states – Germany, France as well as the Benelux countries. These countries are not only founding members of the European Union (EU), but their similar geographic exposure and close connection influence their position in a state system increasingly characterized by 'differentiated membership' (Leuffen *et al.* 2012). As early as the 1970s and 1980s, these five countries started to cooperate outside of the traditional institutional European structures and established basic building blocks on which the Amsterdam Treaty would much later construct the Area of Freedom, Security and Justice (AFSJ). This early mover advantage provided those core member states with the ability to shape the policy domain closely along the lines of their own preferences. In addition, in the following decades, they remained principal drivers of JHA even under changing institutional environments in Europe. However, purely intergovernmental perspectives on these developments fall short because, in the meantime, cooperation on crime, terrorism and migration – originally started as a particular aspect of member states' foreign policy – was transformed into a highly integrated area of European home affairs. The past four decades of intensifying cooperation also had far-reaching consequences for core member states. These included the convergence of basic national problem-solving approaches, the implementation of an increasingly harmonized legal framework and the deep-seated integration of European JHA cooperation even into day-to-day administrative routines.

Research on this relationship between core member states and the EU has been structured along two major research interests – popularly coined as the 'gap hypothesis' and the 'convergence hypothesis' (Hollifield *et al.* 2014) – which both occupied scholars also outside Europe. Before discussing the consequences of the recent crises for future research avenues, this chapter offers an overview about major studies approaching these two research interests. The first hypothesis provides a basic rationale for European cooperation in the JHA domain. On the one hand, it posits discrepancies between the stated interests of politics and publics principally being in favor of more restrictive and security-oriented JHA policies, and the actual reality of more expansive and liberal state practices on the other. Whereas this 'gap' was explained by the more liberal interests of capitalist economic systems, national legal systems or the international human rights regime, it was European cooperation which provided core member states a retreat from those self-imposed constraints upon national sovereignty. The popular 'Fortress Europe' image resulted from strategic decisions of national governments regaining autonomy by escaping to Brussels. The increasing supranationalization of this policy area has only more recently questioned whether or not this European venue has developed into a 'new limit of control', increasingly mirroring the institutional environments on the national level.

The second hypothesis structuring research on core member states starts from the assumption that similar constellations of international security and migration problems result from an increasing convergence of JHA policies in the Western world. Comparative policy studies, Europeanization studies, scholars of policy transfer and diffusion as well as compliance research have all started to analyze the trajectories of JHA policies in core member states. Whereas, traditionally, clearly separable national models structured national justice systems and governed responses to immigration or international terrorism, in their more recent explanatory models about convergence, persistence and divergence, the European Union plays an increasingly important role.

European justice and home affairs and the autonomy of core member states

In a first period, academic analyses about shifting JHA competences from the national to the supranational level followed established theories of European integration and many of the pertinent studies developed their theoretical arguments with empirical reference to one or several of the core member states (e.g., Guiraudon 2000; Lavenex 2002). The specific national interest constellations among core member states may have differed at that time and their policy-shaping initiatives were hardly based on a shared agenda. Nevertheless, an overview about their role in these processes shows principally that the dynamic incorporation of JHA policies into the general process of European integration hardly qualifies as an indication of the erosion of the nation-state. Early neo-functionalist interpretations, which explained the emergence of European JHA policies as functional spill-overs from the Single European Market, were quickly dashed (Turnbull and Sandholtz 2001). Although the expansion of free movement rights curtailed national controls over the mobility of EU citizens, the capacities to control refugees and to provide national security have increased. During this first period, scholarly analyses converged mainly on constructivist and intergovernmental readings, arguing that the deliberate decision of core member states to shift sovereignty to Brussels actually intended to strengthen the nation-state and provided them with greater autonomy over JHA (for an overview, see Bossong and Rhinard 2016).

Securitization, venue-shopping and the hardening of control

The constructivist explanatory approach points to the importance of discourses and the role of ideas and norms for the integration of JHA. Representatives of this approach in particular show how refugees and immigrants in Europe have been reframed, moving from humanitarian and economic objects into security objects. Focusing either on the discursive or on the practice dimension of securitization (Balzacq *et al.* 2016; see also Kaunert and Yakubov, Chapter 3, this volume), studies in this area concentrate empirically mainly on the European level and demonstrate how the creation of an internal security problem was used to establish a close link between the abolition of internal border controls and the necessity to strengthen the control of refugees and migrants as well as the external borders of the EU in order to guarantee a sufficient level of control (Huysmans 2000). The events of 9/11 have particularly reinforced the security–migration nexus, but have also shifted the securitization framework towards other issues like terrorism or cyber security. In her seminal study, Lavenex (2002) demonstrated with the French and German cases how this link has been subsequently used to justify national asylum reforms that would not have otherwise been considered legitimate.

From a completely different theoretical angle, intergovernmental reasoning about two-level games explains the development of JHA by the empowering effects European cooperation has for national executives, permitting them to loosen domestic constraints. Under the label of 'venue-shopping', Guiraudon (2000) demonstrated with the German, French and Dutch cases how the shift to the European level provided national governments with alternative decision-making procedures, allowing them to avoid judicial control as well as parliamentary oversight. With a focus on Germany, Monar (2003: 322) argued that the European integration of JHA is consequently best understood as a strictly 'government-led and controlled process'. Based on empirical analyses of different core member states, scholars have shown that despite an increasing supranationalization of JHA, state-centric motives for European cooperation prevailed and continued to provide national home affairs ministries with extra political resources by offering alternative justifications for policies and greater control over the domestic agendas (e.g., Givens and Luedtke 2004; Menz 2011).

Constructivist as well as intergovernmental approaches explain how the 'hardening of the tools of control' (Guild 2006) has developed into a general characteristic of this policy area. The outcomes of JHA policies closely followed the restrictive agenda of core member state executives generally favoring security and control measures to the detriment of civil rights and freedom. The following example draws upon the development of policies addressing irregular migration to illustrate the working of such securitization and venue-shopping processes. The origins of these policies are found in the early 1990s when core member states started integrating the forced removal of irregularly staying foreigners into their overall national migration control strategies. As a consequence, these countries were soon confronted with a 'deportation gap' (Ellermann 2006: 294) describing the discrepancies between the number of principally deportable migrants and actual deportations carried out. Although they quickly established national legislative and infrastructural abilities to deport increasing numbers of irregular migrants, following the Amsterdam Treaty there was increasing demand for European cooperation to develop a more comprehensive and effective set of policies and institutions consisting of three basic dimensions.

The first dimension concerns the identification of irregular migrants by the implementation of shared technical infrastructures. The Schengen Information System (SIS) was originally agreed upon by Belgium, France, Germany, Luxembourg and The Netherlands, and marks the oldest of these infrastructures. In the meantime, these systems have multiplied and now also include the Eurodac database, the Visa Information System as well as additional infrastructures like Eurosur as a border surveillance system (Broeders 2007). The current refugee and security crises have provided additional opportunities to extend those infrastructures. These include in particular the adoption of the European Passenger Name Records system following the erosion of Germany's previous commitment to data protection (Ripoll Servent and MacKenzie 2016). In addition, new proposals for a European Travel Information and Authorisation System (ETIAS) have been tabled and – following a German initiative in early 2016 – existing systems like SIS will likely be extended for new purposes.

The second dimension concerns policies addressing the missing cooperation of countries of origin or transit for readmitting irregular migrants. Previously only a purely bilateral endeavor by France and other core member states, today it is the European Commission which is the major actor in negotiating readmission agreements on behalf of all member states, particularly in those cases where unilateral strategies are doomed to fail. These agreements work to increase the principal disposition of countries of origin to readmit irregular migrants. Following a French initiative, this principal externalization strategy was enhanced to also include the negotiation of mobility partnerships. In the context of the recent refugee crisis, it was particularly German efforts – motivated by an interest in a common European solution combined with domestic constraints – that prepared the EU–Turkey deal of March 2016 and which now serves as a potential blueprint for the prospective return of irregular migrants.

Finally, a third dimension concerns existing administrative hurdles in enforcing the forced return of irregular migrants. Here, the EU has become an important venue to facilitate operational cooperation among member states by establishing common administrative standards and procedures. Of greatest importance in this respect has been the development of Frontex, the European border agency, an initiative by five member states including Belgium, France and Germany that today provides an important supportive structure for member states (Léonard 2010). Its activities on return cooperation have increased rapidly and, following a proposal from the Commission in December 2015 – supported by France and Germany – the newly created European Border and Coast Guard with its Returns Office as well as a pool of more than 600 return experts will likely accelerate this role.

In all three dimensions of this policy addressing the forced removal of irregular migrants, core member states have been the main actors shaping common European solutions. The relevance of these policies has been documented in a number of recent studies demonstrating how these new European policies have considerably changed the national administrative practices – particularly in core member states – which are using those new structures most extensively (Ette 2017; Slominski and Trauner 2014). The overall developments in this policy area closely follow the venue-shopping predictions. Today, the policies addressing the forced removal of irregular migrants in those member states are characterized by dualist systems combining older national structures with new European ones. Together, these dualist systems have reduced some of the previously existing enforcement constraints, increased the executives' autonomy, and reduced the political, diplomatic and financial costs of this policy.

Supranationalization and the 'new limits of control'

In the early days of European JHA cooperation, securitization and venue-shopping approaches were seen as nearly universal approaches explaining the political dynamics and respective policy outcomes in core member states. A second period developed after the turn of the millennium, as there were some institutional and substantive changes that challenged those dominant explanations and resulted in a greater diversity of theoretical approaches. More recent contributions (e.g., Ette 2017; Kaunert and Léonard 2012) argue that the applicability of venue-shopping has become more limited and that policy areas still meeting the approaches' original assumptions have decreased. Although previously established intergovernmental modes of cooperation have not disappeared and JHA has developed into a prime example of 'new intergovernmentalism' (Maricut 2016), those reforms of the past decade shifted the policy area towards supranationalization and now provide for a new institutional context of cooperation. Whereas the European integration of JHA was originally an escape from national limits of control curtailing core member states in introducing more effective policies, the European level has itself in the meantime developed into a 'new limit of control' (Ette 2017). Empirical examples of European membership increasing refugee and migrant rights are already well documented for southern and eastern member states (cf. Finotelli, Chapter 20, this volume). For core member states, however, only the last few years have witnessed similar unintended consequences demonstrating that European cooperation does not necessarily follow the venue-shopping predictions.

An already well-established example illustrating such new policy-making dynamics refers to the family policy reforms in France, Germany and The Netherlands after the turn of the millennium. In the beginning, the Family Reunification Directive of 2003 resulted in only minor domestic effects in those states. In the long run, however, the Directive developed into an important instrument resulting in liberal rulings by the Court of Justice and locking in existing national policies by the minimum standards prescribed in European legislation (cf. Bonjour, Chapter 18, this volume).

A second example refers to the Common European Asylum System (CEAS) whose early precursors have started a race to the bottom with regard to refugee rights. Following the Amsterdam Treaty, developments at the European and national level demonstrated that policies have either remained at the status quo or have seen a rise in standards (Thielemann and El-Enany 2011; Zaun 2015). In an analysis of the dynamics in Germany's asylum policy since the late 1990s, Ette (2017) rejects venue-shopping as an explanatory mechanism. European institutions, not national executives, initiated the constitutionalization of refugee rights, and despite governmental interests in preserving existing policy frameworks, European cooperation reversed a previously existing restrictive policy trend in Germany. Liberal reforms included, for example, the recognition of non-state persecution, the termination of the 'religious subsistence level' doctrine as well as steps towards reducing restrictive aspects of Germany's deterrence regime. The underlying political processes of these reforms played out in different institutional venues: the legislative process, the judicial venue as well as lobbying by civil society actors. But in all cases the initiatives of the European Commission – and in subsequent policy processes also by the European Court of Justice and the European Parliament – and not two-level games of national governments constituted the crucial factor tipping domestic political forces. These examples do not add up to a liberal family or refugee policy in core member states. The altered institutional environment at the European level nevertheless resulted in some policy outcomes which indicate that during this second period 'the pendulum between security and liberty […] tentatively starts to move back' (Trauner and Lavenex 2015: 220).

Globalization, Europeanization and convergence in core member states

The second research question structuring much of the available literature on core member states is interested in the broad trajectories of JHA during recent decades. Because of the supranationalization of this policy area and the density of common regulations, an increase in the similarity between policies during recent decades is more likely to take place among European member states compared to other world regions. The overview focuses first on the description of policy trajectories among core member states before discussing available findings on major mechanisms driving convergence, persistence or divergence of policies.

From national towards European models

Justice and home affairs are generally deeply entrenched in national political and judicial systems and their culturally specific understandings of sovereignty and state security. Particularly pronounced in the area of citizenship and migration studies, European core member states were regularly seen as belonging to different national models. The French republican model, the Dutch multicultural model, a regionalized model in Belgium as well as an ethnic model characterizing Germany have all dominated the debates. Whether these ideal types, which are based on strong internal consistence and coherence, ever existed as an actual societal and political phenomenon is open to debate, but overall consensus exists that during the past two decades these models have changed fundamentally and lost some of their heuristic potential (for an overview about this debate see Finotelli and Michalowski 2012). Since the early 2000s, for example, The Netherlands experienced a turn towards assimilation, most recently followed by a shift towards policy mainstreaming embedding immigrant integration within more general welfare state policies (Breugel and Scholten 2017). Similarly, Germany has seen far-reaching reforms during the same time frame. These include the *ius soli* amendments to its citizenship policy as well as the development of comprehensive immigration and integration legislation shifting the country away from former ethnic conceptualizations (Faist 2007).

In the analysis of national JHA policy trajectories, the selection of countries or other jurisdictions together with the time frame and the different policy areas under investigation, irrespective of the actual methodology to measure convergence, all have a major impact upon the final results. With respect to the influence of case selection, the most prominent examples of convergence in the JHA domain have been catching-up processes of new or potential future member states aiming at conformity with the existing acquis of the traditional EU member states (Faist and Ette 2007). But also in the case of core member states, the selection of country cases determines final conclusions. An example may be seen in the case of civic integration policies, which include obligatory language and country knowledge requirements with tests and contracts for new immigrants. Such policies did not exist until the late 1990s, and several studies focusing on the example of The Netherlands and Germany describe an obviously convergent trend. Taking into account other cases like Belgium or studying the details of policy instruments studies result in more differentiated conclusions (Goodman 2010).

Similarly, time and timing affect the trend of the dependent variable. In particular, scholars with a legal background or who are interested in the compliance of member states with European regulations often adopt relatively restricted approaches on the timing of national responses. Methodologically they are regularly based on official statistics about transposition notifications or infringement proceedings and lack information about national adaptation during the protracted preparation phases of European instruments as well as their potential long-term consequences. In addition, the time period has a major impact upon results of convergence in the JHA domain. Whereas earlier studies on core member states regularly focused on the approximation of the previously existing different national models and 'philosophies', more recent studies concentrate on the harmonization of legislative frameworks and administrative routines.

Finally, disparate developments in different areas of the JHA domain also lead to inconsistent findings about convergence among core member states. One obvious explanation could be discrepancies with respect to the level and scope of supranationalization: Whereas police cooperation and asylum policies are both highly integrated, integration and citizenship policies are still dominated by intergovernmental modes of cooperation, but the reality is even more complex with police cooperation actually constituting an area with a comparatively low level of convergence. Police cooperation is one of the areas of JHA where European cooperation started first with an impressive legislative output and increasing expectation of similarities among member state practices. Similarly, the existence of numerous executive European agencies, such as Europol, Eurojust and the European Police Academy, in this field would bolster the same conclusion (Occhipinti 2015). In her studies, den Boer (2014) argues instead that policing remains far removed from supranational politics and explains the existing implementation gap as a lack of trust among national administrations. But even within individual policy areas, the case selection of specific policy instruments has an impact on final conclusions. When scholars focus on specific aspects like the codification of terrorist offenses, aviation security or terrorism financing – instead of police cooperation or counter-terrorism policies in their totality – they find greater degrees of convergence and a catching-up process by Germany and The Netherlands to an already existing French approach (Nohrstedt and Hansen 2010).

The Common European Asylum System (CEAS) constitutes a policy area with a higher level of convergence. Converging policy trends among core member states started no later than the 1990s, when The Netherlands, for example, copied the experiences of their neighbors and introduced restrictive asylum reforms closely in line with the developments in Germany. With the supranationalization of this policy area, the legislative frameworks increasingly conform to each other even in areas where no strict European policy templates exist. The introduction of accelerated asylum procedures based on safe country of origin policies is an example of those informal governance arrangements. Whereas in 1990 hardly any EU member state had a safe country of origin policy in place, in 2013 only four EU member states remained without such a policy and there is an increasing similarity within this policy in its everyday practice (Engelmann 2014). Following a fundamentally different methodological approach, Toshkov and Haan (2013) also found evidence of a convergent effect of CEAS focusing on the major outcome indicators of asylum policy. They show that European countries have become more alike in terms of the percentage of people to whom they offer protection. Nevertheless, CEAS is still based on different national asylum systems and, despite the comparatively high level of harmonization, these converging trends do not hide the remaining discrepancies in refugee protection, even among core member states.

Mechanisms of convergence

In addition to the description of cross-national policy reforms towards convergence, persistence or divergence among core member states, it is similarly appealing to study the causal factors of those changes. Two major lines of debate can be differentiated, with the first discussing whether these convergent policy trends are caused solely by internal factors or also by external ones. In the case of counter-terrorism policy, for example, Lehrke and Schomaker (2014) argue that for nineteen OECD countries convergent trends may be caused by a general trend of emergency in the Western world or a specific US influence instead of a purely European response. Koopmans and Michalowski (2017) end up with similar conclusions in their analysis of twenty-nine countries worldwide, highlighting that being a member state of the EU has no significant impact upon the level of immigrant rights. These findings only partly apply to policy trajectories among core member states and are hardly surprising. The original presentation of the 'convergence hypothesis' already pointed to strong factors pushing policies in the Western world in a similar direction. Nevertheless, qualitative evidence on the trend towards highly skilled labor migration policies in Europe's core member states also provides conflicting findings. Based on the developments in Germany, France and The Netherlands, recent studies dispute the causal relevance of European-level policies compared to different varieties of capitalism or domestic politics frameworks (e.g., Cerna 2016; Paul 2015).

The second line of debate on the causal factors of convergence highlights the differences between vertical and horizontal mechanisms of Europeanization. The vertical logic describes the central penetration of national policies by adapting to a common European framework. In the context of the EU-28, such a mechanism particularly shaped the most recent enlargement processes where new member states were coerced into adapting to the existing JHA acquis. But also within the core member states, the EU has the resources to make member states comply – particularly in highly supranationalized areas. Next to the previously discussed CEAS, there are many empirical examples across all areas of JHA. In the case of integration policies, the introduction of European anti-discrimination policies in the year 2000 resulted in a widespread adoption of this policy framework and fundamentally reoriented previously existing national models governing equality in core member states like France or Germany (Bell 2008). Similarly, the European Arrest Warrant (EAW) marks a major example in the area of police cooperation. Its underlying Framework Decision replaced traditional extradition procedures and countries now receiving an EAW are supposed to search and surrender the wanted person. Den Boer and Wiegand (2015: 399) show that in France, Germany and The Netherlands the EAW has developed into a widely used instrument, which has resulted in a high level of procedural convergence and the spread of standard administrative routines.

In policy areas, which only recently switched to supranational modes of cooperation, such vertical logics are hardly convincing. More horizontal mechanisms are highlighted by policy transfer and diffusion studies analyzing the influence of policy decisions made in other member states through softer mechanisms (Gilardi 2010). In such cases, the EU functions as a forum supporting horizontal convergence by developing and spreading new perspectives and understandings. Empirical examples include the exchange of knowledge by organizations like the European Migration Network (Geddes and Scholten 2015). The introduction of pre-departure integration requirements for family migrants again provides an appropriate example. While most available studies claim that the EU has spread those policies, Bonjour (2014) shows that the EU has only functioned as a platform for the exchange of ideas. The Commission even attempted to obstruct this process and it was the German and French governments which – in this case in line with the venue-shopping predictions – wanted to present such measures as European practice to build legitimacy for restrictive national reforms.

The European crises as test cases for theory development

Recent years have witnessed a fundamentally changing context for Europe's core member states and their hitherto existing policy-shaping tradition. Whereas the collapse of the Warsaw Pact and the East–West confrontation originally gave rise to the dynamic development of JHA since the late 1980s, the most recent developments potentially offer a comparable challenge. The protests in North Africa and the Middle East from 2011 onward resulted in unprecedented levels of forcibly displaced people and growing numbers of refugees from these regions into Europe. In addition to this 'refugee crisis', there has been a recent increase in Islamic terrorism, with Belgium, France, Germany and other European and non-European countries having experienced major attacks as spill-overs from the civil wars in Syria and Iraq. These 'crises' have brought JHA back to the top of political and public agendas in core member states. The economic recession since 2008 has shown that such crises are not only policy-making challenges, but also provide major research avenues to test and refine existing theories of European integration (e.g., Tosun et al. 2014). Similarly, the recent crises affecting JHA raise expectations of scientifically based policy advice, but also provide formidable test cases to push recent thinking further. For moving the research agenda on core member states forward (Bonjour et al. 2017), the 'gap hypothesis' as well as the 'convergence hypothesis' will continue to structure major research avenues even under changing contexts.

The European responses to these crises in JHA have been inconsistent from the very beginning. On the one hand, fundamentally different political interests and a renationalization trend have shaped these responses, including controversial negotiations of common responses and their half-hearted national implementation. On the other hand, the past few years have witnessed sweeping policy reforms that were unthinkable only months before. This applies to the establishment of the European Border and Coast Guard Agency as well as proposals for a European Union Agency for Asylum, both increasing the operational resources of CEAS.

Furthermore, the introduction of a relocation mechanism of asylum-seekers from Greece and Italy together with the hotspot approach provides a more direct approach to sharing responsibility.

Confronted with such dynamic but inconsistent policy trends, scholars have to keep track of the trajectories of these policies with converging policies being a major precondition for greater solidarity among member states. Methodologically, citizenship and migration studies have seen recent progress for measuring and quantifying policy changes (Bjerre et al. 2015; Koopmans and Michalowski 2017). The study of policy convergence in Europe's core member states will profit enormously from those endeavors. Quantitative measures over long time periods will allow for assessing the impact of the recent crises upon actual policy developments. But in advancing this research agenda, one also has to keep its caveats in mind and extend the thematic scope of the available quantitative measures to additional areas like data protection or counter-terrorism.

The current crises in JHA not only affected the outcomes of policies but also altered the underlying multi-level political processes. On the national level, this particularly concerns the increasing politicization of the JHA domain in all core member states. The reinforced security-migration nexus as well as a general globalization backlash allowed populist parties to successfully mobilize against migration issues. On the European level, the resurgence of intergovernmental modes of cooperation has also contributed to a change in the institutional environment with an abundance of European summits shifting the European Council into a key actor in day-to-day decision-making in JHA. In this changed political context, core member states strongly shaped the unfolding of the 'refugee crisis'. This had already started years before with their non-response to enduring calls by Southern European member states for more burden-sharing and a reform of the Dublin System. In the years since 2015, Germany in particular has been taking the lead. The suspension of the Dublin rules for Syrian refugees in September 2015, the adoption of the relocation mechanism against the objection of four Eastern European countries in the European Council only weeks later as well as the negotiation of the EU–Turkey agreement of March 2016 were all only weakly coordinated with Germany's European partners. These unilateral activities contributed to a swelling critique about the hegemonic role of Germany, and the imminent exit of the United Kingdom will even increase the central role of core member states in the EU, all exacerbating necessary compromises in Europe. Not least because of the historically close relationship with the Visegrád countries, Germany has a particular responsibility for finding a new balance between these increasing cleavages of core and Eastern member states, but also for establishing a more fundamental solution with Southern European countries going beyond the provisional relocation mechanisms. These European crises together with the policy-shaping tradition of core member states have reinforced 'new intergovernmentalism' in JHA. They are likely to contribute to a lack of transparency and legitimacy of European policy-making known from earlier periods of cooperation and will likely decrease rights for citizens and migrants alike. But the actual impact of the crises in JHA can only be assessed on the basis of detailed analyses about the trajectories of policies in core member states as well as their underlying multi-level political processes.

Bibliography

Balzacq, T., Léonard, S. and Ruzicka, J. (2016). 'Securitization' Revisited: Theory and Cases. *International Relations*, 30(4), pp. 494–531.

Bell, M. (2008). The Implementation of European Anti-discrimination Directives: Converging towards a Common Model? *The Political Quarterly*, 79(1), pp. 36–44.

Bjerre, L., Helbling, M., Römer, F. and Zobel, M. (2015). Conceptualizing and Measuring Immigration Policies. A Comparative Perspective. *International Migration Review*, 49(3), pp. 555–600.

Bonjour, S. (2014). The Transfer of Pre-departure Integration Requirements for Family Migrants among Member States of the European Union. *Comparative Migration Studies*, 2(2), pp. 203–226.

Bonjour, S., Ripoll Servent, A. and Thielemann, E. (2017). Beyond Venue Shopping and Liberal Constraint: A New Research Agenda for EU Migration Policies and Politics. *Journal of European Public Policy*, OnlineFirst, pp. 1–13.

Bossong, R. and Rhinard, M. (2016). Alternative Perspectives on Internal Security Cooperation in the European Union. In Bossong, R. and Rhinard, M. (eds), *Theorizing Internal Security in the European Union*. Oxford: Oxford University Press, pp. 3–27.

Breugel, M. V. and Scholten, P. (2017). Mainstreaming in Response to Superdiversity? The Governance of Migration-related Diversity in France, the UK and the Netherlands. *Policy and Politics*. doi: 10.1332/030557317X14849132401769.

Broeders, D. (2007). The New Digital Borders of Europe: EU Databases and the Surveillance of Irregular Migrants. *International Sociology*, 22(1), pp. 71–92.

Cerna, L. (2016). *Immigration Policies and the Global Competition for Talent*. Basingstoke: Palgrave Macmillan.

Den Boer, M. (2014). Police, Policy and Politics in Brussels: Scenarios for the Shift from Sovereignty to Solidarity. *Cambridge Review of International Affairs*, 27(1), pp. 48–65.

Den Boer, M. and Wiegand, I. (2015). From Convergence to Deep Integration: Evaluating the Impact of EU Counter-terrorism Strategies on Domestic Arenas. *Intelligence and National Security*, 30(2–3), pp. 377–401.

Ellermann, A. (2006). Street-level Democracy: How Immigration Bureaucrats Manage Public Opposition. *West European Politics*, 29(2), pp. 293–309.

Engelmann, C. (2014). Convergence against the Odds: The Development of Safe Country of Origin Policies in EU Member States (1990–2013). *European Journal of Migration and Law*, 16(2), pp. 277–302.

Ette, A. (2017). *Migration and Refugee Policies in Germany. New European Limits of Control?* Opladen: Barbara Budrich.

Faist, T. (2007). *Dual Citizenship in Europe: From Nationhood to Societal Integrations*. Aldershot: Ashgate.

Faist, T. and Ette, A. (eds) (2007). *The Europeanization of National Policies and Politics of Immigration. Between Autonomy and the European Union*. Basingstoke: Palgrave Macmillan.

Finotelli, C. and Michalowski, I. (2012). The Heuristic Potential of Models of Citizenship and Immigrant Integration Reviewed. *Journal of Immigrant and Refugee Studies*, 10(3), pp. 231–240.

Geddes, A. and Scholten, P. (2015). Policy Analysis and Europeanization: An Analysis of EU Migrant Integration Policymaking. *Journal of Comparative Policy Analysis*, 17(1), pp. 41–59.

Gilardi, F. (2010). Who Learns from What in Policy Diffusion Processes? *American Journal of Political Science*, 54(3), pp. 650–666.

Givens, T. and Luedtke, A. (2004). The Politics of European Union Immigration Policy: Institutions, Salience, and Harmonization. *The Policy Studies Journal*, 32(1), pp. 145–165.

Goodman, S.W. (2010). Integration Requirements for Integration's Sake? Identifying, Categorising and Comparing Civic Integration Policies. *Journal of Ethnic and Migration Studies*, 36(5), pp. 753–772.

Guild, E. (2006). Danger – Borders under Construction: Assessing the First Five Years of Border Policy in an Area of Freedom, Security and Justice. In Zwaan, J.W. d and Goudappel, F. (eds), *Freedom, Security and Justice in the European Union: Implementation of the Hague Programme*. The Hague: Asser Press, pp. 45–72.

Guiraudon, V. (2000). European Integration and Migration Policy: Vertical Policymaking as Venue-shopping. *Journal of Common Market Studies*, 38(2), pp. 251–271.

Hollifield, J.F., Martin, P.L. and Orrenius, P.M. (2014). The Dilemmas of Immigration Control. In Hollifield, J.F., Martin, P. and Orrenius, P. (eds), *Controlling Immigration: A Global Perspective*. Stanford, CA: Stanford University Press, pp. 3–34.

Huysmans, J. (2000), The European Union and the Securitization of Migration. *Journal of Common Market Studies*, 38(5), pp. 751–777.

Kaunert, C. and Léonard, S. (2012). The Development of the EU Asylum Policy: Venue-shopping in Perspective. *Journal of European Public Policy*, 19(9), pp. 1396–1413.

Koopmans, R. and Michalowski, I. (2017). Why Do States Extend Rights to Immigrants? Institutional Settings and Historical Legacies across 44 Countries Worldwide. *Comparative Political Studies*, 50(1), pp. 41–74.

Lavenex, S. (2002). *The Europeanisation of Refugee Policies: Between Human Rights and Internal Security*. Farnham: Ashgate.

Lehrke, J.P. and Schomaker, R. (2014): Mechanisms of Convergence in Domestic Counterterrorism Regulations: American Influence, Domestic Needs, and International Networks. *Studies in Conflict & Terrorism*, 37(8), pp. 689–712.

Léonard, S. (2010). EU Border Security and Migration into the European Union: FRONTEX and Securitisation through Practices. *European Security*, 19(2), pp. 231–254.

Leuffen, D., Rittberger, B. and Schimmelfennig, F. (2012). *Differentiated Integration. Explaining Variation in the European Union.* Basingstoke: Palgrave Macmillan.

Maricut, A. (2016). With and Without Supranationalisation: The Post-Lisbon Roles of the European Council and the Council in Justice and Home Affairs Governance. *Journal of European Integration*, 38(5), pp. 541–555.

Menz, G. (2011). Stopping, Shaping and Moulding Europe: Two-level Games, Non-state Actors and the Europeanization of Migration Policies. *Journal of Common Market Studies*, 49(2), pp. 437–462.

Monar, J. (2003). Justice and Home Affairs: Europeanization as a Government-controlled Process. In Dyson, K. and Goetz, K. (eds), *Germany, Europe and the Politics of Constraint*. Oxford: Oxford University Press, pp. 309–324.

Nohrstedt, D. and Hansen, D. (2010). Converging under Pressure? Counterterrorism Policy Developments in the European Union Member States. *Public Administration*, 88(1), pp. 190–210.

Occhipinti, J.D. (2015). Still Moving Toward a European FBI? Re-examining the Politics of EU Police Cooperation. *Intelligence and National Security*, 30(2–3), pp. 234–258.

Paul, R. (2015). *The Political Economy of Border-drawing: Arranging Legality in European Labor Migration Policies.* New York: Berghahn.

Ripoll Servent, A. and Mackenzie, A. (2016). Eroding Germany's Commitment to Data Protection: Policy Entrepreneurs and Coalition Politics in EU Passenger Name Records. *German Politics*. doi: 10.1080/09644008.2016.1250889.

Slominski, P. and Trauner, F. (2014). Die Europäisierung der Abschiebepolitik Österreichs: Mehr Handlungsoptionen für staatliche AkteurInnen oder mehr Schutz für Betroffene? *Österreichische Zeitschrift für Politikwissenschaft*, 43(2), pp. 151–168.

Thielemann, E.R. and El-Enany, N. (2011). The Impact of the EU on National Asylum Policies. In Wolff, S., Zwaan, J.W. d. and Goudappel, F. (eds), *Freedom, Security and Justice after Lisbon and Stockholm*. The Hague: TMC Asser Press, pp. 97–116.

Toshkov, D. and Haan, L. de (2013). The Europeanization of Asylum Policy: An Assessment of the EU Impact on Asylum Applications and Recognitions Rates. *Journal of European Public Policy*, 20(5), pp. 661–683.

Tosun, J., Wetzel, A. and Zapryanova, G. (2014). The EU in Crises: Advancing the Debate. *Journal of European Integration*, 36(3), pp. 195–211.

Trauner, F. and Lavenex, S. (2015). A Comparative View. Understanding and Explaining Policy Change in the Area of Freedom, Security and Justice. In Trauner, F. and Ripoll Servent, A. (eds), *Policy Change in the Area of Freedom, Security and Justice. How EU Institutions Matter*. London: Routledge, pp. 219–240.

Turnbull, P. and Sandholtz, W. (2001). Policing and Immigration: The Creation of New Policy Spaces. In Stone Sweet, A., Sandholtz, W. and Fligstein, N. (eds), *The Institutionalization of Europe*. Oxford: Oxford University Press, pp. 194–220.

Zaun, N. (2015). Why EU Asylum Standards Exceed the Lowest Common Denominator: The Role of Regulatory Expertise in EU Decision-making. *Journal of European Public Policy*. doi: 10.1080/13501763.2015.1039565.

20
SOUTHERN EUROPE
Twenty-five years of immigration control on the waterfront

Claudia Finotelli

Introduction

Southern Europe's most recent migration history is closely linked to Europe's major immigration crises. It was the migration crisis caused by the breakdown of the Soviet Union and the war in ex-Yugoslavia that first highlighted the crucial role played by Southern European countries in protecting Europe's external borders. As the new 'guardians' of the border following the implementation of the Schengen Agreement, they were confronted *prima facie* with tensions between 'internal security considerations and humanitarian issues' (Lavenex 2001: 852) by having to stop the entry of unwanted migrants while simultaneously guaranteeing humanitarian protection standards for refugees. As Schuster (2011: 17) put it, a heavy burden fell on the member states 'least equipped to cope' with the new migration challenge due to their recent migration history and lack of efficient asylum regimes.

The adaptation of Mediterranean control regimes to the imperatives of a common European border has been met with widespread skepticism about their ability to manage such a challenge. Southern European migration countries were considered to have lax migration regimes with weak border controls, large irregular migration flows and few guarantees for asylum-seekers and refugees (e.g., Baldwin-Edwards 1997). The lack of adequate regulation systems to manage immigration flows quickly became the hallmark of what has been labeled the 'Southern model of migration' (King *et al.* 2000; King and De Bono 2013). The large number of irregular migrants compared with the small number of refugees in Southern Europe has also often been used to highlight the North–South divide between weak and strong control regimes across the European immigration panorama (e.g., Thränhardt 2003). In particular, large flows of irregular migrants and frequent regularization processes turned these regimes into the most evident example of the gap between 'restrictive policy goals and expansionist outcomes' within the European Union (Cornelius *et al.* 2014). Furthermore, low asylum figures in Southern Europe underpinned the so-called 'welfare-magnet thesis', according to which asylum-seekers who first arrive in Southern Europe decide to migrate further on to Northern Europe, where they expect to obtain higher welfare benefits (e.g., Bloch and Schuster 2002).

However, more recent studies claim that Southern European countries have improved their regulation frameworks and control capacity over time (e.g., Peixoto *et al.* 2012; Pastore 2014). Second, it has been proven that Southern and Northern European countries do not differ on account of the existence or absence of irregular flows, but in the way they manage their presence (Finotelli 2009; Bommes and Sciortino 2011; Echeverría 2016). Third, it is also the case that structural differences challenge the perceived homogeneity of Southern European regimes (Baldwin-Edwards 2012).

This notwithstanding, the most recent Mediterranean crisis, this time caused by the collapse of Arab states and the civil war in Syria, revived the image of Southern European countries as ports of entry to Europe due to the increasing numbers of refugees and immigrants landing on the Southern European shores of the EU. Media images of obsolete and overcrowded reception structures in Italy and Greece suggested that Southern European countries are still ill prepared to face the new migration challenge. It appears that Southern European countries still have trouble shaking off their reputation as 'transit countries' with porous borders and extremely unattractive asylum systems. Does this mean that very little has changed in Southern Europe since the first migration crisis in the 1990s? Or does the idea of a North–South divide in immigration and asylum still bias the public perception of Southern European migration regimes?

The aim of this chapter is to discuss these questions by analyzing the evolution of Southern European control systems since the migration crisis of the 1990s. The challenge represented by the migration crisis of 2015, the strategic position of Southern European countries in its management and public anxiety regarding their control capacity all generate a need to highlight improvements as well as persisting weaknesses at the Southern European border. To this end, our analysis will focus on Italy, Spain, Greece and Malta. The reason for this choice is that irregular migration is a structural feature of their migration regimes (e.g., Baldwin-Edwards and Arango 1999; King and Thomson 2008; Peixoto et al. 2012). Moreover, all four countries share the Mediterranean border and have islands (or are islands themselves), which makes them particularly exposed 'blue borders' (Cutitta 2014; Bernardie-Tahir and Schmoll 2014).[1]

The analysis presented in this chapter is structured into three key themes. In the first theme, the main pillars of border management (visa policy, border policing and bilateral cooperation) are discussed. In the second theme, an overview is given of Southern European asylum systems and their functioning mechanisms. Finally, the third theme deals with internal controls and their relevance to the struggle against irregular migration. The chapter concludes with an outline of some of the most significant research gaps which, when closed, may facilitate a better assessment of the role of Southern European control regimes in the control of Europe's external borders.

Managing the external border

The management of Southern European borders has certainly been one of the core issues of the European Justice and Home Affairs (JHA) Council since the beginning of the 1990s. The implementation of the Schengen Agreement in 1995 was accompanied by increasing pressure on Southern European member states to improve the performance of their external control systems to adequately protect the EU's southern borders. Initial efforts involved the introduction of more restrictive visa regulations, as visa policies are a fundamental pillar of European harmonization on immigration and asylum. The evidence available to date shows that Southern European countries have significantly strengthened their visa regimes since the 1990s in order to meet the imperatives of EU membership (Sciortino and Pastore 2004). Moreover, analysis of visa implementation has called into question the reputation of Southern European countries as lax entry avenues to Europe. Indeed, Southern European countries have been far more restrictive in issuing visas to non-EU Eastern European citizens than Northern EU members (Finotelli and Sciortino 2013). The strengthening of border policing has helped improve Southern European border management even further. Funding allocated by individual member states as well as by the EU for the 'security' of its southern border has grown significantly over the past ten years. Moreover, Southern European governments have been requesting greater involvement on the part of the European Union in the control of its Southern European borders and have repeatedly asked the EU for more financial resources and personnel to face the migration challenges of Europe's 'blue borders' (Wolff 2008). In this respect, Spain was certainly one of the countries that most actively supported the creation of Frontex, the European border agency which has coordinated or participated in several joint operations in the Mediterranean Sea since its creation in 2004 (Bialasiewicz 2012; Carrera 2007).

However, if the commitment to more restrictive visa policies and more intensive border policing is deeply embedded in the imperatives of European membership, the degree of such a commitment is often markedly national. Spain, for instance, has significantly lower visa rejection rates for Latin Americans and Moroccans than Italy. In addition, there is evidence that French consular representatives are also more generous than their Italian counterparts in issuing visas to Moroccan immigrants (Infantino 2014). Not surprisingly, Southern European member states, like other European countries, pursue a de facto 'selective liberalization' of visa policy implementation, which depends on different geopolitical, economic and historical relationships with the countries of origin involved (Finotelli and Sciortino 2013). Remarkable cross-country differences have also been observed in the case of border policing. Here, Spain acts as the 'model student' in Southern European border management, thanks to the implementation of sophisticated border technologies, such as the Sistema Integrado de Vigilacia Exterior (SIVE), an integrated system of external surveillance, or the 'Berlinization' of the border in Ceuta and Melilla by constructing and reinforcing fences between Spain and Morocco (Godenau 2014; Gabrielli 2014). Border sealing in the case of Greece appears to have been less successful, in spite of some improvement thanks to the support provided by Frontex (Lauth Bacas 2010; Kasimis 2012). Italy is the only country that has attempted to combine border policing with rescue operations of immigrants detected on the high seas (e.g., Mare Nostrum)[2] to prevent large numbers of migrants from drowning in the Mediterranean (Pastore and Roman 2014). Finally, it must be said that, especially in emergency cases, current (and often ambiguous) European legislation leaves considerable room for national responses and interpretations, often leading to tensions among the member states involved. This is what occurred, for instance, when France reintroduced border controls during the Lampedusa crisis of 2011 (McMahon 2012) or in the conflict between Malta and Italy on the disembarkation location of migrants rescued on the high seas (Mainwaring 2012).

The focus on the national component of border controls inevitably draws attention to bilateral cooperation, which represents the most prominent example of the intersection between common control goals and national strategies. The proliferation of bilateral agreements shows that the European control imperative went beyond intra-EU cooperation involving third countries in the control of Europe's external borders, As Gil-Bazo (2006: 600) noted in a pointed manner,

> [T]he policies of northern European States in the field of migration shape those of their southern neighbours, as well as their own relations with third countries, whether within a formal framework (like in the case of Morocco) or by means of ad hoc measures (as it is the case with Libya).

It therefore comes as no surprise that bilateral cooperation has played a pivotal role in Southern European border management.

Already in the 1990s, Italy actively pursued bilateral cooperation with Albania to reduce immigration pressure from that country. Since then, Italian governments have continuously strengthened bilateral cooperation with countries of origin, offering legal entry quotas for nationals of countries that have cooperated in the struggle against irregular migration (Pastore 2008; Finotelli and Sciortino 2009). Spain also seems to have been relatively successful in relying on bilateral agreements to control unwanted migration flows. Most agreements signed between 2004 and 2008 provided legal immigration channels for labour migrants from countries that actively cooperated with the Spanish government in the struggle against irregular migration and the readmission of irregular migrants (Ferrero-Turrión and López-Sala 2009). However, migrants and smugglers are perfectly able to adapt their strategies to those of states, changing routes very quickly (Monzini et al. 2006; Monzini 2007). Therefore, bilateral agreements that proved successful for one country produced negative externalities for others. For example, Spain's bilateral cooperation with Morocco, or Italy's agreements with Libya before the Arab Spring, resulted in the redirection of certain migrant flows from Africa to Greece (Godenau 2014; Kasimis 2012). However, Greece initially had fewer opportunities to address such a challenge by implementing bilateral cooperation strategies due to Turkey's reluctance to cooperate in the struggle against irregular migration (Triandafyllidou and Ambrosini 2011).

As such, bilateral cooperation efforts by Southern European member states demonstrate that a major challenge in controlling external borders does not lie with the Southern European countries themselves, but also with the willingness of third countries to engage in such cooperation. In fact, Southern European countries are not the only element of the game, since relationships with countries of origin represent a significant piece in the border management puzzle. Spain's bilateral cooperation with Morocco and the Italy–Libya negotiations, for instance, show that bilateral cooperation in matters of readmission depends to a great extent on the country of origin's geopolitical and economic interests (Carrera et al. 2016; Ferrer-Gallardo 2008). In this respect, Klepp (2010) has argued that bilateral cooperation actually reflects a 'bottom-up' pattern (country of origin versus EU), in which countries of origin often set the negotiating conditions. Paoletti and Pastore have further developed this argument, using Libya–Italy relations to claim that Europe's migration–security nexus must not be understood as the outcome of a 'hegemonic model of interaction' (2010: 27), but rather as a 'supralateral' dialectic process involving several levels of governance at the same time and in which 'security ideas and practices originating from Italy, Libya and the EU are put forward and agreed upon on the basis of a larger give-and-take framework' (Paoletti and Pastore 2010: 24–25). A detailed analysis of such a complex interaction puzzle should help us understand why highly controversial cooperation with countries lacking in basic humanitarian standards is tolerated by certain European institutions and rejected by others. In this respect, it has even been argued that ad hoc decisions or practices currently pursued by Southern European countries within bilateral agreements may one day even become part of the EU legal framework, eroding the current humanitarian standards of the EU (Klepp 2010). Although such an argument certainly deserves more in-depth analysis, there is no doubt that bilateral cooperation promoted by Southern European countries is part of a 'passing-the-buck' strategy in which guaranteeing humanitarian standards seems to play second fiddle to the EU's commitment to secure its borders more effectively.

Asylum and refugee protection: still too weak?

The Mediterranean migration crisis of 2015 has narrowed the focus on the humanitarian challenge posed by refugee flows from the Middle East to Southern European asylum systems. Inefficient asylum systems and low welfare provisions for refugees were considered to be one of the main weaknesses of Southern European migration regimes. For this reason, Northern European countries have always been concerned about the fact that most irregular migrants arriving at Southern European shores would inevitably end up applying for asylum in Northern European member states, which have much more generous welfare regimes and more efficient asylum systems (e.g., Bloch and Schuster 2002). In this context, the implementation of the Dublin Regulation[3] to determine a country's responsibility for examining an asylum application is certainly to be seen as Northern European member states' answer to the 'transit challenge' from Southern Europe. In light of such agreements, and considering that most asylum routes start in Africa and the Middle East, Southern European countries became the first countries of asylum for many refugees. Inevitably, the implementation of the Dublin Regulation became controversial for all parties involved. While Southern European countries claimed that the Dublin rules contradicted the principle of burden-sharing within the EU, serious concerns also existed about the capacity of Southern European countries in their new role as 'first countries of asylum' to cope with the new challenges, due to their lack of asylum legislation or efficient reception systems. For example, neither Italy nor Greece, two major countries of arrival, had any asylum legislation until 2007 and 2011, respectively,[4] which stood in clear contrast with the better organized asylum systems in traditional Northern European asylum countries (Thränhardt 2003; Finotelli 2007).

The 'lack of an asylum tradition' (Pastore and Roman 2014: 41) in Southern Europe has clearly influenced the public perception of the asylum channel, since both public opinion and political discourse 'tend to frame asylum simply as "another way for migrants to get in" rather than a right granted to people who flee war and persecution' (ibid.). From this perspective, the harmonization of asylum standards within the EU, despite all the criticism, was considered to be a good chance to bring Southern European countries to the level of their North European partners in order to guarantee equal burden-sharing (Schuster 2000). Arguably, EU harmonization has had a certain positive impact upon the development of Southern European asylum systems. It cannot be denied, for instance, that the EU directives on asylum approved to date currently constitute the backbone of the current Italian asylum regulation framework. As Paolo Bonetti (2008: 13) highlighted,

> 60 years after the enforcement of the Italian Constitution and thanks to the implementation of those two European directives (n. 2004/83/CE on minimum standards for the qualification of third country nationals as refugees and n. 2005/85/CE on minimum standards on procedures for granting and withdrawing refugee status/A/N), Italian legislation experiences such important changes that it is possible to say that the asylum right granted by art. 10(3) of the Italian Constitution has been eventually completely implemented.

Moreover, external pressure and increasing exposure to refugee flows has contributed to an improvement in the reception standards of a system that used to be very poorly organized (Finotelli 2009). Finally, the image of Southern European countries as mere transit countries has become increasingly less realistic due to their gradual transformation into settlement countries (Finotelli 2009; Peixoto et al. 2012; Ponzo and Finotelli 2017).

The refugee crisis of 2015, however, has refueled the debate on Southern European asylum systems. Even though Southern European countries have become settlement countries, transit to Northern Europe undoubtedly remains an attractive option for certain groups of asylum-seekers. As noted in a recent report on refugee protection in Southern European countries, a large number of Syrian refugees who arrived on Italian shores in 2013/2014 did not apply for asylum in Italy (Pastore and Roman 2014). Reasons for transit, however, seem to be embedded in a complex mix of factors where the quality of protection represents one but by no means the only input to transit. In the case of Eritrean refugees in Italy, for example, the decision to further migrate to another country depends on the interplay of several factors that downplay the dissuasive potential of restrictive policies. Particularly relevant in this respect are migrants' perceptions of the risk implied by moving to another country, the lack of integration measures in the first country of asylum, or the type of social expectations that relatives or friends in the country of origin demand from migrants (Belloni 2016). This is also why transit is an option even for refugees who have obtained a relatively secure status. This occurs, for instance, in the case of refugees with subsidiary protection in Malta who decide to leave the island northbound due to their social exclusion *despite* having obtained legal status (Skov 2016).

The persistence of the transit phenomenon has also drawn attention to the heterogeneity of Southern European asylum systems, which exhibit a wide range of protection standards in spite of harmonization (Pastore and Roman 2014). Italy in particular seems to have noticeably improved its reception systems since the 1990s, whereas the poor quality of second reception in Greece in particular remains a highly critical issue (Cabot 2012). Italy has also taken a step forward by giving greater priority to search-and-rescue operations, whereas its Southern European colleagues prefer a control-based approach. However, the increasing challenge for Southern European asylum systems not only stems from the weaknesses of their own asylum systems, but also from the complexity of current mixed migration flows, which make it increasingly difficult to differentiate between forced and economic migrants (Roman 2015). In fact, the screening phase of Southern European asylum systems plays a crucial role to this end, and it is this very phase that still exhibits major shortcomings (Pastore and Roman 2014). These may be due to the absence of implementation structures, as well as their difficulties to manage such a large number of arrivals (as in the case of Italy) or the reluctance of certain groups of refugees to be identified on their arrival, since their goal is to travel north.

Shortcomings in the screening phase during the current crisis have revived tensions between Southern and Northern European countries, whose political representatives have claimed that their Southern European counterparts, and Italy in particular, are intentionally delaying screening operations in order to promote transit and hence lighten the refugee burden (Müller 2014). This is also the reason why countries such as Austria and Germany considered suspending Schengen to stop the entry of Syrian refugees, as occurred during the Kosovo crisis in 1997 (Finotelli 2007). Bilateral cooperation with sending or transit countries led to further criticism of Southern European asylum systems, as they prevent potential asylum-seekers from having direct access to a legal asylum procedure, as occurred in the case of Italy–Libya cooperation (Andrijasevic 2010). In this respect, Spain is currently viewed as the 'bad guy' of the Southern European asylum systems since it appears to enforce 'push-back' operations along the Moroccan border before immigrants have any possibility of applying for asylum, deactivating de facto the principle of *non-refoulement* (CEAR 2015; Pastore and Roman 2014). In fact, the return of potential asylum-seekers to Morocco before they can actually apply for asylum is considered to be one of the reasons for the extremely low asylum figures in the Spanish case, even at the height of the refugee crisis (CEAR 2015). Restrictive asylum and visa policies together with inefficient legal entry channels have inevitably promoted irregular entry and residence. In this way, irregular migration has been turned into an internal issue that has had to be tackled at the internal level and far from the reach of JHA guidelines.

The role of internal controls

The relevance of irregular migration systems for Southern European migration regimes inevitably raises the question of the role played by internal controls. In fact, since the 1990s, Southern European countries have exhibited a striking contradiction between the implementation of increasingly restrictive border controls on the one hand, and the persistence of weak internal controls on the other (Sciortino 1999; Triandafyllidou and Ambrosini 2011). Even though scholars have observed a certain increase in internal controls in countries such as Spain (López-Sala 2015), most Southern European countries show significant gaps in the numbers of ordered and implemented detentions. According to data provided by the Spanish Border Police for the period 2003 to 2013, the yearly percentage of expulsions executed by the Spanish Police never went over 28 percent of the expulsion orders filed during the same year (Sainz de la Maza 2016).[5]

The situation seems to be quite similar for the Italian case, where the percentage of expulsions actually enforced between 2003 and 2009 never exceeded 30 percent of all expulsions ordered (Colombo 2011).[6] As Asher Colombo (2013: 8) remarks regarding the Italian case, 'administrative detention is practically reserved for a relatively small number of irregular immigrants, based on discretionary decisions by a variety of state police officials'. Like Italy, in Spain the relatively low number of expulsions executed also seems to depend on a wide range of factors, which are deeply embedded in the administrative routine of policemen and judges (Sainz de la Maza 2016). Along these lines, a recent comparison of irregular migration situations in Amsterdam and Madrid has shown that, in spite of a slight increase in internal controls following the economic crisis in Spain, these remained relatively intermittent, and immigrants felt that the lack of a residence permit in Spain was not sufficient grounds for being deported following detention (Echeverría 2016). Another shortcoming of Southern European control systems is certainly the small number of labor market inspections for controlling an extensive and constantly booming informal economy (e.g., Reyneri 2003; Maroukis et al. 2011). This seems to be the case in all Southern European countries, although it should be noted that, at least in the case of Spain, some (limited) efforts have been made to tackle this issue (Finotelli 2011).

Weak workplace and border controls have inevitably favored the development of regularizations as *ex-post* control instruments (Sciortino 1999), which allowed Southern European countries to 'postpone' control in terms of time and space (Moffette 2014). In most Southern European countries, regularizations enabled them to regain control of the presence of irregular foreigners, contributing to a stabilization of foreign populations (e.g., Finotelli and Arango 2011). As available data show, long-term residents currently represent more than half of the immigrant population in Southern European countries, most of them having obtained their first residence permit following a regularization process (Ponzo et al. 2015). Even though regularizations are usually identified as a specific feature of the Southern European model, there are exceptions. The government of Malta, for example, turned the detention of immigrants (and not their regularization) into its main instrument of migration internal control (King and Thomson 2008). The extremely long periods of detention on the island have understandably been the subject of sharp criticism by NGOs and scholars. However, this has not prevented the government from continuing its strict detention policy in order to strengthen the country's image of being a vulnerable spot in Brussels (De Bono 2013; Lemaire 2014).

Interestingly, regularizations and detention policies have had the opposite effect at the EU level. On the one hand, regularizations have been a source of discord, as they were deemed to reflect a laissez-faire attitude toward irregular migration. Consequently, Southern European EU member states were forced to give up the execution of mass regularization processes while de facto keeping more individual or 'hidden' regularization procedures. Spain, for instance, has recently introduced an ongoing regularization formula, called *arraigo* ('rootedness'), which somehow 'corrects' irregularity on an individual basis (e.g., Finotelli and Arango 2011; Sabater and Domingo 2012).[7] By contrast, Malta's strict detention policy has ultimately managed to gain more support from the EU for the control of its external border, in spite of the small number of asylum-seekers and migrants who land on the island (Mainwaring 2012). Despite such differences, both examples show that Southern European countries have balanced JHA imperatives on external controls with 'national' internal control strategies to correct the dysfunctionalities arising from their status as external border watchers.

Conclusions and future research avenues

Things have unquestionably changed in Southern Europe since the migration crisis of the 1990s. Southern European control regimes have introduced visa restrictions, strengthened border control technology and intensified bilateral cooperation. Asylum systems such as that in Italy have also benefitted, at least to a certain extent, from European harmonization, leading to an improvement in their legal frameworks. Southern European countries have also partially succeeded in fulfilling a more influential role in European control policies, as demonstrated by Spain's insistence on creating Frontex, or the leading role played by Malta in negotiations to amend the Schengen Border Code (Mainwaring 2012). Bilateral agreements with immigrants' countries of origin, promoted by Southern European countries, are now seen as 'laboratories' for future developments in the EU legal framework (Klepp 2010). All in all, the available evidence indicates that Southern European migration regimes have improved the 'bad' reputation they had from the 1990s, and that there is a need to review the alleged North–South divide between 'strong' and 'weak' control regimes in Europe.

This notwithstanding, the evidence to date also points to significant knowledge gaps that should be addressed by future research to gain a better understanding of how Southern European regimes function and the impact they have upon Europe's JHA. This initially concerns control practices both at the EU and the national level. It has been noted, for instance, that the readmission of detected irregular migrants in the context of Frontex missions has often been negotiated ad hoc by security and military officials when clear operational guidelines are lacking, as occurred in the case of readmission negotiations between Libya and Malta or Italy (Klepp 2010). As this chapter shows, recent scholarly works on the detention of immigrants in Spain and Italy also point to the significant role played by state bureaucracies in shaping internal state controls. However, knowledge on how bureaucracies operate at distinct levels and in different countries remains scant. In fact, only very few researchers have as yet drawn attention to this shortcoming, arguing that a top-down approach to policy implementation fails to reflect the complex interplay of actors, norms, discourses and practices that now characterize border controls (Côté-Boucher et al. 2014; Bommes and Sciortino 2011). Such a research approach, for example, may be useful for understanding the contradiction between the existence of minimum asylum standards set by asylum directives on the one hand and their heterogeneous implementation at the country level on the other. This is particularly the case for screening procedures at the border, which are essential for managing increasingly complex flows and for understanding the mechanisms behind the South–North transit patterns of certain groups of refugees.

If future research devoted greater attention to the practices of street-level bureaucrats, deeper insight would also be gained into the often overlooked differences within Southern European countries. Even though the idea of a homogeneous Southern European model of migration is still very widespread in current migration studies, the evidence available to date indicates that this model is far less homogeneous than was first assumed. While Spain, for instance, is often presented as the 'clever guy' in border management, Greece is still considered the most porous maritime border of the EU, despite having benefitted from the support of Frontex operations. Visa policy implementation analysis further indicates that Southern European embassies operate according to different *modi operandi* with regard to the same national groups. Differences also exist in Southern European asylum systems. Italy's reception system for asylum-seekers, for instance, has become more efficient than the Greek system. Overall, the research suggests that the implementation of immigration controls is embedded in a complex mix of structural constraints, which differ from country to country and may depend, among other things, on different political constellations, bureaucratic traditions and geopolitical interests. This may explain why a commitment to a common border may co-exist with pure national strategies when it comes to managing unexpected immigration in emergency situations. This is the reason why Southern European migration regimes must be analyzed from a more dynamic perspective. In this regard, targeted cross-country comparison rather than single-country analysis would enable us to gain a much better grasp of the structural constraints in which European control systems are embedded.

A final consideration, but by no means the least important, is the relationship between Southern European control regimes and the perceived weaknesses of European common border management. As was seen, bilateral cooperation concerning readmission agreements does not always take into account the lack of humanitarian standards in the third countries involved. In fact, detected immigrants are often sent back to countries where they will probably have no chance of applying for asylum. And it is also a sad fact that stricter border controls have not prevented the increasing number of deaths in the Mediterranean; nor have they deterred the development of alternative migration routes (Carling 2007; Andersson 2013). Through the analytical lens of Southern European migration regimes we can observe that tensions between the struggle for internal security and the guarantee of humanitarian standards in the European Union are far from having been resolved. However, it remains highly questionable whether the burden of such tensions should remain a predominantly Southern European problem.

Acknowledgments

I wish to thank Maria Caterina La Barbera and Gabriel Echeverría for their comments on the first version of this chapter.

Notes

1 For the same reason, Portugal has been excluded from this comparative analysis, despite usually being included in the countries belonging to the so-called 'Southern European model' of immigration.
2 'Mare Nostrum' was a military and humanitarian operation under the auspices of Frontex, and was coordinated and mainly financed by the Italian government. Its goal was to combine the control of sea borders with rescue actions of immigrants on the high seas. It remained operational between October 2013 and November 2014, and helped save almost 150,000 immigrants' lives.
3 The Dublin Convention (Dublin I) was signed in 1990 and came into force in 1997. It was then followed and modified by Dublin Regulation n. 343/2003 (Dublin II) and Regulation n. 604/2013 (Dublin III).
4 The Greek asylum system was only reformed and modernized in 2011 by l. n. 3907/2011, which established a fairer asylum procedure. Further amendments were introduced by l. n. 4357/2016 on common procedures for granting and withdrawing international protection in order to accomplish the readmission agreement between the European Union and Turkey. In turn, Italy's asylum regulation is based on law decree n. 251/2007 and n. 25/2008, modified by law decree n. 159/2008 and law n. 59/2009, which transpose EU directives n. 2004/83/CE and 2005/85/CE, respectively.

5 For instance, of the almost 80,000 expulsion orders filed in 2009, only about 12,000 were ultimately carried out (Sainz de la Maza 2016).
6 Even though the Italian Ministry of Interior has not published any data on expulsions since 2010, the gap between the number of expulsions ordered vis-à-vis those implemented seems to persist. According to information provided by the Head of the Italian Police, Alessandro Pansa, to the Italian Parliament in January 2016, fewer than half of the 34,107 migrants with an expulsion order in 2015 have left Italian territory (Camera dei deputati 2016).
7 In such a case, a residence permit is issued if the immigrant can demonstrate social ties in Spain over the past three years or having been employed irregularly by a Spanish employer for at least one year prior to the application.

Bibliography

Andersson, R. (2013). Europe's Failed 'Fight' against Irregular Migration: Ethnographic Notes on a Counterproductive Industry. *Journal of Ethnic and Migration Studies*, 42(7), pp. 1055–1075.

Andrijasevic, R. (2010). Deported: The Right to Asylum at EU's External Border of Italy and Libya. *International Migration*, 48(1), pp. 148–174.

Baldwin-Edwards, M. (1997). The Emerging European Migration Regime: Some Reflections on Implications for Southern Europe, *Journal of Common Market Studies*, 35(4), pp. 497–519.

Baldwin-Edwards, M. (2012). The Southern European Model of Immigration: A Sceptical View. In M. Okolski (ed.), *European Immigrations. Trends, Structures and Policy Implications*. Amsterdam: Amsterdam University Press, pp. 149–158.

Baldwin-Edwards, M. and Arango, J. (eds) (1999). *Immigrants and the Informal Economy in Southern Europe*. London: Frank Cass.

Belloni, M. (2016). Refugees as Gamblers: Eritreans Seeking to Migrate Through Italy. *Journal of Immigrant & Refugee Studies*, 14(1), pp. 104–119.

Bernardie-Tahir, N. and Schmoll, C. (2014). Islands and Undesirables: Introduction to the Special Issue on Irregular Migration in Southern European Islands. *Journal of Immigrant & Refugee Studies*, 12(2), pp. 87–102.

Bialasiewicz, L. (2012). Off-shoring and Out-sourcing the Borders of Europe: Libya and EU Border Work in the Mediterranean. *Geopolitics*, 17(4), pp. 843–866.

Bloch, A. and Schuster, L. (2002). Asylum and Welfare: Contemporary Debates. *Critical Social Policy*, 22(3), pp. 393–414.

Bommes, M. and Sciortino, G. (eds) (2011). *Foggy Social Structures. Irregular Migration, European Labour Markets and the Welfare State*. Amsterdam: Amsterdam University Press.

Bonetti, P. (2008). Il diritto d'asilo in Italia dopo l'attuazione della direttivacomunitaria sulle qualifiche e sugli status di rifugiato e di protezione sussidiaria. *Diritto, immigrazione e cittadinanza*, 1, pp. 13–53.

Cabot, H. (2012). The Governance of Things: Documenting Limbo in the Greek Asylum Procedure. *Political and Legal Anthropology Review*, 35(1), pp. 11–29.

Camera dei deputati (2016). Resoconto stenografico n. 37. *Atti Parlamentari*, seduta 20 gennaio.

Carling, J. (2007). Migration Control and Migrant Fatalities at the Spanish–African Borders. *International Migration Review*, 41(2), pp. 316–343.

Carrera, S. (2007). *The EU Border Management Strategy. Frontex and the Challenges of Irregular Migration in the Canary Islands*. Brussels: CEPC. Available at www.ceps.eu/publications/eu-border-management-strategy-frontex-and-challenges-irregular-immigration-canary (accessed November 6, 2016).

Carrera, S., Cassarino, J.P., El Qadim, N., Lahlou, M. and den Hertog, L. (2016). *EU–Morocco Cooperation on Readmission, Borders and Protection: A Model to Follow?* Brussels: CEPC. Available at www.ceps.eu/publications/eu-morocco-cooperation-readmission-borders-and-protection-model-follow (accessed November 6, 2016).

Colombo, A. (2011). *Fuori controllo? Miti e realtà dell'immigrazione in Italia*. Bologna: Il Mulino.

Colombo, A. (2013). Foreigners and Immigrants in Italy's Penal and Administrative Detention System. *European Journal of Criminology*, 10(6), pp. 746–759.

Comisión de Ayuda al Refugiado (CEAR) (2015). Las personal refugiadas en Espana y en Europa. Available at www.cear.es/wp-content/uploads/2015/06/Informe-2015-de-CEAR2.pdf (accessed August 19, 2016).

Cornelius, W., Martin, P.L. and Hollifield, J. (eds) (2014). *Controlling Immigration. A Global Perspective.* Stanford, CA: University Press.

Côté-Boucher, K. (2014). Border Security as Practice: An Agenda for Research. *Security Dialogue*, 45(3), pp. 195–208.

Cutitta, P. (2014). 'Borderizing' the Island Setting and Narratives of the Lampedusa 'Border Play'. *ACME: An International E-Journal for Critical Geographies*, 13(2), pp. 196–219.

De Bono, D. (2013). 'Less than Human': The Detention of Irregular Immigrants in Malta. *Race & Class*, 55(2), pp. 60–81.

Sabater, A. and Domingo, A. (2012). A New Immigration Regularization Policy. The Settlement Programme in Spain. *International Migration Review*, 46(1), pp. 191–220.

Echeverría, G. (2016). Living at the Margins of the State: Ecuadorian Irregular Migrants in Amsterdam and Madrid. PhD thesis, Universiad Complutense de Madrid.

Ferrer-Gallardo, X. (2008). The Spanish Moroccan Border Complex: Processes of Geopolitical, Functional and Symbolic Rebordering. *Political Geography*, 27, pp. 301–321.

Ferrero-Turrión, R. and López-Sala, A. (2009). Nuevas dinámicas de gestión de las migraciones en España: el caso de los acuerdos bilaterales de trabajadores con los países de origen. *Revista del Ministerio de Trabajo e Inmigración*, 80, pp. 119–132.

Finotelli, C. (2007). *Illegale Einwanderung, Flüchtlingsmigration und das Ende des Nord Süd-Mythos. Zur funktionalen Äquivalenz des deutschen und des italienischen Einwanderungsregimes.* Münster: LIT.

Finotelli, C. (2009). The North–South Myth Revised: A Comparison of the Italian and German Migration Regimes. *West European Politics*, 32(5), pp. 886–903.

Finotelli, C. (2011). Regularisation of Immigrants in Southern Europe: What Can Be Learned from Spain? In M. Bommes and G. Sciortino (eds), *Foggy Social Structures. Irregular Migration, European Labour Markets and the Welfare State.* Amsterdam: Amsterdam University Press, pp. 189–210.

Finotelli, C. and Ponzo, I. (2017). Integration in times of economic decline. Migrant inclusion in Southern European societies: trends and theoretical implications. *Journal of Ethnic and Migration Studies*, published online August 2017, doi: 10.1080/1369183X.2017.1345830.

Finotelli, C. and Arango, J. (2011). Regularisation of Unauthorised Immigrants in Italy and Spain: Determinants and Effects. *Documents d'Analisi Geografica*, 57(3), pp. 495–515.

Finotelli, C. and Sciortino, G. (2009). The Importance of Being Southern. The Making of Policies of Immigration Control in Italy. *European Journal of Migration and Law* (Special Issue on Immigration Policy Making), 11, pp. 119–138.

Finotelli, C. and Sciortino, G. (2013). Through the Gates of the Fortress: European Visa Policies and the Limits of Immigration Control. *Perspectives on European Politics and Society*, 14(1), pp. 80–101.

Gabrielli, L. (2014). Securitarization of Migration and Human Rights: Frictions at the Southern EU Borders and Beyond. *Urban People*, 16, pp. 311–322.

Gil-Bazo, M.T. (2006). The Practice of Mediterranean States in the Context of the European Union's Justice and Home Affairs External Dimension. The Safe Third Country Concept Revisited. *International Journal of Refugee Law*, 18(3–4), pp. 571–600.

Godenau, D. (2014). Irregular Maritime Immigration in the Canary Islands: Externalization and Communitarisation in the Social Construction of Borders. *Journal of Immigrant & Refugee Studies*, 12, pp. 123–142.

Infantino, F. (2014). State-bound Visa Policies and Europeanized Practices. Comparing EU Visa Policy Implementation in Morocco. *Journal of Borderland Studies*, 31, pp. 171–186.

Kasimis, C. (2012). Greece: Illegal Immigration in the Midst of Crisis, Washington. Available at www.migrationpolicy.org/article/greece-illegal-immigration-midst-crisis (accessed November 6, 2016).

King, R. and De Bono, D. (2013). Irregular Migration and the 'Southern European Model of Migration'. *Journal of Mediterranean Studies*, 22, pp. 1016–3476.

King, R. and Thomson, M. (2008). The Southern European Model of Immigration: Do the Cases of Malta, Cyprus and Slovenia Fit? *Journal of Southern Europe and the Balkans Online*, 10(3), pp. 265–291.

King, R., Lazaridis, G. and Tsardanidis, C. (eds) (2000). *Eldorado or Fortress? Migration in Southern Europe.* Basingstoke: Macmillan.

Klepp, S. (2010). A Contested Asylum System: The European Union between Refugee Protection and Border Control in the Mediterranean Sea. *European Journal of Migration and Law*, 12, pp. 1–21.

Lauth Bacas, J. (2012). No Safe Haven: The Reception of Irregular Boat Migrants in Greece. *Ethnologia Balkanica*, 14, pp. 147–167.

Lavenex, S. (2001). The Europeanisation of Refugee Policies: Between Human Rights and Internal Security. *Journal of Common Market Studies*, 39(5), pp. 851–874.

Lemaire, L. (2014). Islands and a Carceral Environment: Maltese Policy in Terms of Irregular Migration. *Journal of Immigrant & Refugee Studies*, 12, pp. 143–160.

López-Sala, A. (2015). Exploring Dissuasion as a (Geo)Political Instrument in Irregular Migration Control at the Southern Spanish Maritime Border. *Geopolitics*, 20(3), pp. 513–534.

Mainwaring, C. (2012). Resisting Distalization? Malta and Cyprus' Influence on EU Migration and Asylum Policies. *Refugee Survey Quarterly*, 31(4), pp. 38–66.

Maroukis, T., Iglicka, K. and Gmaj, K. (2011). Irregular Migration and Informal Economy in Southern and Central-Eastern Europe: Breaking the Vicious Cycle? *International Migration*, 49(5), pp. 129–156.

McMahon, S. (2012). North African Migration and Europe's Contextual Mediterranean Border in Light of the Lampedusa Migrant Crisis of 2011. EU Working Paper, SPS 2012/07. Available at http://cadmus.eui.eu/handle/1814/24754 (accessed November 6, 2016).

Moffette, D. (2014). Governing Immigration through Probation: The Displacement of Borderwork and the Assessment of Desirability in Spain. *Security Dialogue*, 45(3), pp. 262–278.

Monzini, P. (2007). Sea-border Crossings: The Organization of Irregular Migration to Italy. *Mediterranean Politics*, 12(2), pp. 163–184.

Monzini, P., Pastore, F. and Sciortino, G. (2006). Schengen's Soft Underbelly? Irregular Migration and Human Smuggling across Land and Sea Borders to Italy. *International Migration*, 44(4), pp. 95–119.

Müller, P. (2014). CDU fördert Kontrolle an der Grenze zu Österreich. Spiegel online, 9/9/2014. Available at www.spiegel.de/politik/deutschland/asyl-csu-macht-vorschlaege-zur-fluechtlingspolitik-und-grenzkontrollen-a-990500.html (accessed November 6, 2016).

Pastore, F. (2008). Italy. In J. Doomernik and M. Jandl (eds), *Modes of Migration Regulation and Control in Europe*. Amsterdam: Amsterdam University Press, pp. 105–123.

Pastore, F. (2014). The Governance of Migrant Labour Supply in Europe, Before and During the Crisis. *Comparative Migration Studies*, 2(4), pp. 385–415.

Pastore, F. and Roman, E. (2014). Implementing Selective Protection. A Comparative Review of the Implementation of Asylum Policies at National Level Focusing on the Treatment of Mixed Migration Flows at EU's Southern Maritime Borders. FIERI Working Paper. Available at http://fieri.it/wp content/uploads/2014/11/WP_FIERI_FINAL_Implementing-Selective Protection_PastoreRoman_Oct-20141.pdf (accessed November 6, 2016).

Paoletti, E. and F. Pastore. (2010). Sharing the Dirty Job on the Southern Front? Italian–Libyan Relations on Migration and their Impact on the European Union. Available at www.imi.ox.ac.uk/publications/wp-29-10 (accessed November 6, 2016).

Peixoto, J., Arango, J., Bonifazi, C., Finotelli, C., Sabino, C., Strozza, S. and Triandafyllidou, A. (2012). Immigrants, Markets and Policies in Southern Europe: The Making of an Immigration Model? In M. Okolski (ed.), *European Immigrations: Trends, Structures and Policy Implications*. Amsterdam: Amsterdam University Press, pp. 107–146.

Ponzo, I., Finotelli, C., Malheiros, J., Fonseca, L. and Salis, E. (2015). Is the Economic Crisis in Southern Europe Turning into a Migrant Integration Crisis? *Politiche Sociali*, 1, pp. 59–88.

Reyneri, E. (2003). Immigration and the Underground Economy in New Receiving South European Countries: Manifold Negative Effects, Manifold Deep-rooted Causes. *International Review of Sociology*, 13(1), pp. 117–143.

Roman, E. (2015). Mediterranean Flows into Europe. Refugees or Migrants? In *IEMED Mediterranean Yearbook*. Available at www.iemed.org/observatori/arees-danalisi/arxius-adjunts/anuari/med.2015/IEMed_MedYearbook%202015_Mediterranean%20Flows%20into%20Europe_Emanuela%20Roman.pdf (accessed November 6, 2016).

Sainz de la Maza, E. (2016). Ultima ratio. El proceso de expulsión de inmigrantes en situación irregular en España. PhD thesis, Universidad Complutense de Madrid.

Schuster, L. (2000). A Comparative Analysis of the Asylum Policy of Seven European Governments. *Journal of Refugee Studies*, 13(1), pp. 118–132.

Schuster, L. (2011). Dublin II and Eurodac: Examining the (Un)intended(?) Consequences. *Gender, Place and Culture*, 18(3), pp. 401–416.

Sciortino, G. (1999). Planning in the Dark. The Evolution of the Italian System of Migration Controls. In T. Hammar and G. Brochmann (eds), *Mechanisms of Immigration Controls*. Oxford: Berg, pp. 233–260.

Sciortino, G. and Pastore, F. (2004). Immigration and European Immigration Policy: Myths and Realities. In J. Apap (ed.), *Justice and Home Affairs in the EU. Liberty and Security Issues after Enlargement*. Cheltenham; Northampton, MA: Edward Elgar, pp. 191–209.

Skov, G. (2016). Transfer Back to Malta: Refugees' Secondary Movement Within the European Union. *Journal of Immigrant & Refugee Studies*, 14(1), pp. 66–82.

Thränhardt, D. (2003). Where and Why? Comparative Perspectives on Asylum in the OECD World. In J. Doormenik and H. Knippenberg (eds), *Immigration and Immigrants: Between Policy and Reality, A Volume in Honor of Hans van Amersfoort*. Amsterdam: Aksant, pp. 18–41.

Triandafyllidou, A. and Ambrosini, M. (2011). Irregular Immigration Control in Italy and Greece: Strong Fencing and Weak Gate-keeping Serving the Labour Market. *European Journal of Migration and Law*, 13, pp. 251–273.

Wolff, S. (2008). Border Management in the Mediterranean: Internal, External and Ethical Challenges. *Cambridge Review of International Affairs*, 21(2), pp. 253–271.

21
DIFFERENTIATED INTEGRATION AND THE BREXIT PROCESS IN EU JUSTICE AND HOME AFFAIRS

Steve Peers

Introduction

EU justice and home affairs (JHA) law has attracted more forms of differentiated integration than any other area of EU law (Stubb 2002; Tuytschaever 1999). They occur as cooperation outside of the EU framework, different specific rules inside the EU framework, use of ordinary enhanced cooperation, as well as special 'fast-track' enhanced cooperation rules. There is also a series of special rules applicable to associated non-member states: Norway, Iceland, Switzerland and Liechtenstein. These rules may be relevant when the time comes to develop a framework for the UK's continued connection with EU law in this field after Brexit. To what extent can the issues raised by Brexit simply be addressed by using the templates already in force as between the EU and non-EU countries? Or will it be necessary to agree an additional set of special rules?

Legal framework

The framework for differentiated integration in this field concerns Schengen rules; specific opt-outs for certain countries; and enhanced cooperation. I will outline each in turn.[1]

Schengen acquis

The initial reference to differentiated integration in the JHA field was in Article K.7 of the Maastricht version of the EU Treaty, later repealed by the Treaty of Amsterdam, which expressly permitted member states to engage in bilateral or multilateral action as long as this did not 'conflict with, or impede' third-pillar cooperation.[2] Unusually, this concerned cooperation outside of the EU legal order, notably the development of the Schengen acquis, in the form of the 1985 Schengen Agreement, the 1990 Schengen Convention and the measures implementing the Convention.[3] From the outset, the Schengen rules applied only to certain member states, and this has been the case ever since. In particular, the 1990 Convention came into force on September 1, 1993 in seven member states (France, Germany, the Benelux states, Spain and Portugal), but was not applied until March 26, 1995. Italy and Austria later acceded; but by the entry into force of the Treaty of Amsterdam in May 1999, accession treaties with Greece and Scandinavian member states were not yet fully in force.

In order to reconcile the overlap between the Schengen acquis and JHA cooperation among all member states, the Treaty of Amsterdam integrated the Schengen rules into the framework of the EC and EU Treaties. This was accomplished by means of a Protocol on the Schengen acquis, attached to the EC and EU Treaties ('the Schengen Protocol'), which was subsequently amended by the Treaty of Lisbon. The Protocol gave the Council the power to decide on when the Schengen provisions would be fully extended to the EU member states which were not yet fully participating in the Schengen rules at the time of the entry into force of the Treaty of Amsterdam.[4] This power was used in 1999 to extend the Schengen rules fully to Greece as from March 2000 (Decision 1999/848),[5] and again in 2000 to extend the Schengen rules fully to Denmark, Sweden and Finland as from March 2001 (Decision 2000/777).[6]

As for later member states, the Protocol specified that all future member states were to be bound by the entire Schengen acquis.[7] This was implemented first of all by the 2003 Accession Treaty,[8] which specified that the ten new member states which joined the EU pursuant to that Treaty were not covered by the Schengen rules until a unanimous Council decision by the representatives of the member states fully applying the Schengen acquis at that time and the member state(s) seeking to participate fully.[9] However, a number of Schengen rules immediately applied upon accession, namely on external border controls, except for checks in the Schengen Information System (SIS); certain aspects of visas (particularly the common visa list and visa format); irregular migration; policing (other than cross-border hot pursuit and surveillance); criminal law cooperation (except for references to the SIS); drugs; firearms; and data protection (to the extent that the other Schengen rules apply). Conversely, the rules on the abolition of internal border controls, other aspects of the common visa policy, freedom to travel, cross-border hot pursuit and surveillance by police officers, and the SIS did not apply in practice until the later Council decision. Ultimately, nine of the ten member states due to join the EU in 2004 participated in the full Schengen system as from December 2007, and from March 2008 as regards air borders.[10] Only Cyprus was left out of the extension of the Schengen zone, owing to the practical difficulties in controlling the borders as long as the country is divided. The model set out in the 2003 Treaty of Accession was largely copied in the 2005 Treaty of Accession with Romania and Bulgaria, in force from January 1, 2007,[11] and again for the Accession Treaty with Croatia, in force from July 1, 2013.[12] However, so far the full Schengen acquis has not yet been extended to those states.

A different set of rules applied to the UK and Ireland. The Protocol extended to them the possibility of applying to participate in only part of the Schengen acquis, subject to a decision in favor by the Council, acting with the unanimous approval of the Schengen states.[13] The Council accepted the UK's application for partial participation in Schengen in 2000, and the parallel Irish application in 2002 (Decisions 2000/365/EC and 2002/192/EC), although the partial participation of these member states in the Schengen rules only took effect (for the UK) or will take effect (for Ireland) when the Council approved or later approves it separately (Art. 6 and Art. 4 from the respective Decisions).[14] Both member states participate (or will participate) in almost all of the criminal law and policing provisions of Schengen,[15] as well as the provisions on the control of irregular migration.[16] However, they do not, or will not, participate in any of the rules relating to visas, border controls or freedom to travel. Following this distinction, they participate in the SIS to the extent that it applies to policing and judicial cooperation,[17] but not as it applies to immigration.

What about future measures building on the Schengen acquis? The UK and Ireland adopted the view that the general rules for JHA opt-ins applied if they wished to opt into such measures (i.e., they did not need the Council's approval to opt in). Conversely, the Council and Commission took the view that the UK and Ireland could not opt into Title IV proposals where these measures built on those provisions of the acquis which the UK and Ireland had not opted into. This dispute was ultimately settled by the Court of Justice, when the UK challenged its exclusion from the EU legislation on security features for EU passports and the creation of Frontex, the EU borders agency.[18] The UK also challenged its exclusion from access to the Visa Information System (VIS) by UK law enforcement officials.[19] The Court rejected the UK's position, holding that the Commission and Council were correct: in order to preserve the 'effectiveness' of the rules on the UK and Ireland's participation in the Schengen acquis, there was a necessary link between their participation in the original acquis and their participation in measures building on it. Moreover, the Court adopted a broad interpretation in these cases, ruling that both measures built on the acquis, even though they did not actually amend it, because they were sufficiently linked to the control of external borders. This broad approach was followed in the VIS case, where even a policing measure was held to build on the Schengen acquis rules relating to visas.

The Treaty of Lisbon did not amend the provisions of the Schengen Protocol dealing with this issue, so presumably the Court's case law continues to apply. However, the Treaty did amend the rules governing the position if the UK and Ireland wish to opt out of a measure building on a provision of the acquis.[20] In that case there are complex rules which provide for the removal of the UK or Ireland from the portions of the Schengen rules which they apply already, 'to the extent considered necessary' by the EU institutions, which must also 'seek to retain the widest possible measure of participation of the Member State concerned without seriously affecting the practical operability of the various parts of the Schengen acquis, while respecting their coherence'.[21]

Next, there are specific rules on Denmark. Although it participates in the Schengen acquis, it is subject to special rules to this effect. Denmark has six months to decide whether new measures which build on the Schengen acquis apply within its national law.[22] If it does so, this decision creates 'an obligation under international law' between Denmark and the other member states participating in the measure. If Denmark fails to apply such a measure, the other Schengen states and Denmark 'will consider appropriate measures to be taken'.[23] In practice, Denmark has consistently opted into all such measures building on the Schengen acquis.

Finally, the Schengen association of Norway, Iceland, Switzerland and Liechtenstein is set out in a series of treaties.[24] The Schengen area was extended to Norway and Iceland in March 2001, while Switzerland joined in 2008.[25] There are related treaties associating these states with EU rules on asylum responsibility,[26] the borders agency (Frontex), the EU's borders funds legislation, and participation in comitology committees connected to the Schengen acquis. These treaties require the associated states to apply the relevant EU rules, as they existed when those treaties were agreed. A Mixed Committee established by each treaty is a forum for discussions about implementation of the acquis.[27] If the associates do not accept a measure building on the EU rules, the Treaty is terminated regarding them, although the Mixed Committee may decide to retain it in force.[28] The parties must keep the judgments of the Court of Justice, and of associated states' courts, under close review.[29] If a 'substantial difference' develops in judicial interpretation or national application of the agreement, and the Mixed Committee cannot agree a measure to ensure uniform interpretation or application of the Treaty, or if a dispute relating to the agreement otherwise develops, then the Mixed Committee has a fixed period in which to settle the dispute; otherwise the agreement is terminated.[30] In practice, this legal framework has entailed the associated states' acceptance of most EU measures concerning visas, border control and irregular migration, certain measures concerning policing and criminal law, and amendments to the EU rules on asylum responsibility and Frontex (Lavenex and Wichmann 2009).

General JHA rules

The complex rules on this issue result from a compromise among those member states who wanted EU rules to apply fully to JHA issues, and those who felt this was an infringement of their sovereignty, but who nonetheless wanted the facility to opt in on an individual basis. The following overview addresses in turn issues specific to the UK and Ireland; to Denmark; and to Schengen associates.

The UK and Ireland are both covered by a specific Protocol on border controls, a specific Protocol on the possibility of opting into any Title IV measure, and to specific rules as regards the Schengen acquis. There is also a specific criminal and policing law opt-out for the UK. First, when it comes to border controls, a Protocol attached to the Treaty of Amsterdam entitles the UK and Ireland to maintain the 'Common Travel Area' in force between them and to check individuals coming from other member states. This Protocol also specifically exempts the UK and Ireland from any EU legislation requiring the abolition of border controls, thus overlapping with their general exemption from JHA and Schengen rules. However, this is not an exemption from EU rules on free movement of EU citizens, as confirmed by the CJEU.[31]

Second, the UK and Ireland were granted an opt-out from all of the JHA issues transferred to Title IV of the EC Treaty (immigration, asylum and civil law) under another Protocol attached to the Treaty of Amsterdam. This Protocol was amended by the Treaty of Lisbon to extend it to policing and criminal law measures, and also to set out a procedure for opting out of measures that amend acts by which the UK and Ireland are already bound. As noted above, the Court of Justice has ruled that this Protocol does not apply to measures that build on the Schengen acquis, which are instead governed by the Schengen Protocol rules on participation by the UK and Ireland.

While the default position pursuant to the Title V Protocol is that the UK and Ireland opt out of each individual JHA proposal (Arts 1 and 2), the UK and Ireland can instead choose to opt into each measure. To do this, they must tell the Council within a period of three months of receiving an initial proposal that they wish to take part in it. However, the Protocol provides that if it is not possible to obtain the agreement with the participation of the UK and Ireland after 'a reasonable period of time', the Council may go ahead and adopt the measure without them (Art. 3). Even if they do not opt into a proposed measure within the deadline (or if they opted in, but it was adopted without them), the UK and Ireland may then join in later under the general conditions applying to enhanced cooperation in the Treaties.[32]

In practice, the UK and Irish governments have opted into most or all of the first-phase measures establishing the Common European Asylum System, but only a few of the second-phase measures; a small number of measures on irregular migration, visas, border controls and legal migration; and a significant chunk of the post-Lisbon criminal and policing law measures (Peers 2016). The approach of the two governments has been largely, but not entirely, consistent. There have been no cases where the Council went ahead and adopted JHA measures without their participation. There have been several occasions when the UK or Ireland initially did not participate in a proposal, but then opted in after its adoption.[33]

A significant new provision in the Title V Protocol introduced by the Treaty of Lisbon concerns the proposals made to amend a measure by which the UK and Ireland are already bound.[34] Essentially, it allows them to opt out of the new measure while remaining subject to the old measure. However, it is possible for the Council, acting on a proposal from the Commission, to 'expel' them from participation in the earlier measure, if that measure becomes 'inoperable' for other member states, or for the EU as a whole. It is even possible to agree financial sanctions as a consequence of non-participation. These provisions have not yet been applied in practice, although the UK and Ireland have opted out of several measures which amended asylum legislation in which they already participated.

In addition, the UK (but not Ireland) had the possibility (which it used) of invoking a 'block opt-out' from all pre-Lisbon EU criminal law and policing law, at the end of the transitional period of five years established by the Treaty of Lisbon, which expired on December 1, 2014. The opt-out only applied to acts which had not been amended during that transitional period.[35] Equally, it did not apply to acts adopted after the entry into force of the Treaty of Lisbon to which the UK had opted in. However, these rules allowed the UK to opt back into any of the relevant measures, which it chose to do immediately for thirty-five of these measures.[36] In effect, then, the UK only opted out of part of its pre-existing third-pillar commitments.

The final issue with regard to the JHA opt-outs of the UK and Ireland (which is potentially also relevant to Denmark) is the question of what happens when the UK or Ireland are bound by an existing JHA measure, but when that measure is repealed (not simply amended) by a later measure in which they do not participate. Could it be argued that since the original JHA measure has been repealed as regards most member states, its repeal is also effective for those which did not participate in its repeal? This has already occurred in the case of the original measure establishing the EU's visa list,[37] as well as much of the EU's first-phase asylum legislation.[38] In practice, the Council has consistently repealed JHA measures only with regard to the member states which participate in the measure repealing it, leaving the existing measure in force with regard to the UK and/or Ireland.[39]

The non-participation of Denmark in JHA matters formally began with the Treaty of Amsterdam, which set out a general 'Protocol on the position on Denmark' (the 'Danish Protocol') governing Denmark's status as regards measures concerning, *inter alia*, immigration, asylum and civil law (the former Title IV EC). The Treaty of Lisbon has since extended this Protocol to cover policing and criminal law. There are also special rules related to Denmark's participation in Schengen, discussed above. Unlike the UK or Ireland, Denmark does not have the ability to opt into specific JHA measures (other than measures building on Schengen), either when they are initially adopted or at a later date. If Denmark wishes to change this position, it has two options. First, it could denounce 'all or part' of the Danish Protocol, in which case it has to immediately apply all measures adopted in the relevant field without any need for the Commission or Council to approve its intention to apply those measures.[40] Second, it may decide to replace the rules concerning its JHA opt-out with a different set of rules, which is almost identical to the Title V opt-outs for the UK and Ireland.[41]

In practice, Denmark held a referendum in December 2015 to decide on whether to apply the second option and then opt into a number of civil, criminal and policing law measures (Ibolya 2015), but the Danish public voted against. Although there is no formal possibility for Denmark to opt into JHA measures, the EU and Denmark have nevertheless agreed to Danish participation in some measures by other means. First, there are treaties on participation in measures concerning responsibility for asylum applications, civil and commercial jurisdiction, and service of documents.[42] Second, it was agreed that Denmark could continue a limited form of participation in Europol, despite the latter body being reconstituted by means of a post-Lisbon measure which Denmark could not opt into as such.[43]

Finally, when it comes to the Schengen associates, Norway and Iceland have signed up by means of treaties to apply certain EU laws outside the scope of Schengen and Dublin. In particular, they have signed up to a Treaty on a 'surrender procedure' very similar to the European Arrest Warrant. This Treaty requires them to keep their case law under review and sets up a committee that can discuss and settle disputes. There are no provisions on what happens if the EU legislation is amended.[44] Another Treaty provides that Norway and Iceland apply the EU

Convention on Mutual Assistance in Criminal Matters; it has similar rules on dispute settlement and review of case law.[45] Finally, Norway and Iceland have agreed to apply the EU's 'Prüm' legislation on cross-border exchange of national police data. In this case, the usual rules on dispute settlement and review of case law are supplemented by a clause providing for potential termination of the Treaty if the associated states do not agree with an amendment to the underlying legislation.[46]

Enhanced cooperation

The treaties include general rules on 'enhanced cooperation', which in principle allow for the adoption of measures across most areas of EU law, including JHA law, without the full participation of all member states. They have been applied to JHA measures several times. These rules also apply whenever the UK or Ireland wishes to opt into a JHA measure which either initially opted out of.

Such general rules were first introduced in the Treaty of Amsterdam, and were then amended by the Treaty of Nice.[47] These rules were never in fact used, except (as noted above) in the context of the UK and Ireland opting into immigration, asylum and civil law measures after those measures had already been adopted. Subsequently, the Treaty of Lisbon amended the rules again[48] in that a group of member states may establish enhanced cooperation among themselves, within the context of the EU's non-exclusive competences, by 'applying the relevant provisions of the Treaties'.[49] In other words, once enhanced cooperation has been approved, the normal rules on competence and decision-making (for example, unanimity as regards family law measures) apply. Enhanced cooperation is authorized by the Council 'as a last resort, when it has established that the objectives of such cooperation cannot be attained within a reasonable period by the Union as a whole', and at least nine member states must participate.[50] Furthermore, enhanced cooperation must 'aim to further the objectives of the Union, protect its interests and reinforce its integration process'; 'comply with the Treaties and Union law'; not 'undermine' the internal market or 'distort' competition and so on; and 'respect the competences, rights and obligations of those Member states which do not participate in it'. In return, the non-participants 'shall not impede its implementation by the participating Member States'.[51] The treaties are silent on the question of enhanced cooperation outside the EU legal framework, but of course there are prior examples of this taking place in the JHA field, notably the Schengen and Prüm Conventions (cf. Monar 2001).

Member states that wish to establish enhanced cooperation must address a request to the Commission, which 'may' then make a proposal for enhanced cooperation. If the Commission does not make a proposal, it must tell the requesting member states why.[52] If the Commission proposes authorization of enhanced cooperation, it must then be approved by the Council (by QMV, with all member states voting) and consent of the EP to go ahead.[53] The measure implementing enhanced cooperation is then adopted by whichever procedure usually applies, although only the participating member states can vote. The Treaty provides that enhanced cooperation must 'be open at any time to all Member States', and sets out a procedure for joining.[54] Finally, the participants in enhanced cooperation can decide, acting unanimously, to change the decision-making rules governing the adoption of the substantive measures concerned from unanimity into QMV, or from a special legislative procedure into an ordinary legislative procedure. Unlike the general *passerelle clause*,[55] there is no requirement for consent of the EP or control by national parliaments. In the JHA area, this provision would permit a shift to QMV and/or the ordinary legislative procedure as regards, for instance, passports. To date the use of enhanced cooperation has been modest, and it seems likely to remain confined to areas where unanimous voting applies – meaning that in the field of immigration and asylum law it could only be applied in practice as regards passports.

There are also special rules on enhanced cooperation in several JHA areas linked to special decision-making rules: the 'emergency brake' and the 'pseudo-veto' (Peers 2008). The emergency brake applies to decisions regarding domestic criminal procedure and substantive criminal law,[56] while the pseudo-veto applies to decisions regarding the European Public Prosecutor and operational police cooperation (except for measures building on the Schengen acquis).[57] In each case, it is necessary to distinguish between the legal bases which are subject to these special rules, and those legal bases which are not.[58] Both of these special procedures could lead to a discussion of a draft proposal or initiative at the level of the European Council (the EU leaders) and, in both cases, one possible outcome is a 'fast-track' approval for a group of member states to adopt the relevant measure without the participation of other member states. This would take the form of enhanced cooperation and thus circumvent the substantive or procedural requirements (discussed above) which would normally apply before enhanced cooperation could be authorized. All that is necessary is that at least nine member states want to proceed with enhanced cooperation as regards the relevant proposal.

There are differences between the two procedures: in particular, a veto is distinct from an emergency brake because there are no limitations to the grounds on which a member state could exercise the former, whereas an emergency brake can only be pulled on specified grounds – namely if a proposal 'would affect fundamental aspects of [a member state's] criminal justice system'. Even if an emergency brake could be challenged or overridden, a veto cannot. Moreover, the dynamics are different: a pseudo-veto triggers enhanced cooperation in a positive way (i.e., a group of member states wanting the adoption of a proposal refer the issue to the European Council), whereas the emergency brake would trigger enhanced cooperation in a negative way, because it would be invoked by a single member state objecting to a measure. In addition, the member states invoking the pseudo-veto process would have comparative 'safety in numbers'. Of course, it also follows that a different voting rule applies to the participating member states after fast-track enhanced cooperation is authorized (QMV for the emergency brake; unanimity for the pseudo-veto). Finally, where the pseudo-veto applies, participants in the enhanced cooperation would be able to change the decision-making rules, to shift unanimity to QMV and to shift a special legislative procedure to an ordinary legislative procedure.[59] In practice, the pseudo-veto has been used to move forward on the proposal relating to the European Public Prosecutor's Office.[60] In contrast, the emergency brake has never been pulled, although its existence may have influenced negotiations.

Conclusion and avenues for future research

This complex framework necessarily leads to important questions about the interpretation and application of the rules – and how it might be adapted to deal with the specific issue of Brexit.

As regards Schengen, the distinction between what the UK and Ireland can opt into has been clarified by the ECJ – although later case law allows forms of cooperation outside of participation in the legislation as such. There are also several member states which are obliged to join Schengen but which cannot, or have been prevented from doing so, in practice. An important question is how the dividing line between full and partial participation works in practice, and in particular a comparison among those member states obliged to join and those which have exercised the option not to join. More broadly, should the EU continue to insist upon participation in Schengen as a condition of enlargement – given that it may raise the perception that enlargement poses a security risk and increases the prospect of irregular migration? Is it possible to address public concerns about these issues through a form of differentiation among existing Schengen participants, with some fully applying the abolition of border controls and others (with greater perceived risks regarding security and irregular migration) allowed a form of 'light-touch' internal border control? This has already been the de facto situation since 2015, with the EU authorizing several member states to apply internal border checks.

As for the specific opt-outs, a significant question is whether the Protocol relating to the common travel area imposes obligations on the EU side as regards the Brexit negotiations, limiting its negotiating position owing to the legal requirement to keep the common travel area effective. Could the Protocol also be relevant if an independent Scotland sought to join the EU – given that the common travel area currently applies to Scottish/Irish travel? In that case the implicit consequence may be to exempt Scotland from the usual requirement to join Schengen.

As regards enhanced cooperation, it is notable that there is no clear division between old and new member states in their participation, and no consistent group of member states who always participate. Enhanced cooperation has always been an ad hoc decision, rather than a systematic attempt of a core group to forge ahead with EU integration in general without the unwilling states. There are no longer express rules on cooperation outside of the EU framework. In principle, it should follow from the division of competences between the EU and the member states that this is permissible as regards all issues outside the scope of the EU's exclusive competences (i.e., all JHA matters), provided that the participating member states comply with the relevant EU law. However, the Pringle judgment suggests that they may be limited in the same way as member states signing treaties with non-EU states: they cannot sign a deal which 'affects the scope' of existing EU law within the meaning of the relevant ECJ case law. There are also questions as to when member states can – or may – use the EU institutions if they go down this route (Peers 2013). Although so far the use of the process as regards the European Public Prosecutor has been unproblematic, the two forms of fast-track to enhanced cooperation in areas of criminal law raise certain questions: Could a state which referred a proposal to the European Council under the pseudo-veto process then choose not to participate? Could a state which stayed aloof participate? Can the emergency brake process be judicially reviewed, in particular with regard to the allegedly abusive use of the ground that there was a 'fundamental threat' to that state's criminal justice system?

Overall, the EU's rules on differentiated integration and JHA appear to have squared some circles, reconciling the positions of those who are fully in favor of Schengen and who wish to pursue ambitious EU measures in this field with those who oppose the key aspects of Schengen and have reservations about signing up to all JHA measures. A series of different rules apply to this end, some of them highly customized and some relatively general. All this is diverse enough to discourage member states from cooperation outside of the EU framework – absorbing the Schengen process eventually, the Prüm process at an early stage and preventing further such measures in practice. The question may arise whether the rules on differentiated integration should be even more flexible – or whether the 'fast-track' for certain criminal law measures should be generalized, perhaps with certain limits, to cover other parts of EU law. Certainly the JHA field provides many possibilities for a group of member states which want to go ahead without unwilling participants, perhaps as part of a broader process of relaunching EU integration led by Eurozone states in general and France and Germany in particular.

To what extent could these rules – and in particular the EU's relations with the Schengen associates – provide a model for Brexit? At present, the EU's negotiation guidelines specify the goal of agreeing (1) transitional rules for cases or proceedings pending on Brexit Day; (2) a possible time-limited transitional agreement agreed before Brexit Day to avoid a 'cliff edge' where

EU rules suddenly cease to apply without a replacement; and (3) a future relationship which would be concluded after Brexit Day, including cooperation on security (European Council 2017, par. 22). The rules in category (1) are very dependent upon what applies in the context of (2) – as there is only a need for transitional rules if the applicable legal rules are going to change. For the transitional agreement, the EU says this must be 'subject to effective enforcement mechanisms'. Moreover paragraph 6 indicates that should a time-limited prolongation of Union acquis be considered, this would require existing Union regulatory, budgetary, supervisory, judiciary and enforcement instruments and structures to apply. However, for the post-Brexit deal, the EU guidelines state (par. 23): 'The future partnership must include appropriate enforcement and dispute settlement mechanisms that do not affect the Union's autonomy, in particular its decision-making procedures.' Thus there are two issues here. First, the EU's expectation that if EU rules still apply to the UK for a short transitional period following Brexit, the usual EU rules (including implicitly the role of the ECJ) will still apply. While the (current) UK government is opposed in principle to the role of the ECJ, a short-term continuation of its role may be less problematic. But what happens as regards amendments to EU legislation during the transitional period? Could the 'guillotine' clauses in some of the Norway/Iceland treaties apply by analogy if the UK does not agree to those changes? If the UK successfully resists the ECJ's jurisdiction, what happens as regards case law developments? Would a clause modeled on the Norway/Iceland deal be sufficient?

Second, after that point, if the EU seeks some unspecified dispute settlement system, that does not affect its own decision-making. This sounds similar to the arrangements already in place for Norway and Iceland, as discussed above: discussion in the event of case law divergence, and political dispute settlement, with (in some cases) a guillotine clause in the event that the associates do not accept changes to EU law. So the questions are: (1) which elements of EU law will the UK still seek to participate in; (2) will the UK seek to stay connected to EU law as such (cf. Norway/Iceland and Schengen/Prüm) or a variant upon it (similar to the agreements with Norway/Iceland on extradition), or perhaps some combination; and (3) will the models already used for Norway/Iceland be simply copied over for the UK?

The answers to these questions may result in a framework for differentiated integration with a non-EU state that will add a significant new chapter to the complex saga of convoluted compromises in this area.

Notes

1 Parts of this summary of the framework are adapted from Peers (2016, ch. 2 of both volumes).
2 See also the parallel Art. 100c(7) EC, which was also repealed by the Treaty of Amsterdam.
3 See [2000] OJ C 239.
4 Previous Art. 2(2). The Council had to act with the unanimous vote of the Schengen states.
5 See Declaration [1999] OJ C 369/1.
6 See Declaration [2000] OJ L 309/28. Note that distinct rules apply to Denmark (see below).
7 Art. 8, Schengen Protocol, renumbered Art. 7 by the Treaty of Lisbon.
8 See [2003] OJ L 236/33 (Act of Accession).
9 See Art. 3(3), Act of Accession.
10 See [2007] OJ L 323/34.
11 See Art. 3 and Annex I to Act of Accession ([2005] OJ L 157/203).
12 See [2012] OJ L 112.
13 See Art. 4, Schengen Protocol.
14 The UK's part participation in the Schengen acquis applied from January 1, 2005, except with regard to the SIS (which was subject to a later decision). No such decision has yet been adopted with regard to Ireland.

15 Art. 1 of each Decision. The exceptions are cross-border police hot pursuit (for the UK) and cross-border police hot pursuit and surveillance (for Ireland).
16 Arts 26 and 27 of the Convention.
17 This was put into effect for the UK in 2015: [2015] OJ L 36/8.
18 Cases C-77/05 *UK v. Council* [2007] ECR I-11459 and C-137/05 *UK v. Council* [2007] ECR I-11593. The UK can, however, cooperate with other member states as regards EU laws within the scope of the Schengen acquis to a limited extent: Case C-44/14 *Spain v. Council and EP* ECLI:EU:C:2015:554.
19 Case C-482/08 *UK v. Council* [2010] ECR I-10413.
20 Art. 5(2) to (5), Schengen Protocol.
21 Art. 5(3) ibid.
22 Art. 4(1).
23 Art. 4(2). There is no indication of the voting rule applicable or what the 'appropriate measures' may entail.
24 See [1999] OJ L 176/35 and [2000] OJ L 15/1 (Norway and Iceland); [2008] OJ L 53/13 and 52 (Switzerland); [2011] OJ L 160 (Liechtenstein).
25 See [2000] OJ L 309/24 (Norway and Iceland); [2008] OJ L 327/15 (Switzerland).
26 See [2001] OJ L 93/38.
27 See, for instance, Arts 2–5 of the EU/Norway/Iceland Treaty on Schengen Association.
28 Art. 8 of the Schengen Association Treaty (ibid.).
29 Art. 9 of the Schengen Association Treaty (ibid.).
30 Arts 10 and 11 of the Schengen Association Treaty (ibid.).
31 Case C-202/13 *McCarthy* ECLI:EU:C:2014:2450.
32 Art. 4.
33 For instance, Ireland opted into Directive 2001/55/EC on temporary protection.
34 Art. 4a, as inserted by the Treaty of Lisbon.
35 Art. 10(4), first sub-paragraph, transitional protocol. For a list of the acts which were amended up until the end of the period, see [2014] OJ C 430/23.
36 Art. 10(5), transitional protocol. See the Council and Commission decisions authorizing the UK to opt back into these measures ([2014] OJ L 345/1 and 6). The Council amended the Decisions on the UK's opt-in to the Schengen rules as a consequence: for a consolidated version, see [2014] OJ C 430/1 and 6. For a list of the measures which the UK opted out of, see [2014] OJ C 430/17.
37 Regulation 539/2001/EC.
38 The UK and Ireland participated in the first-phase legislation concerning asylum procedures and the 'qualification' of refugees and persons needing subsidiary protection, and the UK participated in the first-phase legislation on reception conditions for asylum-seekers, but they have opted out of the legislation which repealed those measures.
39 For example, see Regulation 1231/2010/EU on social security for third-country nationals.
40 Art. 7.
41 Art. 8(1).
42 For the text of the treaties, see [2006] OJ L 66/38 (asylum responsibility), [2005] OJ L 299/61 (jurisdiction rules) and [2005] OJ L 300/53 (service of documents).
43 For the text, see Council doc 7078/1/17, March 17, 2017.
44 See [2006] OJ L 292/1, Arts 36 and 37. There is no provision for termination if a dispute is not settled, although Art. 41 provides for termination in general.
45 See [2004] OJ C 26/3, Arts 2 and 4.
46 See [2009] OJ C 353/1, Arts 3 to 5.
47 See Arts 11 and 11a EC and Arts 43–45, previous TEU. There were specific rules for the third pillar in the prior Arts 40, 40a and 40b TEU. For an overview of issues relating to enhanced cooperation and further references, see Peers (2017).
48 Art. 20, revised TEU and Arts 326–334 TFEU.
49 Art. 20(1), revised TEU, first sub-paragraph. All JHA matters are shared competences, and so are therefore non-exclusive: see Art. 4(2)(j) TFEU.
50 Art. 20(2), revised TEU.
51 Art. 20(1), revised TEU, second sub-paragraph, and Arts 326 and 327 TFEU.
52 Art. 329(1) TFEU, first sub-paragraph. There is no time limit set for the Commission's decision as to whether to propose enhanced cooperation or not.
53 Art 329(1) TFEU, second sub-paragraph.

54 Art. 20(1), revised TEU, second sub-paragraph. See also Arts 328 and 331 TFEU.
55 Art. 48(7), revised TEU.
56 Arts 82(3) and 83(3) TFEU, referring to Arts 82(2) and 83(1) and (2) TFEU. However, where the adoption of 'Community criminal law' measures pursuant to Art. 83(2) TFEU requires unanimous voting (for instance, as regards tax or racism), the emergency brake procedure would implicitly not apply, since it may only be used to suspend the ordinary legislative procedure (Art. 83(3) TFEU), which always entails QMV.
57 Arts 86 and 87(3) TFEU.
58 Notably Arts 82(1) (cross-border mutual recognition measures), 85 (Eurojust), 87(2) (other forms of police cooperation), 88 (Europol) and 89 (cross-border police operations).
59 Art. 333 TFEU.
60 Conclusions of the President of the European Council, March 9, 2017.

Bibliography

European Council (2017). *European Council (Art. 50) Guidelines for Brexit Negotiations – Consilium*, April 29. Available at www.consilium.europa.eu/en/press/press-releases/2017/04/29-euco-brexit-guidelines/ (accessed June 2017).

Ibolya, T. (2015). *A Vote of No Confidence: Explaining the Danish EU Referendum*, December 17, open Democracy. Available at www.opendemocracy.net/can-europe-make-it/tam-s-ibolya/vote-of-no-confidence-explaining-danish-eu-referendum (accessed June 2017).

Lavenex, S. and Wichmann, N. (2009). The External Governance of EU Internal Security. *Journal of European Integration*, 31(1), pp. 83–102.

Monar, J. (2001). The Dynamics of Justice and Home Affairs: Laboratories, Driving Factors and Costs. *Journal of Common Market Studies*, 39(4), pp. 747–764.

Peers, S. (2008). EU Criminal Law and the Treaty of Lisbon. *European Law Review*, 33(4), pp. 507–529.

Peers, S. (2013). Towards a New Form of EU Law? The Use of EU Institutions outside the EU Legal Framework. *European Constitutional Law Review*, 9(1), pp. 37–72.

Peers, S. (2016). *EU Justice and Home Affairs Law: EU Immigration and Asylum Law* (4th edn). Oxford: Oxford University Press.

Peers, S. (2017). Enhanced Cooperation: The Cinderella of Differentiated Integration. In B. De Witte, E. Vos and A. Ott (eds), *Between Flexibility and Disintegration: The Trajectory of Differentiation in EU Law*. Cheltenham: Edward Elgar, pp. 76–91.

Stubb, A. (2002). *Negotiating Flexibility in the European Union: Amsterdam, Nice and Beyond*. Basingstoke: Palgrave Macmillan.

Tuytschaever, F. (1999). *Differentiation in European Union Law*. Oxford: Hart Publishing.

22
CENTRAL AND EASTERN EUROPE
The EU's struggle for rule of law pre- and post-accession

Ramona Coman

Introduction

At the beginning of the 1990s, the first post-communist governments in Central and Eastern Europe initiated far-reaching reforms to dismantle the communist legal order and to accelerate the transition to democracy and a market economy. New constitutions had been adopted to restore democratic rights, norms and principles such as the separation of powers and the independence of the judiciary. The collapse of communism was celebrated in the region and the international support for democracy was expected to solve global problems such as economic stagnation, poverty and political instability (Piana 2010: 2). To this end, various international organizations offered policy prescriptions to support this process of change and put forward the rule of law as a precondition to attract investment and to ensure citizens' rights and equality before the law. In doing so, judicial reforms weighed heavily on the transition process as both democracy and economic development imply that judges are impartial and independent of political influence and committed to upholding the law. Thus, drawing from previous democratic transitions in Latin America and Southern Europe, the World Bank and the International Monetary Fund as well as the Council of Europe and the Organization for Economic Development and Cooperation came up with global prescriptions for fast and smooth transitions from communism to capitalism, devoting particular attention to the independence, efficiency and accountability of the judiciary.

Regardless of the international support for judicial reforms and the rule of law in the 1990s, academic interest in this topic was relatively marginal within EU studies. With the exception of some works devoted to the constitutional courts in the democratization and comparative politics literature, scholars paid little attention to the functioning of the judiciary in Central and Eastern Europe. Research in European studies developed slowly when the EU established the criteria for membership at the European Council in Copenhagen and initiated its enlargement policy, conditioning accession to the existence of stable democratic institutions and respect for the rule of law. Thus, starting in the 2000s, a few scholars scrutinized judicial reforms in the region by looking primarily at the ability of the EU to transform domestic institutions in the candidate countries for the 2004/2007 enlargements. The literature on Europeanization inspired them to elaborate research designs and theoretical frameworks that capture the interactions among domestic, European and international actors, and to explain differential outcomes at the domestic level. Most of the accounts on the influence of the EU in shaping judicial reforms in the enlargement context stopped here. The topic has regained academic attention in recent years when the governments of certain new member states planned to review the attributions of some judicial institutions, putting at risk their independence and respect for the rule of law.

Against this backdrop, the aim of this chapter is three-fold: (1) to shed light on how the EU in general and the European Commission in particular sought to shape judicial reforms in order to strengthen the rule of law in the 2004 and 2007 enlargements; (2) to scrutinize the paths of reforms undertaken in Central and Eastern Europe to consolidate the independence of the judiciary in the pre-enlargement context; (3) to discuss the EU's ability to safeguard the rule of law following accession when at the domestic level political actors seek to increase political power over judicial institutions. Organized into three sections, the chapter provides an overview of the literature and in conclusion suggests new avenues of research that can refresh academic and political debates on the conflicts at the EU level generated by judicial reforms at the domestic level.

The EU as a community of common values based on the rule of law

The political changes in the international order following the collapse of communism in Central and Eastern Europe required the EU to rethink its legitimacy and *raison d'être*, and to develop a new rhetoric with regard to its role in the world. The prospect of enlarging the EU to include the former communist countries strengthened the idea that the EU has an obligation to promote democracy through its policies, both internally and externally. Therefore, in 1993, by offering the former communist countries the opportunity to become member states and by defining the associated political conditionality at the European Council in Copenhagen, the EU outlined the contours of its normative power (Manners 2002): democracy, the rule of law, human rights and the principles of international law became one of the explicit aims of the EU in its relations with the rest of the world (Cremona 2011). By incorporating these values into the treaties, the EU was firmly committed to their preservation inside its own legal order as well as inside the national legal orders of its member states. Adherence to these common values was not only a condition for EU membership; Article 7 TEU stipulates sanctions against member states in case of a serious and persistent breach of the common values referred to in Article 2 TEU.

From common values to concrete policy recommendations in the EU's external action

The prospect of enlargement and conditionality for membership gave the EU significant 'leverage in transferring to the applicant countries its principles, norms, and rules' as well as in shaping their institutions (Grabbe 2002: 93). Nonetheless, the conditions set by the European Council in 1993 provided little guidance as to how political criteria should be implemented at the domestic level to restore the legitimacy of democratic institutions and to reduce the political influence inherited from the communist regimes over the judiciary (Grabbe 2002; Kochenov 2004; Coman 2009; Fleck 2011: 795). Thus, at the inception of enlargement, the EU's approach to the rule of law relied mainly on the *savoir-faire* of the international rule of law community (Piana 2010). The European Commission borrowed ideas and tools from the flourishing international community of rule of law promotion that brought together a wide range of actors, both American and European (see Bergling 2006; Carothers 2006; Piana 2010; Dezalay and Garth 2005, 2011).

Involved in the management of enlargement, the European Commission gradually translated the political conditionality defined by the European Council in 1993 into concrete prescriptions for reforms to support the candidate countries in their attempts to establish democratic institutions that resonate with the EU's acquis and values (Kochenov 2004; Grabbe 2002; Coman 2009). Priority was given to building up new institutions and strengthening the formal rules in the former communist countries (Pech 2010: 359). Considering the weaknesses of judicial institutions in Central and Eastern Europe in the transition context, and in some cases the high levels of judicial corruption as well as the interference of political parties in judicial decisions, EU officials and civil servants within the Commission asserted that the independence and efficiency of the judiciary are essential ingredients for the functioning of the market and for the establishment of a European space of freedom and security. As a result, judicial reforms had been seen as urgent priorities and a *sine qua non* condition for accession, weighing heavily on the enlargement process (Kochenov 2004).

Although the rule of law is a multi-layered concept, the European Commission gave it a more narrow definition in reference to the independence of the judiciary, seeking to limit the political influence inherited from the communist regime over the judiciary. The consolidation of the guarantees of judicial independence stood at the core of the process, in particular 'the (re)organization of the judicial systems and the insertion of institutional mechanisms that ensure the independence of the judicial bodies and the impartiality of adjudication' (Piana 2010: 17). Thus, in the regular reports on the progress made by each candidate country, the Commission called for the adoption of new laws on the organization and functioning of the judiciary and recommended a series of measures concerning the selection and career path of judges and prosecutors (Coman 2009). Particular attention was devoted to the establishment of new institutions such as judicial councils – established in several Western democracies after World War II as a guarantee for the independence of the judiciary. Overall, the Commission recommended enhancing the independence, impartiality, efficiency and accountability of the judiciary as overarching principles that support the rule of law (Kochenov 2004; Ginsburg and Garoupa 2009).

Horizontal policy instruments to strengthen the independence of the judiciary

However, providing recommendations on how to strengthen the independence of judicial institutions was not an easy task for a bureaucratic administration like the Commission. The organization of the judiciary is part of the sovereign power of the state. As it went beyond the competence of the Commission in the enlargement process, its recommendations gave rise to tensions with domestic governments (Coman 2009); on the other hand, on the European continent there are several institutional models that sustain the independence of the judiciary (Ginsburg and Garoupa 2009). As Heidbreder (2011: 8) writes, the Commission had 'extraordinary discretion in how to interpret and to implement the accession criteria and was endowed with far-reaching independence in developing and applying steering instruments vis-à-vis the candidate states'.

Scrutinizing periodically the reforms undertaken in twelve candidate countries, and more importantly in a field in which the EU did not have prior expertise and *savoir-faire*, the Commission managed to develop its own approach to judicial reforms and the rule of law supported by a series of tools and instruments conceived to strengthen the independence of the judiciary. At the end of the 1990s, the programs TAIEX (Technical Assistance and Exchange of Information) and Twinning were launched to involve Western experts in institutional change in the region. These two tools became important vectors of socialization and a laboratory of ideas to design judicial reforms. The twinning programs became the main 'instruments of policing the EU's conditionality', implying a horizontal circulation of ideas from member states to candidate countries (Papadimitriou and Phinnemore 2004, 624; Tulmets 2005; Coman 2009; Piana 2010:

37; Trauner 2011). By bringing together civil servants from the old member states and the former communist countries in twinning programs, the aim was not to create legally binding norms but to allow governments to maintain their national specificities while ensuring that they remain compatible with EU requirements.

The establishment of judicial councils is an illustrative example of this process through which civil servants from the old member states provided support in the drafting of new legislation and the establishment of new institutions in the former communist countries (Papadimitriou and Phinnemore 2004). Due to the diversity of judicial traditions on the European continent, there was no consensus among experts and academics about how to reduce the political power inherited from the communist regime on the organization and functioning of the judiciary. What was at stake was the degree of independence that was to be granted to the judicial councils vis-à-vis elected branches of power (Ginsburg and Garoupa 2009: 202; Piana 2010). Prior to accession, this recommendation generated heightened tensions between political and judicial actors at the domestic level.

The absence of clear prescriptions on how to strengthen the independence of the judiciary prompted the Commission to involve a wide range of domestic civil servants from older member states to support institutional change at the domestic level. In other words, the EU offered an 'important legitimizing force for "selling" these reforms to the CEEC's electorate' (Papadimitriou and Phinnemore 2004: 622; Dallara 2014), but the choice of institutional models through which the conditions were to be achieved remained very much in the hands of domestic political elites (Trauner 2011; Mendelski 2013; Dallara 2014; Coman 2014: 899). The rule of law in general and judicial reforms in particular were promoted and implemented through horizontal mechanisms of Europeanization, with the European Commission playing the role of the facilitator of policy transfer.

The subtle empowerment of the Commission

In scrutinizing how the EU sought to shape judicial reforms in Central and Eastern Europe in the context of the 2004 enlargement, scholars documented not only the evolution of the EU's approach to the rule of law and its prescriptions on how to strengthen the independence of the judiciary, but also the subtle institutional empowerment of the European Commission. As Heidbreder (2011) demonstrated, the enlargement policy designed for the Eastern enlargement strengthened the role and action capacity of the European Commission vis-à-vis member states and candidate countries. The enlargement policy revealed the Commission's ability to act as a policy entrepreneur in its attempts to develop credible policy ideas with regard to the independence of the judiciary (Heidbreder 2011). While at the beginning of the 1990s the Commission borrowed ideas and policy tools from other international actors to promote judicial independence, it gradually managed to define its own approach, namely to identify standards to be reached, to determine benchmarks for evaluation and to justify the importance of the judicial reforms in normative terms (Piana 2010; Nicolaidis and Kleinfeld 2012; Pech 2010). This body of research allowed scholars to observe how norms and ideas travel from one international actor to another and how competing or converging understandings on the rule of law emerge.

The quest for judicial independence in Central and Eastern Europe

While some scholars focused on the top-down dimension of the rule of law as underlined in the previous section, others have elaborated research designs to capture the influence of the EU and domestic actors in reforming judicial institutions (Coman 2009, 2014; Dallara 2014; Piana 2010;

Trauner 2011; Kmezić 2017). Thus, the processes and outcomes of judicial reforms have been analyzed from different perspectives, drawing upon the rich literature on Europeanization (Exadaktylos and Radaelli 2012; Börzel and Risse 2012; Goetz 2001). Putting forward historical, sociological and rationalist explanations, scholars of Europeanization have shown how different causal mechanisms such as socialization and domestic empowerment have shaped institutional change in the former communist countries. Thus, conditionality, benchmarking, monitoring, advice, twinning and technical assistance have all received ample attention in the literature to understand how these tools designed by the Commission alter the functioning and organization of the judiciary in different national contexts (Grabbe 2002; Papadimitriou and Phinnemore 2004; Coman 2009; Piana 2010; Trauner 2011; Dallara 2014).

The depoliticization of the judiciary in the pre-accession context

With regard to the ability of the EU to shape domestic change, scholars are unanimous in maintaining that the mechanisms put forward by the Commission for the Eastern enlargement led to concrete institutional change in the region. There is incontestably a first-order change (Hall 1993) that is reflected in the creation of new institutions and the incorporation of new norms and ideas at the domestic level. The establishment of judicial councils mentioned in the previous section is an illustrative example of this formal adaptation of the EU's requirements (Piana 2010: 41; Coman 2014: 894; Kosar 2016: 18). The diffusion of this institutional model of self-administration of the judiciary determined scholars to confirm the influence of the EU in designing judicial reforms in the region.

Thus, while Romania and Bulgaria re-established their pre-communist judicial councils at the beginning of the 1990s, Hungary witnessed the most radical change in terms of judicial independence in 1997 through the empowerment of the National Judicial Council (Bobek 2007; Fleck 2011). Similarly, in Poland, the competences of the judicial council – established as a result of round-table talks in 1989 – had been extended in 1997, 2001 and 2003, without altering the roles of the Ministry of Justice (Bodnar and Bojarski 2011; Kuhn 2004). Slovakia and Slovenia established independent judicial councils with wide powers in 1997. Estonia and Lithuania followed the same path in 2002, and Latvia established a similar institution in 2010 (Kosar 2016: 5). By contrast, the Czech Republic remained the 'black sheep', following a different model of administration of the judiciary (Bobek 2007). Although the European Commission promoted the idea of the self-administration of the judiciary and the creation of judicial councils, this option did not find any overwhelming support in the Czech Republic. Here, the traditional model of state administration and the role of the Ministry of Justice had been maintained over time because 'politicians did not consent to the transfer of such broad powers to the judiciary' (Kosar 2010: 17).

Attempts to limit judicial power in the post-accession context

In spite of these reforms, scholars remained divided with regard to their substantive outcome, arguing that the pre-enlargement institutional change has not resulted in a substantial transformation (Mendelski 2013). Moreover, following accession, domestic actors in the new member states deplored the shortcomings generated by the model of self-administration of the judiciary and the establishment of judicial councils (Schonfelder 2005: 61; Fleck 2011). The empowerment of these bodies expected to prevent the politicization of the judiciary gave rise to mitigated results and opinions, since in some countries judges were still perceived as 'unreliable, inefficient and corrupt' (Schonfelder 2005: 61). Adopting a more critical stance, experts deplored that the radical reforms undertaken in Hungary, Poland, Romania and Bulgaria prior to EU accession moved power and undue influence from one bureaucratic institution (the Ministry of Justice) to another (the judicial councils) (Bobek 2007: 112; Parau 2011). Analyzing the Romanian case, Parau (2011: 647) argued that following the consolidation of the prerogatives of the Superior Council of Magistracy in the pre-accession period, this institution no longer performs its mandate 'as the representative of judges but rather as someone who own(ed) the judiciary, made the rules for the judiciary and ruled the judiciary'. As a result, Romania and Bulgaria saw their accession to the EU for 2007 postponed and conditioned to the obligation to follow the benchmarks of the Mechanism of Cooperation and Verification – an instrument established by the Commission in 2006 to assess ongoing progress on judicial reforms, corruption and organized crime in these two countries.

Following accession, Poland, Hungary and the Czech Republic witnessed heightened tensions between judicial and political actors as the latter sought to adopt measures to reduce the powers of the recently empowered judicial councils and of the constitutional courts. Scholars deplored the 'growing governmental disdain for the rule of law' in Poland and Hungary, and sought to understand how and why political parties seek 'to capture the state for their own ideological or economic gains by dismantling key rule of law institutions' (Bugaric and Ginsburg 2016: 69–70). For example, in Poland, one year after the country's accession to the EU, President Kaczynski repeatedly voiced his hostility towards judges (Bodnar and Bojarski 2011: 729); in 2005 he sought to establish a political coalition to amend the Constitution and to reduce the power of the judiciary. The aim of the Polish executive was to empower the Ministry of Justice and to reduce the role of the National Judicial Council (NCJ). While in 2005 the government failed to review the attributions of the NCJ, in 2015 the conservative Polish government led by Law and Justice passed new laws to extend political control over the Constitutional Tribunal and to limit its checks on governmental power. In an opinion released in October 2016, the Venice Commission of the Council of Europe stated that Poland's new Act on the Constitutional Tribunal did not meet two essential standards of balance of power, namely the independence of the judiciary and the position of the Constitutional Court as the final arbiter in constitutional issues (Venice Commission 2016).

Similarly, in Hungary in 2011, the Parliament, in which the FIDESZ had a majority of two-thirds of votes, passed new laws on the organization of the judiciary and the National Council of Judiciary (NCJ). The government contended that the NCJ's decisions were influenced by particular interests and created a new institution – the National Judicial Office (OBH). The president of the latter was elected for a nine-year term and was granted the power to 'reassign specific cases from the courts where they are assigned by law to any other court in the country' (Bankuti et al. 2012: 143). Another area of contention in the Hungarian judicial reform of 2011 was the decision of the government to retire 274 judges and the premature termination of the mandate of the former president of the Supreme Court in 2011, who was elected for six years in June 2009. As Bankuti and colleagues (2012: 143) wrote, 'the ordinary judiciary has lost a great deal of its independence'. The Hungarian government changed the rules for nominating judges at the Constitutional Court and restricted the jurisdiction of the Court over fiscal matters (Bugaric and Ginsburg 2016: 73). Against this backdrop, Bugaric and Ginsburg conclude that the Constitutional Court, which had been 'respected' and 'powerful' in the first years of the democratic transition in Hungary, has been eliminated from the political scene as a result of the reforms promoted by Viktor Orban (ibid.).

Controversies and challenges at the EU level

The constitutional and judicial reforms undertaken in Poland and Hungary revealed the following paradox: while the enlargement process empowered the Commission in its relations with candidate countries (Heidbreder 2011), its prerogatives with regard to member states' commitment to the rule of law following accession remain weak (Müller 2013). Article 7 TEU stipulates sanctions in cases of serious and persistent breach of the common values by member states. However, it has never been used. Although it enables the European Council to determine the existence of a serious and persistent breach by a member state of principles mentioned in Article 2 and to suspend the voting rights of the country in question, many have argued that sanctions are not the most appropriate way to deal with such cases, as they provide for the insulation of one member state from the rest of the EU rather than for a solution to prevent a breach of common values. In addition, Article 7 requires unanimity for the sanctioning of a member state and four-fifths of votes for the alert procedure. Thus, this mechanism is rather 'impracticable' at the EU level (Batory 2016: 687; Muller 2013).

Against this backdrop, the reforms in Poland and Hungary generated strong demands to if not improve then at least to clarify the action capacity of the EU to safeguard the rule of law within its member states (Muller 2013; Kochenov and Pech 2016; Batory 2016). EU institutional actors called for new mechanisms to safeguard common values at the supranational level (Coman 2015). As Blauberger and Kelemen (2016: 2) argue, 'more can be done to maximize the effectiveness of existing judicial mechanisms'. Since 2011, the search for new mechanisms has become 'a pressing issue' at the EU level (Batory 2016: 697). Normative and legal questions have been addressed both in the academic and political milieu such as: How to put pressure on errant member states (Batory 2016: 688)? Does the EU have the authority to protect values referred to in Article 2 (Müller 2013)? Which mechanisms and tools have to be established to safeguard the EU's values at the supranational level (Van Bogdandy and Ioannidis 2014; Coman 2015)? How well is the EU equipped, legally and politically, to defend democracy and the rule of law within its member states (Bugaric and Ginsburg 2016: 75)?

The new rule of law framework to complement Article 7 TEU

Thus, following the Hungarian decision in 2011 to reform the powers of the National Judicial Council, some member states and representatives of the European Parliament required the Commission to clarify its role in this field. Given that the rule of law issue touches the core of national sovereignty, diverging views have been expressed. In 2013 the Commission organized a consultation on the rule of law entitled *Les assises de la justice* (Coman 2015: 2). This brought together a wide range of participants, including lawyers, judges, academics, NGOs, representatives of member states, EU agencies, the Council of Europe, etc. To the question on how the EU should react to similar challenges, the consultation offered a mix of solutions, alternating between politically ambitious proposals and legally feasible frameworks. While some suggested the revision of the treaties and the creation of new legislation at the EU level, others put forward the need to strengthen cooperation among the European Commission, the European agencies, networks and other bodies in the monitoring of the rule of law in member states. The Commission, the EP and the Council sought to find a balance between member states' reluctance to strengthen the powers of the Commission and the need of supranational mechanisms to effectively safeguard common values at the EU level (Coman 2015: 9).

Drawing upon this consultation, in 2014 the Commission proposed a new framework for the rule of law conceived to be complementary to both infringement procedures and Article 7

(European Commission 2014). It introduces clarity on three points: first, it is designed to deal with threats to the rule of law which are of a 'systemic nature'; this means that the framework is activated by the Commission when national rule of law safeguards do not seem capable of effectively addressing those threats; second, it clarifies the political and administrative role of the Commission. In this regard, Jean-Claude Juncker nominated Frans Timmermans, First Vice-President of the Commission, to be responsible for rule of law issues. In addition, the framework establishes a dialogue between the Commission and the member state concerned, which takes place in three stages: assessment, recommendation and follow-up to the recommendation. Each stage places the Commission at the center of the procedure. The third novelty of the new framework is that it institutionalizes the collaboration of the Commission with the Council of Europe (CoE) and with two of its main bodies: the European Commission for Democracy through Law (the Venice Commission) and the European Commission for the Efficiency of Justice (CEPEJ). In so doing, the aim is to provide an objective, non-partisan and evidence-based evaluation of the threats to the rule of law as the Council of Europe's expertise and moral authority as producer of democratic standards and norms is undisputed and recognized at the international level. Although the new rule of law framework empowers the Commission in its political and administrative role, it relies heavily on data for monitoring and opinions for assessment delivered by the CEPEJ and the Venice Commission of the CoE.

Two years after the establishment of the rule of law framework, scholars remain divided with regard to its strengths and limitations. According to Bugaric and Ginsburg (2016: 78), the framework offers 'little in the way of viable sanctions'. For Kochenov and Pech (2016: 1066), it is 'a modest step in the right direction'. For Sedelmeier (2016: 2), the new rule of law framework 'has potential because it meets the criteria of formalization, publicity and impartiality' in the monitoring and assessment of the state of the rule of law in member states. Being a new instrument, most of the accounts in the literature stop here. However, considering its political implications, it deserves increased academic attention, as the tensions generated by judicial reforms at the domestic level are illustrative cases in understanding the limitations of EU political and legal integration.

Conclusion

This chapter has aimed to provide an overview of how the EU sought to shape judicial reforms in Central and Eastern Europe in order to strengthen the independence of the judiciary in the enlargement context and how the paths of reforms taken in some new member states following accession have challenged EU institutional actors and the integration process itself. The chapter has shown that in its enlargement policy the Commission has embraced a narrow definition of the rule of law. Given the risks of politicization of the judiciary in the former communist countries, the Commission has emphasized in its regular reports the need to limit the political power over the organization and functioning of the judiciary. From the onset, judicial reforms stood at the center of political conditionality as pillars of democratic, legal and economic integration. The enlargement experience empowered the Commission vis-à-vis candidate countries. As the first section showed, the management of the enlargement gave rise to new policy-making capacities of the Commission in shaping the path of judicial reforms in the region and this, as Heidbreder (2011: 22) put it, 'without creating new formal powers of the EU'. By contrast, the second and third sections show that the political authority of the Commission and its power to deal with rule of law crises remained precarious following accession. Judicial reforms undertaken recently in Poland and Hungary undermined the independence of the judiciary and challenged EU institutional actors, as their room for maneuver in dealing with such cases seemed to the limited. Although invoked by many, Article 7 TEU was not a solution. Infringement proceedings had been initiated, but only on issues covered by EU law, which excluded the attempts to limit the power of judicial institutions. Considering the political implications of triggering Article 7, many have called for a more flexible framework. Thus, a new procedure was adopted in 2014 which takes the form of a political dialogue between the Commission and the member state whose domestic reforms in the field of the judiciary represent a systemic threat to the rule of law. As the third section underlines, the new framework strengthens the political and administrative power of the Commission and institutionalizes the collaboration with the Council of Europe and its bodies, which enjoy moral prestige and expert authority for their expertise in providing opinions and recommendations on constitutional and judicial matters.

Recent attempts to limit the power of judicial institutions in the new member states have given rise to new political dilemmas and intellectual puzzles. Beyond the scope of recent domestic reforms and the motivations of their promoters, two main avenues for research may be identified:

1. The EU's new mode of governance in dealing with rule of law crises. The debates that led to the establishment of the rule of law framework in 2014 revealed, on the one hand, a strong tension between the preferences of member states to design intergovernmental mechanisms of compliance, and, on the other, supranational attempts to strengthen the political and administrative role of the Commission. Considering the rise of intergovernmentalism in EU decision-making as a way to rapidly react to multiple crises, how does the Commission perform these new political and administrative roles? Moreover, the new rule of law framework implies an intensified collaboration with the Council of Europe and its bodies. Although the Venice Commission has attracted intensive media coverage over the past few years, research on this expert body has remained scarce. How does the Venice Commission reach consensus in its interactions with domestic governments and how does it produce its opinions and recommendations on judicial and constitutional matters? How does the Council of Europe as a producer of norms and standards shape the EU's Area of Freedom, Security and Justice?

2. The usages of the rule of law as a common value. In their quest for legitimacy, EU institutional actors incessantly invoke the rule of law. In discourses it is an end in itself, since it pertains to an ideal of legality, justice, equity and fairness. It is also a tool, since the rule of law is used as a benchmark to create new institutions and legal cultures to facilitate economic and political integration. Overall, as a common value, the adherence to this principle is supposed to create consensus among political actors at the EU and domestic level. However, recent developments show that it generates conflicts and challenges to EU integration. Thus, what do these recent tensions tell us about the structure of conflict in EU politics? How is the conflict over the rule of law framed? What are its implications for the Area of Freedom, Security and Justice and ultimately for the *finalité* of the EU as a political community?

To conclude, these two research perspectives invite scholars to scrutinize conflicts over the rule of law at the domestic and supranational level and to examine how they shape the EU's modes of governance and, as a result, give rise to new understandings of sovereignty, legitimacy and power.

Bibliography

Bankuti, M., Halmai, G. and Scheppele, K.L. (2012). Hungary's Illiberal Turn. Disabling the Constitution. *Journal of Democracy*, 23(3), pp. 138–146.

Batory, A. (2016). Defying the Commission: Creative Compliance and Respect for the Rule of Law in the EU. *Public Administration*, 94(3), pp. 685–699.

Bergling, P. (2006). *Rule of Law on the International Agenda. International Support to Legal and Judicial Reforms in International Administration, Transition and Development Co-operation*. Antwerp: Intersentia.

Blauberger, M. and Kelemen, D. (2016). Can Courts Rescue National Democracy? Judicial Safeguards against Democratic Backsliding in the EU. *Journal of European Public Policy*, pp. 1–17.

Bobek, M. (2007). Iudex Ex Machina: Institutional and Mental Transitions of Central and Eastern European Judiciaries. In *Judicial Reforms in Central and Eastern European Countries*, ed. R. Coman and J.M. De Waele, pp. 107–135. Bruges: Vanden Broele.

Bodnar, A. and Bojarski, L. (2011). Judicial Independence in Poland. In *Judicial Independence in Transition*, ed. A. Seibert-Fohr, pp. 667–738. New York; Dordrecht; London: Springer.

Börzel, T. Risse, Th. (2012). From Europeanisation to Diffusion: Introduction. *West European Politics*, 35(1), pp. 1–19.

Bugaric, B. and Ginsburg, T. (2016). The Assault on Post-Communist Courts. *Journal of Democracy*, 27(3), pp. 69–82.

Carothers, T. (2006). The Rule-of-law Revival. In *Promoting the Rule of Law Abroad. In Search of Knowledge*, ed. T. Carothers, pp. 3–15. Washington, DC: Carnegie Endowment for International Peace.

Coman, R. (2009). *Reformer la justice dans un pays post-communiste. Le cas de la Roumanie* [Reforming the Judiciary in a Post-communist Country. The Case of Romania]. Brussels: Editions de l'Université.

Coman, R. (2014). Quo Vadis Judicial Reforms? The Quest for Judicial Independence in Central and Eastern Europe. *Europe-Asia Studies*, 66(6), pp. 892–924.

Coman, R. (2015). Strengthening the Rule of Law at the Supranational Level: The Rise and Consolidation of a European Network. *Journal of Contemporary European Studies*, 24(1), pp. 171–188.

Cremona, M. (2011). Values in EU Foreign Policy. In *Beyond the Established Legal Orders*, ed. M. Evans and P. Koutrakos, pp. 275–315. Oxford: Hart Publishing.

Dallara, C. (2014). *Democracy and Judicial Reforms in South-east Europe. Between the EU and the Legacies of the Past*. Cham Heidelberg; New York; Dordrecht; London: Springer.

Dezalay, Y. and Garth, B.G. (2005). *Global Prescriptions. The Production, Exportation and Importation of a New Legal Orthodoxy*. Ann Arbor: The University of Michigan Press.

Dezalay, Y. and Garth, B.G. (2011). *Lawyers and the Rule of Law in an Era of Globalization*. Abingdon, Oxon: Routledge.

European Commission (2014). Communication from the Commission to the European Parliament and the Council. A New EU Framework to Strengthen the Rule of law, COM(2014)158.

Exadaktylos, T. and Radaelli, C.M. (eds) (2012). *Research Design in European Studies. Establishing Causality in Europeanization*. New York: Palgrave.

Fleck, Z. (2011). Judicial Independence in Hungary. In *Judicial Independence in Transition*, ed. A. Seibert-Fohr, pp. 793–835. Heidelberg: Springer.

Ginsburg, N. and Garoupa, T. (2009). Guarding the Guardians. Judicial Councils and Judicial Independence. *American Journal of Comparative Law*, 57, pp. 201–232.

Goetz, K. (2001). Making Sense of Post-communist Central Administration: Modernization, Europeanization or Latinization? *Journal of European Public Policy*, 8(6), pp. 1032–1051.

Grabbe, H. (2002). European Union Conditionality and the Acquis Communautaire. *International Political Science Review*, 23(3), pp. 249–268.

Hall, P. (1993). Policy Paradigms, Social Learning, and the State: The Case of Economic Policymaking in Britain. *Comparative Politics*, 25(3), pp. 275–296.

Heidbreder, E.G. (2011). *The Impact of Expansion on European Institutions. The Eastern Touch on Brussels*. Basingstoke: Palgrave Macmillan.

Kmezić, M. (2017). *EU Rule of Law Promotion. Judiciary Reform in the Western Balkans*. London: Routledge.

Kochenov, D. (2004). Behind the Copenhagen Façade: The Meaning and the Structure of the Copenhagen Political Criterion of Democracy and the Rule of Law. *European Integration Online Papers*, 8(10), pp. 1–36.

Kochenov, D. and Pech, L. (2016). Better Late than Never? On the European Commission's Rule of Law Framework and its First Assessement. *Journal of Common Market Studies*, 54(5), pp. 1062–1074.

Kosar, D. (2010). Judicial Accountability in the (Post)transitional Context: A Story of the Czech Republic. In *Transitional Justice, Rule of Law and Institutional Design*, ed. A. Czarnota and S. Parmentier, pp. 307–363. Antwerp: Intersentia.

Kosar, D. (2016). *Perils of Judicial Self-government in Transitional Societies*. Cambridge: Cambridge University Press.

Kuhn, Z. (2004). Worlds Apart: Western and Central European Judicial Culture at the Onset of the European Enlargement. *The American Journal of Comparative Law*, 52(3), pp. 531–567.

Manners, I. (2002). Normative Power Europe: A Contradiction in Terms? *Journal of Common Market Studies*, 40(2), pp. 235–258.

Mendelski, M. (2013). Where Does the European Union Make a Difference. Rule of Law Development in the Western Balkans and Beyond. In *European Integration and Transformation in the Western Balkans. Europeanization or Business as Usual?*, ed. A. Elbasani, pp. 101–118. London and New York: Routledge.

Müller, J.W. (2013). *Safeguarding Democracy inside the EU. Brussels and the Future of the Liberal Order*. Washington, DC: Transatlantic Academy.

Nicolaidis, K. and Kleinfeld, R. (2012). Rethinking Europe's Rule of Law and Enlargement Agenda: The Fundamental Dilemma. *The Jean Monnet Working Papers Series*, no. 12/12, pp. 1–91.

Papadimitriou, D. and Phinnemore, D. (2004). Europeanization, Conditionality and Domestic Change: The Twinning Exercise and Administrative Reform in Romania. *Journal of Common Market Studies*, 42(3), pp. 619–639.

Parau, C. (2011). The Drive for Judicial Supremacy. In *Judicial Independence in Transition*, ed. A. Seibert-Fohr, pp. 619–667. Heidelberg: Springer.

Pech, L. (2010). 'A Union Founded on the Rule of Law': Meaning and Reality of the Rule of Law as a Constitutional Principle of EU Law. *European Constitutional Law Review*, 6, pp. 359–396.

Piana, D. (2010). *Judicial Accountabilities in New Europe. From Rule of Law to Quality of Justice*. Burlington, VT: Ashgate.

Schonfelder, B. (2005). Judicial Independence in Bulgaria: A Tale of Splendour and Misery. *Europe-Asia Studies*, 57(1), pp. 61–92.

Sedelmeier, U. (2016). Political Safeguards against Democratic Backsliding in the EU: The Limits of Material Sanctions and the Scope of Social Pressure. *Journal of European Public Policy*, pp. 1–15.

Trauner, F. (2011). *The Europeanization of the Western Balkans. EU Justice and Home Affairs in Croatia and Macedonia*. Manchester: Manchester University Press.

Tulmets, E. (2005). The Management of New Forms of Governance by Former Accession Countries of the European Union: Institutional Twinning in Estonia and Hungary. *European Law Journal*, 11(5), pp. 657–674.

Venice Commission (2016). New Polish Law on Constitutional Tribunal Gives Excessive Power to Parliament and the Executive Over the Judiciary. Available at: https://wcd.coe.int/ViewDoc.jsp?p=&id=2443325&Site=DC&BackColorInt%0Dernet=F5CA75&BackColorIntranet=F5CA75&BackColorLogged=A9BAC%0DE&direct=true (accessed December 19, 2016).

Von Bogdandy, A. and Ioannidis, M. (2014). Systemic Deficiency in the Rule of Law: What It Is, What Has Been Done, What Can Be Done. *Common Market Law Review*, 51, pp. 2014–2059.

23
THE WESTERN BALKANS
Decreasing EU external leverage meets increasing domestic reform needs

Florian Trauner and Zoran Nechev

Introduction

The Western Balkans are a prime target for EU action in justice and home affairs (JHA). With Croatia joining in 2013, the EU's Stabilization and Association Process for the Western Balkans now encompasses Albania, Bosnia and Herzegovina, Serbia, Kosovo, Montenegro, and Macedonia. These states have particularly close relations with the EU under the enlargement framework, and strive towards full membership (for an overview of the state of relations, see Kmezić 2015; Damjanovski *et al.* 2016). At the same time, they continue to struggle with bilateral conflicts, open constitutional questions, authoritarian tendencies and entrenched organized crime networks. The region was also at the forefront of the refugee crisis of 2015 and early 2016. Most newly arrived migrants crossed the Western Balkans on their route from Greece to Northern European states. Tackling these security-, migration- and rule of law-related challenges has become a priority for the EU, also with a view to realizing the Area of Freedom, Security and Justice within the EU (e.g., Trauner 2011; Geddes *et al.* 2012; Mungiu-Pippidu 2011; Nechev 2013).

This chapter investigates the issues at stake with regard to the EU's engagement in JHA in the Western Balkans. It introduces the main elements of the EU's policy strategy and outlines the key scholarly debates dealing with the subject. It ends by presenting some future avenues of research in relation to JHA in the Western Balkans.

The EU's objectives in justice and home affairs in the Western Balkans

In May 1999, the EU launched the Stabilization and Association Process and provided the Western Balkan countries with the status of 'potential candidate for EU membership' (European Council 2000: point 67). The field of justice and home affairs has been an important element in the EU's enlargement policy for two reasons: it should help improve the situation in the Western Balkans and prevent insecurity spill-overs from the region.

Rule of law and EU-driven institutionalization in the Western Balkans

When the Stabilization and Association Process was launched, a key issue was 'weak statehood' (Anastasakis and Bechev 2003). More effective and accountable state institutions should contribute to regional stability and prosperity. The JHA dimension to this challenge has been 'non-professional and corrupt security forces, an inefficient and overly politicized judiciary, weak borders without efficient border controls and no professional and specialized anti-trafficking forces that could prohibit illegal migration and trans-border crime activities' (Luif and Riegler 2006: 7). The EU has therefore been interested in assisting the Western Balkan countries in creating new or reforming existing border control and migration management policies. The police and judicial structures should function more efficiently and be more accountable.

The Western Balkan countries have made progress in strengthening their institutional arrangements. However, the EU has increasingly been concerned with preventing local elites from 'capturing' state institutions and structures, thereby neglecting the separation of powers and undermining the rule of law. For instance, 'politics of state capture led to growing tensions in Macedonia, which resulted in the complete breakdown of legitimate institutions and enormous political polarization' (Kmezić 2015: 8). A wire-tapping scandal revealed extensive political pressure on and control over the judiciary exerted primarily through informal networks (Preshova *et al.* 2017). The Macedonian government under Prime Minister Nikola Gruevski has been accused of mass surveillance, corruption and government interference in the judiciary system. Even the European Commission spoke openly of 'state capture' in its 2016 report:

> Democracy and rule of law have been constantly challenged, in particular due to state capture affecting the functioning of democratic institutions and key areas of society. The country suffers from a divisive political culture and a lack of capacity for compromise.
>
> *(European Commission 2016a: 4)*

The Macedonian crisis has been a case *in extremis*, with the European Commission ascertaining 'backsliding' in terms of separation of powers and an independent judiciary (European Commission 2015c: 5, 2016a: 5). However, the European Commission considers 'political interference' in the work of the judiciary and a weak track record in terms of fighting high-level political corruption to be problems for most Western Balkan countries in its 2016 reports.

Preventing insecurity spill-overs from the Western Balkans

The prevention of insecurity spill-overs from the region is closely interrelated with the situation of rule of law and fundamental rights in the region – but it is not entirely the same interest. According to the EU's 'Global Strategy', 'the challenges of migration, energy security, terrorism and organized crime are shared between the EU, the Western Balkans and Turkey. They can only be addressed together. Yet the resilience of these countries cannot be taken for granted' (European Union 2016: 24).

Since the advent of the Stabilization and Association Process, the EU has engaged the Western Balkan states in tackling migration- and security-related challenges that originate from or are linked to the region (for more details, see Ioannides and Collantes-Celador 2011). Organized crime networks have been involved in the illicit trafficking of human beings, weapons and drugs, and most notably heroin. Due to the growing awareness of terrorist threats, the EU and the Western Balkans have also agreed to intensify their cooperation on counter-terrorism, in particular with regard to 'the fight against arms trafficking, financing of terrorism, radicalization and its prevention and border control' (Paris Western Balkan Summit 2016). The Western Balkans potentially play an important strategic role in preventing jihadists seeking to return from Syria and Iraq from entering the EU. In addition, a radicalization of Balkan youth – often disillusioned with economic hardship – should be avoided (e.g., European Commission 2015b). According to data compiled by Radio Free Europe/Radio Liberty, Bosnia and Herzegovina, Kosovo and Albania have proportionally more foreign fighters in Syria and Iraq than any other European state.[1] The EU emphasized not only a need for law enforcement cooperation but also for more anti-radicalization efforts, and an 'intercultural dialogue with and within the countries of the Western Balkans' (Council of the EU 2015: 25).

Since 2010, the EU's border management agency Frontex has established a 'Western Balkans Annual Risk Analysis' to better grasp the phenomenon of irregular migration from and through the region. The Western Balkan route gained prominence in 2015, when most migrants *en route* from Turkey and Greece made their way via Macedonia and Serbia into Hungary and Croatia further north. Of the more than one million refugees and migrants arriving in the EU in that year, around 764,000 have used the Western Balkan route. The irregular border crossings by migrants in the region have seen a sixteen-fold increase compared to 2014.[2] The number of transit migrants using the southeastern corridor has decreased following the EU–Turkey deal of March 2016 and the introduction of stricter border controls in Serbia and Macedonia.

In 2015, around 2 percent (or 38,000) of detected irregular border crossings were made by regional migrants (Frontex 2016: 12). The focus has since shifted to (non-regional) migrants using the Western Balkans as a transit route to the EU. Yet the question of irregular migration in the EU from within the region was a salient one in the wake of the EU's visa liberalization process. The number of Balkan asylum applications in the EU increased significantly once visa-free travel was installed for Serbia, Macedonia and Montenegro in 2009, and for Bosnia and Herzegovina and Albania in 2010 (Trauner and Manigrassi 2014). Few of them actually received international protection (Frontex 2011: 23–30). Due to a mix of policy reforms both in the EU and Balkan countries of origin (e.g., accelerated asylum procedures, more return operations and stricter exit border controls), the issue of asylum-seeking from the Western Balkans has lost salience. However, a side effect of this new approach is that minorities, notably Roma, seem to have increasing difficulties leaving their countries for whatever purposes (see, e.g., Council of Europe 2011; Kacarska 2012).

The EU's approach towards JHA in the Western Balkans

The framework provided by the Stabilization and Association Process outlines common political and economic objectives for the countries from the region, with the aim to generate closer ties with the EU. Tailor-made Stabilization and Association Agreements (SAA) were signed between the EU, on one side, and each Western Balkan country on the other (Phinnemore 2003).[3] All of these agreements foresee a close cooperation on JHA issues, usually under the headings 'reinforcement of institutions and rule of law'; 'protection of personal data'; 'visa, border management, asylum and migration'; 'prevention and control of illegal immigration'; 'readmission'; 'money laundering and terrorism financing'; 'cooperation on illicit drugs, preventing and combating organized crime and other illegal activities', and 'combating terrorism'.

The 1993 Copenhagen criteria defined in preparation for the 2004/2007 enlargements with the countries of Central and Eastern Europe are also central for the Western Balkans. Still, the accession requirements have evolved and expanded in comparison to previous enlargements (Pippan 2004; Bieber 2011; Blockmans 2007; Renner and Trauner 2009).

Croatia was the first country in which the negotiation framework put a stronger emphasis on justice and home affairs-related matters. Based on Bulgaria's and Romania's unsatisfactory compliance with rule of law-related conditions at the time of their accession (Spendzharova 2003), the EU split the JHA policy field into two distinct chapters. Croatia hence negotiated thirty-five instead of the thirty-three chapters of previous enlargements. The policies relating to the independence and the efficiency of the judiciary, as well as the laws and institutional set-up to fight corruption and ensure fundamental rights, were put in the newly established chapter twenty-three entitled 'Justice and Fundamental Rights'. All migration- and internal security-related policies such as border control, visas, migration, asylum, police cooperation, the fight against organized crime and terrorism, cooperation in the field of drugs, customs cooperation and judicial cooperation in criminal and civil matters became part of chapter twenty-four entitled 'Justice, Freedom and Security'. Both chapters are relevant to assess the Copenhagen criteria for EU membership.

A so-called 'benchmarking system' became an additional quality check for aspiring countries (Council of the European Union 2005: point 26). To better monitor and track the reform efforts, the Commission introduced benchmarks for the opening and/or closure of chapters. Only with a positive assessment regarding compliance with the closing benchmarks could the negotiations for a specific chapter be provisionally closed.

In 2012, the EU undertook another reform aiming to place 'rule of law' at the very center of the enlargement policy (European Commission 2012: 2). The new approach aims to reinforce the EU's conditionality approach by opening chapters twenty-three and twenty-four at the initial phase of the accession negotiations, keeping them open during the entire negotiation period and closing them at the very end. JHA should become a key priority during every phase of the enlargement process. This approach is supposed to improve compliance and implementation – essential elements for making reforms sustainable.

To improve the monitoring and tracking of reforms, the Commission also introduced interim benchmarks. If progress in the rule of law chapters is absent and/or lags behind the progress of the overall negotiations, the Commission may recommend not to open and/or close any other negotiating chapters (Council of the EU 2012: 25). This 'imbalance' or 'equilibrium clause' has been a novelty in the negotiation framework for Montenegro and will be incorporated into all countries starting accession negotiations. The new conditionality approach is hence meant to exercise political influence and steer political reforms, especially on politically highly sensitive issues such as rule of law, corruption and internal security (Nechev et al. 2013).

A background to this reform was the experience of the EU in negotiating with Croatia. Chapter twenty-three was opened rather late in the negotiations with Croatia. It then needed to be closed quite quickly when member states decided to move towards a conclusion of the whole of negotiations. As a matter of fact, many reforms had not had the time to mature and be implemented in a sufficient manner (Damjanovski et al. 2016: 25). However, the Commission was not keen to reintroduce a 'Cooperation and Verification Mechanism' such as it had done for Bulgaria and Romania. This would have been seen as a sign that Croatia is in fact not ready. As a compromise, the Commission continued to monitor Croatia's implementation record related to chapter twenty-three even after the formal closure of the negotiation and the signing of the Accession Treaty up until the country's accession in 2013 (European Council 2011: point 31).

The Commission also modified the assessment methodology for the progress made by each candidate country in 2015. In a symbolic gesture, it changed the title of these reports from 'Progress Reports' to 'Annual Reports'. The reports now report extensively on the core issues relating to rule of law, fundamental rights and democratic institutions. The Commission (2015a) developed harmonized assessment tables that are piloted in a number of key chapters and policy areas. They look at key chapters and provide an assessment of the current state of affairs across all enlargement countries in addition to their individual level of progress. The focus has initially been on rule of law and fundamental rights (functioning of the judiciary, corruption, organized crime, freedom of expression). In 2016, other policy areas from chapter twenty-four were added to this assessment exercise, including migration, asylum, border control and the fight against terrorism. Standard five-tier assessment scales indicate different levels of preparedness, from 'early stage' to 'well advanced'. Corresponding grades are given for the progress of each candidate country (from 'backsliding' to 'some progress' to 'very good progress') (European Commission 2015a). Furthermore, the Commission's 'enlargement strategy' is no longer annually revised, and has become a medium-term, multi-annual document. The 2015 strategy is supposed to cover the whole term of the Juncker Commission (2014–2019).

Currently most advanced in the Stabilization and Association Process, Montenegro was the first country subject to this new conditionality approach. As of February 2017, the country has opened twenty-four chapters for negotiations out of a total of thirty-three negotiating chapters (chapters thirty-four and thirty-five are currently not applicable to Montenegro). Two have been provisionally closed (European Commission 2016b). The number of intermediate benchmarks assigned for chapter twenty-three and twenty-four amounts to a total of eighty-three – forty-five for the chapter on judiciary and fundamental rights and thirty-eight for the chapter on justice, freedom and security. In comparison, the closing benchmarks for all of the other twenty chapters under negotiations add up to no more than fifty-five (own calculations, based on European Commission 2016b). Serbia has opened six negotiating chapters, including the JHA-related ones, and provisionally closed two (see Table 23.1).

The enlargement process with Macedonia has reached an impasse due to the bilateral dispute with Greece over the name of the country; the process is only slowly progressing with Albania, Bosnia and Herzegovina and Kosovo. For these countries that have not yet started negotiations, the Commission initiated a series of country- and policy-specific dialogues. The rule of law is the common denominator in all of these dialogues (see Table 23.2).

Research dealing with JHA in the Western Balkans

Scholars have followed the engagement of the EU in the Western Balkans, focusing on issues such as the degree of external influence and on processes of national adaptation, transformation and contestation.

Table 23.1 State of play of the Western Balkan countries with regard to the EU accession process (as of February 2017)

Country	Candidate status (since)	Accession negotiations
Albania	2014	No negotiations
Bosnia and Herzegovina	Potential candidate	No negotiations
Kosovo	Potential candidate	No negotiations
Macedonia	2005	No negotiations
Montenegro	2010	Twenty-four negotiation chapters opened, two provisionally closed
Serbia	2012	Six negotiation chapters opened, two provisionally closed

Table 23.2 Country- and policy-specific dialogues in the Western Balkans (as of February 2017)

Country	Date initiated	Topics covered
Bosnia and Herzegovina • Justice Dialogue	June 2011	Judiciary, human rights, fight against corruption and discrimination, prevention of conflict of interests, police reforms
Kosovo • Structured Dialogue on the Rule of Law	May 2012	Judiciary, fight against organized crime and corruption
Macedonia • High-level Accession Dialogue	March 2012	Freedom of expression, rule of law and ethnic relations, challenges for electoral reform, public administration reform, strengthening of the market economy, good neighborly relations
Albania • High-level Dialogue	November 2013	Fight against organized crime and corruption, judiciary, administrative reform, human rights

External governance and Europeanization

Building on the rich body of literature on transformation and adaption processes in Central and Eastern Europe (for an overview, see Sedelmeier 2011; Schimmelfennig and Sedelmeier 2005), scholars have increasingly applied concepts building on 'Europeanization' and 'external governance' also in the Western Balkans. A guiding research interest of this literature has been under which conditions the EU can transfer its rules and norms to the candidates or potential candidates in the Western Balkans.

In theoretical terms, the Europeanization literature has been dominated by rational-choice and constructivist approaches. According to an influential model, the 'external incentives model', the most crucial mechanism employed by the EU to make candidate countries accept its rules is the use of conditionality, meaning that the EU sets its rules as conditions that the applicant country has to fulfill in order to receive rewards (Schimmelfennig et al. 2003: 496f.). The successful adoption of EU rules depends on whether the (rationally thinking) actors perceive the external EU rewards to be higher than the costs of domestic adaptation (Schimmelfennig and Sedelmeier 2004: 663–667). The most prominent alternative explanation to this argument derives from constructivist thinking (e.g., Kelley 2004; Schimmelfennig and Sedelmeier 2004: 667f.; Checkel 2001). Constructivists argue that the EU may apply strategies other than conditionality to affect domestic change. Candidate countries would accept the EU's influence due to socialization and persuasion processes in which domestic actors internalize identities, values and norms.

Influenced by the 'external incentives model', scholars have asked if the EU would exert a similar influence in the Western Balkans given that its 'rewards' are less credible and tangible. A certain enlargement fatigue, discussions on the EU's integration capacities, the 'Brexit' issue and several other factors have contributed to the lack of clarity concerning when or even whether the aspiring candidates of Southeastern Europe will make it into the EU (Nechev 2016: 5). In addition, the domestic point of departure is different for the Western Balkans. The countries face 'problems of limited statehood' (Börzel 2011). The momentum for enlargement has not only been lost, but a 'negative momentum has set in' (de Borja Laheras and Tcherneva 2015). It is also obvious that the EU is pursuing its enlargement to the Western Balkans with a lower level of commitment compared to the Eastern enlargement. The rather blunt statement by Jean-Claude Juncker, then newly elected President of the European Commission, that no candidate country will accede the EU during his term, was a case in point.[4] The announcement was ill received in the Western Balkans. Given all of these contextual factors, how strong has the EU's influence been in Southeast Europe?

The literature points to the fact that the EU has struggled to exert influence on sensitive political questions in the countries that are still riddled by post-conflict and post-socialist political dynamics (e.g., Elbasani 2012; Radeljić 2013; Keil 2013; Economides and Ker-Lindsay 2015). Noutcheva (2009), for instance, argued that the EU's political conditions regarding constitutional questions of statehood were perceived to lack legitimacy due to their normative justification, thereby opening up space for contestation. The Western Balkan states embarked on 'fake', 'partial' or 'non-compliance' with regard to changes in the statehood structures. Economides (2015: 1028) highlights that the normalization of Serbia's policy vis-à-vis Kosovo has taken place due to material concerns and rational cost–benefit calculations, rather than 'embedded changes to identity and normative value systems'. Freyburg and Richter (2010) argue that in cases where 'national identity issues' are contradicting EU's political requirements, Western Balkan states tend to abstain from achieving compliance (such as the prosecution of war crimes).

The impact of the EU in the field of JHA

Yet the literature also highlights that the Europeanization processes differ. The level of contestation is not the same in all countries and across all policies. JHA has been presented as a policy field in which the EU managed to exert a comparatively high level of influence. Trauner (2009, 2011) points out the importance of 'policy conditionality' in understanding the impact of the EU. By linking an expansive list of conditions to the incentive of visa-free travel, the EU has been able to compensate for a rather weak 'membership conditionality' and to trigger far-reaching reforms in areas such as document security, border and migration management. The visa issue has also remained important even after Serbia, Macedonia and Montenegro received visa-free travel in 2009, and Albania and Bosnia and Herzegovina in 2010. By installing post-visa liberalization monitoring and establishing a new visa safeguard clause, the EU is more able to keep track of JHA-related reforms and push for changes post-visa liberalization (Trauner and Manigrassi 2014).

Border security and migration management in the Balkans have also been the focus of other scholars. Applying a social network analysis, Geddes *et al.* (2012) highlight that the networks underlying the EU–Western Balkans relationship in this field tend to be relatively hierarchical and are managed from the EU's center. Scholars have also zoomed in on the particular aspects of the EU's JHA approach in the Western Balkans, such as the EU's police mission in Macedonia as a test case for a '"European" approach on building peace' (Ioannides 2006) or the impact of the EU on reforming the police in Bosnia (Tolksdorf 2013).

Overall, the EU seems to be relatively effective in terms of aligning the Western Balkans with its standards on migration, border security and crime fighting. Yet the picture becomes different when one looks at research focusing on rule of law and judicial independence. Kmezić (2017) draws attention to a lack of clarity in the EU's rule of law demands (caused, among others, by the absence of a single EU model on this issue), which negatively affects the EU's external influence. He suggests that the EU should take more into account the peculiarities and historical legacies of the judiciary systems of each Western Balkan state and develop country-tailed rule of law approaches. Collantes-Celador and Juncos (2012) make a similar argument with regard to EU police reform. The EU's demands would mainly follow logics deriving from EU internal security policy-making than 'functional imperatives and local realities' (2012: 415).

Scholars – not unlike NGOs such as Freedom House and international actors including the European Commission and World Bank – point to a lack of progress or even a backsliding of rule of law standards in the region. If the judiciary has been reformed, the reforms have concerned more efficiency-related aspects (such as judicial capacity) than power-related ones (such as judicial impartiality) (Mendelski 2010). By investigating Turkey, Croatia and Albania, Noutcheva and Aydin-Düzgit (2012) maintain that state capacity and the level of empowerment of local elites explain whether or not the domestic institutional and legislative structures underlying rule of law have been changed. In line with rational choice institutionalism, these elites have weighed up costs and benefits deriving from the EU's conditional offer.

The question of judicial independence is closely interlinked with high-level political corruption and state capture. Comparing the Western Balkans' anti-corruption policies with a 'house of cards', Mungiu-Pippidu (2011) highlights the deficiencies of both the EU's rule of law promotion and the demand side of recipient countries. For instance, the EU's approach was lacking a unitary rule of law model and was too bureaucratic. 'Countries were judged in the monitoring process not by the effectiveness of their reforms or even by their real potential for change, but by the number of "prescription pills" taken' (Mungiu-Pippidu 2011: 161). Satisfying the demands put forward in the monitoring reports has become more important than tackling the corruption problems at their root.

In many instances, the institutions and laws created to satisfy the EU have been unconnected from local realities and 'ways-of-doing-things'. 'Informal institutions' in the Western Balkans are believed to flourish, as people perceive them to be more effective than the 'formal' procedures and rules (Marcic 2015; Kostovicova and Bojicic-Dzelilovic 2008; Mungiu-Pippidu 2005). A project entitled 'Closing the gap between formal and informal institutions in the Balkans' is currently funded under the EU's Horizon 2020 program and led by Eric Gordy. Starting in early 2016, the project aims to better understand the interplay of formal institutions brought about by the EU integration process and informal 'rules of the games' existing in the Western Balkans.[5]

Conclusions and avenues for further research

This chapter has shown that the EU has high stakes in terms of security and stability in the Western Balkans. The Union faces a difficult balance of a growing EU-internal opposition towards further enlargement (post-financial crisis, post-Brexit vote and in view of high migratory pressures) and a persistent need for external engagement. Without the prospect of joining the EU, bilateral and ethnic conflicts that have never ceased to simmer in the Balkans may escalate again. The EU's main approach has been to refine its *modus operandi* of enlargement, in particular by putting rule of law and other justice and home affairs-related matters to the forefront. These aspects are covered in chapters twenty-three and twenty-four and are now at the center of the accession process. There have also been other efforts to compensate for a lack of momentum for enlargement and a hostile political environment. The Commission has launched 'dialogues' on rule of law with those Western Balkan countries that lag behind.

Scholars have drawn a mixed picture regarding the effectiveness of the EU to transfer its JHA rules to the Western Balkans. Whereas the EU has been relatively influential in the areas of migration, border control and crime fighting, the picture becomes different with regard to rule of law and fundamental rights. Here, there seems to be a growing gap between what is written in law and what is done in practice. The reasons for this are manifold and include weak institutional capacities to implement the reforms triggered by the EU accession process, a polarized political landscape and a growing reluctance of incumbent governments to step back from power and resources. It will be an avenue of further research to better understand the dynamics of 'state capture' and the role of 'informal institutions' in the Western Balkans – and how effective EU and other efforts are to counter this development.

Other avenues of research include a better understanding of the altering dynamics of decision-making. The enlargement process has become more political compared to previous rounds, most likely at the expense of the Commission's standing. Factors such as the Western Balkans' willingness to prevent irregular migrants from entering the EU may empower these countries' governments and may outweigh other EU concerns such as political interference in the work of the judiciary and curtailing media freedom. Individual EU member states are taking a lead in the enlargement. The 'Berlin Process' organizing regular summits between the Western Balkans and certain EU member states is a case in point. The initiative was taken by the German Chancellor Angela Merkel and Foreign Minister Frank-Walter Steinmeier to highlight the persisting importance of the Western Balkans for the EU in a situation where the accession of any of these countries is a rather distant one (Nicič et al. 2016). The Commission's Directorate-General for Neighbourhood and Enlargement Negotiations (DG NEAR) seems to have become more of a project implementer and manager of the enlargement process, strongly relying on external institutions to gain expertise or even to enforce its conditions (see Economides and Ker-Lindsay 2016).

At a policy level, avenues of research are the consequences of a growing agentification of policing and judiciary work in Southeast Europe (mirroring EU-internal developments). The regional agencies and bodies include the Regional Cooperation Council (based in Sarajevo), the Migration, Asylum, Refugees Regional Initiative (MARRI), the Southeast European Cooperation Initiative (SECI Regional Centre), the Southeast European Prosecutors Advisory Group and the Southeast Europe Police Chiefs Association. What is the exact role and impact of these institutions? It will also be of high interest to follow how the Western Balkans respond to particular JHA challenges, such as the threat of radicalization of disillusioned young Muslims, a shrinking population, and growing international pressure to host and integrate migrants from the Middle East and elsewhere.

Acknowledgment

The authors would like to thank Frank Schimmelfennig, Lora Ujkaj and Ariadna Ripoll Servent for useful comments on earlier versions of this chapter.

Notes

1 See RFE/RL website 'Foreign Fighters In Iraq & Syria – Where do they come from?', available at: www.rferl.org/a/foreign-fighters-syria-iraq-is-isis-isil-infographic/26584940.html (accessed January 30, 2017).
2 See Frontex website, 'The Western Balkan route', available at: http://frontex.europa.eu/trends-and-routes/western-balkan-route/ (accessed January 30, 2017).
3 Following the Lisbon Treaty and the EU becoming a legal entity, the SAA with Kosovo was signed between EU and Kosovo, without member states as signatories to the Agreement.
4 Jean-Claude Juncker (2014). European Parliament. Plenary Session. Strasbourg, July 15, 2014, available at: https://ec.europa.eu/commission/publications/president-junckers-political-guidelines_en (accessed January 30, 2017).
5 For more information see the project website, available at: www.formal-informal.eu/en/ (accessed January 30, 2017).

Bibliography

Anastasakis, O. and Bechev, D. (2003). *EU Conditionality in South East Europe: Bringing Commitment to the Process*. South East European Studies Programme. Oxford: University of Oxford.

Bieber, F. (2011). Building Impossible States? State-building Strategies and EU Membership in the Western Balkans. *Europe-Asia Studies*, 63(10), pp. 1783–1802.

Blockmans, S. (2007). *Tough Love: The European Union's Relations with the Western Balkans*. The Hague: TMC Asser Press.

Börzel, T. (2011). *When Europeanization Hits Limited Statehood. The Western Balkans as a Test Case for the Transformative Power of Europe*. Berlin: KFK Working Paper No. 30.

Checkel, J.T. (2001). Why Comply? Social Learning and European Identity Change. *International Organization*, 55(3), pp. 553–588.

Collantes-Celador, G. and Juncos, A.E. (2012). The EU and Border Management in the Western Balkans: Preparing for European Integration or Safeguarding EU External Borders? *Southeast European and Black Sea Studies*, 12(2), pp. 201–220.

Council of Europe (2011). *The Right to Leave One's Country should be Applied without Discrimination*. Strasbourg. press release – CommDH037.

Council of the European Union (2005). *Negotiating Framework, Croatia*. Luxembourg, October 3.

Council of the EU (2012). *Negotiating Framework for Montenegro*. Brussels, June 27.

Council of the EU (2015). *Follow-up to the Statement of the Members of the European Council of 12 February 2015 on Counter-terrorism: Report on Implementation of Measures*. Brussels, 9422/1/15, June 10.

Damjanovski, I., Nechev, Z., Schimmelfennig, F. and Zhelyaskova, A. (2016). *New Approach, Old Obstacles? EU Enlargement Strategy and Compliance with Rule of Law Provisions in Croatia, Macedonia and Serbia*. Paper presented at the Conference of the ECPR Standing Group on the European Union, Trento. Available at: https://ecpr.eu/Events/PaperDetails.aspx?PaperID=26742&EventID=105 (accessed February 3, 2017).

de Borja Laheras, F. and Tcherneva, V. (2015). *Is the EU Losing the Western Balkans? What Local Experts Think*. London: European Council on Foreign Relations. Available at: www.ecfr.eu/article/is_the_eu_losing_the_western_balkans_what_local_experts_think3093 (accessed on February 1, 2017).

Economides, S. and Ker-Lindsay, J. (2015). Pre-accession Europeanization: The Case of Serbia and Kosovo. *Journal of Common Market Studies*, 53(5), pp. 1027–1044.

Economides, S. and Ker-Lindsay, J. (2016). 'Outsourced Conditionality': The Problems and Pitfalls of Incorporating External Bodies into the EU Accession Process. UACES 46th Annual Conference, London. Available at: http://uaces.org/events/conferences/london/papers/abstract.php?paper_id=423#.WLRYnpVwXcs (accessed February 1, 2017).

Elbasani, A. (ed.) (2012). *European Integration and Transformation in the Western Balkans: Europeanization or Business as Usual?* London: Routledge.

European Commission (2012). *Enlargement Strategy and Main Challenges 2012–2013*. Brussels. COM(2012) 600 final, October 10.

European Commission (2015a). *EU Enlargement Strategy*. COM(2015) 611 final, November 10.

European Commission (2015b). *The European Agenda on Security*. Strasbourg. COM(2015) 185 final, April 28.

European Commission (2015c). *The Former Yugoslav Republic of Macedonia. Report 2015*. SWD(2015) 212 final, November 10.

European Commission (2016a). *The Former Yugoslav Republic of Macedonia 2016 Report*. Brussels. SWD(2016) 362 final, November 9.

European Commission (2016b). *Montenegro: Accession Negotiations – Summary Chapter Status*. Brussels. January 8.

European Council (2000). *Presidency Conclusions*. Santa Maria da Feira, June 19 and 20.

European Council (2011). *Presidency Conclusions*. Brussels, June 22/24.

European Union (2016). *Shared Vision, Common Action: A Stronger Europe. A Global Strategy for the European Union's Foreign and Security Policy*. Brussels, June.

Freyburg, T. and Richter, S. (2010). National Identity Matters: The Limited Impact of EU Political Conditionality in the Western Balkans. *Journal of European Public Policy*, 17(2), pp. 263–281.

Frontex (2011). *Western Balkan Annual Risk Analysis 2011*. Warsaw: European Agency for the Management of Operational Cooperation at the External Borders of the Member States of the European Union. Available at: http://frontex.europa.eu/assets/Attachments_News/wb_ara_2011_for_public_release.pdf (accessed February 10, 2017).

Frontex (2016). *Western Balkans Annual Risk Analysis 2016*. Warsaw.
Geddes, A., Lees, C. and Taylor, A. (2012). *The European Union and South East Europe. The Dynamics of Europeanization and Multilevel Governance*. London: Routledge.
Ioannides, I. (2006). EU Police Mission Proxima: Testing the 'European' Approach to Building Peace. In Agnieszka Nowak (ed.), *Civilian Crisis Management: The EU Way*. Chaillot Paper No. 90. Paris: Institute for Security Studies, pp. 62–87. Available at: www.iss.europa.eu/uploads/media/cp090.pdf (accessed February 10, 2017).
Ioannides, I. and Collantes-Celador, G. (2011). The Internal–External Security Nexus and EU Police/Rule of Law Missions in the Western Balkans. *Conflict, Security and Development*, 11(4), pp. 415–445.
Kacarska, S. (2012). *Europeanisation through Mobility: Visa Liberalisation and Citizenship Regimes in the Western Balkans*. CITSEE Working Paper Series 2012/21, Edinburgh. Available at: https://papers.ssrn.com/sol3/papers2.cfm?abstract_id=2115563 (accessed February 10, 2017).
Keil, S. (2013). Europeanization, State-building and Democratization in the Western Balkans. *Nationalities Papers*, 41(3), pp. 343–353.
Kelley, J.G. (2004). *Ethnic Politics in Europe: The Power of Norms and Incentives*. Princeton, NJ: Princeton University Press.
Kmezić, M. (2015). *The Western Balkans and EU Enlargement: Lessons Learned, Ways Forward and Prospects Ahead*. Report for the European Parliament EP/EXPO/B/AFET/FWC/2013-08/Lot1/03. Available at: www.europarl.europa.eu/RegData/etudes/IDAN/2015/534999/EXPO_IDA(2015)534999_EN.pdf (accessed February 10, 2017).
Kmezić, M. (2017). *EU Rule of Law Promotion. Judiciary Reform in the Western Balkans*. London: Routledge.
Kostovicova, D. and Bojicic-Dzelilovic, V. (2008). *Transnationalism in the Balkans*. London: Routledge.
Luif, P. and Riegler, H. (2006). *The External Dimension of the EU's Area of Freedom, Security and Justice in Relation to the Western Balkan Countries*. Briefing Paper for the European Parliament, Strasbourg: Directorate-General for External Policies of the European Union. Available at: www.europarl.europa.eu/RegData/etudes/note/join/2006/348588/EXPO-JOIN_NT(2006)348588_EN.pdf (accessed February 10, 2017).
Marcic, S. (2015). Informal Institutions in the Western Balkans: An Obstacle to Democratic Consolidation. *Journal of Balkan and Near Eastern Studies*, 17(1), pp. 1–14.
Mendelski, M. (2010). *Where Does the European Union Make a Difference? Rule of Law Development in Southeastern Europe*. APSA 2010 Annual Meeting Paper. Available at: https://papers.ssrn.com/sol3/papers2.cfm?abstract_id=1644729 (accessed February 16, 2017).
Mungiu-Pippidu, A. (2005). Deconstructing Balkan Particularism: The Ambigious Social Capital of Southeastern Europe. *Southeast European and Black Sea Studies*, 5(1), pp. 45–65.
Mungiu-Pippidu, A. (2011). A House of Cards? Building the Rule of Law in the Balkans. In J. Rupnik (ed.), *The Western Balkans and the EU: 'The Hour of Europe'*. Paris: Chaillot Papers of the European Union Institute for Security Studies, pp. 145–162.
Nechev, Z. (2013). *Bolstering the Rule of Law in the EU Enlargement Process towards the Western Balkans*. Clingendael Policy Brief No 22, Clingendael Institute. Available at: www.clingendael.nl/publication/bolstering-rule-law-eu-enlargement-process-towards-western-balkans (accessed February 16, 2017).
Nechev, Z. (2016). Reinstating the Transformative Power of the European Union in the Western Balkans. European Fund for the Balkans Paper Series. Available at: http://balkanfund.org/wp-content/uploads/2016/10/Reinstating-the-Transformative-Power-of-the-European-Union-in-the-Western-Balkans.pdf (accessed February 16, 2017).
Nechev, Z., Vidovic Mesarak, G., Saranovich, N.B. and Nikolov, A. (2013). *Embedding Rule of Law in the Enlargement Process: A Case for EU Political Conditionality in the Accession of the Western Balkan Countries*. Skopje: Konrad Adenauer Stiftung. Available at: www.kas.de/wf/doc/kas_36352-544-2-30.pdf?131211140824 (accessed February 18, 2017).
Nicič, J., Nechev, Z. and Mameledžija, S. (2016). *The Berlin Process: Crystallisation Point for the Western Balkans. A Regional Study on the Implementation of the Commitments from the 2015 Vienna Western Balkans Summit*. Belgrade: Group for Development Policy. Available at: https://wbc-rti.info/object/document/15248/attach/GDP-Vienna-Summit-Berlin-Process-Commitments-Implementation-Study.pdf (accessed February 18, 2017).
Noutcheva, G. (2009). Fake, Partial and Imposed Compliance: The Limits of the EU's Normative Power in the Western Balkans. *Journal of European Public Policy*, 16(7), pp. 1065–1084.
Noutcheva, G. and Aydin-Düzgit, S. (2012). Lost in Europeanisation: The Western Balkans and Turkey. *West European Politics*, 35(1), pp. 59–78.

Paris Western Balkan Summit (2016). *Final Declaration by the Chair of the Paris Western Balkans Summit*. Paris, July 4.

Phinnemore, D. (2003). Stabilisation and Association Agreements: Europe Agreements for the Western Balkans? *European Foreign Affairs Review*, 8(1), pp. 77–103.

Pippan, C. (2004). The Rocky Road to Europe: The EU's Stabilisation and Association Process for the Western Balkans and the Principle of Conditionality. *European Foreign Affairs Review*, 9, pp. 219–245.

Preshova, D., Damjanovski, I. and Nechev, Z. (2017). *The Effectiveness of the 'European Model' of Judicial Independence in the Western Balkan*. CLEER Working Paper 2017/1, T.M.C. Asser Institute. Available at: www.asser.nl/media/3475/cleer17-1_web.pdf (accessed February 18, 2017).

Radeljić, B. (2013). Democratising and Europeanising the Western Balkans: Context, Challenges and Prospects. *East European Politics and Societies*, 29(2), pp. 245–251.

Renner, S. and Trauner, F. (2009). Creeping EU-membership in Southeast Europe: The Dynamics of EU Rule Transfer to the Western Balkans. *Journal of European Integration*, 31(4), pp. 449–465.

Schimmelfennig, F. and Sedelmeier, U. (2004). Governance by Conditionality: EU Rule Transfer to the Candidate Countries of Central and Eastern Europe. *Journal of European Public Policy*, 11(4), pp. 661–679.

Schimmelfennig, F. and Sedelmeier, U. (eds) (2005). *The Europeanisation of Central and Eastern Europe*. Ithaca, NY, and London: Cornell University Press.

Schimmelfennig, F., Engert, S. and Knobel, H. (2003). Costs, Commitment and Compliance: The Impact of EU Democratic Conditionality on Latvia, Slovakia and Turkey. *Journal of Common Market Studies*, 41(3), pp. 495–518.

Sedelmeier, U. (2011). Europeanisation in New Member States and Candidate Countries. *Living Reviews in European Governance*, 6(1). Available at: http://europeangovernance.livingreviews.org/Articles/lreg-2011-2011/ (accessed February 16, 2017).

Spendzharova, A.B. (2003). Bringing Europe In? The Impact of EU Conditionality on Bulgarian and Romanian Politics. *Southeast European Politics*, 4(2–3), pp. 141–156.

Tolksdorf, D. (2013). Police Reform and EU Conditionality. In T. Flessenkemper and D. Helly (eds), *Ten Years After: Lessons from the EU Police Mission in Bosnia 2002–2012*. Paris: EU Institute for Security Studies, pp. 20–26.

Trauner, F. (2009). From Membership Conditionality to Policy Conditionality: EU External Governance in South Eastern Europe. *Journal of European Public Policy*, 16 (5), pp. 774–790.

Trauner, F. (2011). *The Europeanisation of the Western Balkans: EU Justice and Home Affairs in Croatia and Macedonia*. Manchester: Manchester University Press.

Trauner, F. and Manigrassi, E. (2014). When Visa-free Travel Becomes Difficult to Achieve and Easy to Lose: The EU Visa Free Dialogues after the EU's Experience with the Western Balkans. *European Journal of Migration and Law*, 16(1), pp. 125–145.

24
JUSTICE AND HOME AFFAIRS IN EU–TURKEY RELATIONS
Mutual interests but much distrust

Alexander Bürgin

Introduction

Cooperation in justice and home affairs (JHA) is of mutual interest to the EU and Turkey. For the EU, cooperation is important because Turkey has become one of the main transit routes for irregular migration to the EU. In 2013 and 2014, arrivals to the EU directly from Turkey numbered 25,121 and 52,994 respectively. In 2015, this number increased almost sixteen-fold, to 888,457. Around 98 percent of irregular entries occurred via the Greek islands from the nearby Turkish Aegean coast, often facilitated by smugglers. The remaining 2 percent entered via Turkey's land border with Greece and Bulgaria (European Commission 2016a: 79–80). In addition, cooperation is also important in the fight against organized crime and terrorism. For Turkey, in turn, this cooperation is important for burden-sharing reasons, since the country's transformation from a migrant-sending country into a transit and immigration country (Içduygu 2011) has generated high costs. Up until October 2015 Turkey spent $8 billion on hosting almost three million Syrian refugees, of which international contributions comprise less than half a billion, with the EU's share constituting only one-third of this sum (Kirişci 2015). Consequently, Turkey has an interest in deeper cooperation with the EU.

This chapter looks at three venues for EU–Turkey cooperation: (1) the accession process; (2) the initiated visa liberalization process in December 2013; and (3) the March 2016 EU–Turkey refugee statement. For each venue, developments and main scholarly debates are summarized.

Turkey's EU accession process

The EU accession process begun on October 3, 2005 is characterized by slow progress, reciprocal mistrust and increasing alienation (Aydın-Düzgit and Kaliber 2016). Regarding justice and home affairs, there has been no progress on opening chapter twenty-four which deals with issues such as border control, illegal migration, drug smuggling and money laundering, organized crime, and police and judicial cooperation. In particular, the Republic of Cyprus has remained determined to block this chapter due to Ankara's refusal to extend the customs union to the Greek part of the island. Consequently, while Turkey completed the screening process for all negotiation chapters on October 13, 2006, the benchmarks to be fulfilled for the opening of chapter twenty-four have never been delivered to Ankara.

Despite the stalemate in the accession process, the European Commission acknowledges Turkey's partial convergence with EU policy priorities in the field of justice and home affairs. In particular, the new law on foreigners and international protection, adopted by the Turkish Parliament on April 4, 2013, has been praised as a comprehensive framework for protecting and assisting all asylum-seekers and refugees, regardless of their country of origin, in line with international standards (European Commission 2013: 64). For instance, the law includes an accentuated commitment to the principle of non-refoulement, and regulates *inter alia* the timely processing of applications, access to translators and lawyers, the right to appeal against rejected asylum applications, access to primary and secondary education and to health services, as well as provisions concerning work permits. Furthermore, it provides for the establishment of a Directorate General of Migration Management at the Ministry of Interior to be responsible for the status determination of asylum-seekers, a competence previously exercised by the Foreigners Department of the National Police. According to the European Commission, this 'establishment of a civilian institution suggests a shift away from the security-oriented approach followed in this field until now' (European Commission 2013: 64).

However, the new law did not lift the geographical limitation of the 1951 Geneva Convention on the Status of Refugees. By becoming a signatory of the Convention, Turkey accepted international obligations concerning asylum and refugees, but maintained a geographical limitation on the origin of persons seeking protection. Consequently, non-European asylum-seekers can only apply for a subsidiary protection status, resulting in their inevitable removal: either to resettle in a third country if their applications are accepted, or to return to their country of origin if rejected. The status determination procedure is conducted by the Directorate General for Migration Management of the Interior Ministry; however, since their provincial Directorates have only very recently become fully operational, the UNHCR still continues to undertake its own refugee status determination activities, grounded in UNHCR's mandate, and to make resettlement referrals – 'in tandem' with the recently introduced 'international protection' procedure of the government. Yet, the UNHCR decisions have no direct binding effect (Asylum Information Data Base 2016).

A key scholarly debate concerns the main drivers for Turkey's recent reforms in migration management. Overall, the EU's impact upon Turkey's reforms in the field of asylum and migration policy has been acknowledged, at least for the period between 1999 and 2006 (Bürgin 2016a, 2012; İçduygu 2007; Kirişci 2012; Özcürümez and Şenses 2011; Tolay 2012). For instance, for Kirişci (2012), the incorporation of EU demands in national action and strategy plans on migration and asylum illustrates the success of the EU's conditionality strategy. He argues that the EU's *Accession Partnership* documents of 2001 and subsequent years were responsible for Turkish officials recognizing that

> Turkey would have to adopt structural, institutional and legislative reforms in order to open the negotiation chapter on migration. [Accordingly] in 2002 the government formed a task force that brought together officials from various agencies, possibly for the first time in their history, to actually discuss what needed to be done to meet the conditions set by these documents.
>
> *(Kirişci 2012: 73)*

In addition to the impact of the conditions set by the EU, it is also acknowledged that the EU was successful in triggering socialization and learning processes in twinning projects dealing with asylum policy and border management (Bürgin 2016a; Bürgin and Aşikoğlu 2015; Kirişci 2012; Tolay 2012). An important step towards legislative reform in this field was the adoption of a National Action Plan on Asylum and Migration in 2005, and a National Action Plan on Integrated Border Management the following year. Both plans were prepared during twinning projects with EU member states, and each envisaged the establishment of a specialized institution for migration management and border management, respectively. The first step towards the creation of such specialized institutions was the creation, under the under-secretariat of the Ministry of Interior on October 15, 2008, of two Bureaus: the Integrated Border Management Bureau, and the Asylum and Migration Bureau. Both received mandates to prepare the draft laws in the relevant policy areas. Based on interviews with officials from the European Commission, Bürgin and Aşikoğlu (2015) argue that the preparations of the laws provide evidence for the adoption of a more Europeanized approach, including active civil society involvement and comprehensive communication with other ministries and parliamentarians, which may be attributed to the necessary groundwork having been carried out during previous IPA-financed projects.

In spite of these developments, the EU's impact upon Turkish domestic politics has weakened, with worsening EU–Turkey relations since 2006. In addition to a growing pessimism in Turkey as regards EU membership prospects, Turkish officials were increasingly concerned that the EU intended to shift the responsibility of controlling migration and dealing with asylum applications to the periphery (İçduygu 2008: 15; Kirişci 2014). This concern has also been raised by scholarly work beyond specifically EU–Turkey relations, pointing more generally to the EU's externalization of migration control via readmission agreements as a new EU foreign policy tool (Lavenex 2006; Sterkx 2008). In particular, the EU's adoption of the asylum procedures Directive in December 2005, which opened the way for asylum-seekers to be transferred to a neighboring country if characterized as a safe third country, led to concern that Turkey would become a buffer zone for irregular immigrants (Tokuzlu 2010: 2).

The continuation of reforms in justice and home affairs, in spite of such obstacles, has been attributed to the impact of other international actors. In particular, the long-term engagement of the UNHCR in formal training programs for governmental officials, as in the status determination process, has been identified as a factor contributing to the socialization of Turkish officials in international refugee norms (Kaya 2009: 21; Kirişci 2012). Furthermore, recent unfavorable rulings of the European Court of Human Rights (ECtHR) have been named as another important driver of the reform of the Turkish asylum policy and practice (Tolay 2012: 47).

In addition, domestic factors explaining the transformation of Turkey's migration policies have been highlighted. A significant rise in the number of asylum applications since the mid-1990s increased the pressure for reform. It was recognized that Turkey hosted the largest refugee population worldwide in both 2014 and 2015, mainly because of its 2.54 million Syrian refugees, but there was also a significant rise in the number of asylum claims from other countries (UNHCR 2016a). The UNHCR registered 133,300 new claims in 2015 compared with 87,800 in 2014, making Turkey the fifth-largest recipient of individual new asylum claims (UNHCR 2016a). Moreover, the need for a general reform of Turkey's migration policy is also reflected in Turkey's transformation from a sending and transit country to a country of destination of legal and illegal migration, a development which is to a certain extent explained by Turkey's prospering economy. This is illustrated by the fact that of the total of 797,000 irregular immigrants apprehended in Turkey between 1995 and 2009, although nearly 58 percent were considered as potential transit migrants, as many as 42 percent intended to stay permanently (İçduygu 2011: 4).

Finally, the activities of non-governmental organizations (NGOs) are considered to be another relevant domestic factor in the reform process, due to their frequent criticism of denial of international protection rights to asylum-seekers. The recent increase in the numbers and influence of Turkish NGOs in the field of asylum and migration is partly explained by the support they receive from the EU. The EU has not only directly financed several NGO projects but has also supported capacity-building projects for Turkish bureaucracy with an important emphasis on promoting the consultation and participation of NGOs working in this field (Tolay 2012: 48). Furthermore, the UNHCR was also actively involved in training and seminars for Turkish NGOs, enabling them to develop expertise in filing complaints with local courts as well as the ECtHR (Kirişçi 2012: 69).

Readmission agreement and visa liberalization process

With the Amsterdam Treaty, the European Commission received the competence to conclude readmission agreements on behalf of all Schengen EU member states. These agreements set out clear obligations and procedures for the return of those residing irregularly in the EU. As one of the important transit routes for illegal immigrants, Turkey was invited by the European Commission to begin negotiations on a draft text of a readmission agreement in March 2003, which was eventually implemented in March 2004. However, as with most third countries with which the Commission was holding negotiations, Turkey was unwilling to commit to a readmission agreement without clear incentives, due to concerns that it would become the final destination for third-country nationals and stateless persons. Finally, the member states accepted the Commission's demand to link readmission agreements to the prospect of a visa waiver for the Balkan countries (Trauner and Kruse 2008: 11). Consequently, Bosnia-Herzegovina, Serbia, Macedonia, Moldova and Montenegro signed agreements in January 2008 and the EU lifted the visa obligation for Serbs, Macedonians and Montenegrins in December 2009, and for Albania and Bosnia-Herzegovina the following year. Turkey insisted on a procedure identical to that offered to the Balkan countries, in which a readmission agreement was the starting point for a visa liberalization process, based on a roadmap clearly setting out conditions to be fulfilled leading to the abolition of the visa duty. The Commission finally offered Turkey a visa dialogue with the goal of visa liberalization in return for the signing of a readmission agreement. In the interests of maintaining the credibility of the EU, the Commission argued that, in the light of the abolition of the visa obligation for the Balkan countries, and visa liberalization talks with Russia and Ukraine, it was no longer defensible to deny the linkage between readmission and visa waiver to Turkey. This commitment of the Commission paved the way for negotiations on a readmission agreement text, accepted by Turkey on January 27, 2011 (Bürgin 2012).

However, due to the insistence of opponents of a visa liberalization process, on February 24, 2011, the Justice and Home Affairs Council only invited the Commission to start a dialogue with Turkey on visa facilitations; the target of general visa exemption was excluded (Council of the European Union 2011). Ahmet Davutoğlu, then Turkish Foreign Minister, responded by stating that Ankara would not put into effect the agreement until the EU launched talks aimed at visa liberalization. In the aftermath, the Commission, in close cooperation with the Danish Council Presidency, elaborated a strategy to overcome the resistance of reluctant member states. Their approach was to incorporate into the Council Conclusions about the visa liberalization process a broader dialogue and cooperation framework between the EU and Turkey. This dialogue would include the full range of justice and home affairs policy fields such as, *inter alia*, the combat against terrorism, money laundering and drug trafficking. Reluctant governments had to reconsider two conflicting policy goals: on the one hand, the return of illegal immigrants and the benefits of cooperation with Turkey in justice and home affairs, and, on the other, the security concerns regarding Turkish nationals who overstay the ninety-day period of visa-free travel. Eventually, in June 2012 the Commission received the backing of the member states to launch a visa liberalization process with Turkey, in exchange for a readmission agreement obliging Ankara to readmit irregular immigrants who passed through Turkey as a transit country. The agreement envisaged an application only to Turkish citizens in the first stage of the implementation, and an extension to third-country nationals three years after the agreement's enactment (Bürgin 2013).

The visa liberalization process was based on a roadmap specifying approximately seventy conditions for the visa waiver, including a functioning readmission agreement and reforms in areas of document security, border management, asylum, human rights and cooperation with EU member states and EU agencies. At a EU–Turkey Summit on November 29, 2015, both sides agreed that the readmission agreement would become fully applicable from June 2016, anticipating the entry into application of the provisions related to third-country nationals, thus fulfilling an important condition for the completion of the visa liberalization process and lifting visa requirements for Turkish citizens in the Schengen zone by October 2016. Turkey's progress in fulfilling the benchmarks has been acknowledged by the European Commission. In its second progress reports on March 4, 2016 the Commission (European Commission 2016b) noted that especially after the EU–Turkey Summit on November 29, 2015, Turkey has accelerated the reform process aimed at fulfilling the requirements of the roadmap. The report highlighted four main improvements. First, refugees from Syria have been given access to the labor market, which is expected to facilitate their social inclusion and self-reliance. Second, schooling has been made available for refugee children. Third, stricter visa and admission rules have been introduced regarding nationals coming from countries which are sources of significant irregular onward migration from Turkey to the EU. Finally, there have been continued efforts to strengthen overall border surveillance and management capacities. The report also identifies the measures Turkey should take in order to fulfill all roadmap requirements. Among others, Turkey needs to adopt passports that carry fingerprints, in line with EU standards. The report also calls on Turkey to reduce backlogs in implementing asylum procedures, to intensify cooperation with all member states with shared borders, notably concerning readmission, police and judicial matters, and to intensify efforts to combat corruption and organized crime. Other necessary steps in the roadmap are the adoption of legislation on personal data protection in line with EU standards and the conclusion of cooperation agreements with Europol and Eurojust, as well as the development of comprehensive measures to facilitate the social inclusion of its Roma population. The report further underlined the need for Turkey to align its legislation on terrorism with EU and Council of Europe standards (European Commission 2016b).

Regarding the consequences of a possible visa waiver, skeptical voices in some EU member states are worried about the potential for a significant increase in illegal permanent migration, due to the expectation that many Turkish visitors will ignore the maximum stay of 90 days in a 180-day period. Moreover, the earlier experience with the Balkan countries has led to the expectation of a rise in unfounded asylum requests once the visa requirement is abolished. Another concern is the threat from free travel for terrorists of Turkish origin. However, the basis for these concerns has largely been rejected by scholarly work. According to Kirişci and Ekim (2015: 2), the fear of a significant increase in illegal migration lacks evidentiary support, arguing that while Turkish immigration into EU countries continued until around the mid-2000s, since then migration movements have turned in the opposite direction, with Turkey serving as an immigration destination for Europeans. One reason for this development is Turkey's positive economic development. The doubling in size of the Turkish economy between 2004 and 2014 reduced migration pressure due to economic reasons. In addition, Bürgin (2016b) argues that the problem of overstayers could be addressed by the introduction of a EU-wide entry/exit system, which is currently in preparation, making it easier to detect overstayers. Furthermore, the concern of unfounded asylum claims could be eased by the more efficient processing of asylum requests, obliging those who failed to qualify as refugees to be immediately returned to Turkey. Rather than focusing on possible risks of the visa waiver, researchers have highlighted the economic advantages for the EU, with an increase in revenue from Turkish tourists, and improved business relations (Kirişçi and Ekim 2015; Stiglmayer 2012). Furthermore, it has been argued that the granting of visa-free travel could lead to new trust in the EU and motivate the Turkish government to combat irregular transit migration with greater conviction (Kirişçi and Ekim 2015: 3).

EU–Turkey refugee statement

The EU–Turkey statement of March 18, 2016 is another milestone in their cooperation in the management of irregular migration (European Council 2016). Ankara agreed to readmit all new irregular migrants and asylum-seekers arriving from Turkey to the Greek islands, and whose applications for asylum have been declared inadmissible by the Greek authorities. This step will serve as a signal to all potential refugees of the futility in following the route offered by the smugglers. In return, the EU has offered Turkey four main rewards. First, the EU will resettle a Syrian currently resident in Turkey to the EU for every Syrian returned to Turkey from the Greek islands. Priority is given to migrants who have not previously entered or tried to enter the EU irregularly within the framework of the existing commitments. Second, the fulfillment of the visa liberalization roadmap would be accelerated with a view to lifting the visa requirements for Turkish citizens at the latest by the end of June 2016, provided that the remaining benchmarks have been fulfilled. Third, the EU will increase its financial support under the Facility for Refugees in Turkey from three to six billion euro. Finally, the accession process will be re-energized, with chapter thirty-three to be opened during the Dutch Presidency of the Council of the European Union and preparatory work on the opening of other chapters to continue at an accelerated pace.

Thus far the statement has reached its goals, reducing the number of attempts to cross the Aegean and associated deaths. According to a European Commission report (European Commission 2016c), published on September 28, 2016, around 1740 migrants made the Aegean crossing to the Greek islands daily in the weeks before the implementation of the Statement. By contrast, since March 21, this figure is down to 94 and the number of lives lost in the Aegean Sea has fallen to 11, compared to 270 in 2015. Furthermore, the European Commission sees no evidence that new routes are developing directly as a result of the EU–Turkey Statement. So far, 1614 Syrian refugees have been resettled from Turkey to Europe, and 578 irregular migrants have been returned from the Greek islands. The organization of the resettlement requires that an initial list of resettlement candidates is prepared by the Turkish authorities on the basis of vulnerability criteria. This list is then assessed by the UNHCR in order to identify the cases that meet the criteria for application to EU member states for resettlement. Member states make the final decision on UNHCR submissions and carry out their own security checks. Of the overall €3 billion, €2.239 billion was allocated in September 2016, divided between humanitarian and non-humanitarian assistance, and €1.252 billion of this amount has been contracted. Of this contracted €1.252 billion, €467 million has been disbursed to date. Accession negotiations on chapter thirty-three (Financial and Budgetary Provisions) were opened on June 30 in accordance with the EU–Turkey Statement (European Commission 2016c).

However, one key demand by Turkey, namely visa liberalization, has not been realized at the time of writing (July 2017). In May 2016, the Commission proposed the lifting of the visa duty, provided that the few remaining requirements will be fulfilled by Turkey. The European Parliament stressed that the proposal will be dealt with only after the fulfillment of all benchmarks, in particular the requirement to change anti-terror laws, which the EP considers are being exploited to constrain the freedom of expression (European Parliament 2016a). The visa waiver has to be approved by a qualified majority in the Council and a simple majority in the EP. The Turkish President has responded by stressing that no changes will be made to antiterror legislation, and, should the visa waiver not be realized in the near future, has threatened to withdraw from the commitment to readmit irregular immigrants from the EU (*The Guardian* 2016a).

The attempted coup in Turkey on July 15, 2016, and the reaction of the Turkish government, have further increased political tensions between the two sides, reducing the chances of a prompt realization of a visa waiver. In its 2016 Turkey report, the Commission expressed its concerns over the functioning of democracy: 'There has been backsliding in the past year, in particular with regard to the independence of the judiciary. The extensive changes to the structures and composition of high courts are of serious concern and are not in line with European standards' (European Commission 2016d). Regarding the freedom of expression, the Commission attests a similarly serious reversal in the past year:

> Selective and arbitrary application of the law, especially of the provisions on national security and the fight against terrorism, is having a negative impact on freedom of expression. Ongoing and new criminal cases against journalists, writers or social media users, withdrawal of accreditations, high numbers of arrests of journalists as well as closure of numerous media outlets in the aftermath of the July attempted coup are of serious concern.
>
> *(European Commission 2016d)*

In the EP, in turn, a broad coalition of MEPs voted for a suspension of the accession talks on November 23, 2016, condemning the 'disproportionate repressive measures' taken by the Turkish government since the failed coup attempt in July 2016 (European Parliament 2016b). The resolution is non-binding; a temporay freeze of accession negotiations has to be initiated either by the Commission or one-third of the MS, who need to secure a qualified majority in favor of taking such a step. So far, both the Commission and the majority of the member states prefer a continuation of the dialogue. Subsequently, the Turkish President announced his intention to drop the refugee deal should the Council follow the EP's recommendation (*The Guardian* 2016b).

The statement has also triggered a debate about the legal nature of the deal. According to the Commission, the deal fully respects EU and international law, as requests for asylum are individually assessed (European Commission 2016c). However, EU asylum rules allow, in certain clearly defined circumstances, member states to declare an application 'inadmissible'; that is to say, to reject the application without examining the substance, after a fast-track procedure, and thereby accelerate application processing. There are two legal criteria that may be used for declaring asylum applications inadmissible in relation to Turkey: (1) first country of asylum (Article 35 of the Asylum Procedures Directive): where the person has already been recognized as a refugee in that country or otherwise enjoys sufficient protection there; (2) safe third country (Article 38 of the Asylum Procedures Directive): where the person has not already received protection in the third country but the third country can guarantee effective access to protection to the readmitted person. The Commission regards Turkey as a safe third country, as the Turkish authorities have provided assurances that all returned Syrians will be granted temporary protection; and that each non-Syrian who seeks international protection in Turkey will enjoy protection from refoulement, in line with international standards and in accordance with the applicable Law on Foreigners and International Protection (European Commission 2016c).

Nevertheless, civil society organizations, legal experts, the Council of Europe and the UNHCR have all criticized the application of the safe third-country principle with respect to Turkey, especially due to cases of refoulement (Carrera and Guild 2016; Greene and Kelemen 2016; Parliamentary Assembly of the Council of Europe 2016; UNHCR 2016b). Furthermore, criticisms have been made of the Syrian refugees' temporary protection status, which leaves them in a state of uncertainty (Baban et al. 2016). Finally, it has been argued that non-Syrian asylum-seekers are subject to a largely dysfunctional international protection procedure. It has been stated that despite recent reforms, the Directorate General for Migration Management still lacks the capacity to process asylum applications, while numerous barriers to state funded legal aid, coupled with resource constraints upon NGOs, leave asylum-seekers without legal representation or advice (European Council on Refugees and Exiles 2016).

Another debate emerged about the appropriateness of reviving the accession process through the opening of new accession chapters. It has been argued that upgrading Turkey's relationship with the EU by opening new negotiation chapters is undeserved due to Ankara's deviation from the EU's political values, reflected in regressive steps regarding freedom of speech and freedom of the press (Paul 2016). From this perspective, the EU's readiness to accelerate accession negotiations represents an unacceptable compromise over European values. Hakura (2016) argues that Turkey's lack of reliable alternative partners and its struggling economy, and long-term stagnation would actually have afforded the EU a tougher bargaining position.

The defenders of the deal reject the claim that the EU is kowtowing to President Erdoğan. It has been argued that, while the EU has lost its leverage on Turkish domestic politics in recent years, the opening of new negotiation chapters dealing with sensitive issues such as the freedom of the press or the independence of the judiciary would bring the EU a renewed influence over Turkish domestic politics, and could therefore contribute to a *rapprochement* between the EU and Turkey (Gedikkaya 2016). Consequently, the opening of new chapters cannot be said to represent a retreat by the EU on political standards (Bürgin 2016b). Furthermore, the closing of a chapter is more significant than its opening, and it is impossible to make progress in an accession process without reform and concrete improvements (Seufert 2016: 7).

Conclusion

The overview of EU–Turkey relations in the field of justice and home affairs has shown that the mutual benefits of cooperation have triggered positive results, despite an overall political atmosphere characterized by mutual mistrust. With EU support, Turkey has improved its asylum standards and border management capacities. After ten years of negotiations, in 2013, a readmission agreement was finally concluded. The 2016 EU–Turkey refugee statement has contributed to a significant decrease in the numbers of irregular immigrants reaching the EU via Turkey.

In particular, the most recent refugee statement represents interesting avenues for further research, which could address the following issues. From a theoretical perspective, it would be valuable to explore what this deal represents for the normative power of the EU (for a discussion of the normative power concept see Diez 2005; Manners 2002). Does it represent a break with a norm-based relationship with Turkey? If so, does it signify that Turkey is now considered more as a strategic partner rather than as a candidate country? Another avenue for further research is the role of the Commission in the EU's relationship with Turkey. The Commission's agency in the visa liberalization process illustrates a critical but fair approach towards Turkey by ensuring that both sides abide by the rules. However, there is still a lack of investigation into the extent to which the European Commission is able to establish mutual trust and lasting policy networks in its frequent interactions with officials in Turkish ministries, and the extent to which the Commission is able to influence Turkey-related positions in the European Parliament and in the Council.

Finally, linked to the topic of the Commission's agency, softer mechanisms of EU influence, such as policy learning and socialization, deserve more attention. In the face of the stalled EU accession talks, policy learning processes outside of the framework of official accession negotiations represent an opportunity to keep the Europeanization process in Turkey alive. Such studies would also attract stronger attention to the role of Turkish bureaucracy, NGOs and policy networks at local and national level. These factors are often neglected by the Europeanization literature on Turkey, which rather tends to focus on the behavior of the political elite and the ruling party in particular when discussing the successes and failures of Europeanization processes. From an empirical perspective, the effects of the refugee statement could be investigated to determine whether the statement actually leads to fewer refugees, or rather to a shifting of refugee routes. Other questions include: Have the EU funds improved the situation of refugees in Turkey? Will Turkey continue taking back refugees from the Greek islands in the event that visa liberalization for Turkish citizens is not realized in the near future? If so, what are the reasons, and if not, what will be the consequences for EU–Turkey relations?

Bibliography

Asylum Information Data Base (2016). Introduction to the Asylum Context in Turkey. www.asylumineurope.org/reports/country/turkey/introduction-asylum-context-turkey (accessed December 4, 2016).

Aydın-Düzgit, S. and Kaliber, A. (2016). Encounters with Europe in an Era of Domestic and International Turmoil: Is Turkey a De-Europeanising Candidate Country? *South European Society and Politics*, 21(1), pp. 1–14.

Baban, F., Ilcan, S. and Rygiel, K. (2016). Syrian Refugees in Turkey: Pathways to Precarity, Differential Inclusion, and Negotiated Citizenship Rights. *Journal of Ethnic and Migration Studies*, published online June 8.

Bürgin, A. (2012). European Commission's Agency Meets Ankara's Agenda: Why Turkey is Ready for a Readmission Agreement. *Journal of European Public Policy*, 19(6), pp. 883–899.

Bürgin, A. (2013). Salience, Path Dependency and the Coalition between the European Commission and the Danish Council Presidency: Why the EU Opened a Visa Liberalization Process with Turkey. *European Integration Online Papers*, 17(9), pp. 1–19.

Bürgin, A. (2016a). Why the EU Still Matters in Turkish Domestic Politics: Insight from Recent Reforms in Migration Policy. *South European Society and Politics*, 21(1), pp. 105–118.

Bürgin, A. (2016b). Why the EU Should Accept Ankara's Demands. *Euractiv*, March 16. www.euractiv.com/section/global-europe/opinion/why-the-eu-should-accept-ankaras-demands/ (accessed December 9, 2016).

Bürgin, A. and Aşikoğlu, D. (2015). Turkey's New Asylum Law: A Case of EU Influence. *Journal of Balkan and Near Eastern Studies*, published online November 13.

Carrera, S. and Guild, E. (2016). EU–Turkey Plan for Handling Refugees is Fraught with Legal and Procedural Challenges. *CEPS*. www.ceps.eu/publications/eu-turkey-plan-handling-refugees-fraught-legal-and-procedural-challenges (accessed December 9, 2016).

Council of the European Union (2011). Press Release 307 1st Justice and Home Affairs Council Meeting, February 25. www.consilium.europa.eu/uedocs/cms_data/docs/pressdata/en/jha/119497.pdf (accessed December 9, 2016).

Diez, T. (2005). Constructing the Self and Changing Others: Reconsidering 'Normative Power Europe', Millenium. *Journal of International Studies*, 33(3), pp. 613–636.

European Commission (2013). *Turkey 2013 Progress Report*, SWD(2013) 417 final. Brussels.

European Commission (2016a). *Turkey Report 2016*, SWD(2016), 366 final, November 9. http://ec. europa.eu/enlargement/pdf/key_documents/2016/20161109_report_turkey.pdf (accessed December 8, 2016).

European Commission (2016b). Commission Visa Progress Report: Turkey Makes Progress towards Visa Liberalisation, March 4. http://europa.eu/rapid/press-release_IP-16-582_en.htm (accessed December 8, 2016).

European Commission (2016c). Implementing the EU–Turkey Statement – Questions and Answers, September 28. http://europa.eu/rapid/press-release_MEMO-16-3204_en.htm (accessed December 8, 2016).

European Commission (2016d). Key Findings of the 2016 Report on Turkey, Memo/16/3639. http://europa.eu/rapid/press-release_MEMO-16-3639_en.htm (accessed December 8, 2016).

European Council (2016). EU–Turkey Statement, March 18. www.consilium.europa.eu/en/press/press-releases/2016/03/18-eu-turkey-statement/ (accessed December 9, 2016).

European Council on Refugees and Exiles (2016). ECRE Memorandum to the European Council Meeting, March 17–18, 2016. www.statewatch.org/news/2016/mar/eu-ecri-right-asylum.pdf (accessed December 4, 2016).

European Parliament (2016a). Visa Liberalisation for Turkey: EU Criteria Must Be Met, Say MEPs, May 10. www.europarl.europa.eu/news/en/news-room/20160509IPR26368/Visa-liberalisation-for-Turkey-EU-criteria-must-be-met-say-MEPs (accessed December 8, 2016).

European Parliament (2016b). Freeze EU Accession Talks with Turkey Until it Halts Repression Urge MEPs, November 24. www.europarl.europa.eu/news/en/news-room/20161117IPR51549/freeze-eu-accession-talks-with-turkey-until-it-halts-repression-urge-meps (accessed December 8, 2016).

Gedikkaya, P. (2016). The Effects of the Refugee Crisis on the EU–Turkey Relations: The Readmission Agreement And Beyond. *European Scientific Journal*, 12(8), pp. 14–35.

Greene, M. and Kelemen, R.D. (2016). Europe's Lousy Deal with Turkey. *Foreign Affairs*, March 2.

The Guardian (2016a). Turkey Threatens to Block EU Migration Deal without Visa-free Travel, May 24. www.theguardian.com/world/2016/may/24/turkey-eu-migration-deal-visa-free-travel-recep-tayyip-erdogan (accessed December 8, 2016).

The Guardian (2016b). Turkey Threatens to End Refugee Deal in Row Over EU Accession, November 25. www.theguardian.com/world/2016/nov/25/turkey-threatens-end-refugee-deal-row-eu-accession-erdogan (accessed December 8, 2016).

Hakura, F. (2016). The EU–Turkey Refugee Deal Solves Little, April/May, *Chatham House*. www.chathamhouse.org/publications/twt/eu-turkey-refugee-deal-solves-little (accessed December 4, 2016).

Içduygu, A. (2007). EU-ization Matters: Changes in Immigration and Asylum Practices in Turkey. In T. Faist and A. Ette (eds) *The Europeanization of National Policies and Politics of Immigration. Between Autonomy and the European Union*. Basingstoke: Palgrave Macmillan, pp. 201–222.

Içduygu, A. (2008). Rethinking Irregular Migration Management in Turkey: Some Demo-economic Reflections, *European University Institute*. http://cadmus.eui.eu/handle/1814/10117 (accessed December 9, 2016).

Içduygu, A. (2011). The Irregular Migration Corridor between the EU and Turkey: Is it Possible to Block it with a Readmission Agreement? *European University Institute*. http://cadmus.eui.eu/handle/1814/17844 (accessed December 9, 2016).

Kaya, I. (2009). Reform in Turkish Asylum Law: Adopting the EU Acquis? *European University Institute*. http://cadmus.eui.eu/bitstream/handle/1814/11849/CARIM_RR_2009_16.pdf?sequence=2 (accessed December 9, 2016).

Kirişçi, K. (2012). Turkey's New Draft Law on Asylum: What to Make of it. In S.P. Elitok and T. Straubhaar (eds) *Turkey, Migration and the EU: Challenges and Opportunities*. Hamburg: University Press of Hamburg, pp. 63–83.

Kirişçi, K. (2014). Will the Readmission Agreement Bring the EU and Turkey Together or Pull Them Apart. *Brookings*, February 4. www.brookings.edu/research/opinions/2014/02/04-readmission-agreement-eu-turkey-kirisci (accessed December 4, 2016).

Kirişçi, K. (2015). What the New Turkey–EU Cooperation Really Means for Syrian Refugees. *Brookings*, October 19. www.brookings.edu/blogs/order-fromchaos/posts/2015/10/19-turkey-europe-action-plan-syrian-refugees-kirisci (accessed December 4, 2016).

Kirişçi, K. and Ekim, S. (2015). EU–Turkey Visa Liberalization and Overcoming the 'Fear of Turks': The Security and Economic Dimensions. *German Marshall Fund of the United States*, February 13. www.

gmfus.org/publications/eu-turkey-visa-liberalization-and-overcoming-fear-turks-security-and-economic (accessed December 4, 2016).

Lavenex (2006). Shifting Up and Out: The Foreign Policy of European Immigration Control. *West European Politics*, 29(2), pp. 329–350.

Manners, I. (2002). Normative Power Europe: A Contradiction in Terms? *Journal of Common Market Studies*, 40(2), pp. 235–258.

Özcürümez, S. and Şenses, N. (2011). Europeanization and Turkey: Studying Irregular Migration Policy. *Journal of Balkan and Near Eastern Studies*, 13(2), pp. 233–248.

Parliamentary Assembly of the Council of Europe (2016). The Situation of Refugees and Migrants under the EU–Turkey Agreement of 18 March 2016, Resolution 2109, April 20. http://assembly.coe.int/nw/xml/XRef/Xref-XML2HTML-en.asp?fileid=22738&lang=en (accessed December 9, 2016).

Paul, A. (2016). Turkey Makes a Mockery of Europe's Claim to Uphold Democratic Values. *European Policy Centre*, March 16. www.epc.eu/pub_details.php?cat_id=4&pub_id=6403 (accessed December 4, 2016).

Seufert, G. (2016). Turkey as Partner of the EU in the Refugee Crisis: Ankara's Problems and Interests. *German Institute for International and Security Affairs*, January. www.swp-berlin.org/fileadmin/contents/products/comments/2016C01_srt.pdf (accessed December 9, 2016).

Sterkx, S. (2008). The External Dimension of EU Asylum and Migration Policy: Expanding Fortress Europe. In J. Orbie (ed.) *Europe's Global Role: External Policies of the European Union*. Ashgate: Farnham, pp. 117–156.

Stiglmayer, A. (2012). Visa-free Travel for Turkey: In Everybody's Interest. *Turkish Policy*, 11(1), pp. 99–109. http://turkishpolicy.com/dosyalar/files/2012-1-AlexandraStiglmayer.pdf (accessed December 4, 2016).

Tokuzlu, L.B. (2010). Burden-sharing Games for Asylum Seekers between Turkey and the EU. *Robert Schuman Institute for Advanced Studies*, EUI Working Papers No. 5. http://cadmus.eui.eu/bitstream/handle/1814/13096/RSCAS_2010_05.pdf?sequence=1, (accessed December 4, 2016).

Tolay, J. (2012). Turkey's 'Critical Europeanization': Evidence from Turkey's Immigration Policies. In S.P. Elitok and T. Straubhaar (eds) *Turkey, Migration and the EU: Challenges and Opportunities*. Hamburg: University of Hamburg Press, pp. 39–61.

Trauner, F. and Kruse, I. (2008). EC Visa Facilitation and Readmission Agreements: Implementing a New EU Security Approach in the Neighbourhood. *Centre for European Policy Studies*, Working Document No. 290.

UNHCR (2016a). Global Trends, June 20. www.unhcr.org/cgi-bin/texis/vtx/search?page=&comid=4146b6fc4&cid=49aea93aba&keywords=Trends (accessed December 4, 2016).

UNHCR (2016b). Legal Considerations on the Return of Asylum-seekers and Refugees from Greece to Turkey, March 23. www.unhcr.org/56f3ec5a9.pdf (accessed December 4, 2016).

25
THE EASTERN PARTNERSHIP COUNTRIES AND RUSSIA
A migration-driven cooperation agenda with the European Union

Oleg Korneev and Peter Van Elsuwege

Introduction

Migration and mobility as well as cooperation in the broader area of justice and home affairs (JHA) is an increasingly important topic in the relations between the EU and its East European neighbors. The bilateral Partnership and Cooperation Agreements concluded with the post-Soviet countries in the first half of the 1990s already included a title devoted to 'cooperation on prevention of illegal activities' as well as a declaration regarding the issuing of visas and the prospective conclusion of readmission agreements. The EU's Eastward enlargement as well as its expanding competences regarding the Area of Freedom, Security and Justice (AFSJ) intensified the need for close cooperation on issues such as the tackling of organized crime, the management of migration and the fight against terrorism. It is, therefore, no coincidence that questions of internal security and migration figure high on the agenda of the EU's relations with its Eastern neighbors.

From the end of the 1990s onward, most notably following the entry into force of the Amsterdam Treaty, the EU has gradually developed an external dimension of its cooperation in the field of JHA (Wolff *et al.* 2009) and, later, the AFSJ (O'Neill 2016). Within this context, constructive cooperation with the EU's Eastern neighborhood in general and the Russian Federation in particular was a key policy objective. For instance, the EU's Common Strategy on Russia (European Council 1999) already defined irregular immigration as a 'major preoccupation' in EU–Russia relations and announced further actions to fight organized crime, corruption, money laundering, trafficking in human beings and drug trafficking. This resulted in the adoption in April 2000 of an EU Action Plan 'on common action for the Russian Federation on combating organized crime' (Council of the EU 2000).

The very first Strategy Papers of the European Neighbourhood Policy (ENP), adopted in 2003 and 2004, further acknowledged that prospects for lawful migration and movement of persons, on the one hand, and common efforts to combat irregular migration as well as the establishment of efficient mechanisms for return, on the other, are crucial determinants for successful cooperation with the EU's neighboring countries. Ever since, the EU has developed several specific initiatives and policy instruments vis-à-vis its Eastern neighbors. In this respect, a basic distinction can be made between the countries taking part in the Eastern Partnership, i.e., the specific policy framework for the Eastern ENP countries (Ukraine, Moldova, Belarus,

Georgia, Armenia and Azerbaijan) on the one hand, and the Russian Federation, on the other. From the outset, the Russian Federation made clear that it was not interested in the conditionality-based approach of the ENP. Instead, it preferred to work within the framework of a 'Strategic Partnership' based on the principle of equality with the elaboration of roadmaps for the establishment of four common spaces (devoted to economic cooperation; external security; freedom, security and justice; and research and education) as its most visible manifestation.

Proceeding from this basic distinction, this contribution aims to take stock of the relevant policy evolutions and academic research regarding the EU's internal security and migration policies in relation to its Eastern neighborhood. By establishing the state of the art in this field, this chapter devotes specific attention to (1) the evolution of migration policy instruments such as visa facilitation and readmission agreements, on the one hand, and the establishment of visa liberalization dialogues, on the other, and (2) the challenge of coherence in the EU's JHA policies towards the Eastern neighborhood, including the challenge of reconciling values and interests in these policies against the backdrop of an increasing competition in this region between the EU and Russia, also with regard to migration issues.

The evolution of EU migration policy instruments in relation to the EU's Eastern neighbors

Based on a policy instrument approach, a distinction may be made between legally binding instruments, non-legally binding (soft law and policy) instruments as well as operational and cooperation instruments (Trauner and Wolff 2014; Van Elsuwege and Vankova 2017).

Legally binding instruments

So far as the legally binding instruments are concerned, it is noteworthy that all bilateral framework agreements between the EU and its Eastern neighbors include specific provisions devoted to cooperation in the field of migration and mobility. Whereas the first generation of Partnership and Cooperation Agreements, concluded in the first half of the 1990s, only generally proclaimed the parties' intention to explore options for cooperation in the field of migration management, agreements concluded after 1999 define cooperation on prevention and control of irregular migration as one of the primary objectives of the established partnership. These differences do not necessarily reflect a differentiated level of ambition in the bilateral relationship; nor does the differentiation depend upon the strategic importance of the partner country. Rather, the timing of the agreement's negotiation and signature explains whether or not rather basic or more sophisticated migration clauses have been incorporated.

As observed by Coleman (2009), there is a direct correlation between the EU's expanding competences in relation to migration and mobility and the evolution of migration-related provisions in bilateral framework agreements.[1] From this perspective, it is no surprise that the latest generation of Association Agreements signed in 2014 with Ukraine, Moldova and Georgia all include broadly defined migration clauses *inter alia* providing for an in-depth dialogue on migration, cooperation on border management, the joint establishment of a preventive policy against irregular migration and the exchange of views on the informal employment of migrants.[2] Remarkably, there are small differences among the three agreements. For instance, the preambles to the Association Agreements with Moldova and Georgia refer explicitly to 'circular migration' as an integral part of the migration dialogue. Such a reference is absent in the Association Agreement with Ukraine. On the other hand, the EU–Ukraine Association Agreement is significantly more developed in the sense that it also has articles devoted to 'mobility of workers' and 'treatment of workers', which are absent in the agreements with Moldova and Georgia.[3] The potential direct effect of those provisions in the legal order of the EU member states is still an open question (Van der Loo 2016: 197).

The Association Agreements all cross-refer to more specific readmission and visa facilitation agreements as far as the implementation of concrete engagements is concerned. The parallel conclusion of readmission and visa facilitation agreements with the EU's Eastern neighbors has been regarded as 'a means for mitigating the negative side effects of the eastern enlargement' (Trauner and Kruse 2008: 412). The latter process – more specifically the requirement to implement the EU's Schengen acquis – led to the introduction of visa requirements between the new EU member states from Central and Eastern Europe and their Eastern neighbors (Grabbe 2002). In relation to Russia, the peculiar situation of the Kaliningrad enclave created a significant security challenge and it was only after long-standing negotiations that a compromise solution on facilitated transit to Kaliningrad could be found (Potemkina 2003; Van Elsuwege 2008: 399–462). In this context, in August 2002, Vladimir Putin proposed to reciprocally abolish the visa requirement between Russia and the EU. Even though this proposal did not yield any immediate results, it nevertheless opened the gates to more profound discussions on strengthened cooperation in the field of justice and home affairs.

On the occasion of the May 2003 Saint Petersburg EU–Russia Summit, the EU and Russia established a new, non-legally binding framework for their bilateral cooperation in the form of four so-called Common Spaces, namely a Common Economic Space; a Common Space of Freedom, Security and Justice; a Common Space of External Security, and a Common Space of Research and Education, including Cultural Aspects (Van Elsuwege 2008). A roadmap for the implementation of the Common Spaces, adopted at the 2005 Moscow EU–Russia Summit, provided a mutually agreed agenda for further action. Within this framework, visa liberalization was recognized as a 'long-term' objective of EU–Russia cooperation whereas in the 'short term' the aim was to facilitate the visa application procedures as much as possible.

Significantly, the visa facilitation agreement between the EU and Russia was the first to be negotiated and signed in parallel with a readmission agreement. This approach, defined as the 'readmission–visa facilitation nexus' (Hernández i Sagrera 2010), shaped the EU's relations with the entire region, since it became virtually impossible for the EU to block similar initiatives with other countries (Korneev 2008). As observed by Trauner and Kruse (2008), the combined use of visa facilitation and readmission agreements quickly developed into a new standard EU foreign policy tool. The offer of more relaxed travel conditions turned out to be instrumental in the acceptance of readmission practices and to press for reforms in domestic justice and home affairs. Despite the offer of visa facilitation, the EU's Eastward enlargement resulted in strengthened border regimes between the EU and its Eastern neighbors (ibid.).

Even though the evaluation of the European Commission (2009) has generally been positive, research shows that the real impact of the Visa Facilitation Agreements is limited – it does not remedy the complex application procedure, its length and the limited issuance of multi-entry visas (Andrade et al. 2015; Weinar et al. 2012; Van Elsuwege 2013). Moreover, the amended Visa Facilitation Agreements with Moldova and Ukraine, concluded in 2013, do not provide for much improvement. Notwithstanding an extension of the personal scope of the agreement, concerns relating to the documentary evidence needed for visa applications of bona fide travelers have not been addressed (Andrade et al. 2015: 41).

The launch of the Eastern Partnership (EaP) in May 2009 provided new impetus for close cooperation between the EU and its Eastern neighbors on matters related to migration and mobility. The EaP's founding document, adopted at the Prague EaP Summit, not only confirmed the importance of the visa facilitation–readmission nexus as a tool for promoting mobility of citizens of the partner countries but also unequivocally defined 'visa liberalization in a secure environment' as an important aspect of the established partnership (Council of the EU 2010). For this purpose, the EU introduced Visa Liberalisation Dialogues with three EaP countries, i.e., Moldova, Ukraine and Georgia. The officially declared purpose of the Visa Liberalisation Dialogues is to help the partner countries in improving their legal and policy framework in the realm of justice and home affairs. However, as Zhyznomirska (2016: 139) points out:

> [V]isa dialogue and a roadmap to a visa-free regime function as leverage for the EU to demand compliance with its norms and rules, and hence allow it to intervene into third states' governance capacities in migration and border management. Facilitating mobility for the neighbouring countries' nationals (that was restricted in the first place due to the introduction of strict visa rules by the EU for these potentially 'risky' nationals) emerges as a tool to secure third countries' co-operation on irregular migration.

In particular, there is a requirement to demonstrate effective implementation within the ambit of four thematic areas: (1) document security, including the introduction of biometric passports; (2) border management, including irregular migration and readmission, asylum and migration management; (3) public order and security; and (4) external relations and fundamental freedoms (Hernández i Sagrera 2014b). The dialogues may be compared to a mini-accession process, with a high degree of leverage on behalf of the EU (Andrade et al. 2015: 30).

The reforms that a country aspiring to achieve a visa-free regime with the EU needs to undertake are included in a Visa Liberalisation Action Plan. The Commission monitors the progress of candidate countries on the basis of a set of benchmarks in these four areas. A distinction is made between 'two tiers of benchmarks', dealing with planning and legislative alignment, on the one hand, and the actual implementation of those reforms, on the other. The introduction of this two-phased approach in the visa dialogue with the EaP countries is an important evolution in comparison with the visa liberalization process with the Western Balkan countries. As explained by Trauner and Manigrassi (2014), the sudden increase of Balkan asylum-seekers following the abolition of a visa requirement for persons coming from this region significantly affected the EU's approach with, on the one hand, an increased focus on implementation of internal reforms and an increasing politicization of the Visa Liberalization Dialogues and, on the other hand, the introduction of a 'post-visa liberalization monitoring mechanism'. This allows the EU to closely monitor the continued implementation of the expected reforms following the abolition of the visa requirement and, if necessary, to start a procedure leading to the suspension of visa-free travel. For this purpose, the European Parliament and the Council introduced a safeguard clause in Council Regulation 539/2001 (European Parliament and Council 2013). A further revision of the suspension mechanism was a precondition for the introduction of a visa-free regime with Ukraine and Georgia. For the latter countries, the European Commission issued positive progress reports at the end of 2015 (European Commission 2015). In the course of 2016, the Commission formally presented a proposal for amending Regulation (EC) No. 539/2001 in order to lift visa requirements for short-term travels (maximum ninety days) for Goergian and Ukrainian holding a biometric passport (European Commission 2016). The visa-free regime with Georgia entered into force on 28 March 2017 and with Ukraine on 11 June 2017. With Moldova, a visa-free regime for holders of biometric passports had already been introduced in 2014.

Significantly, the visa liberalization process with Russia differs from the approach adopted in the context of the EaP. For instance, in relation to Russia there is no Visa Liberalization Action

Plan. Rather, the dialogue is based on a list of 'Common steps towards visa-free short term travel for Russian and EU citizens', adopted in December 2011 (European Commission 2011). This document contains four 'blocks' of issues under discussion (document security, irregular migration, public order, security and judicial cooperation and external relations). Even though this appears somewhat comparable to the content of the Visa Liberalisation Action Plans, the entire process proceeds from the concept of reciprocity and, therefore, lacks the same conditionality approach (Van Elsuwege 2013). Nevertheless, the dialogue with Russia has been suspended in the wake of the Ukraine crisis (European Council 2014).

Non-legally binding instruments

Apart from the legally binding framework agreements and the combination between bilateral visa facilitation and readmission agreements, cooperation with the EU's East European neighbors has to a large extent been based on non-legally binding instruments. In relation to Russia, reference could be made to the 2000 Action Plan on combatting organized crime, the 2005 roadmap for the establishment of a Common Space of Freedom, Security and Justice, and, from 2010 onward, the Partnership for Modernization. Whereas such instruments create a flexible framework for pragmatic cooperation, a different understanding of concepts and objectives frequently impedes the actual implementation of the shared agenda for cooperation (Romanova and Pavlova 2014: 500). This is for instance the case in the fight against corruption (Pavlova 2015) and the discourse regarding visa liberalization (Mäkinen et al. 2016).

Also in the context of the ENP, the use of soft law instruments turned out to be a remarkable trend (Van Vooren 2009). With regard to migration, Mobility Partnerships have gradually developed into one of the principal bilateral frameworks for facilitating policy dialogue and operational cooperation with the EU's Eastern neighbors. The Mobility Partnerships are non-legally binding political declarations signed by the EU and the participating member states and a third country (Parkes 2009). They were introduced in 2007 as part of the Commission's novel approach to improve regular migration management between the EU and third countries, which are committed to the fight against irregular migration. This *quid pro quo* tactic has since become the *modus operandi* of Mobility Partnerships, meaning in practice that third countries, which cooperate with the EU on the prevention of irregular migration, are offered regular migration opportunities, such as participation in circular migration schemes (Reslow 2015). Even though the Mobility Partnership is not exclusively used in relation to the EaP countries, the EU's Eastern neighborhood has always been a preferential region for testing this migration policy instrument. Moldova served, together with Cape Verde, as a 'pilot' country before Mobility Partnerships were signed with other countries. In 2016, eight joint declarations on Mobility Partnerships had been signed, half of them with EaP countries (Moldova, Georgia, Armenia and Azerbaijan). It is noteworthy that to date there is no Mobility Partnership with Ukraine. According to Guild and colleagues (2014), this is due to the low interest on behalf of EU member states and the reluctance of Ukraine to allow further emigration of Ukrainian workers to the EU through the establishment of more legal channels.

Despite the successful negotiation of Mobility Partnerships within the EaP, the added value of this policy instrument in terms of creating labor mobility opportunities for the participating third countries remains questionable (Carrera and Hernández i Sagrera 2009; Parkes 2009; Reslow and Vink 2015). An initial review of the available scoreboards of the EaP countries reveals that the greater part of the projects funded under Mobility Partnerships aim at least partially to prevent irregular migration, including readmission, reintegration and border security.[4] Moreover, despite the *quid pro quo* tactic, the greater emphasis on irregular migration initiatives does not necessarily lead to more options for regular migration. The circular migration opportunities are limited to small-scale pilot projects in most cases (Kalantaryan 2015). Recent ethnographic studies have documented profound incoherence in the design and implementation of Mobility Partnerships. For instance, Brouillette (2016) shows that the Mobility Partnership with Moldova lacks opportunities for a genuine increase in regular migration and, instead, remains focused on countering irregular migration. It has been argued that the European Commission is well aware of this misbalance but it has very limited leverage on member states keeping their sovereignty over labor migration regulation. On a more conceptual level, looking at how Mobility Partnerships reveal general trends in EU external migration governance, Lavenex and Stucky (2011: 116) demonstrate that 'whereas a certain widening of the understanding of international migration towards a more comprehensive vision has taken place, the notion of "partnership" becomes less and less tangible, the farther the practical operationalization of the concept proceeds'.

Operational cooperation instruments

The EU and its Eastern partners have developed a number of operational instruments related to migration governance and the broader field of justice and home affairs. These include various formats of institutional cooperation among relevant internal security bodies, such as working dialogues on counter-terrorism cooperation, implementation of Working Arrangements between the European Agency for Operational Cooperation at the External Border of the member states of the EU (Frontex) and individual Eastern European countries or the activity of the EU Border Assistance Mission to the Republic of Moldova and to Ukraine (EUBAM) at the Ukrainian–Moldovan border. Arguably, joint efforts aimed at border management form the core of operational cooperation instruments in the JHA field. This is not surprising, since the focus on borders is quintessential not only for EU migration-related concerns but also for its wider EU internal security regime. The mutual fixation on border-related challenges has been explored in various studies covering EU–Russia relations (Golunov 2013; Prozorov 2006). On the one hand, EU–Russia cooperation on border management and, specifically, the interaction between Frontex and the Russian Federal Border Service has been praised as a success story (Hernándes i Sagrera and Potemkina 2013). On the other hand, the EU has received a portion of scholarly criticism for orchestrating management of the Ukrainian–Russian border through, among others, 'privatization' of this sphere leading to increased tensions between the EU and Russia (Gatev 2008).

The EU, indeed, has been very active concerning the management not only of its own borders with its Eastern neighbors but also of *their* borders with each other. Frontex has been promoting the famous Integrated Border Management scheme – designed to reach EU standards in the absence of a genuine EU common border service – and relevant 'best practices' through its operational cooperation with Moldova and Ukraine. This dimension of EU JHA external action, as in the case of Russia, relies heavily on operational cooperation developed between Frontex and border services of the countries in question. However, specific scholarly attention has been paid to the EU's massive engagement in border management *between* Moldova and Ukraine (Hernándes i Sagrera 2014a; Jeandesboz 2015; Kurowska and Tallis 2009). Empirical research has shown that the EUBAM has used Integrated Border Management promotion as a platform 'to extend its territorial scope well beyond the remits of the common Moldovan–Ukrainian border', which 'raises concerns over the legitimacy of the actual territorial scope of EUBAM activity' (Hernándes i Sagrera 2014a: 12). Moreover, despite – or, rather, because of – the EUBAM relative 'success story' in bringing practices of the Ukrainian and Moldovan border and customs services in line with 'European' standards, questions have been raised about the normative dimension of the EU's intervention (Kurowska and Tallis 2009: 59).

The challenge of coherence in the EU's relations with its Eastern neighbors

EU JHA policies towards its Eastern neighbors have been recurrently analyzed within the prominent conceptual framework of Europeanization (Grabbe 2002; Lavenex 2007; Makaryan and Chobanyan 2014; Mananashvili 2015; Wunderlich 2011). A popular way to examine Europeanization in this field is to unpack it as a process that should lead to greater cohesion between the AFSJ (gradually developing within the EU) and the relevant internal security and migration regimes of its Eastern neighbors. This ultimate goal of cohesion within the – potentially emerging – pan-European security community with the EU at its core (Korneev 2007) has presumably required a certain degree of coherence across EU policies towards countries in the region. However, such coherence has proved difficult to achieve in practice, at least for two major reasons. First, the European Commission has seen the need to come up with differentiated JHA policies towards its various Eastern ENP partner countries to avoid the blame for its 'one size fits all approach' (Börzel and Risse 2004). Second, the EU has had to make a clear – be it sometimes symbolic – distinction between policies towards ENP countries and those towards Russia. This paradoxical policy trap – inherent tension between coherence and differentiation – has attracted serious scholarly attention, resulting in nuanced and very insightful analyses of the ENP and the EaP, as well as of the external dimension of EU JHA (Delcour 2007; Lavenex and Wichmann 2009; Zhyznomirska 2011, 2016).

Building on a then unprecedented comparison of EU policies, including in the sphere of JHA, towards Ukraine and Russia, Delcour concludes that 'four years after the ENP was launched, policy patterns do not significantly differ, in spite of discursive differentiation' (2007: 148). Similarly, it has been shown that the building blocks of EU relations with Russia and ENP partners in this field and the concrete mechanisms used by the EU to foster its JHA agenda externally – action plans, roadmaps, instruments, incentives and conditionality patterns – are virtually the same (Korneev 2008). In relation to the South Caucasus, Makaryan and Chobanyan (2014: 62) argue that the EU umbrella framework and common mechanisms such as MPs, visa facilitation and readmission agreements or practices of IBM beyond promoting

> 'the establishment of biometric passports, integrated border management, automated information systems, approximation of legislation and of institutional capacity' also 'create a common policy space, not only between those states and the EU but also among these states at the regional level'.

However, other analyses indicate significant problems with coherence of policy implementation faced by the EU, exacerbated by different policy reception on the part of the target countries (Börzel and Pamuk 2012; Delcour 2007; Zhyznomirska 2016). The artificial nature of homogenized policies towards 'the East' and, hence, their predisposition to variegated implementation has also been signaled by scholars critically examining EU policies in relation to an 'invented neighborhood'.[5] The strive for coherence becomes particularly problematic in the context of increasing EU–Russia competition in the shared neighborhood. It has clearly spilled over from the economic sphere into the field of migration governance. In some cases, this competition is implicit and manifests itself only through unexpected externalities of EU–Russia deals on migration issues (Ademmer and Börzel 2013). However, in other cases, prospects of visa liberalization signaled by the EU – and intertwined with its frames of 'good governance' in the migration sphere – put Eastern Partnership countries in a position of uneasy choices between potential advantages of more open borders with the EU and the actual benefits of the existing visa-free regimes with Russia (Ademmer and Delcour 2016).

The lack of coherence – and a clear discrepancy between declared values and goals of JHA cooperation and actual policies of the EU – has also been obvious in the very conceptualization of the EU migration regime and its external dimension, in particular in relations with Russia (Korneev 2012). It has been argued that normative concerns constitute an instrument of negative conditionality in EU external dialogues on more interest-oriented issues, such as migration management. However, putting into practice a model of 'concentric circles' (Lavenex and Uçarer 2002), the EU has proceeded in a way that has been characterized as a 'closed security community' (Korneev 2007). This ambivalent approach has been an important element in the accumulation of mistrust between the EU and some of its partners, in particular, between the EU and Russia (Potemkina 2002, 2010). The EU has even been reproached for not practicing what it preaches when it comes to cooperation on visas and broader migration-related issues (Salminen and Moshes 2009).

The tension between the promotion of values and protection of EU interests defined in security terms is also obvious when one analyzes 'the externalities' (Lavenex and Uçarer 2002) of EU cooperation with its Eastern neighbors for the 'wider neighborhood'. A certain shift of the EU migration management burden onto Russia has produced a domino effect in the region: additional restrictive mechanisms have been introduced into cooperation on migration management between Russia and Central Asian countries as well as within Central Asia (Korneev and Leonov 2016). This has raised concerns that

> externalities of EU policies creating a web of readmission agreements, enforcing readmission practices and developing relevant detention infrastructure without prior establishing proper legislative and practical safeguards can potentially endanger the position of migrants in Eurasia – the region where human rights of migrants and persons seeking international protection are already at risk.
>
> *(Korneev and Leonov 2016: 170)*

Hence, the broader implications of the EU's migration and other JHA policies for the wider neighborhood and for the coherence of the EU's external action deserve further consideration.

Concluding remarks

Since the early 2000s, research on the external dimension of EU JHA has focused increasingly on the EU's relations with its wider Eastern neighborhood. In this context, cooperation with respect to internal security challenges and migration management has been defined as a key priority of the EU's relations with its East European neighbors. This is to a large extent the natural and unavoidable consequence of the EU's Eastward enlargement and the EU's expanding competences in relation to the AFSJ. Since the end of the 1990s, a number of significant tendencies and evolutions have been discerned.

First, whereas the EU's initial policies focused almost exclusively on the prevention of illegal activities, the perspective of visa facilitation and visa liberalization is increasingly used as an incentive to foster cooperation with the neighboring countries. The combined conclusion of visa facilitation and readmission agreements with the Russian Federation has become a model for the entire Eastern neighborhood. Despite the remarkable difference in terms of methodology as far as relations with Russia are concerned, on the one hand, and the associated EaP countries, on the other, the process of visa liberalization is embedded in a broader approach essentially aiming at protecting the EU's security interests and export of the EU's values and norms. Second, the EU's approach towards its Eastern neighborhood cannot be disconnected from general developments in the EU's migration and asylum policy. Most notably, such instruments as the Mobility Partnerships were introduced in the framework of the Global Approach to Migration and Mobility and later developed into a standard tool of the EaP. The same is valid for the EU's involvement in third countries' border management policies. The transfer of EU 'best practices' in this field has been based on the Integrated Border Management concept and its application to the management of the EU's own external borders, whereas the institutional basis for such external cooperation has been provided by the rapidly developing Frontex.

Third, several studies question the actual impact of instruments such as visa facilitation agreements and Mobility Partnerships on the mobility of persons and point to the security bias of the EU's initiatives. Consequently, the process of visa liberalization has gained increased importance and is a key objective for the EU's Eastern neighbors. This provides the EU with significant leverage to intervene in the neighboring countries' governance capacities in migration and border management and to demand compliance with its norms and values (Zhyznomirska 2016). The inherent tension between values and interests within the external dimension of EU JHA policies has triggered questions about the coherence of the EU's strategy. Such ambiguity of the EU's approach against the background of security-linked interdependence has also stimulated academic interest in the mechanism of conditionality in the EU's relations with its Eastern neighbors. The methodology of the visa liberalization process gradually developed to maximize the EU's influence while at the same time ensuring sufficient guarantees for the EU's internal security and migration management. The introduction and amendment of safeguard measures in the EU's visa regulation, allowing for the reintroduction of the visa requirement in exceptional circumstances, is a clear reflection of this approach. Further research is needed to analyze the actual impact of these developments. Moreover, the correlation between the (evolution of) legal requirements for visa applications and the economic relations with the neighboring countries requires further interdisciplinary research. Arguably, more theoretical research is needed to transcend binary oppositions such as neighbors–non-neighbors, interests–values, conditionality–interdependence in order to better reflect on goals, challenges and prospects of EU internal security and migration policies towards the Eastern Partnership countries and Russia.

Notes

1 However, even in the 1990s, there have been significant differences in the EU's approach to Russia and other Eastern neighbors. They have been explained, *inter alia*, by such factors as the length of the common border and, importantly, the evolving status of Russia as an increasingly important immigration country that the EU wanted to see an important part of its remote control strategy (Korneev 2007, 2008).
2 Art. 16 of the Association Agreement with Ukraine, OJ, 2014, L 161/11, Art. 14 of the Association Agreement with Moldova, OJ, 2014, L 260/11; Art. 15 of the Association Agreement with Georgia, OJ, 2014, L 261/11.
3 Arts 17 and 18 of the Association Agreement with Ukraine.
4 The scoreboards for the Mobility Partnership with Georgia, Armenia and Azerbaijan were accessed through official requests for information at the end of 2015.
5 The concept of the 'invented neighborhood' in relation to EU migration policies was elaborated by the team of the Migration Policy Centre at the European University Institute, in particular by Agnieszka Weinar and Philippe Fargues, during their work on the CARIM-East project (2011–2013). See also Jeandesboz (2007).

Bibliography

Ademmer, E. and Börzel, T. (2013). Migration, Energy and Good Governance in the EU's Eastern Neighbourhood. *Europe-Asia Studies*, 65(4), pp. 581–608.

Ademmer, E. and Delcour, L. (2016). With a Little Help from Russia? The European Union and Visa Liberalization with Post-Soviet States. *Eurasian Geography and Economics*, 57(1), pp. 89–112.

Andrade, P.G., Martín, I. and Mananashvili, S. (2015). *EU Cooperation with Third Countries in the Field of Migration*. Study for the LIBE Committee, European Parliament.

Börzel, T. and Pamuk, Y. (2012). Pathologies of Europeanization. Fighting Corruption in the Southern Caucasus. *West European Politics*, 35(1), pp. 79–97.

Börzel, T. and Risse, T. (2004). One Size Fits All! EU Policies for the Promotion of Human Rights, Democracy and the Rule of Law. Paper presented at the Workshop on Democracy Promotion, Stanford University, October 4–5.

Brouillette, M. (2016). Du discours à la pratique: trajectoire dune politique européenne de gestion des migrations mise en œuvre dans les pays frontaliers à l'Union européenne. In D. Duez and F. Delmotte (eds) *Les frontières et la communauté politique. Faire, défaire et penser les frontiers*. Brussels: Université Saint-Louis, pp. 121–153.

Carrera, S. and Hernández i Sagrera, R. (2009). The Externalisation of EU's Labour Immigration Policy: Towards Mobility or Insecurity Partnerships. CEPS Working Document 321/2009.

Coleman, N. (2009). *European Readmission Policy. Third Country Interests and Refugee Rights*. Boston, MA, and Leiden: Martinus Nijhoff.

Council of the EU (2000). Action Plan on Common Action for the Russian Federation on Combating Organised Crime. OJ (2000) C 106/5.

Delcour, L. (2007). Does the European Neighbourhood Policy Make a Difference? Policy Patterns and Reception in Ukraine and Russia. *European Political Economy Review*, 7, pp. 118–155.

European Commission (2009). Evaluation of the Implementation of the European Community's Visa Facilitation Agreements with Third Countries (Commission Staff Working Document). SEC (2009) 1401 final.

European Commission (2011). EU–Russia: Common Steps Towards Visa-free Regime. https://ec.europa.eu/home-affairs/what-is-new/news/news/2013/20130311_02_en (accessed January 6, 2017).

European Commission (2015). Three Reports on Visa Liberalisation: Ukraine, Georgia and Kosovo. https://ec.europa.eu/home-affairs/what-is-new/news/news/2015/20151218_3_en.htm (accessed January 6, 2017).

European Commission (2016). Proposal for a Regulation of the European Parliament and of the Council amending Regulation (EC) No. 539/2001 listing the third countries whose nationals must be in possession of visas when crossing the external borders and those whose nationals are exempt from that requirement. COM (2016) 277 final.

European Council (1999). *Council Conclusions*. Cologne.

European Council (2014). Statement of the Heads of State or Government on Ukraine. Brussels, March 6.

European Parliament and Council of the EU (2013). Regulation No. 1289/2013 of 11 December 2013 Amending Council Regulation (EC) No 539/2001 listing the third countries whose nationals must be in possession of visas when crossing the external borders and those whose nationals are exempt from that requirement. OJ (2013) L 347/74.

Gatev, I. (2008). Border Security in the Eastern Neighbourhood: Where Bio-politics and Geopolitics Meet. *European Foreign Affairs Review*, 13(1), pp. 97–116.

Golunov, S. (2013). *EU–Russian Border Security: Challenges, (Mis)perceptions and Responses*. London and New York: Routledge.

Grabbe, H. (2002). Stabilizing the East While Keeping Out the Easterners: Internal and External Security Logics in Conflict. In S. Lavenex and E. Uçarer, *Migration and the Externalities of European Integration*. Lanham, MD: Lexington Books, pp. 91–104.

Guild, E., Carrera, S. and Parkin, J. (2014). 'What Role for Migration Policy in the Ukraine Crisis?' CEPS Commentary. www.ceps.eu/publications/what-role-migration-policy-ukraine-crisis (accessed January 6, 2017).

Hernández i Sagrera, R. (2010). The EU–Russia Readmission–Visa Facilitation Nexus: An Exportable Model for Eastern Europe? *European Security*, 19(4), pp. 569–584.

Hernández i Sagrera, R. (2014a). Exporting EU Integrated Border Management beyond EU Borders: Modernization and Institutional Transformation in Exchange for More Mobility? *Cambridge Review of International Affairs*, 27(1), pp. 167–183.

Hernández i Sagrera, R. (2014b). *The Impacts of Visa Liberalisation in Eastern Partnership Countries, Russia and Turkey on Trans-border Mobility*. Study for the LIBE Committee, European Parliament. www.europarl.europa.eu/thinktank/nl/document.html?reference=IPOL-LIBE_ET%282014%29493050 (accessed January 6, 2017).

Hernández i Sagrera, R. and Korneev, O. (2012) Bringing EU Migration Cooperation to the Eastern Neighbourhood: Convergence beyond the Acquis Communautaire? European University Working papers, RSCAS 2012/22. http://cadmus.eui.eu/handle/1814/21989 (accessed January 6, 2017).

Hernández i Sagrera, R. and Potemkina, O. (2013). *Russia and the Common Space on Freedom, Security and Justice*. Study for the LIBE Committee, European Parliament. www.europarl.europa.eu/RegData/etudes/etudes/join/2012/474394/IPOL-LIBE_ET(2012)474394_EN.pdf (accessed January 6, 2017).

Jeandesboz, J. (2007). Labelling the 'Neighbourhood': Towards a Genesis of the European Neighbourhood Policy. *Journal of International Relations and Development*, 10(4), pp. 387–416.

Jeandesboz, J. (2015). Intervention and Subversion: The EU Border Assistance Mission to Moldova and Ukraine. *Journal of Intervention and Statebuilding*, 9(4), pp. 442–470.

Kalantaryan, S. (2015). *Migrant Support Measures from an Employment and Skills Perspective: Armenia*. Report for the European Training Foundation. www.etf.europa.eu/web.nsf/pages/MISMES_Armenia (accessed January 6, 2017).

Korneev, O. (2007). The EU Migration Regime and Its Externalization in the Policy Toward Russia. InBev-Baillet Latour Working Paper No. 31. Leuven: Catholic University of Leuven. https://soc.kuleuven.be/web/files/11/74/WP31-Korneev.pdf (accessed January 6, 2017).

Korneev, O. (2008). Primus Inter Pares? The EU's Justice and Home Affairs Policies in its Eastern European Neighbourhood. InBev-Baillet Latour Working Paper No. 32. Leuven: Catholic University of Leuven. https://soc.kuleuven.be/web/files/11/74/WP32-Korneev.pdf (accessed January 6, 2017).

Korneev, O. (2012). Deeper and Wider Than a Common Space: EU–Russia Cooperation on Migration Management. *European Foreign Affairs Review*, 17(4), pp. 605–624.

Korneev, O. and Leonov, A. (2016). Eurasia and Externalities of Migration Control: Spillover Dynamics of EU–Russia Cooperation on Migration. In R. Zaiotti (ed.) *Externalizing Migration Management: Europe, North America and the Spread of 'Remote Control' Practices*. London: Routledge, pp. 154–176.

Kurowska, X. and Tallis, B. (2009). EU Border Assistance Mission: Beyond Border Monitoring? *European Foreign Affairs Review*, 14(1), pp. 47–64.

Lavenex, S. (2007). The External Face of Europeanization: Third Countries and International Organizations. In T. Faist and A. Ette (eds) *The Europeanization of National Policies and Politics of Immigration: Between Autonomy and the European Union*. New York: Palgrave Macmillan, pp. 246–264.

Lavenex, S. and Stucky, R. (2011). 'Partnering' for Migration in EU External Relations. In R. Kunz, S. Lavenex and M. Panizzon (eds) *Multilayered Migration Governance: The Promise of Partnership*. London: Routledge, pp. 116–142.

Lavenex, S. and Uçarer, E. (2002). *Migration and the Externalities of European Integration*. Lanham, MD: Lexington Books.

Lavenex, S. and Wichmann, N. (2009). The External Governance of EU Internal Security. *Journal of European Integration*, 31(1), pp. 83–102.

Makaryan, S. and Chobanyan, H. (2014). Institutionalization of Migration Policy Frameworks in Armenia, Azerbaijan and Georgia. *International Migration*, 52(5), pp. 52–67.

Mäkinen, S., Smith, H. and Forsberg, T. (2016). With a Little Help from my Friends: Russia's Modernisation and the Visa Regime with the European Union. *Europe–Asia Studies*, 68(1), pp. 164–181.

Mananashvili, S. (2015). The Diffusion of the EU Asylum Acquis in the Eastern Neighbourhood: A Test for the EU's Normative Power. *European Foreign Affairs Review*, 20(2), pp. 187–206.

O'Neill, M. (2016). The Development of the External Dimension of the AFSJ – New Challenges of the EU Legal and Policy Framework. *European Politics and Society*, 17(2), pp. 166–180.

Parkes, R. (2009). EU Mobility Partnerships: A Model of Policy Coordination? *European Journal of Migration and Law*, 11(4), pp. 327–345.

Pavlova, E. (2015). The Russian Federation and European Union against Corruption: A Slight Misunderstanding? *European Politics and Society*, 16(1), pp. 111–125.

Potemkina, O. (2002). Russia's Engagement with Justice and Home Affairs: A Question of Mutual Trust. CEPS Policy Brief No. 16. www.ceps.eu/publications/russias-engagement-justice-and-home-affairsa-question-mutual-trust (accessed January 6, 2017).

Potemkina, O. (2003). Some Ramifications of Enlargement on the EU–Russia Relations and the Schengen Regime. *European Journal of Migration and Law*, 5(2), pp. 229–247.

Potemkina, O. (2010). EU–Russia Cooperation on the Common Space of Freedom, Security and Justice – A Challenge or an Opportunity? *European Security*, 19(4), pp. 551–568.

Prozorov, S. (2006). *Understanding Conflict between Russia and the EU: The Limits of Integration*. New York and Basingstoke: Palgrave Macmillan.

Reslow, N. (2015). EU 'Mobility' Partnerships: An Initial Assessment of Implementation Dynamics. *Politics and Governance*, 3(2), pp. 117–128.

Reslow, N. and Vink, M. (2015). Three-level Games in EU External Migration Policy: Negotiating Mobility Partnerships in West Africa. *Journal of Common Market Studies*, 53(4), pp. 857–874.

Romanova, T. and Pavlova, E. (2014). What Modernisation? The Case of Russian Partnerships for Modernisation with the European Union and its Member States. *Journal of Contemporary European Studies*, 22(4), pp. 499–517.

Salminen, M. and Moshes, A. (2009). Practice What You Preach. The Prospects for Visa Freedom in Russia–EU Relations. FIIA Report. www.fiia.fi/assets/events/FIIA_Report_18_2009.pdf (accessed January 6, 2017).

Trauner, F. and Kruse, I. (2008). EC Visa Facilitation and Readmission Agreements: A New Standard EU Foreign Policy Tool? *European Journal of Migration and Law*, 10(4), pp. 411–438.

Trauner, F. and Manigrassi, E. (2014). When Visa-free Travel Becomes Difficult to Achieve and Easy to Lose: The EU Visa-free Dialogues after the Experience with the Western Balkans. *European Journal of Migration and Law*, 16(1), pp. 125–145.

Trauner, F. and Wolff, S. (2014). The Negotiation and Contestation of EU Migration Policy Instruments – A Research Framework. *European Journal of Migration and Law*, 16(1), pp. 1–18.

Van Der Loo, G. (2016). *The EU–Ukraine Association Agreement and Deep and Comprehensive Free Trade Area*. Leiden, and Boston, MA: Brill.

Van Elsuwege, P. (2008) *From Soviet Republics to EU Member States. A Legal and Political Assessment of the Baltic States' Accession to the EU*. Leiden, and Boston, MA: Martinus Nijhoff.

Van Elsuwege, P. (ed.) (2013). EU–Russia Visa Facilitation and Liberalisation. State of Play and Prospects for the Future. EU–Russia Civil Society Forum, September 2013. http://eu-russia-csf.org/fileadmin/Docs/Visa/Draft_Visa_Report.pdf (accessed April 5, 2016).

Van Elsuwege, P. and Vankova, Z. (2017). Migration and Mobility in the EU's Eastern Neighbourhood: Mapping out the Legal and Political Framework. In F. Ippolito, G. Borzoni and F. Casolari (eds) *Bilateral Relations in the Mediterranean: Prospects for Migration Issues*. Cheltenham: Edward Elgar, forthcoming.

Van Vooren, B. (2009). A Case Study of Soft Law in EU External Relations: The European Neighbourhood Policy. *European Law Review*, 34(5), pp. 696–719.

Weinar, A., Korneev, O., Makaryan, S. and Mananashvili, S. (2012). Consequences of Schengen Visa Liberalisation for the Citizens of Ukraine and the Republic of Moldova. Migration Policy Centre Research Report 2012/01. http://cadmus.eui.eu/handle/1814/23497 (accessed January 6, 2017).

Wolff, S., Wichmann, N. and Mounier, G. (2009). *The External Dimension of Justice and Home Affairs. A Different Security Agenda for the European Union*. London: Routledge.

Wunderlich, D. (2011). Europeanization through the Grapevine: Communication Gaps and the Role of International Organizations in Implementation Networks of EU External Migration Policy. *Journal of European Integration*, 34(5), pp. 485–503.

Zhyznomirska, L. (2011). The European Union's 'Home Affairs' Model and its European Neighbours: Beyond the 'Area of Freedom, Security and Justice'? *Comparative European Politics*, 9(4/5), pp. 506–523.

Zhyznomirska, L. (2016). At a Distance: The European Union and the Management of Irregular Migration in Eastern Europe. In R. Zaiotti (ed.) *Externalizing Migration Management: Europe, North America and the Spread of 'Remote Control' Practices*. London: Routledge, pp. 134–153.

26

THE SOUTHERN MEDITERRANEAN

A testing ground and a litmus test for EU JHA policies and research?

Sarah Wolff and Patryk Pawlak

Introduction

Since the launch of the Barcelona Process in 1995 and later the European Neighbourhood Policy (ENP) in 2003, the European Union's (EU) relationship with Southern Mediterranean countries has been in constant flux. Today, the EU's Southern neighborhood has shifted from Romano Prodi's idealized status of a 'ring of friends' to a 'ring of fire'. Instead of expected reforms, democratization and an easing in the relationship, the Middle East and North Africa (MENA) region has been plagued by conflict and violence, providing an image of regional disorder and uncertainty. Since the Arab uprisings, restrictions to mobility, changes in the control of EU borders and the stepping up of counter-terrorism and counter-radicalization efforts have moved to the top of the EU policy agenda. Overall, Justice and Home Affairs (JHA) expenses have never been so high, with an increase in spending of 163 percent between 2006 and 2011 (Sgueo 2016). Yet, according to Europol, terrorist attacks (either failed, foiled or completed) in the EU are on the rise, from 151 attacks in 2013 to 211 in 2015 (Europol 2016).[1] Simultaneously, although the EU has spent more than €1 billion on over 400 external migration projects worldwide (García Andrade and Martin 2015: 10), its capacity to deal with an increase in migratory fluxes is still limited, raising questions about the efficiency and effectiveness of the EU's response.

The EU's crisis narrative is at odds with the history of mobility and migration in the Mediterranean (Wolff and Hadj-Abdou 2017). The Mediterranean as a 'space of mobility' depicted by historian Fernand Braudel was at the heart of the EU's idealized vision of the region that underpinned the Euro–Mediterranean Partnership (EMP)/Barcelona Process. Following the terrorist attacks across Europe and faced with the growing fear of jihadi terrorism, EU internal security interests and stability in the neighborhood are nonetheless the main drivers of the EU JHA policies towards the region. Prior to the Arab uprisings, the external dimension of JHA had suffered from the co-optation of authoritarian regimes in the management of the EU's external borders. This was at odds with the popular protests that swept across the region from 2010 onward which resulted in a varied geometry of approaches embodied in the EU's 'more for more' doctrine. The underlying assumption of the new approach was that countries in which democratization processes occur at a faster pace should also receive a more substantial 'reward'. The processes launched on the basis of the new approach were quickly hijacked by security concerns linked to the conflicts in Syria and Libya, the risk posed by returning European terrorist fighters, as well as the rising number of irregular migrants crossing the Mediterranean. The persistence of authoritarian or quasi-authoritarian regimes in Egypt and Turkey once again exposed the EU's weakness when confronted with the dilemma of organizing its relations with governments that do not necessarily subscribe to the same values as the EU.

This chapter reviews the external dimension of JHA policies towards the Southern neighborhood from both policy development and research perspectives. First, the pre-Arab uprising literature wave is analyzed. The governance and securitization approaches that have dominated the study of this subject since the early 2000s are discussed and their weaknesses analyzed. Second, the chapter delves into the post-Arab uprisings literature which focuses more on foreign policy approaches and new security-seeking practices. It also embraces new concepts of societal and state resilience. Third, this chapter discusses trends and the future of the discipline. In doing so, this chapter addresses the underlying assumptions about the internal–external security nexus and security–development nexus as organizing concepts and the recent shift towards state and societal resilience as preconditions for regional security and stability.

Pre-Arab uprisings wave: the governance and securitization approaches

The governance and securitization scholarship constitutes the first wave of research on the topic. In the late 1990s and 2000s, it was driven by the EU's internal agenda and the EU's expanding involvement in international affairs following the Maastricht Treaty and the Treaty of Amsterdam. Simultaneously, as part of The Hague and Stockholm Programmes and the ensuing externalization of EU JHA policies towards its Southern neighbors – initially aimed at the control of migration and the fight against terrorism and transnational crime – the research grew to better understand the EU's policies and approaches towards the region.

Governance literature

Drawing from institutionalist, multi-governance and Europeanization approaches, the governance literature focuses on the types of channels, formal or informal, mobilized by the EU to influence its Southern partners (Wunderlich 2012; Freyburg 2011; Lavenex and Uçarer 2004). The literature has scrutinized whether the EU uses soft or hard policy instruments and the diversity of EU institutions and actors active in promoting JHA policies and norms abroad (Trauner and Wolff 2014; Trauner and Carrapico 2012; Reslow 2012; Cassarino 2007). This research appeared alongside two policy frameworks governing EU relations with its Southern neighbors: the EMP/Barcelona Process and the ENP. When the EMP was launched in 1995, JHA matters were absent from the agenda as cooperation focused mostly on confidence-building measures, which were later incorporated into the 2001 Charter for Peace and Stability. This changed as Mediterranean partners became countries of transit for migrants at the beginning of the 2000s and when the EMP stumbled upon hard security with the start of the Second Intifada (Wolff 2012). Soft security issues such as terrorism and migration were swiftly integrated into the EMP with the Marseille Summit conclusions (European Council 2000). Furthermore, the 2002 Valencia Action Plan led to the creation of the first regional Euromed Police, Justice and Migration programs. Counter-terrorist clauses were included in Association Agreements (Wolff 2012). Later on, bilateral ENP action plans established detailed cooperation on the issues of justice, security and migration through the holding of subcommittees.

The EU's multi-level governance setting, which has greatly altered since the Lisbon Treaty, has proven to be central to the analysis of the EU's JHA policies towards the Southern Mediterranean. In spite of extended competences for supranational EU institutions, member states remain the main gatekeepers of the external dimension of JHA towards Southern partners. For instance, bilateral ad hoc informal readmission agreements signed between EU member states and Southern partners have sapped the efforts of the European Commission to negotiate EU readmission agreements. These agreements allow the EU to return irregular migrants back to neighboring third countries based solely on whether a migrant is a national of that country or has merely transited through its territory (European Commission 2011). In the case of the EU's Southern partners, this would mean also readmitting sub-Saharan African migrants, an idea that many have resisted (Wolff 2014). Bilateral agreements signed outside of the EU framework allow for more informal, ad hoc agreements beyond any scrutiny by national parliaments (Cassarino 2007, 2009). Not only do these actions compete with the initiatives of the European Commission or the European External Action Service (EEAS), but they also pose certain ethical challenges. Before the Arab uprisings, Italy–Libya cooperation allowed Gadhafi to threaten that Europe was becoming a 'black continent' in the absence of more means to fight irregular migration (Paoletti 2010; Andrijasevic 2010). The intensification of flows through the Central Mediterranean route in the mid-2000s, with an increase from 15,527 arrivals in 2005 on Lampedusa to 31,252 in 2008, led Italy and Libya to conclude an agreement in 2008 to stop migration. As numbers fell sharply, down to 459 in 2010 (Council of Europe 2011), it came at the cost of violations of migrants', refugees' and asylum-seekers' rights. Italy was condemned for violating migrants' rights and forcing them to return to Libya in spite of the principle of non-refoulement. Article 33(1) of the 1951 Convention relating to the Status of Refugees states:

> [N]o Contracting State shall expel or return ('refouler') a refugee in any manner whatsoever to the frontiers of territories where his life or freedom would be threatened on account of his race, religion, nationality, membership of a particular social group or political opinion.
>
> *(United Nations 1951)*

The European Court of Human Rights in the case *Hirsii Jamaa vs. Italy* found that the interception of a group of Somali and Eritrean migrants at sea by Italian authorities constituted a violation of this principle (European Court of Human Rights 2012). Nonetheless, Italy–Libya bilateral cooperation was so effective that at some point Lampedusa's reception center closed down and international organizations withdrew from the island (Council of Europe 2011).

A key concern of governance scholars has been the extent to which the EU can exert some conditionality on its Southern neighbors in the absence of any accession prospect. Even though Morocco, Tunisia and Jordan gained an 'advanced status' which should have facilitated trade opportunities and cooperation with some EU agencies and programs, the EU has enjoyed less leverage than with candidate countries (Lavenex and Uçarer 2004: 436). The network literature has proved useful in assessing the EU's impact. Socialization through implementation networks has indeed led to policy diffusion and/or transfer. In the case of Morocco, even though the implementation of formal migration rules remains weak, the EU has indirectly been able to promote basic democratic governance features such as transparency, accountability and participation (Freyburg 2012). Thus, analyzing the practice of EU external governance in the field of JHA has led researchers to study not only substantive JHA rules and acquis, but 'also procedural rules on how decisions are to be made' (Freyburg 2012: 127).

Securitization literature

Moving beyond the institutional focus, the securitization literature investigates EU discourses and practices (Balzacq 2009) and border management practices (Léonard 2010) in particular. Building on the work of the Copenhagen School, securitization is the result of a 'securitizing actor [who] uses a rhetoric of existential threat and thereby takes an issue out of what under those conditions is "normal politics"', or, in other words, 'securitization is constituted by the intersubjective establishment of an existential threat with a saliency sufficient to have substantial political effects' (Buzan et al. 1998: 24–25). A 'speech act' by policy-makers is a discursive practice that transforms issues like migration into security questions. The discourse of EU actors regarding the influx of Syrian refugees to Europe since 2014 has been built as a 'crisis' narrative, which overlooks the broader historical reality of mobility, mainly in the field of labor migration in the Mediterranean until the mid-1970s, and epitomizes two decades of securitization of migrants coming from the EU's Southern neighborhood (Wolff and Hadj-Abdou 2017). The images of groups of migrants crossing the Mediterranean or the Western Balkans are exploited to justify the adoption of exceptional measures such as the reintroduction of Schengen internal border controls. Another example is how security *rapprochement* became a shared organizing frame for cooperation between the EU and its Southern partners. Before the Arab uprisings, JHA cooperation, in particular efforts made through the EMP and the ENP to cooperate on counter-terrorism, was favored by Southern authoritarian regimes eager to fight their domestic Islamist opposition (Wolff 2012). The EU's normative ambitions of democratization and credibility in the region were thus severely hampered by its preference for internal security.

The Paris School, on the other hand, argues that securitization is about the routinization of security practices. In the field of border and migration control, a rich body of literature has investigated the impact of these security practices upon EU islands such as Lampedusa and Malta, which are the first point of arrival for many migrants traveling the Central Mediterranean route by boat (Orsini 2016; Mountz 2015; Mainwaring 2012; Lutterbeck 2006). Research has shown how border control has become a modern technology of government that creates insecurities for migrants and local populations (Orsini 2016). The political pressure put on member states at the EU's periphery to deal with migrants has led them to find strategies to cope with this situation which may create further insecurities for migrants. For instance, up until 2016, Malta had the longest detention term for migrants and strategically built a crisis narrative to gain more financial resources and equipment from other EU member states (Mainwaring 2012). The line between humanitarian and security practices is also blurred. The 'saving lives' narrative developed by agencies like Frontex, the EU border management agency created in 2004 that later became the European Border and Coast Guard in 2016, is used to justify their actions and existence when confronted with the criticism that these agencies contributed to increased insecurities in the EU's Southern borderlands (Del Sarto and Steindler 2015; Pallister-Wilkins 2015).

Drawing from the field of bio-politics, the changing functions and characteristics of internal and external security agencies have been extensively analyzed (Vaughan-Williams 2015; Bigo 2006, 2014; Lutterbeck 2006). Labeled 'militarization of policing' or 'border militarization', the literature describes the progressing tendency to rely on military technologies – such as systems of radars, sensors and cameras – for policing and securing borders as well as on the direct involvement of the military in border management operations; for example, through the EU's military Operation Sophia, also known as EUNAVFORMED, operating in the Southern, Central Mediterranean. However, the involvement of the armed forces in border management is not a new phenomenon: Spain has regularly deployed military units to curb undocumented immigration into Ceuta and Melilla, and the North Atlantic Treaty Organization (NATO)'s Mediterranean fleet was dispatched in the Eastern Mediterranean in 2002 under operation 'Active Endeavour' (Lutterbeck 2006). With the growing involvement of the military in what used to be civilian tasks (e.g., policing, border protection or counter-terrorism), EU policy-makers have progressively started to explore synergies between JHA and the Common and Security Defence Policy (CSDP) at both a functional and an institutional level (Argomaniz 2012; Wolff and Mounier 2012).

Pitfalls of the first-wave approaches

The governance and securitization approaches, albeit useful in explaining the institutional and geographic dynamic expansion of JHA policies beyond EU borders, have ignored domestic developments among the EU's Southern partners to a large extent. As a consequence, the first wave of predominantly EU-centered scholarship on the external dimension of JHA has proven to have its limits when confronted with post-2010 developments in the Arab world.

First, the literature tends to treat MENA agency, governmental or non-governmental, as passive recipients of the external dimension of JHA. MENA actors are often seen as being on the receiving end of JHA policies and 'victims' of EU-centered agendas (Cassarino 2007). This vision was certainly true before the Arab uprisings when regional negotiations were driven by an EU agenda that aimed at creating EU interlocutors and then responsibilizing them in the common management of migration (Lavenex and Panizzon 2013: 9). These realities are still true, but are rapidly evolving. For instance, the 'geopolitics of migration' is making a comeback as instantiated by the EU–Turkey deals from October 2015 and March 2016. State actors are increasingly mobilizing migration as a bargaining chip in their negotiations with the EU. Consequently, the 'crisis' narrative promoted by internal security actors like the Directorate-General Home is increasingly counterbalanced by the 'new normal' narrative adopted by the EEAS that deals primarily with the external relations with specific countries. At the same time, the perception of migrants is shifting from passive victims of their circumstances towards actors capable of actively influencing their situation. The 'geopolitics of migration' approach, for instance, presents migrants as being capable of reshaping policies through socio-political practices and changing patterns of migration (Collyer 2012). For example, sending money back home can also contribute to democratization (Piper 2009).

Second, little attention has been devoted to the third-country perspective, resulting in suggestions that it is time to 'de-colonize' the study of migration and JHA more broadly (El Qadim 2014). This involves decentering the focus of analysis on Southern partners and delving into the domestic, political and regional dynamics at hand. The public consultation conducted by the European Commission in relation to the 2015 ENP review revealed that it is viewed by some partners as too prescriptive and does not sufficiently reflect their respective aspirations. Research has shown, however, that domestic factors are crucial for explaining policy implementation (Pressman and Wildavsky 1984). How is it possible to explain the diversity of cooperation with MENA countries? From Egypt to Morocco, Tunisia or Lebanon, the domestic political context conditions MENA countries' cooperation and the efficiency of JHA policies. For instance, the negotiations on the EU–Morocco readmission agreement were suspended following disagreements on trade negotiations in 2014. In 2016, all relations with the EU were suspended due to a case law delivered by the European Court of Justice (Case T-512/12) that annulled a trade agreement on fisheries and agricultural products and was perceived as acknowledging the Western Sahara's long-standing claims of independence.

Post-Arab uprisings wave: building state and societal resilience

Instability and the growing number of populations affected by conflicts and terrorism have adversely affected the region, leading to displacement or causing people to live in conflict-torn areas. The ensuing humanitarian crisis and the flow of refugees have once again tested Europe's relationship with its Southern neighbors and brought to the fore discussions about the root causes of migration, conflicts and instability. This has prompted new policy and research developments. First, there is a clearer foreign policy focus in JHA since the creation of the EEAS. Second, a new stream of research has developed focusing on building state and societal resilience as a potential remedy for the fragmentation that undermined the sustainability and effectiveness of efforts undertaken by peacebuilding, humanitarian and development communities.

New life of the internal–external security nexus

Following the Arab uprisings, the external dimension of JHA gained a renewed dynamism. Several initiatives that were blocked in the Council or the European Parliament since the mid-2000s, concerning the strengthening of the EU's border management policies, were eventually finalized. In addition, in 2016, the European Commission proposed a set of measures aimed at the creation of 'an effective and genuine Security Union' through improving cross-border cooperation in the fight against terrorism and organized crime with the support of EU agencies, preventing and fighting radicalization, improving information exchange and enhancing security at the external border (European Commission 2016). Cooperation with third countries also became more dynamic due to the increasing involvement of the EEAS and the activism of the EU Counter Terrorism Coordinator Gilled de Kerchove. The Foreign Affairs Council of February 2015 put forward an extensive agenda for strengthening partnerships and capacity-building with countries in the region and ultimately aiming at enhancing the EU's internal security (Council of the European Union 2015). Some of the most innovative measures included security and counter-terrorism dialogues with Algeria, Egypt, Morocco and Tunisia. In addition, counter-terrorism action plans were developed, starting with Morocco, Tunisia, Algeria, Egypt, Jordan and Lebanon, including measures to dissuade and disrupt foreign terrorist fighters' travel and manage their return as well as measures to curb the financing of terrorism. Beyond capacity-building in various areas of JHA, it is noticeable that the document mentions improving strategic communication and developing an outreach strategy to the Arab world, including through the proposal of counter-narratives to terrorist propaganda and the promotion of fundamental rights (Pawlak 2016). This agenda also demonstrates that the 'more for more' logic has spilled over into the area of security, resulting in the emergence of a group of 'darling countries' such as Tunisia, Jordan and Morocco (due to their relative progress with reforms) with which cooperation on counter-terrorism and security issues is pursued as a matter of priority.

Although securitization theories thus far have focused on the EU's physical internal security, the EU's ontological-seeking security practices that derive from JHA have received little scholarly attention. Ontological security, as defined by Giddens, refers to 'the need for actors such as states to have a consistent and stable identity or sense of self' (Agius 2016: 2). Security practices then provide 'a sense of continuity of self-identity' (Agius 2016: 3). In the EU's Southern neighborhood, JHA policies and their external dimension have participated in the securitization of religion, more specifically Islam, as part of a threat to the EU's liberal-secular values. This in turn has created new ontological-seeking security practices which aim to provide the EU with a security about its own 'self'. Thus, European foreign affairs ministries, the EEAS and the

European Parliament have placed religious engagement at the center of EU–MENA relations (Mandeville and Silvestri 2015; Wolff 2015; Hurd 2015). Since 2013, with the introduction of the Guidelines on the Freedom of Religion or Belief (Council of the EU 2013), European diplomats are trained in religion, EEAS delegations have been instructed to engage with religious actors and a European Parliament intergroup publishes an annual report on the State of Freedom of Religion or Belief in the World. These ontological-seeking security practices vis-à-vis Islam include counter-radicalization initiatives, inter-civilizational dialogues and religious engagement, and have contributed to the global politics of the moderation of Islam (Wolff 2017).

These practices are increasingly becoming particularly relevant in light of the threat posed by terrorist groups like Daesh, which managed to attract significant numbers of foreign fighters from third countries – including European citizens. In response, the EU has stressed the need for engagement with Muslim communities across Europe to counter the jihadi narrative and violent extremism more broadly. At the same time, the rise of Islamist parties across the region has revived the discussion about political Islam (Mamdani 2005; Esposito 1997) and brought to the fore the debate about the role of religion in shaping those countries' political landscapes (Fadel 2011; El-Ghobashy 2005), its potential link to international stability (Esposito 1997), and its impact upon relations with the EU. Looking inside the countries themselves, many authors questioned whether democracy and Islam are compatible (Brown 1997) or whether Islamist politics is inherently anti-Western (Tibi 1998). Islamist political actors, ranging from the Salafists to more mainstream parties, have nonetheless entered the MENA political landscape. Although the Muslim Brotherhood was taken down in Egypt in 2013 and Ennahda lost the elections in Tunisia, they are in power in Morocco with the PJD and made a comeback in the Jordanian Parliament in the 2016 legislative elections. Engagement with the Muslim community or Islam thus offers multiple challenges for securitization theories. This includes researching the extent to which the external dimension of JHA pursues physical security and ontological security objectives, but also the extent to which JHA policies contribute to defining the role and identity of the EU as a global security provider.

Societal and state resilience

The EU has consistently highlighted the need to address fragility, conflict and security in a holistic way. The Council Conclusions on Security and Development (2007) acknowledged that 'there cannot be sustainable development without peace and security', just as there will be no sustainable peace without development and poverty eradication. The EU Approach to Resilience and the Action Plan for Resilience in Crisis-prone Countries for 2013 to 2020 have further recognized the need to address the root causes of crises and to incorporate a number of key elements, including risk assessment, risk reduction, prevention, mitigation and preparedness, and swift responses to and recovery from crises.

The need to move from declarations to actions became evident with the increase in numbers of migrants arriving at EU borders. The June 2016 Global Strategy for the EU's foreign and security policy identified building state and societal resilience as one of its priorities in responding to fragility and instability and building sustainable growth and societal development. According to the strategy, 'a resilient state is a secure state, and security is key for prosperity and democracy'. Foreign policy analysis has integrated the concept of resilience and assesses the EU's discourse as a 'pragmatist turn' that takes into account the 'practical consequences of [EU] actions and local practices' (Juncos 2016: 2). It has the advantage of taking into account the structural conditions of EU policies in third countries as well their sustainability. Although resilience can really substantiate EU external relations and opens up new ways of working and thinking among international organizations (Wagner and Anholt 2016), it is unclear 'how the EU should build resilience, what kind of resilience and whose resilience' (Juncos 2016: 16).

While the 'resilience turn' in policy-making may be perceived as lacking substance, Chandler (2014) sees its particular value in the rejection of modernist or liberal approaches to governance where policy-making is constructed in 'top-down' ways. Chandler also demonstrates that while neoliberalism sought to govern complexity through intervening in social processes to adjust or transform them, resilience thinking asserts that governance is only possible in non-instrumental ways. In addition, resilience approaches imply a shift in the placement of agency: from one focused on the role of 'international interveners' as external saviors and judges to putting the agency of those most in need of assistance at the center and hence stressing a program of empowerment and capacity-building (Chandler 2012).

The EU's narrative about building resilience in third countries suggests a two-fold approach whereby the EU's internal security concerns are 'internalized' by third countries and its policies serve to transform third countries' institutions and societies through a mix of state-building mechanisms and financial incentives. This strategy has been particularly visible in relation to the Syrian crisis wherein the EU has heavily invested in various forms of support to countries in the neighborhood that were most affected by high numbers of Syrian refugees. Initial steps taken by the EU were focused primarily on reducing the pressure of the increasing migration flows at the EU's borders through proposals like safe countries of origin, and providing incentives for transit countries to tighten their border controls. On the basis of the agreement between the EU and Turkey from March 2016, the EU provided €3 billion for the Facility for Refugees in Turkey for concrete projects and committed to advancing talks on visa liberalization in exchange for Turkey's cooperation in controlling migration flows to Greece (Collett 2016). At the same time, the EU launched new Partnership Priorities with individual countries with the aim of providing a strategic framework for coordinating political, security and cooperation efforts in areas such as security, countering terrorism, governance, rule of law, migration, mobility and fostering growth and job opportunities. The 'compacts' accompanying each of the Partnership Priorities provide a detailed list of concrete initiatives to be undertaken by both sides involved in the agreement.

Trends and the future of ED JHA research

Over the past fifteen years, the study of the external dimension of JHA has undergone a significant evolution from a policy area whose existence was called into question as a mere 'add-on' to the study of foreign policy to a broader discipline interested in the link between conflict, security and development. The MENA region has proven to be a particularly useful laboratory for the study of a range of domestic and international factors that ultimately influence JHA policies, such as unemployment, income shocks, terrorism, and tensions among ethnic, religious or social groups. Recent developments across the region, their impact upon the EU's security and the EU's response to them have led to several observations concerning the future evolution of this policy area.

Broadening and deepening of the policy area

One of the main conclusions from the research on the external dimension of JHA in the MENA region is the progressive broadening of research in terms of subjects and countries as well as its deepening in terms of analysis. It has shifted from purely institutional and Eurocentric analysis in the early 2000s to analysis that increasingly looks into disciplines such as development, economics, climate and/or resources in order to better understand the factors shaping the external dimension of JHA. As such, the exclusive focus on the traditional internal–external security nexus or security–development nexus may prove to be insufficient to grasp the complexity of processes shaping the EU's policies towards the region and those influencing their impact. This shift in the understanding of the security environment – its spatial and temporal distribution – is one of the key drivers for the emergence of the concept of resilience as one of the organizing principles. In that vein, the research on the impact of migration from MENA upon the EU, for instance, needs to increasingly reach out to other disciplines and look at trends in order to identify potential triggers of instability. The analysis of trends shaping the security environment around the Mediterranean basin suggests that the occurrence of other crises is just a matter of time. For instance, as a consequence of extreme temperatures across the MENA region and increasing air pollution by windblown desert dust, living conditions in parts of the region will become intolerable by 2050, and may lead to a 'climate exodus' migration (most likely to Europe) and social unrest (Lelieveld et al. 2016).

Progressing militarization

The growing recognition of the internal–external security nexus has provided an impulse for an increasing reliance on development instruments in addressing security challenges through crisis management within the framework of CSDP missions and operations. Due to their focus on strengthening state institutions through support for security sector reform and judiciary and public administration reforms, JHA policies have de facto become an integral element of the EU's engagement in the region, expressed through the launch of CSDP missions and operations, and an increasing focus on capacity-building, including for the military. The EU Integrated Border Management Assistance Mission (EUBAM) in Libya – launched in May 2013 – had the goal of providing support to the Libyan authorities in developing the security of the country's borders through training, mentoring and advice on an integrated border management strategy. In June 2016, the Council expanded the operation's mandate to include two additional supporting tasks: training the Libyan coastguard and navy and contributing to the implementation of the UN arms embargo on the high seas off the coast of Libya. The expanding scope of the operations and their links with JHA policies has attracted the interest of other research communities looking into politics and practices relating to migration and border control (Jeandesboz and Pallister-Wilkins 2016; Vaughan-Williams 2015), but still require further investigation, particularly with respect to the impact of new initiatives such as increasing the link between the military and law enforcement through capacity-building initiatives.

Mercantilization of JHA

Issues that have remained under the radar in the study of ED JHA are the reliance of JHA on financial and trade incentives, a growing link between the economic and social development of a country and a potential link to the EU's security. This thinking has been present in the EU's policies towards the region since the early days following the Arab uprisings with initiatives such as the Deauville Partnership or the 'Three Ms' concept built around money, mobility and markets as elements to incentivize a positive change across the region. In the case of Jordan, for instance, assistance was provided through, among others, Macro-Financial Assistance operations and is a part of the so-called EU–Jordan Compact that contains precise commitments from both sides, including political reforms to strengthen parliamentary democracy and the rule of law.

Respect for effective democratic mechanisms such as a multi-party parliamentary system, the rule of law and respect for human rights are preconditions for granting the Union's Macro-Financial Assistance. The announcement of the European External Investment Plan in 2016 is further confirmation of this trend, whereby the EU hopes to resolve its security problems through strengthening trade and investment relations with countries in the region.

Role for new technologies

The wave of terrorist attacks on European soil since 2014 has shown that the destabilization of and state failure in the MENA region had direct implications inside the EU. It has been quite striking to see that most of the attacks perpetrated in Europe were conducted by 'home-grown' terrorists who trained in Syria as 'foreign fighters'. This phenomenon is directly linked to radicalization via the Internet and has been affecting European countries as much as MENA countries, with Morocco and Tunisia supplying the most important contingent of foreign fighters. The use of new technologies by criminal groups and terrorist organizations is not a new phenomenon. However, the increasing complexity of this phenomenon and the rapid proliferation of policy responses – ranging from institutional solutions such as the establishment of an internal referral unit (IRU) at Europol to legislative changes significantly increasing the powers of intelligence and law enforcement services – bring to the fore a new set of questions about balancing fundamental rights like freedom of expression online with security priorities like fighting radicalization and extremist propaganda on the Internet. The multi-stakeholder character of the digital environment – where resources and responsibilities are distributed among public and private actors – points to another set of governance challenges that need to be explored.

As this chapter has demonstrated, the external dimension of JHA policy has evolved into a vibrant field of research. The EU's relations with its Southern neighbors play a particular role in pushing the scholarship further. First, the EU's Southern neighborhood is by no means a homogeneous group of countries. While they may share a religion and common heritage, there is also much that distinguishes them, which is the main reason why projects like the Barcelona Process have never really picked up. Second, the willingness of these countries to work with the EU varies. While some – like Morocco, Tunisia or Jordan – consider the EU an important actor in ensuring their societal and economic development, countries like Egypt are wary of the potential political cost of Europe's 'goodwill'. In that sense, the region is the ultimate test for the attractiveness of European values and ideals, many of which are defended under the EU's JHA policy. Finally, from the research perspective, the region represents a goldmine for scholars keen to reach beyond the conceptual limitations of their own discipline and courageous enough to venture into the uncertain ground between the studies of political science, sociology, development and religion.

Note

1 These attacks were reported by six member states and, according to the TE-SAT, 'almost half of them (103) were reported by the UK'. This number includes not only jihadist attacks, but also ethno-nationalist and separatist terrorism such as Dissident Republican groups in Northern Ireland or Euskadi ta Askatasuna in the Basque Country.

Bibliography

Agius, C. (2016). Drawing the Discourses of Ontological Security: Immigration and Identity in the Danish and Swedish Cartoon Crises. *Cooperation and Conflict*, p. 0010836716653157.

Andrijasevic, R. (2010). DEPORTED: The Right to Asylum at EU's External Border of Italy and Libya. *International Migration*, 48(1), pp. 148–174.

Argomaniz, J. (2012). A Rhetorical Spillover? Exploring the Link between the European Union Common Security and Defence Policy (CSDP) and the External Dimension in EU Counterterrorism. *European Foreign Affairs Review*, 17(2), pp. 35–52.

Balzacq, T. (ed.) (2009). *The External Dimension of EU Justice and Home Affairs – Governance, Neighours, Security*. Basingstoke: Palgrave.

Bigo, D. (2014). The (In)securitization Practices of the Three Universes of EU Border Control: Military/Navy–Border Guards/Police–Database Analysts. *Security Dialogue*, 45(3), pp. 209–225.

Bigo, D. (2006). Internal and External Aspects of Security. *European Security*, 15(4), pp. 385–404.

Brown, N. (1997). Sharia and State in the Modern Muslim Middle East. *International Journal of Middle East Studies*, 29(3), pp. 359–376.

Buzan, B., Wæver, O. and De Wilde, J. (1998). *Security: A New Framework for Analysis*. Boulder, CO: Lynne Rienner Publishers.

Cassarino, J.P. (2007). Informalising Readmission Agreements in the EU Neighbourhood. *The International Spectator*, 42, pp. 179–196.

Cassarino, J.P. (2009). The Co-operation on Readmission and Enforced Return in the African-European Context. In Trémolières, M. (ed.), *Regional Challenges of West African Migration: African and European perspectives*. Paris: OECD, pp. 49–72.

Chandler, D. (2012). Resilience and Human Security: The Post-interventionist Paradigm. *Security Dialogue*, 43(3), pp. 213–229.

Chandler, D. (2014). Beyond Neoliberalism: Resilience, the New Art of Governing Complexity. *Resilience*, 2(1), pp. 47–63.

Collett, E. (2016). *The Paradox of the EU–Turkey Refugee Deal*. Migration Policy Institute: Commentary, March.

Collyer, M. (2012). Migrants as Strategic Actors in the European Union's Global Approach to Migration and Mobility. *Global Networks*, 12(4), pp. 505–524.

Council of Europe (2011). Report on the Visit to Lampedusa (Italy) 1 (23–24 May 2011). Committee on Migration, Refugees and Population Ad hoc Sub-Committee on the large-scale arrival of irregular migrants, asylum seekers and refugees on Europe's southern shores. AS/MIG/AHLARG (2011) 03 REV 2, September 30.

Council of the European Union (2013). *EU Guidelines on the Promotion and Protection of Freedom of Religion or Belief*. Foreign Affairs Council meeting, Luxembourg, June 24.

Council of the European Union (2015). *Council Conclusions on Counter-terrorism*. Foreign Affairs Council, Brussels, February 9.

Del Sarto, R.A. and Steindler, C. (2015). Uncertainties at the European Union's Southern Borders: Actors, Policies, and Legal Frameworks. *European Security*, 24(3), pp. 369–380.

El-Ghobashy, M. (2005). The Metamorphosis of the Egyptian Muslim Brothers. *International Journal of Middle East Studies*, 37(3), pp. 373–395.

El Qadim, N. (2014). Postcolonial Challenges to Migration Control: French–Moroccan Cooperation Practices on Forced Returns. *Security Dialogue*, 45(3), pp. 242–261.

Esposito, J. (1997). *Political Islam: Revolution, Radicalism or Reform?* Boulder, CO: Lynne Riener.

European Commission (2011). *Communication from the Commission to the European Parliament and the Council. Evaluation of EU Readmission Agreements*. Brussels, February 23.

European Commission (2016). *Communication from the Commission to the European Parliament, the European Council and the Council on Delivering on the European Agenda on Security to Fight against Terrorism and Pave the Way towards an Effective and Genuine Security Union*. Brussels, April 20.

European Council (2000). Fourth Euro–Mediterranean Conference of Foreign Ministers, Presidency's Formal Conclusions. Marseille, European Council.

European Court of Human Rights (2012). Jamaa, Hirsi. Others v. Italy: Application no. 27765/09, February 23.

Europol (2016). *European Union Terrorism Situation and Threat Report 2016*. Available at: www.europol.europa.eu/content/211-terrorist-attacks-carried-out-eu-member-states-2015-new-europol-report-reveals (accessed October 7, 2016).

Fadel, M. (2011). Modernist Islamic Political Thought and the Egyptian Revolutions of 2011. *Middle East Law and Governance*, 2, pp. 94–104.

Freyburg, T. (2011). Transgovernmental Networks as Catalysts for Democratic Change? EU Functional Cooperation with Arab Authoritarian Regimes and Socialisation of Involved State Officials into Democratic Governance. *Democratization*, 18(4), pp. 1001–1025.

Freyburg, T. (2012). The Janus Face of EU Migration Governance: Impairing Democratic Governance at Home – Improving It Abroad? *European Foreign Affairs Review*, 17(5), pp. 125–142.

García Andrade, P. and Martin, I. (2015). *EU Cooperation with Third Countries in the Field of Migration*. Brussels: Study for the European Parliament.

Hurd, E.S. (2015). *Beyond Religious Freedom. The New Global Politics of Religion*. Princeton, NJ: Princeton University Press.

Jeandesboz, J. and Pallister-Wilkins, P. (2016). Crisis, Routine, Consolidation: The Politics of the Mediterranean Migration Crisis'. *Mediterranean Politics*, 21(2), pp. 316–320.

Juncos, A.E. (2016). Resilience as the New EU Foreign Policy Paradigm: A Pragmatist Turn? *European Security*. doi: 10.1080/09662839.2016.1247809.

Lavenex, S. and Panizzon, M. (2013). Multilayered Migration Governance: The Partnership Approach in the EU and Beyond. Geneva: United Nations Research Institute for Social Development, draft paper.

Lavenex, S. and Uçarer, E.M. (2004). The External Dimension of Europeanization. The Case of Immigration Policies. *Cooperation and Conflict*, 39(4), pp. 417–443.

Lelieveld, J., Proestos, Y. and Hadjinicolaou, P. (2016). Strongly Increasing Heat Extremes in the Middle East and North Africa (MENA) in the 21st Century. *Climatic Change*, 137(1), pp. 137–245.

Léonard, S. (2010). EU Border Security and Migration into the European Union: FRONTEX and Securitization through Practices. *European Security*, 19(2), pp. 231–254.

Lutterbeck, D. (2006). Policing Migration in the Mediterranean. *Mediterranean Politics*, 11(1), pp. 59–82.

Mainwaring, C. (2012). Constructing a Crisis: The Role of Immigration Detention in Malta. *Population, Space and Place*, 18(6), pp. 687–700.

Mamdani, M. (2005). *Good Muslim, Bad Muslim: America, the Cold War, and the Roots of Terror*. London: Harmony Books.

Mandeville, P. and Silvestri, S. (2015). *Integrating Religious Engagement into Diplomacy: Challenges and Opportunities*. Brookings Institute, Issues in Governance Studies, No. 65.

Mountz, A. (2015). In/visibility and the Securitization of Migration Shaping Publics through Border Enforcement on Islands. *Cultural Politics*, 11(2), pp. 184–200.

Orsini, G. (2016). Securitization as a Source of Insecurity: A Ground-level Look at the Functioning of Europe's External Border in Lampedusa. *Studies in Ethnicity and Nationalism*, 16(1), pp. 135–147.

Pallister-Wilkins, P. (2015). The Humanitarian Politics of European Border Policing: Frontex and Border Police in Evros. *International Political Sociology*, 9(1), pp. 53–69.

Paoletti, E. (2010). *The Migration of Power and North–South Inequalities: The Case of Italy and Libya*. Basingstoke: Palgrave Macmillan.

Pawlak, P. (2016). *EU Strategic Communication with the Arab World*. Briefing, European Parliamentary Research Service, May.

Piper, N. (2009). Temporary Migration and Political Remittances: The Role of Organisational Networks in the Transnationalisation of Human Rights. *European Journal of East Asian Studies*, 8(2), pp. 215–243.

Pressman, J.L. and Wildavsky, A.B. (1984). *How Great Expectations in Washington are Dashed in Oakland*. Berkeley: University of California Press.

Reslow, N. (2012). The Role of Third Countries in EU Migration Policy: The Mobility Partnerships. *European Journal of Migration and Law*, 14, pp. 393–415.

Sgueo, G. (2016). *Counter-terrorism Funding in the EU Budget*. Briefing, European Parliamentary Research Service, April.

Tibi, B. (1998). *The Challenge of Fundamentalism: Political Islam and the New World Disorder* (Vol. 9). Berkeley: University of California Press.

Trauner, F. and Wolff, S. (2014). The Negotiation and Contestation of EU Migration Policy Instruments: A Research Framework. *European Journal of Migration and Law*, 16(1), pp. 1–18.

Trauner, F. and Carrapico, H. (2012). The External Dimension of EU Justice and Home Affairs after the Lisbon Treaty: Analysing the Dynamics of Expansion and Diversification. *European Foreign Affairs Review*, 17(5), pp. 143–162.

United Nations (1951). *Convention Relating to the Status of Refugees*. Geneva: United Nations.

Vaughan-Williams, N. (2015). *Europe's Border Crisis: Biopolitical Security and Beyond*. New York: Oxford University Press.
Wagner, W. and Anholt, R. (2016). Resilience as the EU Global Strategy's New Leitmotif: Pragmatic, Problematic or Promising? *Contemporary Security Policy*, 37(3), pp. 414–430.
Wolff, S. (2012). *The Mediterranean Dimension of European Union's Internal Security*. London: Palgrave.
Wolff, S. (2014). The Politics of Negotiating EU Readmission Agreements: Insights from Morocco and Turkey. *European Journal of Migration and Law*, 16(1), pp. 69–95.
Wolff, S. (2015). *U.S. and EU Engagement with Islamists in the Middle East and North Africa*. Transatlantic Academy, Paper Series, 2014–2015, No. 3.
Wolff, S. (2017). EU religious engagement in the MENA region: much ado about nothing? *Mediterranean Politics*, http://dx.doi.org/10.1080/13629395.2017.1358905.
Wolff, S. and Hadj-Abdou, L. (2017). Mediterranean Migration and Refugee Politics between Continuities and Discontinuities. In Volpi, F. and Gillespie, R., *The Routledge Handbook of Mediterranean Politics*. Abingdon: Routledge.
Wolff, S. and Mounier, G. (2012) A Kaleidoscopic View on the External Dimension of Justice and Home Affairs after Lisbon. *European Foreign Affairs Review*, 17(5), pp. 143–162
Wunderlich, D. (2012). The Limits of External Governance: Implementing EU External Migration Policy. *Journal of European Public Policy*, 19(9), pp. 1414–1433.

27
AFRICA–EU RELATIONS ON ORGANIZED CRIME

Between securitization and fragmentation

Judith Vorrath and Verena Zoppei

Introduction[1]

With growing awareness about organized crime (OC) as a threat at the interface of internal and external security, combatting OC has emerged as a driver for the justice and home affairs (JHA) external action of the EU. This chapter looks in particular at Africa–EU relations on OC.

While the literature on the EU externalization of the fight against OC is substantial (e.g., Carrapico 2013; Cremona 2011; Longo 2003; Mitsilegas 2007, 2009, 2011), little academic work deals specifically with Africa–EU relations in combatting OC (Aning 2009; Monar 2012). It may be common sense that internal and external security are inseparable today, but for actual EU policy as well as for research, bridging these two dimensions has proven difficult. The focus of Africa–EU relations has long been in development, meaning the ACP (Africa, Caribbean and Pacific countries)–EU Partnership Process, which only more recently – particularly in the 2010 revision of the Cotonou Agreement – made reference to OC as a security-related issue.

Overall, Africa–EU relations on OC have become more relevant. In order to better understand how and why relations have evolved, the following section outlines theoretical approaches on the external dimension of the EU JHA agenda. These are used in the third section to interpret Africa–EU relations to combat OC, in particular actual EU cooperation formats and programs with Africa and the role which OC plays as part of those. The final section presents a brief case study of EU cooperation with West Africa in combatting drug trafficking in order to discuss the relevance of different explanations of how relations have evolved.

The external dimension of the EU JHA agenda: what to expect for Africa–EU relations?

This section deals with the literature debating the external action of the EU in the field of JHA, and particularly of the fight against OC. It focuses on critical literature on the EU's external governance as an expression of a security-driven agenda and as the result of fragmented forms of governance and a patchwork of partnerships.

The EU's external action on JHA: patterns of remote policing and securitization

There are different explanations for the EU's external action in the field of JHA. Some argue that it was triggered by the cross-border nature of threats like OC, which have blurred the boundaries of the traditional division between national security and external security. In addition, the abolition of border controls within the Union exacerbated the blending of the two dimensions and led to the necessity of safeguarding internal security by protecting the Union's external borders (Lavenex 2011: 119; Poli 2011: 74). There is also evidence of an opposite trend, namely of the perceived external origin of OC in setting the internal agenda (Monar 2012; Poli 2011: 73). Scholars have also argued that a driver for the EU's external governance of JHA can be the pursuit of completely different goals, such as EU foreign policy or military matters (Koutrakos 2011: 147; Carrapico and Trauner 2013).

The first generation of policy instruments was concluded with a view to strengthen internal security more than the pursuit of goals outside the Union (Poli 2011: 74; Tocci 2007: 23). In addition, the Treaty of Lisbon specified that the Union's external action in the Area of Freedom, Security and Justice was aimed at ensuring a high level of security for its citizens. This pattern of externalization, called 'remote policing', has also been observed in other fields, such as migration control, in which the EU exports internal migration control tools to origin and transit countries (Trauner and Deimel 2013: 21) with the goal of moving border controls away from EU frontiers (Bigo and Guild 2005).

With specific regard to combatting OC, scholars have criticized the hierarchical imposition of domestic definitions and perceptions of OC, and the export of instruments to counteract the phenomenon to other national contexts (Irrera 2013: 225). From the third countries' perspective, cooperation in the field of JHA is challenged by the asymmetry of interests between the EU and Africa (Lavenex 2011: 131). The Stockholm Programme advocated for a switch from a hierarchical approach to horizontal forms of cooperation with third states through the establishment of regional networks of functional experts. Such forms of cross-border regional cooperation projects, like joint police or customs centers, were supposed to avoid overarching political divides (Council of the European Union 2010a: 5, 7). Yet, this rather technical approach has also been criticized as leading to depoliticization and insulating cooperation from political debates and institutions, and thus distancing security-driven cooperation from the values of democracy, rule of law and human rights (Lavenex 2011: 137).

Some scholars primarily describe the externalization process of JHA policies as securitization. For example, it has been observed that EU cooperation with the Mediterranean in the area of migration policies has shifted from the social and economic agenda to the security agenda, and that the enhancement of neighboring countries' law enforcement and border control capabilities is aimed at reducing security risks inside the Union (Monar 2011: 423). Thus, it has been argued that the relations between the neighboring countries and the EU have become largely based on security concerns of the Union while the commitment to human rights, freedom of persons and shared values has remained rhetorical (Longo 2011: 385). In this context, the contribution of Frontex, the agency in charge of managing operational cooperation at the external borders of the EU, is seen as part of the securitization process of asylum and migration (e.g., Léonard 2010; Vollmer and von Boemcken 2014).

Yet, the literature is far from unanimous. While the JHA agenda may follow a short-term perspective of border management and migration controls, the broader foreign and security policies have also been assessed as a contribution to reducing the root causes of migration in a long-term perspective (Parkers 2010). Overall, what the European agenda primarily looks like in this field may be explained by securitization or depoliticization processes, but also by the mutual impact of internal and external (security) considerations.

The EU's external action on OC as an expression of a fragmented institutional landscape?

The potential pitfall of looking at the EU's external action on OC through the above-elaborated lenses is that there is the assumption of a coherent agenda or at least a main scheme. However, one of the most debated aspects of the EU external agenda is the co-existence of different policies and documents vis-à-vis third countries or other regions. In this particular field, the overlapping of policies is connected to the multifaceted nature of OC and to the ever-expanding range of partners involved.

In many African states the term OC can be difficult to apply, since criminal networks tend to 'transcend the state/non-state boundary in ways that are hardly subsumed in standard concepts of organized crime' (Ellis and Shaw 2015). At the EU level itself, it is difficult to unequivocally define the phenomenon of OC, due partly to its rapid evolvement (Allum and Den Boer 2013: 136). Despite having a transnational dimension, the topic remains within the domestic field of law enforcement and thus reflects national diversities. At the same time, OC is not confined to the area of JHA. Reference to OC has become commonplace in development, trade, foreign and security policy documents – whether at the EU or member state level – and a whole range of departments and bodies are more or less directly engaged in dealing with it. This reflects the dynamic sectorial dimension of external JHA policies of the EU.

The multi-sectoral approach may be interpreted as a way to use all available frameworks for cooperation with partners for preventing and combatting OC (Koutrakos 2011: 143). But from a governance perspective, the absence of a fully integrated approach for tackling OC can potentially lead to framework fragmentation of policies, which has been referred to as a 'policy patchwork' (Carrapico 2013).

Moreover, the rising number of members and the inclusion of ever-new OC-related matters triggered by the 'shifting EU borders' (Bachmann and Stadtmuller 2011), among other things, have increased the concurrence of neighborhood policies. Yet, the more distant from the EU the concerned regions are, the less concrete the related EU plans (Trauner and Carrapico 2012: 6, 11). This can potentially affect the EU's capacity to act coherently on OC in external affairs.

Another source of fragmentation is the overlap of strategic partnerships between the member states, the EU and the different agencies acting in JHA fields, and the third countries (e.g., Wolff and Mounier 2012: 160–161). The debate on strategic partnerships in the external relations of the EU is particularly vivid (Husar et al. 2010). It is argued that strategies with geographically wide areas, such as the EU–Africa Strategy, may be compensating for the inability of the EU to select specific partners (Bendiek and Kramer 2010: 30, 41). While the external dimension of EU JHA is of growing importance, the EU is still struggling to become a relevant partner in international relations (Renard 2016: 33). This is partly due to the lack of operational capability of the Union, the perpetually strong position of single member states in the international arena, and the difficulty of converging on certain issues (e.g., Monar 2011: 418). The EU's promotion of a multi-layered approach against OC in the international arena is considered by Renard to be an interesting attempt to adopt an 'effective multilateralism' (2014: 11). The downside remains that some actors continue to neglect the EU as a partner and prefer to cooperate directly with member states. Moreover, these multiple layers and simultaneously engaged channels may well increase fragmentation and the unclear profile of the EU's activities.

For all of these reasons, it may be expected that EU–Africa relations – rather than following one specific thread or agenda – display the fragmentation of the policies and actors involved.

EU–Africa cooperation in tackling organized crime: a strategic partnership?

The EU recognized the importance of the strategic partnership with Africa in combatting OC and especially drug trafficking in West Africa in the Action Oriented Papers adopted by the Council of the EU (Council of the European Union 2010a, 2010b).

There can be different levels and formats for pursuing such a partnership. The EU may interact with African regional organizations and countries or groups of countries in different frameworks – from international fora to (inter)regional cooperation schemes or agreements with specific countries. There is also a whole set of instruments which the EU can apply to support combatting OC outside of the Union. The following section provides an overview of the main features of Africa–EU relations[2] in tackling OC.

Global fora and Africa–EU partnerships

A major reference point in the global fight against OC is the United Nations Convention on Transnational Organized Crime and its Protocols. While all EU member states and the EU itself as well as most African countries have signed the convention, it has not served as a main platform for common policy formulation or concrete cooperation between the EU and African states for various reasons. This largely holds true for other, more specialized international fora as well. The process leading to the UN General Assembly Special Session on Drugs (UNGASS) 2016 has shown that even when common EU and African Union (AU) positions are formulated and converge in several respects,[3] this is not necessarily a basis for strong cooperation. In this case, the participation by African countries in the negotiations on the draft of the UNGASS outcome document conducted by the Commission on Narcotic Drugs in Vienna was very weak, and South Africa presented a far more restrictive and, in many respects, inconsistent position on behalf of the Africa Group. Thus, the reach of the relationship in international fora is rather weak.

As part of longer established regional cooperation formats and partnerships, OC and different types of trafficking have increasingly been mentioned. For example, the 2000 Cotonou Agreement of the EU with the ACP simply refers to drugs and OC including money laundering as fields of mutual concern and regional cooperation (Cotonou Agreement 2000). While the revision in 2005 brought no significant change, the 2010 revised version mentions 'organized crime, piracy and trafficking of, notably, people, drugs and weapons' as 'new or expanding security threats' that need to be addressed (Cotonou Agreement 2010: 25). Apart from the previous paragraphs, the joint declaration on migration and development (Article 13) also stresses the strengthening and deepening of cooperation regarding illegal migration, 'including smuggling and trafficking of human beings and border management' (Cotonou Agreement 2010: 217). However, while EU–ACP cooperation has shown a stronger reference to OC and its multiple facets over time, it is still mainly driven by the development agenda.

The intercontinental EU–Africa strategic partnership – initiated particularly to create a more equitable relationship – made extended reference to OC and related activities from the beginning. The Joint Africa–EU Strategy (JAES) adopted at the Lisbon Summit in 2007 largely frames transnational OC as well as human and drugs trafficking and all types of illicit trade in natural resources as peace and security challenges. Yet no specific activities related to those challenges have been foreseen under the Partnership on Peace and Security. Rather, the partnership on democratic governance and human rights foresaw increased cooperation in the prevention of and fight against drugs and OC, mostly by enhancing dialogue in international fora – which, as mentioned above, is still very limited.

Enhancing cooperation by regional action plans

A more concrete priority action named in the Joint Africa–EU Strategy at the inter-regional level is the implementation of the EU–Africa Plan of Action on Trafficking of Human Beings. In fact, the activities related to tackling human trafficking and smuggling have become more extensive. Among other things, the African Union Commission has launched a campaign to drive the implementation of the Ouagadougou Action Plan and regional action plans have been developed below the AU level with EU support. Moreover, the Human Trafficking Initiative under the Second Action Plan (2011–2013) of the Joint Africa–EU Strategy also covered AU and EU support to Regional Economic Communities in Africa for monitoring and evaluation at the regional level.[4] Based on the intercontinental partnership and regional policies, the Khartoum process was initiated in 2014 to address the issue of migration from the Horn of Africa, including specific projects to address trafficking in human beings and the smuggling of migrants. The process has often been criticized for being narrowly focused on security and providing technical assistance to East African countries with a poor human rights record and authoritarian leadership, particularly Sudan and Eritrea (e.g., Grinstead 2016).

The Khartoum Process is also an expression of a general feature of Africa–EU relations in the field, namely the (sub)regional focus and different reach within Africa – despite the intercontinental framework of the Joint Africa–EU Strategy. Along the Western migratory route the Rabat Process was launched in 2006 to address irregular migration and strengthen the synergies between migration and development. While officially promoting a balanced approach, it has been argued that the activities of the process largely serve the purpose of preventing irregular migration to Europe rather than assisting victims of trafficking and tackling the roots of the problem (Rees 2008: 104; Rijken 2011: 209).

More specifically in relation to OC, the Instrument for Stability (IfS) – started in 2007 and renamed the Instrument contributing to Stability and Peace in 2014 – has a (sub)regional focus, for instance, on West Africa (European Union 2014). The Annual Action Programmes 2014 and 2015 contain specific work programs for fighting OC and refer to strategies by the EU, the AU and African regional economic communities. However, the actual activities like the EU Cocaine Route Programme and the Critical Maritime Routes Programme focus on specific areas and subregions, which means setting priorities on where and what type of OC to tackle (European Commission 2014b, 2015). Indeed, both can be linked to regional strategies and action plans; for example, the European Union's Strategy for Security and Development in the Sahel from March 2011. Despite its title, the EU Sahel Strategy focuses strongly on security while OC is almost exclusively mentioned in connection with terrorism, and drug trafficking is the only specified type of trafficking cited (EEAS 2011). While the Cocaine Route Programme focuses largely on the coastal states of West Africa, there are also program components in Mali and Niger. In addition, the EU has deployed civilian Common Security and Defence Policy (CSDP) missions under the regional strategy, namely EUCAP Sahel Niger and EUCAP Sahel Mali. These were launched in 2012 and 2015 respectively with a focus on advice to and training of security forces in order to strengthen their capabilities, particularly in fighting terrorism and OC.

The Gulf of Guinea Action Plan (2015–2020) was adopted by the Council of the European Union for cooperating with Western and Central African coastal states and the region in tackling maritime crime. The actions named included 'piracy and armed robbery at sea, illegal fishing, smuggling of migrants and trafficking of human beings, drugs, and arms, and [...] the underlying causes to foster long-term security and stability in the region' (Council of the European Union 2015a: 2). In contrast to the EU Naval Force Operation Atalanta deployed under the CSDP to combat piracy off the coast of Somalia, the Gulf of Guinea process relies on supporting regional efforts, such as the Yaoundé process based on a Memorandum of Understanding and a Code of Conduct on maritime security adopted in June 2013 by West and Central African countries and regional organizations (International Maritime Organization 2013). The Action Plan stresses the EU Comprehensive Approach, and besides supporting regional dialogue and information sharing, it foresees capacity- and institution-building, training, equipment and joint operations, as well as development aid projects and coordinated actions supported through Sustainable Fisheries Partnership Agreements (Council of the European Union 2015a: 16–18). At the same time, tackling OC in the maritime domain introduces a stronger military component and raises the question of cooperation not just with development actors, but also with police and civil actors in the Area of Freedom, Security and Justice.

A EU-driven, fragmented agenda instead of strategic partnership

The only EU strategic partnership at the country level is with South Africa,[5] and even this one is marginal overall (Renard 2014: 20, 24). The Partnership Framework with third countries under the European Agenda on Migration launched in 2015 refers to measures for tackling human smuggling and increasing border security in some African countries and regions (European Commission 2015). As a comprehensive strategy it combines external and internal policies and continental, regional and bilateral (especially with Niger, Mali and Nigeria) levels of cooperation. Yet it remains to be seen how it will be implemented.

Europol is monitoring the continent, especially West and North Africa, in order to assess cyber, criminal and terrorist threats (Europol 2011, 2016). Joint operations between Europol and its liaison officers in third countries in Africa have been successfully conducted, in particular to tackle human trafficking originating from Western Africa.[6] Yet, relations remain relatively limited, including in judicial cooperation. Only two out of thirty contact points established by Eurojust in third countries are in Africa (Cape Verde and Tunisia).[7] There may be increased cooperation in the future with the African police body Afripol – newly created as an AU entity based in Algiers. But even though Europol has pledged to support Afripol in building its structures to effectively deal with security threats like terrorism, human and drug trafficking and cyber crime, it will take years to see whether this can be a new basis for an intensified partnership.

So far, an overall strategy in Africa–EU relations on OC is not visible. The issue comes up increasingly in core policy documents, but usually neither the challenges nor possible responses are clearly laid out. It has generally been questioned whether the Joint Africa–EU Strategy really lives up to building a strategic partnership (Tardy 2016); with regard to OC, it is certainly a tool for intensified dialogue at best. The framework for EU engagement tends to be (sub)regional, while specific actions tackling OC in Africa are most commonly undertaken at the country level; EU member states certainly have various relevant projects in the field as well. So, there is a lot of area- and issue-specific variation below the continental level. But is this due to dominant EU interests or differences in OC patterns across Africa?

Overall, notwithstanding the efforts for a more equitable relationship beyond a simple donor–recipient logic, the funding for actual activities basically comes from the EU side. This also holds true for the development of action plans and policies at the (sub)regional level in Africa, which have often been supported by the EU. However, while the EU has de facto been in the driver's seat in terms of putting OC on the agenda in relations with African regions and countries, it is difficult to clearly identify a predominant agenda.

A closer look at the EU Sahel Strategic Regional Action Plan (2015–2020) can be revealing in this regard. The document makes very strong reference to irregular migration, trafficking in human beings and the smuggling of migrants, while the reference to drug trafficking is marginal. The Action Plan identifies 'border management and fight against illicit trafficking and transnational organized crime' as one of four areas that have to be further developed in terms of strategic focus (Council of the EU 2015b: 13). Moreover, there is a significantly stronger focus on border management, referring, among other things, to the implementation of integrated border management projects in the Sahel region as well as around Lake Chad. This surely mirrors a shift in EU concerns compared to the strategy document of 2011. With regard to the underlying approach, the document emphasizes action in the fields of development and security. The recommended actions, however, seem to support the securitization argument, for example, the focus on 'development programs on specific geographic areas/communities where radicalization and recruitment are concentrated' (Council of Europe 2015b: 25) and the funding of security-relevant activities through the European Development Fund. Yet, the picture is not clear-cut for OC, since the main recommended actions relate more to issues like terrorism and migration. There is a vague reference to alternative development for youths engaged in illegal activities, but looking at current and planned actions OC still seems to be tackled mostly by capacity-building in criminal justice and law enforcement.

However, the Action Plan is very recent, so it remains difficult to say to what extent programs and actions are mostly security-driven or depoliticized and, even if so, whether they are really about tackling organized crime or serve other purposes. Moreover, there will naturally be a fragmented picture when looking at Africa as a whole in relation to the EU. There can hardly be one clear EU strategy with regard to fifty-four countries, let alone the multitude of fora and partnerships and different issues of OC. Therefore, the final section of this chapter will look at a specific example of cooperation in order to gain some more concrete insights on what drives Africa–EU relations in the field.

The EU's cooperation with West Africa on fighting international drug trafficking

Beginning in about 2005, UNODC noticed a strong increase in the number of seizures of cocaine *en route* from South America to Europe via West Africa (UNODC 2008: 3). With a rising market in Europe, a decline in demand in the United States and a better controlled Caribbean route, South American cocaine traffickers started to use West African countries as transit zones more extensively.[8] Other drugs, such as heroin and methamphetamine, have also been found to come from the region, and there is significant cultivation, trade and consumption of cannabis. Yet, cocaine smuggling seemed to reach alarming levels at the time, with some very prominent cases of cocaine trafficking in West Africa detected between 2004 and 2009. Not all countries were equally affected, but several hubs were identified, most notably around Guinea-Bissau and Guinea going up to Senegal and around Nigeria, including Benin, Togo and Ghana, and, for air shipments, Mali and parts of Mauritania (UNODC 2013: 11).

An overview on actions and programs

Since most of the cocaine was going to Europe, there was a particularly strong interest there to interrupt the flows before they reached their markets of destination. The EU Drug Strategy

(2005–2012) clearly stated that 'the efforts of the EU should be based [...] on the relevance of the particular country or region to the drugs problem in the Union' (Council of the European Union 2004: 18). However, it also referred to the impact upon sustainable development in a particular country or region as a criterion for deciding on concrete action. While this Drug Strategy paid particular attention to cooperation with countries on the Eastern border of the Union, the Balkan states, Afghanistan and its neighbors, Latin American and Caribbean countries as well as Morocco (Council of the European Union 2004: 19), the EU later intensified its focus on West Africa. Therefore, the EU Drugs Action Plan (2013–2016) names Africa, particularly West Africa, as a priority region for reinforcing cooperation (Council of the European Union 2013: 15). The most important expression of that engagement was probably the start of the EU Cocaine Route Programme in 2009, financed under the Instrument contributing to Peace and Stability. It comprises projects along the route from Latin America and the Caribbean to Africa, especially West Africa, to enhance (trans)regional cooperation and build the capacities of law enforcement and judicial bodies. The components of the program involving West African states are AIRCOP,[9] SEACOP,[10] AML-WA[11] and WAPIS,[12] mirroring the overall strong focus on the interception of illicit flows of drugs but also the financial flows linked to it. As such, it was in line with efforts inside the EU during this phase, namely the installation of the Maritime Analysis and Operations Centre-Narcotics (MAOC-N) as a European law enforcement unit based in Lisbon, that became operational in 2007 with the aim of suppressing illicit drug trafficking by sea and air.

The regional ministerial conference that took place in Praia, Cape Verde in 2008, which was supported, among others, by the EU, led to the adoption of a political declaration against illicit drug trafficking and the Praia Plan of Action. Subsequently, the EU strongly supported this regional process and provided substantial financing from the tenth European Development Fund (EDF), also for tackling security-related issues. The European pact to combat international drug trafficking adopted at the JHA Council meeting in 2010 confirmed the philosophy of regional partnerships and technical assistance to source and transit countries like those in West Africa. It even pushed for intensifying and streamlining this philosophy.

Controversial aspects

Despite the ECOWAS Action Plan, EU–West Africa cooperation on tackling OC and drug trafficking was often seen as strongly driven by European interests since there was hardly a market for drugs like cocaine in West Africa. By imposing standards and priorities in the fight against OC, Western powers should have influenced African national and regional agendas. In addition, the typology of responses adopted by West African governments, which are mostly security-centered, have been perceived as imposed by Western governments, the USA in particular. In this context, the absence of reliable data justifies the diplomatic pressure by outside governments to tackle specific types of crimes based on alarming estimates (Alemika 2013: 131–132).

This raises the question about what the actual threat within the region is. The EU Sahel Strategy strongly emphasizes the link to terrorist groups, and the establishment of EUCAP Sahel is certainly an expression of this assumption. While some armed groups have profited from cocaine trafficking, for example, in Mali, this was not initially their major source of income. Often, the links were rather indirect (e.g., through transit fees), and other actors were equally or more important in the smuggling (Lacher 2013). The West Africa Commission on Drugs (WACD) initiated by the Kofi Annan Foundation in 2013 rather stresses the growing consumption of hard drugs in the region as well as political and governance challenges, referring to the complicity of government officials, security personnel and the judiciary as the biggest threats. The Commissioners from ten different West African countries chaired by former Nigerian President Obasanjo concluded that despite increasing regional efforts, most responses have focused on controlling the flows of drugs and strengthening law enforcement while rarely addressing high-level corruption and public health (WACD 2014: 17).

Looking at the activities outlined for tackling cocaine trafficking, this also seems to hold true for EU–West Africa cooperation efforts. At the same time, the EU Cocaine Route Programme was evaluated in 2013 and the respective conference in Rome concluded that a multifaceted response relating to the peace, security and development nexus in which the OC debate is now located is necessary, as well as addressing corruption and impunity (EUC/EEAS/It. 2013: 3). Moreover, Africa–EU relations provide several bases for cooperation. The roadmap adopted at the 2014 EU–Africa Summit alone makes ample reference to all types of illegal flows and OC. Yet, whether and how a more comprehensive and equitable approach will be implemented remains to be seen.

Looking at more recent documents like the Sahel Regional Action Plan, tackling drug trafficking seems to have been downgraded on the agenda while human smuggling and trafficking have become more prominent due to their link with irregular migration. However, one may also argue that programs like the EU Cocaine Route Programme have contributed to reducing cocaine trafficking in particular through West Africa so that other priorities may be set. Indeed, the amount of seizures in the region has been going down, but it is unclear whether this is due to less trafficking taking place or to adapted modes of moving the drugs through the region. Moreover, the shift in priorities so far seems to be more rhetoric. At least the Sahel Regional Action Plan clearly confirms the continuation of support for enhanced regional and transregional cooperation along the Cocaine Routes to Europe (Council of EU 2015b: 28).

Conclusion

The description of concrete patterns of Africa–EU relations on combatting drug trafficking shows a mixed picture. It is questionable whether the rhetoric of partnership has been translated into action. The EU has largely been setting the agenda and has been financing many activities.[13]

The awareness of the (potential) impact of OC may have increased on the African continent, but (sub)regional processes are not necessarily sustainable; for example, the ECOWAS Regional Action Plan has long been awaiting renewal. Addressing the prominent issue of state complicity and a protection economy going far beyond armed groups has proven to be particularly difficult. In general, it has been argued that African elites tend to accept the funding of activities, particularly when the focus is on strengthening the security apparatus, but they do not necessarily share the same interests and do not really buy into the aims of the outside agenda (e.g., Tull 2011). It is difficult to generalize what the real intentions of EU and African actors actually are in tackling OC. The EU struggles to have a coherent strategy for the whole continent. Tackling OC as part of the external dimension of the EU's JHA is scattered along different budget lines and funds.

Looking at the concrete actions taken, there is clearly a fragmentation, since EU support differs greatly in terms of regional/country focus and the types of OC addressed. The securitization perspective is challenged, since the EU has also supported initiatives financially, such as the West Africa Commission on Drugs, which go beyond a mere repressive focus and rather address the drug issue from a public health and governance perspective. EU activities also cannot be seen as merely being a replication of the war on drugs. Yet, they tend to focus on capacity-building of criminal justice and law enforcement institutions. This may partially confirm scholars applying a securitization perspective, particularly when socio-economic and other issues related to OC are only treated as an accessory to such activities and/or funds from other policy fields are used. In addition, there is a trend of designing policies to tackle both the phenomena of OC and terrorism together (den Boer 2011; Bossong 2014).

In short, the criminal justice focus may simply be an expression of internal security interests finding their way onto the external security agenda. Equally the preferred instruments used hint at a possible depoliticization. The effects of capacity-building in strengthening the response to OC are controversial. For example, it has been observed that OC activities increased in northern Mali when the country received support from the EU to counter terrorism and foster state capacity (Lacher 2013: 16). This indicates that a technical approach tends to neglect – whether purposefully or not – the political challenges.

Looking beyond drug trafficking, the picture is also not clear-cut. Counter-piracy efforts represent an example of a security-focused approach, but they also raise the question of the military's role in law enforcement and tackling maritime crime. Similarly, initiatives like the Khartoum Process address migration largely from a security angle. They may be less driven by the aim of combatting criminal networks, for example, in human smuggling and trafficking, than by related concerns such as a reduction of irregular migration or countering terrorism. Furthermore, a variety of EU activities may address OC, its impact or environment without openly naming this as a prime goal. For example, EU initiatives to improve tax justice to Africa, by imposing higher transparency and compliance standards, may also indirectly affect OC activities on the continent (Cobham 2014).

Therefore, the response to OC outside of Europe may be more comprehensive than the fragmented picture of partnerships, strategies and programs suggest at first glance. Overall, Africa–EU relations on OC are likely to become more important in the future.

In order to identify real underlying motives more systematically, further research will have to be conducted on the recently emerging programs and activities, including those of the EU member states. An extension of research in the field also needs to look into the evolution of OC and political agendas in Africa in order to better understand the policy-making processes and the nature of the relationship.

Notes

1 The authors would like to thank Moritz Gruban and Simona Autolitano for their contributions to this chapter.
2 This section will not include an analysis of bilateral programs and activities by EU member states.
3 See European Union, European Union Common Position on UNGASS 2016. Available at: www.unodc.org/documents/ungass2016/Contributions/IO/EU_COMMON_POSITION_ON_UNGASS.pdf; Common African Position for UNGASS 2016. Available at: www.unodc.org/documents/ungass2016/Contributions/IO/AU/Common_African_Position_for_UNGASS_-_English_-_final.pdf.
4 For an overview, see the Africa–EU Partnership website at: www.africa-eu-partnership.org/en/areas-cooperation/migration-mobility-and-employment/irregular-migration.
5 Council of the European Union, The South Africa–European Union Strategic Partnership. Joint Action Plan, 2007.
6 See, for instance, the Joint Action to Tackle West African Human Trafficking Networks. Press release. Available at: www.europol.europa.eu/newsroom/news/joint-action-to-tackle-west-african-human-trafficking-networks-0.
7 See Eurojust, Issue in focus no. 3, 'Cooperation with Third States', 2014, p. 4. Available at: www.eurojust.europa.eu/doclibrary/Eurojust-framework/caseworkdrugtraffickingactionplan2015/Addendum%203%20-%20Cooperation%20with%20Third%20States/drug-trafficking-report_addendum3-thirdstates_2015–01–16rev_EN.pdf (November 25, 2016); The contact point in Egypt is listed under 'Middle East'.

8 For 2010, UNODC estimated that 10 percent of European seizures – meaning 18 tons of pure cocaine worth about $1.25 billion – may have passed through West Africa; see UNODC, *Transnational Organized Crime in West Africa: A Threat Assessment* (Vienna: UNODC, February 2013), p. 17.
9 Airport Communication Programme to strengthen anti-drug capacities at selected airports in Africa, the Caribbean and Latin America.
10 Seaport Cooperation Project, strengthening cooperation in addressing maritime trafficking in West Africa and the Eastern Caribbean.
11 Supporting Anti-money Laundering and Financial Crime Initiatives in West Africa.
12 Facilitating the collection, centralization, management, sharing and analysis of police information in West Africa.
13 See, e.g., the program launched in 2015 in the context of the EU's partnership with the African continent under the Joint Africa–EU Strategy (JAES), with the goal of 'Enhancing African capacity to respond more effectively to transnational organized crime (TOC)'. Commission Implementing Decision on the Annual Action Programme 2015 of the DCI Pan-African Programme Action Document, 2015.

Bibliography

Alemika, E.O. (ed.) (2013). *The Impact of Organized Crime on Governance in West Africa*. Abuja: Friedrich Ebert Stiftung.
Allum, F. and Den Boer, M. (2013). United we Stand? Conceptual Diversity in the EU Strategy against Organized Crime. *Journal of European Integration*, 35(2), pp. 135–150.
Aning, E.K. (2009). *Organized Crime in West Africa: Options for EU Engagement*. Stockholm: International Institute for Democracy and Electoral Assistance (IDEA).
Bachmann, K. and Stadtmuller, E. (2011). *Shifting Borders in the European Union: Theoretical Approaches and Policy Implications in the New Neighbourhood*. Abingdon: Routledge.
Bendiek, A. and Kramer, H. (2010). The EU as a 'Strategic' International Actor: Substantial and Analytical Ambiguities. *European Foreign Affairs Review*, 4, pp. 453–474.
Bigo, D. and Guild, E. (2005). *Controlling Frontiers: Free Movement into and within Europe*. London: Ashgate.
Bossong, R. (2014). Countering Terrorism and Organized Crime: EU Perspectives. Policy Paper Series.
Carrapico, H. (2013). The Exporting of EU Organized Crime Approaches in the Context of the External Dimension of the Area of Freedom, Security and Justice. *Journal of Contemporary European Research*, 9(3), pp. 460–476.
Carrapico, H. and Trauner, F. (2013). Europol and its Influence on EU Policy-making on Organized Crime: Analyzing Governance Dynamics and Opportunities. *Perspectives on European Politics and Society*, 14(3), pp. 357–371.
Cobham, A. (2014). The Impacts of Illicit Financial Flows on Peace and Security in Africa. Study for Tana High-level Forum on Security in Africa 2014. Available at: www.tanaforum.org/y-file-store/Discussion_Papers/2014/iscussionillicit_financial_flows_conflict_and_security_in_africal.pdf (accessed July 31, 2016).
Cotonou Agreement (2000, 2005, 2010). The Cotonou Agreement. Available at: www.europarl.europa.eu/document/activities/cont/201306/20130605ATT67340/20130605ATT67340EN.pdf (accessed July 31, 2016).
Council of the European Union (2004). EU Drugs Strategy (2005–2012) (15074/04). Available at: www.emcdda.europa.eu/html.cfm/index6790EN.html (accessed July 31, 2016).
Council of the European Union (2010a). The Stockholm Programme – An Open and Secure Europe Serving and Protecting the Citizens. 16484/1/09 REV 1 JAI 866 + ADD 1. Available at: https://ec.europa.eu/antitrafficking/sites/antitrafficking/files/the_stockholm_programme_-_an_open_and_secure_europe_en_1.pdf (accessed July 31, 2016).
Council of the European Union (2010b). Implementing the Strategy for the External Dimension of Justice and Home Affairs Action-oriented Paper: Strategic and Concerted Action to Improve Cooperation in Combating Organized Crime, Especially Drug Trafficking, Originating in West Africa.
Council of the European Union (2013). EU Action Plan on Drugs 2013–2016 (2013/C 351/01). Available at: http://ec.europa.eu/taxation_customs/resources/documents/customs/customs_controls/drugs_precursors/drug_precursors/action_plan_2013_2016_en.pdf (accessed July 31, 2016).
Council of the European Union (2015a). Council Conclusions on the Gulf of Guinea Action Plan 2015–2020, March 16. No. prev. doc.: 7082/15.

Council of the European Union (2015b). Council conclusions on the Sahel Regional Action Plan 2015–2010, April 20. No. prev. doc.: 7776/15.

Cremona, M. (2011). EU External Action in the JHA Domain. A Legal Perspective. In M. Cremona, J. Monar and S. Poli (eds), *The External Dimension of the European Union's Area of Freedom, Security and Justice*. Brussels: P.I.E. Peter Lang, College of Europe Studies.

Den Boer, M. (2011). Soft, Smart and Strategic. The International Dimension of EU Action in the Fight against Terrorism. In M. Cremona, J. Monar and S. Poli (eds), *The External Dimension of the European Union's Area of Freedom, Security and Justice*. Brussels: P.I.E. Peter Lang, College of Europe Studies.

Ellis, S. and Shaw, M. (2015). Does Organized Crime Exist in Africa? *African Affairs*, 114(457), pp. 505–528.

European Commission (2014a). Action Document for the 2014–2016 Action Programme of the African Peace Facility. Available at: http://ec.europa.eu/europeaid/sites/devco/files/apf-ad-2-measure-2014_en.pdf (accessed July 31, 2016).

European Commission (2014b). Action Document for Fighting Organised Crime and Protecting Critical Infrastructure. Available at: http://ec.europa.eu/transparency/regcomitology/index.cfm?do=Search.getPDF&dG4sCqeuyrC0HcZ+29KN6aDbby3gYP7DoFPCzj0pZY5pwdiRD711AhJs7+5RXcm37kGvLzo2Pu5uyjPyPE0HGhn1Yyu8a5hceFqN5ixnqYI= (accessed July 31, 2016).

European Commission (2015). Communication from the Commission to the European Parliament, the Council, the European Economic and Social Committee and the Committee of the Regions. A European Agenda on Migration. Available at: http://ec.europa.eu/dgs/home-affairs/what-we-do/policies/european-agenda-migration/background-information/docs/communication_on_the_european_agenda_on_migration_en.pdf(accessed September 30, 2016).

European Commission/European External Action Service/Italian Ministry of Foreign Affairs (EUC/EEAS/It.) (2013). Improving Responses to Organised Crime and Drug Trafficking along the Cocaine Route. Report of the Conference, May 28–30, Rome.

European External Action Service (2011). European Union External Action Service Strategy for Security and Development in the Sahel. Available at: https://eeas.europa.eu/africa/docs/sahel_strategy_en.pdf (accessed July 31, 2016).

European Union (2014). Regulation (EU) No. 233/2014 of the European Parliament and of the Council Establishing a Financing Instrument Contributing to Stability and Peace. Available at: http://ec.europa.eu/dgs/fpi/documents/140311_csp_reg_230_2014_en.pdf (accessed July 31, 2016).

Europol (2011). EU Organized Crime Threat Assessment (OCTA). Available at: www.europol.europa.eu/content/publication/octa-2011-eu-organised-crime-threat-assesment-1465 (accessed September 30, 2016).

Europol (2016). Internet Organised Crime Threat Assessment (IOCTA). Available at: www.europol.europa.eu/content/internet-organised-crime-threat-assessment-iocta-2016 (accessed September 30, 2016).

Grinstead, N. (2016). The Khartoum Process: Shifting the Burden. *Clingendael*, February 22. Available at: www.clingendael.nl/publication/khartoum-process-shifting-burden (accessed July 31, 2016).

Husar, J., Maihold, G. and Mair, S. (eds) (2010). *Europe and New Leading Powers*. Baden-Baden: Nomos.

International Maritime Organization (2013). West and Central Africa Regional Agreements and Information Sharing. Available at: www.imo.org/en/OurWork/Security/WestAfrica/Pages/Code-of-Conduct-against-illicit-maritime-activity.aspx (accessed July 31, 2016).

Irrera, D. (2013). The Externalisation of the EU Internal Security Strategy in the Framework of Multilateralism: The Case of the Fight against Transnational Organised. In M. O'Neill, K. Swinton and A. Winter (eds), *New Challenges for the EU Internal Security Strategy*. Newcastle: Cambridge Scholars Publishing.

Koutrakos, P. (2011). The External Dimension of the AFSJ and Other EU External Policies. An Osmotic Relationship. In M. Cremona, J. Monar and S. Poli (eds), *The External Dimension of the European Union's Area of Freedom, Security and Justice*. Brussels: P.I.E. Peter Lang, College of Europe Studies.

Lacher, W. (2013). Challenging the Myth of the Drug–Terror Nexus in the Sahel. Kofi Annan Foundation, WACD Background Paper No. 4.

Lavenex, S. (2011). Channels of Externalisation of EU Justice and Home Affairs. In M. Cremona, J. Monar and S. Poli (eds), *The External Dimension of the European Union's Area of Freedom, Security and Justice*. Brussels: P.I.E. Peter Lang, College of Europe Studies.

Léonard, S (2010). EU Border Security and Migration into the European Union: FRONTEX and Securitisation through Practices. *European Security*, 19(2), pp. 231–254.

Longo, F. (2003). The Export of Fight against Organised Crime Policy Model and the EU's International Actorness. In S. Prince and M. Knodt (eds), *Understanding the EU's International Presence*. Abingdon: Routledge.

Longo, F. (2011). The Mediterranean Dimension of the Areas of Freedom, Security and Justice. In M. Cremona, J. Monar and S. Poli (eds), *The External Dimension of the European Union's Area of Freedom, Security and Justice*. Brussels: P.I.E. Peter Lang, College of Europe Studies.

Mitsilegas, V. (2007). The External Dimension of EU Action in Criminal Matters. *European Foreign Affairs Review*, 12, pp. 457–497.

Mitsilegas, V. (2009). *EU Criminal Law*. Oxford, and Portland, OH: Hart Publishing.

Mitsilegas, V. (2011). The European Union and the Implementation of International Norms in Criminal Matters. In M. Cremona, J. Monar and S. Poli (eds), *The External Dimension of the European Union's Area of Freedom, Security and Justice*. Brussels: P.I.E. Peter Lang, College of Europe Studies.

Monar, J. (2011). The Outcomes of the External Dimension of the AFSJ. Form, Effectiveness, Prospects and Specificity. In M. Cremona, J. Monar and S. Poli (eds), *The External Dimension of the European Union's Area of Freedom, Security and Justice*. Brussels: P.I.E. Peter Lang, College of Europe Studies.

Monar, J. (2012). Justice and Home Affairs. *Journal of Common Market Studies*, 50, pp. 116–131.

Parkes, R. (2010). When Home Affairs becomes Foreign Policy: Lessons from EU Immigration Policy towards North Africa and Eastern Europe. SWP Comments 32, December.

Poli, S. (2011). The Institutional Setting and the Legal Toolkit. In M. Cremona, J. Monar and S. Poli (eds), *The External Dimension of the European Union's Area of Freedom, Security and Justice*. Brussels: P.I.E. Peter Lang, College of Europe Studies.

Rees, W. (2008). Inside Out: The External Face of EU Internal Security Policy. *Journal of European Integration*, 30(1), pp. 97–111.

Renard, T. (2014). Partners in Crime? The EU, its Strategic Partners and International Organized Crime. ESPO Working Papers No. 5.

Renard, T. (2016). Partnering for Global Security: The EU, its Strategic Partners and Transnational Security Challenges. *European Foreign Affairs Review*, 21(1), pp. 9–34.

Rijken, C. (2011). The External Dimension of EU Policy on Trafficking in Human Beings. In M. Cremona, J. Monar and S. Poli (eds), *The External Dimension of the European Union's Area of Freedom, Security and Justice*. Brussels: P.I.E. Peter Lang, College of Europe Studies.

Tardy, T. (2016). The EU and Africa: A Changing Security Partnership. *European Union Institute for Security Studies*, EUISS Brief 5/2016, February.

Tocci, N. (2007). *The EU and Conflict Resolution. Promoting Peace in the Backyard*. Abingdon: Routledge.

Trauner, F. and Carrapico, H. (2012). The External Dimension of EU Justice and Home Affairs after the Lisbon Treaty: Analysing the Dynamics of Expansion and Diversification. *European Foreign Affairs Review*, 17, pp. 1–18.

Trauner, F. and Deimel, S. (2013). The Impact of EU Migration Policies on African Countries: The Case of Mali. *International Migration*, 51(4), pp. 20–32.

Tull, D.M. (2011). Weak States and Successful Elites: Extraversion Strategies in Africa. *Stiftung Wissenschaft und Politik/German Institute for International and Security Affairs*. SWP Research Paper 2011/RP 09, Berlin, August.

UNODC (2008). *Drug Trafficking As a Security Threat in West Africa*. Vienna: UNODC, November.

UNODC (2013). *Transnational Organised Crime in West Africa: A Threat Assessment*. Vienna: UNODC, February.

Vollmer, R. and von Boemcken, M. (2014). Europe off Limits: Militarization of the EU's External Borders. In I-J. Werkner, J. Kursawe, M. Johannsen, B. Schoch and M. von Boemcken (eds), *Friedensgutachten 2014*. Münster: LIT.

West Africa Commission on Drugs (2014). *Not Just in Transit: Drugs, the State and Society in West Africa*. An Independent Report of the West Africa Commission on Drugs, June. Available at: www.unodc.org/documents/ungass2016/Contributions/IO/WACD_report_June_2014_english.pdf (accessed July 31, 2016).

Wolff, S. and Mounier, G. (2012). A Kaleidoscopic View on the External Dimension of Justice and Home Affairs after Lisbon. *European Foreign Affairs Review*, 2(1), pp. 143–162.

28
THE EVOLUTION OF TRANSATLANTIC LEGAL INTEGRATION
Truly, madly, deeply? EU–US justice and home affairs

Elaine Fahey

Introduction

Well over a decade after the September 2001 (9/11) terrorist attacks, there are many EU–US justice and home affairs (JHA) agreements in force and under development. Transatlantic JHA cooperation has had a vibrant agenda during this period, in particular in the area of law enforcement. It is arguably one of the most active fields of EU–US cooperation and, as a result, the focus of consideration here. They have variable degrees of success or failure and comprise public and private spheres, variable actors and activities. JHA lawmaking continues to evolve through widening and deepening, and indeed now autonomously sets a global agenda to some extent. While the relationship between the EU and USA is conventionally viewed as a 'law-light' and 'institutionally light' scientific entity and historically (Pollack 2005), JHA cooperation is in some senses quite law dependent albeit still sharing many of the characteristics of other areas of transatlantic cooperation.

This chapter explores this deepening and widening agenda beginning with the development of Extradition and Mutual Legal Assistance from a legal perspective. Such agreements demonstrate a high level of cooperation and settled effective practice. There are further indications of deeper bilateral cooperation sometimes outside of the strictly legal parameters of the relationship (e.g., as regards the death penalty). This deepening agenda generally appears to have facilitated further and broader forms of cooperation, for example, in cyber-crime with specifically global ambitions.

In recent times, the ambitions of EU–US JHA have expanded and increasingly attempt to adopt a global approach albeit in many different forms. For example, Passenger Name Records (PNR) and cyber crime cooperation appear to have spurred further global cooperation. The idea of a EU global approach to EU–US JHA and its contextual or broader understanding is outlined here as a result. EU–US justice and home affairs during the post 9/11 period has been subject to broad critique for its scant attention to questions of fundamental rights, their lack of transparency or their problematic governance. The effects of the Snowden revelations concerning the US National Security Agency (NSA) now remain the most significant challenge ahead with respect to the appropriate place of human rights and in data privacy in all new areas of regulation, cooperation and lawmaking.

This chapter thus describes the evolution and status quo of many cooperation and integration mechanisms in a variety of areas of JHA. It begins with an overview of the deepening and widening of EU–US JHA. It examines the evolution from extradition and MLA to contemporary cooperation in PNR and the significance of the shifts. Thereafter, there is an analysis of the unfolding of the global approach of EU–US justice and home affairs, looking at the areas of PNR and cyber crime and security, and then the chapter reflects upon a right-centric approach to EU–US JHA, followed by concluding reflections.

This chapter considers the key features of the first transatlantic cooperation mechanisms in criminal law post-9/11 in the prominent subject areas of cooperation, extradition and mutual legal assistance.

Deepening and widening cooperation

First major criminal law enforcement cooperation

The analysis here may logically begin with an attempt to outline widening then deepening cooperation, but this is not necessarily the exact narrative applicable. In June 2003, the EU and USA signed two treaties on extradition and mutual legal assistance so as to simplify the extradition process and promote better prosecutorial cooperation as part of efforts to improve transatlantic security cooperation following the 9/11 atrocities. The agreements were historic, as they were the first law enforcement agreements conducted between the EU and USA and the first cooperation agreements to be negotiated by the Council in criminal matters (Mitsilegas 2003; Peers 2011: 751). Their negotiation surpassed the debate on whether the EU had legal personality at this time to so act. As a result, many suggested that the agreement appeared to be a step towards the EU being a global player in the area of criminal law or at least a precedent of the EU speaking globally with one voice in criminal matters (Mitsilegas 2003: 533). The secrecy of the negotiation of the agreements and their limited review by parliaments in both jurisdictions gave rise to concerns about the democratic character of the agreements (Mitsilegas 2009, 2014). Similarly, the omission of human rights protections from the scope of the agreements provoked concerns, as did the prospect of joint investigation teams working together, not least the place of personal data within the scope of the agreements (Peers 2011: 751). Nevertheless, in practice their evaluation appears to have been viewed positively with respect to the ability of the EU to speak with one voice (Mitsilegas 2003: 516).

As regards implementation, there were also some variations in the form of the bilateral instruments across the member states. A majority of member states opted for an instrument containing an annex clearly stating the changes made by the EU–US agreements, but there are considerable variations in a minority of states. The member states are bound to the provisions of each EU–US agreement as a matter of law and also have separate but parallel international obligations with the USA under the bilateral instruments. At the time of writing, there were in excess of fifty agreements in place between the EU and USA on extradition and mutual legal assistance, a significant number indeed. This leads to a more specific analysis of extradition.

Deepening: the EU–US Extradition Agreement

The EU–US Extradition Agreement was the centerpiece of the first EU–US Summit held since the Iraqi War, in the aftermath of failed US attempts to extradite an accused flight instructor of the 9/11 hijackers on the grounds of proof of the US claim. The Extradition Agreement is viewed as having significantly widened the list of extradition offenses and thereby deepened EU–US cooperation in a key area. It introduced provisions *inter alia* simplifying the transmission of documents, furnishing additional information, the temporary surrender of persons already in custody, competing requests for extradition, simplifying procedures where the fugitive consented to extradition, the treatment of sensitive information, the transit of fugitives and the exclusion of death penalty fugitives. The definition of the grounds for extradition therein is credited with modernizing its definition through applying a dual criminality analysis. Where there is already a dual criminality approach in the existing bilateral extradition treaty with a member state, the Agreement's provisions do not apply, given that it is perceived as preferable to continue to apply existing and well-functioning provisions. Nevertheless, it is a notable development of the nature of EU–US cooperation as a joint effort. A more specific analysis of mutual legal assistance arrangements follows.

EU–US Mutual Legal Assistance Agreement

The EU–US Mutual Legal Assistance (MLA) Agreement has its origins in several provisions in the EU Mutual Assistance Convention of 2000 and its Protocol of 2001, and is another cooperation mechanism of note (Denza 2003). The MLA Agreement was designed as an assistance mechanism between law enforcement authorities and does not confer rights upon private parties (e.g., defendants). The EU–US Mutual Legal Assistance Agreement amended bilateral treaties where it existed with regard to the supply of banking information, joint investigative teams, video conferencing of witnesses/experts, expedited transmission of requests, the extension of mutual assistance rules to administrative authorities, the protection of personal data and request confidentiality provisions. Article 4 in particular was significant for placing the parties under an obligation to search for the existence of bank accounts and financial transactions unrelated to specific bank accounts and also including provisions on banking secrecy. It was significant for including within its scope evidence sharing for criminal investigations and prosecutions, streamlining of extradition arrangements, central points of contact between US and EU judicial authorities and the sharing of sensitive data, such as that related to bank accounts and terrorist financing. The MLA has been criticized for its provisions on fundamental rights grounds and these concerns are significant but possibly also difficult to discern further for reasons of transparency and accountability, discussed further below (see Mitsilegas 2003, 2009). It has received less attention during recent times in light of the turn to specific rather than generalized forms of cooperation agreements for the transfer of data. This leads to a consideration of the notion of changing cooperation.

EU–US death penalty cooperation: 'soft power' cooperation?

Another legal provision of note but with significantly less legal prominence in theory unlike in practice is death penalty cooperation. While there is a long-standing opposition by the EU to capital punishment and all EU member states are party to the ECHR Protocol 13 on the abolition of the death penalty (Fahey 2014), during the negotiation of the EU–US Extradition and Mutual Assistance Agreements, the death penalty proved a specific challenge for negotiations so as to accommodate EU–US variations, i.e., the EU prohibition on the death penalty within its legal mores. As a result, the Agreement contains a clause permitting the requested state to make non-application of the death penalty a condition of extradition. The USA as a general rule agrees to the condition that the death penalty is not imposed upon EU citizens. Nevertheless, what is of note is that the European External Action Service (EEAS) delegation in Washington, DC has a specific official charged with furthering the EU's campaign against the death penalty for over a decade at the time of writing – thus preceding and post-dating the Treaty of Lisbon with its innovations in legal personality and fundamental rights (Fahey 2014: 374–376). The EU has recently made many *amicus curiae* submissions before the US Supreme Court in death penalty cases, arguing against its application in high-profile cases. It did so in several cases, even those with no application to the EU, thereby showing its efforts to engage in soft power diplomacy in such a prominent setting (Fahey 2014: 374–376). The clause was a significant development in cooperation terms, even if not a strict legal obligation. Instead, its broader institutionalized development in Washington, DC demonstrates the forms of strategic legal development that are possible at the highest possible level of the legal system and in some senses a very entrenched and deepened form of engagement with a close partner. This leads to a discussion of the most significant EU–US JHA cooperation in recent times as to data transfer.

PNR and SWIFT: a one-sided deepening?

Two of the most prominent forms of agreements entered into by the EU with the USA during the post 9/11 period, designed to communicate air passenger data and to target the financing of terrorism, are the EU-US Passenger Name Records (EU–US PNR) Agreements and EU–US Terrorist Financial Tracking Program (EU-US TFTP) Agreements (2004, 2007, 2012, 2010). These agreements, even in later evolutions, have generated much controversy on account of their limitations on redress and their uneven application of US law to EU citizens, not enabling the latter to fully realize their rights to redress and review. The formulation of the character of rights, remedies and redress is distinctively replicated in both agreements in a broad time frame, extending well after a decade post 9/11. As a result, they are perceived to form very prominent examples of the limits of deeper attempts at the mutual recognition of justice in transatlantic relations (Fahey 2013).

One may argue that this cooperation involved an era of deepening cooperation but with certain imbalances of significance. The legal goals of these agreements, especially TFTP, have been explicitly orientated towards US objectives on EU territory, suggesting some dispersal of authority. The agreements seem to contain many non-standard accountability mechanisms in the form of 'New Accountability' mechanisms, a fuller discussion of which is outside the scope of this chapter. Suffice it to say that, for example, the 'Eminent Person' review or EU overseer review constitutes the use of distinctive actors that have operated against the interests of citizens. On the one hand, EU–US Joint Reviews of these agreements have used many information sources, with the EU and US acting horizontally as peers. However, challenging 'oversight' in EU–US PNR appears to entail that a EU citizen is seriously hampered in seeking judicial review through complex layers of oversight at least until very recently, and became a significant issue for the EP (De Goede 2012; Curtin 2014; Fahey 2013; Ripoll Servent and MacKenzie 2012; Argomaniz 2009). The most recent EU–US PNR Agreement is explicitly drafted on the basis that no new rights are created there. EU citizens have also been historically excluded from alleging privacy violations under US law, despite provisions in the EU–US PNR Agreement on onward transfer of data. Similarly, the TFTP subjects rights to broad state-oriented exceptions. It notably masks the EU oversight of the Agreement for reasons that are not explicit or transparent (Fahey 2013). There are considerable legal challenges as a result in assessing the effectiveness of security agreements shrouded in secrecy, discussed below. This account will now move to consider the second theme, namely the global approach to EU–US JHA.

EU–US JHA and a 'global' approach to legal integration between legal orders

Overview

The phenomenon of the global approach of EU law is a complex and uncertain one, with many meanings and possible understandings across policy fields (Fahey 2016). It may indicate relative forms of taking and receiving and the push and pull of law. A distinctive feature of certain EU–US JHA measures has been their global reach and effects, their common purpose in advancing the global regulatory environment and their general efforts at a regulatory push. This account limits itself to consideration of two diverse forms of global approaches to the JHA with significant EU–US dimensions: one a very literal and explicit global endeavor of the EU and US acting bilaterally, and the other also a literal and explicit effort to engage in a global approach to lawmaking, but instead emanating from the EU as a consequence of its lawmaking with the USA.

The global approach and EU Passenger Name Records (PNR)

Following the decision of the CJEU to strike down the EU–US PNR Agreement in 2004, the EP began to press the Commission for a global strategy on external PNR with the USA, Canada and Australia which emphasized better redress and effective legal safeguards, and the Commission's 'global approach' is an important starting point in understanding the development of PNR (Fahey 2016; Commission 2010). Whether the EU–US agreements have actually generated a global approach is a difficult question. It may perhaps be more correct to say that they have ignited here a series of bilateral agreements with substantial imprints of the initial and evolving EU–US agreements such that the transatlantic arrangements form a significant part therein. Thereafter, negotiation of a revised EU–US PNR Agreement with the USA followed suit, and a 'Second Generation' Agreement was agreed upon in 2011 (PNR 2011). It has been described by the European Commission as an 'improved' agreement, enhancing data protection mechanisms therein, limiting the use of data, purporting to fight crime more effectively, placing obligations on the USA to share data with the EU and setting out a detailed description of the circumstances for when PNR may be used (*Schrems*, CJEU 2015). Not without controversy, the EU has been developing its own internal EU PNR system and various atrocities in the EU have driven the development of a EU PNR Directive (Fahey 2016). Several member states, particularly the UK, have meanwhile been developing their own PNR systems, albeit with considerable variations. Significant similarities are to be found in all subsequent EU third-party agreements on a wide variety of clauses and provisions as to rights, review and redress (Monar 2015; Fahey 2013). However, little is yet known as to the judicial view to be taken on the global approach to PNR, however viewed or formulated. An agreement reached with Canada in 2014 has been referred by the EP to the Court of Justice on the basis of its possible non-compliance with the Data Retention Directive decision, substantially similar to the EU–US PNR Agreement (Opinion 1/15). Other third countries such as Mexico, South Korea and the United Arab Emirates all now urgently seek a PNR Agreement with the EU (Fahey 2016). This form of global approach arises from EU–US cooperation rather than explained as a transatlantic global approach. However, it is notable the extent to which EU–US agreements have influenced the content in subsequent arrangements. A very different form of global approach arising from EU–US JHA cooperation may be in the form of EU–US cyber crime and security cooperation, considered next.

The global approach and EU–US cyber crime and cyber security cooperation

The latest transatlantic cooperation in JHA is in cyber crime and cyber security in the form of the EU–US Working Group on Cybercrime and Cybersecurity (WGCC) was established following the EU–US Summit in November 2010 (WGCC Concept Paper 2011). However, the origins of this cooperation date date back a decade earlier to the Joint EC–US Task Force on Critical Infrastructure Protection (Commission 2000). Also around this time, the Council of Europe Cybercrime Convention was adopted, which now forms a central legal element of EU–US cooperation. The EU–US cooperation goals have been predominantly in four areas: the expansion of cyber incident management response capabilities jointly and globally, through a cooperation program culminating in a joint-EU–US cyber incident exercise at the end of 2011, to broadly engage the private sector using public–private partnerships, sharing good practices with industry and to launch a program of joint awareness-raising activities, to remove child pornography from the Internet and to advance the international ratification of the Council of Europe Convention by the EU and Council of Europe member states and to encourage non-European countries to become parties. This came as no surprise, given the commitment of EU–US senior JHA officials that the EU and USA would work together in the UN to avoid dilution of the body of international law on cyber crime (Council 2011).

It seems apparent that the WGCC had first and foremost 'global' rule-making objectives. The WGCC mentions specific countries to be 'encouraged' to become parties to the Convention, countries within and outside of the EU (WGCC Concept Paper 4; Carrapico and Farrand 2015). Another goal of EU–US cooperation includes the endorsement of EU–US 'deliverables' in cyber crime by the Internet Corporation for Assigned Names and Numbers (ICANNs). This latest EU–US cooperation may be said to indicate new boundaries in the transatlantic relationship on account of their global rule-making ambitions, notwithstanding formal limitations on the conduct of the USA as an actor outside of the Council of Europe (Fahey 2014). Unlike earlier bilateral rule-making, this newer rule-making appears to have joint-shared 'global' objectives. The goals of the WGCC suggest that they will lead eventually to the adoption of a global-like cyber policy, or, at the very least, global standard-setting, through their promotion of the primacy of external norms. Instead, this newer bilateral rule-making is distinctive because it does not seek to engage in mutual recognition in justice and home affairs but rather has 'larger' global-like legal goals. This leads to an analysis of the final area studied here, namely fundamental rights in EU–US JHA.

Fundamental rights in EU–US JHA and legal integration challenges

Overview

As the account above in respect of evolving cooperation has demonstrated, not all agreements are viewed in the same light. In the post-9/11 context, the place of fundamental rights in EU–US JHA cooperation has also been thorny. While the US Attorney General Eric Holder claimed before the European Parliament in 2011 that no human rights violations have *ever* resulted from EU–US JHA cooperation, by contrast, certain members of the European Parliament have claimed that the secrecy surrounding the transmission of data under certain transatlantic agreements makes it virtually impossible to assess their operation (Holder 2011; in 't Veld 2014). The Ombudsman has experienced significant difficulties in obtaining access to EU–US governance materials (e.g., as to SWIFT; European Ombudsman 2013). Many civil and administrative proceedings have been successfully conducted by the Dutch MEP Sophie in 't Veld in respect of EU–US agreements on data transfer for security/counter-terrorism purposes (See *in 't Veld vs. Department of Homeland Security* 2008) (2008 No. 1151, US District of Columbia District Judge Collyer) (December 15, 2008); see also T-529/09 *in 't Veld vs. Council*, Judgment of the General Court of May 4, 2012 [2012] ECR II-000; Case C-350/12, *Council vs. in 't Veld*) (Fahey 2016). These developments demonstrate the significance of oversight and accountability and the complexity of discerning fundamental rights violations in the absence of transparency.

The recent NSA surveillance saga has once more placed EU–US JHA affairs cooperation center stage. The outbreak of the NSA/Snowdon/PRISM surveillance saga in the midst of the rule-making processes has in fact operated to place EU citizens' fundamental rights and data protection centrally in *all* rule-making of the EU with the USA, from trade to security (Council 2013). It notably caused the EP to vociferously call into question a range of existing EU–US JHA agreements (EP Resolution 2013). This resistance has now achieved legal significance going forward given the place of the EP in international agreements negotiations pursuant to Article 218 TFEU (Ripoll Servant 2014). For example, high-profile litigation, such as the recent *Data Retention Ireland*, *Google vs. Spain* and the landmark *Schrems* decisions, demonstrates that the CJEU is not afraid to put the EU's fundamental rights centrally in this context (2013, 2014). The Court and its President have been highly vocal, inside and outside of the courtroom, about its role in protecting EU citizenships from the effects and consequences of the US legal order (Lenaerts 2015). These developments have started to have more significant repercussions for the content of EU–US JHA cooperation. For example, these particular developments appeared to have spurred the development of a significant new agreement, namely the EU–US Umbrella Agreement, predicated upon stronger protection of citizens' rights, considered next. Another very significant new EU–US agreement, the Privacy Shield, is not considered here for reasons of its specific content and application, which fall outside of this chapter.

A new era of EU–US JHA agreements?

EU–US negotiations on a harmonized data protection agreement have been on slow-burn for some time until the NSA revelations, arising in particular from a high-level contact group established in 2009. The negotiations were premised upon its legal anchor being a framework agreement to protect personal data transferred between the EU and USA for law enforcement purposes which would be an international agreement for the purposes of Article 218 TFEU and ensure a measure of harmonized rights protections. The lack of equivalent protection for EU nationals under US privacy law was also a significant hurdle to a finding of adequacy or adequate protection of fundamental rights under EU law. The above revelations appear to have had a significant effect. A EU–US Umbrella Agreement was signed on June 2, 2016. The main functions of the Agreement are to put an onus on authorities to do so appropriately or risk considerable sanctions. It strives to develop a system to facilitate claims in the event of misconduct and thus constitutes some form of looser institutionalization. EU citizens recently qualified for protection in the 1974 Privacy Act under changes to US law, which represents a tremendous shift in EU–US relations. The Agreement has not been enacted pursuant to Article 218 TFEU thus far and the role of the EP is currently legally ambiguous. While this must be seen as of significance, fundamental rights still remain at the forefront of this newer form of EU–US JHA cooperation. This puts coherent integration between the legal orders as a key principle thereof.

Conclusions on a future research agenda

EU–US JHA agreements have been shown here to have formed a prolific area of legal integration. They have evolved through a deepening enforcement agenda. The evolution of EU–US JHA agreements must be viewed as having taken effect in waves of deepening and widening cooperation but not necessarily always logically so post-9/11. Cooperation appears to have become embedded in different ways. The significant data transfer agreements (PNR and TFTP) signaled new shifts in the manner and form of cooperation, appearing to give scant attention to the place of citizens' rights therein. The evolution of the integration agenda however has moved on in many ways. Moving on to the question of a global approach to EU–US JHA, this account has considered its multiple meanings, for example, as to PNR and cyber crime and security, and significant shifts are evident here as to the EU's changing ambitions in the world. EU–US JHA cooperation signifies very different levels and forms of legal integration in this context, despite the same global approach goals. Finally, the account considered the developments as to the place of fundamental rights in EU–US JHA and major shifts recently evident in law and practice. While the secrecy and shortcomings vis-à-vis fundamental rights of transatlantic cooperation in security continue to be of concern, the Umbrella Agreement represents an important new departure as to the place of fundamental rights in EU–US JHA relations and a welcome turn in EU–US JHA agreements.

Acknowledgment

The author is grateful to Sarah Lovelace for her research assistance.

Bibliography

Publications

Argomaniz, J. (2009). The Passenger Name Records Agreement and the European Union Internalisation of US Border Security Norms. *Journal of European Integration*, 31(1), pp. 119–136.

Carrapico, H. and Farrand, B. (eds) (2015). *The Governance of Online Expression in a Networked World: Free-speech, Surveillance and Censorship*. New York, London: Routledge.

Council of the European Union (2000). (2000/C 197/01) of May 29. Council Act establishing in accordance with Article 34 of the Treaty on European Union the Convention on Mutual Assistance in Criminal Matters between the Member States of the European Union.

Council of the European Union (2008). 9831/08 of May 28. Final Report by EU–US High Level Contact Group on information sharing and privacy and personal data protection.

Council of the European Union (2011). 16726/10 of November 20. EU–US Summit, Joint Statement Press 315, Presidency Conclusions of the Cybercrime Conference, Budapest Conclusions (April 13).

Council of the European Union (2013). 16987/13 of November 27. Report on the Findings by the EU Co-chairs of the Ad Hoc EU–US Working Group on Data Protection, Rebuilding Trust in EU-US Data Flows.

Council of the European Union (2013). 16682/13 of November 18. Summary of Conclusions of the EU–US JHA Ministerial Meeting.

Cremona, M. (2011). Justice and Home Affairs in a Globalised World: Ambitions and Reality in the Tale of the EU–US SWIFT Agreement, No. 4. Institute for European Integration Research.

Curtin, D. (2014). Challenging Executive Dominance in European Democracy. *Modern Law Review*, 77(1).

De Goede, M. (2012). The SWIFT Affair and the Global Politics of European Security. *Journal of Common Market Studies*, 50(2), pp. 214–230.

Denza, E. (2003). The 2000 Convention on Mutual Assistance in Criminal Matters. *Common Market Law Review*, 40, pp. 1047–1074.

European Commission (2010). Communication from the Commission on the Global Approach to Transfers of Passenger Name Record (PNR) Data to Third Countries.

European Commission (2016). Proposal for a Council Decision on the signing, on behalf of the European Union, of an Agreement between the United States of America and the European Union on the Protection of Personal Information Relating to the Prevention, Investigation, Detection, and Prosecution of Criminal Offenses, COM(2016) 238 final, April 29; Commission, Annex I (Agreement between the United States of America and the European Union on the Protection of Personal Information Relating to the Prevention, Investigation, Detection, and the Prosecution of Criminal Offenses) accompanying the Proposal for a Council Decision on the signing, on behalf of the European Union, of an Agreement between the United States of America and the European Union on the Protection of Personal Information Relating to the Prevention, Investigation, Detection, and Prosecution of Criminal Offenses, COM(2016) 238 final, April 29.

European Ombudsman (2013). Refused access to a document on the implementation of the EU–US Terrorist Finance Tracking Program (TFTP) Agreement Ombudsman. Available at: www.ombudsman.europa.eu/en/cases/summary.faces/en/57623/html.bookmark (accessed July 20, 2016).

European Parliament Resolution (2013). 2013/2831 of October 23 on the suspension of the TFTP agreement as a result of US National Security Agency (NSA) surveillance.

Fahey, E. (2013). Law and Governance as Checks and Balances in Transatlantic Security. *Yearbook of European Law*, 32, pp. 1–21.

Fahey, E. (2014a). On the Use of Law in Transatlantic Relations: Legal Dialogues between the EU and US. *European Law Journal*, 20(3), pp. 368–384.

Fahey, E. (2014b). EU's Cybercrime and Cyber Security Rule-making: Mapping the Internal and External Dimensions of EU Security. *European Journal of Risk Regulation*, 5(1), pp. 46–60.

Fahey, E. (2016). *The Global Reach of EU Law*. Abingdon and New York: Routledge.

Holder, E.H. (2011). US Attorney General: 'We All Want to Protect Privacy, but in our Own Ways'. *European Parliament News*, Press release, REF. 20110919IPR26958. Available at: www.europarl.europa.eu/news/en/news-room/20110919IPR26958/us-attorney-general-we-all-want-to-protect-privacy-but-in-our-own-ways (accessed March 31, 2017).

in 't Veld, S. (2014). Transatlantic Relations and Security – Reflections from a Politician, Practitioner and Litigator. In E. Fahey and D. Curtin (eds), *A Transatlantic Community of Law*. Cambridge: Cambridge University Press.

Lenaerts, K. (2015). ECJ President on EU Integration, Public Opinion, Safe Harbor, Antitrust. *Wall Street Journal*, October 12.

Mitsilegas, V. (2003). EU–US Co-operation in Criminal Matters post-9/11: Extradition, Mutual Legal Assistance and the Exchange of Police Data. *European Foreign Affairs Review*, 8(4), pp. 515–536.

Mitsilegas, V. (2009). *EU Criminal Law*. Oxford: Hart Publishing.

Mitsilegas, V. (2014). Transatlantic Counter-terrorism Cooperation and European Values: The Elusive Quest for Coherence. In E. Fahey and D. Curtin (eds), *A Transatlantic Community of Law: Legal Perspectives on the Relationship between the EU and US Legal Orders*. Cambridge: Cambridge University Press, ch. 14.

Mitsilegas, V. (2016). *EU Criminal Law after Lisbon Rights. Trust and the Transformation of Justice in Europe*. Oxford: Hart Publishing.

Monar, J. (2015). Extending Experimentalist Governance: The External Dimension to the EU's Area of Freedom, Security and Justice. In J. Zeitlin (ed.), *Extending Experimentalist Governance: European and Transnational Regulation*. 2nd edn. Oxford: Oxford University Press, ch. 10.

Peers, S. (2011). *Justice and Home Affairs Law*. Oxford: Oxford University Press.

Pollack, M. (2005). The New Transatlantic Agenda at Ten: Reflections in an Experiment in International Governance. *Journal of Common Market Studies*, 43(5), pp. 899–919.

Ripoll Servent, A. (2014). The Role of the European Parliament in International Negotiations after Lisbon. *Journal of European Public Policy*, 21(4), pp. 568–586.

Ripoll Servent, A. and MacKenzie, A. (2012). The European Parliament as a 'Norm Taker'? EU–US Relations after the SWIFT Agreement. *European Foreign Affairs Review*, 17, pp. 71–86.

Cases

Case C-350/12. *Council vs. in 't Veld*. ECLI:EU:C:2014:2039.

Case C-293/12. *Digital Rights Ireland vs. Minister for Communications*. ECLI:EU:C:2014:238.

Case C-131/12. *Google Spain SL and Google Inc. vs. Agencia Española de Protección de Datos (AEPD) and Mario Costeja González*. ECLI:EU:C:2014:317.

Case C-362/14. *Schrems vs. Data Protection Commissioner.* ECLI:EU:C:2015:650.
T-529/09. *in 't Veld vs. Council*, Judgment of the General Court of May 4, 2012 [2012]. ECR II-000.
in 't Veld vs. Department of Homeland Security, 2008 (2008 No. 1151, US District of Columbia District Judge Collyer) (December 15, 2008).

EU–US JHA agreements

Agreement between the European Union and the United States of America on the Processing and Transfer of Financial Messaging Data from the European Union to the United States for the Purposes of the Terrorist Finance Tracking Program (hereafter TFTP) [2010] OJ L 195.
Agreement on Extradition between the United States and EU [2003] OJ L 181/27.
Agreement between the United States of America and the European Union on the Use and Transfer of Passenger Name Record Data to the United States Department of Homeland Security of November 17, 2011; COM (2011) 807 final.
Agreement between the United States of America and the European Union on the Use and Transfer of Passenger Name Record Data to the United States Department of Homeland Security of November 17, 2011; OJ L 215/5.
EU–Canada PNR Agreement was signed by the EU Council of Ministers and Canada on June 25, 2014.

Other

Cyber-security Strategy of the European Union: An Open, Safe and Secure Cyberspace JOIN (2013) 1 final, Brussels, February 7, 2013.
Working Group Cybercrime Cybersecurity Concept Paper, Annex 1, April 13, 2011.

29
EU COOPERATION IN JUSTICE AND HOME AFFAIRS WITH AUSTRALIA AND CANADA*
New ties that bind?

Agnieszka Weinar

Introduction

Throughout the history of the European Union, both Canada and Australia have cooperated first and foremost with the UK. For both countries, the UK was a channel connecting them with possible EU policies of interest. The introduction of the EU justice and home affairs (JHA) pillar, from which the UK had a number of opt-outs, did not improve the situation. As a result, neither Australia nor Canada voiced any clear interest in that policy domain for a long time. However, since the mid-2000s, Canada, and to a lesser extent Australia, have become more open to working with the EU in the JHA domain. Still, the differences in policy definitions and the conceptualizations of security and justice allow for adhoc cooperation at most, while more efforts are actually spent on building a common understanding of risks, legal frameworks and political cultures. In addition, there has also not been much scholarly or public attention given to cooperation with these two states. In fact, because Canada and Australia do not strike an anti-American chord in the EU, several policy items that would have caused a major outburst of criticism in the case of EU–US cooperation have gone through unnoticed (e.g., Passenger Name Record (PNR) agreements). Indeed, the focus of almost all scholars working on the external dimensions of JHA has been on cooperation with either neighboring countries or the USA.

In this chapter I will outline the main areas of current and possible future cooperation. Since the topic is new, literature that would provide a relevant analytical lens is very scarce. I will start with a brief description of the relevant debates in Canada and Australia. I will then discuss the patchy EU cooperation framework relating to both countries and reflect upon the main common areas of interest. As the major gap in literature calls for an ambitious research plan, I will propose one such plan at the end of the chapter.

Current debates on JHA issues in Canada and Australia

Both Canada and Australia are post-colonial federal states. The fact that the responsibilities for internal security, policing, juridical systems and migration are divided among various levels of government makes it difficult to compare them with the EU's responsibilities in the same areas.

Generally speaking, most of the issues in JHA that do not relate to national security or international cooperation are provincial responsibilities in Canada and Australia. Issues requiring more internal coordination and cooperation with international partners (e.g., cyber crime, organized crime, counter-terrorism and migration) are a federal prerogative. This situation makes it difficult for Canada and Australia to enter into cooperation with any other international partner on justice or policing, for instance, since detailed and binding agreements would also have to be signed, or at least authorized, by the provinces.

The federal character of these states is the main focus of the debates in the JHA area. The division of responsibilities, the efficacy of inter-provincial policing and cross-border policing between the provinces are some of the main issues (Cunningham 1998; Finnane 1994; Hufnagel 2012). Another territorial jurisdiction issue, quite exotic from the European perspective, is the policing of native lands. These vast swathes of land (ex-reservations or territories assigned by a treaty to autochthon groups, i.e., the aboriginal tribes of Australia or the First Nations in Canada) often cross provincial borders and may be located in two or three provinces. They also have their own policing forces (the result of self-government rights), which face a variety of issues (Hufnagel et al. 2012; Jones et al. 2013). Support and coordination of policing in these areas requires innovative approaches, but it also stirs up many legal arguments (Daly and Marchetti 2012; Hufnagel et al. 2012; King 1997; McNeil and Centre 2001). There are similar debates concerning overlapping territorial jurisprudence prerogatives (Bayley 1992). In Canada, the difference between the legal cultures of Quebec (codified law) and other provinces (case law) adds to these debates (Schertzer 2016; Tetley 2003). Both Canada and Australia have had intense debates on gun control. However, the resulting policy solutions have differed: in Australia the gun buyback program resulted in restricted ownership of heavy weapons (Norberry et al. 1996; Reynolds 1998). In Canada, the regulation of gun ownership was strengthened; as a result, the country is seen as a model for gun regulation (Jacobs 1994).

Most known Canadian and Australian debates that sit squarely in the JHA field concern border control and immigration.[1] These are also the debates that seem to resonate most with European policy-makers, which can be a source of some cross-learning. Both Australia and Canada are cases of immigration countries which were able to retain strict control of their borders and pursue regulated immigration policies. Public trust in the border management system is seen as necessary to keep the gates open. In the history of both countries, any perceived loss of control over immigration and borders was immediately followed by an anti-immigration backlash (Knowles 2016; Ozdowski 1985). As a consequence, when it comes to border control and immigration management in Canada and Australia, human rights issues may take a back seat, while pragmatic solutions focused on avoiding domestic backlashes against immigration are prioritized. The next sections will give a more detailed view of both cases.

Border control and immigration in Canada

Canada's geographic position makes it virtually impossible to reach by boat or on foot. Sea journeys from any place other than Siberia or Greenland are long and dangerous. The scarcity of roads leading from the shores inland makes such a journey too risky and too unprofitable for smugglers. The long southern borders are managed by a set of bilateral mechanisms with the USA (e.g., safe third-country agreement). Undocumented immigration in Canada is not a major concern, as it is rather small. Only twice in recent Canadian history did a boat arrive on its shores, causing general (but short-lived) mayhem and prompting some scholars to draw comparisons with Australia (Taylor 2014).

Canada's approach to legal immigration is choice-based. Its legal immigration program has oscillated around 250,000, but as of 2015 it allows for over 300,000 landed immigrants per year (almost 1 percent of the total population). The immigration targets set by the government each year represent a range for each immigration class and are widely accepted by the population. It is a result of many years of policy formation and of the trust Canadians have in the immigration management competence of the government. Any deviation from the planned trajectory can result in an electoral backlash in both directions. The quota system, in which immigrants apply for a place in one of the three categories, is built in a balanced way (from the economic needs perspective): economic class immigrants constitute around 60 percent of arrivals; family class, around 30 percent; and refugees, 10 percent.[2] A decrease in the quota for a given group can result in a backlog of applications and longer processing times. The past Conservative governments' decisions to decrease targets complicated the screening procedures (for security reasons), causing a significant backlog for permanent residence applications in all groups. These Conservative governments, in power until 2015, kept the refugee resettlement targets relatively low, below 10 percent, focusing on economic immigration. Canadians saw this as highly inadequate during the Syrian refugee crisis; Canadian voters demanded higher refugee intake in the election of 2015, which helped bring the Liberal government to power. Since 2016, Canada has decided to share its experience with the private sponsorship model globally within the framework of the Global Refugee Sponsorship Initiative.[3]

As regards border management, Canada's greatest concern is assuring its sovereignty while working with the USA (Smith 2007; Sokolsky and Lagassé 2006; Topak et al. 2015; Longo 2016). Historically, Canada has built its identity in opposition to the USA, often reflected in a more proclaimed openness than its southern neighbor (Pottie-Sherman and Wilkes 2016). Nevertheless, there have been many moments in Canadian history when the dramatic reality of 'sleeping with an elephant' swept the country out of balance.[4]

In the aftermath of 9/11, US authorities made a series of cooperation requests to their Canadian counterparts on border security and counter-terrorism. Even if none of the terrorists entered the USA from Canada, the country came to be seen as a security threat to the USA, mainly because of its perceived lax immigration and border policies. Some scholars have referred to the Mexicanization of Canada–US border politics after 9/11 (Andreas 2004). Only cooperation and an overhaul of border policies could have reassured Canada's southern neighbor. For example, a Smart Border Declaration (signed in December 2001) led to a Thirty-point Action Plan. It had four goals: (1) the secure flow of people; (2) the secure flow of goods; (3) secure infrastructure and coordination; and (4) information-sharing to facilitate the enforcement of these objectives. Canada agreed to a series of solutions that reflected American legislation and resulted in a more impenetrable border, transforming it into a security perimeter (Roach 2003; Topak et al. 2015). Many human rights concerns were voiced by scholars, who saw the plunge into the US war on terror as a threat to Canadian values (Arbel 2013; Smith 2007; Salter 2004). An important example of Canadian–US cooperation is the ETA system (Electronic Travel Authorization). Canada tried to work out its own system and then ended up building a system compatible with the US ESTA (Electronic System for Travel Authorization), thus becoming an extension of the US national security apparatus. This however has not prevented Canada from imposing its own rules for cross-border mobility with the EU.

Border management and immigration control in Australia

Australian immigration policy is based on a pragmatic approach to various migration flows and the ability to set clear immigration quotas for each of them. Over the past decade, Australia has set quotas at around 1 percent of its own population, which is slightly over 200,000 annually. Nearly 70 percent of the arrivals are in the category of skilled and business immigration. Less than 30 percent of the quota is reserved for family reunification, while around 6 percent is for refugees and people in refugee-like situations.[5] Australia is one of the four top refugee-resettling countries and its population generally cherishes the humanitarian aspect of the country's immigration policy. However, popular support for immigration policy comes at a price.

Australia's geographical location is characterized both by its 'tyranny of distance' from the Western world and its central position between Asia and Oceania. Australia has no dominant neighbor, and thus its border management choices are largely its own. Australia is reachable by a boat from the shores of Indonesia and it has experienced arrivals of unauthorized boats carrying immigrants and asylum-seekers. The last two waves that had the biggest impact on Australian policy occurred from 1999 to 2001 and from 2008 to 2014, with peaks of 5561 and 25,173 people arriving in one year, respectively. Over time, the majority of these people received refugee status. Yet, it was problematic for the integrity of the system. Anybody who travels illegally and in the end receives refugee status enters this quota, chipping at the number of spaces available for formal resettlement. Consequently, asylum-seekers-turned-refugees were seen by a majority of the population as 'queue-jumpers', whose rapid receipt of status was unfair to other refugees waiting to be resettled (McKay *et al.* 2012). A backlash against immigration and diversity would have dire consequences in a nation where over 25 percent of residents were born abroad (Ozdowski 2012). To prevent a political outburst, subsequent Australian governments (regardless of political colors) engaged in a controversial policy of deterrence as early as the 1990s, developing and testing each of its components: mandatory detention; temporary protection visas (TPVs); and offshore processing. Currently, the detention of unsuccessful asylum-seekers arriving on boats – if they cannot be returned or do not depart – is indefinite. This policy has been heatedly debated in Australia by human rights scholars (Bhabha 2002; Sampson 2015) and other scholars putting the policy in a broader context of state sovereignty (Gelber and McDonald 2006; Wilson and Weber 2002). Indeed, the High Court of Australia upheld the constitutionality of this solution in the case of *Al-Kateb vs. Godwin* (Curtin 2005).

The Temporary Protection Visa corresponds largely with the European version of subsidiary protection or the humanitarian permit. It gives the recipient the right to work, but not to family reunification, and no access to social welfare benefits. After 2001, it also became virtually impossible to apply for permanent status when holding a TPV. The solution has been criticized as a way for the government to avoid taking responsibility, effectively putting people's lives on hold (Momartin *et al.* 2006). Some also say that it damages the fabric of Australian society because it leaves people without real prospects for establishing themselves as full members of Australian society (Barnes 2003). In 2007, a new Labor government scrapped the TPV temporarily in an effort to overturn the policy of deterrence. It reintroduced the TPV in 2014 following a new wave of unauthorized arrivals, confirming that political divide is not always clear in this policy area.

Offshore processing has so far been the most controversial but effective measure to stop boat arrivals. The policy excises the Pacifica islands belonging to Australia, and, since 2013, the whole mainland Australian territory from immigration jurisdiction for boat people (Foster and Pobjoy 2011). Arrivals with valid visas and permits are not affected. Australia also signed a number of agreements with neighboring countries that allow for the operation of processing centers from their territories. Importantly, asylum-seekers were intercepted by the Australian navy and then transferred to centers in Nauru or Papua New Guinea, where they would await the outcome of their asylum applications. This 'Pacific Solution' limited arrivals to the mainland, where removal is usually more difficult (for example, because the Australian legal framework on human rights legislation applies). The solution became largely unpopular and was criticized by academia and international organizations alike (Evans 2003; McKenzie and Hasmath 2013). In addition, several reports on children and living conditions in those offshore centers brought about a public outcry (Human Rights and Equal Opportunity Commission 2004). Over time, the 'Pacific Solution' lost its public appeal and in 2007 it was dismantled by the new government. As a result, the number of arrivals by boat rose dramatically, forcing subsequent governments to return to previous strategies. Operation Sovereign Borders (OSB), which was introduced in 2013, adopted an even harsher stance. Under this program, asylum-seekers arriving by boat can be turned around and returned to international or Indonesian waters, or escorted to the offshore processing centers (which are currently operated nationally by Nauru and Papua New Guinea, since they both signed the Geneva Convention). The operation uses a number of other instruments to implement its 'zero-tolerance policy', such as bounty payments (for information leading to the conviction of people smugglers), the provision of intelligence to Indonesian police, communication campaigns, diplomatic efforts and a program that buys up smuggling boats (Fleay *et al.* 2016). The OSB has been widely described as breaching the human rights of asylum-seekers and as an erroneous interpretation of sovereignty (Bui 2015; van Berlo 2015). It has also been protested by the High Commissioner on Human Rights, Amnesty International, Human Rights Watch and Statewatch (Human Rights Watch 2016; Maley 2003). The Australian government managed to agree with the US administration to resettle some of the asylum-seekers from the islands to the USA. No such agreement has even been tried with the EU.

EU cooperation with Canada and Australia on JHA issues

Canada and Australia have been treated differently regarding the external relations of the European Union for two reasons: geography and politics. Geography is quite a simple marker of relations: because of its geographic position (neighboring the USA and Europe), Canada is a part of transatlantic relations, hosting a wide variety of European diasporas and mobile Europeans. It is also a direct EU neighbor via the Arctic. Australia is a remote destination, with far fewer non-British European influences (a smaller variety of Europeans have emigrated or moved temporarily there) and no shared border. Trade as a measure of proximity and interdependence is also telling: in 2015, Canada was the EU's eleventh trading partner, while Australia ranked twentieth.

Politics has also played a role in establishing relations. Both countries were prompted to acknowledge the relative importance of the European Communities following the accession of the UK. The EC opened its mission in Ottawa in 1976 and in Canberra in 1981. Since then, Canada, with the strong pro-French voice of Quebec, was able to balance the typical Euroskeptic views emanating from its relationship with the UK. This mixed attitude allowed Canadian governments to invest in understanding the EU as a political being. In addition, since the early 2000s, the European Union seemed for some a possible counterbalance to Canada's dependency on the USA. For Europeans, Canada gained importance mainly owing to French and British ties. In contrast, Australia has always been rather ambivalent about the EU, buying into skeptical British views of the block. Australian governments have not been interested in investing in the relationship with a political being that is seen as complex and impenetrable (Murray 2016). And for Europeans, Australia has been too remote to stir serious political interest. It is still largely perceived as an exotic place.

Both countries have been involved in political dialogues with the European Union on various JHA topics within multilateral fora; for example, migration and asylum are themes of the

Intergovernmental Consultations[6] that take place several times a year and are limited to the main Western countries of destination. In this chapter I will not refer to these multilateral frameworks, which are not specific to Canada or Australia. It is, however, important to keep in mind that EU cooperation with those countries has been traditionally set in a multilateral context and that bilateral relations are in fact something new and emerging.

Canada–EU relations

The EU established its formal cooperation framework with Canada in 1976; it was the first OECD country with which the EU signed an agreement. Back then, Canada was considered an important part of the transatlantic relations puzzle and its inclusion in the wider policy context of the European Communities was seen as necessary (not least because the UK had just joined in 1973). Still, that first framework was very general and vague, focusing on cultural and economic relations. The subsequent political declarations of 1990 and 1996 did not bring about any substantive change to the relationship. It was only in the 2004 EU–Canada Partnership Agenda that both parties decided on a closer relationship, this time including guidelines for cooperation on justice and home affairs issues. In practice, that cooperation was limited largely to political dialogues on various levels. However, Canada was welcomed to work with EU agencies and signed a cooperation agreement with Europol in 2005. On this basis, Canada can deploy liaison officers to Europol and exchange data and information. In contrast to the Europol–US agreement, the Canadian agreement has been seen as unproblematic (Alegre 2008).

Joint Consultations on Asylum and Migration are annual meetings between heads of Canadian ministries/departments responsible for immigration and border control, and the head of DG HOME. They have tackled JHA issues that are strictly related to these areas: migration, asylum, border control, integration, and to a lesser extent, radicalization. The meetings are devoted to exchanges on recent developments on migration and asylum in both territories, and policy solutions and issues to be tackled. An important topic during these meetings was the situation of EU nationals in Canada. The discussions had two aspects: visa obligations and the deportation of irregular citizens of the European Union.

Visa policy has become an important element of EU–Canada relations, especially following the enlargement of 2004, which added many new member states whose citizens were subject to visa obligations when traveling to Canada. At the same time, the new prerogatives on short-term visas becoming a EU competency (introduction of the Schengen framework) made the Commission the right interlocutor on this dossier. Canadian views on visa obligations are relatively straightforward: it is a tool the government uses to control inflows of unplanned (read: unwanted) immigrants. Between 2006 and 2008, Canada lifted the visa obligation for biometric passport holders from all the countries that became EU members in 2004. Nevertheless, the visa-free mobility between Canada and the EU was tested in the so-called Canada–Czech visa dispute (Eggenschwiler 2010). Following visa liberalization, Canada saw a substantial increase in applications from the Czech Roma: in the first year alone, Canada received 3000 applications. As discussed above, the Canadian system is not geared to cope with spontaneous asylum applications, and for this reason it became overburdened. In 2008, out of 196 cases analyzed, 43 percent were accepted. Then, in the first half of 2009, 22 percent of cases were accepted (European Commission 2009). The dispute ended in 2013, when Canada was able to change its legislation and introduce a notion of a 'designated country of origin' which mirrors the European 'safe country of origin'. That was one of the proposed solutions championed by the Czech Republic during the dispute. The European influence on the Canadian refugee policy is discernible in this case. Hungary also brought about a similar issue of increased Roma applications, but the 'designated country of origin' policy allowed Canadians to control the inflow more efficiently. Nevertheless, the introduction of that new concept was widely criticized by Canadian scholars. It was seen as transplanting the worst practices from Europe (widely seen as mismanaging migration) and betraying Canadian values (Reynolds and Hyndman 2014; Taylor 2014). It was also argued that the Romas' limited access to asylum constituted global discrimination (Stefanova 2014).

In 2006, Canada and the EU signed the first PNR agreement. In contrast to the much-criticized EU–US agreement, the first agreement with Canada was deemed to be less controversial, and was even seen as 'a model agreement' (Hobbing 2010). Indeed, its privacy protection mechanisms were seen as solid. That agreement had to be renewed in 2014. The second agreement, with slightly different legal mechanisms on privacy protection, was signed on September 23, 2014. However, the agreement itself has not entered into force because of a more global development: in 2014 the European Parliament sent the agreement to the European Court of Justice (ECJ) asking for its opinion on the compatibility of certain parts of the agreement with the European Charter of Fundamental Rights and the EU Treaties. On July 26, 2017, the ECJ issued a negative opinion, which means that the EU will have to renegotiate the agreement.[7]

All in all, up until 2016, cooperation between the EU and Canada on JHA matters has been rather fluid and unstructured. Alegre (2008) has best described the lack of formal structures and channels in her working paper on the EU's external cooperation in criminal justice and counter-terrorism. Cooperation seemed to take place in a relatively informal sphere of people-to-people contacts and working relations. It is important that Canadian and European officials have been able to coordinate their position on a number of international issues regarding human rights (e.g., the International Criminal Court). As is often the case with unstructured cooperation, it fell victim to the political choices of the subsequent Canadian Conservative governments led by Stephen Harper and was thus nearly phased out. The return of the Liberals to power in 2015 gave new impetus to EU–Canada cooperation on various levels. An example of this was the coordination of positions at the UN Summit in September 2016 on refugees and the situation in Syria.

Also in 2016, the Partnership Agenda was upgraded to the status of a EU–Canada Strategic Partnership (signed on October 30, 2016).[8] Its Title V is devoted to justice and home affairs. This is the first time that EU–Canada cooperation in this field has received guidelines in a legal form. Topics included in the title reflect the EU's definitions of JHA. The chapters of Title V are: Judicial cooperation; Cooperation against illicit drugs; Law enforcement; Cyber crime; and Migration, asylum and border management. Counter-terrorism is a chapter in Title III devoted to international peace, security and effective multilateralism. To put the cherry on the cake, the Joint Declaration of the Summit has also clearly stated several elements of the way forward, which includes the creation of a Platform on Migration and Asylum.[9] One important element that arose during the negotiations of the agreement was the issue of the clause on human rights, the rule of law and democracy. The EU requests this clause in each international agreement it signs and the EU makes cooperation conditional upon this. Canadians felt offended by that requirement. In order to meet their objections, the EU came up with a different version of the clause, accepted by the Canadian side, which is now used in agreements with other countries with a good human rights record.

Australia–EU relations

If cooperation on JHA matters between the EU and Canada has been fluid, EU cooperation with Australia should be called ephemeral. In her account of the budding partnership, Philomena Murray (2016) underlines the reciprocal distrust and antipathy that blocked more formal cooperation for decades. While informal cooperation in international relations or science was getting some traction in the 1980s, it was only in the late 1990s that Australia and the EU decided to issue a political statement on cooperation. The Joint Declaration of 1997 was the basis of growing cooperation until 2003. The Agenda for Cooperation of 2003 included a long list of fields of common interest for the first time, including some JHA domains: immigration and security (albeit defined in more international terms). Historical events pushed the cooperation further and more quickly than anticipated. Terrorist attacks on Australians in Bali in 2002 and the bombing of the Australian Embassy in Jakarta in 2004 opened up new avenues of cooperation. The Australian government stepped up its international efforts in counter-terrorism, which included ad hoc cooperation with the European Union. The Australian–Indonesian initiative, the Jakarta Center for Law Enforcement Cooperation, received funding from the EU's criminal justice program (2009), while the Bali Process on trafficking and smuggling was supported by EU funds in 2005.

Since 2003, there have been Senior Official Dialogues on Migration, with meetings being devoted to issues such as border management, asylum, visa reciprocity, integration, and more recently, radicalization. The Australian approach to immigration, and especially the Pacific Solution, was of special interest considering the EU's own soft borders on the Mediterranean. Resettlement was also an issue: for example, Australians were quite vocal about policies pursued by European newcomers to the scheme, who focused on resettlement of Christian refugees from the UNHCR camps in Iraq. But apart from comparing each country's experiences with immigrants, the interlocutors also engaged in a visa dialogue. Australia took a different approach than Canada to visa liberalization for all EU nationals. In its two-tier electronic system, it granted ETA (Electronic Travel Authorization) to all travelers from EU visa-waiver countries under the 'auto-grant system', while holding the citizens of several member states, which entered the EU in 2004 and 2007, under the so-called e676 tourist visa system. In 2008, a new eVisitors system introduced equal treatment of all EU travelers.

The EU–Australia Partnership Framework signed in 2008 reflected the closer bilateral relations of the two partners and the need to provide a better political context for many initiatives in various fields. The closer links ranged from more regular bilateral consultations on high levels to new sectoral agreements. For example, as regards JHA, Australia signed an agreement with Europol in 2007 allowing for the exchange of data and intelligence to fight terrorist-related trafficking and human smuggling. Nevertheless, Australia has long been seen as not sharing exactly the same values with the EU (Murray 2016). The country was perceived as a promoter of ultra-liberal economic policy and with a contentious discrimination record. It was only in 2008 that this attitude changed (following the election of the Labor government) and a series of more structured collaboration mechanisms were put in place. Among these, the Partnership Framework was the most comprehensive; it also allowed for closer cooperation in JHA fields.

In 2008, the EU and Australia signed the agreement on the processing and transfer of Passenger Name Record data by air carriers to the Australian Customs and Border Protection Service. The Australian agreement was then renewed and signed in 2011. It is seen as a model agreement, assuring even more privacy rights than its Canadian counterpart. In 2010 another agreement was signed regarding the exchange of classified information, opening up even more avenues for a common fight against terrorism and organized crime.

The most recent development in EU–Australia relations is the signature of the Framework Agreement in 2016. However, despite agreeing on closer cooperation, the process left participants with a bitter aftertaste: during the negotiations, the Australian side was offended by the clause on human rights. The clause was even seen as mismatched with Australia's legal system (Murray 2016). Finally, the model (Canadian) clause was accepted.

Australia's cooperation with the EU in JHA is still in the early stages compared with Canada's. However, the Framework Agreement, with a whole title on JHA that is identical to the text in the agreement with Canada, opens up a new road for cooperation: it covers judicial cooperation; cooperation against illicit drugs; law enforcement; cyber crime; and migration, asylum and border management. It also includes a chapter on counter-terrorism in Title III. Nevertheless, we will have to wait in order to assess its implementation.

A way forward

The EU's relationships with Canada and Australia in JHA have been insufficiently developed for decades, for a variety of reasons. Importantly enough, the scholarship on these relations has also been underdeveloped. The EU, Canada and Australia have embarked upon formal cooperation only on non-controversial issues and in a non-controversial manner, and therefore, much of the more controversial collaboration occurred under the public radar (and under the academic radar as well).

What is crucial for our future comparative work is to first understand the different interests and topics of controversy in JHA areas, while also searching for possible areas of common interest. Three such areas seem to be quite obvious. First is the relationship with the USA and the way in which US security concerns have shaped EU, Canadian and Australian policies in the JHA field. We know a great deal about the EU's balancing act between rights and security under American pressure. Indeed, there has also been work on the Canadian and (to a much lesser extent) Australian cases. But a systematic comparative approach has never been tried. At the same time, this approach may tell us a great deal about the power of persuasion, policy learning and rebuttal in a clearly asymmetric world.

Second is the comparative view of immigration policies. Several scholars have already attempted to compare the EU and Australia's maritime immigration controls following the EU refugee crisis (Glynn 2016; Little and Vaughan-Williams 2016). It seems that the obvious topic of interest has been border control. And yet there is much more to examine with regard to mutual learning and policy diffusion in other areas of immigration management; for instance, legal migration, integration and refugee accommodation.

The third clear research gap is on the common interpretation of human rights between the EU and Canada and the EU and Australia, which forms the foundation of renewed cooperation post-2016. It is clear that both Australia and Canada have rather different approaches to human rights, and that they also have differences in this field when it comes to the EU. It would be interesting to see how the parties negotiate the fundamental values of cooperation in JHA and what it might reveal in terms of diverse value systems at the core of the so-called 'Western world'.

Other areas of interest include systematic empirical research on EU–Canada and EU–Australia relations in the area of the judiciary, cyber crime and fighting organized crime (which is also related to emigration from Europe). For the time being, it is a patchy series of disconnected chapters in only a few edited volumes; the growing importance of the EU in these fields calls for a new encompassing research agenda.

Notes

* This work was supported by the 7th FP of the European Commission through the Marie Curie Outgoing Fellowship [grant no 624433].
1 I decided not to include the debates on citizenship revocation for foreign fighters or international terrorists in this chapter, as national citizenship sits squarely outside of the EU's competence.

2 In 2016, the targets were adjusted to 55 percent, 27 percent and 18 percent, respectively, to reflect the public's wish to accept more refugees from Syria.
3 See www.unhcr.org/news/press/2016/12/58539e524/global-refugee-sponsorship-initiative-promotes-canadas-private-refugee.html.
4 This metaphor of Canada–US relations (where the USA is the elephant and Canada a mouse) was used first by the Canadian Prime Minister Pierre Trudeau in 1969 in his Washington Press Club speech.
5 In 2013, in the response to the surge in boat arrivals, the humanitarian quota was increased to 20,000; and in 2015, the Australian government committed to an extraordinary measure to accept 12,000 Syrian and Iraqi refugees in addition to the quota of 13,750.
6 The IGC is an informal, non-decision making forum for intergovernmental information exchange and policy debate on issues of relevance to the management of international migratory flows. The IGC brings together 16 Participating States, the United Nations High Commissioner for Refugees, the International Organization for Migration and the European Commission.

(https://igc.ch/)

7 https://curia.europa.eu/jcms/jcms/p1_402881/en/.
8 At the time of writing, the Agreement had been sent to the European Parliament for consent and its ratification was forecast for December 2016.
9 Moreover, Chapter 10 of the Canada–Europe Trade Agreement, signed at the same time, includes some mobility mechanisms for nationals of the partner jurisdictions.

Bibliography

Alegre, S. (2008). The EU's External Cooperation in Criminal Justice and Counter-terrorism: An Assessment of the Human Rights Implications with a Particular Focus on Cooperation with Canada. *CEPS Special Reports*, September.
Andreas, P. (2004). Mexicanization of the US–Canada Border – Asymmetric Interdependence in a Changing Security Context, The. *International Journal*, 60, p. 449.
Arbel, E. (2013). Shifting Borders and the Boundaries of Rights: Examining the Safe Third Country Agreement between Canada and the United States. *International Journal of Refugee Law*, 25(1), pp. 65–86.
Barnes, D. (2003). A Life Devoid of Meaning: Living on a Temporary Protection Visa in Western Sydney. WSROC and Dr Diane Barnes.
Bayley, D.H. (1992). Comparative Organization of the Police in English-speaking Countries. *Crime and Justice*, pp. 509–545.
Berlo, P. van (2015). Australia's Operation Sovereign Borders: Discourse, Power, and Policy from a Crimmigration Perspective. *Refugee Survey Quarterly*, 34(4), pp. 75–104.
Bhabha, J. (2002). Internationalist Gatekeepers: The Tension between Asylum Advocacy and Human Rights. *Harvard. Human Right. Journal*, 15, p. 155.
Bui, T-M. (2015). Asylum Seeker Policy: Why Australia Must End Operation Sovereign Borders and Build towards a Durable Regional Cooperation Framework. *Ethos*, 23(4), p. 18.
Cunningham, A.H. (1998) North of the 49th Parallel: The Criminal Justice System of Canada. *Criminal Justice*, 13, p. 21.
Curtin, J. (2005). Never Say Never: Al-Kateb v. Godwin. *Sydney Law Review*, 27, p. 355.
Daly, K. and Marchetti, E. (2012). Innovative Justice Processes: Restorative Justice, Indigenous Justice, and Therapeutic Jurisprudence. *Crime and Justice: A Guide to Criminology*, pp. 455–481.
Eggenschwiler, A. (2010). The Canada–Czech Republic Visa Affair: A Test for Visa Reciprocity and Fundamental Rights in the European Union. *CEPS Liberty and Security in Europe*, November.
European Commission (2009). *Report from the Commission to the Council on the Re-introduction of the Visa Requirement by Canada for Citizens of the Czech Republic in Accordance with Article 1(4)(c) of Council Regulation (EC) No. 539/2001 […]*, COM/2009/0562 final.
Evans, C. (2003). Asylum Seekers and 'Border Panic' in Australia. *Peace Review*, 15(2), pp. 163–170.
Finnane, M. (1994). *Police and Government: Histories of Policing in Australia*. Oxford: Oxford University Press.
Fleay, C., Cokley, J., Dodd, A., Briskman, L. and Schwartz, L. (2016). Missing the Boat: Australia and Asylum Seeker Deterrence Messaging. *International Migration*, 54(4), pp. 60–73.

Foster, M. and Pobjoy, J. (2011). A Failed Case of Legal Exceptionalism? Refugee Status Determination in Australia's 'Excised' Territory. *International Journal of Refugee Law*, 23(4), pp. 583–631.

Gelber, K. and McDonald, M. (2006). Ethics and Exclusion: Representations of Sovereignty in Australia's Approach to Asylum-seekers. *Review of International Studies*, 32(2), pp. 269–289.

Glynn, I. (2016). Boat People and Migration Theory. In *Asylum Policy, Boat People and Political Discourse*. New York: Springer, pp. 17–48.

Hobbing, P. (2010). Tracing Terrorists: The EU–Canada Agreement in PNR Matters. In M.B. Salter (ed.), *Mapping Transatlantic Security Relations: The EU, Canada and the War on Terror*. London; New York: Routledge, pp. 73–97.

Hufnagel, S. (2012). Harmonising Police Cooperation Laws in Australia and the European Union: The Tension between Local/National and National/Supranational Interests. *Australian Journal of Forensic Sciences*, 44(1), pp. 45–62.

Hufnagel, S., Harfield, C. and Bronitt, S. (2012). *Cross-border Law Enforcement: Regional Law Enforcement Cooperation – European, Australian and Asia-Pacific Perspectives*. Abingdon: Taylor & Francis.

Human Rights and Equal Opportunity Commission (2004). *A Last Resort? National Inquiry into Children in Immigration Detention*. Sydney.

Human Rights Watch (2016). *Australia is no Longer a Human Rights Leader*. Human Rights Watch.

Jacobs, S. (1994). Toward a More Reasonable Approach to Gun Control: Canada as a Model. *NYL School Journal of International and Comparative Law*, 15, p. 315.

Jones, N.A., Ruddell, R., Nestor, R., Quinn, K. and Phillips, B. (2013). First Nations Policing – A Review of the Literature. Collaborative Centre for Justice and Safety, Regina, Canada.

King, M. (1997). Policing and Public Order Issues in Canada: Trends for Change. *Policing and Society*, 8(1), pp. 47–76.

Knowles, V. (2016). *Strangers at Our Gates: Canadian Immigration and Immigration Policy, 1540–2015*. Toronto: Dundurn.

Little, A. and Vaughan-Williams, N. (2016). Stopping Boats, Saving Lives, Securing Subjects: Humanitarian Borders in Europe and Australia. *European Journal of International Relations*. doi: 10.1177/1354066116661227.

Longo, M. (2016). A '21st Century Border'? Cooperative Border Controls in the US and EU after 9/11. *Journal of Borderlands Studies*, 31(2), pp. 187–202.

Maley, W. (2003). Asylum-seekers in Australia's International Relations. *Australian Journal of International Affairs*, 57(1), pp. 187–202.

McKay, F.H., Thomas, S.L. and Kneebone, S. (2012). 'It Would Be Okay if They Came through the Proper Channels': Community Perceptions and Attitudes toward Asylum Seekers in Australia. *Journal of Refugee Studies*, 25(1), pp. 113–133.

McKenzie, J. and Hasmath, R. (2013). Deterring the 'Boat People': Explaining the Australian Government's People Swap Response to Asylum Seekers. *Australian Journal of Political Science*, 48(4), pp. 417–430.

McNeil, K. and Centre, U. of S.N.L. (2001). *Emerging Justice? Essays on Indigenous Rights in Canada and Australia*. Native Law Centre, University of Saskatchewan.

Momartin, S., Steel, Z., Coello, M., Aroche, J., Silove, D.M. and Brooks, R. (2006). A Comparison of the Mental Health of Refugees with Temporary versus Permanent Protection Visas. *Medical Journal of Australia*, 185(7), p. 357.

Murray, P. (2016). EU–Australia Relations: A Strategic Partnership in All but Name? *Cambridge Review of International Affairs*, 29(1), pp. 171–191.

Norberry, J., Woolner, D. and Magarey, K. (1996). *After Port Arthur: Issues of Gun Control in Australia*. Department of the Parliamentary Library.

Ozdowski, S.A. (1985). The Law, Immigration and Human Rights: Changing the Australian Immigration Control System. *International Migration Review*, pp. 535–554.

Ozdowski, S. (2012). Australia – Emergence of a Modern Nation Built on Diversity and 'Fair Go'. *Political Crossroads*, 19(1), pp. 25–46.

Pottie-Sherman, Y. and Wilkes, R. (2016). Visual Media and the Construction of the Benign Canadian Border on National Geographic's Border Security. *Social and Cultural Geography*, 17(1), pp. 81–100.

Reynolds, C. (1998). Issue Management and the Australian Gun Debate. *Public Relations Review*, 23(4), pp. 343–360.

Reynolds, J. and Hyndman, J. (2014). A Turn in Canadian Refugee Policy and Practice. *Whitehead Journal of Diplomacy and International Relations*, 16, p. 41.

Roach, K. (2003). *September 11: Consequences for Canada*. Montreal: McGill-Queen's Press-MQUP.

Sampson, R. (2015). Mandatory, Non-reviewable, Indefinite. In Nethery, A. and Silverman, S.J. (eds), *Immigration Detention: The Migration of a Policy and Its Human Impact*. London: Routledge, p. 104.

Schertzer, R. (2016). Quebec Justices as Quebec Representatives: National Minority Representation and the Supreme Court of Canada's Federalism Jurisprudence. *Publius: The Journal of Federalism*, 46(4), pp. 539–567.

Smith, P.J. (2007). Anti-terrorism in North America: Is There Convergence or Divergence in Canadian and US Legislative Responses to 9/11 and the U–Canada Border? In Brunet-Jailly, E. (ed.), *Borderlands: Comparing Border Security in North America and Europe*. University of Ottawa Press/Les Presses de l'Université d'Ottawa, pp. 277–310.

Sokolsky, J.J. and Lagassé, P. (2006). Suspenders and a Belt: Perimeter and Border Security in Canada–US Relations. *Canadian Foreign Policy Journal*, 12(3), pp. 15–29.

Stefanova, M. (2014). Safe Need Not Apply: The Effects of the Canadian and EU Safe Country of Origin Mechanisms on Roma Asylum Claims. *Texas International Law Journal*, 49, p. 121.

Taylor, L. (2014). Designated Inhospitality: The Treatment of Asylum Seekers Who Arrive by Boat in Canada and Australia. *McGill Law Journal*, 60, p. 333.

Tetley, W. (2003). Nationalism in a Mixed Jurisdiction and the Importance of Language (South Africa, Israel, and Quebec/Canada). *Tulane Law Review*, 78, p. 175.

Topak, Ö.E., Bracken-Roche, C., Saulnier, A. and Lyon, D. (2015). From Smart Borders to Perimeter Security: The Expansion of Digital Surveillance at the Canadian Borders. *Geopolitics*, 20(4), pp. 880–899.

Wilson, D. and Weber, L. (2002). Surveillance, Risk and Preemption on the Australian Border. *Surveillance and Society*, 5(2), pp. 124–141.

30
THE EU AND LATIN AMERICA
A real security and development nexus or a superficial one?

Arantza Gómez Arana

Introduction

Latin America as a region has suffered long periods of unrest for centuries that has consequently affected its regional stability to a high degree. During the twentieth century, several dictatorships in South America divided the countries internally, provoking lengthy transitions towards full democracies and the implementation of the rule of law in the 1980s. Moreover, Central America suffered various civil wars, resulting in more political and social instability. This led many Latin American countries to establish 'Commissions of the truth' with the aim of reconciling and healing their societies. Consequently, the development of governmental justice and home affairs institutions was confronted with numerous challenges simultaneously. Another key variable for understanding the difficulties in strengthening these institutions is the deep degree of economic inequality. Relative poverty, alongside high levels of corruption inherited from dictatorships, has fostered the proliferation of organized crime groups. Honduras has the highest murder rate in the world (UNODC 2013), and Mexico and Colombia are, to some extent, considered security failures – not failed states – due to the power accumulated by organized crime groups and the lack of control over regions within the state (Kenny and Serrano 2012). At the same time, the European Union has not demonstrated any considerable interest in the region, mostly because it is geographically far away. This created a generalized perception, at least until recently, that justice and home affairs issues in Latin America did not affect Europe directly.

However, over the past few years there has been a change in the degree of EU involvement in Latin American matters relating to home affairs and security issues more generally. If the amount of activity and economic investment implies interest, one might suggest that, on the EU side, the key priority is to tackle the rise of Latin American organized crime groups and their activities on European soil. Therefore, it may be argued that the sudden interest of the EU relates to the impact organized crime is having on EU member states and surrounding areas such as West Africa.

There is a clear tendency in the EU to frame ongoing efforts and past involvements under the security–development nexus. Javier Solana explained the 'new' approach and its policy implications as early as 2003: 'More active in pursuing our strategic objectives. This applies to the full spectrum of instruments for crisis management and conflict prevention at our disposal, including political, diplomatic, military and civilian, trade and development activities' (Solana 2003: 11).

According to the Conclusions adopted by the Council a few years later,

> Increasing coherence between security and development, both at a policy and an operational level, is a process that requires short-term improvements and longer term action. As a step in this process the Council has identified initial pragmatic actions for increased coherence in some of the areas spanning the security–development nexus: strategic planning, Security Sector reform, partnerships with regional and sub regional organizations, and humanitarian aid and security. This is without prejudice to other important areas of the nexus, where work also should be taken forward in the future.
> (Council of the European Union 2007: 3)

In 2009, this nexus was used explicitly for Africa (European Commission 2009). In relation to Latin America, this nexus was first mentioned in 2014 (EEAS 2014).

This chapter argues that, to some extent, the label 'security–development nexus' is more fabricated than real. This, however, does not necessarily signify that the EU is not moving towards a more structured plan involving development and security, which could become a strategy around that nexus. Nevertheless, that will require a coherent strategy developed by the EU institutions with a clear set of policies, achievable goals and a realistic budget.

The remainder of the chapter is divided into several sections: the first covers the conceptual framework and the second is a literature review on EU–LA relations. The rest of the sections focus on the different programs developed in the area of justice and home affairs with an emphasis on the policies in place to tackle drug trafficking since they achieved more funding and planning from the EU side than any other policy in this area.

Theoretical approaches to EU–LA cooperation in justice and home affairs

Relations between the EU and LA draw from broader approaches to the external dimension of JHA policies. Some authors have put more emphasis on the institutional structure and evolution, while others focus more on the type and role of actors.

Institutional approaches: examining the internal–external nexus

Other chapters in this volume discuss the internal–external nexus extensively; therefore, a brief summary will be defined in this chapter. The 2004 Hague Programme created the necessary provisions for developing the working structure of the EU's external dimension in JHA; the Council's strategy aimed to improve the lack of consistency in this policy area. It set objectives that followed a principle of 'geographical prioritization' whereby geographically close countries were considered a priority, while others such as those in Latin America would be considered only for specific issues such as drugs (Wolff *et al.* 2009).

It could be said that, in its external dimension, JHA has experienced an 'issue expansion', whereby the core policy area has developed beyond the traditional actors and issues. Now all three key European Union institutions are involved (Wolff *et al.* 2009). Scholars supportive of critical security studies have denied the existence of a distinction between external and internal issues whenever JHA cooperation is considered (Wolff *et al.* 2009). They underline processes of functional integration that have increased the external development of JHA over time as a consequence of its internal integration, concluding that the higher the level of internal integration, the more likely it is that the EU will behave as a united actor. In the case of drug trafficking, for example, the fact that there are non-EU countries of origin and transit exemplifies the de facto connection between internal and external drug policies. More importantly, the understanding of the need for cooperation between EU and non-EU countries/institutions helps to develop that connection even further to the point where the line separating internal from external policies becomes blurred.

Wolff et al. (2009) attempted to use the model created by Ginsberg (1999) to analyze the input and output dimension of European foreign policy. The central argument here is the consideration of the external dimension of JHA as a system where the different interests of EU members and institutions and the international arena produce a demand that is transformed into a EU policy. The key aspect of this model is the constant improvement of policies by the improvement of inputs. In relation to Latin America, this model may be applied in the area of drug policies, since they have been developed and improved over a period of time considering the views of different EU states and institutions, i.e., the Cooperation Programme on Drugs Policies with EU (COPOLAD). In relation to other JHA issues, EU actions may be considered 'ad hoc' (i.e., the arrest of Pinochet in the UK) and with unexpected consequences that may provoke new EU actions. This means that the EU has not tried intentionally to provoke this input–output reaction but that this reaction has rather been inadvertent and a result of unexpected consequences.

International security network

The concept of the *international security network* (Gerspacher and Dupont 2007) is relevant for explaining the type of set-up that consciously or unconsciously is created when developing cooperation among regions in the area of justice and home affairs. Following the conceptualization of Gerspacher and Dupont (2007: 352–353), this type of network includes four types of actors: first, international actors and professionals whose presence fosters interstate cooperation. In this case, these actors are the European Union in general and Europol and the European Extern Action Service (EEAS) (2014) in particular, together with Interpol and Latin American regional groups such as Mercosur (Common Market of the South), Unasur (Union of South American Nations) and even the OAS (Organization of American States). Similar to Europol, Interpol has contributed to the multilateral approach against transnational crime (Gerspacher and Dupont 2007). In the instance of Interpol, cooperation between both sides of the Atlantic is cultivated for pragmatic reasons and because it is necessary for avoiding the constant use of different criminal justice systems and sovereignty by criminals. The second types of actors are national policy-making actors in charge of establishing and providing security at the local and international level. In this case, this refers to both the governments of different EU countries and Latin American countries in general and their Ministries of Home Affairs in particular. It may also include diplomatic bodies such as embassies in other countries and even national Ministries of Foreign Affairs when cooperation involves other third countries. The third types of actors are subnational police and law enforcement actors who are in charge of enforcing security. This includes law enforcement agencies in different countries, which can be particularly complicated in countries with a federal structure, like Brazil or Germany, or with different sub-regional police agencies (Spain, the UK). Finally, private security companies may come to replace the state in the provision of security and may also provide services to private corporations, such as transnational businesses, particularly in countries that lack political stability. Also, private security companies are becoming more relevant, as the use of private companies such as G4S during the Olympic Games in London 2012 demonstrates.

Cooperation in this domain has shown a weakness in the lack of legal resources for facilitating EU-LA assistance in this area. The legal obligations in relation to data protection for

Europol must also be respected when cooperating with Latin America. In the case of Latin America, the only one is with Colombia (Europol 2009). Colombia has used this status as a bridge between both regions. The creation of AMERIPOL (Comunidad de Policías de América, the Police Community of the Americas) to develop cooperation among police agencies across Latin America with the headquarters in Colombia (Europol 2014) demonstrates the bridge role of Colombia. Another example is the collaboration on malware analysis; in February 2016, a workshop organized by Colombia, EMAS (Europol Malware Analysis Solution), was discussed in front of law enforcement representatives from other AMERIPOL countries (Europol 2016). The use of EMAS is constricted only to EU members and law enforcement from countries outside the EU if they have signed the operational agreement, as is the case with Colombia (Europol 2016). Consequently, Computer Emergency Response Teams (CERT) and the private industry from Colombia and AMERIPOL countries do not have direct access to EMAS; they have to cooperate with the representative of Colombia at the Joint Cybercrime Action Taskforce (J-CAT) based in The Hague, Europol's Headquarters (Europol 2016).

Review of EU-LA relations over time in the area of justice and home affairs

Academic discussions of EU–LA topics tend to include the role of the USA as a consequence of the shadow that this North American country still retains over the rest of the continent. The EU would traditionally avoid going against the USA's security agenda in Latin America for this reason. Therefore the competition between the EU and the USA over Latin America can only be understood from an economic point of view (Smith 1998; Smith 2003: 80). Moreover, according to Dinan (1999), traditional relations between the EU and Latin America since 1960 are the result of the close socio-historical and cultural links between the two regions.

Several authors agree that there has been a clear change in EU–Latin American relations since the mid- to late 1980s (e.g., Aldecoa Luzarraga 1995; Laporte Galli 1995; Ayuso 1996; Dauster 1996; Piening 1997; CEPAL 1999; Hoste 1999; Freres 2000; Youngs 2000; Sanahuja 2003; Cienfuegos 2006). At a political level, the EU's involvement in Latin America started with its involvement in Central America to support and help with the peace process initiated in the region to deal with regional instability. The EU relied on the Contadora group for this involvement. The Contadora group was created in January 1983 to support Central America, and initially included Venezuela, Colombia, Panama and Mexico; later the Lima group joined – Argentina, Uruguay, Brazil and Peru (Stedman et al. 2002). 'Contadora emphasized regional support for an involvement in the peace process. It also focused on economic and social inequality in each country, rather than East–West tensions, as the primary cause of conflict in the region' (Stedman et al. 2002: 357). A year later, in September 1984, the San Jose dialogue took place between the EU and six Central American countries – Costa Rica, El Salvador, Nicaragua, Guatemala, Honduras and Panama. Their dialogue was upgraded the following year with meetings at the ministerial level.

> The key objective of the dialogue […] was to find – with the support and encouragement of the Contadora Group – a peaceful, regional, comprehensive and negotiated solution in order to put an end to violence and instability in the region and to foster social justice and economic development and respect for human rights and democratic freedoms.
>
> *(European Commission 1995: 2)*

Out of this collaboration, a financial contribution from the EU was agreed on in 1985 and implemented in 1987 (European Commission 1995). In 1995, the Commission explained: 'The

Community has always recognized the critical link between the region's stabilization and its socioeconomic development' (1995: 2). Therefore, the concept behind the security-development nexus is not a new one, but its implementation across Latin America is at best, superficial.

The Contadora group eventually evolved into the Rio Group in 1986, and the EU had informal dialogues with them until they requested the institutionalization of their meetings. This took place in December 1990 with the Declaration of Rome (European Commission 1993). The annual meetings between the groups helped build a forum in which the two sides could develop their relationship further. Within the Declaration of Rome, the following areas were included for discussion: commerce, general economic cooperation, science and technology, investment, debt, aid for development, regional cooperation and integration, environment, drugs, terrorism, consultation on global issues, and cooperation projects. Although it was a forum with no legal obligations, it was an important step for the relationship, since Latin American countries at least had a permanent channel of communication. The involvement in Central America should be seen as the exception to EU–LA relations. Traditionally, the USA was the one focusing on security prior to the crisis in Central America, especially during the Cold War and nowadays with the War on Drugs. The EU focused mainly on the trade side of their relations, at least until the twenty-first century.

The role of Spain and Portugal also has to be taken into consideration. Even before they joined the EU, Spain in particular put pressure on the EU's involvement in Central America. Grabendorff (1987–1988), an expert in EU–Latin America relations since the 1970s, wrote about the importance of Spain and Portugal as early as 1987. In any case, when the EU decided to deal with Latin American issues, it was generally accepted that Spain would lead this process, since the other countries had other priorities and key areas of interest (Nolte 2004).

In the area of aid and cooperation, and primarily in the area of drugs, the first steps took place in 1984, when the Council demonstrated interest in the problem and gave the first grants to fund workshops and seminars in different places, such as Brazil in 1987 (Blanco Garriga 1992: 287). Clearly these workshops and seminars do not appear to have been very ambitious, but it is relevant to mention them in order to highlight that even though drug trafficking was causing massive problems in Latin America at that time, the EU acknowledged the problem but its involvement was only superficial. In the twenty-first century, however, there was a change of attitude in the EU, which decided to enhance the intensity of its involvement in the region because it was increasingly feeling the effects of these Latin American issues. In other words, the EU was aware of ongoing problems in Latin America, but its degree of involvement increased only when they became a concern for Europe.

Institutionalization of EU–Latin American cooperation

In order to understand the real impact of EU–LA relations in justice and home affairs, it is crucial to examine the type of cooperation that has developed since the 1990s, as explained in the introduction.

Latin American countries participate in the European Union Development Cooperation Instrument (DCI). The first regional programs were launched over twenty years ago in the 1990s. The 2014 to 2020 Multiannual Indicative Regional Programme for Latin America is currently being implemented (EEAS 2014). The aim is to improve relations between both regions and to contribute to Latin American efforts in the area 'of respect for human rights, the rule of law, democracy and other key elements of good governance' (EEAS 2014: 1) These issues are dealt with at regional, subregional or national levels. For the period 2002 to 2013, the EU provided €4 billion for the development of Latin America (EEAS 2014). The current program has two components. The first component relates to EU–Latin American issues (€805 million), while the second component focuses on Central America (€120 million) (EEAS 2014) (see Table 30.1) Regional Cooperation (EEAS 2014: 2–23). Even though the EU's Development Cooperation Instrument (DCI) for the Pan-African program has a budget of €845 million which is similar to the Latin American budget for the same period, namely 2014 to 2020, it is important to highlight that the African Peace Facility established in 2004 received €1.45 billion until 2014 from the EU (European Commission 2007). Moreover, the European Union together with the member states give around €20 billion in Official Development Assistant to Africa *every year* (European Commission 2007).

As mentioned in the introduction and explained above, Central America had to face worse challenges than South America as a consequence of the conflicts in the 1970s and 1980s. Central American countries are also in a more unstable economic position than South American countries, and the region's use as a drug corridor for traffickers from South America to the USA (UNODC 2010) has created an even more complex picture.

Considering the security–development nexus, the Multiannual Indicative Regional Programme for Latin America aims to support states by focusing on the improvement of justice services for Latin American citizens alongside the improvement of policies in the area of crime prevention, drugs and migration (EEAS 2014). Consequently, the main actions are: 'Support for regional reform efforts, mutual learning and regional benchmarking in the field of integrated

Table 30.1 Regional cooperation

Allocation for the 2014–2020 Regional Programme for Latin America	€925 million
Component 1: Continental Programme Argentina, Bolivia, Brazil, Chile, Colombia, Costa Rica, Cuba, Ecuador, El Salvador, Guatemala, Honduras, Mexico, Nicaragua, Panama, Paraguay, Peru, Uruguay and Venezuela.	€805 million
• Security–development nexus: Reinforcing the capacity of states to effectively ensure security conditions conducive for inclusive development.	€70 million
• Good governance, accountability and social equity: Reinforcing the accountability and capacity of institutions and public administrations to provide high-quality public services.	€42 million
• Inclusive and sustainable growth for human development: Poverty reduction through more inclusive and sustainable economic growth in Latin America.	€215 million
• Environmental sustainability and climate change: Reducing poverty of most vulnerable populations by fostering environmentally sustainable development and improving the capacity to cope with climate change and disasters.	€300 million
• Higher education: Promoting higher education exchanges and cooperation between the EU and Latin America.	€163 million
• Support measures.	€15 million
Component 2: Sub-regional Programme for Central America focussing on: Costa Rica, El Salvador, Guatemala, Honduras, Nicaragua and Panama.	€120 million
• Regional economic integration: Contributing to sustainable and inclusive growth in Central America through an improved regional economic integration.	€40 million
• Security and rule of law: Contributing to the reduction of violent crime and impunity while respecting human rights and promoting a culture of peace.	€40 million
• Climate change and disaster management: Contributing to building more resilient and sustainable societies through better preparation of the region to address climate change.	€35 million
• Support measures.	€5 million

Source: Adapted from EEAS (2014: 2–23).

and Justice and Security-Sector Reform (JSSR), respecting human rights principles'; 'in the field of drugs policies, particularly with respect to their coherence, balance and impact, including statistical information on crime and criminal justice'; and 'in the field of migration and border management' (EEAS 2014: 6). The programs, which will be explained below, are part of this theme: *COPOLAD I (2010–2015), COPOLAD II (2016–2019)* and *EU-CELAC Project on Migration (2010–2015)* (EEAS 2014). The use of the already mentioned security–development nexus by the European Union in this program seems superficial; since the budget is small, these activities do not have a long-term strategic plan and do not create a narrative that demonstrates clear links between the improvements of development by improvements to the security of the region/country.

Another program directly linked to the development of sectors of justice and home affairs is called EUROsociAL, a multi-sectorial program that includes different policies to improve the social cohesion in Latin America. It was created in 2004 during the Summit of Head of States of the countries of the European Union and Latin America (EUROsociAL 2016). Improving social cohesion in the region should help to improve instability, in particular in the cities.

The first phase lasted for five years (2005–2010) and was considered successful enough to continue. The second phase started in 2011 and attracted a budget of €40 million. This program brings together eighty public institutions because the main tool is the implementation of public policies (EUROsociAL 2016); the eighty partners are led by the Spanish Foundation Fundación Internacional e Iberoamericana Internacional en Materia de Administración y Políticas Públicas (FIIAPP 2017). This budget for the entire region is more symbolic than realistic, especially considering the budgets that organized crime groups manage in the region. The role of Spain is again significant. Tables 30.2 and 30.3 (EUROsociAL 2016: 2–6) show just a sample of the types of activities covered. When looking at all the activities included in EUROsociAL, it facilitates the perception of a soft and pragmatic EU approach avoiding complex justice and security issues.

In the area of democratic governance (see Table 30.3; EUROsociAL 2016: 2–6), one of the main topics has been the need for transparency (i.e., Chile).

Cooperation in the field of transnational organized crime

As explained in the introduction, the most developed area of JHA cooperation between the European Union and Latin America is the fight against drug trafficking caused by transnational organized crime groups. After several decades of Latin American countries promoting the shared responsibility between countries that produce and consume drugs, together with those considered to be transit countries, there has been some progress. Europe has agreed with this discourse (Chanona 2015). Indeed, an important step towards the understanding of drug trafficking as an international problem is the acceptance that it is not merely the responsibility of countries of origin, transit and destination to sanction, but that it also requires the cooperation of both regions – an idea that was eventually confirmed in the Declaration of EU-CELAC (Community of Latin American and Caribbean States) of 2013 in Quito (Chanona 2015; Nolte 2004). For instance, in the case of Mexico, one of the Latin American countries most affected by drug trafficking and organized crime, the dialogue regarding citizens' security has created the opportunity to discuss Europe's pursuit of the decriminalization of drugs in Mexico (Gratius 2012). The EU not only agreed upon the need to share responsibility, but it also considered Mexico to be a strategic associate and, as a result, they work together on tackling drug trafficking and organized crime (Rodríguez Pinzón 2014).

However, the EU has avoided an approach similar to the US War on Drugs. For example, when Plan Colombia was being prepared and military aid was requested from Europe, members

Table 30.2 A sample of the types of programs that are being funded by country in the area of justice

Argentina	National training of justices of the peace and mediators in restorative and community justice.
Bolivia	Bolivia is part of a group of nine countries working to create a regional model for access to justice for vulnerable groups.
Brazil	Preparation and introduction of a protocol to reduce barriers to accessing justice for young black people in situations of violence.
Chile	Preparation of an attention and legal guidance protocol for migrants and trafficking victims. Dissemination of the rights of trafficking victims and creation and implementation of action guidelines to orient professional teams intervening in the socio-legal area.
Colombia	Improved inter-agency work for reintegration for persons deprived of liberty.
Costa Rica	Support for the Comprehensive and Sustainable Policy on Public Security and the Promotion of Social Peace (POLSEPAZ).
Ecuador	Creation of a unit for the sentence enforcement phase in the Public Defender's Office and implementation of a regional guide in order to guarantee access to justice by incarcerated people.
El Salvador	Preparation of an initial training module and a continuous training module on the subject of social-labor reintegration aimed at prison employees.
Guatemala	Support to the Public Defender's Office, providing it with a specialized entity for monitoring the penal execution phase through definition of a comprehensive model for attention to incarcerated persons.
Honduras	Design of the Criminal Conciliation Centre model and its implementation in a pilot court.
Nicaragua	Creation and implementation of three protocols for comprehensive attention to victims of gender-based violence: (1) investigation of cases of gender-based violence in Public Prosecutor's Offices; (2) improving attention to victims by the Ministry of Justice; and (3) coordinating the interventions of all the stakeholders in victim protection.
Panama	Preparation and implementation of three protocols for investigation of cases of gender-based violence in Public Prosecutor's Offices; improving attention to victims by the Ministry of Justice; coordinating the interventions of all the stakeholders in victim protection.
Paraguay	Approval and implementation of a protocol to ensure effective access to justice for incarcerated persons.
Peru	Support for building a system of intercultural justice. Three protocols: (1) coordination of judicial stakeholders at the local level for legal aid to indigenous communities; (2) coordination between the special and ordinary justice systems; (3) attention to the indigenous population.
Uruguay	Support for implementation of the Community and Restorative Justice Programme.

Source: Adapted from EUROsociAL (2016: 2–6).

Table 30.3 A sample of activities in the area of democratic governance linked to JHA by country

Brazil	• Creation of a Legal Aid Centre for Corruption Whistleblowers (pilot).
Chile	• Support for the law on data protection and transparency in the financing of political parties.
Colombia	• Approval of the CONPES Comprehensive Anti-corruption Policy document.
Costa Rica	• Definition of an inter-agency coordination model between the government bodies involved in fighting corruption and institutions in the justice sector.
Ecuador	• Creation of a corruption whistleblower protection system and a system for monitoring compliance with the Law on Public Access to Information.
El Salvador	• Support to the Under-secretariat for Transparency and Anti-corruption for institutional strengthening and consolidation and promoting implementation of the Access to Public Information Law.
Honduras	• Inter-agency coordination for implementation of the National Policy on Violence.
Mexico	• Support to the Transparency Network, of which IFAI is a promoter and active member. • Support in the area of parliamentary transparency and political parties in Mexico.
Peru	• Inter-agency coordination mechanism to combat corruption linked to economic-financial crimes.

Source: Adapted from EUROsociAL (2016: 2–6).

of the European Parliament expressed their opposition to the Plan Colombia (Roy 2001), only offering aid in the areas of education, health, justice and infrastructure (Malamud 2004). The heads of state of European countries would not provide military aid for several reasons, including concerns about human rights issues. For instance, the former president of Colombia, Álvaro Uribe, received criticism from European governments and NGOs as a consequence of his policies against drug trafficking due to concerns regarding practices such as the spraying of herbicides to kill plants of coca, arguing that it could affect the health of citizens and that it would not create a substitute source of income (Nolte 2004). Instead, alternative development – such as the reduction of the cultivation of coca crops to grow licit agricultural products – has been promoted since the 1990s in the Andean region by the EU with limited success (Wigell and Romero 2013).

At around the same time that Plan Colombia was being negotiated in 1998, the 'EU–LAC Coordination and Cooperation Mechanism on Drugs' was formally launched in order to develop bi-regional cooperation (Chanona 2015: 163). The idea was to improve cooperation between both regions (Wigell and Romero 2013). Over a decade after this mechanism was created, the European Union took a step further with programs such as COPOLAD (see Table 30.4; Chanona 2015: 165). The increasing connections of Latin American organized crime groups with Europe came to be seen as a threat (Wigell and Romero 2013). However, the EU could be seen as having a slightly contradictory plan, since supply reduction could have been promoted by facilitating EU trade of agricultural products with the region which consequently would have helped to promote alternative development. However, the EU Common Agricultural Policy has traditionally had other goals.

In 2009, after the acknowledgment on both sides of the limitations of their collaboration, the EU and LA launched specific programs to contribute to the EU–LAC (European Union–Latin American and Caribbean) dialogue. This was intended to increase the sharing of information and cooperation, and in surveying maritime areas, customs and money laundering in both regions (Wigell and Romero 2013); also to increase the strength of national and regional drug observatories, as well as to increase capacity-building in relation to demand and supply reduction (Rodríguez Pinzón 2014; Chanona 2015: 164). Transnational organized crime groups in general, and drug trafficking in particular, became a major issue, not just in Latin America but also in Europe, which explains the intensification of the relations and the budget assigned by the EU (see Tables 30.4 and 30.5; Chanona 2015: 165).

The Cocaine Route Programme was launched in 2009 and, considering the budget, it seems to be a priority for the EU when compared to other programs. It includes thirty-six countries from Latin America and the Caribbean as well as some African nations (Chanona 2015). In comparison, COLACAO (Cooperation against cocaine trafficking from Latin America to West Africa) also represents a multi-regional approach, but the focus is mainly on interdiction (Table 30.5). The threat of these transnational organized crime groups in fragile areas close to Europe such as the Sahel, as well as the perception of an inter-regional threat, may explain these programs

Table 30.4 Cooperation programs on drugs between the European Union and Latin America from 2004 to 2015

Program	Objectives	Budget (€)
COPOLAD 42 months from December 2010	To strengthen capacities and encourage the process of elaborating drugs policies in LAC.	6,574,786.74 from the EU
PRELAC I March 2009 to February 2012	To strengthen trans-regional capacities to prevent the diversion of chemical substances. Supporting international cross-border cooperation.	Total; 2,437,075 90% from the EU 10% from the UNODC
EU-LAC Intelligence Sharing Working Group 2006–2009	To increase the exchange of operational intelligence.	514,504 from the EU
PRELAC II February 2012 to February 2015	To strengthen the relationship between the private sector and control authorities. Complement other EU initiatives.	Total: 3,061,300 98% from the EU 2% from the UNODC
EU–LAC Cities in Partnership 2007–2010	To improve policy decisions at the city level on the quality and coverage of drug treatment, rehabilitation and harm reduction.	1,400,000 from the EU

Source: Adapted from Chanona (2015: 165).

Table 30.5 Cooperation programs on drugs between the European Union and Latin America from 2004 to 2015 at the multi-regional level

Program	Objectives	Budget (€)
COLACAO 2006–2010	Law enforcement and intelligence cooperation to reduce the amount of cocaine destined for or transiting Africa (interdiction capabilities).	800,000
Cocaine Route from 2009 to the present	Law enforcement to fight international criminal networks. Thirty-six countries.	50,000,000

Source: Adapted from Chanona (2015: 165–166).

and the inclusion of African countries at this stage. Considering the instabilities and insecurity issues created in the Maghreb, the use of drug revenues for dangerous purposes and the proximity with Europe, transnational organized crime groups could be perceived as a security threat to Europe (Wigell and Romero 2013).

Conclusion and research agenda for the future

As the introduction explains, the European Union is starting to create a narrative about the security–development nexus to justify its actions. However, an overview of its relations since the 1980s demonstrates that the EU only did something that can be linked to that nexus during its involvement in the Central American crisis in the 1980s. In fact, the EU focused mainly on the trade side of its relations with Latin America during the last three decades of the twenty-first century. Only in the past decade has there been a clear emphasis on tackling drug trafficking but the EU's actions do not represent a security–development nexus in this area. Moreover, it has been argued that it is difficult to see a clear plan around that nexus and in fact it resembles a long list of programs and actions with extremely low budgets.

A future research agenda should include an examination of the real impact of EU-funded programs in Latin America. Moreover, it should include a comparison of the type of cooperation Latin American countries have been demanding and the actual offer from the European Union to reveal the real commitment of the latter. As in the case of the African Peace Facility, African leaders requested EU support (European Commission 2007) and they received a considerable amount: €1.45 billion.

The study of the evolution of drug policies that include the coasts of the Mediterranean will have to be analyzed together with the actions of the EU in North and West Africa, the Sahel and, of course, the Mediterranean in relation to other types of crimes that are sometimes committed by the same individuals (i.e., human trafficking and human smuggling). The complexity of drug trafficking when it reaches Africa must be taken into consideration.

The role the new US Administration will have in Mexico in relation to drug trafficking and human trafficking will have an impact upon the EU's approach to this Latin American country. The EU does not want to and cannot compete with the USA over Mexico. In general terms, the emblematic triangle created between the EU, Latin America and the USA in the area of justice and home affairs will have to be persistently studied.

Bibliography

Aldecoa Luzarraga, F. (1995). El acuerdo entre la Unión Europea y el Mercosur en el marco de la intensificación de relaciones entre Europa y América Latina. *Revista de Instituciones Europeas*, 22(3), pp. 761–792.

Ayuso, A. (1996). La relación Euro-latinoamericana a través del proceso de integración regional europea. *Revista Cidob d'Afers internacionals*, 32, pp. 147–164.

Blanco Garriga, T. (1992). Brasil y la Comunidad Europea en el marco de las relaciones CE América Latina. *Revista CIDOB d'Afers Internacionals*, 23–24(Enero), pp. 267–290.

CEPAL (1999). *América Latina en la agenda de transformaciones estructurales de la Unión Europea*. Santiago de Chile: CEPAL.

Chanona, A. (2015). The European Union and Latin America: Facing the Drug-trafficking Challenge. In J. Roy (ed.), *A New Atlantic Community: The European Union, the US and Latin America*. Miami-Florida European Union Center/Jean Monnet Chair. Available at: www.as.miami.edu/media/college-of-arts-and-sciences/content-assets/euc/docs/books/Atlantic2015.pdf (accessed March 28, 2017).

Cienfuegos, M. (2006). *La asociación estratégica entre la Unión Europea y el Mercosur, en la encrucijada*. Barcelona: CIDOB.

Council of the European Union (2007). Brussels, November 20, 15097/07 DEVGEN 243 POLMIL 14 ACP 230 RELEX852. Available at: http://register.consilium.europa.eu/doc/srv?l=EN&f=ST%20 15097%202007%20INIT (accessed March 28, 2017).

Dauster, J. (1996). União Européia: rumo à associação inter-regional. *Política Externa*. São Paulo: Paz e Terra, 4(4), pp. 35–48.

Dinan, D. (1999). *Ever Closer Union? An Introduction to the European Community*. Basingstoke: Palgrave Macmillan.

European Commission (1993). Press Release. European Council in Brussels – October 29, Presidency Conclusions. Available at: http://europa.eu/rapid/press-release_DOC-93-7_en.htm (accessed April 5, 2017).

European Commission (1995). Communication from the Commission to the Council on the Renewal of the San Jose Dialogue between the European Union and Central America. Brussels COM(95) 600 final. Available at: http://aei.pitt.edu/2786/1/2786.pdf (accessed March 28, 2017).

European Commission (2007). Joint Africa–EU Strategy. Available at: www.africa-eu-partnership.org/en/about-us/financing-partnership (accessed March 28, 2017).

European Communities (2009). European Report on Development 2009, *Overcoming Fragility in Africa*. Robert Schuman Centre for Advanced Studies, European University Institute, San Domenico di Fiesole. Available at: https://ec.europa.eu/europeaid/sites/devco/files/report-development-overcoming-fragility-africa-2009_en_5.pdf (accessed March 28, 2017).

European External Action Service (EEAS) (2014). Development Cooperation Instrument (DCI) 2014–2020, Multiannual Indicative Regional Programme for Latin America. *European Commission – Directorate General for Development and Cooperation – Europeaid*. Available at: https://eeas.europa.eu/sites/eeas/files/multiannual_indicative_regional_programme_for_latin_america.pdf (accessed March 28, 2017).

Europol (2009). Agreement on Operational and Strategic Co-operation between the Republic of Colombia and the European Police Office. Available at: www.europol.europa.eu/partners-agreements/operational-agreements (accessed March 28, 2017).

Europol (2014). Europol and AMERIPOL Strengthen Cooperation against Organised Crime, March 21. Press Release. Available at: www.europol.europa.eu/newsroom/news/europol-and-ameripol-strengthen-cooperation-against-organised-crime (accessed March 28, 2017).

Europol (2016). Workshop in Colombia on Europol Malware Analysis Solution 'News Article', February 26. Available at: www.europol.europa.eu/newsroom/news/workshop-in-colombia-europol-malware-analysis-solution (accessed March 28, 2017).

EUROsociAL (2016). CONOCIENDO EUROSOCIALII Mayo. Available at: http://sia.eurosocial-ii.eu/files/docs/Conociendo_EUROsociAL.pdf (accessed February 1, 2017).

FIIAPP homepage, available at: www.fiiapp.org/en/ (accessed April 5, 2017).

Freres, C. (2000). The European Union as a Global 'Civilian Power': Development Cooperation in EU–Latin American Relations. *Journal of Interamerican Studies and World Affairs*, 42(2), pp. 63–86.

Gerspacher, N. and Dupont, B. (2007). The Nodal Structure of International Police Cooperation: An Exploration of Transnational Security Networks. *Global Governance: A Review of Multilateralism and International Organizations*, July to September, 13(3), pp. 347–364.

Ginsberg, R.H. (1999). Conceptualizing the European Union as an International Actor: Narrowing the Theoretical Capability–Expectations Gap. *Journal of Common Market Studies*, 37(3), pp. 429–454.

Gratius, S. (2012). El Nuevo Sexenio en México y su relación (poco) estratégica con la UE No 84, September, *Policy Brief*. Available at: www.files.ethz.ch/isn/152963/PB_84_El_nuevo_sexenio_en_Mexico.pdf (accessed March 28, 2017).

Hoste, A. (1999). The New Latin American Policy of the EU University of Bradford. DSA *European Development Policy Study Group Discussion Paper* No. 11, February. Available at: www.business.mmu.ac.uk/edpsg/docs/Dp11.pdf (accessed March 28, 2017).

Kenny, P. and Serrano, M. (2012). Introduction: Security Failure Versus State Failure. In P. Kenny, M. Serrano and A. Sotomayor (eds), *Mexico's Security Failure: Collapse Into Criminal Violence*. Abingdon: Routledge.

Laporte Galli, D. (1995). La Union Europea y el Cono Sur emprenden la reconciliación. Fundacio Cidob. *Afers Internacionals*, 31, pp. 63–97.

Malamud, C. (2004). Europa y la Seguridad en América Latina. *Jean Monnet/Robert Schuman Paper Series*, Vol. 4(6), July. Available at: http://aei.pitt.edu/8121/1/malamudfinal.pdf (accessed March 28, 2017).

Nolte, D. (2004). Problems of Latin American Security and its Implications for Europe: A German Perspective. *Jean Monnet/Robert Schuman Paper Series*, 4(11), October.

Piening, C. (1997). *Global Europe: The European Union in World Affairs*. London: Lynne Rienner (esp. ch. 6, The EU and Latin America).

Rodríguez Pinzón, E. (2014). México y la UE: hacia una cooperación estratégica en el control de las drogas ilícitas y el crimen organizado. *Real Instituto Elcano* ARI 38/2014. Available at: www.real institutoelcano.org/wps/portal/rielcano_es/contenido?WCM_GLOBAL_CONTEXT=/elcano/ elcano_es/zonas_es/america+latina/ari38-2014-rodriguezpinzon-mexico-ue-cooperacion-estrategica-control-drogas-ilicitas-y-crimen-organizado (accessed March 28, 2017).

Roy, J. (2001). European Perceptions of Plan Colombia: A Virtual Contribution to a Virtual War and Peace Plan? The Strategic Studies Institute. Available at: www.files.ethz.ch/isn/47536/European_Perceptions_Plan.pdf (accessed March 28, 2017).

Sanahuja, J.A. (2003). De Río a Madrid. Posibilidades y límites de las relaciones Unión Europea-América Latina. Barcelona, *Institut Universitari d'Estudis Europeus, Working Chapters del Observatori de Política Exterior Europea*, No. 45, April.

Smith, H. (1998). Actually Existing Foreign Policy or Not? The EU in Latin and Central America. In J. Peterson and H. Sjursen (eds), *A Common Policy for Europe? Competing Visions of the CFSP*. London: Routledge, ch. 9.

Smith, K.E. (2003). *European Union Foreign Policy in a Changing World*. Cambridge: Polity Press.

Solana, J. (2003). 'A Secure Europe in a Better World – European Security Strategy', 15895/03, PESC787, Brussels, December 12. Available at: www.consilium.europa.eu/uedocs/cmsUpload/78367.pdf (accessed March 28, 2017).

Stedman, J., Rothchild, D. and Cousens, E.M. (eds) (2002). *Ending Civil Wars: The Implementation of Peace Agreements*. Boulder, CO; London: Lynne Rienner.

UNODC (United Nations Office on Drugs and Crime) (2010). Mexico, Central America and the Caribbean World Drug Report 2010. Available at: www.unodc.org/unodc/en/drug-trafficking/mexico-central-america-and-the-caribbean.html (accessed March 28, 2017).

UNODC (United Nations Office on Drugs and Crime) (2013). Global Study on Homicide, Trends, Contexts and Data. Available at: www.unodc.org/documents/gsh/pdfs/2014_GLOBAL_HOMICIDE_BOOK_web.pdf (accessed March 28, 2017).

Wigell, M. and Romero, M. (2013). Transatlantic Drug Trade: Europe, Latin America and the Need to Strengthen Anti-narcotics Coperation. The Finnish Institute of International Affairs Briefing Paper No. 132, June. Available at: www.fiia.fi/en/publication/343/transatlantic_drug_trade/ (accessed March 28, 2017).

Wolff, S., Wichmann, N. and Mounier, G. (2009). The External Dimension of Justice and Home Affairs: A Different Security Agenda for the EU? *Journal of European Integration*, 31(1), pp. 9–23.

Youngs, R. (2000). Spain, Latin America and Europe: The Complex Interaction of Regionalism and Cultural Identification. *Mediterranean Politics*, 5(2), pp. 107–128.

31
THE EU–ASEAN RELATIONSHIP
Cooperation on non-traditional security threats between discourse and practice

Angela Pennisi di Floristella

Introduction

It is a common view among foreign policy analysts and practitioners that trade and investment have long stood at the center of interregional relations between the European Union (EU) and the Association of Southeast Asian Nations (ASEAN) (Yeo 2010; Umbach 2008). However, a changed post-Cold War security landscape compounded by the spread of globalization and the advent of more diverse, less visible and unpredictable threats is driving a redefinition of the EU–ASEAN dialogue and agenda. As the contemporary world system has turned into a 'world risk society' (Beck 2002), which has left states more exposed to new transnational security threats that no single country is able to tackle entirely on its own, there has been a growing tendency towards finding solutions beyond the national level. Thus, regional and interregional cooperation have increasingly become a practical necessity to deal with these new sources of insecurity, generally defined as non-traditional security (NTS) challenges.

Specifically, the concept of NTS has gained growing importance as an analytical tool to broadly categorize new emerging threats arising primarily out of non-military spheres and demanding greater international cooperation due to the scale and speed of their transmission as a result of growing interconnectedness and interdepence (Caballero Anthony 2016). These include challenges spanning the domain of justice and home affairs (JHA), such as terrorism, organized crime, irregular immigration and border control, and other soft security issues like natural disasters, climate change and infectious diseases. NTS emphasizes a new perspective compared to the threats that were experienced in the past. *Inter alia*, the novelty of NTS threats is reflected in their transnational dimension and ability to migrate from one place to another through mechanisms such as spill-over and contagion.

This having been said, cooperation on NTS has steadily risen in significance at the EU and ASEAN level, and both organizations have seen their interregional dialogue evolving along new political–security parameters, which had been neglected up until the 1990s. In particular, the narrative on NTS entered the EU–ASEAN agenda approximately fifteen years ago in the aftermath of large-scale NTS challenges. This development has gone largely undetected, however, because at that time most studies were focused on EU–ASEAN discord and tensions over Myanmar, 'which had been branded by the EU as a rogue state with a terrible human rights record' (Yeo 2013: 3). The recent Joint Communication to the European Parliament and the

Council, 'The EU and ASEAN: a partnership with a strategic purpose' (Join (2015) 22 final) does not truly demarcate a transformation of the EU–ASEAN agenda but is only one of the latest examples of the declared EU commitment to engage ASEAN on managing contemporary NTS risks.

In spite of these trends, it has only been over the past five years that the literature on EU–ASEAN relations has started to reflect a broadening of mutual political engagement and recognition of shared interests and security challenges. In this context, a burgeoning discussion has been opened up on the potential of the EU to raise its security profile in the Southeast Asian region working more closely with ASEAN partners to manage many of the new NTS threats. However, while ASEAN influence on the institutional design and evolution of the EU has thus far been largely disregarded, many have observed the rather unilateral capacity of the EU to transfer cooperative practices and institutions to the Southeast Asian region (Portela and Jetschke 2013; Islam 2015; Yeo and Matera 2015; Wong and Brown 2016). Yet, scant attention has been paid to analyze how the ASEAN–EU NTS discourse has evolved over time, especially since the end of the Cold War and to explore what kind of cooperation has taken place thus far between ASEAN and the EU since the two organizations affirmed their commitment to work together to cope with NTS challenges.

This chapter seeks to address these empirical gaps by focusing on NTS challenges pertaining only to the policy area of JHA. Although the ASEAN–EU NTS menu includes a prolific list of existent and potential threats, JHA is one of the key arenas in which ASEAN and the EU have been mutually engaged given its strong regional and international dimension. By closely examining the EU's cooperation with ASEAN in selected JHA fields, namely terrorism, migration and border management as well as maritime security, this chapter seeks not only to broaden the empirical basis of scholarship, but also to connect JHA issues to the wider debate regarding ASEAN–EU security cooperation. To this end, this chapter commences with a short overview of the scholarly debate to date regarding EU–ASEAN relations in the field of NTS. Next, an analysis of the EU and ASEAN development of a NTS discourse is carried out. The chapter will therefore explore the extent to which ASEAN–EU cooperation on NTS has taken place in counter-terrorism, migration and border management and maritime security. The chapter then concludes by suggesting avenues for further research. Key pieces of evidence in this chapter include official documents, speeches and policy instruments that promote practices of NTS cooperation.

The role of security in EU–ASEAN relations

The EU is one of ASEAN's oldest dialogue partners. In most Southeast Asian countries, it is, however, mostly seen as an economic actor and the biggest provider of foreign direct investment (FDI), accounting for almost a quarter of the total of FDI stock in ASEAN. In comparison, the EU political and military presence is perceived as distant and there is persistent skepticism about the EU's ability to develop a coherent strategy and to be a serious security actor in the region. As argued by Cameron (2010: 289), 'the EU is far from being in the same league as the United States when it comes to hard security'. This is inevitably also reflected in the limited attention devoted to EU–ASEAN cooperation in policy fields related to JHA (Maier Knapp 2015). In recent years however, some EU members have championed closer security ties with Southeast Asia (Islam 2015).

For instance, France has diversified its approach to the region from a simple mercantilist one to a broader security engagement. This is evidenced by the speech of France's Defense Minister, Jean-Yves Le Drian (2016: 5), who told attendees at the fourth plenary session of the Shangri-La

Dialogue, a key Asian security forum, that France would encourage the EU to undertake 'regular and visible patrols' in the South China Sea. Germany remains a critical force for closer ties between the EU and ASEAN. The High Representative of the EU for Foreign Affairs and Security Policy, Federica Mogherini, has recently expressed the European intention to deepen cooperation from trade to security. 'Don't look at the EU only as an economic and trade partner, but also as foreign policy and security partner', she said (as quoted in *The New Straits Times* 2015) in her opening remarks at the forty-eighth ASEAN-EU Ministerial Meeting.

Yet, established scholarship has traditionally seen EU–ASEAN security cooperation as problematic due to differences in EU–ASEAN security approaches, historical experiences and regional identities (Rees 2010; Katzenstein 2005). Overall EU efforts to put human rights issues and democracy promotion at the center of the dialogue created discontent on the ASEAN side, thus prolonging cooperation on soft security issues. Furthermore, although a key driver for both processes of regional cooperation was to create regional spaces for peace and security, ASEAN never intended to acquire elements of supranationalism. In the security realm, the heart of the ASEAN approach was rooted in the *musyawarah* – the practice of consultation derived from Javanese village societies – and *mukafat* – the search for consensus-building among members of the ASEAN community. The ASEAN security framework developed around the so-called principles of the 'ASEAN Way', which reflect a preference for quiet diplomacy, consultation and consensus, non-interference in the affairs of others and respect for national sovereignty. By contrast, processes of regionalism within the EU have run counter to ASEAN's state-centric security concepts, the low level of institutionalization and preference for less controversial issues. Notably, under the framework of the Common Foreign and Security Policy (CFSP), the EU has planned military and civilian operations and has deployed armed personnel, police and civilian response teams to manage global crises (Rees 2010).

Important changes have occurred though over the past decade, and ASEAN has embarked on a gradual evolution of its ideas, norms and practices (Dosch 2003; Pennisi di Floristella 2013). In 1998, Thai Foreign Minister Surin Pitsuwan, supported by the Philippines, proposed that ASEAN's non-interference policy be replaced by 'flexible engagement', which would give ASEAN members permission to publicly raise and collectively discuss domestic issues with cross-border implications. On this point, Dosch (2003: 493) has argued that 'even though the concept was not well received by the majority of ASEAN's Foreign Ministers and was finally re-named "enhanced interaction", it shook up the status quo of foreign relations and security culture in Southeast Asia' and opened up the path for the beginning of a new formal security dialogue between ASEAN and the EU. This was also demonstrated by the subsequent adoption of the Strategy Paper of the European Commission document 'Europe and Asia: A Strategic Framework for Enhanced Partnership'. Even more importantly, in the aftermath of major NTS crises such as the Asian financial crisis in 1997/1978, the terrorist attacks in Bali (2002), and the SARS flu epidemic, a new security discourse gained momentum at the ASEAN level. Although keeping the principles of the 'ASEAN Way' as the main pillars of regional security cooperation, ASEAN has recognized the need for a new regional, holistic, integrated and comprehensive approach to handle concerns that are transborder in nature. The Bali Concord II (ASEAN Secretariat 2003a), and later the ASEAN Charter (ASEAN Secretariat 2007), have underlined a gradual shift away from a dominant state-centric security approach and have put a growing emphasis on NTS concerns. The Bali Concord II states that: 'the ASEAN Security Community shall fully utilize the existing institutions and mechanisms within ASEAN with a view to strengthening national and regional capacities to counter terrorism, drug trafficking, trafficking in persons and other transnational crimes'. With the ASEAN Charter, member states also committed to respond 'effectively, in accordance with the principle of comprehensive security to all forms of threats, transnational crime and transboundary challenges' (Art. 1.8). Meanwhile, with the adoption of the European Security Strategy (Council of the European Union 2003), it was also clear that the EU was attributing growing importance to NTS such as terrorism, organized crime and failed states, and to international cooperation.

The growing tendency from both the EU and ASEAN sides for incorporating issues of NTS into the framework of regional security cooperation has brought new opportunities for EU–ASEAN cooperation beyond the more familiar matters of trade and investment. It is in such a context that the literature has explored the opportunity for the EU to play a stabilizing role in the region in these domains. In particular, according to Maier Knapp (2015), the NTS frame has positively served the EU to advance cooperation and normative influence with and within Southeast Asia in the aftermath of large-scale crises. It has also been argued that the soft contours of NTS perspectives may allow EU–ASEAN interactions in the South China Sea dispute, without jeopardizing EU relations with China (Maier Knapp 2016). Along the same lines, other studies (Yeo and Matera 2015; Wong and Brown 2016) have seen NTS as a suitable entry point to strengthen EU security engagement in the region. Thus, being seen as a non-threatening partner with no hard power in the region, such as the United States and China (Weissman 2013), and having acquired skills and expertise in counter-terrorism, cyber crime, maritime security, humanitarian assistance and disaster relief, there is the belief that ASEAN could benefit from European experience and that in turn selected EU policies and institutions could be exported to the ASEAN region even in the NTS domain (Pennisi di Floristella 2015).

The rise of the NTS and ASEAN–EU security discourse

With the 2015 Joint Communication 'The EU and ASEAN: A Partnership with a Strategic Purpose' (Join (2015) 22 final) the label 'NTS' officially entered the European security lexicon regarding Southeast Asia. The Joint Communication included, in fact, proposals to implement 'an extensive package of new initiatives in the area of NTS'. Inevitably, this development raises one important question: does the explicit reference to 'NTS' mark a turning point in the EU–ASEAN security discourse?

In truth, the year 2012 had seen an intensification of EU–ASEAN relations witnessed by the unprecedented number of visits from EU officials to ASEAN, by EU accession to the Treaty of Amity and Cooperation; which provides the main principles shaping ASEAN security thinking and guiding regional cooperation for conflict avoidance and prevention, and by new commitments for closer cooperation in the realm of NTS. This has led to the suggestion that the EU was announcing its own pivot; or alternatively, demonstrating its increased engagement with Southeast Asia, especially by strengthening cooperation in NTS. Remarkably, the EU High Representative Lady Ashton (2013) has also delivered a speech at the Shangri-La Dialogue calling on Asian partners to consider the EU as being 'a true long-term partner on security issues' and exhorting them to cooperate on the basis of a 'comprehensive approach' to tackle new contemporary security challenges. The EU has also upgraded the 'Guidelines on its Foreign and Security Policy in East Asia' (Council of the European Union 11492/12) and has released the Bandar Seri Begawan Plan of Action for the years 2013 to 2017 (ASEAN Secretariat 2012) listing concrete policy measures to address regional and global challenges of shared concern. As a result, the EU appeared committed to strengthen its presence in the region not only in economic terms but also in the security arena.

By looking more closely at ASEAN–EU official documents it may, however, be reasonably argued that the security discourse has substantially moved along the lines of an agenda set up over a decade ago. There seems, in fact, to be no fundamental change between the new

Guidelines for East Asia and the former document adopted in 2007. In terms of security, the EU reiterated its intention to promote 'cooperative and sustainable policies to meet global challenges' and 'to step up participation in regional "soft security issues"' (Council of the European Union 11492/12). Similarly, the ambitious Bandar Seri Begawan Plan of Action refers to the same values, features and security concerns already encapsulated in 'A new Partnership with Southeast Asia' from 2003.

Compared to the situation in the aftermath of the Cold War when EU foreign policy towards Asia was strongly dominated by economic aspects and by the ambition to ensure and enhance a European presence in a rapidly growing region, the events following the 2002 Bali bombings marked an important transformation in the EU–ASEAN security discourse. Indeed, these events have been the first to signal the advent of NTS, specifically transnational terrorism, on the ASEAN–EU interregional agenda. In the 1990s, in fact, there was the feeling in the European Commission that the United States occupied an excessively strong position vis-à-vis Asia and that 'there was the need to embrace the growth of Asia and to match US diplomatic investment' (Forster 1999: 748). Suffice it to say that in the 1994 European Commission document 'Towards a New Asia Strategy' (COM 94 (314) final), the term 'security' did not even appear among the EU's overall objectives in Southeast Asia. Similarly, the 1996 European Commission policy paper 'Creating a New Dynamic in EU–ASEAN Relations' (COM (96) 314 final) was fundamentally focused on stimulating trade, investment and economic cooperation.

In contrast, following the Bali attacks a shift in the discourse took place. In 2003, the EU and ASEAN signed a 'Joint Declaration to Combat Terrorism' (ASEAN Secretariat 2003b), and declared the intention to enhance cooperation within both the United Nations framework and at a bilateral level through the 'exchange of information on measures in the fight against terrorism' and by 'strengthening links between law enforcement agencies'. A strategy paper from the European Commission entitled 'A New Partnership with Southeast Asia' (European Commission 2003) was also adopted. This acknowledged that the international landscape had substantially changed in comparison to the Cold War era and that 'in the global village the EU and Southeast Asia find themselves more dependent on one another, not only economically but also in addressing global challenges' (European Commission 2003). Under this strategy the fight against terrorism and various issues of JHA, including the control of migratory movements, trafficking in human beings, money laundering and piracy, organized crime and drug trafficking, have been considered as strategic priorities of the EU policy towards Southeast Asia.

Thus, though trade and investment remained the core EU interests in Southeast Asia, NTS acquired salience. After all, as was stated by the High Representative of the CFSP, Javier Solana (2005: 3), 'in the years ahead inter-regional dialogues will steadily reshape the nature of international politics and forge new mechanisms to manage global interdependence and tackle cross-border problems'.

In summary, from a security angle, all major documents adopted since 2003 basically recall the convergence of interests between ASEAN and the EU and the desire to advance closer cooperation in NTS arenas. It is indubitable that issues of JHA have formed what could be called the 'hard shell' of the ASEAN–EU NTS agenda. Again in 2007, the Nuremberg Declaration (Council of the European Union 2007) states that the EU and ASEAN aim for 'closer cooperation in addressing and combating terrorism, trafficking in human beings, drug trafficking, sea piracy, arms smuggling, money laundering, cyber-crime and related transnational crime'. In the same vein, the 2015 Joint Communication (Join (2015) 22 final) recommends mutual engagement on key regional and global issues such as: maritime security, counter-terrorism, human trafficking and migration. Despite this unchanged focus on NTS, 'European foreign ministers remained reserved about the policy-relevance of the NTS concept' (Maier-Knapp 2016: 8) differently than in Asia where both the Declaration of Bali II (ASEAN Secretariat 2003a) and the ASEAN Charter (ASEAN Secretariat 2007) make explicit reference to NTS challenges when discussing the above-mentioned concerns. The NTS label appears, indeed, to be less confrontational and more compatible with the principles of the 'ASEAN Way' of non-interference and respect for national sovereignty and, therefore, is more suitable for allowing greater regional interactions in the Southeast Asian context. Inversely, the recent employment of the NTS concept in the EU security discourse towards ASEAN does not seem to reflect substantial change in the content of the discourse; that is, EU official documents do not reveal a new NTS narrative and particularly an emergence of new issue areas of cooperation. Therefore, the next section examines whether NTS has been translated into practical cooperation over the past decade and whether the new emphasis on NTS is engendering new initiatives. The analysis deals with cases of JHA, which have been at the center of the ASEAN–EU security discourse. To this end, terrorism, immigration and border control and maritime security are placed under closer scrutiny.

NTS cooperation in practice: cases of JHA

Counter-terrorism

In a number of statements, ASEAN and the EU have identified terrorism as a strategic priority and have signaled their willingness to cooperate in counter-terrorism activities. In the 2003 'EU–ASEAN Declaration to Combat Terrorism' they stressed the leading role of the UN and committed to implement UN anti-terrorism resolutions and the work of the UN Terrorism Committee. They also pledged to enhance their cooperation by exchanging information on measures in the fight against terrorism and strengthening links between law enforcement agencies of EU and ASEAN member states; that is to say, between the European Police Office (EUROPOL) and between the chiefs of ASEAN's police (ASEANAPOL). Subsequent Plans of Action, such as the Bandar Seri Begawan Plan of Action and the Plan of Action to Implement the Nuremberg Declaration, have also encouraged a comprehensive exchange of experience- and information-sharing, capacity-building, and enhanced cooperation among relevant governmental agencies and academies/universities. ASEAN and the EU have also committed to set up links among regional counter-terrorism institutions and agencies, including the Jakarta Centre for Law Enforcement Cooperation, the Southeast Asia Regional Centre for Counter Terrorism in Kuala Lumpur and the International Law Enforcement Academy in Bangkok.

Against this background, the EU has constantly tried 'to convince ASEAN to improve its counterterrorism measures and is backing these demands with technical help and capacity building programs' (Beyer 2008: 308). In particular, through the program 'Strengthening the Rule of Law and Security in Indonesia', the EU provided support to the Jakarta Centre for Law Enforcement in counter-terrorism training programs. Launched in 2012, the Joint Initiative from the EU and the UN Office on Drugs and Crime for Supporting Southeast Asian Countries to counter-terrorism has sought to enable countries in the region to achieve effective implementation of the rule of law based on criminal justice responses to terrorism. Under this initiative, technical support and capacity-building programs have been offered in Cambodia, Lao PDR, Indonesia, the Philippines and Vietnam for the adoption of anti-terrorist financing laws and capacity. In the Philippines, the UN–EU joint project engaged all relevant counter-terrorism agencies in a long-term training initiative to foster inter-agency collaboration for the whole cycle of terrorism prevention, including intelligence-gathering, investigation and prosecution of terrorism-related cases. In addition, regional cooperation has taken place under the aegis of the ASEAN Regional Forum Intersession Meeting on Counterterrorism and Transnational Crime at which the EU has disseminated advice and shared its domestic cooperative experience, emphasizing the potential to translate this mode of cooperation to the Asian context. The ASEAN Regional Forum is, however, only a discussion forum serving to identify areas of mutual concern. Thus, the best that can be achieved here are non-binding agreements based on the lowest common denominator.

Despite these efforts, operational cooperation in counter-terrorism is still at a very embryonic stage. Indeed, although both ASEAN and the EU recognize terrorism as a common challenge, they still rely on a different *modus operandi*. The EU has developed a much more sophisticated framework and can claim advanced instruments to improve practical cooperation and information exchange between political and judicial authorities, in particular through EUROPOL and the European Union's Judicial Cooperation Unit, and a set of rules to cut networks that facilitate terrorist activities from financing. Conversely, ASEAN lacks similar instruments and any progress in counter-terrorism is hindered by the diversity of the interests of its members, varied perceptions of threats, different political and legal systems, and diverse levels of state effectiveness, as well as by the principles of non-interference and respect for national sovereignty (Pennisi di Floristella 2013). Therefore, it is inevitable that the EU would have much more to share with those ASEAN states such as Indonesia, Malaysia, Brunei, Singapore, Thailand and the Philippines that have already established well-developed counter-terrorism strategies, including anti-Islamic radicalization programs. Operational cooperation is also handicapped by the difficult links between the EU and ASEAN institutions such as EUROPOL and ASEANAPOL, which play different roles and have different functions. ASEANAPOL is indeed primarily a discussion forum for ASEAN police chiefs (Holmes 2013: 157), whereas EUROPOL retains its own legal powers and autonomous budget. Finally, the practice of cooperation is colored by the lack of a mutually agreed definition of terrorist offenses. The recently adopted ASEAN Convention on Counterterrorism relies on an understanding of terrorism according to thirteen listed UN Treaties, while the EU has clearly defined terrorist offenses within the Framework Decisions of 2002, amended in 2008. Problems are further likely to surface within the ASEAN region for those ASEAN member countries which have not signed all of the thirteen listed UN Treaties.

Migration and border management

Since the end of the Cold War, migratory flows have incrementally troubled European and Southeast Asian states, which have been confronted with difficult political, social and economic issues related to unprecedented migratory inflows from war zones, oppressive regimes or underdeveloped countries. In the case of Europe, the Arab Spring has increased the challenge of migration, security of external borders and asylum. According to Eurostat (2016), in 2014 alone there were an estimated 1.9 million immigrants of non-member countries. In Southeast Asia since the early 1990s, widespread persecutions of the Muslim minority in Myanmar, known as the Rohingya, forced nearly 250,000 Muslims to flee and to seek refuge in other countries, including Indonesia, Malaysia and Thailand (Naushin Parnini 2013). Data from the *Migration and Remittances Factbook 2016* of the World Bank report that both EU (Germany, the UK, France and Italy) and ASEAN states (Thailand, Malaysia and Singapore) figure on the list of top destinations for immigrants in the world.

To secure external borders, the EU has developed a broad range of policies and instruments serving to manage the challenge of migration and border control, including the European Agency for the Management of External Borders (Frontex) to coordinate operational cooperation between member states; the European Border Surveillance System (EUROSUR) to increase border surveillance and to tackle serious crime; and the Schengen Information System

(SIS), which supports external border control and law enforcement cooperation in the Schengen states. Differently, the intergovernmental nature of ASEAN has so far not allowed the development of regional institutions responsible for addressing the migration challenge. Furthermore, the limited magnitude of migratory flows when compared to the crisis in the Middle East, Syria and Libya following the Arab Spring has given the impression among ASEAN members that migration is not such a significant problem (Petcharamesree 2016). Unlike in the EU, most countries in Southeast Asia do not have any legislation regulating the rights of asylum-seekers and refugees, and the traditional countries of resettlement are facing refugee fatigue (Petcharamesree 2016). Yet, the EU has manifested its interest in cooperating with ASEAN on migration and mobility issues and, at the ASEAN–EU Senior Official Meeting on Transnational Crime in Hanoi (2003), it was decided that the mission should focus only on: (1) border management and immigration control, and (2) anti-money-laundering activities (Maier Knapp 2015: 70). After all, for both ASEAN and the EU, migration and border management are increasingly associated with NTS problems such as organized crime, human trafficking and terrorism, and strengthening cross-border cooperation is becoming an essential tool to reduce vulnerability from NTS threats in both Europe and Southeast Asia. Furthermore, the fact that Southeast Asia hosts a number of indigenous regional terrorist groups such as Jemah Islamiah, the Moro Islamic Liberation Front and Abu Sayyaf Group has further stimulated the EU to cooperate with ASEAN on this front, especially with reports of Southeast Asian nationals traveling to join the Islamic State and potentially also carrying out attacks in Europe (Wong and Brown 2016). It is in such a context that the EU has increased its practical collaboration with ASEAN countries. From 2007 to 2010, the EU financed a pilot project (€4.7 million) in the realm of migration and border management. The project, which was partially implemented by INTERPOL, has been aimed at developing a more coherent system of border management at selected border-crossing points in the Southeast Asian region. In this framework, information exchange between INTERPOL local offices and the INTERPOL General Secretariat have improved (EU Delegation in Jakarta 2013). The project has also allowed Cambodia and Vietnam to install advanced technology for law enforcement authorities at border crossings (Kennes 2015: 375). With the financial and technical support of INTERPOL, the EU has also supported the development of an Integrated Border Management System in order to facilitate the legal movement of goods and persons and to better combat transnational crime, irregular immigration and human trafficking across ASEAN. To this end, the EU has stated its support for the implementation of the 'ASEAN Leaders' Joint Statement in Enhancing Cooperation against Trafficking in Persons in Southeast Asia' (ASEAN Secretariat 2011) through measures such as information-sharing and the use of technologies relevant to border management and document security.

Building on the first ASEAN–EU pilot project, a new program for border management has also been designed for the period of 2015 to 2018. The program (€3.4 million) has centered on two main components: capacity-building, training and operational activities; and research into easing visa requirements. Under this framework, training courses have already been held, including the INTERPOL training course on 'Enhancing border security across Southeast Asia' to address transnational crimes such as migrant smuggling and human trafficking, and a training course to develop practical knowledge and skills to enhance border security and to support ASEAN countries against potential criminal and terrorist networks.

Hence, there is evidence that there is nascent cooperation on issues of migration and border control. The EU has supported various initiatives, including training and joint workshops serving to disseminate ideas and best practices in Southeast Asia. Yet, despite these achievements, information exchange between ASEAN–EU law enforcement agencies and authorities remains largely outside of the cooperation process.

Maritime security

Maritime security is a key security priority for both the EU and ASEAN, which share an interest in protecting their member states against NTS threats in the global maritime domain, such as organized crime, trafficking in persons, terrorism, piracy and threats to freedom of navigation. Remarkably for ASEAN, the importance of maritime cooperation is underlined by the fact that the region is home to some of the busiest and most strategically crucial sea lanes in the world. Fuel imports from the Middle East and trade between the economies in East Asia extensively depend on the Malacca Straits and the South China Sea (The Jakarta Post 2012). Energy supplies, raw materials and goods transiting these waters are also of vital importance for the EU. Notably, almost 50 percent of world shipping passes through the South China Sea (Joint 2015 (22) final). It is no wonder that ensuring maritime security in these critical passages and preventing NTS threats that may paralyze trade and supplies is a common EU–ASEAN concern.

Although the importance of cooperating actively in this domain has been highlighted since the ASEAN–EU conference on Maritime Security (2002), and by official documents such as 'The New Partnership in Southeast Asia' (2003), it is the Bandar Seri Begawan Plan of Action that clearly sets out guidelines to move forward the EU's contribution to ASEAN maritime security. These guidelines are, among others: the promotion of the exchange of experience, knowledge-sharing and enterprise in the sustainable joint management of maritime resources, and cooperation in combatting sea piracy, armed robbery against ships and arms smuggling.

However, at the moment ASEAN and the EU have only engaged in extensive discussions on maritime-related issues under the auspices of the EU–ASEAN High-level Dialogue launched in 2013 to facilitate discussion among high-level representatives and experts from ASEAN and the EU. The first forum, which was held in Jakarta, has been an exchange of views, best practices and lessons learned on piracy, maritime surveillance, port security and the joint management of resources. It was followed by a second high-level dialogue with the theme 'Developing Inter-agency and Region Cooperation' held in 2015 in Kuala Lumpur. In September 2016, a third high-level dialogue emphasized the means to strengthen dialogue and cooperation on: how to enhance trust and confidence in maritime areas and the role of preventive diplomacy in reducing tensions; maritime situation awareness; exchanges of information and intelligence; and piracy, robbery at sea, and protection of ports.

Yet, as noted by Youngs (2015: 26), 'participating in a dialogue on maritime security is a welcome advance but hardly constitutes a security strategy'. In 2014, the EU adopted a maritime security strategy and declared its willingness to promote interregional cooperation with ASEAN by promoting exercises and training, capacity-building initiatives and activities in the realm of criminal justice and maritime law enforcement. However, despite this rhetoric, ASEAN–EU maritime cooperation has thus far remained limited if not inexistent. There is no evidence of coordinated training and patrols, nor of information- and intelligence-sharing. The EU does not play a significant role in the South China Sea either in ensuring the freedom of navigation or in the dispute regarding the overlapping territorial claims of China, Vietnam, Taiwan, Malaysia, the Philippines and Brunei. While it rhetorically calls for peaceful means and the rule of law, the EU lacks concrete instruments to back up this call.

Conclusions and further avenues for research

This chapter has shown that NTS is not a novelty in EU–ASEAN security discourse and that strengthening NTS cooperation has been the *leitmotif* of the EU–ASEAN dialogue for more than a decade. The discussion on the three cases of JHA in counter-terrorism, migration and border management and maritime security has demonstrated, however, that though these concerns have formally been on the ASEAN–EU security agenda since the beginning of 2000, in practice they encounter much resistance. Then, although on numerous occasions ASEAN and the EU have announced the political will to cooperate in NTS, their different *modus operandi* and diverse security approaches render it difficult to advance concrete operational measures to ensure cooperation among law enforcement and intelligence agencies, regional militaries and their navies.

Open questions for conducting further research into ASEAN–EU NTS and JHA domains are plentiful. Other impediments to EU–ASEAN NTS cooperation should be investigated. In particular, one should examine the long-term commitment of EU NTS policy in Southeast Asia given that the EU is, indeed, facing huge challenges both within its own borders and its immediate neighborhood, notably North Africa and the Middle East, as well as experiencing limited resources in qualitative and quantitative terms, *inter alia*, insufficient economic resources, inadequate operational capacities, and limited personnel and expertise. Furthermore, work should be carried out to evaluate the consistency between the EU's political declarations towards ASEAN and Mogherini's recently launched EU security strategy entitled 'The European Union in a Changing Global Environment', which mentions ASEAN only twice, thus suggesting that the EU–ASEAN partnership is not a key priority for EU foreign policy. On the other hand, more analysis is also needed to examine opportunities for interregional cooperation in terms of possibilities to transfer best practices of JHA and other NTS concerns. Studies should also theoretically engage with the concept of NTS from a comparative perspective. Recently, NTS has become a catch-all term to denote non-conventional security threats. Its use may however be subject to different interpretations in the EU and ASEAN context.

In conclusion, unless well-conceived training activities, workshops and dissemination of best practices are implemented in concrete operational initiatives and intelligence-sharing, the ASEAN–EU practice will remain a glass half full, inadequate to deal with the urgency of contemporary NTS.

Bibliography

ASEAN Secretariat (2003a). Declaration of ASEAN Concord II. Bali, Indonesia.
ASEAN Secretariat (2003b). Joint Declaration on Co-operation to Combat Terrorism. Fourteenth ASEAN–EU Ministerial Meeting, Brussels.
ASEAN Secretariat (2007). The ASEAN Charter. Jakarta.
ASEAN Secretariat (2011). ASEAN Leaders' Joint Statement in Enhancing Cooperation against Trafficking in Persons in Southeast Asia. Jakarta.
ASEAN Secretariat (2012). Bandar Seri Begawan Plan of Action to Strengthen the ASEAN–EU Enhanced Partnership. Jakarta.
Ashton, C. (2013). Defending National Interests, Preventing Conflict. Speech delivered by the EU High Representative at the Shangri-La Dialogue, Singapore. Available at: www.consilium.europa.eu/uedocs/cms_Data/docs/pressdata/EN/foraff/137368.pdf (accessed July 20, 2016).
Beck, U. (2002). The Terrorist Threat: World Risk Society Revisited. *Theory, Culture Society*, 19(4), pp. 39–45.
Beyer, C. (2008). The European Union as a Security Policy Actor: The Case of Counterterrorism. *European Foreign Affairs Review*, 13, pp. 293–315.
Caballero Anthony, M. (2016). *An Introduction to Non Traditional Security Studies. A Transnational Approach*. London: Sage.
Cameron, F. (2010). The Geopolitics of Asia – What Role for the European Union? *International Politics*, 47(3/4), pp. 276–292.
Council of the European Union (2003). A Secure Europe in a Better World. European Security Strategy, Brussels.

Council of the European Union (2007). Nuremberg Declaration on an EU–ASEAN Enhanced Partnership, 7588/07.
Forster, A. (1999). The European Union in South-East Asia: Continuity and Change in Turbulent Times. *International Affairs*, 75(4), pp. 743–758.
Dosch, J. (2003). Changing Security Cultures in Europe and Southeast Asia. Implications for Interregionalism. *Asia Europe Journal*, 1, pp. 483–501.
EU Delegation in Jakarta (2013). EU–ASEAN Natural Partners. Available at: www.eeas.europa.eu/asean/docs/eu_asean_natural_partners_en.pdf (accessed May 8, 2016).
European Commission (2003). A New Partnership with South East Asia. COM/2003/399 final.
Eurostat (2016) Migration and Migrant Population Statistics. Available at: http://ec.europa.eu/eurostat/statistics-explained/index.php/Migration_and_migrant_population_statistics (accessed October 24, 2016).
Holmes, L. (2013). Dealing with Terrorism, Corruption and Organised Crime: The EU and Asia. In T. Christiansen, E. Kirchner and P.B. Murray (eds), *The Palgrave Handbook of EU–Asia Relations*. Basingstoke: Palgrave Macmillan, pp. 143–164.
Islam, S. (2015). A New Momentum in EU–ASEAN Relations. Drivers, Risks, the Way Forward. In L. Brennan and P. Murray (eds), *Drivers of Integration and Regionalism in Europe and Asia*. London: Routledge, pp. 289–308.
Katzenstein, P. (2005). *A World of Regions. Asia and Europe in the American Imperium*. Ithaca, NY: Cornell University Press.
Kennes, W. (2015). ASEAN and the EU. An Evolving and Solid Partnership. In L. Brennan and P. Murray (eds), *Drivers of Integration and Regionalism in Europe and Asia*. London: Routledge, pp. 366–384.
Le Drian, J-I. (2016). 'Fourth Plenary Session: The Challenges of Conflict Resolution'. Fifteenth Asia Security Summit, the International Institute for Strategic Studies (IISS), the Fifteenth Shangri-La Dialogue.
Maier Knapp, N. (2015). *Southeast Asia and the European Union. Non Traditional Security Crises and Cooperation*. New York: Routledge.
Maier Knapp, N. (2016). The Non-traditional Security Concept and the EU-ASEAN Relationship against the Backdrop of China's Rise. *The Pacific Review*, 29(3), pp. 411–430.
Mogherini, F. (2015). As quoted by the New Straits Times Online, EU–ASEAN Cooperation Must Move beyond Trade. Available at: www.nst.com.my/news/2015/09/eu-asean-cooperation-must-move-beyond-trade (accessed October 20, 2016).
Naushin Parnini, S. (2013). The Crisis of the Rohingya as a Muslim Minority in Myanmar and Bilateral Relations with Bangladesh. *Journal of Muslim Minority Affairs*, 33(2), pp. 282–297.
Pennisi di Floristella, A. (2013). Are Non-traditional Security Challenges Leading Regional Organizations towards Greater Convergence? *Asia Europe Journal*, 11(1), pp. 21–38.
Pennisi di Floristella, A. (2015). Building the ASEAN Center for Humanitarian Assistance. KFG Working Paper No. 62. KFG, The Transformative Power of Europe, Freie Universität Berlin.
Petcharamesree, S. (2016). ASEAN and its Approach to Forced Migration Issues. *The International Journal of Human Rights*, 20(2), pp. 173–190.
Portela, C. and Jetschke, A. (2013). ASEAN–EU Relations: From Regional Integration Assistance to Security Significance. GIGA Focus No. 3, Hamburg.
Rees, N. (2010). EU and ASEAN, Issues of Regional Security. *International Politics*, 47(3/4), pp. 402–418.
Solana, J. (2005). The Future of the European Union as an International Actor, Available at: www.consilium.europa.eu/uedocs/cms_data/docs/pressdata/en/articles/84349.pdf (accessed July 10, 2016).
The Jakarta Post (2012). Maritime Security Cooperation in Southeast Asia. Available at: www.thejakartapost.com/news/2012/02/08/maritime-security-cooperation-southeast-asia.html (accessed August 15, 2016).
Umbach, F (2008). Asian–European Relations: More Security through Inter- and Transregional Relations? In J. Rüland, G. Schubert, G. Schuchert and C. Storz (eds), *Asian–European Relations: Building Blocks for Global Governance?* London: Routledge, pp. 114–142.
Weissman, M. (2013). A European Strategy Towards East Asia. UI Occasional Paper, Swedish Institute of International Affairs, Stockholm.
Wong, R. and Brown, S. (2016). Stepping Up EU–ASEAN Cooperation in NTS. In O. Gipner (ed.), *Changing Waters Towards a New EU Asia Strategy*. LSE Ideas Special Report, London.
Yeo, L.H. (2010). The EU as a Security Actor in Southeast Asia. Panorama: Insights into Asian and European Affairs, Konrad Adenauer Stiftung, Singapore.

Yeo, L.H. (2013). How Should ASEAN Engage the European Union? Reflections on ASEAN's External Relations. Working Paper No. 13, EU–Asia Centre, Singapore.

Yeo, L.H. and Matera, M. (2015). The EU and ASEAN – Seeking a New Regional Paradigm. In L. Brennan and P. Murray (eds), *Drivers of Integration and Regionalism in Europe and Asia*. London: Routledge, pp. 270–288.

Youngs, R. (2015). Keeping EU–Asia Reengagement on Track. Carnegie Endowment for International Peace, Washington, DC.

PART V

EU institutions and decision-making dynamics (the vertical dimension)

32
THE EUROPEAN PARLIAMENT IN JUSTICE AND HOME AFFAIRS

Becoming more realistic at the expense of human rights?

Ariadna Ripoll Servent

Introduction

There is no other EU institution that has changed its shape and functions as much as the European Parliament (EP). From a consultative assembly composed of representatives of national parliaments it has grown into a much larger institution, with 751 members (MEPs) directly elected by EU citizens and a complex internal organization. It now plays a crucial role when deciding on EU legislation, the budget as well as the appointment and accountability of other organs, particularly the Commission.

This process of empowerment has been even swifter in justice and home affairs: when a third pillar dealing with internal security policies was introduced in the Treaty of Maastricht, the European Parliament was excluded from exerting any sort of influence over legislation. It only enjoyed a right to provide a non-binding opinion. This has radically changed over time, with a gradual 'communitarization' of JHA between 2005 and 2009. The European Parliament now enjoys the right to co-decide with the Council over highly sensitive areas, such as migration, data protection and counter-terrorism. It also has the right to have a say over the budget, which has grown increasingly important as the EU has increased its funding of migration and security policies, and over the appointment and control of regulatory agencies acting in the JHA field (see Chapter 37).

Despite this swift process of empowerment, does the EP exert any sort of influence over policy outputs? This chapter examines the major changes in the nature of the European Parliament and considers the theoretical instruments necessary to understand whether and how these institutional changes have an impact on the way it behaves in policy-making. Understanding this is particularly important, since the European Parliament has enjoyed a long-standing reputation for its liberal and rights-enhancing positions (Elsen 2010). I examine here why the EP has struggled lately to maintain this reputation and shifted to more pragmatic behavior that has brought it closer to the restrictive positions of member states.

The European Parliament: from talking shop to co-decider

The European Parliament is a great example of formal and informal institutional change. Its evolution has been gradual, but it has resulted in an institution of a drastically different nature to what had been foreseen in the Treaty of Paris (1951). At the outset, the European Parliament was known as the Assembly of the European Coal and Steel Community and its aim was to provide the new community with more democratic accountability (Rittberger 2009). With the Treaty of Rome (1957), it became the Common Assembly for the three communities, but it was still composed of representatives of national parliaments and had only very limited rights when it came to decision-making. It is, therefore, remarkable that what became known as the 'European Parliament' in 1962 has managed over the years to transform the EU into a bicameral system, where most decisions cannot be passed without its agreement.

This path has been long and rocky, but it has demonstrated a remarkable ability of MEPs to interpret formal norms to expand its influence informally and to use its democratic credentials to claim more powers. The first major turning point spanned the 1970s, when the EP managed to gain some say in budgetary decisions and became the only directly elected EU institution in 1978. This imbued it with a new form of legitimacy that was used to claim further legislative powers in the Single European Act (1986), which introduced two new decision-making procedures: the cooperation procedure, which allowed the EP to propose amendments to new legislation, and the assent procedure, which gave it a right to veto the accession of new member states and the ratification of association agreements.

However, the most important change came with the Treaty of Maastricht (1992), which gave the European Parliament the power to veto legislation with the new co-decision procedure and a say over the appointment of the Commission and its president. The Treaty also marked a turning point in the wider process of European integration: it expanded the European Union beyond purely economic matters, but the inclusion of more sensitive competences required new forms of differentiated integration. The Treaty established a three-pillared structure: the first pillar comprised the traditional EC policies, in particular the Single Market and the Economic Monetary Union (EMU); the second pillar initiated the Common Foreign and Security Policy (CFSP); and the third pillar incorporated the initiatives that had been started outside of the community structures under the Schengen Agreement (1985/1990) in the new field of justice and home affairs (JHA). While the first pillar was mostly regulated by qualified majority voting (QMV) and co-decision, the second and third pillars were mostly intergovernmental. There, the EP had (almost) no say and the Council had to decide under unanimity. In addition, some member states decided not to participate in all policies: the EMU, JHA, defense and social policies included opt-outs by various member states – the UK and Denmark being the two most obvious cases.

Although the Treaty of Amsterdam (1997) is generally seen as less important than Maastricht, it was of the utmost importance for the European Parliament and the field of justice and home affairs. In procedural terms, the Treaty formalized some changes that the EP had introduced informally to the co-decision procedure (Hix 2002). This meant that the Council could not reintroduce a proposal if the Parliament voted it down and that an agreement could be concluded already in the first of the three potential readings contemplated in the procedure. In the area of justice and home affairs, the Treaty contemplated a change in the structure of the three pillars, so that some of the third-pillar policies (asylum, borders, visas, irregular immigration and civil law cooperation, apart from family law) would be 'shifted' to the first pillar. In practice, this meant that the areas that were to be 'communitarized' would be decided under co-decision and with QMV in the Council after a proposal was made by the Commission. However, since member states were reluctant to lose control over these issues, a transitional period was introduced so that the new decision-making rule only entered into force in 2005.

Finally, the Treaty of Lisbon transformed co-decision into the 'ordinary legislative procedure' and brought the EP on a par with member states in the allocation of the annual budget.

It also dissolved the pillar structure, which meant that almost all remaining areas in the JHA pillar – namely police and judicial cooperation in criminal matters and family law – were 'communitarized' and are now also decided under co-decision and with QMV in the Council. Only a few areas have remained under the old regime, namely passports and identity cards, family law, operational police cooperation and the decision to set up a European Public Prosecutor's Office.

In addition, the Treaty expanded the former assent procedure (now known as 'consent'), so that it applied to most international agreements signed by the European Union, including those falling under the JHA domain, such as data-sharing or readmission agreements. At the same time, a new provision contemplates the possibility that national parliaments raise an 'orange' card if they feel that a new EU proposal is infringing their rights of subsidiarity. In practice, national parliaments would need to win a quarter of the votes to support a reasoned opinion on a new proposal, which would force the Commission to review it and consider whether it should be changed or not. The need to reach this threshold within eight weeks makes it difficult for national parliaments to coordinate, and explains why there has only been one single 'orange' card up until now, which showed the concerns of some national parliaments towards the initiative to set up a European Public Prosecutor's Office.

This short overview of the EP's empowerment shows the radical change in its functions and powers. From a chamber of national representatives with only the power to talk, it has evolved into a full co-legislator and the only directly elected EU institution (Rittberger 2005). This shift in formal institutional powers has been particularly swift in the JHA domain, where the EP has come from being a complete outsider to gaining a veto power in internal security matters both inside the European Union and beyond. The question is, thus: do institutional changes actually matter and, if so, how can we assess their impact?

Integration theories and justice and home affairs: from venue-shopping to liberal constraints

The early literature on EU justice and home affairs was characterized by a strong emphasis on the intergovernmental nature of the policy field. As a result, most studies concentrated on classical or 'grand' theories of European integration, notably liberal intergovernmentalism, and to a lesser extent neo-functionalism, to explain the process of integration in a policy area where it was relatively unexpected to see any sort of European cooperation (cf. Niemann 2008; Monar 2012). For instance, Stetter (2000) argued that migration was successfully shifted to the first pillar during negotiations on the Treaty of Amsterdam because member states managed to introduce control mechanisms that allowed them to keep oversight of EU supranational institutions and the speed of integration.

Among these early works, Guiraudon's 'venue-shopping' thesis (2000) used two-level game models to explain why member states cooperated in the field of internal security. She argued that the EU served as an alternative decision-making venue where national governments could upload contested issues to the EU level and thereby escape the constraining effects of national institutions like courts or non-governmental organizations. As long as member states could decide under unanimity and in isolation from supranational EU institutions like the Court or the European Parliament, they enjoyed the isolation of the EU venue and used it to bypass domestic actors with more liberal preferences.

This thesis shaped the academic debate on JHA policy-making for the following years. However, with the treaty changes introduced in Amsterdam and Lisbon, the 'venue-shopping' thesis has largely lost its explanatory power and become increasingly contested (Bendel *et al.*

2011). Indeed, since it was based on intergovernmental assumptions, the thesis largely ignored the role of EU supranational institutions. With the gradual communitarization of justice and home affairs, new research underlined the growing importance of institutions like the Commission and the European Parliament in how decisions were made in this policy area. Generally, it was expected that the empowerment of the EU supranational institutions would erode the restrictive bias that had predominated in EU justice and home affairs (Carrera and Geyer 2007; Elsen 2010). Therefore, this new thesis posited the idea that EU supranational institutions acted as a 'liberal constraint' upon member states, limiting their room for maneuver and shifting decisions to the external domain, where intergovernmental procedures are still the rule (Lavenex 2006). Therefore, although the predicted outcomes of cooperation at the EU level were different from the 'venue-shopping' thesis, both explanations assumed that member states adopt restrictive or security-led policy positions, while the Commission, European Parliament and Court of Justice were seen to favor more liberal or rights-enhancing policies. In the case of the European Parliament, in particular, it was expected that its participation in policy-making would reduce the secrecy enveloping Council decisions and that this would help reinforce the liberal character of this policy area (Carrera and Geyer 2007; Elsen 2010; Maurer and Parkes 2005; Kaunert and Léonard 2012). These expectations have not always been fulfilled, which raises questions about the assumptions used by 'grand' theories and underlines the need to open the 'black box' of institutions in order to examine how intra- and inter-institutional dynamics affect policy-making in justice and home affairs (see also Bonjour et al. 2017).

New institutionalism and justice and home affairs: assessing the EU's political system

We have now experienced over a decade of co-decision in justice and home affairs, particularly in the field of migration and border management. During these years we have seen how the European Parliament has shifted from a vocal advocate of migrants' rights and liberal policies to a more sedate actor often collaborating with the Council in its attempt to reinforce the security aspects of JHA policies (Ripoll Servent 2015; Lopatin 2013). How can we explain this shift in behavior? Have institutional changes had any impact, and if so, in which direction? In order to answer these questions, research has shifted from 'grand' theories to middle-range theories that conceive of the EU as a political system. New institutionalism, in particular, has underlined that 'institutions matter', but different emphases on the effects of time and the meaning of institutions have resulted in the, by now, classical division between rational choice, historical and sociological institutionalism (Hall and Taylor 1996; Immergut 1998). Since historical institutionalism tends to focus on stability rather than on change and does not make an explicit choice between rationalism and constructivism, I will focus here on the other two variants (for more on the use of institutionalism in JHA, see Ripoll Servent and Kostakopoulou 2016).

Rational choice explanations: time horizons and shifting coalitions

The emphasis on structures and formal rules makes rational-choice institutionalism particularly useful to analyze the behavior of actors in situations of uncertainty, when institutions (understood as a configuration of rules that constrain the actions of individuals) can provide the necessary information and rules of procedure to facilitate and evaluate costs and benefits (Elster 1986; North 1990). In this sense, it has been one of the major theoretical approaches to study the European Parliament, especially when it comes to understanding its internal functioning (e.g., Yordanova 2013; Ringe 2010), its voting behavior (e.g., Hix *et al.* 2006) and the balance of power across the main EU institutions (e.g., Thomson 2011; Tsebelis and Garrett 2000).

These insights can also help us understand why the European Parliament has become more prone to supporting the Council in the field of justice and home affairs. If we focus on the formal procedures, the shift from consultation to co-decision has affected two key parameters of intra- and inter-decision-making: time horizons and coalition-building. Indeed, consultation made it relatively easy for the European Parliament to adopt more radical positions that went against the wishes of member states: since the EP was only required to provide a non-binding opinion, it knew that its amendments had very little chance of success, and therefore could express its wishes freely. Since this opinion only needed a simple majority in the Civil Liberties and Justice and Home Affairs Committee (LIBE), it was relatively easy for the liberal and left-wing groups to express their views. This bias was confirmed by Hix and Noury (2007) who examined the EP's voting behavior in the area of migration and showed that the main voting dimension reflected political rather than economic interests; that is, when MEPs focused on the security/liberty cleavage, left-wing and liberal groups had better chances of forming winning coalitions under consultation. On the contrary, when MEPs focused on the restriction or openness of labor markets, the left–right divide blurred and a cleavage across liberal and protectionist political groups emerged (see also Lahav *et al.* 2013). This explains why, in the case of the Blue Card Directive, the EP actually sought to introduce further restrictions to the admission of high-skilled migrants, since it was seen as a potential threat to national workers (Roos 2015).

How would a change in procedural rules alter the behavior of the European Parliament? For one, co-decision changed its time horizons: since its amendments now mattered, the EP became more reluctant to fail – if it antagonized the Council to such an extent that a compromise was not possible, this could affect not only that specific negotiation but also other parallel or future decisions (Farrell and Héritier 2007; Rittberger 2000). The pressure to find a compromise was particularly strong during the period that followed the shift to co-decision and may help us understand why political groups that had been very vocal on civil liberties, particularly the liberal group in the European Parliament, accepted the passage of very controversial laws like the Data Retention Directive, which was ultimately invalidated by the Court of Justice (Ripoll Servent 2013; European Court of Justice 2014).

The formal structure of co-decision made it more difficult to build winning coalitions. The procedure does not impose time limits upon the EP to vote on its report, for which it only needs a simple majority; in contrast, in the second reading, the EP has to vote within a limit of three (extendable to four) months and has to gather an absolute majority of 376 MEPs to pass its resolution. Given the fact that no political group in the EP has ever managed to gather a majority in the chamber, building coalitions is part and parcel of each negotiation. One also has to bear in mind that any winning coalition needs to propose an agreement that is also suitable to the Council (Costello 2011). These formal rules explain why the EP now rarely pushes votes beyond the first reading – the shadow of an absolute majority and the need to find an agreement with Council make it necessary for the EP to propose less extreme amendments than under consultation (Ripoll Servent 2015; Lopatin 2013).

In addition, the political majorities in the EP have changed since 2005: the elections of 2009 and 2014 have seen a rise in center-right and right-wing parties and a decreasing electoral support of liberal parties. In addition, mainstream groups are now surrounded by stronger Euroskeptic and radical parties, which makes it more difficult to build either right-wing or left-wing coalitions. The eighth parliamentary term (2014–2019) has been characterized by the impossibility of escaping a 'grand coalition' of Christian democrats and social democrats, with the liberal group often turning it into a 'super-grand coalition' (Ripoll Servent 2017).

The decline in liberal and left-wing forces explains why the EP was ready to accept very controversial proposals such as the Returns Directive, which introduced common rules on the deportation of migrants that had been denied the right to stay in EU territory (Acosta 2009; Ripoll Servent 2011). The Council has also been very skilled at using divisions inside the EP to co-opt the more conservative groups. This mechanism can help us understand the lack of major policy changes in many areas of justice and home affairs (Trauner and Ripoll Servent 2016). For instance, during the reform of the asylum system concluded in 2013, the EP managed to integrate this area further, but it maintained the restrictive approach at the core of its architecture, which explains why it could not cope with the increase in the number of asylum-seekers in 2015 (Ripoll Servent and Trauner 2014). Similar patterns have also emerged in the field of internal security after Lisbon. We have seen how many negotiations have been spearheaded by conservative MEPs, who have been more ready to reach deals on long-discussed proposals like the EU Passenger Names Record (Votewatch 2016) and to listen to private (security) interests, as was the case in the recently adopted revision of the Firearms Directive (Euobserver 2016).

Constructivist explanations: legitimating norms and the role of actors

Sociological institutionalism is based on a constructivist ontology, which assumes that social entities are constructed through perceptions, norms and discourses. Therefore, institutions are understood as more than formal rules; they may also include social practices, ideas and norms (Checkel 1998; Wendt 1998). This implies a relational character that is sometimes difficult to capture: research has often focused on the content of norms and ideas and looked at how institutions shape the positions of actors, but have forgotten that actors can also shape their institutional context. This has led some authors to emphasize that narrowing institutions to structures constraining the behavior of actors understates the important role that actors play (Saurugger 2013); for instance, by framing discourses or shaping institutional practices in order to legitimize certain policies or their right to intervene in decision-making. In this sense, constructivist approaches can help us understand where ideas come from, how we aggregate individual positions into collective ones or why certain actors are seen as more legitimate than others in the policy-making process.

How can they help us understand the effects of institutional change on the behavior of the EP in JHA? Constructivist explanations help us differentiate between two levels of analysis: the procedural and substantive dimensions of policy-making. If we concentrate on the procedural dimension – that is, how decisions are made – we see how the European Parliament relies extensively on the legitimacy derived from the fact that it is the only directly elected EU institution. These democratic 'credentials' have helped it in its quest to extend its procedural powers over the years (Rittberger 2005). For instance, the decision to shift border and migration policies from the third to the first pillar in the Treaty of Amsterdam responded as much to a need for more efficient decision-making as to the perceptions that these highly sensitive policies were not subjected to any form of democratic accountability (Huber 2015). Indeed, the EP has repeatedly used its role as representative of EU citizens to claim more powers to scrutinize and hold the other institutions accountable. This argument was used extensively on the first occasion in which it could use its right to consent over an internal agreement. During the ratification of the EU–US SWIFT Agreement, the EP blocked the deal on the basis that it had not been consulted. Despite the fact that it only had a right to say yes or no to the final agreement, it interpreted the formal rules in such a way that it managed to participate fully in the formulation of the Commission's negotiation mandate and had a direct say on the content of the final agreement (Ripoll Servent 2014). It has also been used repeatedly to increase its oversight over regulatory agencies in the JHA field – particularly those that are perceived as having a more direct impact upon policy implementation like Frontex and Europol (Trauner 2012; Ekelund 2014).

This understanding of its institutional role, however, may also explain why the EP has become more prone to supporting the Council in co-decision negotiations. If the EP's legitimacy rests on its ability to represent the interests of EU citizens, this means that as a co-legislator it now has to bear responsibility for policy outputs. This has been used extensively by the Council, which has requested a change in the EP's behavior towards a more 'responsible' and 'mature' institution. This has had a direct effect on the internal dynamics of the EP, since its political groups have often felt the need to sacrifice their substantive positions in order to reach a compromise with other groups or with the Council; consensus, therefore, has become a procedural norm that generally prevails over substantive interests (Ripoll Servent 2015; Roos 2015; Huber 2015).

Constructivist approaches also help us understand how substantive norms shift over time by focusing on the role of policy entrepreneurs. In this sense, individual actors are essential in understanding how problems are framed and which solutions are seen as legitimate. For instance, the growth in conservative forces has made it easier for some MEPs from the Christian democratic or conservative groups to reframe policies that had long been opposed by the Parliament. When specific instruments entered into the realm of counter-terrorism, policy entrepreneurs from these groups managed to frame the protection of EU citizens as a more legitimate policy solution than preserving high data protection standards (Ripoll Servent and MacKenzie 2011; Ripoll Servent 2013). Frames have also affected the area of regular migration, where the level of liberalism or restrictiveness has often depended on whether actors have been able to frame a problem as affecting human or labor rights rather than bearing on domestic labor markets. Therefore, it is important to look at the issues on which actors base their arguments, which policy rationales they use and whether other (international) norms enhance or undermine the legitimacy of a potential solution (Roos and Zaun 2014; Roos 2013; Cerna and Chou 2014).

As may be seen, the two approaches are not incompatible, and, in combination, can provide richer and deeper answers to questions that have complex sources. While rational-choice approaches focus more on (formal) structures and may help us understand the institutional context, constructivism sheds light on actors and how they may be shaped by this context, but also how they actively seek to manipulate it.

Conclusion: has the European Parliament become more influential?

The area of justice and home affairs illustrates like no other the effects of institutional changes on the EP's behavior. We have seen how the EP has become a more important actor in policy-making, gaining significant powers to decide over most legislation in this policy field. However, has the participation of the EP made any difference? There is still disagreement on whether and how much the EP has had an impact on policy outputs. In general, we can say that the EP has often emphasized the importance of integrating JHA policies further; for instance, defending the importance of Schengen as an area free of internal borders when member states have wished to reintroduce internal controls (Huber 2015). However, a comparative analysis has shown that the shift to co-decision has not led to any major policy changes in a majority of cases – the EP may not have contributed to securitizing JHA further, but it has also not managed to change the restrictive rationale prevailing in many of its policy areas (Trauner and Ripoll Servent 2015). These disagreements, however, also point to the need to improve the way we define policy change and how we operationalize it (see also Bonjour et al. 2017).

We also need to further the comparative analysis of different policy fields within JHA and also with other policy domains. Our knowledge is too often focused on one specific area, such as asylum or counter-terrorism, which makes it difficult to draw wider patterns of behavior. For instance, when it comes to the EP's impact upon international agreements, we know that the EP has become more relevant and can now shape to a certain extent the content of negotiations, but these findings are based largely on the field of data protection and counter-terrorism – which have seen particularly notorious episodes, like the EU–US PNRs, SWIFT and ACTA (Suda 2013; MacKenzie et al. 2015; Ripoll Servent 2014). It would then be interesting to see whether these patterns of behavior also extend to other fields, like readmission and visa liberalization agreements, which are based on a different set of problems (migration) and a different type of external partner (e.g., neighboring countries). Indeed, we have some examples already of how improving our comparisons could help us further our understanding of the conditions under which the EP enjoys more influence over the policy-making process. For instance, by examining instances of deeper policy change, we have seen that there are conditions under which the EP can prevail over the Council. In cases like data protection or criminal law, where the policy core had not been yet defined by member states deciding under unanimity, the EP managed to appear united around issues like human trafficking, where it is normatively difficult for member states to go against the EP. The EP has also learned to use existing jurisprudence by the various European courts to enhance the legitimacy of its proposals so as to ensure that they are incorporated into new EU legislation (Trauner and Ripoll Servent 2016).

Hence, we need to pay more attention to the role of the EP within the wider framework of European governance. We have often tended to either focus on specific EU institutions in isolation or to consider them as a unitary actor (a 'black box') in their interactions with other EU institutions. However, we need to make an effort to situate members of the European Parliament in a complex system of governance formed by domestic actors, European and national political parties as well as citizens and private organizations. By opening the black box and linking it to the outside world, we may come to understand the behavior of MEPs and the way positions are aggregated inside the EP much better. For instance, we know relatively little about the role of NGOs and interest groups (although see Hoffmann 2012 and Chapter 38, this volume). Their role, however, is particularly relevant for the Parliament, especially in an area where it is extremely difficult to obtain expertise that does not originate from national authorities. Technology is also becoming increasingly important, especially in the domain of databases and border management, and it remains unclear to what extent and with what success companies try to contact and put pressure on MEPs. We also know that domestic events, like elections or a change in government, have an influence on EU negotiations, but the links among domestic actors, national representatives in EU institutions and MEPs is still unclear. For instance, we saw how a change in the German position on a EU Passenger Name Record was actively used by policy entrepreneurs inside the European Parliament to convince reluctant members to vote in favor (Ripoll Servent and MacKenzie 2016). We also know that member states continue to use their expertise and their role in the actual implementation of JHA policies to prevail over the wishes of the European Parliament (Trauner and Ripoll Servent 2016). However, we do not know much about how national governments 'lobby' their MEPs, how they actually try to co-opt their members and to what extent MEPs can also frame and influence their national colleagues (although see Chapter 36). This link between Europe and home is still tenuous and needs to be explored further, especially in an area as sensitive as JHA, where events at the domestic level can shift European agendas in a radical manner.

Finally, these last years have seen informal changes in the inter-institutional balance of power that need to be kept under careful observation. The formalization of the European Council in the Treaty of Lisbon and the creation of a new president have given member states an even more important role in day-to-day decision-making. Indeed, although the Treaty charged the European Council with providing the political directions in legislative and budgetary terms, the informal interpretation made of these rules means that the European Commission and the European Parliament have very limited room for maneuver to innovate and change existing policy rationales (see also Chapters 34 and 35, this volume). As we have seen with the migration crisis, the European Parliament has been largely excluded from the major political deals and has been put between a rock and a hard place when it comes to implementing the most controversial parts of the EU–Turkey deal. This questions the overall role of the European Parliament in the EU's political system and forces us to reconsider to what extent it has reached the end of the road in its constant quest for more powers.

Bibliography

Acosta, D. (2009) The Good, the Bad and the Ugly in EU Migration Law: Is the European Parliament Becoming Bad and Ugly? (The Adoption of Directive 2008/15: The Returns Directive). *European Journal of Migration and Law*, 11(1), pp. 19–39.

Bendel, P., Ette, A. and Parkes, R. (eds) (2011) *The Europeanization of Control: Venues and Outcomes of EU Justice and Home Affairs Cooperation*. Münster: LIT Verlag.

Bonjour, S., Ripoll Servent, A. and Thielemann, E. (2017) Beyond Venue Shopping and Liberal Constraint: A New Research Agenda for EU Migration Policies and Politics. *Journal of European Public Policy*, forthcoming.

Carrera, S. and Geyer, F. (2007) The Reform Treaty and Justice and Home Affairs – Implications for the Common Area of Freedom, Security. *CEPS Policy Brief*.

Cerna, L. and Chou, M-H. (2014) The Regional Dimension in the Global Competition for Talent: Lessons from Framing the European Scientific Visa and Blue Card. *Journal of European Public Policy*, 21(1), pp. 76–95.

Checkel, J.T. (1998) The Constructivist Turn in International Relations Theory. *World Politics*, 50(2), pp. 324–348.

Costello, R. (2011) Does Bicameralism Promote Stability? Inter-institutional Relations and Coalition Formation in the European Parliament. *West European Politics*, 34(1), pp. 122–144.

Ekelund, H. (2014) The Establishment of FRONTEX: A New Institutionalist Approach. *Journal of European Integration*, 36(2), pp. 99–116.

Elsen, C. (2010) Personal Reflections on the Institutional Framework of the Area of Freedom, Security and Justice. In Monar, J. (ed.) *The Institutional Dimension of the European Union's Area of Freedom, Security and Justice*. Brussels: Peter Lang, pp. 255–265.

Elster, J. (ed.) (1986) *Rational Choice*. Oxford: Blackwell.

Euobserver (2016) EU Reaches Deal on Contested Gun Laws. December 20.

European Court of Justice (2014) The Court of Justice Declares the Data Retention Directive to Be Invalid. Press release No. 54/14.

Farrell, H. and Héritier, A. (2007) Introduction: Contested Competences in the European Union. *West European Politics*, 30(2), pp. 227–243.

Guiraudon, V. (2000) European Integration and Migration Policy: Vertical Policy-making as Venue Shopping. *Journal of Common Market Studies*, 38(2), pp. 251–271.

Hall, P.A. and Taylor, R.C.R. (1996) Political Science and the Three New Institutionalisms. *Political Studies*, 44(5), pp. 936–957.

Hix, S. (2002) Constitutional Agenda-setting Through Discretion in Rule Interpretation: Why the European Parliament Won at Amsterdam. *British Journal of Political Science*, 32(2), pp. 259–280.

Hix, S. and Noury, A. (2007) Politics, Not Economic Interests: Determinants of Migration Policies in the European Union. *International Migration Review*, 41(1), pp. 182–205.

Hix, S., Noury, A. and Roland, G. (2006) Dimensions of Politics in the European Parliament. *American Journal of Political Science*, 50(2), pp. 494–520.

Hoffmann, U. (2012) Lobbying for the Rights of Refugees: An Analysis of the Lobbying Strategies of Pro-migrant Groups on the Qualification Directive and Its Recast. *Journal of Contemporary European Research*, 8(1), pp. 21–39.

Huber, K. (2015) The European Parliament as an Actor in EU Border Policies: Its Role, Relations with Other EU Institutions, and Impact. *European Security*, 24(3), pp. 420–437.

Immergut, E.M. (1998) The Theoretical Core of the New Institutionalism. *Politics and Society*, 26(1), pp. 5–34.

Kaunert, C. and Léonard, S. (2012) The Development of the EU Asylum Policy: Venue-shopping in Perspective. *Journal of European Public Policy*, 19(9), pp. 1396–1413.

Lahav, G., Messina, A.M. and Vasquez, J.P. (2013) Were Political Elite Attitudes toward Immigration Securitized after 11 September? Survey Evidence from the European Parliament. *Migration Studies*, 2(2), pp. 212–234.

Lavenex, S. (2006) Shifting Up and Out: The Foreign Policy of European Immigration Control. *West European Politics*, 29(2), pp. 329–350.

Lopatin, E. (2013) The Changing Position of the European Parliament on Irregular Migration and Asylum under Co-decision. *Journal of Common Market Studies*, 51(4), pp. 740–755.

MacKenzie, A., Kaunert, C. and Léonard, S. (2015) *The EU as a Global Counter-terrorism Actor: Spillovers, Integration, and Institutions*. Cheltenham: Edward Elgar.

Maurer, A. and Parkes, R. (2005) Democracy and European Justice and Home Affairs Policies under the Shadow of September 11. *SWP Berlin Working Paper FG 1*.

Monar, J. (2012) Justice and Home Affairs: The Treaty of Maastricht as a Decisive Intergovernmental Gate Opener. *Journal of European Integration*, 34(7), pp. 717–734.

Niemann, A. (2008) Dynamics and Countervailing Pressures of Visa, Asylum and Immigration Policy Treaty Revision: Explaining Change and Stagnation from the Amsterdam IGC to the IGC of 2003–04. *Journal of Common Market Studies*, 46(3), pp. 559–591.

North, D.C. (1990) *Institutions, Institutional Change and Economic Performance*. Cambridge: Cambridge University Press.

Ringe, N. (2010) *Who Decides, and How? Preferences, Uncertainty, and Policy Choice in the European Parliament*. Oxford: Oxford University Press.

Ripoll Servent, A. (2011) Co-decision in the European Parliament: Comparing Rationalist and Constructivist Explanations of the Returns Directive. *Journal of Contemporary European Research*, 7(1), pp. 3–22.

Ripoll Servent, A. (2013) Holding the European Parliament Responsible: Policy Shift in the Data Retention Directive from Consultation to Codecision. *Journal of European Public Policy*, 20(7), pp. 972–987.

Ripoll Servent, A. (2014) The Role of the European Parliament in International Negotiations after Lisbon. *Journal of European Public Policy*, 21(4), pp. 568–586.

Ripoll Servent, A. (2015) *Institutional and Policy Change in the European Parliament: Deciding on Freedom, Security and Justice*. Basingstoke: Palgrave Macmillan.

Ripoll Servent, A. (2017) *The European Parliament*. Basingstoke: Palgrave Macmillan, forthcoming.

Ripoll Servent, A. and Kostakopoulou, D. (2016) Institutionalism: Shaping Internal Security Cooperation in the EU. In *Theorizing Internal Security in the European Union*. Oxford: Oxford University Press, pp. 153–175.

Ripoll Servent, A. and MacKenzie, A. (2011) Is the EP Still a Data Protection Champion? The Case of SWIFT. *Perspectives on European Politics and Society*, 12(4), pp. 390–406.

Ripoll Servent, A. and MacKenzie, A. (2016) Eroding Germany's Commitment to Data Protection: Policy Entrepreneurs and Coalition Politics in EU Passenger Name Records. *German Politics*. doi: 10.1080/09644008.2016.1250889.

Ripoll Servent, A. and Trauner, F. (2014) Do Supranational EU Institutions Make a Difference? EU Asylum Law before and after 'Communitarization'. *Journal of European Public Policy*, 21(8), pp. 1142–1162.

Rittberger, B. (2000) Impatient Legislators and New Issue-dimensions: A Critique of the Garrett-Tsebelis 'Standard Version' of Legislative Politics. *Journal of European Public Policy*, 7(4), pp. 554–575.

Rittberger, B. (2005) *Building Europe's Parliament*. Oxford: Oxford University Press.

Rittberger, B. (2009) The Historical Origins of the EU's System of Representation. *Journal of European Public Policy*, 16(1), pp. 43–61.

Roos, C. (2013) How to Overcome Deadlock in EU Immigration Politics. *International Migration*, 51(6), pp. 67–79.

Roos, C. (2015) EU Politics on Labour Migration: Inclusion versus Admission. *Cambridge Review of International Affairs*, 28(4), pp. 536–553.

Roos, C. and Zaun, N. (2014) Norms Matter! The Role of International Norms in EU Policies on Asylum and Immigration. *European Journal of Migration and Law*, 16(1), pp. 45–68.

Saurugger, S. (2013) Constructivism and Public Policy Approaches in the EU: From Ideas to Power Games. *Journal of European Public Policy*, 20(6), pp. 888–906.

Stetter, S. (2000) Regulating Migration: Authority Delegation in Justice and Home Affairs. *Journal of European Public Policy*, 7(1), pp. 80–103.

Suda, Y. (2013) Transatlantic Politics of Data Transfer: Extraterritoriality, Counter-extraterritoriality and Counter-Terrorism. *Journal of Common Market Studies*, 51(4), pp. 772–788.

Thomson, R. (2011) *Resolving Controversy in the European Union: Legislative Decision-making Before and After Enlargement*. Cambridge: Cambridge University Press.

Trauner, F. (2012) The European Parliament and Agency Control in the Area of Freedom, Security and Justice. *West European Politics*, 35(4), pp. 784–802.

Trauner, F. and Ripoll Servent, A. (2015) *Policy Change in the Area of Freedom, Security and Justice: How EU Institutions Matter*. London: Routledge.

Trauner, F. and Ripoll Servent, A. (2016) The Communitarization of the Area of Freedom, Security and Justice: Why Institutional Change Does Not Translate into Policy Change. *Journal of Common Market Studies*, 54(6), pp. 1417–1432.

Tsebelis, G. and Garrett, G. (2000) Legislative Politics in the European Union. *European Union Politics*, 1(1), pp. 9–36.

Votewatch (2016) EU Parliamentarians Adopt the Long Awaited EU-PNR Directive.

Wendt, A. (1998) On Constitution and Causation in International Relations. *Review of International Studies*, 24(5), pp. 101–118.

Yordanova, N. (2013) *Organising the European Parliament: The Role of Committees and Their Legislative Influence*. Colchester: ECPR Press.

33

THE EUROPEAN COURT OF JUSTICE AS A GAME-CHANGER

Fiduciary obligations in the area of freedom, security and justice

Ester Herlin-Karnell

Introduction

There are few areas in EU integration law and policy in which the Court of Justice of the European Union ('the EU Court') has not played a major role as a vehicle of integration, and the Area of Freedom, Security and Justice (AFSJ) is no exception. One could even go so far as to say that the AFSJ represents a field of law in which the EU Court has been a particularly important player and in which the judicial process has helped constitutionalize and transform this area into a central EU integration site.

The European mission of establishing an AFSJ is an interesting case study on the activity of the EU Court in its endeavors to construct a policy framework with legal implications across twenty-eight member states (alas, the United Kingdom is about to leave through its Brexit negotiations). In the same way as the Court was a central player in mainstreaming the former third pillar, it continues to remain at the very apex of this development (Fichera 2016). With the Treaty of Maastricht era starting in 1993, the famous 'third pillar' was established, which created a European system of criminal law cooperation as well as civil law cooperation, and asylum and immigration law. The Treaty of Amsterdam of 1999 clarified the EU's objectives with regard to the fight against crime and the concept of an AFSJ was generated. While asylum matters, immigration and civil law cooperation were moved to Title IV of the former EC Treaty, criminal law cooperation and security remained the hallmark of the third-pillar regime under the Amsterdam Treaty (Peers 2015). However, as is often pointed out, the third pillar to a large extent excluded the Court of Justice from policing this area as its jurisdiction was based on a voluntary declaration of the member states. From a EU law perspective, this was a prime example of judicial deficit and lack of oversight, which was remedied with the Treaty of Lisbon.

The AFSJ is a very broadly defined field of law dealing with a EU-wide policy area that ranges from security and criminal law to border control and civil law cooperation. However, the third pillar allowed for limited involvement by the European Parliament in the legislative process, and was criticized for having a democratic deficit and for a lack of transparency. The Treaty of Lisbon has now recast this whole framework by incorporating the AFSJ acquis into the Treaty of the Functioning of the European Union (TFEU). One of the most significant changes introduced by the Lisbon Treaty was the extension of the Court's jurisdiction to cover also the former third-pillar area (Lenaerts 2010; Lenaerts and Gutiérrez-Fons 2016; Hinarejos 2009). Thus, the Lisbon Treaty stipulates in Article 267 TFEU that (summarized):

> The Court of Justice of the European Union shall have jurisdiction to give preliminary rulings concerning: (a) the interpretation of the Treaties; (b) the validity and interpretation of acts of the institutions, bodies, offices or agencies of the Union; Where such a question is raised before any court or tribunal of a Member State, that court or tribunal may, if it considers that a decision on the question is necessary to enable it to give judgment, request the Court to give a ruling thereon. *If such a question is raised in a case pending before a court or tribunal of a Member State with regard to a person in custody, the Court of Justice of the European Union shall act with the minimum of delay.*[1]
>
> *(Emphasis added)*

Hence, this chapter will focus on what I consider to be the most important judicial developments in AFSJ law and the role played by the Court of Justice in this European process, and as a 'game-changer' in this area of former third-pillar law. The specific focus of this chapter is the role of the Court as a guardian of constitutional rights and as an integrationist court. The chapter is structured as follows. The next section charts the trajectory of the AFSJ and the function of the Court in this story. In the following I focus on the tactics of mutual recognition and how this has been a particularly successful method in the AFSJ as an expression of negative integration through the Court's case law. In doing so, I will zoom in on a number of pertinent cases for the development of, in particular, EU criminal law and EU asylum law. Thereafter, I will discuss the relationship between the EU Court of Justice and other courts. Finally, I will tentatively ask to what degree the Court is acting as a trustee court for establishing and maintaining the AFSJ and streamlining it with the Charter of Fundamental Rights.

The Court of Justice and the AFSJ: the path to constitutionalization

This section will seek to demonstrate some of the judicial highlights of the centrality of the Court's function as a 'game-changer' in this area. I will try to demonstrate the importance of the Court of Justice as a legal and political agent in the AFSJ. The outcome of the Court's active role as an agent of integration in the AFSJ is an extension of European law, values and objectives into the national arena. This seems particularly important in the times of crises (writing in 2016), as the Schengen system with its borderless travel in Europe is under severe strain, and the increased terrorism threat as well as the migration crisis on top of the financial crisis are no easy components for the EU to deal with. The core question for the purposes of this chapter is to what extent the Court of Justice is a sufficient agent for this institutional reformation and the many challenges caused by the various crises (Ripoll Servent and Trauner 2014).

The AFSJ is rapidly expanding and becoming one of the newest policy domains in contemporary EU integration. Any discussion of the constitutional basis of an AFSJ means first examining Article 3 TEU. This sets out the EU's mission in this area by promising that the EU will offer its citizens an AFSJ. Article 4j TFEU confirms this mission by explicitly acknowledging the EU's competence and the fact that, in seeking to achieve such a constitutional space, the EU shares its competence with the member states. Article 67 TFEU adds to this by setting out the AFSJ objectives in further detail. Article 67 TFEU states that the Union will 'endeavour to ensure a high level of security' and that this is to be achieved through measures to prevent and combat crime, racism and xenophobia, and through measures for coordination and cooperation between police and judicial authorities and other competent authorities, as well as through the mutual recognition of judgments in criminal matters and, if necessary, through the approximation of criminal laws.

The Lisbon Treaty changed the institutional battleground by abolishing the complex pillar structure and extending the Court of Justice's previously constrained jurisdiction to include the former third pillar. The changes brought about by this Treaty are of great importance for the credibility of the AFSJ project, as they enhance its democratic legitimacy. All is not well, however, with AFSJ law. The problem is that the main driver in this area has, to date, evidently been preventive regulation through a strong security focus, whereas the creation of the AFSJ was closely associated with the more general promotion of EU values at the EU level. I have previously argued that the EU's ongoing fight against crime, and in particular against money laundering and the financing of terrorism, is an example of a risk-based approach in which linking effectiveness with security is problematic owing to too much emphasis being placed on preventive regulation (Herlin-Karnell 2016).

Therefore, the starting-point when discussing the influence of the Court of Justice on the development of an AFSJ is the safeguarding of the rule of law at the EU level. The Court of Justice sets, as one of its main priorities, the safeguarding of this principle. The rule of law is a constitutional principle of the EU, as recognized in Article 2 TEU. Central to the rule of law is the idea of bounded government retrained by law from acting outside of its powers (Kumm 2012). Therefore, given the public law nature of the AFSJ, controlling coercive power and respecting human rights, the rule of law is of crucial importance when discussing the AFSJ. It should be recalled that, in *Les Verts* (Case C-294/83), the Court of Justice stated that the community had a basic constitutional charter based on the rule of law inasmuch as neither the member states nor its institutions can avoid a review of the question of whether the measures adopted by them are in conformity with the basic constitutional charter of the Treaty. In the *Kadi* case (Case C-415/05P) concerning the right to judicial review in an asset-freezing case, the Court of Justice went further and referred to the 'constitutional principles of the EU' (Halberstam). According to the Court, the autonomous structure of EU law applies not only vis-à-vis member state law, but also vis-à-vis international law. As a consequence, no international legal obligation can alter the core principles of EU constitutional law, and the rule of law is the very backbone of the EU's constitutional structure.[2]

However, despite its importance as a EU constitutional axiom, the rule of law (in a formal sense) had possibly been side-tracked in the former third pillar. It could be argued that the Court stretched the boundaries of consistent interpretation in the context of criminal procedural law to an area in which the Treaty excluded it (the former third pillar). This was the case in the *Pupino* judgment (Case C-105/03), where the national court had asked the Court of Justice whether it was required to interpret Italian law in the light of a Framework Decision that enabled minors to give evidence by alternative means (for example, video conference). Framework Decisions did not have a direct effect (according to ex-Article 34 EU) and supremacy was not an established notion in the former third pillar. Nonetheless, the Court made it clear that the principle of consistent interpretation and loyalty applied to the former third pillar. In the wake of the *Pupino* case, a number of decisions were delivered, each adding to the understanding of the third pillar, and demonstrating how EU legal principles were being imported to the former third pillar as a way of fixing problems which the unsuccessful Constitutional Treaty had failed to achieve (Peers 2007).

In line with these developments, the principle of effectiveness has, in many ways, been the driving principle for the evaluation of the AFSJ, and in particular the criminal law domain. The story of EU criminal law has been noteworthy because it has challenged the previous assumption that the EU has no legislative competence in that field. In the environmental crimes case (Case C-176/03), the Court of Justice made it clear that, when

> the application of effective, proportionate and dissuasive criminal penalties by the competent national authorities is an essential measure for combating serious environmental offences from taking measures which relate to the criminal law of the Member States which it considers necessary in order to ensure that the rules which it lays down on environmental protection are fully effective.
>
> *(Par. 48)*

Thus, a lot of weight in this case was placed on the full effectiveness of the EU and its application in national law when asserting the EU's competence. Hence, the principle of effectiveness has been one of the most important tools for the Court when applying its reasoning. Certainly, the Court had early on insisted upon effective sanctions against breaches of EU law (the effective, proportionate and dissuasive criteria stipulated in *Greek Maize* and other cases), but in the environmental crimes case, the Court concluded that criminal law could fall within the EU sphere of competence if it was necessary for the full effectiveness of EU law. The classic principle of effectiveness is often held to stem from the more general loyalty obligation, Article 4(3) TEU (formerly Article 10 EC), and the Court has played a crucial role in shaping the contours of the effectiveness of EU law (Lang 2008). For example, the doctrines of indirect effect, state liability and supremacy are also imbued with 'effectiveness' thinking (Craig 2012). The effectiveness of EU law is part of the Court's core vocabulary and is, therefore, of no surprise in the AFSJ context.

As noted above, EU criminal law has offered a good example of how the Court set out to handle things in the absence of this Treaty and thereby set out to shape the development of the AFSJ. After all, this Treaty introduced an explicit legal basis for effective judicial protection, so use of the principle of effectiveness in the area of judicial protection is more legally settled. Article 19 TEU, which codifies the existing case law, states that member states are to provide sufficient remedies to ensure effective legal protection in the fields covered by EU law. In addition, Article 47 of the EU Charter of Fundamental Rights ('the Charter') states that everyone has the right to an effective remedy. Therefore, it seems clear that the contextualization is the important aspect here.

The extensive reach of the Court's jurisdiction was demonstrated in the famous *Kadi* cases (Case C-402/05). While in *Kadi I* the Court of Justice famously extended the jurisdiction of the EU to review, albeit indirectly, UN measures, and while this was a ground-breaking development in the context of sanctions, the adoption of the Lisbon Treaty means that the previous jurisdictional shortcomings have been resolved thanks to a specific legal basis in the Treaty (Article 75 TFEU). In *Kadi II* the Court of Justice made it clear that the reasons given by the UN for having listed Kadi as an alleged terrorist were not reasonable, since they only contained a summary of claims (C-584/10 P; C-593/10 P and C-595/10 P). The Court required a more sophisticated way of reasoning. In both Kadi cases the internal and external were blurred. The difficulty of distinguishing between the internal and external aspects of EU action with regard to sanctions in the fight against terrorism is reflected in the recent judgment in *European Parliament* vs. *Council* (Case C-130/10). In this ruling, the European Parliament challenged Council Regulation 1286/2009 amending Council Regulation 881/2002 by imposing certain specific restrictive measures directed against targeted persons and entities associated with the Al-Qaeda network. The Parliament argued that, with regard to the aim and content of the regulation, the correct legal basis should have been Article 75 TFEU, and not Article 215 TFEU. With regard to the contested regulation, the Court of Justice made it clear that this was based on a Security Council measure and intended to preserve international peace and security, which implies that the measure at stake had a clear Common Foreign and Security Policy (CFSP) character. In addition, the Court stated in the argument that it was impossible to distinguish between the combatting of 'internal' terrorism on the one hand, and the combatting of 'external' terrorism on the other, and did not matter for the choice of the legal basis and for the scope of Article 215(2) TFEU as the legal basis of the contested regulation. The Court, therefore, stressed the political considerations behind the drafting of the Lisbon Treaty and accepted that, when choosing between legal bases, it is not just the role of the European Parliament and the increased democratic input that are the decisive factors (Case C-300/89). The Court did not specify what these critical factors entailed, but it seems reasonable to conclude that the choice of sanctions, and thereby also the legal basis, mattered at the political level as much as the effectiveness of the actual enforcement or the definition of a sanction. While the *European Parliament* vs. *Council* is a case which mainly concerns the dividing line between the internal and the external fight against terrorism, it is also a case which arguably highlights the choice by the legislator to fight terrorism by the means of the administrative model and not the criminal law model.

The *Kadi* cases, discussed above, offer a well-known example of how the EU places the values of EU law at the center of the discussion by stressing the importance of the autonomous legal order of the EU for the safeguarding of fundamental rights. In doing so, the Court emphasized the significance of a EU that not only respects fundamental rights, but also actively safeguards them in a legal order based on the rule of law and respect for due process rights (Murphy 2012). Hence, the *Kadi* case is an example of the Court as an agent of European values.

The Court and mutual recognition in the AFSJ

The Court of Justice has been a prominent game-changer in the AFSJ and especially in the area of mutual recognition (Lenaerts 2015). The application of mutual recognition and trust in the AFSJ raises familiar questions about the implications of free movement within the area of EU criminal law cooperation as well as the constitutional dimension of citizenship in EU criminal law. It could, perhaps, be argued that the most essential aspect has been of a symbolic nature, i.e., simply recognizing the relevance of citizenship. After all, it could be argued that there was a need to recognize that a system based on enforcement and mutual recognition also needed the other side of the coin, namely substantial principles of non-discrimination and the recognition of citizenship rights.

The European Arrest Warrant (EAW) turned out to be a particularly useful test case.[3] Notoriously, the EAW replaced the traditional extradition procedures with ones which secured 'surrender' in accordance with the theme of mutual recognition and in which the previous requirement of dual criminality was abolished. The purpose of the EAW was to speed up criminal law cooperation and to fight terrorism more effectively. In short, the EAW litigation saga started with an assumption that mutual trust was the prevailing condition for upholding the legality of the EAW (Rijken 2010; Peers 2015). *Advocaten voor de Wereld* (Case C-303/05) was the first test case of the validity of the EAW that was brought before the Court of Justice. To recap, *Advocaten voor de Wereld* was a non-profit-making association that brought an action in Belgium for the annulment of the EAW Framework Decision. One of the questions asked by the national court[4] was whether the EAW and its abolition of dual criminality breached the principle of legality in criminal law. This judgment insisted that the underlying idea of the EAW and the rule to abolish the notion of dual criminality did not breach the principle of legality, since the Framework Decision was concerned with procedural law and not with substantive law. The main reason for such a conclusion was, according to the Court of Justice, the high degree of trust and solidarity among the member states.

As noted above, the area of mutual recognition has been one of the most important playing fields for the Court of Justice (de Waele 2016). Indeed, much of the EU's cooperation in the AFSJ has been built on the principle of mutual recognition as underpinning cooperation in matters of justice and home affairs. Indeed, the concept of mutual recognition constitutes the main rule-of-thumb in the structure, as provided by the Lisbon Treaty in AFSJ matters, where 'trust' plays an increasingly important role (Moreno-Lax 2012; Costello 2015). It is often suggested that the main problem with mutual recognition in the AFSJ is the absence of sufficient trust in the AFSJ, and that this is problematic, as Article 67 TFEU presupposes that mutual recognition plays the key role in this area. Hence, the notion of trust in this area has worked as a quasi-constitutional standard for justifying EU action.

The Court of Justice has used the notion of trust in the area in order to overcome the lack of uniformity in national systems. For example, in the *NS* case, the Court held that the *raison d'être* of the EU and its creation of an AFSJ, and in particular the Common European Asylum System, is based on mutual confidence and a presumption of compliance by other member states and must be in compliance with fundamental rights (C-411/10). The Court set the ball rolling on mutual recognition of criminal law in the judgment of *Gözütok and Brügge* (C-187/01). The key provision in this area is Article 54 CISA that set out the fundamentals of *ne bis in idem*. In *Gözütok and Brügge*, the Court stated that there is a necessary implication that the member states have mutual trust in their criminal justice systems and that each recognizes the criminal law in force in other member states even when the outcome of a case would be different if its own national law were applied.

Thus, the mutual recognition of judicial decisions across the member states presupposes a level of trust between the domestic legal orders that appears particularly difficult to achieve in an area as sensitive as criminal law. In general, criminal law deals with the deprivation of liberty, which contrasts with the imperative of the EU's freedom of movement. Furthermore, a common problem which arises when discussing the notion of EU criminal law cooperation, and as such one that is frequently highlighted by academic commentary, is that there is no definition of 'mutual trust' in the field of criminal law (Walker 2002). This lack of conceptualization has been considered a significant *lacuna* in EU criminal law cooperation. In this regard, there is currently insufficient mutual trust among the member states and no adequate European regime for the protection of human rights within the former third pillar to justify such an analogy with the internal market and mutual recognition (Peers 2015). The notion of trust has also played an important role in the civil law area (Storskrubb 2016). For example, in the case of *Grasser* (Case C-116/02), in connection with the Lugano Convention, the Court concluded that the hypotheses of mutual trust must prevail over conflicting considerations such as when a member state faces difficulties in dealing with a case effectively.

Indeed, several recent cases on the limits of mutual recognition in the AFSJ demonstrate that the concept of mutual trust is not an absolute requirement, but can be set aside if necessary for the adequate protection of human rights (Case C-123/08). In the *NS* (Case C-411/10) case regarding EU asylum law, the Court of Justice asserted that, if there are substantial grounds for believing that there are systematic flaws in the asylum procedure in the member state responsible, then the transfer of asylum-seekers to that territory would be incompatible with the Charter of Fundamental Rights.

Furthermore, the recent case of *Stefano Melloni* was concerned with the application of the principle of mutual recognition to trial *in absentia*. The message of *Melloni*, according to the recent Opinion 2/13 on the accession to the ECHR, is to protect the supremacy of the EU from divergent (stricter) application of fundamental rights. In Opinion 2/13, the Court held that the principle of mutual trust requires, particularly with regard to the AFSJ, 'each of those States, save in exceptional circumstances, to consider all the other Member States to be complying with EU law and particularly with the fundamental rights recognized by EU law'. Hence, the EU's accession to the ECHR was seen as potentially weakening the EU enforcement project. This unilateral approach may appear to be a contradictory message against the background of the struggle to achieve better enforcement in criminal law.

Yet, in the recent *Aranyosi and Căldăraru* case (C-404/15 and C-659/15 PPU), concerning the execution of a EAW and the risk of inhumane and degrading treatment, the Court emphasized Article 4 of the Charter of Fundamental Rights that prohibition is absolute in that it is closely linked to respect for human dignity (Gáspár-Szilágyi 2016). The Court held that the executing judicial authority must postpone its decision on the surrender of the individual concerned until it obtains the supplementary information that allows it to exclude the existence of such a risk.

The Court has interwoven the AFSJ and the different areas that it entails. In the project of asylum law, the judgment of *El Dridi* (Case C-61/11) is instructive. Here, the Court held that the principle of proportionality must be complied with when deciding on the return procedure. In this case, the principles of proportionality and effectiveness were relied upon by the CJEU to define the competence and margin of appreciation of member states concerning the coercive measures they can implement in the context of the procedure for the return of illegally staying third-country nationals.[5] The first principle was employed by the Court to examine the lawfulness of such measures (which include, for example, detention in a facility and deportation) (Case C-61/11). The second principle restricted national competence in the sense that the member state must not prevent the achievement of the objectives of the Return Directive,[6] with regard to the implementation of an efficient policy of removal and repatriation of irregularly staying third-country nationals. The obligation to ensure compliance with EU law implies that the national court has the power to refuse to apply a custodial sentence which is imposed for the mere reason that the third-country national continues to stay in the territory of the member state after the expiry of the period established for him or her to leave the country.

Moreover, as indicated above in the *NS* case, in the context of the EU asylum system, the Court of Justice asserted that, if there are substantial grounds for believing that there are systematic flaws in the asylum procedure in the member state responsible, then the transfer of asylum-seekers to that territory would be incompatible with the Charter of Fundamental Rights. For the CJEU, there is no doubt that where there is a serious risk that the applicant's rights, as guaranteed by the Charter of Fundamental Rights, may be breached, member states should enjoy a wide 'margin of discretion'. This permits the member state in which the application was lodged to examine it even when the criteria set out in Chapter III of the Dublin III Regulation[7] do not apply, in particular when the state that should be responsible is deemed to be 'dangerous'. The question is the extent to which this margin of appreciation should operate in light of potential political or ideological conflicts (Fichera and Herlin-Karnell 2013). The Court has yet to respond to this question.

Cooperation with other courts?

The EU Court has to ensure consistency between the rights under the EU Charter of Fundamental Rights and the European Convention on Human Rights (ECHR).[8] This means that it often looks at the case law of the Strasbourg Court for guidance.

For example, prior to the *NS* case discussed above, in 2011, the European Court of Human Rights, in the case *M.S.S.* vs. *Belgium and Greece*, held that the conditions of detention and the living conditions of asylum-seekers in Greece were to be regarded as a violation of Article 3 of the ECHR (Leczykiewicz 2016).[9] Likewise, in the area of EU criminal law, the Court 'copies' the ECHR with regard to the minimum standard adopted, which was both the case in *Melloni* (Case C-399/11) (the ECHR does not give a wider protection, but leaves it often to the margin of appreciation test whether to allow trial *in absentia*) and in *Aranyosi and Căldăraru* (Cases C-404/15 and C-659/15 PPU) (on the prohibition of degrading treatment). In spite of this, the Court of Justice continues to conduct a rather complicated relationship with Strasbourg, and the European Convention on Human Rights in particular. In its recent Opinion 2/13 on the EU's accession to the ECHR, the Court of Justice rejected the possibility of EU accession to the ECHR partly on the grounds that as 'EU law imposes an obligation of mutual trust between those Member States, accession is liable to [...] undermine the autonomy of EU law' (Halberstam 2015).

The Court has adopted a 'yo-yo'-like approach with regard to its relationship with national courts. Sometimes the Court has maintained its *Solange* doctrine, and at other times it has simply focused on the enforcement of EU law at all costs. The case law, if you like, is contextualized, albeit sometimes a little unclearly, as to why some cases are different from others. Apart from the importance of consistency as a value in shaping legal drafting, and as such a prominent theme in the case law of the Court of Justice, consistency theoretically plays an important part in judicial decision-making (Levenbook 1984). In Opinion 2/13 the Court held that:

> In so far as the ECHR would require a EU Member State to check that another Member State has observed fundamental rights, even though EU law imposes an obligation of mutual trust between those Member States, accession [to the ECHR] is liable to upset the underlying balance of the EU and undermine the autonomy of EU law.

Regarding the relationship between the Court of Justice and the European Convention Court, the ECtHR's case law has been rather more solicitous of asylum-seekers' fundamental rights, as in *M.S.S.* vs. *Belgium and Greece* mentioned above. According to Halberstam (2015), by asking for an express exemption for member states' Convention violations caused by EU law's mutual confidence obligations, the EU Court is trying to mimic the existence of a federal state in international law. On the other hand, cases such as *Kadi* confirm that the Court of Justice sometimes gives more protection than does the ECtHR. A challenge for the EU Court of Justice is then to convince the highest national courts that, despite the non-accession, the EU system of rights is, at a minimum, as good as that offered by the ECHR. In a recent article, Anneli Albi (2015) has argued that what is really needed in AFSJ matters (and, more generally, in EU constitutional law) is a turn to 'substantive co-operative constitutionalism'. By this, she means that the Court needs to adopt a conceptual approach through which scholars, courts, and national and transnational institutions would be able to explore how to develop European and global governance in a way that would seek to uphold and enhance the achieved standards of the classic, substantive, more 'guarantistic' and democratically responsive version of constitutionalism. Clearly, this is work in progress. It is also an area in which the Court of Justice is likely to continue to be a game-changer in the future, with either more cooperation on the table or by promoting a 'closed-door' approach. What, then, does all this tell us about the Court at the apex of AFSJ integration?

The Court of Justice as a trustee court in the area of freedom, security and justice?

Arguably, the Court considers itself to be not only at the top of the judicial integration chain, but also as a court with fiduciary obligations to protect rights ensured by EU law in all member states via its extensive case law on trust in the autonomous European legal order.

Therefore, according to Alec Stone Sweet and Thomas Brunell (2013), the Court of Justice is not a simple agent of the member states, but instead it is the latter that are the trustees of its regimes, i.e., of EU law at large (Criddle and Fox-Decent 2016). In reaching this conclusion, the authors mention three criteria. First, that the Court is recognized as the authoritative interpreter of the regime's law, which is the case of the EU Court of Justice. Second, that the Court's jurisdiction with regard to state compliance is compulsory. Third, that it is virtually impossible, in practice, for contracting states to reverse the Court's important rulings on treaty law. A trustee court is a kind of 'super-agent', empowered to enforce the law against the member states themselves.

Does this description then fit the Court of Justice with regard to the AFSJ? A tentative expression of trusteeship may be found in the AFSJ where the Court has to balance freedom, security and justice. An example of the Court of Justice acting as a successful guardian of the AFSJ can, perhaps, be found in the recent case of *Digital Rights* (Case C-293/12), which is instructive as a touchstone of justice-inspired reasoning in the European Court. The Court annulled the 2006 Data Retention Directive, which was aimed at fighting crime and terrorism, and which allowed data to be stored for up to two years. It concluded that the measure breached proportionality on the grounds that the Directive had a too sweeping generality and therefore violated, *inter alia*, the basic right of data protection as set out in Article 8 of the Charter of Fundamental Rights. The Court pointed out that access by the competent national authorities to the data retained was not made dependent on a prior review carried out by a court or by an independent administrative body whose decision sought to limit access to the data to what was strictly necessary for the purpose of attaining the objective pursued. Nor did it lay down a specific obligation on member states designed to establish such limits. According to the Court, there was not a sufficiently good enough justification provided by the EU legislator.

Subsequently, in *Schrems* (C-362/14 *Schrems* vs. *Data Protection Commissioner*), the Court ruled, in effect, that US law allows US intelligence services to access the personal data of EU citizens without sufficient privacy safeguards as a matter of EU law. The EU law in question was the so-called Commission 'Adequacy Decision' 2000/520, adopted pursuant to Article 25 of the Data Protection Directive 95/46. Under Directive 95/46, the transfer of personal data outside the European Economic Area to a third country is only permissible when the third country de facto ensures an 'adequate level of protection'. The Commission may find that a third country meets this standard through its domestic law or international commitments, and by taking into account all of the circumstances surrounding the data transfer. The Court declared the Adequacy Decision invalid. It did so 'without there being any need to examine the content of the safe harbour principles' (Fletcher and Herlin-Karnell 2016) on the basis that the Commission had not stated in the Adequacy Decision that the United States did, in fact, 'ensure' an adequate level of protection through its domestic law or its international commitments. This approach was confirmed in the recent *Telia 2 Sverige* (Joined Cases C-203/15 and C-698/15) case concerning the retention of traffic and location of data in relation to subscribers and registered users, which was in breach of the Charter. The Swedish Post and Telecom Authority required Telia 2 to retain traffic and location data in relation to its subscribers and registered users. The measure was disproportionate and in breach of data protection (pars 95–96 of the judgment).

Another example of the Court's active reading of fundamental rights, and therefore an attempted trusteeship, may arguably be found in the case of *Åkerberg Fransson* concerning the compatibility with the *ne bis in idem* principle of a national system involving two separate sets of proceedings to penalize the same wrongful conduct (Case C-617/10). I think this is not just a case about extending the reach of the Charter, but one of genuine concern about the individual. The Court of Justice adopted a very broad reading of the Charter. It held that, although the national rules in question did not, *stricto sensu*, involve any implementation, it was clear from Article 325 TFEU that the member states are required to fight fraud against the EU and thereby supply the same level of penalties for EU and domestic fraud respectively. Moreover, the Court observed that EU law precludes a judicial practice which makes the obligation for a national court to disapply any provision contrary to a fundamental right guaranteed by the Charter conditional upon that infringement, made clear by the text of the Charter or the case law relating to it. According to the Court, such an interpretation would withhold from the national court the power to assess fully whether that provision in question was compatible with the Charter (par. 48).

As seen above, the idea of 'balancing mechanisms' of state action has for a long time been a touchstone for the EU and, as such, has been elevated to a golden rule in EU lawmaking in terms of the proportionality principle. At a minimum, it has always been a key message of the European Court of Justice's case law, and its insistence on proportionality has functioned as a way of either preventing member states from derogating from EU law obligations or, by contrast, of granting them some leeway when asked to enforce supranational EU principles in the national arena. Thus, the potential for the Court to act as a trustee court could arguably be found in an ambitious reading of the proportionality principle, and one such avenue, if read in the light of the fundamental rights, may be seen as being safeguarded by the Charter of Fundamental Rights.

Avenues for future research

The AFSJ era has only just begun and is no longer viewed in isolation from the rest of the EU acquis, but should instead be viewed holistically, without denying the special features of AFSJ law. The creation of trust is a long-term, fundamental project for the EU and the Court plays a key role in pinning down what is precisely meant by it, and clarifying when this notion can be rebutted. For obvious reasons, the refugee and Schengen crises of 2015/2016, along with the increased terrorist threat, the long-standing financial crisis and the consequences of Brexit, will all be challenges for the construction of the AFSJ and its monitoring by the Court of Justice. Clearly, with the UK actually leaving, the opt-out issue from the AFSJ still remains, but the UK relationship will be a challenge. Ireland and Denmark have negotiated a unique approach to the AFSJ project via opt-outs. This poses challenges not only for those trying to analyze the current state of play, but also for national courts, as well as for the Court of Justice, when applying the constitutional principles of the EU.

As is evident from the case law on mutual recognition in the AFSJ, such as the European Arrest Warrant, the Court of Justice has been highly experimental. Although the progress has been slow in many respects, it is nonetheless a Court that has a lot to offer, as it has the toolkit to achieve this aim. Still a great challenge for the Court of Justice in the future is the external dimension of the AFSJ and the growing importance of agencies in decision–making, since they are generally excluded from the Court's jurisdiction. As the Commission has put it: 'Steps taken to ensure freedom, security and justice in Europe are also influenced by events and developments outside the EU.'[10] In other words, the external agenda shapes the internal agenda and is likely to remain a burning issue for the future of AFSJ law. The AFSJ is not immune from the global landscape and societal setting. As a result of current non-accession to the ECHR, the unified level of human rights protection is likely to remain a key task for the Court of Justice when developing the AFSJ further and maintaining a robust level of fundamental rights protection in Europe. Likewise, an interesting avenue for future research is the potential for the Court to act as a trustee court as well as the implications of a proportionality test and the notion of solidarity in this area.

Acknowledgments

Thanks to the editors for their useful comments on this chapter, and to Chris Engert for his excellent help with lingustic corrections and proofreading. The useful disclaimer applies.

Notes

1 The Court will not have the power to review the validity or proportionality of operations carried out by the police or other law enforcement agencies of a member state or the exercise of responsibilities incumbent upon member states with regard to the maintenance of law and order and the safeguarding of internal security. This limitation seems rather artificial and begs the question of to what extent this treaty-based limitation will be fulfilled in practice.
2 COM (2014) 158 final, Communication from the Commission. A new EU framework to strengthen the rule of law.
3 Council Framework Decision 2002/584/JHA of June 13, 2002 on the European arrest warrant and the surrender procedures between member states [2002] OJ L 190/1.
4 The other questions asked were whether the EAW should have been adopted as a Convention rather than as a Framework Decision and whether the EAW breached the principles of equality and non-discrimination.
5 See in this regard points 13 and 16 Preamble and Article 8 (4) of the Directive 2008/115/EC of the European Parliament and of the Council of December 16, 2008 on common standards and procedures in member states for returning illegally staying third-country nationals, OJ L 348 24.12.2008.
6 Directive 2008/115/EC *supra*.
7 Dublin Regulation No. 604/2013.
8 See, in particular, Charter of Fundamental Rights of the European Union [2000] OJ C364/01, Article 52(3):

> In so far as this Charter contains rights which correspond to rights guaranteed by the Convention for the Protection of Human Rights and Fundamental Freedoms, the meaning and scope of those rights shall be the same as those laid down by the said Convention. This provision shall not prevent Union law providing more extensive protection.

9 Article 3 ECHR: 'No one shall be subjected to torture or to inhuman or degrading treatment or punishment.'
10 'An open and secure Europe: making it happen', COM (2014) 154 final and A European Agenda on Security COM(2015) 185 final.

Bibliography

Albi, A. (2015). Erosion of Constitutional Rights in EU Law: A Call for 'Substantive Co-operative Constitutionalism'. *Vienna Journal of International Law*, 9, p. 151.
Costello, C. (2015). *The Human Rights of Migrants and Refugees in European Law*. Oxford: Oxford University Press.
Craig, P. (2012). *EU Administrative Law*. Oxford: Oxford University Press.
Criddle, E. and Fox-Decent, E. (2016). *Fiduciaries of Humanities*. Oxford: Oxford University Press.
de Waele, H. (2016). Entrenching the Area of Freedom, Security and Justice: Questions of Institutional Governance and Judicial Control. In M. Fletcher, E. Herlin-Karnell and C. Matera (eds), *The European Union as an Area of Freedom, Security and Justice*. Abingdon: Routledge, ch.19.

Fichera, M. (2016). Sketches of a Theory of Europe as an Area of Freedom, Security and Justice. In M. Fletcher, E. Herlin-Karnell and C. Matera (eds), *The EU as an Area of Freedom, Security and Justice*. Abingdon: Routledge, ch. 3.

Fichera, M. and Herlin-Karnell, E. (2013). The Margin of Appreciation Test and Balancing in the Area of Freedom Security and Justice: A Proportionate Answer for a Europe of Rights? *European Public Law*, 19, p. 759.

Fletcher, M. and Herlin-Karnell, E. (2016). Is There a Transatlantic Security Strategy? Area of Freedom, Security and Justice Law and its Global Dimension. In M. Fletcher, E. Herlin-Karnell and C. Matera (eds), *The European Union as an Area of Freedom, Security and Justice*. Abingdon: Routledge, ch. 16.

Gáspár-Szilágyi, S. (2016). Converging Human Rights Standards, Mutual Trust and a New Ground for Postponing a European Arrest Warrant. *European Journal of Criminal law and Criminal Justice*, 24, pp. 197–219.

Halberstam, E. (2015). 'It's the Autonomy, Stupid!' A Modest Defence of Opinion 2/13 on EU Accession to the ECHR, and the Way Forward. *German Law Journal*, 16, p. 105.

Herlin-Karnell, E. (2016). The EU as a Promoter of Preventive Criminal Justice and the Internal Security Context. *European Politics and Society*, 17, pp. 215–225.

Hinarejos, A. (2009). *Judicial Control in the European Union*. Oxford: Oxford University Press.

Kumm, M. (2012). Constitutionalism and the Moral Point of Constitutional Pluralism. In P. Eleftheriadis and J. Dickson (eds), *Philosophical Foundations of EU Law*. Oxford: Oxford University Press, ch. 9.

Lang, J.T. (2008). The Developments of the Court of Justice on the Duties of Cooperation of National Authorities and Community Institutions Under Article 10 EC. *Fordham International Law Journal*, 31, p. 1483.

Leczykiewicz, D. (2016). Human Rights and the Area of Freedom, Security and Justice. In M. Fletcher, E. Herlin-Karnell and C. Matera (eds), *The EU as an Area of Freedom, Security and Justice*. Abingdon: Routledge, ch. 3.

Lenaerts, K. (2010). The Contribution of the European Court of Justice to the Area of Freedom, Security and Justice. *ICLQ*, 59. p. 255.

Lenearts, K. (2015). The Principle of Mutual Recognition in the Area of Freedom, Security and Justice. Talk delivered at the Fourth Annual Sir Jeremy Lever Lecture, All Souls College, University of Oxford, January 30 (on file with the author).

Lenaerts, K. and Gutiérrez-Fons, J. (2016). The European Court of Justice and Fundamental Rights in the Field of Criminal Law. In M. Bergstrom, V. Mitsilegas and T. Konstadinides (eds), *Research Handbook on EU Criminal Law*. Cheltenham: Edward Elgar, ch. 1.

Levenbook, B. (1984). The Role of Coherence in Legal Reasoning. *Law and Philosophy*, 3, p. 355.

Moreno-Lax, V. (2012). Dismantling the Dublin System: M.S.S. v Belgium and Greece. 14 *European Journal of Migration and Law*, 14, p. 1.

Murphy, C. (2012). *EU Counter Terrorism Law*. Oxford: Hart Publishing, p. 224.

Peers, S. (2007). Salvation Outside the Church: Judicial Protection in the Third Pillar after the Pupino and Segi Judgments. *Common Market Law Review*, 44, p. 883.

Peers, S. (2015). *EU Justice and Home Affairs*. Oxford: Oxford University Press; for an extensive overview of the history of the former third pillar, see ch. 1.

Rijken, C. (2010). Re-balancing Security and Justice: Protection of Fundamental Rights in Police and Judicial Cooperation in Criminal Matters. *Common Market Law Review*, 47, p. 1455.

Ripoll Servent, A. and Trauner, F. (2014). Do Supranational EU Institutions Make a Difference? EU Asylum Law Before and After 'Communitarization'. *Journal of European Public Policy*, 21, pp. 1142–1162.

Storskrubb, E. (2016). Civil Justice – Constitutional and Regulatory Issues Revisited. In M. Fletcher, E. Herlin-Karnell and C. Matera (eds), *The EU as an Area of Freedom, Security and Justice*. Abingdon: Routledge, pp. 303–326.

Stone Sweet, A. and Brunell, T.L. (2013). Trustee Courts and the Judicialization of International Regimes: The Politics of Majoritarian Activism in the ECHR, the EU, and the WTO. *Journal of Law and Courts*, p. 61.

Walker, N. (2002). The Problem of Trust in an Enlarged Area of Freedom, Security and Justice: A Conceptual Analysis. In M. Anderson and J. Apap (eds), *Police and Justice Cooperation and the New European Borders*. The Hague: Kluwer Law International, p. 22.

Cases

Case C-294/83, *Les Verts* [1986] ECR 1339.
Case C-300/89, *Commission* vs. *Council* [1991] ECR I-2867.
C-187/01 and C-385/01, *Gözütok and Brugge* [2003] ECR I-1354. See also C-436/04 *Van Esbrock* [2006] ECR I-2333.
Case C-116/02, *Gasser*, ECR I-000.
Case C-105/03, *Pupino* [2005] ECR I-05285.
Case C-176/03, *Commission* vs. *Council* [2005] ECR I-07879.
Case C-303/05, Advocaten voor de Wereld VZW vs. Leden van de Ministerraad [2007] ECR I-03633.
Case C-415/05P, *Kadi* [2008] ECR I-6351.
Case C-123/08, *Wolzenburg* [2009] ECR I-09621, C-411/10 and C-493. Judgment of December 21, 2011, nyr.
Case C-411/10, NS judgment of December 21, 2011, nyr.
Case C-130/10, *European Parliament* vs. *Council*. Opinion of AG Bot delivered on January 31, 2012.
Case C-617/10, *Åkerberg Fransson*. Judgment of February 26, 2013 nyr.
C-61/11, *El Dridi*. Judgment of April 28, 2011.
M.S.S. vs. *Belgium and Greece*. Judgment of January 21, 2011. Application No. 30696/09.
Case C-399/11, Criminal proceedings against *Stefano Melloni*, judgment of February 26, 2013, nyr.
Case C-293/12, judgment of April 8, 2014.
Opinion 2/13 of the Full Court, *Accession to the ECHR*, December 18, 2014.
Kadi II, Joined Cases C-584/10 P, C-593/10 P and C-595/10 P, judgment of July 18, 2013 (not yet reported).
C-362/14, *Schrems* vs. *Data Protection Commissioner*. Judgment of Court (Grand Chamber) of October 6, 2015, nyr.
Joined Cases C-404/15 and C-659/15 PPU, *Aranyosi and Căldăraru*. Judgment of the Court of Justice (Grand Chamber) of April 5, 2016.
Joined Cases C-203/15 and C-698/15, Telia 2 Sverige. Judgment December 21, 2016.

34
THE EUROPEAN COMMISSION IN JUSTICE AND HOME AFFAIRS
Pushing hard to be a motor of integration

Natascha Zaun

Introduction

The European Commission is often considered the motor of European integration. Ernst B. Haas (1964: 11), most prominently, conceived of the Commission as an institution which aimed at 'upgrading the common interest' and which constantly provided new policy ideas implying further integration. As a non-partisan institution, the Commission is, moreover, perceived as an honest broker providing policy solutions that reconcile the member states, the European Parliament (EP) and civil society (Nugent and Rhinard 2015: 18).

This chapter assesses the Commission's specific role in the area of justice and home affairs (JHA) and compares it to findings from the literature on the European Commission more generally. In doing so, I shed light on a number of pivotal questions on the role of the Commission in JHA. In the second section, I analyze how influential the Commission is in the area of JHA as compared to the other EU institutions and to what extent it was able to leave a mark on European Union (EU) legislation in the field. To this end, I will investigate how the competences of the Commission in this policy area have changed over time and compare competences across the individual subfields of JHA, including cooperation in judicial matters, police cooperation, and immigration and asylum policies. Subsequently, I assess the positions advanced by the Commission in the area of JHA and compare them to those proposed by the other EU institutions. I analyze to what extent the Commission has acted as a supporter of enhanced integration in the area and whether the Commission promotes individual rights or whether it focuses rather on collective security against potential threats.

The role of the Commission in JHA is a heavily under-researched topic. While there is a growing body of literature dealing specifically with the European Parliament in JHA (e.g., Hix and Noury 2007; Lopatin 2013; Ripoll Servent 2014, 2015) or the Council in JHA (e.g., Aus 2006; Maricut 2016; Zaun 2016, 2017), the Commission has rarely been the research focus of a study but has rather been studied *en passant* (with two notable exceptions; see Kaunert 2010a; Uçarer 2001). Research on the role of the Commission in EU policy-making more generally or on the inner functioning of this institution (e.g., Kassim *et al.* 2013; Nugent and Rhinard 2015) has not focused on its role in the area of JHA. Thus, we have little systematic analysis of the Commission's positions and its impact in the field. Given this lacuna, this chapter collects the existing knowledge on the Commission's role in the field and tries to draw tentative general conclusions. More research will be needed to further substantiate these claims.

Impact of the Commission

Determining the impact of the Commission in JHA is methodologically not an easy task, as the Commission is not – like the EP or the Council – a co-legislator with concrete powers in EU legislative processes. Instead, the Commission submits a legislative proposal which is the basis of discussions in both the Council and the EP. Moreover, it mediates between these institutions should they hold different opinions on a legislative proposal. The Commission's influence is therefore based on its potential to steer debates from early on through setting the agenda and framing policies with its proposals (Héritier 1996: 152–153). Pollack (2000) has argued that the Commission tends to be most influential: (1) if it has a clear treaty mandate; (2) if decisions in the Council are taken under qualified majority voting (qmv), and (3) if member states are unwilling or unable to effectively sanction the Commission in case it embarks on a policy pathway that they do not like. A clear mandate allows the Commission to legitimately submit legislative proposals. Qmv in the Council enables the Commission to push through policies against reluctant minorities among the member states in the Council. Member states are usually unwilling or unable to sanction the Commission if they profit heavily from EU legislation and if they are hence more impatient for it to be in place than the Commission is. Patience is generally considered a key power resource in negotiations (Knight 1992: 135). In addition, the Commission has been demonstrated to use the Court of Justice of the EU (CJEU) strategically in its rhetoric to strengthen its own position. For instance, the Commission has repeatedly threatened the Council to bring an issue to court or has followed up on judgments in its legislative proposals (Schmidt 2000).

In the following, I will analyze to what extent the Commission had these power resources and in how far it was able to use them in JHA. A particular focus will be given to the peculiar institutional design of JHA policies, which evolved from a purely intergovernmental setting into a more communitarized one in most policy areas. Following an overview of the institutional evolution of this policy area, I will draw conclusions on its influence and impact more generally.

The Commission in early cooperation on JHA

Early European cooperation on JHA was characterized through a purely intergovernmental mode of decision-making outside of the European architecture. Points in case are fora such as TREVI (short for *Terrorisme, Radicalisme et Violence Internationale;* translation: Terrorism, Radicalism and International Violence), created in 1975, and STAR (short for *Ständige Arbeitsgemeinschaft Rauschgift*, translation: Permanent Working Group on Drugs), created in preparation of the Schengen Agreement. Both were composed of senior officials from national JHA ministries, and they aimed at combatting either terrorism or drug trafficking respectively.

With the Maastricht Treaty in 1992, JHA made it into the so-called third pillar of the EU. Although issues such as immigration and the combat against organized crime and drug trafficking had now made it into EU primary law, decisions were still made in an intergovernmental mode and did not lead to directives or regulations but to less binding instruments such as common positions or joint actions. This implied that the Commission shared the right to initiative with the member states that were the only ones entitled to submit proposals in areas such as police cooperation and judicial cooperation in criminal matters. Since JHA deal with sensitive issues, decisions in the Council were taken unanimously, and only implementing measures could be passed by qmv, provided there was a previous unanimous agreement among the member states. The EP was not part of this decision-making process in any way. Given these circumstances, the Commission remained 'a potentially awkward actor' with extremely limited possibilities to take influence (Uçarer 2001: 1).

Newly gained competences with the Amsterdam Treaty

Since the mid-1990s the Commission had pleaded for an enhanced integration of all issues that were part of the third pillar, proposing in particular the Commission's right to initiative in all areas and qualified majority voting (Uçarer 2001: 9). Indeed, the lack of integration in the field had produced unsatisfying results, as policies were barely enforceable. This became particularly obvious for the area of immigration and asylum policies which had been in the spotlight ever since large numbers of immigrants had come to Europe subsequent to the disintegration of the Soviet Union and Yugoslavia in the early 1990s. The Amsterdam Treaty therefore introduced immigration and asylum policies into the first pillar of the EU (Stetter 2000).

Yet, policy-making in this field was still not fully communitarized. For an interim period of five years, the Commission continued to share its right to initiative with the member states, decisions in the Council were taken under unanimity, the EP was only consulted and the CJEU had only very limited jurisdiction. Still, this implied a strengthening of the Commission, which was now able to initiate binding legislation. In the remaining areas of JHA the Commission did not receive any additional rights. With the Tampere summit, the Commission received the sole right to initiative in the area of asylum policies, an area in which member states wanted to see quick results following the mass influx of refugees from former Yugoslavia since the mid-1990s, while competences in other areas of immigration policies remained mixed (Uçarer 2001: 14). Overall, the Commission's potential impact was enhanced significantly with the Amsterdam Treaty and the Tampere summit – at least in the area of asylum (and to some extent immigration) policies. In this area the Commission had a clear treaty mandate to initiate secondary legislation and in the case of asylum policies was even the sole actor possessing this competence. Thus, the Commission was able to frame debates from early on.

Yet, as studies of the decision-making processes after Amsterdam have shown for the area of asylum policies, the Commission did not leave a strong mark on EU legislation. Instead, the suggestions in its proposals were significantly watered down (Zaun 2017: 176–183). With unanimity vote in the Council, the Commission had to accommodate every member state that voiced a concern. Where it did not take into account all of these concerns, it received substantial criticism from the member states and even had to redraft its legislative proposal, as the cases of the Asylum Procedures Directive (see European Commission 2002), the recast Asylum Procedures (see European Commission 2011a) and the recast Reception Conditions Directive (see European Commission 2011b) demonstrate. While some member states in Northwestern Europe had initially wanted enhanced cooperation to ensure a more even distribution of asylum-seekers across Europe, this was no longer a priority when negotiations on EU legislation took place, as the numbers of asylum applications were decreasing in Europe at that time. Thus, member states were rather reluctant to change tried-and-tested national policies for the sake of EU harmonization and did not accept any Commission proposals that they would deem too ambitious (Zaun 2017: 176–183, 190–200). This heavily constrained the Commission's possibility for action.

Full communitarization of most policies with the Lisbon Treaty

After the first round of asylum directives had been passed in 2005, decision-making in the Council moved to qualified majority voting. This also applied to the areas of judicial cooperation in civil matters (excluding family law) and irregular immigration. With the Lisbon Treaty, the decision-making in legal immigration policies, judicial cooperation in criminal matters, Europol, visa policies and residence permits, civil protection and non-operational police cooperation also became fully communitarized. In these areas the EP is a co-legislator and the CJEU has full jurisdiction (Council of the European Union 2009). While the Commission has the sole right to initiative in immigration and asylum policies, a quarter of the member states may also initiate legislative proposals in criminal matters and police cooperation (Art. 76 TFEU). In areas like family law and operational police cooperation, consultation procedure and unanimity voting in the Council still apply (Council of the European Union 2009).

This may be assumed to have substantially strengthened the role of the Commission, at least in most areas of JHA. Indeed, the following example from the area of asylum policies shows that the Commission has been more effective in promoting its own policy suggestions than before the Lisbon Treaty. Both in its proposals on the Reception Conditions Directive (post-Amsterdam) and the Recast Reception Conditions Directive, the Commission suggested labor market access for asylum-seekers within six months after their application. In the negotiations on the original Directive this suggestion was entirely undermined by two restrictive outliers, Germany and France, which could only agree to labor market access after one year. In the negotiations on the Recast Directive, these two restrictive outliers no longer had a veto and thus, with the backing of the EP and the remaining member states in the Council, a compromise was found proposing labor market access after nine months which is much closer to the initial Commission proposal. This is a case in point for the enhanced agenda-setting powers the Commission has gained through full communitarization in the area (Thielemann and Zaun 2013: 11–12).

Evaluating the influence of the Commission

While the Commission has been able to draw legislative output closer to its proposal on a number of issues in the area of asylum policies since their full communitarization, this does not imply that the Commission is no longer heavily dependent on close cooperation with the member states and the EP to get its proposals accepted. The fact that two of the Commission's proposals on recast asylum directives had to be amended shows that the Commission has little leverage when proposing policies that are incompatible with (at least the majority of) member states' interests. In this regard the situation has barely changed from the pre-Lisbon context. In 2005 the introduction of European Border Guards had also failed due to ideological tensions between member states and eventually resulted in a less integrated agency, known under the name of Frontex (Parkes 2015: 64).

Situations of crisis, however, are windows of opportunity for successful policy activism by the Commission. According to MacKenzie et al. (2015), the Commission needs to 'seize [...] windows of opportunities' to be influential in JHA (MacKenzie et al. 2015: 93). A case in point for a demand of member states strengthening the Commission's ability to shape EU law according to its preferences is the European Arrest Warrant (EAW). The Commission had been working on a proposal for a EAW as an instrument of police cooperation since 2000, and some member states had opposed the idea of a EAW altogether. Yet, following 9/11 the Commission was able to frame the EAW as an instrument of counter-terrorism which was welcomed by many member states, as it allowed them to demonstrate to the USA that they were supporting them in the 'War on Terror'. Italy was even pressured by member states and the Commission to revise its law so that it would be able to agree to the EAW. Moreover, the adoption of the EAW implied more significant transfers of sovereignty than initially foreseen (Kaunert 2007: 396; MacKenzie et al. 2015: 102). Overall, this demonstrates that the Commission had strong leverage in this situation of crisis. Another recent example for the Commission seizing a window of opportunity is related to the European Boarder and Coast Guards Agency which was launched on October 6, 2016 (European Commission 2016a). The Commission 'recycled' this idea from the early 2000s and presented it as a response to the so-called EU refugee crisis. It succeeded in doing so due to the urgent need to address the influx of refugees (Interview Commission 1) and because it was successfully linked to EU counter-terrorism. While this shows that crisis situations are windows of opportunity for policy activism by the Commission, its success still strongly depends on the willingness of member states. The idea of a refugee quota system which was also meant to address the refugee crisis, for example, failed due to lack of support from the Visegrad countries and the high degree of politicization of the proposal, particularly in Central and Eastern Europe (Zalan 2016).

In the absence of an urgent demand for common EU policies, member states will usually prioritize their national sovereignty and draw upon unilateral action in the highly sensitive policy field of JHA. This weakens the position of the Commission substantially. For instance, following the Arab Spring, France and Denmark resorted to unilateral border closings and blocked an initiative of the Commission which wanted to be asked for its consent before any border closings. Subsequently, the Commission only needed to be notified in case a state suspended Schengen (Parkes 2015: 66). This, of course, also had important repercussions in the so-called refugee crisis, where member states lost their confidence in their neighbors' adherence to the Dublin Regulation and many of them, including Sweden, Germany, Austria and Denmark, closed their borders unilaterally (Taynor 2016). The fact that member states can do so without having to consult the Commission sets a low threshold for Schengen suspensions and severely weakens the European integration project in one of its key areas, namely internal freedom of movement.

Apart from seizing crisis situations, the Commission has used other strategies to pursue its aims in JHA. Roos (2013) has demonstrated in the area of labor migration policies that the Commission has partitioned its proposals so they would only focus on aspects that member states could agree on. While this, of course, led to less ambitious policies, it helped the Commission to safeguard policy ideas that would not have made it into EU legislation otherwise. In addition to that, the Commission has also strategically used the Court to constrain the Council, as described by Schmidt (2000) in the area of competition law. For instance, the Commission has drawn extensively upon case law by the CJEU (and the European Court of Human Rights) when drafting the recast asylum directives and initiated more than forty infringement procedures at the height of the 'refugee crisis' in 2015 when it became obvious that many member states, including those whose asylum systems had proven particularly poor at this time, had not implemented the Common European Asylum System (CEAS) (Carrera et al. 2015: 14). Arguably, the crisis situation provided the Commission with the necessary political backing for doing so, as it had previously shied away from initiating such a large amount of infringement procedures, although widespread non-implementation was identified as a key problem lying at the heart of the malfunctioning of the CEAS (Interview PermRep Germany).

After I have demonstrated that the Commission has assumed a relatively stronger role with each step of further integration while still depending widely on the consent of the member states and the EP, I will now assess the content of positions advanced by the Commission.

Positions of the Commission in JHA

Usually, the Commission is assumed to have a strong pro-integrationist stance, as this is its mandate and as more integration strengthens its own role (Kassim et al. 2013: 19). However, as it has always to take into consideration member states' concerns, it tends to water down its own proposals in anticipation of potential reservations of the member states. Regarding the content of its positions, the Commission is often described as a neutral and technocratic actor. At the same time, it has been both described as promoting 'neoliberal' policies undermining the welfare state or – more closely related to the policy area under investigation here – as a fervent supporter of minority rights (Hartlapp et al. 2014: 1). This section will assess to what extent these expectations can be confirmed in the area of JHA.

The Commission as a promoter of enhanced integration

While the Council has been quite cautious in accepting a deeper integration of policies in the area of JHA, the Commission has generally proposed policies that would ensure more competences for the EU. This is as true for data protection and police cooperation as it is in the areas of immigration policies and border control. In the area of border control, the Commission twice proposed the highly integrated concept of European Border Guards, which implies that European officials protect the EU's external borders. Its first attempt was only partly successful and the proposal was later watered down in the Council, resulting in the adoption of Frontex, which is much less integrated, as it is an agency coordinating national border guards (Parkes 2015: 64). The same may be said about the EAW where the Commission went for a much more integrated version that virtually abolished all political decisions in extraditions, when it had the opportunity to do so following 9/11 (Kaunert 2010b: 75; MacKenzie et al. 2015: 106–107). As mentioned earlier, the Commission had proposed full communitarization of JHA since the mid-1990s (Uçarer 2001: 9). This all supports the expectation that the Commission has a strong interest in a high degree of integration of JHA.

The Commission as a promoter of individual freedoms or security?

By design, the Area of Freedom, Security and Justice, as JHA were previously called, tries to balance two public goods, namely freedom and security, using law (justice) as a mediator. Since its early beginnings, scholars were therefore highly interested in whether JHA tilted towards individual freedoms or collective security. Some scholars came to the conclusion that this policy area was highly securitized (Bigo 2001), while others did not share this perspective (see, e.g., Boswell (2007) for the absence of securitization after 9/11).

This section addresses the question whether the Commission advances more security-oriented positions or whether the Commission is an advocate of freedom rights. In contrast to the question whether the Commission is a promoter of more integration, there is no straightforward answer to the question of the political leaning of the Commission. While the Commission has proposed comparatively liberal policies in the areas of immigration and asylum which had the potential to enhance individual rights of migrants (Thielemann and Zaun 2013), it also advanced relatively security-oriented policies in the area of border policies or counter-terrorism

(Parkes 2015). This leads to the conclusion that the Commission is an 'opportunistic' actor when it comes to the normative underpinnings of its proposals and corresponds well with the concept of the Commission as an unideological, technocratic actor. The Commission proposes policies which are generally in line with its core policy aim and mandate, namely to strengthen EU integration, as I will show in the following. I will now assess how the Commission's content-related positions vary both between policy areas and over time.

Variance between policy areas

Whereas the Commission proposes policies oriented towards individual freedoms in some policy areas, it suggests security-oriented policies in others.

In the area of asylum policies, the Commission has usually submitted legislative proposals which were much too liberal in the eyes of the Council. Thus, the Commission gradually watered down these proposals to ensure member states' consent and the passage of the Directive. Cases in point are the already mentioned original and recast asylum directives. There are three reasons why the Commission is a relatively liberal actor in the area of asylum policies. First, when minimum standards or even common standards are negotiated, agreeing on a high level of protection immediately implies agreeing on a high level of harmonization. Policies on a low level of protection that allow for more liberal policies (as is the case in the asylum area) means de facto little harmonization. If the EU agrees on a high level of protection member states falling below this protection standard need to adjust their policies to be compliant. Agreeing on a high level of protection thus ensures a high degree of harmonization and implies deeper integration. While the Commission is usually described as a neutral technocrat, it does see itself as a visionary and therefore not only tries to fulfill its duties but also proposes policy solutions that provide an added value for states and refugees (Interview Commission 3; Interview Commission 2). Second, besides the member states, NGOs and UNHCR are important contacts for the Commission that provide it with the expertise to write legislative proposals. This expertise is essential for the Commission, as expertise usually lies with the operating institutions in the member states (Interview Consultant). These, however, do not provide information as openly as do UNHCR and NGOs. In comparison to member states, NGOs and UNHCR are considered less biased towards a specific system, but oriented towards best practices. Third, the Commission is a non-elected or non-majoritarian institution which does not consider itself responsible to any specific electorate. Instead its positions are based on technocratic expertise (Thielemann and Zaun 2013). In addition, research has repeatedly shown that Commission officials belong to an elite which is arguably much more open to universalist ideas of human rights than to particularistic interests and national immigration laws (see Kassim *et al*. 2013: 31–54). While, of course, it is questionable to what extent Commission officials can follow their own preferences and ignore member states' concerns, their training may prejudice the arguments they find convincing.

In other policy areas, however, the Commission has put forward policies that are likely to sacrifice individual freedoms for the sake of security. One example is that of the European Border and Coast Guards (EBCG), mentioned previously, which should ensure a more effective border protection. Its predecessor, Frontex, has already been heavily criticized for human rights violations (Fischer-Lescano *et al*. 2009). In a similar vein the EAW is controversial, among others, given the highly diverse legal practices and detention conditions across Europe (Chakrabarti 2014). Subsequent to the terrorist attacks in Paris on November 13/14, 2015 and in Brussels on March 22, 2016, the Commission has launched a number of highly security-oriented projects, including the Security Union. The EBCG Agency was introduced as a measure of the Security

Union and thus clearly links irregular border crossings to issues such as terrorism (European Commission 2016a). In addition, the Security Union envisages the introduction of European Travel Information and Authorisation System (ETIAS), comparable to the US Electronic System for Travel Authorization (ESTA) (European Commission 2016b).

Variance of positions in comparison to other EU institutions and over time

Whereas the Commission was usually considered less liberal than the EP in the first phase of the CEAS, it was probably the most liberal actor compared to the other two institutions (Council and EP) in its second phase (Ripoll Servent and Trauner 2014; Zaun 2017: 179–180). This was for various reasons. First, the EP had become notably more restrictive. One reason for the EP becoming more restrictive was that the EP was an elected body and, with enhanced powers, considered itself more strongly as representer of the interests of its national electorate and ideological gaps among parties became more visible. During the first phase this had played a much smaller role, since the EP had little influence as an institution and so concentrated more on giving a single message to be heard at all (Interview Caritas Europa). Interestingly, this finding seems to be consistent across policy areas. For instance, Ripoll Servent and MacKenzie (2009) demonstrate for the case of the EU–US SWIFT agreement, that with increasing powers following the Lisbon Treaty the EP had to take into account security concerns of member states, whereas previously it had been free to advocate strong data protection. The Commission, as a fully non-majoritarian institution, was not subject to the aforementioned political pressures. Neither did it face the constraints that the EP was confronted with resulting from becoming a co-legislator and suddenly being in the spotlight. This leads to the conclusion that the Commission's positions were probably indeed more stable over time. Yet, more systematic research (across JHA policy areas) is needed to provide evidence for this conjecture.

With the EP becoming more restrictive and the Commission maintaining a stable (non)-ideology, the Commission has now turned into the most liberal among the EU institutions in the legislative process, at least in the area of asylum policies where high standards are closely related to its key interest of enhanced integration. But even in asylum policies, the Commission did not depart from the restrictive policy core that is underlying asylum policies in all European member states (Ripoll Servent and Trauner 2014: 1142). The focus of these policies still lies in the control and management of asylum, and the Commission rather proposes best practices from member states than radical innovations. It has often been questioned whether even these best practices are always in line with international law (e.g., Peers 2011; Trauner and Ripoll Servent 2015). The reason for adopting such a conservative approach is, again, that the Commission needs the support of the member states for any policy proposal it submits. Nevertheless, the Commission became more self-confident with its newly acquired powers in the second phase of the CEAS and at times adopted a more confrontational style, trying to link up with the EP against the Council. For instance, the Commission warned the Council not to resume negotiations on the Dublin III Regulation before the revised Eurodac Regulation was finalized. The Commission was aware that Northwestern European member states were not ready to accept the suspension of transfers it had proposed in the Dublin III Regulation and therefore tried to use Dublin as leverage for negotiations on the Eurodac Regulation, which member states had dropped (Interview Council). However, member states later turned the tables on the Commission, saying they would not discuss Eurodac until Dublin was passed (Interview PermRep Germany) and were more successful than the Commission had been.

Conclusion

This chapter has demonstrated that the Commission has always tried to deepen integration in all areas of JHA. This is a general feature of the Commission and is not related to any policy area. However, member states have been extremely reluctant to transfer competences to the EU in this field and only did so in times of crisis when they felt that enhanced cooperation was the only way to ensure effective policies that can be enforced. Cases in point are the partial communitarization of asylum policies with the Amsterdam Treaty, which was prompted by the high refugee influx from the former Soviet states and Yugoslavia in the early 1990s, the introduction of the EAW as a tool of counter-terrorism shortly after 9/11, and the recent introduction of the EBCG Guards as a response both to the 'refugee crisis' and recent terrorist attacks in Europe.

While most policy areas of JHA have been fully communitarized with the Lisbon Treaty, member states are still very reluctant to agree on policies which could potentially interfere with their national sovereignty and do not accept proposals by the Commission which they deem 'too ambitious'. Unless there is a real situation of crisis, the Commission has little to offer member states and has a stronger interest in EU policies than the member states, as this is its mandate. In situations of crisis, however, the Commission can act as a provider of policy solutions to predefined problems.

While the Commission has continuously been a fervent supporter of stronger European integration, the leaning of its normative underpinnings is more mixed. On the one hand, the Commission has promoted rights-enhancing policies in the area of immigration and asylum policies; on the other hand, it has also fostered securitarian policies, potentially reducing individual rights in the areas of police cooperation or border policies. The core focus of the Commission still seems to lie in strengthening integration and the Commission does not follow a clear ideological line in its proposals. Overall, this fits very well with its mandate and its role as a technocratic actor.

While the analysis has shown certain trends, the Commission in JHA still remains a highly under-researched topic. To date, there is no systematic research comparing the role of the Commission in the different subfields of JHA or research that focuses on the Commission as an actor in one of them, linking its findings to the general discussions on the role of the Commission in EU policy-making. Interesting avenues for further research include the systematic assessment of whether the liberal policy ideas promoted by the Commission in areas such as asylum policies are really a result of its focus on enhanced integration, or whether the Commission does follow normative or ideological considerations under specific circumstances. Further research should consider how institutional developments within the Commission, such as the separation of DG Justice, Freedom and Security into two DGs, one for Justice and Consumers and one for Migration and Home Affairs, as well as different Commissioners, have influenced policy-making processes and policy output. In addition, research in the field should address the question how the introduction of comitology into JHA with the Lisbon Treaty has changed the Commission's impact in its implementation and whether this has provided more leverage to the Commission, as has been demonstrated in other areas (Ballmann *et al.* 2003).

Table 34.1 List of interviewees

Cited as	Institutional affiliation of interviewee	Date of interview
Interview Caritas Europa	Caritas Europa	November 21, 2012
Interview Commission 1	European Commission, DG Migration and Home Affairs, Asylum Unit	October 5, 2016
Interview Commission 2	European Commission, DG Migration and Home Affairs, Asylum Unit	November 21, 2012
Interview Commission 3	European Commission, formerly DG Migration and Home Affairs, Asylum Unit	November 20, 2012
Interview Consultant	Freelance consultant on asylum refugee policies	March 24, 2013
Interview Council	Secretariat of the Council of the EU	April 10, 2012
Interview PermRep Germany	Permanent Representation of Germany to the EU	November 22, 2012

Bibliography

Aus, J.P. (2006). Decision-making under Pressure: The Negotiation of the Biometric Passports Regulation in the Council. Oslo: ARENA Working Paper No. 11/2006. www.ciaonet.org/attachments/9674/uploads.

Ballmann, A., Epstein, D. and O'Halloran, S. (2003). Delegation, Comitology, and the Separation of Power in the European Union. *International Organization*, 56(3), pp. 551–574.

Bigo, D. (2001). Migration and Security. In V. Guiraudon and C. Joppke, *Controlling a New Migration World*, pp. 121–149. London and New York: Routledge.

Boswell, C. (2007). Migration Control in Europe After 9/11: Explaining the Absence of Securitization. *Journal of Common Market Studies*, 45(3), pp. 589–610.

Boswell, C. (2008). The Political Functions of Expert Knowledge: Knowledge and Legitimation in European Union Immigration Policy. *Journal of European Public Policy*, 15(4), pp. 471–488.

Carrera, S., Blockmans, S., Gros, D. and Guild, E. (2015). The EU's Response to the Refugee Crisis. Taking Stock and Setting Policy Priorities. Brussels: CEPS Essay No. 20/2016. www.ceps.eu/system/files/EU%20Response%20to%20the%202015%20Refugee%20Crisis_0.pdf.

Chakrabarti, S. (2014). It's Not Just Eurosceptics Who Think the European Arrest Warrant is Rotten. *The Guardian*, November 9. www.theguardian.com/commentisfree/2014/nov/10/eurosceptics-think-european-arrest-warrant-rotten.

Council of the European Union. (2009). The Lisbon Treaty's Impact on the Justice and Home Affairs Council: More Co-decision and New Working Structures. Brussels. www.consilium.europa.eu/uedocs/cms_data/docs/pressdata/en/ec/111615.pdf.

European Commission. (2002). Amended Proposal for a Council Directive on Minimum Standards on Procedures in Member States for Granting and Withdrawing Refugee Status. COM (2002) 326 final. Brussels. http://eur-lex.europa.eu/legal-content/EN/TXT/?uri=COM:2002:0326:FIN.

European Commission. (2011a). Amended Proposal for a Directive of the European Parliament and of the Council on Common Procedures for Granting and Withdrawing International Protection Status (Recast). Brussels. http://eur-lex.europa.eu/legal-content/EN/TXT/?uri=COM:2011:0319:FIN.

European Commission. (2011b). Amended Proposal for a Directive of the European Parliament and of the Council Laying Down Standards for the Reception of Asylum Seekers (Recast). COM (2011) 319 final. Brussels. http://eur-lex.europa.eu/legal-content/EN/TXT/PDF/?uri=CELEX:52011PC0320&from=EN.

European Commission. (2016a). Securing Europe's External Borders: Launch of the European Border and Coast Guard Agency. Press release. Brussels. http://europa.eu/rapid/press-release_IP-16-3281_en.htm.

European Commission. (2016b). European Agenda on Security: Second Report on Progress towards an Effective and Sustainable Security Union. Press release. Brussels. http://europa.eu/rapid/press-release_IP-16-3681_en.htm.

Fischer-Lescano, A., Tillmann, L. and Tohidipur, T. (2009). Border Controls at Sea: Requirements under International Human Rights and Refugee Law. *International Journal of Refugee Law*, 21(2), pp. 256–296.

Guiraudon, V. (2000). European Integration and Migration Policy: Vertical Policy-making as Venue Shopping. *Journal of Common Market Studies*, 38(2), pp. 251–271.

Haas, E.B. (1964). *Beyond the Nation State: Functionalism and International Organization*. Palo Alto, CA: Stanford University Press.

Hartlapp, M., Metz, J. and Rauh, C. (2014). *Which Policy for Europe? Power and Conflict inside the European Commission*. Oxford: Oxford University Press.

Héritier, A. (1996). The Accommodation of Diversity in European Policy-making and its Outcomes: Regulatory Policy as a Patchwork. *Journal of European Public Policy*, 3(2), pp. 149–167.

Hix, S. and Noury, A. (2007). Politics, Not Economic Interests: Determinants of Migration Policies in the European Union. *International Migration Review*, 41(1), pp. 182–205.

Kassim, H., Peterson, J., Bauer, M.W., Connolly, S., Dehousse, R., Hooghe, L. and Thompson, A. (2013). *The European Commission of the Twenty-first Century*. Oxford: Oxford University Press.

Kaunert, C. (2007). 'Without the Power of Purse or Sword': The European Arrest Warrant and the Role of the Commission. *Journal of European Integration*, 29(4), pp. 387–404.

Kaunert, C. (2010a). The Area of Freedom, Security and Justice in the Lisbon Treaty: Commission Policy Entrepreneurship? *European Security*, 19(2), pp. 169–189.

Kaunert, C. (2010b). *European Internal Security: Towards Supranational Governance in the Area of Freedom, Security and Justice?* Manchester: Manchester University Press.

Knight, J. (1992). *Institutions and Social Conflict*. Cambridge: Cambridge University Press.

Lopatin, E. (2013). The Changing Position of the European Parliament on Irregular Migration and Asylum under Co-decision. *Journal of Common Market Studies*, 51(4), pp. 740–755.

MacKenzie, A., Kaunert, C. and Léonard, S. (2015). Counter-terrorism. Supranational EU Institutions Seizing Windows of Opportunities. In F. Trauner and A. Ripoll Servent (eds), *Policy Change in the Area of Freedom, Security and Justice. How EU Institutions Matter*, pp. 93–113. London: Routledge.

Maricut, A. (2016). With and Without Supranationalisation: The Post-Lisbon Roles of the European Council and the Council in Justice and Home Affairs Governance. *Journal of European Integration*, 38(5), pp. 541–555.

Nugent, N. and Rhinhard, M. (2015). *The European Commission*. Basingstoke: Palgrave Macmillan.

Parkes, R. (2015). Borders. EU Institutions Fail to Reconcile Their Agendas Despite Communitarisation. In F. Trauner and A. Ripoll Servent (eds), *Policy Change in the Area of Freedom, Security and Justice. How EU Institutions Matter*, pp. 53–72. London: Routledge.

Peers, S. (2011). Revised EU Asylum Proposals: 'Lipstick on a Pig'. www.statewatch.org/analyses/no-132-asylum.pdf.

Pollack, M.A. (2000). The Commission as an Agent. In N. Nugent (ed.), *At the Heart of the Union: Studies of the European Commission*, pp. 111–130. New York: St. Martin's Press.

Ripoll Servent, A. (2014). The Role of the European Parliament in International Negotiations After Lisbon. *Journal of European Public Policy*, 21(4), pp. 568–586.

Ripoll Servent, A. (2015). *Institutional and Policy Change in the European Parliament – Deciding on Freedom, Security and Justice*. London: Routledge.

Ripoll Servent, A. and MacKenzie, A. (2009). Is the EP Still a Data Protection Champion? The Case of SWIFT. *Perspectives on European Politics and Society*, 12(4), pp. 390–406.

Ripoll Servent, A. and Trauner, F. (2014). Do Supranational EU Institutions Make a Difference? EU Asylum Law before and after 'Communitarization'. *Journal of European Public Policy*, 21(8), pp. 1142–1162.

Roos, C. (2013). How to Overcome Deadlock in EU Immigration Politics. *International Migration*, 51(6): pp. 67–79.

Schmidt, S.K. (2000). Only an Agenda Setter? The European Commission's Power over the Council of Ministers. *European Union Politics*, 1(1), pp. 37–61.

Stetter, S. (2000). Regulating Migration: Authority Delegation in Justice and Home Affairs. *Journal of European Public Policy*, 7(1), pp. 80–103.

Taynor, I. (2016). Is the Schengen Dream of Europe without Borders Becoming a Thing of the Past? www.theguardian.com/world/2016/jan/05/is-the-schengen-dream-of-europe-without-borders-becoming-a-thing-of-the-past.

Thielemann, E. and Zaun, N. (2013). Escaping Populism – Safeguarding Human Rights: The European Union as a Venue for Non-majoritarian Policy-making in the Area of Refugee Protection. Paper presented at the Annual Meeting of the American Political Science Association, Chicago, August 29 to September 1.

Trauner, F. and Ripoll Servent, A. (2015). *Policy Change in the Area of Freedom, Security and Justice: How Institutions Matter*. London: Routledge.

Uçarer, E. (2001). From the Sidelines to Center Stage: Sidekick No More? The European Commission in Justice and Home Affairs. *European Integration Online Papers*, 5(5), pp. 1–20.

Zalan, E. (2016). EU Migrant Quota Idea Finished, Fico Says. euobserver, September 27. https://euobserver.com/migration/135245.

Zaun, N. (2016). Why EU Asylum Policies Exceed the Lowest Common Denominator: The Role of Regulatory Expertise in EU Decision-Making. *Journal of European Public Policy*, 23(1), pp. 136–154.

Zaun, N. (2017). *EU Asylum Policies: The Power of Strong Regulating States*. Basingstoke: Palgrave Macmillan.

35
THE COUNCIL AND EUROPEAN COUNCIL IN EU JUSTICE AND HOME AFFAIRS POLITICS

Christof Roos

Introduction

Research on the EU policy area of justice and home affairs (JHA) almost inevitably touches upon the 'Council'. The Council is the most influential EU institution and is the gatekeeper for member state interests (Lewis 2015: 221), particularly with regard to JHA issues and their sovereignty relevance. Therefore, almost any study on legislative politics in the EU policy area of JHA includes an analysis of one or more governing bodies that comprise the Council. The bodies are the European Council and its permanent president in which heads of state or government decide and define the JHA agenda, the JHA Council headed by the respective member state holding the rotating six-month Council presidency as part of the Council of the European Union where the home affairs ministers negotiate and make the decisions, the Committee of Permanent Representatives (COREPER) where ambassadors (COREPER II for JHA) from member states take preparatory decisions for the ministers, and, at the lowest level, the eighteen working parties consisting of national experts and JHA counselors that channel Commission proposals into the Council bodies for a decision (A-point) or further discussion (B-point) to the higher levels (de Schoutheete 2006; Puetter 2012; Maricut 2016).

This review of scholarly work on the Council in JHA departs from a counter-intuitive observation. Despite the Council's key position in the policy area, it has largely remained a 'black box' in the academic literature concerned with JHA. A few notable exceptions to this general claim are the works of Maricut (2016), Smeets (2013) and Aus (2008). Compared to the broader political science debates on the Council, the JHA Council is under-researched with regard to themes such as the voting behavior of member states or alliances among member states, as well as on questions regarding possible shifts of power within the Council, from lower to higher levels of decision-making. The reasons for these research gaps relate to the fact that the member states and the Council are often not considered as analytically distinct units. This has the effect of obscuring dynamics within the EU institution that can originate from specific procedures at play within the body. In addition, research on the JHA policy area is dominated by issue-specific case studies that aim at understanding policy output in the respective policy subfields of police cooperation, asylum, immigration and justice matters, rather than identifying general patterns in policy-making.

One more reason for these research gaps may also be the methodological choices of scholars and the challenge of data access that working on the Council poses. Scholars have shown a preference for single or comparative case studies and qualitative methods. Mixed or quantitative methods are rarely applied in the JHA field. This limits the range of questions that can be tackled as well as the generalizability of the findings. However, any choice for a specific method faces the problem of data access (Häge 2008: 538). The documentation of decision-making in this EU institution is less transparent and accessible than that of the Commission, the European Parliament (EP) or the European Court of Justice (EUCJ). Research on the Council, in particular research on the process dimension of negotiations, calls for the triangulation of data. Among other possible sources, researchers can revert to the minutes of Council meetings, the Council agenda, European Council conclusions, the negotiation proceedings from the Commission, the EP or national governments, and expert interviews.

The chapter proceeds by discussing the three major theoretical approaches and their respective research questions and empirical findings that are dominant in studies on the Council in general and JHA in particular. First, I focus on the work that applies an intergovernmental and state-centered perspective in explaining whether and why member states would pool sovereignty in the Council in this specific policy area. Second, the application of new institutionalism, its rational choice as well as sociological accounts has allowed scholars to solve puzzles that could not be explained by intergovernmental theory. For example, member states' changing their preferences during Council negotiations is explained by the impact of decision-making rules and norms that are specific to the Council. The institutional procedures at work within the Council is a research area that is still barely explored by scholars of JHA. Third, the review suggests attention be paid to to the research paradigm of 'new intergovernmentalism' (Bickerton *et al.* 2015). The research paradigm shifts emphasis from the Council as a lawmaking institution to a EU institution that takes on executive power and facilitates policy coordination. In light of the evolution of the policy area, I suggest critically reflecting upon whether or not intergovernmental modes of policy-making persisted in JHA despite recent moves in communitarizing the policy area. Thus, the observation of changes in EU decision-making at the expense of the community method may apply to other EU policy areas but not to JHA (Maricut 2016). The chapter concludes with a summary of the main research gaps that this review on the Council in JHA identified.

State-centered approaches to member state cooperation in the Council

Intergovernmental theory, stressing the interests of member states in EU cooperation, dominates the study of policy-making on JHA in the Council. The evolution of this EU policy area as one of the last to become communitarized explains why researchers first looked at state motivations for cooperation in the Council. In fact, the involvement of the Council in the cooperation of member states on JHA policies first began with the entry into force of the Maastricht Treaty in 1993 (Title VI TEU). The Council as a EU institution has existed since the adoption of the Treaty of Rome in 1957, but member states preferred other EU-level venues for collaboration. Scholars who observed the inclusion of JHA issues into the newly created third pillar described the working methods of the JHA Council. At first, the member states largely continued an intergovernmental legacy from the TREVI bodies that preceded JHA cooperation within the Council. However, the Council framework and its procedures were also considered to have significantly changed the flexible and informal character of the former TREVI cooperation. The literature that documents this early phase of Council involvement in the JHA policy area ascertains the socialization of member state officials into the formalized environment of EU procedures (Stetter 2000: 91; Monar 2012: 727–728). According to Lavenex and Wallace, 'intensive transgovernmental networks' emerged from cooperation among member state officials

(Lavenex and Wallace 2005: 463). Along this line, the post-Maastricht phase is considered to be the 'decisive intergovernmental gate opener' for the facilitation of member state cooperation. It prepared further communitarization of the policy area with the implementation of the Amsterdam Treaty in 1999 (Monar 2012).

Scholars also assessed that, initially, the transfer of JHA cooperation to the Council would not go along with significant policy output. Cooperation in the Council remained intergovernmental and excluded the serious delegation of oversight over commitments and the implementation of common policy to a supranational institution. This would not resolve the 'decision-making dilemma' in JHA (Maurer et al. 2003: 58) and led to 'regulatory failure' (Stetter 2000: 92). In the absence of delegation to the Commission or the EP, authors argued, no claimable objectives for cooperation could be set. In addition, the limited commitment promoted by policy instruments such as resolutions and joint decisions would be insufficient in dealing with transaction costs arising from the abolition of internal border control and the free movement of persons in the Single Market (Stetter 2000). Accordingly, functional spill-over from the Single Market, EU enlargements and a growing legitimacy deficit called for the delegation of oversight to supranational institutions such as the Commission and the Court as well as more democratic participation by involving the EP (Lavenex and Wallace 2005; Niemann 2008).

In contrast, scholars such as Geddes, Guiraudon and Lavenex came to a slightly different conclusion in assessing the policy output of the post-Maastricht phase of JHA cooperation. Basically, they stressed that intergovernmental cooperation within and outside of the Council created a venue where national law and order officials could elaborate a restrictive security agenda for the EU (Lavenex 1999: 45; Geddes 2000: 93). 'Shopping' intergovernmental venues, the Council included, allowed for the adoption of 'restrictive control policies' away from national veto players and judicial constraints that could prevent a more restrictive agenda (Guiraudon 2000: 261). In fact, the JHA Council adopted 335 binding and non-binding measures between 1993 and the entry into force of the Amsterdam Treaty in 1999 (Nilsson 2004: 121). In this light, a reassessment of the JHA Council's policy output, including its content, restrictive or expansive, for the post-Maastricht period, could bring clarity to the contradictory findings proposed by the literature.

An intergovernmental, state-centered approach to explaining member state preferences in JHA defines a dominant research paradigm. Largely, scholars attribute domestic politics and interests as driving member state positions in the Council (Guiraudon and Lahav 2000; Lavenex 2001; Givens and Luedtke 2004; Luedtke 2009). Such state-centered approaches highlight variables such as issue salience of border control, migration and crime prevention, the political partisanship of the government negotiating in the Council, or domestic veto players providing incentives for EU-level policy. Accordingly, the hypothesis was put forward that an increase in the domestic salience of JHA issues motivated EU policy that puts emphasis on law and order as well as on immigration control. In addition, parties of the center right in power would be more likely to push for such measures than parties left of center (Givens and Luedtke 2004: 152–153). Along the lines of 'venue shopping for restriction' (Guiraudon 2000), state-centered approaches explained the policy output of the Council as a result of member states using the EU level mainly for the purpose of restricting domestic policy. Decision-making rules would work in favor of this rationale. Accordingly, decisions based on unanimity gave each member state the power to veto a policy. This made policy output of the lowest common denominator more likely. The later transposition and implementation of the lowest common denominator EU legislation would allow for undermining comparatively higher domestic standards in some member states (Maurer and Parkes 2007).

Actors, institutions and interactions in Council negotiations

Conversely to the predicted outcomes of the venue-shopping hypothesis, scholars discovered that policy output in the intergovernmental setting did not necessarily define decisions on the lowest common denominator for all member states (Aus 2008; Roos 2013; Thielemann and El-Enany 2010; Zaun 2015). Member states accepting policy output that seemingly contradicts their preferences is a major puzzle in EU studies as well as in JHA. In this regard, the concept of multi-level governance, but also attention to the impact of Council-specific rules and norms on JHA politics, opens up an alternative research paradigm.

Alternatives to venue-shopping: regulatory competition, lock-in and misfit

By applying the concept of multi-level governance and regulation theory, the puzzle of negotiation outcomes above the lowest common denominator could be explained (Majone 1996). For example, the 'misfit model' holds that member states prefer to maintain the status quo of their legislation rather than policy changes that would entail administrative costs (Börzel and Risse 2000). By uploading policy to the EU level, governments 'lock in' policy preferences that most often resemble their domestic choices. Negotiation outcomes in the Council may also depend on the capacity of a member state in terms of its expertise in regulating a certain issue effectively. According to these variables, member states in the JHA Council may be categorized as strong, medium or weak regulators, leading to different positions in EU decision-making. Strong regulators occupy an advantageous position in the Council, since they have expertise on the issue being debated. Usually, they also push for EU legislation in order to avoid regulatory competition with weak regulators (Héritier 1996; Zaun 2015). Counter-intuitively, member states did not engage in competition for the lowest standards in asylum or immigration legislation. Rather, they tried to halt a 'race to the bottom in protection standards in the EU' (Thielemann and El-Enany 2010: 216).

With regard to EU asylum politics, Zaun showed that strong regulators succeeded in locking in their comparatively higher standards in EU legislation. Weak regulators agreed to high EU standards, factoring the option of non-implementation into their position. As a result, policy output did not necessarily meet all of the preferred positions from member states or allow for restrictive changes in domestic legislation (Zaun 2015). The strategic non-compliance of member states with EU legislation is a likely negotiation scenario in JHA considering the evidence brought forward by implementation studies (Falkner et al. 2005). At the same time, the viability of such a negotiation strategy may be short-lived. The 'benefits' of premeditated non-compliance must be weighed against the loss in the reputation of a member state as a reliable partner and contractor for international agreements (Hayes-Renshaw et al. 2006: 172; Aus 2008: 115).

Diffuse reciprocity and appropriate behavior in Council negotiations

The understanding of member states as actors that are affected by the institutional environment at the EU level allows for a more nuanced understanding of member states' changing preferences and their behavior during negotiations in the Council. In this regard, variants from new institutionalism such as rational-choice institutionalism and perspectives borrowing from sociological institutionalism answer these research questions.

Rational-choice institutionalism starts from the assumption that states are goal-oriented actors that seek to maximize the utility of policy outcome. The preferences of states may be set endogenously or be determined exogenously by the rules and norms, aka the institutions with which the member state interacts. In this setting, the 'logic of consequentialism' applies. It explains why member states refrain from short-term *quid pro quo* bargaining in the Council and its likely consequence of policy deadlock. Rather, they consider compromise and consensus as providing for long-term gains that acknowledge the 'diffuse reciprocity' of EU policy-making (Lewis 2015: 225). In contrast, 'the logic of appropriateness' highlights collectively held expectations of what defines appropriate behavior among actors in the Council (Lewis 2005: 938). To the detriment of actors' strategic interests, social norms and the desire to conform to rules such as consensus and compromise can determine member state negotiations in the Council (March and Olsen 1989: 160–162; Lewis 2005).

Both approaches apply to understanding JHA politics in the Council. Aus (2008) has shown that member states negotiating the *Dublin II* Regulation went through distinct processes in adopting the legislation. At the beginning of negotiations, an intergovernmental bargaining phase pushed actors to seek outcomes that could maximize their interest. At the brink of deadlock, member states considered the diffuse reciprocity of their veto with regard to other policies under negotiation. The logic of consequentialism would apply and a compromise of positions was the result (Aus 2008: 114). The Council negotiations on *Dublin II* followed a sequence. Compromise positions were not only possible due to reciprocal bargaining, but also because member states adhered to 'Council-specific informal rules' that allowed for a consensus (Aus 2008: 116). After the exchange of all arguments and the realization that opposition would not lead to bargaining success, member states resigned themselves to consensual decision-making rather than be isolated in opposition (ibid.). The example of negotiations on the *Dublin II* Regulation shows that institutions can impact actor behavior with regard to their bargaining strategies as well as normative orientation.

Changing decision-making rules: voting or consensus in the Council?

Attention to how institutional procedures determine member state positions in the Council became even more relevant with regard to changes in the decision-making rules in the JHA Council. The entry into force of institutional change with the adoption of the Amsterdam (1999), Nice (2003) and Lisbon (2009) Treaties transferred JHA to communitarized decision-making step-by-step. The prevalent unanimity rule was replaced by decisions that were based on qualified majority vote (QMV). Following the Nice Treaty and the EU enlargement from fifteen to twenty-five member states, a weighted vote system was applied. For a decision to be adopted, a majority of member states had to cast 72 percent of weighted votes (sixty-two votes out of a total of eighty-seven). Compared to their actual share in the EU population, this system disproportionately favored small and medium-sized member states. With the adoption of the Lisbon Treaty, the rule of the double majority was introduced in 2014. A coalition wins if it casts 55 percent of member states which represent 65 percent of the EU's population. Four countries representing 35 percent of the EU population can form a blocking minority. Interestingly, the member states not participating in the Euro nor the ten Eastern European countries could possibly form a blocking minority within this latest set of rules, whereas under the old rules they were able to do so (Fleishman Hillard 2014). As a baseline, QMV according to the weighted vote system as well as the double majority rule increases the likelihood that individual or groups of countries are outvoted. Accordingly, scholars expected qmv to become the norm with the effect of making EU decision-making more efficient and less prone to deadlock (Héritier 1999; Niemann 2008).

Despite these institutional options, member states seem to prefer consensus, the 'adoption of a collective decision without contesting votes' rather than voting and coalescing (Häge 2013:

482). This is also supported by the Commission, which usually does not propose legislation that cannot be agreed upon by member states consensually (Heisenberg 2005: 71). At its core, consensus tries to balance the interests of member states regarding more or less EU integration. It is the major informal rule in EU decision-making and dates back to the 'Luxembourg compromise' from 1966. Since then, the informal rule co-exists with the formal treaty obligations and has survived many attempts for its repeal (Heisenberg 2005: 68). Consensus among member states does not, however, mean that unanimity is continued. Building consensus within qmv considers the probability of a vote; the so-called 'shadow of the vote' (Golub 1999). This shadow influences negotiations and facilitates consensus (Häge 2013). Under these conditions, consensus means that a minority should in some way be appeased but does not have to be won completely (Heisenberg 2005: 79). Consensus does not necessarily indicate that 'agreement' has been reached. It is possible that a qualified majority was secured in the absence of a formal vote and explicit opposition (Novak 2013: 1092). If a vote is cast, formal abstentions count as 'nos' to a proposal, since a quorum needs to be met for the adoption of a proposal (Van Aken 2012: 20). Accordingly, abstentions may be considered implicit opposition whereas negative votes may be understood as explicit opposition. In contrast to the unanimity rule, opposition counts and becomes visible in qmv.

From a purely rationalist perspective, the maintenance of consensus is puzzling because it raises the question as to why member states do not use the institutional rules for maximizing their interests. New institutionalism and its rationale as well as sociological variant address this question. Both approaches suggest that consensus continues because member states adhere to a culture of consensus (Lewis 2003: 997); consensus facilitates individual compensation and transactions across issue areas (Heisenberg 2005); consensus emerges as a by-product of coalition-building processes (Häge 2013); and member states try to avoid the blame that goes along with being outvoted in the Council. Thus, appropriate behavior in Council decision-making may also mean that member states adhere to 'the norm of non-public dissent' (Novak 2013: 1094). Surprisingly, these hypotheses about decision-making in the Council have not yet been put to the test with regard to the JHA Council. As a matter of fact, future academic research on JHA may therefore focus on the motivations of member states to cast a vote or to agree on a decision by consensus. Even though voting may rarely apply in JHA, we don't know much about its underlying conditions.

The limited data that have been collected thus far by *Vote Watch Europe*, a Brussels-based think-tank, confirms the general claim of the literature that some 70 percent of all decisions taken in the Council were voted upon but were based on consensus (Hayes-Renshaw *et al.* 2006: 161; Vote Watch Europe 2015: 5). Consensus appears to prevail less in issue areas such as the common agricultural or fisheries policy (Hayes-Renshaw *et al.* 2006: 177). Mattila worked with a dataset comprising voting records from the 1990s and excluded the then third-pillar JHA Council. He identified patterns that hint at why member states vote against the majority in the Council. Accordingly, '[t]he most likely "no" voter is a right-wing government from a large member country with a Eurosceptical voter base. The opposite case is a leftist government from a small country' (Mattila 2004: 47). However, these assumptions are not confirmed by *Vote Watch* data on the sixty-two decisions that the JHA Council took between 2009 and 2014. A clearly identifiable voting pattern of big versus small or right- versus left-governed member states does not appear (Vote Watch Europe 2015). As the qualified majority vote is a fairly recent institutional innovation, a larger sample is not yet available. In addition, a qualitative analysis into the justifications of member states opposing the majority in the JHA Council still needs to be done.

Related to voting behavior is the question of whether and how coalitions among member states matter in the area of JHA. This question has not yet been addressed in the literature.

On the general level, stable coalitions in Council decision-making across policy areas seem to be the exemption (Hayes-Renshaw et al. 2006: 177). Despite the inconsistency of the preferences of member states, studies point to a stylized 'North–South' divide that stands for interests built on socio-economic (rich and poor) and regulatory (protectionism and liberalization) cleavages between member states (Zimmer et al. 2005: 403–404). No systematic account exists that shows whether and how member states group on general cleavages or match their issue-specific interests when forming groups in the JHA Council. Considering the variance in member state approaches in dealing with refugee and border protection, cleavages between member states with more or less of a humanitarian orientation could possibly be observable. In addition, a cleavage between member states located in the center and those at the periphery of the EU may be identifiable in Council decision-making. In this regard, the large body of case studies on JHA issues points to a recurring coalition among Austria, Germany and The Netherlands in pushing for EU policy that respects their sovereignty concerns and puts emphasis on law enforcement and control. Another country grouping builds on the member states that have negotiated a voluntary opt-in, namely the UK and Ireland, or Denmark, which opted for a full opt-out from JHA. Despite their special status in JHA, they try and manage to shape policy according to their preferences (Adler-Nissen 2009: 76–77).

A systematic, qualitative and quantitative analysis of votes taken in the JHA Council would be needed in order to overcome the research gaps outlined above. The question of the willingness of member states to agree to more or less EU integration becomes most evident in terms of the relocation of refugees and the redistribution of resources for their support. The JHA Council is the venue where this core conflict will be negotiated. How the cleavage becomes evident in more voting or coalition-building among groups of member states needs to be observed.

The role of the Council's bureaucracy and presidency

Research on the dynamics among the various bodies in the JHA Council is rare. In accordance with the Council hierarchy, most research in this area focuses on the higher levels, the Council of Ministers and the European Council. The level of decision-making is an issue that is empirically disputed and normatively charged. Hayes-Renshaw and collaborators hold that 85 percent of decisions are made before they reach the Council of Ministers (2006: 50; see also Nilsson 2004: 131). Häge contradicts these findings and shows that at least one-third of decisions are taken at the ministerial level (2008: 535). With regard to JHA, he shows that, in 2003, more than 40 percent of decisions were taken by ministers directly rather than at the lower levels of the Council bureaucracy (Häge 2008: 546). Smeets finds himself between these two positions by showing that Council decisions are often the result of interplay between levels. In this regard, the lower levels, the Permanent Representatives and the working parties perform more than just preparatory functions. It is at these levels where a policy can become stuck or deals may be struck (Smeets 2013: 16–18). Determining the level of decision-making is important, since it speaks to debates on the legitimacy of decision-making in the Council as well as the different 'constituencies' of Council bodies. Arguably, decisions have less legitimacy if they are made by bureaucrats rather than by elected politicians. In addition, home affairs ministers and their respective national bureaucracies have been among those most entrenched in national structures and traditions. In JHA, law enforcement and justice need to cooperate within and across national delegations (Lavenex and Wallace 2005: 462–463). Thus, national rivalries among ministries as well as the corresponding government can easily translate into the respective Council bodies.

The Council bureaucracy, with over thirty committees and working parties, plays a distinct role in how decisions on JHA come about (Monar 2012: 499). For example, the process of creating *Eurojust* at the end of the 1990s exemplified how the Council secretariat increased the efficiency of intergovernmental decision-making in the Council. While this function may be expected from an institution, the secretariat's role allegedly expanded to become the 'motor, legal drafter and initiative taker' (Nilsson 2004: 137) in JHA by strategically diffusing ideas and compromise through its network of officials (Beach 2008: 233–234). In fact, the secretariat is instrumental in supporting the respective Council presidency in taking up its leadership function. The Council secretariat provides information on long-term policy developments and assists the chairing presidency in building consensus among member states. The secretariat was found to use this role to exert decisive influence on the policy process (Beach 2008: 234–235; Christiansen 2002). Whether the entry into force of the Lisbon Treaty and the creation of the institution of a permanent president of the European Council has changed the role of the Council secretariat still needs to be assessed. The institution of a permanent president of the European Council probably reduces rather than strengthens the dependence of the respective member state holding the presidency of the Council on the secretariat (Christiansen 2002: 94).

The rotating presidency offers member states opportunities for agenda-setting and its management, as well as country representation (Tallberg 2006). Drafting and finalizing Council conclusions is a key resource in promoting certain member state agendas (Alexandrova and Timmermans 2013: 320). At the same time, the agenda-setting powers of a member state are limited by behavioral norms such as the call for neutrality and the presidency's function of reinforcing consensus-building (Niemann and Mak 2010). Therefore, evidence for member states using the Council presidency systematically for the promotion of their specific agendas could not be found. Influence on the Council's agenda seems to be related more to actual power relationships among member states rather than to exertion through the institution of the presidency (Alexandrova and Timmermans 2013: 323). The finding that member states succeeded in influencing the Council agenda on JHA issues during their turn in the presidency (Roos 2013; Nilsson 2004: 138) may be related to the general intergovernmental set-up of the Council and not to the institution of the presidency as such. This suggests further research into how member states make use of their presidency in promoting JHA issues on the Council's agenda.

'New' or old patterns of intergovernmentalism in the Council?

'New intergovernmentalism' argues that EU integration is promoted outside the community method. By intensifying policy coordination within the European Council, member states are said to promote EU integration without the involvement of genuinely supranational institutions (Bickerton *et al.* 2015: 704). These forms of cooperation allow for more voluntary policy coordination among member states without the full inclusion of the Commission or the Court at the supranational level.

Recent studies show that the European Council evolved from a body that used to set general priorities for the EU to an institution that is increasingly involved in the day-to-day policy-making of the Council (Carammia *et al.* 2016: 14). Apparently, heads of state set the agenda and increasingly 'reserve the right to finalize decision making processes among themselves' (Puetter 2012: 162–163). Since 2009, the European Council has been chaired by a permanent president elected on a 2.5-year mandate. This further increases the role of the European Council as the EU's intergovernmental executive. At the same time, the influence of individual member states holding the six-month EU presidency has diminished (Alexandrova and Timmermans 2013). An indicator of this development is not only more policy coordination occurring directly among member states in the European Council facilitated by its president, but also the delegation of specific functions to so-called *de novo bodies* (Bickerton *et al.* 2015; Puetter 2012). The latter are

EU agencies, semi-autonomous bodies that allow for collective action without empowering supranational institutions (Bickerton *et al.* 2015: 713).

Empirical research on 'new intergovernmentalism' has focused on member state policy coordination during the financial crisis. In governing the EURO, Puetter shows convincingly how intergovernmentalism in the Council and European Council had the effect of downplaying the role of the Commission as a crisis manager (Puetter 2012: 172–173). The analysis of member state policy coordination during the migration crisis of 2015 and 2016 shows how the European Council took on the role of crisis manager in JHA. Yet, differing preferences of member states regarding crisis solutions, such as voluntary or obligatory relocation schemes for refugees, led to a paralysis in problem-solving capacity. Along the lines of Puetter, Maricut finds that in JHA the majority of member states indeed prefer 'integration without (rather than with) supranationalisation' (2016: 546). At the same time, she argues that despite gradual supranationalization after Lisbon, 'new intergovernmentalism' is observable in JHA in a way that strongly resembles old patterns of intergovernmental decision-making (Maricut 2016: 542).

The European Council plays a decisive role in defining JHA. Heads of government have regularly met at this highest-level intergovernmental body since 1975. It has the function of giving long-term political guidance, resolving stalled legislative processes, and developing the institutional design of the EU (de Schoutheete 2006).

The literature documents three influential five-year programs on JHA issues that resulted from meetings of the European Council in Tampere (1999), The Hague (2004) and Stockholm (2009). Among others, the Tampere program formulated under the Finnish Council presidency in 1999 conceptualized the 'Area of Freedom, Security and Justice' and had a lasting influence on motivating policy development in JHA. Equally as important, the Tampere European Council also laid the groundwork for the later adoption of the EU's Charter of Fundamental Rights. The Seville and Thessaloniki European Council meetings in 2002 and 2003 decisively pushed the Tampere objectives further (Nilsson 2004; Lavenex and Wallace 2005: 469; Geddes 2008).

With the termination of the Stockholm program in 2014, the member states discontinued defining JHA objectives in five-year programs. This suggests changes in the intentions of member states to systematically develop and partly control the agenda for JHA (Maricut 2016: 543). It may mean that the member states constrained the Commission's function to oversee implementation rather than promote further integration in JHA. In addition, turning away from long-term strategies allows for more flexibility and ad hoc policy response to current events. In this regard, the discontinuation could indicate that the member states are developing the European Council, also in JHA, to become more of the executive power of the EU (Carammia *et al.* 2016; Puetter 2012).

The discussion on new intergovernmentalism goes beyond studying the European Council. The establishment of agencies in JHA is highly relevant to the discussion on *de novo bodies* as a means for member states to strengthen the EU's executive power (Bickerton *et al.* 2015: 713; see Chapter 37). Among others, the EU border agency (Frontex) and the European law enforcement agency (Europol) are built on EU secondary law but have a strong intergovernmental element in their governance structure (Lavenex and Wallace 2005: 470–472; Trauner 2016). Beyond the description of the functioning of these semi-autonomous EU agencies, there is a gap in research in scrutinizing how EU agencies co-exist with supranational institutions and national bodies. This raises questions of accountability, inter-agency rivalries for resources and effectiveness. 'New intergovernmentalism' is a recent research paradigm in EU studies. It remains to be seen whether the perspective can offer an added value to the study of JHA policy. The area has always been dominated by member states and has functioned in a rather intergovernmental mode since the 1990s (Lavenex and Wallace 2005: 498; Ripoll-Servent and Trauner 2014). A policy area so closely related to issues touching upon the core of national sovereignty could only become communitarized by assuring a central role for the European Council and the Council. Accordingly, JHA may be considered a hybrid policy area in which supranational and intergovernmental decision-making modes exist side by side (Maricut 2016: 552).

The Council 'sharing power' with the Commission and the EP

Whether the gradual increase in influence of supranational actors during the 2000s has been short-lived and is already in decline will need further scholarly attention. In the light of various treaty changes during the 2000s, scholars have debated whether and how the Council shares power in JHA with the EP and the Commission. The research puts an emphasis on the role of supranational actors in JHA and scrutinizes relations among EU institutions.

For example, the Commission was found to be a 'policy entrepreneur' that skillfully frames the EU agenda and thus has an impact on negotiations and policy output (Geddes 2008; Boswell 2009: 195ff.; Kaunert 2010; Roos 2013; Cerna and Meng-Hsuan 2013). The introduction of the EP as co-legislator in JHA put the effects of treaty change on power relations between the Council and the EP on the research agenda. Contrary to the expectation that EP involvement in JHA decision-making would bring substantial changes to policy-making and output, observations from the areas of asylum policy and data protection suggest otherwise (Ripoll Servent 2012; Ripoll Servent and Trauner 2014). Instead of maximizing its powers conferred by co-decision, the LIBE Committee of the EP has refrained from seriously opposing the Council. Findings hold that political factions in the EP prefer an 'efficient' and 'responsible' working relationship with the Council to maintaining their own policy positions (Ripoll Servent 2012: 981).

While this EP position may change due to the growing maturity of the EU institution in the co-decision procedure, little or nothing is known about the Council and how it adapted to the EP at the negotiation table. For example, in formulating amendments to a Commission proposal, it is not yet known whether the Council already considers the positions of dominant factions in the EP. Along this line, knowledge on the Council's behavior in trialogues with the Commission and the EP is also scarce. If the Council aims at limited power-sharing with the Commission and the EP, we should observe these EU institutions being sidelined in negotiations (Winnwa 2016). As trialogues are informal and non-transparent, it will be hard to systematically detect the Council's behavior or strategy in this specific setting.

Conclusions

This review of academic work on the Council in JHA has shown how 'old' and 'new' intergovernmentalism as well as accounts from new institutionalism in its rational and sociological variants can answer pertinent questions on the decision-making dynamics and output of the JHA Council. State-centered perspectives allow for disentangling the various interests factoring into member state positions with regard to JHA at the EU level. The institutional angle focuses the perspective on procedures and social norms at play within the various bodies of the EU institution. Therefore, current research can build on a solid theoretical foundation in researching the Council. In terms of empirical studies on JHA and the Council, the review showed which factors determine why member states agree to EU policy that does not completely match their interests in terms of asylum, police and justice cooperation, or immigration. In addition, researchers have looked into certain decision-making dynamics within the Council (e.g., the level of decision-making or the role and influence of particular Council bodies). However, considering the general literature on the Council and the research questions posed, research gaps become apparent.

Concerning the dynamics at play within the Council, little is known about the voting behavior of member states, their alliances and underlying cleavages that drive contestation of Council decisions in JHA. The political science debates on voting or consensus in the Council have delivered assumptions that are still waiting to be assessed in a policy area that is prone to consensus due to its sensitivity to sovereignty. If consensus is the rule, it is all the more relevant to find out about member state motivations for the contestation of EU decisions. In this vein, the application of the most recent shift to the double majority rule awaits researchers' attention as well. Within a larger EU picture, casting a vote also means that decisions could not be made at the lower level of the working group or COREPER. The more politicized EU issues become, the more likely it is that the Council of Ministers must decide. How higher level decision-making in the JHA Council has repercussions on other EU institutions such as the Commission and the EP in trialogues will have to be assessed.

The review departed from and will finish with reflections on old and new intergovernmentalism. The question of how current member state influence through Council bodies differs from previous intergovernmentalism in JHA will have to be assessed. Research on the process dimension of Council decision-making could become important in determining how the community method may become substituted with more voluntary policy coordination. It needs to be observed how voluntary policy coordination and EU agencies can effectively replace the necessity for the delegation of functions in monitoring implementation and accountability to the Commission or Court. Internal and external migration, border management and police and justice cooperation within the Single Market create the need for collective decisions. In the long run, these may be difficult to achieve outside of the community method. As in the early phase of JHA politics, regulatory failure may be on the agenda again if claimable objectives cannot be defined in community law and long-term goals cannot be overseen by a neutral broker such as the Commission. The Council is the EU institution in which the course will be set for whether and how the challenges posed to JHA motivate member states to create alternative decision-making and governing tools.

Bibliography

Adler-Nissen, R. (2009). Behind the Scenes of Differentiated Integration: Circumventing National Opt-outs in Justice and Home Affairs. *Journal of Euopean Public Policy*, 16(1), pp. 62–80.

Alexandrova, P. and Timmermans, A. (2013). National Interest versus the Common Good: The Presidency in European Council Agenda Setting. *European Journal of Political Research*, 52(3), pp. 316–338.

Aus, J.P. (2008). The Mechanisms of Consensus: Coming to Agreement on Community Asylum Policy. In D. Naurin and H. Wallace (ed.), *Unveiling the Council of the European Union. Games Governments Play in Brussels*. Basingstoke: Palgrave, pp. 99–118.

Beach, D. (2008). The Facilitator of Efficient Negotiations in the Council: The Impact of the Council Secretariat. In D. Naurin and H. Wallace (ed.), *Unveiling the Council of the European Union. Games Governments Play in Brussels*. Basingstoke: Palgrave, pp. 219–237.

Bickerton, C.J., Hodson, D. and Puetter, U. (2015). The New Intergovernmentalism: European Integration in the Post-Maastricht Era. *Journal of Common Market Studies*, 53(4), pp. 703–722.

Börzel, T. and Risse, T. (2000). When Europe Hits Home: Europeanization and Domestic Change. *European Integration online Papers (EIoP)*, 4(15). Available at: www.eiop.at.

Boswell, C. (2009). *The Political Uses of Expert Knowledge. Immigration Policy and Social Research*. Cambridge: Cambridge University Press.

Carammia, M., Princen, S. and Timmermans, A. (2016). From Summitry to EU Government: An Agenda Formation Perspective on the European Council. *Journal of Common Market Studies*. doi: 10.1111/jcms.12346, pp. 1–17.

Cerna, L. and Meng-Hsuan, C. (2013). The Regional Dimension in the Global Competition for Talent: Lessons from Framing the European Scientific Visa and Blue Card. *Journal of European Public Policy*, 21(1), pp. 76–95.

Christiansen, T. (2002). Out of the Shadows: The General Secretariat of the Council of Ministers. *The Journal of Legislative Studies*, 8(4), pp. 80–97.

de Schoutheete, P. (2006). The European Council. In J. Peterson and M. Shackleton (eds), *The Institutions of the European Union*. Oxford: Oxford University Press, pp. 37–59.

Falkner, G., Treib, O., Hartlapp, M. and Leiber, S. (2005). *Complying with Europe: EU Harmonisation and Soft Law in the Member States*. Cambridge: Cambridge University Press.

Fleishman Hillard (2014). *New Council Voting Rules*. Analysis and Insight, October. Brussels. Available at: fleishman-hillard.eu.

Geddes, A. (2000). *Immigration and European Integration. Towards Fortress Europe?* Manchester: Manchester University Press.

Geddes, A. (2008). *Immigration and European Integration. Beyond Fortress Europe?* Manchester: Manchester University Press.

Givens, T. and Luedtke, A. (2004). The Politics of European Union Immigration Policy: Institutions, Salience, and Harmonization. *The Policy Studies Journal*, 32(1), pp. 145–165.

Golub, J. (1999). In the Shadow of the Vote? Decision Making in the European Community. *International Organization*, 53(4), pp. 733–764.

Guiraudon, V. (2000). European Integration and Migration Policy: Vertical Policy Making as Venue Shopping. *Journal of Common Market Studies*, 38(2), pp. 251–271.

Guiraudon, V. and Lahav, G. (2000). A Reappraisal of the State Sovereignty Debate. The Case of Migration Control. *Comparative European Politics*, 33(2), pp. 163–195.

Häge, F. (2008). Who Decides in the Council of the European Union? *Journal of Common Market Studies*, 46(3), pp. 533–558.

Häge, F. (2013). Coalition Building and Consensus in the Council of the European Union. *British Journal of Political Science*, 43(8), pp. 481–504.

Hayes-Renshaw, F. (2006). The Council of Ministers. In J. Peterson and M. Shackleton (eds), *The Institutions of the European Union*. Oxford: Oxford University Press, pp. 60–80.

Hayes-Renshaw, F., Van Aken, W. and Wallace, H. (2006). When and Why the EU Council of Ministers Votes Explicitly. *Journal of Common Market Studies*, 44, p. 1.

Heisenberg, D. (2005). The Institution of 'Consensus' in the European Union: Formal versus Informal Decision-making in the Council. *European Journal of Political Research*, 44(1), pp. 65–90.

Héritier, A. (1996). The Accommodation of Diversity in European Policy-making and its Outcomes: Regulatory Policy as a Patchwork. *Journal of European Public Policy*, 3(2), pp. 149–176.

Héritier, A. (1999). *Policy-making and Diversity in Europe. Escape from Deadlock*. Cambridge: Cambridge University Press.

Kaunert, C. (2010). *European Internal Security: Towards Supranational Governance in the Area of Freedom, Security and Justice?* Manchester: Manchester University Press.

Lavenex, S. (1999). *Safe Third-countries. Extending EU Asylum and Immigration Policies to Central and Eastern Europe*. Budapest and New York: Central European University Press.

Lavenex, S. (2001). The Europeanization of Refugee Policies: Normative Challenges and Institutional Legacies. *Journal of Common Market Studies*, 39(5), pp. 851–874.

Lavenex, S. and Wallace, W. (2005). Justice and Home Affairs. Towards a 'European Public Order'? In H. Wallace, W. Wallace and M.A. Pollack (eds), *Policy-making in the European Union*. Oxford: Oxford University Press, pp. 437–480.

Lewis, J. (2003). Informal Integration and the Supranational Construction of the Council. *Journal of European Public Policy*, 10(6), pp. 996–1019.

Lewis, J. (2005). The Janus Face of Brussels: Socialization and Everyday Decision Making in the European Union. *International Organization*, 59(4), pp. 937–971.

Lewis, J. (2015). The Council of the European Union and the European Council. In J.M. Magone (ed.), *Handbook of European Politics*. London: Routledge, pp. 219–234.

Luedtke, A. (2009). Uncovering European Union Immigration Legislation: Policy Dynamics and Outcomes. *International Migration*, 49(2), pp. 1–27.

Majone, G. (1996). *Regulating Europe*. London: Routledge.
March, J.G. and Olsen, J.P. (1989). *Rediscovering Institutions. The Organizational Basis of Politics*. New York: Free Press.
Maricut, A. (2016). With and Without Supranationalisation: The Post-Lisbon Roles of the European Council and the Council in Justice and Home Affairs Governance. *Journal of European Integration*, 38(5), pp. 541–555.
Mattila, M. (2004). Contested Decisions: Empirical Analysis of Voting in the European Union Council of Ministers. *European Journal of Political Research*, 43(1), pp. 29–50.
Maurer, A. and Parkes, R. (2007). The Prospects for Policy-change in EU Asylum Policy: Venue and Image at the European Level. *European Journal of Migration and Law*, 9(2), pp. 173–205.
Maurer, A., Mittag, J. and Wessels, W. (2003). National Systems' Adaptation to the EU System: Trends, Offers, and Constraints. In B. Kohler-Koch (ed.), *Linking EU and National Governance*. Oxford: Oxford University Press, pp. 53–81.
Monar, J. (2012). Justice and Home Affairs: The Treaty of Maastricht as a Decisive Intergovernmental Gate Opener. *Journal of European Integration*, 34(7), pp. 717–734.
Niemann, A. (2008). Dynamics and Countervailing Pressures of Visa, Asylum and Immigration Policy Treaty Revision: Explaining Change and Stagnation from the Amsterdam IGC to the IGC of 2003–04. *Journal of Common Market Studies*, 46(3), pp. 559–591.
Niemann, A. and Mak, J. (2010). How Do Norms Guide Presidency Behaviour in EU Negotiations. *Journal of European Public Policy*, 17(5), pp. 727–742.
Nilsson, H.G. (2004). The Justice and Home Affairs Council. In M. Westlake and D. Galloway (eds), *The Council of the European Union*. London: Harper, pp. 113–142.
Novak, S. (2013). The Silence of Ministers: Consensus and Blame Avoidance in the Council of the European Union. *Journal of Common Market Studies*, 51(6), pp. 1091–1107.
Puetter, U. (2012). Europe's Deliberative Intergovernmentalism: The Role of the Council and European Council in EU Economic Governance. *Journal of Euopean Public Policy*, 19(2), pp. 161–178.
Ripoll Servent, A. (2012). Playing the Co-decision Game? Rules' Changes and Institutional Adaptation at the LIBE Committee. *Journal of European Integration*, 34(1), pp. 55–73.
Ripoll Servent, A. and Trauner, F. (2014). Do Supranational EU Institutions Make a Difference? EU Asylum Law before and after 'Communitarization'. *Journal of European Public Policy*, 21(8), pp. 1142–1162.
Roos, C. (2013). How to Overcome Deadlock in EU Immigration Politics. *International Migration*, 51(6), 67–79.
Smeets, S. (2013). How Issues Move or Get Stuck: Or How to Be Effective in the EU Council of Ministers. *European Integration Online Papers (EIoP)*, 17(1). Available at: www.eiop.at.
Stetter, S. (2000). Regulating Migration: Authority Delegation in Justice and Home Affairs. *Journal of European Public Policy*, 7(1), pp. 80–103.
Tallberg, J. (2006). *Leadership and Negotiation in the European Union*. Cambridge: Cambridge University Press.
Thielemann, E. and El-Enany, N. (2010). Refugee Protection as a Collective Action Problem: Is the EU Shirking its Responsibilities? *European Security*, 19(2), pp. 209–229.
Trauner, F. (2016). Asylum Policy: The EU's 'Crises' and the Looming Policy Regime Failure. *Journal of European Integration*, 38(3), pp. 311–325.
Van Aken, W. (2012). *Voting in the Council of the European Union. Contested Decision-making in the EU Council of Ministers (1995-2010). Sieps 2012/2. Swedish Institute for European Policy Studies*, Stockholm.
Vote Watch Europe (2015). EU Governments' Power Game with Freedom of Movement for European Citizens: Who is Losing?, February 23. Available at: www.votewatch.eu/blog/eu-governments-power-game-with-freedom-of-movement-for-european-citizens-who-is-losing/ (last accessed July 27, 2017).
Winnwa, I. (2016). Schengen under Pressure? Instrumentalisation of Freedom of Movement in the Council of Ministers. Council for European Studies, twenty-third International Conference of Europeanists, Philadelphia, April 14–16.
Zaun, N. (2015). Why EU Asylum Standards Exceed the Lowest Common Denominator: The Role of Regulatory Expertise in EU Decision-making. *Journal of European Public Policy*, 23(1), pp. 136–154.
Zimmer, C., Schneider, G. and Dobbins, M. (2005). The Contested Council: Conflict Dimensions of an Intergovernmental EU Institution. *Political Studies*, 53(2), pp. 403–422.

36
THE ROLE OF NATIONAL PARLIAMENTS IN THE AREA OF FREEDOM, SECURITY AND JUSTICE

High normative expectations, low empirical results

Angela Tacea

Introduction

The role of national parliaments in the Area of Freedom, Security and Justice (AFSJ) has been a conspicuously understudied research field. If the neglect of national parliaments by political science scholars of EU justice and home affairs may be surprising considering the numerous legal studies flagging the problems of accountability and the perceived democratic deficit of the AFSJ (Boswell 2010: 279), it also reflects the limited scrutiny powers of national representative assemblies in justice and home affairs matters. Although national parliaments entered the EU law concomitantly with the beginning of the EU's formal involvement in security matters marked by the Maastricht Treaty (1993), it was only with the Lisbon Treaty that their role was constitutionalized in connection with the AFSJ. The Treaty of Lisbon has added to the traditional indirect way of scrutiny – through the *ex-ante* and *ex-post* accountability of governments – a direct role of national parliaments in the AFSJ, allowing them to interfere directly in the EU legislative process.

Several formal changes, introduced by the Lisbon Treaty, enforced national parliaments' prerogatives in the AFSJ: national parliaments can oppose measures related to cross-border service of judicial and extra-judicial documents (Article 81 TFEU), they are taking part in the evaluation mechanisms for the implementation of the Union policies in this area and they are involved in the political monitoring of Europol and the evaluation of Eurojust's activities (Article 85 TFEU; Article 88 TFEU). To strengthen their scrutiny power, national parliaments were also granted better information rights in the AFSJ field: they will be informed by member states' authorities of the content and results of the evaluation of the implementation of the Union policies in the AFSJ (Article 70 TFEU) and of the activities of the standing committee (COSI) in charge of ensuring that operational cooperation on internal security is promoted and strengthened within the Union (Article 71 TFEU). Moreover, Article 6 of Protocol No. 2 on the Application of the Principles of Subsidiarity and Proportionality introduced the early warning mechanism (EWM). This mechanism enables national parliaments to control the respect of the subsidiarity principle by the draft EU legislative acts and to oppose them on those grounds. Within eight weeks from the date of transmission of the draft EU legislative act, national parliaments may send to the Presidents of the European institutions a reasoned opinion explaining the reasons why the draft in question does not comply with the principle of subsidiarity. Two procedures may result from the EWM (Article 7 of Protocol No. 2): (1) The 'Yellow card': where the reasoned opinions stating the non-compliance of a draft legislative act with the principle of subsidiarity represent at least one-third (one quarter in the AFSJ) of all the votes allocated to the national parliaments (each national parliament has two votes), the legislative initiator may decide to maintain, amend or withdraw the draft, but should motivate its decision; (2) the 'Orange card': where reasoned opinions on the non-compliance of a proposal for a legislative act with the principle of subsidiarity represent at least a simple majority of the votes allocated to the national parliaments (50 percent), the European legislator shall decide whether or not to block the Commission's proposal.[1]

Following the developments in the AFSJ policy process, scholars have mainly studied the role of national parliaments from two perspectives: a formal institutional one, gathering information on national parliaments' constitutional scrutiny provisions (Evangelisiti 1999; Keulen and Mittendorff 2011; Monar 1995) and an inter-parliamentary cooperation perspective, assessing how the collaboration between European parliaments can contribute to an enhanced scrutiny of the AFSJ (Mitsilegas 2007; De Garibay Ponce 2010, 2014; Pokki 2016). However, compared to the study of other EU institutions, research on the role of national parliaments in the AFSJ reveals certain specificities. First, similar to the study of the European Parliament (EP), research on the role of national parliaments bears important normative implications. Most studies claim that parliaments should play an important role in the AFSJ for two reasons: they cannot only reduce the perceived democratic deficit of the AFSJ, but they can also support a more balanced approach to a hitherto security-oriented policy field. Second, very little attention has been payed to developing theoretical explanations of the role of national parliaments in the AFSJ. Thus far, most academic studies (see below) were rather descriptive and focused on presenting variations in the institutional adaptation of national parliaments to the EU integration in the security field.

After reviewing the state of the art, I will suggest some avenues for research in this area, pointing out how scholars of the AFSJ can engage with the broader literature on the EU decision-making process. The first section of the chapter will present the normative debate about the involvement of national parliaments in the AFSJ decision-making process, before summarizing the empirical research on national parliaments. Inter-parliamentary cooperation in the AFSJ is addressed in the third section of this chapter. The concluding section presents avenues for future research.

Normative assumptions about the role of the parliamentary scrutiny of the AFSJ

Most studies about the role of national parliaments in EU affairs claim that the enforcement of scrutiny prerogatives is desirable because their involvement could reduce the democratic deficit of the European Union and restore citizens' confidence in European integration (Rozenberg and Hefftler 2015). This statement becomes even more urgent in the AFSJ, which was considered before the Treaty of Lisbon as an area where the democratic deficit was 'one of the most pronounced and the most difficult to overcome' (Monar 1995: 244). This lack of parliamentary accountability and the perceived democratic deficit was before the Treaty of Lisbon a recurrent theme in the JHA legal academic literature (Neuwahl 1995; Barrett 1997; Peers 2011), which criticized the highly intergovernmental character of cooperation in the third pillar and the 'informal, low-profile and professionally dominated cooperative culture of pre-Maastricht years' (Walker 2004: 24).

Indeed, the long heterogenic intergovernmental aspect of cooperation and decision-making in the AFSJ, involving different ministerial administrations (justice, interior, finance, transport, foreign affairs), made democratic control more difficult than in other policy areas mainly for two reasons. First, because senior officials are not directly responsible to parliaments; second, because the problems of coordination among ministries diluted ministerial responsibility (Monar 1995: 245–246). In addition, internal security allows a higher degree of secrecy and urgency compared to other policy areas (except foreign and security policy). If ministers accepted to report *ex-post* to the parliaments the results of the Councils of ministers on justice and home affairs, they were reluctant to open up the possibility for national parliaments to influence the decision-making process *ex-ante* (House of Lords 1993). At the same time, some political important issues (e.g., the European Arrest Warrant) imposed a tight timetable, which meant that 'national parliaments were given extremely limited time to scrutinize meaningfully the various drafts emanating from the Council working groups' (Mitsilegas 2007: 3). If the secrecy and urgency arguments are justifiable for reasons of operational efficiency and effectiveness and often invoked by ministers themselves, scholars considered that they harm the transparency of the decision-making process (Peers 2006; Monar 1995) and, in the end, its legitimacy for the citizens. Considering the far-reaching consequences of decisions in the justice and home affairs field for individual rights and freedoms, it is not surprising that the case for national parliaments had received the almost unanimous support of scholars. In this context, the question was not how much national parliaments should scrutinize or not European security measures, but rather how democratic accountability may be secured without harming police and security experts' capacity to engage 'in operational activities free from the frustrations, delays and confidentiality risks that may attend external monitoring by non experts' (Walker 2004: 27). But despite this preoccupation being related to all the AFSJ policy subfields, except for the 'critical security literature' developed after the 1990s (Bigo 1992, 1996; Huysmans 2006), most of the studies do not cover the full array of JHA issues, but focus on the lack of parliamentary control in different policy subfields (see Guiraudon (2000, 2001), Boswell (2007) for immigration and asylum; Walker (2000), Boer (2002) for police cooperation).

Parliamentary absence from JHA policies not only created a problem of public legitimation, but it was also considered to facilitate restrictions on civil liberties (Ludford 2004) and human rights protection (Peers 2011), and to favor a policy rationale which prioritized security over liberty (Ripoll Servent 2015: 3). European cooperation in justice and home affairs was considered a way for security professionals to expand the security rationale to policy areas that were not previously framed in security terms (e.g., asylum, immigration). The securitization thesis (Bigo 1992; Buzan et al. 1998) claimed that the lack of parliamentary accountability of European justice and home affairs measures aggravated the security bias nature of the EU's Area or Freedom, Security and Justice.

Similar to the securitization literature, the 'venue-shopping' thesis (Guiraudon 2000, 2001) argued that governments had shifted control-oriented policies to the European level in order to escape domestic pressures and obstacles. In a similar manner, Lavenex (2001: 862–863) states that 'the same officials who were driving co-operation at the European level, that is, the ministries of the interior' drove restrictive national asylum policies. She explains the development of EU asylum policies by the 'opaque nature of transgovernmental co-operation' which 'strengthened their [ministries of the interior] domestic position, enabling them to present European agreements to their national parliaments as *faits accomplis* and to frame domestic concerns in terms of European integration'. Thus, the supporters of increasing parliamentary scrutiny of justice and home affairs have most of the time implicitly suggested that increasing national parliaments' competences in the AFSJ would contribute to a better protection of human rights and could result in a move towards more liberal regulations in this area. This statement makes sense if we consider that parliaments have traditionally been established to protect citizens from the abuses of the executive power, coupled with the stances taken by some parliamentary chambers before the Treaty of Lisbon on JHA issues (e.g., the attitude defended by the House of Lords during the PNR Agreements' negotiations with the United States (Mitsilegas 2008)). However, it is also remarkable because it assumes the willingness of parliaments to nudge the negotiation position of the governments towards a more human rights-oriented rationale, which goes against the inherent logic of parliamentary government: the support of the government by the parliamentary majority. From a constitutional perspective it seems theoretically impossible for parliamentary majorities to keep governments in office while systematically taking stances against them in matters related to the AFSJ. Studies on the domestic policy-making of AFSJ politics have challenged the 'venue-shopping' thesis. For example, in an empirical analysis of the European migration policies in the Netherlands, Saskia Bonjour and Maarten Vink show that national parliamentary actors did not oppose the restrictive stance of the Dutch government (Bonjour and Vink 2013: 390) because these kinds of family migration policies in the Netherlands have been generally supported by very broad majorities. Recent studies have also shown that the Europeanization of justice and home affairs policies reinforced the structural solidarity existing in parliamentary regimes between the executive and the legislative and, thus, had only a relative impact upon the security-oriented approach of this policy area (Tacea 2016b).

Empirical research on the role of national parliaments in the AFSJ

The role of national parliaments in the AFSJ has triggered little empirical research. With very few exceptions (Evangelisiti 1999; Keulen 2014; Keulen and Mittendorff 2011; Monar 1995), the topic appears only incidentally either as a case study for the analysis of the role of national parliaments in European affairs (Bergman 1997; Jančić 2011) or for that of domestic policy-making in the fields of migration or police cooperation (Bonjour and Vink 2013; Lavenex 2001; Luedtke 2009).

Most scholarly attention has been dedicated to mapping the formal prerogatives of national parliaments regarding the areas covered by the third pillar/AFSJ and to provide explanations for cross-national variations. In a pioneering article published in 1997, Torbjörn Bergman, shows that only nine out of the fifteen member states had the right to receive information in relation to the third-pillar decisions (the Austrian, the Danish, the Finish, the German, the Irish, the Luxembourgish, the Dutch, the Swedish and the British parliaments) (Bergman 1997: 377–378). In addition, so long as the measures have been kept within the intergovernmental sphere, governments have reserved considerable discretion in respect of which documents should be released to parliaments and when. 'Many parliaments found themselves informed as late as necessary rather than as early as possible' (Maurer and Wessels 2001: 444) and some texts were forwarded to parliaments only after the end of the negotiations (Monar 1995: 250). The contributors to Maurer and Wessels' study of the institutional and procedural developments of the European and member states' parliamentary level claimed that national parliaments were to a certain extent also guilty for the lack of scrutiny of JHA measures, because 'many parliaments suffered from the effects of internal rivalries between foreign affairs, EU and internal affairs committees' (Maurer and Wessels 2001: 445). Indeed, in some parliaments, including France, Italy and the UK, third-pillar measures depended on the competences of foreign affairs committees rather than on those of European affairs committees. The Treaty of Amsterdam started the normalization of the parliamentary scrutiny of JHA policies by opening up this domain to the information of certain parliaments[2] and by transferring the scrutiny from the home affairs/foreign affairs committees to the European affairs committees.[3] The institutional adaptation of national parliaments to the Treaty of Lisbon resulted in a full communautarization of the parliamentary scrutiny procedures of the AFSJ.

The mapping of formal prerogatives of national parliaments focused not only on the evaluation of the scope and timing of the information in AFSJ, but also on the capacity of national parliaments to influence the position of governments during the negotiations in Brussels. The degree of *bindingness* of parliamentary opinions for the governments was prior to the Treaty of Lisbon particularly important in the JHA field. Considering the unanimity required by the decision-making in JHA, those parliaments where the scrutiny process legally bound the government to a particular policy stand (the Danish *Folketinget*, the German *Bundesrat*, the Austrian *Nationalrat* and the Finish *Eduskunta*) were acting in practice as veto players. This applied also to the two houses of the Dutch Parliament, where a '*consent*' procedure, which required ministers to have the tacit or explicit consent of the Parliament before JHA Councils was introduced as part of the ratification of the 1990 Convention implementing the Schengen agreements (Keulen and Mittendorff 2011: 48). If the requirement of parliamentary approval is certainly a proof of the high influence that mandating system parliaments exercised on 'defining the strategic guidelines for legislative and operational planning within the area of freedom, security and justice' (Art. 68 TFEU), it has also been a stimulus for the governments 'to provide a great deal of (even confidential) information at an early stage of EU decision-making' (Keulen and Mittendorff 2011: 49). Nevertheless, although the influence of national parliaments in non-mandating systems was certainly more limited than in the cases where parliaments were able to legally bind the ministers before the negotiations in the Council, their impact should not be underestimated, particularly when it comes to conventions adopted in the JHA area. A case in point is the implementation of the Schengen Convention in France, which took three years owing to the strict conditions imposed by the French Parliament on the executive (Tacea 2017). Although, the extension of the co-decision procedure to the AFSJ suppressed the veto powers of mandating systems' parliaments, formally they are still considered the strongest parliaments in EU decision-making (Auel et al. 2015).

Compared to other European policy areas, the AFSJ is the only area to attract constant parliamentary attention. However, empirical studies on the actual use of parliamentary formal prerogatives found a great heterogeneity of national parliamentary scrutiny of the AFSJ. National parliaments differ both in terms of the level of activity, the type of parliamentary scrutiny practiced and the motivations of MPs to scrutinize AFSJ measures. The main explanation for this heterogeneity lies in the absence of Treaty provisions on the nature of parliamentary scrutiny. If the enforcement of national parliaments' scrutiny powers applying to the AFSJ went hand in hand with the *constitutionalization* of this area, variations in terms of types of documents received do remain: while some parliaments have access to secret and top-secret documents (Austria), others only have access to public documents (Ireland) (COSAC 2012: 10). The action of national parliaments 'stays in the shadow of a largely informal, non-binding and voluntary liaison with EU institutions' (Jančić 2011: 421) and the national constitutional context determines to a large extent the degree and nature of parliamentary scrutiny. However, the structural strength or weakness of national parliaments is rather reflected in the type of scrutiny practiced and not necessarily in their level of activity. In this sense, if the most powerful parliaments (DK, FI, SK) are not, with the exception of the Finish *Eduskunta*, the most active (DE, CZ, IT), patterns of parliamentary behavior do emerge in relation to the type of parliamentary activity. 'Weak' parliaments focus more on the communication with the EU institutions, while 'strong' parliaments focus more on the traditional control of the governments (Tacea 2017). Therefore, the Europeanization of the AFSJ diminished the influence of 'strong' parliaments and opened up ways of expression for parliaments usually dominated by their governments.

Despite this heterogeneity of national parliaments, some common elements are worth emphasizing. Although the Treaty of Lisbon directly involved national parliaments in the decision-making process in the AFSJ, national representative institutions are hardly going beyond their domestic role. Quantitative studies found that parliamentary scrutiny of the AFSJ responds mainly to domestic political and constitutional considerations. National parliaments tend to follow their own agendas, taking into account their own political interests (Grzelak 2014), and their attention follows only relatively the legislative output of the EU institutions. For example, if, between 2010 and 2012, most of the adopted legislative AFSJ acts concerned the free movement of persons, national parliaments focused mainly on police and judicial cooperation in criminal matters and on data protection (Tacea 2017). Moreover, most parliamentary activity in this area focuses on the division of competences between the EU and member states and not on the actual content of the proposals (Keulen and Mittendorff 2011; Strelkov 2015). From January 1, 2010 to December 31, 2013, reasoned opinions concerning AFSJ issues represented 13.3 percent of the total number of parliamentary activities in EU affairs (Tacea 2017). In this context, it comes as no surprise that one of the three yellow cards to be triggered in the framework of the EWM concerned an AFSJ proposal, the European Public Prosecutor's Office. If the prioritization of subsidiarity vouches for the sensitivity of AFSJ issues, it also raises the question of its efficiency for the AFSJ decision-making process, as national parliaments, guardians of national competences and deeply concerned with the preservation of national sovereignty, may appear as the new brake on the deepening of European integration in the AFSJ. Reaching the threshold for a yellow card is obviously not an easy task – as the only yellow card adopted in six years shows; however, including another veto player in the decision-making may endanger an already delicate intergovernmental equilibrium. The success of the early warning mechanism depends, however, on the closer cooperation of national parliaments, which, as we will see in the next section, is often missing.

Inter-parliamentary cooperation in the AFSJ

Inter-parliamentary cooperation in the AFSJ is no better researched than the role of national parliaments in this policy area and a number of authors have developed more prospective studies than analytical assessments of the real practice of inter-parliamentary cooperation (Mitsilegas 2007). The few studies that have looked at the ways in which parliaments cooperate in the AFSJ at the EU level both vertically (between national parliaments) and horizontally (between national parliaments and the EP) have come to rather sobering conclusions (De Garibay Ponce 2010, 2014; Pokki 2016). While inter-parliamentary cooperation in the AFSJ (Article 88 TFEU) was considered a way to fill in the scrutiny gaps that neither the EP nor the national parliaments could have filled alone (Crum and Fossum 2013; Lord 2008; De Garibay Ponce 2014), empirical studies have shown that inter-parliamentary cooperation is very weak in this area compared to other policy areas. Based on a comparison of three policy areas – the CFSP, the environmental policy and the AFSJ – Saara Pokki (2016) concludes that inter-parliamentary cooperation in the AFSJ is the weakest of the three fields studied.

From a theoretical point of view, the research on inter-parliamentary cooperation followed two opposed paradigms: 'the levels paradigm' and the 'multi-level paradigm'. The first is mainly hierarchical and considers national parliaments and the EP as mutually exclusive. Each parliamentary level is part of a different constitutional order and, thus, scrutiny should take place at the national and European level, independently from one another (Besselink 2006). The second one, represented by the concept of a 'multilevel parliamentary field' developed by Crum and Fossum (2009), is mainly egalitarian and considers parliamentary scrutiny as complementary rather than exclusive. The EU and the national channels of representation co-exist side by side; thus parliamentary scrutiny should also be shared between the EU and the national parliaments.

The advantage of the concept of a 'multilevel parliamentary field' is that it allows a study of 'both formal and informal inter-parliamentary interaction along both horizontal (amongst national parliaments) and vertical (EP-national parliaments) lines' (De Garibay Ponce 2014). However, its application to the AFSJ reveals a very poor development of both the vertical and the horizontal inter-parliamentary cooperation.

Regarding vertical inter-parliamentary cooperation, authors have argued that the involvement of national parliaments was seen rather as a threat to the EP's scrutiny competences and made the two parliamentary levels act like competitors and not as cooperators (De Garibay Ponce 2014: 150). Certain parliaments, like Westminster,[4] and to a certain extent the Nordic parliaments (Monar 1995: 254), have always been reluctant to engage in closer cooperation with the EP in this policy area.

Moreover, in spite of some initiatives taken in the 2000s to encourage vertical inter-parliamentary cooperation in AFSJ, such as the Dutch Parliament's PARLOPOL proposal,[5] the EP seems more engaged in the organization of inter-parliamentary meetings than national parliaments. Between January 2010 and December 2016, the EP (mostly LIBE and JURI committees) organized thirteen inter-parliamentary meetings on topical AFSJ issues (e.g., 'Democratic supervision of intelligence services', 'Reform of the EU Data Protection Framework'). In the absence of an institutionalized conference in AFSJ, the EP even suggested in a resolution of September 25, 2009 the creation of a permanent monitoring mechanism of AFSJ issues and a regular annual meeting on issues related to the AFSJ (COSAC 2009). By contrast, national parliaments lack the political will to organize such meetings. For the same time period, only three inter-parliamentary meetings were organized by the parliament of the rotating presidencies (e.g., 'Human trafficking in the digital age' organized in 2016 by the Dutch presidency). Moreover, the national parliamentary delegations to the inter-parliamentary meetings organized by the EP are composed of officials and civil servants instead of MPs. These results seem to confirm that national parliaments are not interested in using their involvement at the EU level to increase their parliamentary control powers (Larhant 2005).

One may have thought along with certain authors (Pokki 2016: 25) that the lack of vertical inter-parliamentary cooperation is caused by the sensitivity of the AFSJ for the national sovereignty and the preference of national parliaments to use horizontal cooperation. As we have seen in the first section of this chapter, the Treaty of Lisbon offered, through a lower threshold to reach the 'yellow card' in the AFSJ, incentives for this horizontal cooperation. While some authors adopted a very optimistic view on this issue, considering the EWS as the possibility of a 'virtual' third chamber made up of national parliaments (Cooper 2012), others remained very skeptical about the possibility of such a collective role because the EWS would blur existing channels of delegation and accountability in the EU (Kiiver 2006; Wilde 2012). Empirical studies seem to give reason to the latter, because national parliaments (and even the houses of the same parliament) do not have similar understandings of the subsidiarity principle. For example, while the French Senate exercises a more depoliticized control of subsidiarity, the *Assemblée nationale* makes political use of a legal instrument aimed at ensuring that 'action at EU level is justified in light of the possibilities available at national, regional or local levels' (Article 5 TEU).

The different understandings of the subsidiarity principle by the two houses of the French parliament, as well as the different objectives the houses are pursuing when issuing a reasoned opinion gives the impression of a split parliament unable to speak with one national voice.

(Tacea 2016a: 269)

This was the case for the European Public Prosecutor's Office proposal (EPPO). Although, in its resolution of January 15, 2013, the Senate supported the EPPO, the senators adopted on October 28 a reasoned opinion explaining that the proposal breaches the subsidiarity principle. On the contrary, the *Assemblée Nationale* issued not only a resolution supporting the Commission's proposal but, on November 6, 2013, in a public communication to Viviane Reding, several members of the Law Committee, together with the chair of the European Affairs Committee, affirmed their support for the proposal (Tacea 2016a: 254).

Concluding remarks

Studying the role of national parliaments in the AFSJ has been of limited salience both for theories of parliamentary accountability of EU affairs and for those interested in European integration in justice and home affairs.

Numerous theoretical and empirical studies have assessed the impact of European integration upon parliamentary institutions and their adaptation, explained national variations of parliamentary capacity to control their executives and, more recently, explained national parliaments' activity in EU affairs. However, most studies approach EU affairs as a homogeneous policy area and rarely look at individual policy sectors in order to analyze the way in which national parliaments deal with the AFSJ in particular. The AFSJ appears only marginally as a case study among other policy sectors. At the same time, research on democratic accountability and legitimacy of ASFJ has mainly focused on the role of the EP, overlooking the role of national parliaments or only mentioning the negative consequences of their absence for the democratic legitimacy of decision-making in AFSJ.

Those observations reveal both an empirical and a theoretical backlog of the study of national parliaments' role in the European integration in the AFSJ. We know now that the Europeanization of AFSJ policies marginalized national parliaments, but we still lack an individual or/and comparative understanding of the strategies national parliaments use after the Lisbon Treaty to influence the decision-making process in AFSJ. The Lisbon Treaty has been seen as a 'momentum' for the parlamentarization of AFSJ, but is this parlamentarization taking place? If so, how? Whether or not national parliaments can contribute to increasing the democratic quality of EU policies depends crucially on *if*, but especially, on *how* they actually make use of their prerogatives in AFSJ. Hence, strengthening their role in EU affairs may have positive effects on the European constitutional democracy. However, if their voice only replicates the positions of national executives or if their involvement in AFSJ weakens the performance of the European regulatory system, for example, by slowing it down (Chalmers and Chaves 2015), then it may lead to questioning their purpose and utility. Such a research enquiry could contribute to a better understanding of the conditions under which national parliaments can provide added value in terms of democratic accountability and effectiveness to the EU policy-making process, filling in an important gap in the current scientific literature.

Another problem with the research on national parliaments and the AFSJ has been its merely descriptive nature. Integrating the study of national parliamentary scrutiny in the broader analysis of how the new institutional arrangements in the AFSJ policy-making process, such as the increased role of the European Commission, the EP and national parliaments altered the institutional actors' power to define and shape AFSJ legislation (Trauner and Ripoll Servent 2015) would have the potential to overcome the insulation of the different sub-areas of research but also to connect research on AFSJ to the wider literature on the EU legislative process. The development of new research tools, such as text-reuse methods based on automated machine-learning algorithms, has the potential to facilitate large N-studies on AFSJ and to make an important contribution to both empirical and theoretical knowledge.

Notes

1 Up until now no orange card and three yellow cards have been triggered: (1) on May 22, 2012 *on* the proposal for a Council regulation on the exercise of the right to take collective action (Monti II); (2) on October 28, 2013 on the proposal for a Council regulation on the establishment of the European Public Prosecutor's Office (EPPO), and (3) on May 10, 2016 on the European Commission's proposal to revise the Posted Workers Directive.
2 The French Parliament opened up the third pillar to parliamentary information in 1998, but only to measures imposing legislative commitments to France (Fromage 2015).
3 Up until the Amsterdam Treaty, the scrutiny of JHA measures was the sole competence of the Home Affairs Committee of the House of Commons in Westminster (Saulnier 2002: 763).
4 See House of Lords. 1993: 17.
5 In 2001 the Dutch Parliament proposed the creation of a network of national and European parliamentarians concerned with police and justice affairs (De Garibay Ponce 2014: 47).

Bibliography

Auel, K., Rozenberg, O. and Tacea, A. (2015). Fighting Back? And if Yes, How? Measuring Parliamentary Strength and Activity in EU Affairs. In Hefftler, C., Neuhold, C., Rozenberg, O., Smith, J. and Wessels, W. (eds), *The Palgrave Handbook on National Parliaments and the European Union*. Basingstoke: Palgrave Macmillan.
Barrett, G. (1997). *Justice Cooperation in the EU: The Creation of a European Legal Space*. Dublin: Institute of European Affairs.
Bergman, T. (1997). National Parliaments and EU Affairs Committees: Notes in Empirical Variation and Competing Explanations. *Journal of European Public Policy*, 4, pp. 373–387.
Besselink, L.F.M. (2006). National Parliaments in the EU's Composite Constitution: A Plea for a Shift in Paradigm. In Kiiver, P. (ed.), *National and Regional Parliaments in the European Constitutional Order*. Groningen: Europa Law Publishing.
Bigo, D. (1992). *Europe des polices et de la sécurité intérieur*. Paris: Editions Complexes.
Bigo, D. (1996). *Polices en réseaux: l'expérience européenne*. Paris: Presse de Sciences Po.
Boer, M.D. (2002). Towards an Accountability Regime for an Emerging European Policing Governance. *Policing and Society*, 12, pp. 275–289.
Bonjour, S. and Vink, M. (2013). When Europeanization Backfires: The Normalization of European Migration Politics. *Acta Politica*, 48, pp. 389–407.
Boswell, C. (2007). Theorizing Migration Policy: Is There a Third Way? *International Migration Review*, 41, pp. 75–100.
Boswell, C. (2010). Justice and Home Affairs. In Egan, M.P., Nugent, N. and Paterson, W.E. (eds), *Research Agendas in EU Studies: Stalking the Elephant*. Basingstoke; New York: Palgrave Macmillan.
Buzan, B., Wæver, O. and Wilde, J.D. (1998). *Security: A New Framework for Analysis*. Boulder, CO: Lynne Rienner.
Chalmers, D. and Chaves, M. (2015). EU Law-making and the State of the European Democratic Agency. In Cramme, O. and Hobolt, S.B. (eds), *Democratic Politics in a European Union Under Stress*. Oxford: Oxford University Press.
Cooper, I. (2012). A 'Virtual Third Chamber' for the European Union? National Parliaments after the Treaty of Lisbon. *West European Politics*, 35, pp. 441–465.
Cosac (2009). *Eleventh Bi-annual Report on EU Practices and Procedures Relevant to Parliamentary Scrutiny*. Forty-first Conference of Community and European Affairs Committees of Parliaments of the European Union, May 11–12. Prague: Cosac Secretariat.

Cosac (2012). *Seventeenth Bi-annual Report: Developments in European Union Procedures and Practices Relevant to Parliamentary Scrutiny*. Copenhagen: Cosac Secretariat.

Crum, B. and Fossum, J.E. (2009). The Multilevel Parliamentary Field: A Framework for Theorizing Representative Democracy in the EU. *European Political Science Review*, 1, pp. 249–271.

Crum, B. and Fossum, J.E. (2013). Practices of Interparliamentary Coordination in International Politics: The European Union and Beyond. In Crum, B. and Fossum, J.E. (eds), *Practices of Interparliamentary Coordination in International Politics: The European Union and Beyond*. Colchester: ECPR Press.

De Garibay Ponce, D.R. (2010). Interparliamentary Cooperation in the EU: A Case Study of Justice and Home Affairs. Sixtieth Political Studies Association Annual Conference, *Sixty Years of Political Studies: Achievements and Futures*. Edinburgh, UK.

De Garibay Ponce, D.R. (2014). *The Development of Interparliamentary Practices: The Case of the Parliamentary Control of Europol*. PhD, Universidad Autónoma de Madrid.

Evangelisiti, F. (1999). The Role of National Parliaments in the Creation of the Area of Freedom, Security and Justice: An Italian Point of View. In O'Keeffe, D. and Twomey, P. (eds), *Legal Issues of the Amsterdam Treaty*. Oxford: Hart Publishing.

Fromage, D. (2015). *Les Parlements dans l'Union Européenne après le Traité de Lisbonne – La Participation des Parlements allemands, britanniques, espagnols, français et italiens*. Paris: Harmattan.

Grzelak, A. (2014). Scrutiny of the European Comission's Legislative Proposals by National Parliaments – Example of COM(2012)10 on Data Protection in Cooperation in Criminal Matters. *PADEMIA Online Papers in Parliamentary Democracy*, 1.

Guiraudon, V. (2000). European Integration and Migration Policy: Vertical Policy-making as Venue Shopping. *Journal of Common Market Studies*, 38, pp. 251–271.

Guiraudon, V. (2001). The Constitution of a European Immigration Policy Domain: A Political Sociology Approach. *Journal of European Public Policy*, 10, pp. 263–282.

House of Lords (1993). House of Lords Scrutiny of the Intergovernmental Pillars of the European Union. In *Communities*, S.C.O.E. (ed.). London: HMSO.

Huysmans, J. (2006). *The Politics of Insecurity: Fear, Migration and Asylum in the EU*. London: Routledge.

Jančić, D. (2011). *National Parliaments and European Constitutionalism: Accountability beyond Borders*. PhD, Utrecht University.

Keulen, M.V. (2014). New Parliamentary Practices in Justice and Home Affairs: Some Observations. In Holzhacker, R.L. and Luif, P. (eds), *Freedom, Security and Justice in the European Union. Internal and External Dimensions of Increased Cooperation after the Lisbon Treaty*. New York: Springer.

Keulen, M.V. and Mittendorff, F. (2011). Justice and Home Affairs 'at Home': Shaping the AFSJ at the National Level. In Wolff, S., Goudappel, F. and Zwaan, J.D. (eds), *Freedom, Security and Justice after Lisbon and Stockholm*. The Hague: T.M.C. Asser Press.

Kiiver, P. (2006). *The National Parliaments in the European Union: A Critical View on the EU Constitution-building*. The Hague: Kluwer Law International.

Larhant, M. (2005). La coopération interparlementaire dans l'UE l'heure d'un nouveau départ? *Notre Europe Etudes et recherches*, Policy Paper No, 16.

Lavenex, S. (2001). The Europeanization of Refugee Policies: Normative Challenges and Institutional Legacies. *Journal of Common Market Studies*, 39, pp. 851–874.

Lord, C. (2008). Is There a Role for Parliamentary Participation in European Security Co-ordination? In Peters, D., Wagner, W. and Deitelhoff, N. (eds), *The Parliamentary Control of European Security Policy*. London: Arena.

Ludford, S. (2004). An EU JHA Policy: What Should It Comprise? In Apap, J. (ed.), *Justice and Home Affairs in the EU: Liberty and Security Issues after Enlargement*. Cheltenham: Edward Elgar.

Luedtke, A. (2009). Uncovering European Union Immigration Legislation: Policy Dynamics and Outcomes. *International Migration*, 49, pp. 1–27.

Maurer, A. and Wessels, W. (2001). National Parliaments on their Ways to Europe: Losers or Latecomers? In Maurer, A. and Wessels, W. (eds), *National Parliaments on their Ways to Europe: Losers or Latecomers?* Baden-Baden: Nomos.

Mitsilegas, V. (2007). Interparliamentary Co-operation in EU Justice and Home Affairs. In Politik, S.W.U. (ed.), *Fifty Years of Interparliamentary Cooperation*. Berlin: Bundesrat.

Mitsilegas, V. (2008). Coopération antiterroriste Etats-Unis/Union européenne: l'entente cordiale. In Bigo, D., Bonelli, L. and Deltombe, T. (eds), *Au nom du 11 septembre: les démocraties à l'épreuve de l'antiterrorisme*. Paris: La Découverte.

Monar, J. (1995). Democratic Control of Justice and Home Affairs: The European Parliament and the National Parliaments. In Bieber, R. and Monar, J. (eds), *Justice and Home Affairs in the European Union: The Development of the Third Pillar*. Brussels: European Interuniversity Press.

Neuwahl, N. (1995). Judicial Control in Matters of Justice and Home Affairs: What Role for the Court of Justice. In Bieber, R. and Monar, J. (eds), *Justice and Home Affairs in the European Union. The Development of the Third Pillar*. Brussels: European University Press.

Peers, S. (2006). From Black Market to Constitution: The Development of the Institutional Framework for EC Immigration and Asylum Law. In Peers, S. and Rogers, N. (eds), *EU Immigration and Asylum Law: Text and Commentary*. Leiden: Martinus Nijhoff.

Peers, S. (2011). *EU Justice and Home Affairs, Third Edition*. Oxford: Oxford University Press.

Pokki, S. (2016). Interparliamentary Cooperation in the European Union – Differences across Policy Areas. *PACO Working Papers*, WP02.

Ripoll Servent, A. (2015). *Institutional and Policy Change in the European Parliament. Deciding on Freedom, Security and Justice*. Basingstoke: Palgrave Macmillan.

Rozenberg, O. and Hefftler, C. (2015). Introduction. In Hefftler, C., Neuhold, C., Rozenberg, O. and Smith, J. (eds), *The Palgrave Handbook of National Parliaments and the European Union*. Basingstoke: Palgrave Macmillan.

Saulnier, E. (2002). *La participation des parlements français et britannique aux communautés et à l'Union européennes: lecture parlementaire de la construction européenne*. Paris: L.G.D.J.

Strelkov, A. (2015). *National Parliaments in the Aftermath of the Lisbon Treaty Adaptation to the 'New Opportunity Structure'*. PhD, University of Maastricht.

Tacea, A. (2016a). Speaking With One Voice? The Use of the Early Warning Mechanism by the Two Houses of the French Parliament. In Cornell, A.J. and Goldoni, M. (eds), *National and Regional Parliaments in the EU Legislative Procedure after Lisbon: The Impact of the Early Warning Mechanism*. Oxford: Hart Publishing.

Tacea, A. (2016b). Towards More Security? The Involvement of the National Parliaments in the Reform of the Schengen Agreements. In Bossong, R. and Carrapico, H. (eds), *EU Borders and Shifting Internal Security – Technology, Externalization and Accountability*. Heidelberg: Springer International.

Tacea, A. (2017). *Governments under the watchful eye of their parliament. The involvement of the French, Italian and the British parliaments in the scrutiny and the decision-making process in the Area of Freedom, Security and Justice*. PhD, Sciences Po Paris.

Trauner, F. and Ripoll Servent, A. (2015). *Policy Change in the Area of Freedom, Security and Justice: How EU Institutions Matter*. London; New York: Routledge.

Walker, N. (2000). *Policing in a Changing Constitutional Order*. London: Sweet & Maxwell.

Walker, N. (2004). *Europe's Area of Freedom, Security, and Justice*. Oxford: Oxford University Press.

Wilde, P.D. (2012). Why the Early Warning Mechanism Does not Alleviate the Democratic Deficit. *OPAL Online Paper*, No. 6.

37

THE EU'S AGENCIES

Ever more important for the governance of the Area of Freedom, Security and Justice

Juan Santos Vara

Introduction

The Area of Freedom, Security and Justice (AFSJ) has gone through a process of agencification, as has happened with many other EU policies. European agencies represent 'an important part of the EU's institutional machinery' (Chiti 2009: 1395). The development of the AFSJ has led to a multiplication of the activities carried by EU agencies, which were created to reinforce operational cooperation among national authorities. The AFSJ agencies have not only offered operational and technical support to the member states, but they have also provided 'useful evidence-based input to the policy debate and the decision process' at the EU level (AFSJ Agencies 2014). The AFSJ agencies are also bound to play a key role in relations with third states and international organizations. In the past years, AFSJ agencies have been called upon by the institutions to increase their cooperation with those third countries considered to be a priority for the EU.

The role of the home affairs agencies in the development of the AFSJ should be framed within the debate on decentralized agencies of the EU, which has taken place over the past years. The significant degree of autonomy enjoyed by agencies in their activities does not, however, mean that they are immune to all controls. Attention has recently been paid to the need to strike a balance between the autonomy of EU agencies and their accountability (Busuioc *et al.* 2011). In 2008, the Commission stated that the varied roles, structure and profile of regulatory agencies raise doubts about their accountability and legitimacy (European Commission 2008). The 2012 Joint Statement of the European Parliament, the Council of the EU and the European Commission on decentralized agencies aims to develop a common framework for the accountability of agencies (European Parliament, Council and Commission 2012). In contrast to the great majority of regulatory agencies, AFSJ agencies' operational activities may have direct or indirect implications for the fundamental rights of individuals, and particularly for third-country nationals and asylum-seekers. Since AFSJ agencies' operational activities may have negative impacts upon human rights, *ex-post* accountability is not an adequate option, and ongoing scrutiny is the only satisfactory mechanism to ensure accountability (Carrera *et al.* 2013: 338). Even though the main focus of this chapter lies in parliamentary and judicial controls over the activities of the AFSJ agencies, the *ex-post* accountability is also taken into account. Accountability is understood in this context as 'a relationship between an actor and a forum, in which the actor has an obligation to explain and to justify his or her conduct, the forum can pose questions and pass judgment, and the actor may face consequences' (Bovens 2007: 450).

As has happened with agencies in general, the establishment and development of agencies in the AFSJ 'has not been accompanied by an overall vision of the place of agencies in the Union' and 'the lack of such a global vision has made it more difficult for agencies to work effectively and to deliver for the EU as a whole' (European Commission 2008: 2). The 2012 Joint Statement of the European Parliament, the Council of the EU and the European Commission on decentralized agencies has adopted a more critical approach towards the creation of new agencies in general. However, it is not possible to understand the development of the AFSJ without the agencies.

The existing AFSJ agencies are Europol, Eurojust, the European Border and Coast Guard Agency (Frontex), the European Police College (CEPOL), the European Asylum Office (EASO) and the EU Agency for large-scale IT systems within the Area of Freedom, Security and Justice (EULISA). The European Union Agency for Fundamental Rights and the European Monitoring Centre for Drugs and Drug Addiction develop some of their activities under the aegis of the AFSJ, but they are not strictly AFSJ agencies. This chapter will mainly focus on the practices of Europol, Frontex and EASO. The three agencies present characteristics which clearly differentiate them from Eurojust and CEPOL due to the fact that their powers are not merely regulatory and have undertaken relevant operational activities. The second section of this chapter will focus on examining the establishment and development of Europol, Frontex and EASO over the years, as well as on the main activities carried out by them. The third section will be devoted to analyzing democratic control over the activities of the AFSJ agencies. The fourth section provides a detailed examination of the mechanisms available to the individuals in case of fundamental rights violations occurring as a result of the AFSJ agencies.

The development of AFSJ agencies

The activities carried out by AFSJ agencies are very diverse, and have continued to expand in recent years. This expansion of competences has taken place not only through the legislative process, but has also developed through dynamic development in the performance of its activities which has allowed them to expand the powers originally granted by the founding legal act. This dynamism has been accepted by member states as new challenges have been raised to which member states in isolation cannot provide a satisfactory answer. As a result, 'their competences and areas of intervention are in constant mutation, struggle and redefinition' (Carrera et al. 2013: 342). The large-scale and uncontrolled arrival of migrants and asylum-seekers to the Union has led to an expansion of the operational powers of Frontex, Europol and EASO beyond original expectations. This section examines the development of the AFSJ agencies and the main activities carried out by them.

In the past, a formal distinction could be made between the agencies that were created within the framework of the former third pillar and the agencies established under the former first pillar. Europol, Eurojust and CEPOL were established under the former third pillar. After the entry into force of the Lisbon Treaty, the Treaties included for the first time an explicit legal basis for the establishment of Europol and Eurojust in Articles 85 and 88 TFEU. With the adoption of Regulation 2016/794, Europol has recently been integrated within the TFEU. Other agencies have been created on the basis of specific policy areas regulated in the Treaties and without a specific legal basis for their creation. The only AFSJ agency that was originally set up under the former first pillar was Frontex. EASO and EULISA were formally established after the entry into force of the Lisbon Treaty. The activities undertaken by Frontex and Europol have recently been expanded through the legislative process. It is expected that the powers of EASO will also be reinforced in 2017.

Europol

Europol was set up by the Council Decision of April 6, 2009 establishing the European Police Office, which legally established it as a EU agency. Europol's objective, as laid out in Article 88 TFEU, is to support and strengthen action by competent authorities of the member states and their mutual cooperation in preventing and combatting organized crime, terrorism and other forms of serious crime affecting two or more member states. The Europol Council Decision of 2009 replaced the Convention of 1995 (see De Moor and Vermeulen 2010; Santos Vara 2010). The operational powers of Europol have been developed through the protocols that modified the Europol Convention. Europol may participate in joint investigation teams and was granted operational powers to help member states conduct or coordinate investigations and to suggest the setting up of joint investigation teams (JITs).

Since the Europol Decision of 2009 was adopted within the framework of the former third pillar, a need arose to fully integrate Europol within the framework of the TEU and TFEU in order to enhance the democratic legitimacy and accountability of Europol to the Union's citizens. Article 88 TFEU provides for Europol to be governed by a regulation to be adopted in accordance with the ordinary legislative procedure. Therefore, the Europol Council Decision was replaced by Regulation 2016/794. The new Europol Regulation has continued the trend to extend the powers of the agency. It reinforces the powers of Europol to participate in JITs, and to initiate and conduct criminal investigations when it considers that it provides an added value. As a consequence of the refugee crisis, Europol's operational efforts to fight criminal activities associated with migration have been reinforced, in particular within the 'hotspots'.

Frontex

Frontex was established with the aim of coordinating and assisting member states' actions in the surveillance and control of the external borders of the EU (see Carrera 2007). Frontex has been characterized as an agency with a dual character (Rijpma 2012: 90). On the one hand, it assists member states in the implementation of a common integrated management of the external borders through the provision of technical support. On the other hand, Frontex is entrusted with the coordination of joint operations between member states' national border guards. Since its establishment, Frontex has coordinated many joint operations covering the air, land and sea borders of the member states. Frontex is the AFSJ agency which has experienced the greatest growth in its powers in past years. The first amendment of Frontex's founding regulation took place in 2007. Frontex was authorized to deploy Rapid Border Intervention Teams (RABITs) to assist member states faced with the arrival of large numbers of third-country nationals trying to cross the external borders irregularly. The reform introduced by Regulation 1168/2011 conferred upon Frontex stronger powers in the coordination of joint operations and in the deployment of Rapid Border Intervention Teams (RABITs), which were renamed European Border Guard Teams (EBGTs).

One of the most relevant proposals presented by the Commission to address the refugee crisis was the establishment of a European Border and Coast Guard (EBCG). The EBCG is a legal fiction comprising the new European agency that replaced Frontex and the national border guards (de Bruycker 2016: 6). Regulation 2016/1624 does not create a true European border and coast guard, understood as a European body replacing national border guards, but rather a

Frontex-plus agency (Carrera and den Hertog 2016: 2). However, the EBCG Regulation substantially expands the powers of the agency over the member states. The agency shall evaluate member states' capacity to control their sections of the external border through a 'vulnerability assessment' (Article 12). The EBCG Regulation contains a provision giving the agency the power to intervene in a member state in the case that it does not implement the corrective measures proposed after a vulnerability assessment or in case of 'disproportionate migratory pressure at the external border risking to jeopardize the Schengen Area' (Article 19).

EASO

The adoption of Regulation 439/2010 in 2010 established the European Asylum Support Office. The EASO's formal objective is to facilitate, coordinate and strengthen practical cooperation among member states in order to improve the implementation of the Common European Asylum System (CEAS). One of its most well-known tasks is to deploy Asylum Support Teams on the territory of a member state affected by particular pressure on their asylum and reception systems. As has happened with Europol and Frontex, the operational tasks undertaken by the EASO have progressively evolved so as to meet the growing needs of member states and of the CEAS as a whole.

As part of the package to reform the CEAS, on May 4, 2016 the Commission presented a proposal to strengthen the role of the EASO. The Commission considers that the agency is one of the tools that may be used to effectively address the structural weaknesses in the CEAS which have been further exacerbated by the large-scale and uncontrolled arrival of migrants and asylum-seekers to the EU in the past years. The new EASO should be able to 'reinforce and complement the asylum and reception systems of Member States' (European Commission 2008: 1). Accordingly, the proposal renames the EASO as the European Union Agency for Asylum. The Regulation would reinforce its operational activities. New tasks will be conferred onto the EASO to ensure a high degree of uniformity in the application of EU asylum law across the Union, to assess compliance with the CEAS and other key tasks such as the provision and analysis of country of origin information, to increase operational and technical support to member states and to enable more convergence in the assessment of applications for international protection across the Union. Member states may seek assistance from the agency 'when their asylum and reception systems are subject to disproportionate pressure' (Article 16). Similarly to Frontex, the new EASO would have the power to intervene in member states subject to disproportionate pressures on their asylum and reception systems when these states do not seek assistance from the agency or do not take sufficient action to address that pressure (Article 22).

The democratic control over AFSJ agencies' activities

The above examination of the development of agencies has shown that the large-scale and uncontrolled arrival of migrants and asylum-seekers to the Union has led to a reinforcement of the operational powers of Frontex, Europol and EASO. The agencies contribute to the achievement of the objectives of the AFSJ. The agencies allow member states to increase their cooperation in policy areas closely linked to their national sovereignty. Furthermore, the operational activities developed by some AFSJ agencies also contribute to the Europeanization of policies not transferred to the EU. Therefore, AFSJ agencies allow the EU to tackle migration and other issues more efficiently. In light of the legislative changes already introduced or proposed, it is necessary to examine whether they have also brought about a reinforcement of democratic control over the activities of these agencies.

The increasing tasks and powers conferred upon AFSJ agencies have been coupled with concerns for democratic accountability (De Witte and Rijpma 2011; Trauner 2012; Santos Vara 2015). In the case of the three agencies set up under the former third pillar, parliamentary control was originally very limited, although as will become clear below, subsequent reforms have improved their accountability. This situation arose because these agencies were set up as the result of an intergovernmental procedure in which the European Parliament and the Commission were left outside of the decision-making process. Even though Frontex was established under the former first pillar, democratic control over its activities was also very weak. EASO and EULISA were established after the Treaty of Lisbon entered into force, which has not in either case led to the introduction of democratic controls adequate for the important roles these agencies fulfill. Despite the fact that the introduction of the community method in most policy areas of the AFSJ after the Lisbon Treaty has not substantially transformed them (Trauner and Ripoll Servent 2016: 1421), the application of the co-decision to the establishment and modification of Frontex, Europol and EASO has led to an improvement in democratic control over the activities of these agencies (Santos Vara 2015: 122). The changes introduced by the Lisbon Treaty have led to 'new and more EU-based accountability structures' (Trauner 2012).

There is no doubt that the most important control the European Parliament has over AFSJ agencies stems from the fact that they are largely financed through the general EU budget. As the Parliament, along with the Council, is the budgetary authority, the Budgets and Budgetary Control Committees are involved in the establishment and monitoring of the agencies' budget. Furthermore, in accordance with the agencies' founding regulations, the Parliament monitors the implementation of agency budgets. The discharge procedure provides the Parliament with the means to control and monitor the implementation of the agencies' budgets, and the debates in the two parliamentary committees in charge provide the Parliament with the chance to demand changes and improvements in the governance of the agencies (Busuioc 2011).

The AFSJ agencies, like others, are required to prepare an annual and a multi-annual working program and to adopt an annual activity report of the agency's activities for the previous year, which must be submitted to the European Parliament for information. Although these documents report on the activities of the agencies and are reviewed by the Civil Liberties, Justice and Home Affairs Committee (LIBE), they do not result in a parliamentary evaluation of the activities of each of the agencies. The LIBE Committee should be more active by requiring relevant information and monitoring the implementation of its demands by the agencies.

Traditionally, one of the main weaknesses in the democratic control of the AFSJ agencies stemmed from the fact that the European Parliament was not involved in the appointment of the directors of the agencies. The Parliament was not consulted in the past during the appointment process for the directors of Europol, Frontex and CEPOL. In the two agencies established after the entry into force of the Lisbon Treaty (EASO and EULISA), the candidate selected by the Management Board has to appear before the relevant parliamentary committee or committees of the Parliament and answer questions put by their members. The 2016 Regulations of Frontex and Europol have also adopted the same system for the appointment of director. The Parliament must emit an opinion on the proposed candidate or candidates and may indicate a preferred candidate. The Management Board of the agency must inform the Parliament of the manner in which its opinion was taken into account, in particular when it appoints a candidate other than the one preferred by the Parliament. This new formula may be interpreted as a positive response to the efforts made to improve the governance and accountability of the agencies. In contrast with other agencies, where the management board depends directly on the Commission, member states control most of the management boards in the case of AFSJ agencies, which makes the choice of director a more intergovernmental decision. The 2016 Europol

Regulation includes highly significant measures to increase the democratic accountability of the agency, with a view to improving the democratic control of the agency's activities. Article 88 TFEU requires the establishment of procedures for the scrutiny of Europol's activities by the European Parliament, together with national parliaments, in order to enhance the democratic legitimacy and accountability of Europol to the Union's citizens. Article 51 of the Europol Regulation foresees the constitution of a Joint Parliamentary Scrutiny Group established together by the national parliaments and the European Parliament. The Joint Parliamentary Scrutiny Group is entrusted to monitor Europol's activities in fulfilling its mission, including the impact of agencies' activities on the fundamental rights and freedoms of natural persons. Europol has to inform and report to the European Parliament and to national parliaments on assessments of threats, strategic analyses and general updates related to the objectives of Europol, the multiannual programming and the annual work program of Europol, the consolidated annual activity report on Europol's activities, as well as on cooperation agreements concluded with third countries and international organizations. Therefore, the Europol Regulation acknowledges the relevance of interparliamentary cooperation in the supervision of the agency. Since national parliaments were conferred an important role after the Lisbon Treaty in the EU institutional framework, the joint supervision of AFSJ policies and agencies is a welcome development (Mitsilegas 2007). The constitution of the Joint Parliamentary Scrutiny Group introduces a positive innovation that alleviates the democratic deficit of a body which performs a role of major importance in the fight against organized crime.

The obligation of the director to inform the Parliament when requested has been included in the founding regulations of the two agencies established after the Lisbon Treaty (EASO and EULISA). The 2016 Regulations of Frontex and Europol also foresee the possibility of inviting the executive director to report to the Parliament on the performance of the agency. In the past, senior Frontex officials have declined to take part in debates organized by the Parliament on the management of maritime borders in Southern Europe (Baldaccini 2010: 236). The regulation establishing the EBCG has provided a satisfactory solution to this weakness in the democratic control over Frontex. According to the regulation establishing the EBCG, the new Frontex is accountable to the European Parliament. The agency also has to report on its activities to the European Parliament and to the Council to the fullest extent, and in particular, regarding the general risk analyses, the results of the vulnerability assessment, the situations at the external borders requiring urgent action and decisions taken in response, the composition and deployment of European Border and Coast Guard teams, and the research and innovation activities relevant for European integrated border management.

One of the difficulties involved in the parliamentary scrutiny of Frontex, as with AFSJ agencies as a whole, is that of access to classified information. In the case of Frontex, the transmission of classified information to the European Parliament has to comply with the rules applicable to the Parliament and the Commission. Access by the European Parliament to Europol's classified information has to be consistent with the Interinstitutional Agreement of March 12, 2014 between the European Parliament and the Council concerning the forwarding and handling of classified information by the European Parliament held by the Council on matters other than those in the area of the Common Foreign and Security Policy. For this purpose, Europol and the Parliament will have to conclude working arrangements regulating the access allowed to Parliament. The creation of a LIBE subcommittee dedicated solely to the parliamentary supervision of AFSJ agencies has been proposed (De Witte and Rijpma 2011). A subcommittee of this type would be the ideal solution to address the weaknesses that characterize the democratic accountability of AFSJ agencies as regards classified information, while at the same time ensuring the confidentiality of information.

As was pointed out in the introduction to this chapter, the issue of the control and accountability of AFSJ agencies should be framed within the debate on the decentralized agencies of the EU, which has taken place in the past few years (Bernard 2012; Comte 2008). In order to improve the existing situation, specifically the coherence, effectiveness, accountability and transparency of these agencies, the Parliament, the Council and the Commission agreed in 2009 to create an inter-institutional working group on decentralized agencies. The results of this inter-institutional dialogue are laid out in the 2012 Joint Declaration on decentralized agencies and the Commission roadmap on the follow-up to the Common Approach. The Joint Declaration includes proposals to harmonize practices of democratic control over all of the agencies. A novel measure was devised to ensure political control over the agencies. If the Commission has serious cause for concern that an agency's Management Board is about to take a decision which contravenes the mandate of the agency or violates EU law, 'the Commission will formally raise the question in the Management Board and request it to refrain from adopting the relevant decision' (European Parliament, Council and Commission 2012: 13). Should the Management Board not follow the Commission's recommendations, the latter will then inform the European Parliament and the Council in order to allow these institutions to react in good time. This warning system confirms that the Commission has significant authority over the supervision of the agencies, and that it may influence their operation through its participation in the management board.

Redress in the case of fundamental rights breaches

The dynamic evolution of the tasks undertaken by the AFSJ agencies, in particular by Frontex, Europol and EASO in the past years, has not led the institutions to admit that the agencies' activities may have potential fundamental rights implications. It is considered that these agencies were set up in order to facilitate and coordinate operational cooperation among the authorities of the member states. Therefore, AFSJ agencies are not granted the powers to make decisions which have a binding legal effect on third parties; nor do they have the power to make operational decisions. However, 'closer examination of these agencies' tasks reveals that they are entitled to act not only as coordinators, but also as the planners and initiators of operational actions' (Carrera *et al.* 2013: 344). The relevance of human rights has been taken into account by the AFSJ agencies themselves in the development of their activities, and new mechanisms have been introduced through the legislative process to ensure accountability. The question remains to what extent the human rights mechanisms devised thus far provide a satisfactory answer to the issues at stake.

Human rights challenges

Since the powers of Frontex are mainly directed towards managing the external borders, its activities have raised many complex issues. The respect for the right of asylum, the right to an effective remedy and the principle of non-refoulement may be at stake in the operations coordinated by Frontex. This discussion has dealt mainly with the treatment that must be granted to persons on board the vessels intercepted on the high seas and in the territorial waters of third states (Santos Vara and Sánchez-Tabernero 2016; Papastavridis 2010; Fischer-Lescano *et al.* 2009; Klepp 2010). Frontex has been severely criticized since its early days for not carrying out sea surveillance operations in full compliance with human rights obligations (Cederbratt 2013). Regulation 1168/2011, which modified the 2004 Frontex Regulation, constantly stated that the agency was fully committed to respecting fundamental human rights both when it was acting independently and when it was in cooperation with third countries and international organizations. Furthermore, Frontex has undertaken a number of initiatives with a view to integrating fundamental human rights in its activities, such as the development of the Frontex Fundamental Rights Strategy and the establishment of the Frontex Consultative Forum on human rights and the appointment of a fundamental rights officer. These amendments did not constitute an effective remedy in the case of fundamental rights breaches, but they have raised awareness and contributed to mainstreaming fundamental rights in the work of the agency (Rijpma 2014: 67).

Frontex and the European Commission have always held that the responsibility for fundamental rights breaches lies exclusively with the member states. In 2012, the European Ombudsman opened an own-initiative inquiry to assess the implementation by Frontex of fundamental rights obligations. The European Ombudsman pointed out the absence of any procedure to deal with human rights infringements that occurred during joint operations coordinated by Frontex (European Ombudsman 2013). The EBCG Regulation introduces a new complaint mechanism to monitor and ensure respect for fundamental rights. According to Article 72, anyone who considers that he or she is the victim of fundamental rights violations committed during an operation coordinated by Frontex may submit a complaint to the agency. The complaints are handled by the fundamental rights officer. If a complaint is admitted by the fundamental rights officer, the member states or the agency will ensure an 'appropriate follow-up' depending on whether the complaint concerns a staff member of the agency or a member state (Article 72 of the EBCG Regulation). The new procedure brings a positive development to deal with human rights violations, since the victims have a complaint mechanism at their disposal. However, it is an administrative procedure that cannot substitute the right to an effective remedy under Article 47 of the Charter of Fundamental Rights (Peers 2015; Rijpma 2016: 30).

As regards Europol, the rules on data protection are very important in achieving the development of European police cooperation while not negatively affecting fundamental rights, and in particular, the right to private life of all citizens (Santos Vara 2010). Even though data protection has been reinforced in the 2016 Europol Regulation, data processing raises very sensitive issues. The activities developed by Europol in its external dimension raise also fundamental rights concerns. The main external activity carried out by Europol is the possibility of interchanging information with third countries within the framework of the agreements concluded by the agency. The exact nature of the cooperation involved depends on the type of agreement reached. While strategic agreements only allow for the exchange of generic information, operational agreements also facilitate the exchange of personal data.

As regards the external dimension of AFSJ agencies, Frontex is the agency which has experienced the greatest growth in its cooperation with third states in the past years. The working arrangements concluded with third countries constitute a very important instrument for the development of Frontex's external relations (Fink 2012: 20). These agreements include undertakings in the field of information exchange and the creation and coordination of joint operational measures and pilot projects, as well as cooperation in risk analysis, technical development of border procedures and training. The agency may deploy liaison officers in third countries and receive liaison officers from third countries on a reciprocal basis, with a view to contributing to the prevention of and fight against irregular immigration and the return of irregular migrants. The agency may also invite observers from third countries to take part in its activities. The Regulation on the EBCG even foresees the possibility that the agency may coordinate operational cooperation among member states and third countries with respect to management of the external borders and even implement operations on the territory of third countries.

Judicial review over AFSJ agencies

Given that, from the perspective of fundamental rights, AFSJ agencies are acting in a particularly sensitive area, it is essential that they are fully accountable for their activities. The substantial autonomy enjoyed by AFSJ agencies in developing their activities does not mean that they are immune to judicial controls. Since AFSJ agencies were created to reinforce operational cooperation among national authorities and to assist them, they can avoid judicial accountability, arguing that the member states are responsible vis-à-vis the individuals. It is necessary to examine the options offered by the European Union's legal order for obtaining redress in case violations occur as a result of the activities undertaken by the AFSJ agencies.

The Treaty of Lisbon expressly introduced the possibility of taking legal action to annul legal acts of the agencies. In Article 263 TFEU, it is stipulated that the Court of Justice 'shall review the legality of acts of bodies, offices or agencies of the Union intended to produce legal effects vis-à-vis third parties'. All EU agencies may be included within the concept of an 'office' or 'agency' outlined in Article 263 TFEU, with the exception of the CFSP agencies, given that the jurisdiction of the Court of Justice is excluded by Article 24 TEU. Therefore, in the case of fundamental rights violations against an individual, he or she may seek legal redress on the basis of Article 263 TFEU. In addition, Article 340 TFEU gives an individual the right to sue an institution or agency seeking compensation for damages.

Before the entry into force of the Lisbon Treaty, the General Court had already accepted the possibility of bringing an annulment action against the act of an agency in *Solgema*. On the basis of the *Les Verts* judgment, the General Court held that 'an act emanating from a Community body intended to produce legal effects vis-à-vis third parties cannot escape judicial review by the Community judicature' (*Solgema*: par. 48). It must also be kept in mind that the Court of Justice interprets the access to its jurisdiction restrictively. Therefore, the applicants that lodge an action for annulment have to demonstrate that an act has been addressed by an agency directly to them. Apart from that, there is also sometimes uncertainty regarding the distribution of responsibility among the different actors involved in the agencies' activities in the AFSJ. A good illustration is the hotspots set up to manage the massive arrival of refugees to Italy and Greece, developed within the framework of the Agenda for Migration of 2015. The EASO, Frontex, Europol and Eurojust work on the ground with the authorities of member states to help them fulfill their obligations under EU law and swiftly identify, register and fingerprint incoming migrants. Frontex joint operations at sea also raise complex issues regarding the allocation of responsibility between the agency and the member states involved in cases of human rights violations, or even among the member states participating in Frontex joint operations. Furthermore, the possibility of developing and coordinating operations on the territory of third countries exacerbates the difficulty in the delimitation of responsibility between the actors involved. The EBCG Regulation does not introduce a clarification on the allocation of responsibility between the actors involved in Frontex joint operations implemented in the territory of third countries (Fink 2016: 3). The broadening powers conferred upon Frontex by the new regulation may exacerbate the problems facing the individuals who are victims of human rights violations and who try to obtain judicial redress.

Conclusions

This chapter has shown that the substantial autonomy enjoyed by AFSJ agencies in developing their activities does not mean that they are immune to political and judicial controls. The development of the AFSJ has resulted in new tasks and powers entrusted to these agencies as well as new concerns for effective accountability and respect of fundamental rights. The AFSJ agencies have been presented as instruments to facilitate or reinforce operational cooperation among the authorities of the member states. The activities performed by Frontex, Europol and the EASO go beyond mere coordination, as they have assumed relevant operational activities which may have negative implications for fundamental rights. The operational activities developed by these agencies contribute to the Europeanization of national actors and policies closely linked to national sovereignty. However, there is still a gap in the literature regarding the practical working of AFSJ agencies and their impact upon operational cooperation among member states.

Democratic control over the activities of these agencies has not been adequately considered in the successive reforms of the treaties and has not been well developed in practice. It must be recognized that despite the limited prerogatives conferred upon the European Parliament regarding AFSJ agencies, the Parliament has been very active in exerting an increasingly strong political influence, especially the need to take into account the implications of the agencies' activities on fundamental rights. The application of the co-decision to the modification of Frontex, Europol and the EASO after the entry into force of the Treaty of Lisbon has led to an improvement of democratic control over the activities of these agencies. In regards to Europol, the constitution of the Joint Parliamentary Scrutiny Group introduces a positive innovation that alleviates the democratic deficit of an agency which performs a role of major importance in the fight against organized crime. The operational activities developed by Frontex in the past years have raised fierce criticism in terms of democratic accountability. The regulation establishing the EBCG has introduced and reinforced obligations to report on the activities of the new Frontex to the European Parliament. It seems that the ongoing scrutiny by the Parliament has been strengthened in the cases of Frontex and Europol. Since the activities carried out by the AFSJ agencies will probably continue to expand through dynamic development in the future, it should be researched whether these new democratic controls can truly offer a satisfactory solution to ensure accountability.

As has been shown in this chapter, the agencies' activities may have implications for fundamental human rights and could lead to fundamental human rights breaches. The relevance of human rights has been taken into account by the AFSJ agencies setting up interesting initiatives to ensure accountability as regards fundamental rights. The Europol and EBCG Regulations and the Proposal on the European Union Agency for Asylum would lead to reinforcing the operational activities undertaken by the agencies. The expansion of activities carried out by the AFSJ agencies would probably continue to raise tensions concerning the right to an effective remedy. Since Frontex, Europol and the EASO have undertaken relevant operational activities, it is not unlikely that in the future the Court of Justice will have to deal with actions for annulment (Article 263 TFEU) and compensation for damages (Article 340 TFEU), in particular regarding its involvement in hotspots. This issue clearly deserves further research in the future. Apart from that, the distribution of responsibility among the different actors involved in the agencies' activities should be further explored by academia. In the case of Frontex, the new complaint procedure brings a positive development in dealing with human rights violations, since the victims have an administrative mechanism at their disposal. It should be further researched to what extent the complaint mechanism provides a satisfactory solution to the main issues at stake.

One of the major avenues of further research is the cooperation among AFSJ agencies. This cooperation is becoming more and more necessary to achieve AFSJ objectives. One of the most relevant developments in the cooperation among agencies are the hotspots. The hotspots will develop an important role in the future as is acknowledged by the EBCG Regulation, which regulates them for the first time and entrusts Frontex to assist the Commission in the coordination among the different agencies on the ground. The need to cooperate is even extended to agencies created outside of the AFSJ. According to the EBCG Regulation, Frontex, the European Fisheries Control Agency and the European Maritime Safety Agency will have to increase their cooperation in the management of external borders.

It should be analyzed whether the strengthening of these AFSJ agencies is well perceived and accepted by national actors. The new supervision role conferred upon the EASO and Frontex in the management of borders and asylum policy respectively deserves special attention in the literature in the future. More attention should also be devoted to examining whether the new tasks allocated to the agencies allow the EU to more efficiently tackle the challenges member states face in areas such as asylum and migration.

Acknowledgment

This chapter has been written within the framework of the research project on 'Democratic Control and EU External Action' (EUDECEXT), DER2015–70082-P (MINECO/FEDER), led by the author.

Bibliography

AFSJ Agencies (2014). The EU Justice and Home Affairs Agencies' Cooperation in 2014: Working Together to Achieve Common EU Objectives.

Baldaccini, A. (2010). Extraterritorial Border Controls in the UE: The Role of Frontex in Operations at Sea. In B. Ryan and V. Mitsilegas (eds), *Extraterritorial Immigration Control: Legal Challenges*. Leiden: Martinus Nijhoff, pp. 229–255.

Bernard, E. (2012). Accord sur les agences européennes: la montagne accouche d'une souris. *Revue du Droit de l'Union Européenne*, 3, pp. 399–446.

Bovens, M. (2007). Analysing and Assessing Accountability: A Conceptual Framework. *European Law Journal*, 13, pp. 447–468.

Busuioc, M., Curtin, C. and Groenleer, M. (2011). Agency Growth between Autonomy and Accountability: The European Policy Office as a Living Institution. *Journal of European Public Policy*, 19, pp. 848–867.

Carrera, S. (2007). The EU Border Management Strategy FRONTEX and the Challenges of Irregular Immigration in the Canary Islands. CEPS Working Document No. 261, Brussels.

Carrera, S. and den Hertog, L. (2016). A European Border and Coast Guard: What's in a Name? CEPS Paper No. 88.

Carrera, S., den Hertog, L. and Parkin, J. (2013). The Peculiar Nature of EU Home Affairs Agencies in Migration Control: Beyond Accountability *versus* Autonomy? *European Journal of Migration and Law*, 15, pp. 337–358.

Cederbratt, M. (2013). *Frontex: Human Rights Responsibilities*. Doc. 13161, April 8. Strasbourg: Parliamentary Assembly of the Council of Europe.

Chiti, E. (2009). An Important Part of the EU's Institutional Machinery: Features, Problems and Perspectives of European Agencies. *Common Market Law Review*, 46, pp. 1395–1442.

Comte, F. (2008). Agences européennes: relance d'une réflexion interinstitutionnelle européenne. *Revue du Droit de l'Union Européenne*, 3. pp. 461–501.

De Bruycker, P. (2016). The European Border and Coast Guard: A New Model Built on an Old Logic. *European Papers: A Journal of Law and Integration*, 2, pp. 1–12.

De Moor, A. and Vermeulen, G. (2010). The Europol Council Decision: Transforming Europol into an Agency of the European Union. *Common Market Law Review*, 47, pp. 1089–1121.

De Witte, B. and Rijpma, J. (2011). Oversight of the European Union's Area of Freedom, Security and Justice (AFSJ): Parliamentary Scrutiny of Justice and Home Affairs Agencies. LIBE Committee of the European Parliament, Thematic Study.

European Commission (2008). *Communication from the Commission to the European Parliament and the Council – European Agencies – The Way Forward*. COM (2008) 135 final.

European Parliament, Council and Commission (2012). Joint Statement of the European Parliament, the Council of the EU and the European Commission on Decentralized Agencies, Brussels.

Fink, M. (2012). Frontex Working Arrangements: Legitimacy and Human Rights Concerns Regarding Technical Relationships. *Utrecht Journal of International and European Law*, 28, pp. 20–35.
Fink, M. (2016). Salami Slicing Human Rights Accountability: How the European Border and Coast Guard Agency May Inherit Frontex' Genetic Defect. *EJIL Analysis*, March 10.
Fischer-Lescano, A., Löhr, T. and Tohidipur, T. (2009). Border Controls at Sea: Requirements under International Human Rights and Refugee Law. *International Journal of Refugee Law*, 21, pp. 256–296.
Klepp, S. (2010). A Contested Asylum System: The European Union between Refugee Protection and Border Control in the Mediterranean Sea. *European Journal of Migration and Law*, 12, pp. 1–21.
Mitsilegas, V. (2007). Interparliamentary Cooperation in EU Justice and Home Affairs. Fifty Years of Interparliamentary Cooperation Conference, Stiftung Wissenschaft und Politik, Berlin.
Papastavridis, E. (2010). Fortress Europe and FRONTEX: Within or Without International Law? *Nordic Journal of International Law*, 79.
Peers, S. (2015). The Reform of Frontex: Saving Schengen at Refugees' Expense? EU Law Analysis.
Rijpma, J. (2012). Hybrid Agencification in the Area of Freedom, Security and Justice and its Inherent Tensions: The Case of Frontex. In M. Busuioc, M. Groenleer and J. Trondal (eds), *The Agency Phenomenon in the European Union: Emergence, Institutionalisation and Everyday Decision-making*. Manchester: Manchester University Press.
Rijpma, J. (2014). Institutions and Agencies: Government and Governance after Lisbon. In D. Acosta Arcarazo and C.C. Murphy (eds), *EU Security and Justice Law: After Lisbon and Stockholm*. Oxford: Hart Publishing.
Rijpma, J. (2016). The Proposal for a European Border and Coast Guard: Evolution or Revolution in External Border Management? Study for the *LIBE Committee of the European Parliament*.
Santos Vara, J. (2010). Las consecuencias de la integración de Europol en el Derecho de la Unión Europea (Comentario a la Decisión del Consejo 2009/371/JAI, de 6 de abril de 2009. *Revista General de Derecho Europeo*, 20, pp. 1–24.
Santos Vara, J. (2015). The External Activities of AFSJ Agencies: The Weakness of Democratic and Judicial Controls. *European Foreign Affairs Review*, 20(1), pp. 118–136.
Santos Vara, J. and Sánchez-Tabernero, R. (2016). In Deep Water: Towards a Greater Commitment for Human Rights in Sea Operations Coordinated by FRONTEX? *European Journal of Migration and Law*, 18(1), pp. 65–87.
Trauner, F. (2012). The European Parliament and Agency Control in the Area of Freedom, Security and Justice. *West European Politics*, 35(4), pp. 784–802.
Trauner, F. and Ripoll Servent, A. (2016). The Communitarisation of the Area of Freedom, Security and Justice: Why Institutional Change does not Translate into Policy Change. *Journal of Common Market Studies*, 54(6), pp. 1417–1432.

Legislation, proposals for legislation and judgements

Regulation (EU) 2016/794 of the European Parliament and of the Council of May 11, 2016 on the European Union Agency for Law Enforcement Cooperation (Europol) and Replacing and Repealing Council Decisions 2009/371/JHA, 2009/934/JHA, 2009/935/JHA, 2009/936/JHA and 2009/968/JHA [2016] OJ L 135/53.
Council Decision of April 6, 2009 establishing the European Police Office (Europol) (2009/371/JHA), OJ L 121/37.
Council Regulation (EC) No. 2007/2004 of October 26, 2004 establishing a European Agency for the Management of Operational Cooperation at the External Borders of the Member States of the European Union [2004] OJ L 349/1.
Regulation (EC) No. 863/2007 of July 11, 2007 establishing a mechanism for the creation of Rapid Border Intervention Teams and amending Council Regulation (EC) No. 2007/2004 as regards that mechanism and regulating the tasks and powers of guest officers [2007] OJ L 199/30.
Regulation (EU) No. 1168/2011 of October 25, 2011 amending Council Regulation (EC) No. 2007/2004 establishing a European Agency for the Management of Operational Cooperation at the External Borders of the Member States of the European Union [2011] OJ L301/1.
Proposal for a Regulation of the European Parliament and of the Council on the European Union Agency for Asylum and repealing Regulation (EU) No. 439/2010, COM(2016) 271 final.
Regulation No. 439/2010 of the European Parliament and of the Council of May 19, 2010 establishing a European Asylum Support Office [2010] OJ L 132/11.

Regulation No. 439/2010 of the European Parliament and of the Council of September 14, 2016 on the European Border and Coast Guard and amending Regulation (EU) 2016/399 of the European Parliament and of the Council and repealing Regulation (EC) No. 863/2007 of the European Parliament and of the Council, Council Regulation (EC) No. 2007/2004 and Council Decision 2005/267/EC [2010] OJ L 251/11.

Inter-institutional Agreement of March 12, 2014 between the European Parliament and the Council concerning the forwarding to and the handling by the European Parliament of classified information held by the Council on matters other than those in the area of the common foreign and security policy [2014] OJ C 95/11.

Judgment of *Sogelma*, T-411/06, ECLI:EU:T:2008.

38
NGOs GO TO BRUSSELS
Challenges and opportunities for research and practice in the Area of Freedom, Security and Justice

Emek M. Uçarer

Introduction

Over the past few decades, non-governmental organizations (NGOs) have increasingly become a subject of inquiry for scholars in a variety of disciplines. This is particularly notable in the field of international relations and political science, disciplines that are historically predominantly preoccupied with studying the state and its interaction with other states. As the recognition of the importance of civil society in democracies took hold, so did acceptance of NGOs as actors in their own right, occasioning research into their work and their interactions with states and intergovernmental organizations (IGOs) (Liebert 2013; Liebert and Trenz 2011; Steffek and Hahn 2010; Sudbery 2010). In the European Union (EU), this new-found interest in NGOs had the additional benefit of working against the long-standing critique of the organization regarding its democratic deficit. Given this critique, consulting and working with NGOs was considered an important way in which the organization could be brought closer to the people within its territory (Cram 2011; Steffek et al. 2008).

In addition to potentially democratizing and pluralizing the multilateral policy process, NGOs are increasingly seen by states and IGOs as vectors for delivery of services to target populations (Batley and Rose 2011). NGOs, in turn, have started looking beyond the national as they gain expertise and strength and expand their networks. The Internet and ease of communications have played into the development of increasingly denser networks among NGOs, creating opportunities to link horizontally across states and vertically up to IGOs. While governments and IGOs have been interested in partnering with NGOs in terms of service delivery, they have not always been as interested in becoming targets of advocacy, especially in instances in which the substance of the advocacy runs counter to their policy interests and preferences, at times turning states, IGOs, and NGOs into strange bedfellows. This dynamic is captured in studies that show a variety of interactions among states, IGOs and NGOs, ranging from NGOs functioning autonomously to complete subordination where control is maintained over NGOs (Young 2000). Some IGOs, like the United Nations, have adopted formal procedures through which NGOs can access and participate in policy conversations, while others, like the EU, have left such conversations informal and unstructured, causing complications in access for NGOs (Joachim and Locher 2009; Uçarer 2009b).

While (Western) Europe is generally considered to be a welcoming place for civil society activity, NGO activity in the EU has only recently become a subject of systematic study.

Scholarly inquiry into EU–NGO interactions in the EU's various competences is uneven, with some policy areas generating much more research than others. The field of justice and home affairs (JHA) in the EU, later renamed the Area of Freedom, Security and Justice (AFSJ), is one area in which research is still lagging. This is partly because this competence is relatively new to the EU, and partly because its subject matter presents challenges for NGO activity and consequently its study. This chapter begins with an overview of the interactions between NGOs and the European Union and the reasons why there is limited research in the field, before moving to a discussion on recent empirical developments in the AFSJ. It concludes with a discussion on avenues for further research.

Studying NGOs in the AFSJ: assessing the state of the art

Studying the role of civil society in EU deliberations is not new. For example, the role which environmental NGOs have played in shaping the EU's policies and the strategies they have employed in the process have been studied in depth (Zito and Jacobs 2009). Human rights are another area in which NGOs, and research inspired by them, have made inroads (Clark 2001). Not surprisingly, NGO studies have advanced the most in this field. By contrast, NGOs are an under-studied area in the AFSJ.

There are a number of studies on the service work done by NGOs in general or in related EU fields, such as social policy (Gatrell 2016; Ahmed and Potter 2006; Davies 2013; Lewis and Opoku-Mensah 2006). Domestic case studies of civil society mobilization on a variety of immigration and asylum issues are typically how research is conducted (Freedman 2009; Hoffmann 2012). These studies usually address how NGOs work in their respective fields. A significant gap in the literature lies in unpacking the specific interface between NGOs and the EU. Existing literature focusing on immigration and asylum governance in the European Union and the role of NGOs within it primarily examines political opportunity structures (POS) that are drawn from the literature on social mobilization, and social movement theory has been used to understand and explain the impact which NGOs may have upon international institutions, their efforts to mobilize, and their capacity to act as norm entrepreneurs (Imig and Tarrow 2001; McAdam et al. 1996; Cullen 2015b). NGOs are embedded in POS that impact various mobilization resources, which in turn are deployed within particular frames to convince others (Joachim and Locher 2009). POS are themselves shaped by the context in which decisions are made (Princen 2011). Scholars have applied political process theory to migrant advocacy, mostly at the domestic/national level, but have not focused specifically on how NGOs engage regional principals (Koopmans and Statham 1999; Statham and Koopmans 2003; Monforte 2014; Schnyder 2015).

Applied specifically to the AFSJ regional context, a handful of studies have highlighted waxing and waning POS for NGOs both at the national and especially at the international level. Factors that contribute to improved POS for NGOs include access to policy circles by gaining attention and building credibility, an ability to frame issues in ways that prompt interest by decision-makers, claiming relevant authority, ensuring resonance with policy-makers, and commanding sufficient resources to achieve these ends, all of which impact their agenda-setting capabilities (Cullen 2015a; Princen 2011; Schnyder 2015; Uçarer 2009b, 2014). Eising rightly observes:

> [T]time, money, staff, and the support of members – are widely regarded as preconditions for an effective representation of interests. In the complex European multi-level setting, actors need profound organizational resources to keep track of policy

developments and to represent their interests continuously at the different levels of government and throughout the policy cycle.

(Eising 2004: 218)

A number of studies show how changes over time to the treaty structure of the European Union have resulted in increased political opportunities for NGOs to gain access to EU institutions. The subtle shifting of the power balance between the European Commission, the European Parliament and the Council of Ministers towards the first two is perceived by NGOs as enhancing their opportunities (Uçarer 2009b, 2014; Thiel and Uçarer 2014). The Commission and especially the pre-Lisbon Treaty Parliament have been keen on working with NGOs to expand their standing in immigration and asylum (Geddes 2000; Uçarer 2014). The venue-shopping literature provides some insight into inter-institutional dynamics by focusing on understanding strategic choices made by NGOs in targeting particular organs of the European Union. This strand of institutionalist research, drawing upon Guiraudon's work, points to efforts to strategically select a particular decision setting which is most conducive to airing grievances and presenting policies and policy alternatives (Guiraudon 2000; Givens and Luedtke 2004; Kaunert and Léonard 2012).

As organizations with typically limited resources, NGOs have an interest in gaining access to key decision-makers in both national and international settings, but this interest is not always met with receptivity on the part of their advocacy targets. Research demonstrates that there are discrepancies among levels of access, openness and receptivity among the different organs of the EU towards NGOs. Typically, the European Parliament is most promising in terms of access, followed closely by the Commission. The Council, on the other hand, is singled out as difficult to penetrate at the regional level. Brussels-based NGOs have thus focused most of their efforts on the Commission and the Parliament, attempting work-arounds for the Council by trying to reach Brussels with the help of their national counterparts (Uçarer 2009b, 2014).

The normalization of the right of initiative of the Commission over the years has meant that, unlike in the early years of JHA, the Commission now has the exclusive right of initiative in most portfolios in the AFSJ. The extension of the ordinary legislative procedure to most decisions taken in the AFSJ has also meant that the European Parliament has a bigger role to play in decision-making. The Parliament is not only a target of advocacy for civil society, but is also known to initiate conversations to tap into the expertise of NGOs both for information and legal interpretations (Hoffmann 2012: 31). An enhancement in the profile of the Parliament would suggest further improvement of the POS for NGOs. This institutional improvement notwithstanding, recent studies also show that, especially after the Lisbon Treaty and the extension of the OLP to the AFSJ, the Parliament, which was up until then generally progressive in its stance on AFSJ matters and pushed back (though with limited success) at the restrictive stance of the Council, became more conservative (Acosta 2009; Ripoll Servent and Trauner 2014; Uçarer 2014). If this is a sustained trend, and everything indicates this to be the case, the improvement in POS (at least with respect to the European Parliament) may perhaps be more in theory than in actual practice.

Research on NGOs in the AFSJ is uneven among its four components. There is some research on NGOs and refugees/asylum-seekers. This field is particularly suited to being framed within human rights terms and NGOs can link their advocacy efforts much more easily to regional and global protection provisions. Immigration also lends itself to advocacy efforts, but perhaps with less direct links to human rights. In the absence of a well-defined global or regional framework that regulates cross-border mobility, NGO advocacy work on immigration is hampered. This is particularly the case in labor migration of non-EU citizens, which continues to fall under national competence. Studies on labor migration tend to be country-specific and when they consider the multi-level context, they tend to focus their analysis on how the state straddles these levels (Menz and Caviades 2010). Menz's work on the political economy of managing migration contends that NGOs in this field are weakly organized at the national and regional level, and are (unlike in asylum) hampered by a lack of consensus, which makes joining forces difficult. NGOs also have limited access to ministries of interior affairs, as these do not typically consult NGOs. Consequently, NGOs do not exert substantial influence over policy and thus cannot serve as countervailing forces to the restrictionist trends in this field (Menz 2008).

There is much less work on judicial cooperation (Piana 2007), and existing literature does not focus on the role of NGOs. There is practically no work on police cooperation that accounts for NGO activity. Setting aside the independence of the judiciary both in national and in regional contexts that may make NGO advocacy overtures towards them moot, one could imagine that the service role played by NGOs as well as the practical expertise derived from such work could position them to be useful in law enforcement by, for example, providing legal assistance. However, as service NGOs typically serve individuals in precarious situations, they have been cautious not to appear to their clientele as being too close to law enforcement. Their work also oftentimes puts them in an adversarial context with law enforcement, critiquing and resisting such commonplace practices as detention and deportation. Judicial and police cooperation, by the state-centered and nationally oriented nature of both the work and the cadres that do the work (Occhipinti 2003, 2015), has been most resistant to Europeanization, and progress in harmonization here has been limited and slow. It is therefore not surprising that the research has not caught up, mostly because what can be studied is still in its infancy.

Bringing NGOs in: a rocky road

The Maastricht Treaty brought JHA/AFSJ cooperation in immigration, asylum, judicial and police cooperation into the EU in 1992, although cooperative work in this area actually dates back to the mid-1980s. Not coincidentally, so do the efforts of a handful of NGOs that started working at the regional level. While NGOs have been working for quite some time now in related fields, especially asylum and immigration, there is remarkably little academic attention paid to their efforts to engage states and the EU. This is a theoretical and empirical puzzle. Why, at a time when the literature on NGOs in the EU is burgeoning in theoretical and empirical terms, is there such a dearth of academic attention to the work that is done by NGOs in the EU's AFSJ? There may be several explanations for this, none of which should completely justify the inattention. The first and most potent explanation is that the policy domains under the AFSJ umbrella have traditionally been resistant to engagement with civil society actors. Immigration, asylum, police and judicial cooperation are seen as the exclusive business of sovereign states, the last remaining vestiges resisting the march of multilateralism. Furthermore, JHA and the AFSJ largely remain securitized fields, constructing migration as threats to security and a potential danger to public order (Bigo 2002; Bigo et al. 2010; Ceyhan and Tsoukala 2002). This security frame typically privileges states and de-emphasizes and/or subordinates NGOs and their agendas to those of the state.

A second explanation flows from the first. From the inception of JHA cooperation in the European Union, member states have been keen to maintain member state supremacy by creating a framework of decision-making that favored intergovernmentalism and relative secrecy, making it difficult for NGOs to remain effectively plugged into the process. Intergovernmentalism likewise downplayed the role of the EU, relegating its institutions to the role of agents of member states as principals. The NGO sector was well aware of the effects of intergovernmentalism in this field and was quick to identify decision-making based on unanimity, and an institutional setting that marginalized their likely allies (European Commission and European Parliament) as highly problematic for their efforts (Gray and Statham 2005: 893; Uçarer 2006). While the institutional developments in the EU have shifted portions of the initial JHA portfolio towards the community method with the Amsterdam and Lisbon Treaties, the AFSJ is still seen as too sensitive for full NGO inclusion.

A third explanation has to do with the position of the constituents of relevant NGOs. The central challenge is captured accurately by Gray and Statham:

> [The] NGO sector [...] faces the difficult task of lobbying on behalf of migrants, aliens, refugees and asylum-seekers without national domestic citizenship, who possess very few resources of rights or cultural legitimacy or belonging within the political environment to promote their own cause.
>
> *(Gray and Statham 2005: 897)*

While the first three explanations speak to the difficulties for NGOs of working in the AFSJ, the last explanation for why there is as yet very little research in this realm has to do with general difficulties in doing research on NGOs. Case studies demonstrate NGO advocacy efforts in a variety of fields, and there is substantial research on advocacy strategies and repertoires used by NGOs to influence decision-making (Cullen 2015a, 2015b; Thiel and Uçarer 2014; Uçarer 2014). This type of research focuses on agenda-setting and various methods used by NGOs to influence the decision-making process and the policy outcomes, and to produce empirically rich narratives that are field-specific. It is much harder, however, to connect the dots from NGO advocacy to NGO impact. Furthermore, the European Union does not have official procedures by which NGOs can be incorporated into policy discussions, making access to the EU ad hoc and dependent on informal ties to staffers in the organization (Uçarer 2009b). These structural barriers to NGO access not only hamper NGOs' substantive work but may also discourage academic studies, as work in this field may not appear promising to scholars. A relatively young field (AFSJ) is likely to suffer from a research lag, especially when intersecting with another relatively young field (NGO studies), suggesting that research will mature eventually.

Yet, there remain important theoretical and empirical questions to be answered. In order to fully understand how IGOs and NGOs engage each other in a given field, we have to study the motivations of IGOs such as the EU to include NGOs in the formulation and delivery of multilateral policies. (Why) does the European Union wish to engage with NGOs? What formal and informal pathways exist for communication and action? How does the EU interface with NGOs? Does it initiate or respond to overtures for collaboration and communication, and under what circumstances? Does it have and use means of leverage against NGOs to achieve its own priorities? What role do the preferences and priorities of the EU play in shaping the work done by NGOs? How does the EU react or respond when its preferences and priorities are challenged or undermined by civil society? Does the EU attempt to organize its interactions with civil society by developing and resourcing networks of civil society organizations? There are passing glimpses that answer some of these questions in the literature, but there is no systematic effort to theorize about or portray why and how the EU reaches out to or incorporates NGOs into its deliberations. What little research exists is mostly about understanding what motivates NGOs to 'go to Brussels'.

NGOs go to Brussels: goals and strategies

The difficulties highlighted above notwithstanding, NGOs working in AFSJ-related domains are increasingly focusing their attention towards the European Union level. Scholarly attention has already started to follow suit. NGO efforts to engage decision-makers in matters of immigration and asylum pre-date Maastricht. Starting in the mid-1980s, concurrent with early efforts by a handful of then-EC member states to converse on immigration, asylum and terrorism, a few NGOs started Europeanizing their efforts by setting up offices in Brussels. As Cullen observes, 'pro-migrant NGOs have resorted to international political contexts including the European Union (EU) and the United Nations (UN) as arenas for mobilization' for the rights of migrants in domestic settings (2009: 105). This engagement with Brussels was spearheaded by Churches' Commission for Migrants in Europe (CCME) and the European Council on Refugees and Exiles (ECRE), and later joined by the Migration Policy Group (MPG). These 'key pioneers' (Gray and Statham 2005: 895) were also crucial in jump-starting research in this area: early work featuring NGOs and their advocacy efforts was therefore not surprisingly produced by academics and staffers working at these NGOs and included accounts of how their NGOs sought to influence both the substantive policy discussions (Niessen 2002), beginning to draw a picture of the advocacy strategies employed. They also played an important role in linking national and subnational organizations vertically to the European level and horizontally to organizations in other European countries (Uçarer 2009b).

These pioneer NGOs thus became purveyors of information to a variety of audiences, academics included, not only on both the substance and tenor of negotiations in Brussels, but also how NGOs were going about reacting to developments. NGOs that were early entrants also sought to interject their voices at key moments in institutional developments, providing rationales for EU institutional reform and appropriate and inclusive decision-making frameworks following Maastricht and Amsterdam (Niessen 2000). In later years, increasing numbers of national NGOs started to set up offices in Brussels or became partners in transnational umbrella organizations such as the ECRE with already established offices in Brussels.

A substantial portion of these EU-level NGOs were ecumenical, including CCME, Caritas and the Jesuit Refugee Service, with close ties to their national counterparts. The NGO network began to take hold in Brussels, coinciding with institutional developments in the EU that were deemed more favorable (or, perhaps, less unfavorable) to NGO efforts. Among these developments was the incremental acceptance of the Europeanization of the AFSJ portfolio. Although still regarded largely in security terms, it was slowly making its way towards the community model (Lavenex and Uçarer 2004; Kostakopoulou 2000). This was accompanied by the improved standing of the European Commission and the European Parliament, which were typically more favorably disposed towards NGOs than the Council (Westlake and Galloway 2006). Continuing challenges in JHA/AFSJ also involved the proliferation of member states after enlargements. Brussels-based NGOs relied heavily on human rights language and advocacy repertoire to establish and advance priorities. Human rights framing was particularly apt for asylum and social inclusion, and to a lesser extent for immigration issues (Uçarer 2009a, 2009b).

NGOs deploy various kinds of expertise to make their claims vis-à-vis the EU. First among these is their relative advantage in gathering and mobilizing information. With the help of their extended network in member countries, Brussels-based NGOs are able to collect and direct relevant information to the EU and media outlets. Frequently, they facilitate testimonial encounters by providing first-hand accounts from the field. They also draw upon their significant legal expertise to interpret and situate the consequences of potential and adopted policy positions of the EU on international and EU law (Uçarer 2014). Church-affiliated NGOs are further able to use their moral authority to advance positions of protection for asylum-seekers and migrants. Moral authority is of course not the reserve of only faith-based NGOs. Peak human rights NGOs, such as Amnesty International, also frequently leverage similar authority that they draw from being principled actors (Clark 2001). Finally, Brussels-based NGOs were able to translate their knowledge of EU institutions and the policy cycle into timely interventions. Existing research demonstrates these strategies, especially for the asylum and immigration field, and to a lesser extent, judicial and political cooperation. The latter two are briefly examined through work on trafficking in human beings, which straddles asylum, police and judicial cooperation (Uçarer 2009b, 2014). Empirical studies that provide these insights are typically case studies of individual policy instruments adopted by or under consideration in the AFSJ and speak to the sophistication and comprehensiveness with which the thoroughly professionalized cadres of Brussels-based NGOs undertake advocacy efforts (Hoffmann 2012).

Studies show that most of the NGOs working in the field (with the exception of major human rights and service organizations such as Amnesty International and Caritas) suffer from significant resource handicaps in terms of funding and especially personnel. NGOs have had to be creative in overcoming these resource handicaps by specializing and networking horizontally across states and vertically from the local to the regional levels. Such networking militates against unfavorable conditions rooted in anti-migration sentiments and weak public support, a restrictive migration regime both nationally and throughout the European Union, and constraints upon capacity in terms of personnel and financial resources (Cullen 2009; Bouget and Prouteau 2002; Uçarer 2009a, 2009b). In addition to their informal networking practices, they have also created the NGO Platform on EU Migration and Asylum Policy to further harness their collective expertise and to coordinate lobbying efforts among member organizations.

Their ability to tie the local to the regional is also quite important in monitoring the implementation of EU legislation at the national level and allows them to mobilize against adverse developments. It also becomes a tool with which they try to 'unclog' blockages in Brussels. When EU institutions, especially the Council, are unresponsive to their overtures at the regional level, Brussels-based NGOs can reach out to their national affiliates to exert pressure on Brussels from below (Uçarer 2014). In short, Brussels-based NGOs are professionalized and sometimes specialized outfits with an excellent command of the EU policy process. They engage the process at each turn using appropriate and sophisticated methods, and are able to connect the local to the regional thanks to their expansive networks.

Avenues for future research

Given the thorough Europeanization of the AFSJ field, the burgeoning of the study of NGOs in international relations and political science, and the salience of the subject matter to both NGOs and the people they serve, increased scholarly attention to the EU–NGO interface in the AFSJ is more than warranted. Future research can go down a number of (concurrent) paths. To enhance theorizing in this field, research could unpack efforts at Europeanization from above (Börzel and Panke 2016), study efforts of the EU, and particularly the European Commission, to foster support, and at times direct the work of NGOs, in part as a legitimacy building exercise for the EU. This avenue could shed light on the motivations of the EU to include NGOs and the methods it employs in shaping the dialogue with NGOs. Research could also focus on Europeanization from below (della Porta and Caiani 2007; Eigmuller 2013; Liebert 2013) as national NGOs develop horizontal and vertical links to advocate at national and international levels. The literature on Europeanization from below will also be useful, as it points to a transfer of competences to the regional level in the related fields of social policy, campaigned for by domestic NGOs against the expressed wishes of national governments. The extent to which this may (or may not) be the case in the AFSJ should be the subject of further inquiry, which would enhance our understanding of the conditions under which NGO advocacy can expand in the AFSJ.

Most of the existing research relies on country or sector case studies. Process-tracing methods typically inform these studies, which yield rich empirical data. What these studies typically do not offer, however, is a bird's-eye view. Using different research methods, such as network analysis, could arguably produce work of a different scale that offers a broader understanding. This would require studies that develop a longitudinal and historical scope across a variety of issues.

There is also much work to be done empirically. Research should move in the direction of developing comparative case studies among the four constituent subfields of the AFSJ (immigration, asylum, police and judicial cooperation) as well as among the AFSJ and other EU fields. Systematic comparative studies that chart changes and continuities in NGO activity after significant institutional developments in the European Union (Maastricht, Amsterdam and Lisbon Treaties bookmarking substantial changes to decision-making rules and/or environments) would further drive research forward. As the European Union is unique in that it has a mandate in fields in which states would otherwise have exclusive decision-making authority, comparisons to other intergovernmental organizations remain difficult.

A more robust research agenda for this field requires moving beyond immigration and asylum (both in a national and regional context). In particular, more (or actually any) work in judicial and police cooperation is acutely necessary. National case studies for these neglected subfields focusing on key member states would be an opportune place to start. Starting empirical work in domestic settings can feed and mature into studies that then consider regional developments. It would also be interesting to study whether and to what extent NGO advocacy in immigration and asylum has or can cause strategy spill-over into judicial and police cooperation, perhaps in the form of resisting developments that could compromise civil liberties and data protection.

Another empirical area that could greatly benefit from scholarly efforts is the differentiated level of NGO work and advocacy between Western, Central and Eastern European countries. The fall of the Berlin Wall roughly coincides with efforts to bring justice and home affairs governance into the European Union. While NGOs have been firmly rooted in the democratic participatory process in Western Europe, they are newer additions to the policy cycles in Central and Eastern Europe, warranting their study. At a time when these countries are becoming transit and/or destination countries for migration, unleashing some significant resistance to migrants and refugees, it would be instructive to study the role of NGOs in responding to these political and societal developments in the newer members of the European Union.

Finally, our understanding would be enhanced by work that applies a multi-level governance approach to the AFSJ and specifically locates NGOs in such a context. Such studies would draw out the interplay between the local, national and regional levels of decision-making and contention, and could trace if and how NGOs are able to work in and navigate these various levels. The fact remains that studying NGOs in the AFSJ is a wide-open endeavor. A variety of theoretical perspectives and methods can and should be brought to bear in this pursuit.

Bibliography

Acosta, D. (2009). The Good, the Bad and the Ugly in EU Migration Law: Is the European Parliament Becoming Bad and Ugly? *European Journal of Migration and Law*, 11(1), pp. 19–39.

Ahmed, S. and Potter, D.M. (2006). *NGOs in International Politics*. Colorado: Kumarian Press.

Batley, R. and Rose, P. (2011). Analysing Collaboration between Non-governmental Service Providers and Governments. *Public Administration and Development*, 31(4), pp. 230–239.

Bigo, D. (2002). Security and Immigration: Toward a Critique of the Governmentality of Unease. *Alternatives*, 27, p. 63.
Bigo, D., Carrera, S., Guild, E. and Walker, R.B.J. (2010). *Europe's 21st Century Challenge: Delivering Liberty*. Farnham: Ashgate.
Börzel, T.A. and Panke, D. (2016). Europeanization. In M. Cini and N. Perez-Soloranzo Borragan (eds), *European Union Politics*, 5th edn. Oxford: Oxford University Press, pp. 110–121.
Bouget, D. and Prouteau, L. (2002). National and Supranational Government–NGO Relations: Anti-discrimination Policy Formation in the European Union. *Public Administration and Development*, 22(1), pp. 31–37.
Ceyhan, A. and Tsoukala, A. (2002). The Securitization of Migration in Western Societies: Ambivalent Discourses and Policies. *Alternatives*, 27(1), pp. 21–39.
Clark, A.M. (2001). *Diplomacy of Conscience: Amnesty International and Changing Human Rights Norms*. Princeton, NJ: Princeton University Press.
Cram, L. (2011). The Importance of the Temporal Dimension: New Modes of Governance as a Tool of Government. *Journal of European Public Policy*, 18(5), pp. 636–653.
Cullen, P.P. (2009). Irish Pro-migrant Nongovernmental Organizations and the Politics of Immigration. *Voluntas*, 20(2), pp. 99–128.
Cullen, P. (2015a). European Union Non-governmental Organizational Coalitions as Professional Social Movement Communities. *Journal of Civil Society*, 11(2), pp. 204–225.
Cullen, P. (2015b). Feminist NGOs and the European Union: Contracting Opportunities and Strategic Response. *Social Movement Studies*, 14(4), pp. 410–426.
Davies, T. (2013). *NGOs: A New History of Transnational Civil Society*. London: Hurst & Company.
Della Porta, D. and Caiani, M. (2007). Europeanization From Below? Social Movements and Europe. *Mobilization*, 12(1), pp. 1–20.
Eigmuller, M. (2013). Europeanization from Below: The Influence of Individual Actors on the EU Integration of Social Policies. *Journal of European Social Policy*, 23(4), pp. 363–375.
Eising, R. (2004). Multilevel Governance and Business Interests in the European Union. *Governance*, 17(2), pp. 211–245.
Freedman, J. (2009). Mobilising against Detention and Deportation: Collective Actions against the Detention and Deportation of 'Failed' Asylum Seekers in France. *French Politics*, 7(3–4), pp. 342–358.
Gatrell, P. (2016). The World-wide Web of Humanitarianism: NGOs and Population Displacement in the Third Quarter of the Twentieth Century. *European Review of History*, 23(1–2), pp. 101–115.
Geddes, A. (2000). Lobbying for Migrant Inclusion in the European Union: New Opportunities for Transnational Advocacy? *Journal of European Public Policy*, 7(4), pp. 632–649.
Givens, T. and Luedtke, A. (2004). The Politics of European Union Immigration Policy: Institutions, Salience, and Harmonization. *Policy Studies Journal*, 32(1), pp. 145–165.
Gray, E. and Statham, P. (2005). Becoming European? The Transformation of the British Pro-migrant NGO Sector in Response to Europeanization. *Journal of Common Market Studies*, 43(4), pp. 877–898.
Guiraudon, V. (2000). European Integration and Migration Policy: Vertical Policy-making as Venue-shopping. *Journal of Common Market Studies*, 38(2), pp. 251–271.
Hoffmann, U. (2012). Lobbying for the Rights of Refugees: An Analysis of the Lobbying Strategies of Pro-migrant Groups on the Qualification Directive and its Recast. *Journal of Contemporary European Research*, 8(1), pp. 21–39.
Imig, D.R. and Tarrow, S.G. (2001). *Contentious Europeans: Protest and Politics in an Emerging Polity*. Lanham, MD: Rowman & Littlefield.
Joachim, J. and Locher, B. (2009). Transnational Activism in the EU and the UN. In J. Joachim and B. Locher (eds), *Transnational Activism in the UN and the EU: A Comparative Study*. New York: Routledge, pp. 3–18.
Kaunert, C. and Léonard, S. (2012). The Development of the EU Asylum Policy: Venue-shopping in Perspective. *Journal of European Public Policy*, 19(9), pp. 1396–1413.
Koopmans, R. and Statham, P. (1999). Challenging the Liberal Nation-state? Postnationalism, Multiculturalism, and the Collective Claims Making of Migrants and Ethnic Minorities in Britain and Germany. *American Journal of Sociology*, 105(3), pp. 652–696.
Kostakopoulou, T. (2000). The 'Protective Union'; Change and Continuity in Migration Law and Policy in Post-Amsterdam Europe. *JCMS: Journal of Common Market Studies*, 38(3), pp. 497–518.
Lavenex, S. and Uçarer, E.M. (2004). The External Dimension of Europeanization: The Case of Immigration Policies. *Cooperation and Conflict: Journal of the Nordic International Studies Association*, 39(4), pp. 417–443.

Lewis, D. and Opoku-Mensah, P. (2006). Moving Forward Research Agendas on International NGOs: Theory, Agency and Context. *International Development*, 18(5), pp. 665–675.

Liebert, U. (2013). *Democratising the EU from Below? Citizenship, Civil Society and the Public Sphere*. Farnham: Ashgate.

Liebert, U. and Trenz, H. (2011). *The New Politics of European Civil Society*. Abingdon: Routledge.

McAdam, D., McCarthy, J. and Zald, M. (1996). *Comparative Perspectives on Social Movements: Political Opportunities, Mobilizing Structures, and Cultural Framings*. New York: Cambridge University Press.

Menz, G. (2008). *The Political Economy of Managed Migration: Nonstate Actors, Europeanization, and the Politics of Designing Migration Policies*. Oxford: Oxford University Press.

Menz, G. and Caviades, A. (2010). *Labour Migration in Europe*. New York: Palgrave.

Monforte, P. (2014). *Europeanizing Contention: The Protest against 'Fortress Europe' in France and Germany*. Oxford: Berghahn Books.

Niessen, J. (2000). The Amsterdam Treaty and NGO Responses. *European Journal of Migration and Law*, 2(2), pp. 203–214.

Niessen, J. (2002). Consultations on Immigration Policies in the European Union. *European Journal of Migration and Law*, 4(1), pp. 79–83.

Occhipinti, J.D. (2003). *The Politics of EU Police Cooperation: Toward a European FBI?* Boulder, CO: Lynne Rienner.

Occhipinti, J.D. (2015). Still Moving Toward a European FBI? Re-examining the Politics of EU Police Cooperation. *Intelligence and National Security*, 30(2–3), pp. 234–258.

Piana, D. (2007). Unpacking Policy Transfer, Discovering Actors: The French Model of Judicial Education between Enlargement and Judicial Cooperation in the EU. *French Politics*, 5(1), pp. 33–65.

Princen, S. (2011). Agenda-setting Strategies in EU Policy Processes. *Journal of European Public Policy*, 18(7), pp. 927–943.

Ripoll Servent, A. and Trauner, F. (2014). Do Supranational EU Institutions make a Difference? EU Asylum Law before and after 'Communitarization'. *Journal of European Public Policy*, 21(8), pp. 1142–1162.

Schnyder, M. (2015). The Domestic Issue-specific Political Opportunity Structure and Migrant Inclusion Organization Activity in Europe. *Social Movement Studies*, 14(6), pp. 692–712.

Statham, P. and Koopmans, R. (2003). How National Citizenship Shapes Transnationalism: A Comparative Analysis of Migrant and Minority Claims-making in Germany, Great Britain, and the Netherlands. In C. Joppke and E. Morawska (eds), *Toward Assimilation and Citizenship: Immigrants in Liberal Nation-states*. London: Palgrave, pp. 195–238.

Steffek, J. and Hahn, K. (2010). *Evaluating Transnational NGOs: Legitimacy, Accountability, Representation*. Balsingstoke: Palgrave Macmillan.

Steffek, J., Kissling, C. and Nanz, P. (2008). *Civil Society Participation in European and Global Governance: A Cure for the Democratic Deficit?* Basingstoke: Palgrave Macmillan.

Sudbery, I. (2010). The European Union as Political Resource: NGOs as Change Agents? *Acta Politica*, 45(1–2), pp. 136–157.

Thiel, M. and Uçarer, E.M. (2014). Access and Agenda-setting in the European Union: Advocacy NGOs in Comparative Perspective. *Interest Groups and Advocacy*, 3(1), pp. 99–116.

Uçarer, E.M. (2006). Burden-shirking, Burden-shifting, and Burden-sharing in the Emergent European Asylum Regime. *International Politics*, 43(2), pp. 219–240.

Uçarer, E.M. (2009a). Negotiating Third-country National Rights in the European Union. In E. Prügl and M. Thiel (eds), *Diversity in the European Union*. New York: Palgrave, pp. 59–75.

Uçarer, E.M. (2009b). Safeguarding Asylum as a Human Right: NGOs and the European Union. In J. Joachim and B. Locher (eds), *Transnational Activism in the UN and the EU*. New York: Routledge, pp. 121–139.

Uçarer, E.M. (2014). Tempering the EU? NGO Advocacy in the Area of Freedom, Security, and Justice. *Cambridge Review of International Affairs*, 27(1), pp. 127–146.

Westlake, M. and Galloway, D. (2006). The Permanent Representative Committee. In M. Westlake and D. Galloway (eds), *The Council of the European Union* (3rd edn). London: John Harper Publishing.

Young, D.R. (2000). Alternative Models of Government–Nonprofit Sector Relations: Theoretical and International Perspectives. *Nonprofit and Voluntary Sector Quarterly*, 29(1), pp. 149–172.

Zito, A.R. and Jacobs, J.E. (2009). NGOs, the European Union and the Case of the Environment. In J. Joachim and B. Locher (eds), *Transnational Activism in the UN and the EU: A Comparative Study*. New York: Routledge, pp. 105–120.

39
INTERNATIONAL ORGANIZATIONS AND THE AREA OF FREEDOM, SECURITY AND JUSTICE

Claudio Matera[1]

Introduction

The Area of Freedom, Security and Justice (AFSJ) is, possibly, one of the most challenging fields of EU competences. Indeed, the integration into an AFSJ directly affects three fundamental aspects of constitutional relevance: the residual extent of national sovereignty, the monopoly of the state to maintain public order and public security, and the vertical relationship between the exercise of public authority against fundamental freedoms and civil liberties. In spite of its predominantly internal nature, the AFSJ has also been steadily growing externally (Monar 2014). The externalization of the AFSJ implies that the EU may *want* or *need* to engage with international organizations (IOs). Indeed, one should bear in mind that the EU legal order is committed to promoting multilateralism and partnership with third countries and international organizations alike (Article 21 TEU). Thus, as Cremona (2008: 9) has argued, 'the EU's support to multilateralism is both one of the principles of EU foreign policy, including its Security Strategy, and an avenue for advancing its AFSJ objectives'. Therefore, because the policy challenges related to the AFSJ such as transnational organized crime, refugee protection and international terrorism are of transnational origin, the only way for the EU to attain its AFSJ agenda is to engage with all of the relevant parties, including IOs.

However, while cooperation in AFSJ matters with third countries often involves operational cooperation, this is not the case with IOs. With the exception of a few organizations like Interpol, IOs do not normally undertake operational and/or enforcement tasks. Rather, IOs relevant to the EU's AFSJ usually perform tasks that relate predominantly to the adoption, promotion and monitoring of international conventions and norms. This means that their actions are usually not directed against individuals. This is the case, for example, in The Hague Conference on Private International Law or, albeit with some differences, the Council of Europe: in both cases the organizations function as promoters of international conventions at global or regional level, but do not possess enforcement powers against individuals. This, of course, has implications for the types of relationships that the EU can establish with other IOs.

The scope of this chapter is to provide an overview of the role that international organizations have played and can play in the development of the AFSJ. From a legal perspective, the notion 'international organizations' usually refers to intergovernmental organizations set up by subjects of international law by means of a treaty in order to perform a set of specific tasks.

However, as this notion is rather restrictive, for the purposes of this chapter international institutions and treaty regimes will also be taken into account. This means that the chapter also covers agencies and bodies created by international organizations such as the United Nations High Commissioner for Refugees (UNHCR) and other forms of treaty regimes such as the United Nations Convention on Transitional Organised Crime (Van Vooren and Wessel 2014: 247). The chapter looks first at the different types of relationships between the EU and other IOs in the area of justice and home affairs. It then looks at the legal principles behind the externalization of the AFSJ and what this means for EU–IOs relations, and concludes with some further reflections on the nature of the field and where academic research should go next.

The relationship between IOs and the AFSJ

Although research has focused on the discursive and normative aspects of the external dimension of the AFSJ, it has not yet provided a full overview of the different patterns through which the relationships between the EU and IOs take place. This section looks at the different forms of cooperation and then focuses on the relationships between EU agencies and IOs, and the specific challenges they present.

Hard law, soft law and hybrid forms of cooperation

The first dimension is the sort of relationship that the EU may establish with an IO, referring to the legally binding nature of a given relationship. From a legal perspective, the distinction between the conclusion of an international agreement and the conclusion of some sort of 'soft law' deal has implications for the choice of procedural rules needed for its adoption. For instance, the most prominent example of a 'hard law' agreement is the accession of the EU to The Hague Conference on Private International Law in 2007.[2] Although the EU has not become a member of other IOs in the field of the AFSJ, it does play an important role in other multilateral fora. The most prominent examples are the negotiations and conclusions of two multilateral conventions promoted by the UN, namely the United Nations Convention on Transnational Organised Crime (UNTOC)[3] and the United Nations Convention against Corruption (UNCAC).[4] Having played an active role in their adoption, the EU has made use of its expertise in these two fields to promote the adoption of EU internal law related to these two conventions. It has promoted the ratification and application of these instruments in bilateral relations with third countries, for instance, during negotiations on the recent Association Agreement with Moldova[5] (Mitsilegas 2011). The EU has also concluded a cooperation and assistance agreement with the International Criminal Court that, however, does not cover the regulation of judicial cooperation and assistance, and instead focuses on intelligence and institutional cooperation.[6]

On the other hand, the EU often establishes 'soft' frameworks of cooperation with IOs such as the memorandum of understanding with the Council of Europe established in 2007. The latter covers topics such as human rights protection, the promotion of the rule of law and legal cooperation. These include the coordination between EU legislation on judicial cooperation and the administration of justice with conventions adopted within the context of the Council of Europe. However, the memorandum does not directly regulate the relationship between the EU acquis on JHA matters and the numerous conventions adopted within the Council of Europe, especially if one considers that not all member states are party to all the different conventions (Peers 2016: 398) and that not all of the instruments adopted at the EU level regulate their relation to the Council of Europe's instruments (Peers 2016: 259).

Recent events suggest the emergence of a third type of cooperation between IOs and the EU: a hybrid form of cooperation whereby the EU and an IO engage with one another, but without having concluded a bilateral agreement. In these hybrid cases, the IO and the EU engage with one another through the means of bilateral arrangements concluded between an IO and a member state or between an IO and a third country with which the EU has concluded some sort of cooperation mechanism. This appears to be the case in the context of the recent EU–Turkey deal on migration, whereby the International Organization for Migration (IOM) helps with the resettlement of asylum-seekers stationed in Turkey to EU countries (European Commission 2017; IOM 2016).

Finally, the relationships of the EU with IOs may also contain a unilateral commitment. Examples thereof are the Council of Europe study on Passenger Name Records legislation or the UNHCR opinion on the EU–Turkey deal of March 2016. In addition, some rulings of the Strasbourg-based European Court of Human Rights – for instance, the judgment on the EU's Dublin Regime (MSS vs. Belgium and Greece)[7] – may also be considered as a sort of unilateral intervention in EU affairs.

Agreements concluded by agencies with IOs

The EU has created a number of specialized agencies in the AFSJ (see Santos Vara, Chapter 37, this volume). The external activities of the agencies of the AFSJ have raised concerns regarding the respect of EU and national rules on data protection whenever the agencies work with foreign partners, including international organizations (Santos Vara 2015).

Table 39.1 provides some examples of the cooperation of JHA agencies with IOs.

It could be argued that, when it comes to cooperation with IOs, some of the concerns may be set aside, since most counterparts to EU agencies do not have operational capacity. Therefore, the agreements between AFSJ agencies and IOs seek mostly to establish partnerships and open channels for the exchange of best practices without any form of operational activities that may directly affect the rights of individuals. However, Table 39.1 shows that, while the cooperation of agencies with IOs is mostly about technical issues and the transfer of knowledge, it may still raise thorny questions with regard to information-sharing and personal data. This is particularly important, since little is known about the concrete use and resulting impacts that these agreements may have upon individuals. A deeper scrutiny of the application of these agreements, especially the one between EU agencies and Interpol, could provide us with more refined knowledge on how cooperation operates in practice.

Understanding EU–IO cooperation in JHA: externalization and multilateralism

When addressing the relationship between the EU, international law and international organizations, the debate often dwells on discourses focusing on the nature of EU action in the external dimension of the AFSJ or on the EU as a normative power, with an emphasis on multilateralism (Eckes 2014; Matera 2013; Mananashvili 2015; Tuominen 2013; Wessel and Blockmans 2013; Whitman 2011). Therefore, this section concentrates on how these two dimensions have evolved in the EU treaties, its main programs, as well as in relations with third countries.

Treaty provisions relevant for relations with IOs

It is widely acknowledged that the EU Treaties call for the EU to respect and promote public international law and multilateralism (e.g., Article 3(5) TEU and in Article 21 TEU). While the

Table 39.1 Examples of the cooperation of JHA agencies with IOs

Europol	Eurojust	Frontex	EASO
Cooperation Agreement with the World Customs Organisation (2002): Main purpose is to establish and maintain cooperation: obligation to consult regularly, prohibition to exchange personal data.	Letter of Understanding on Cooperation with the Office of the Prosecutor of the International Criminal Court (2007): Exchange of experiences and enhancing contact between the two organizations; Explore areas of cooperation; Facilitate access to information about serious types of crime within the competences of the organizations.	Exchange of letters with the UNHCR (2008): contributing to an efficient border management system fully compliant with the member states' international protection obligations; regular consultations; exchange of information and expertise; preparation of training materials and assistance in the delivery of courses.	Working Arrangement with UNHCR (2013): Promotion of EU and international protection standards; Coherence of policies between the UN and the EU and between the EU and MSs; Technical cooperation; Exchange of relevant information; Exchange of training strategies; Cooperation to support EU member states; Exchange of best practices in the field of relocations; Establishment of support mechanisms in times of emergencies; Joint cooperation with third countries; Mutual respect of the rules pertaining classified and personal data.

relationship between the two systems is complex and is in constant evolution (Moreno-Lax and Gragl 2016), the Treaties identify some key characteristics of this relationship.

The Treaties set for the EU ambitious objectives in the fields of international relations. Not only should it promote and uphold its values, but it must also contribute to peace, security and a number of other broad objectives ranging from sustainable development to the protection of human rights (Article 3(5) TEU). Furthermore, Article 21 TEU provides clearer guidelines about the role that the EU may play in foreign relations, including the relationship of the EU with other IOs. In fact, in two separate sections of the same provisions, the EU is called upon to promote multilateralism and good global governance (Article 21(1) and (2)(h) TEU). In such a context, the same provision of the TEU contains a list of specific substantive objectives that the EU should pursue in its external relations. The list is very broad and covers a plurality of issues; from preserving peace and security to fostering sustainable development and support for human rights. Finally, the last paragraph of the same article also affirms that the EU should pursue the objectives enlisted in Article 21 TEU in the development and implementation of the different areas of the Union's external action and of the external aspects of its other policies. This is of particular importance because it creates an obligation of consistency between the general objectives codified in Article 21 TEU with sector-specific external policies and with the external dimension of other EU policies. The result is that this section of Article 21 TEU obliges the EU to respect its foreign relations principles when acting under the AFSJ both internally and externally.

While Article 21(3) TEU bridges the general objectives of the Union's external action with the AFSJ, Article 67 TFEU and Article 3(2) TEU on the AFSJ do not pay attention to foreign affairs (in general) or international organizations (specifically). This is not surprising, since the AFSJ project is largely an internally driven field of Union competences (Wessel *et al.* 2011). However, paragraph one of Article 78 TFEU affirms that the EU's (common) asylum policy must comply with the non-refoulement principle, the Geneva Convention of July 28, 1951 and the Protocol of January 31, 1967 relating to the status of refugees. Because of the way in which Article 78 TFEU is phrased, it may be argued that there is a double reference to IOs codified therein: the first refers to the obligations deriving from the Geneva Convention of 1951 and the subsequent protocol, including the principle of non-refoulment. Through this reference, it may also be argued that Article 78 TFEU makes an express reference to the work of the UNHCR, because of the special mandate that this UN agency has in monitoring the application of the Convention. The second connection to an IO is indirect, in that the reference to the principle of non-refoulment and 'other relevant treaties' can be equally considered as an indirect reference to the European Convention of Human Rights (ECHR), and in particular to Article 3, which protects any person from torture or inhumane or degrading treatment or punishment.

Indeed, the express references to the non-refoulement principle and to 'other relevant treaties' made in Article 78(1) TFEU confirms how the EU legal order is not only committed to the promotion of multilateralism and public international law, but is also open to the influence of obligations stemming from other IOs and international regimes. Despite the nuances that emerge from the case law of the Court of Justice of the European Union (CJEU), it has been argued that the EU legal order has adopted a maximalist approach when enforcing obligations stemming from international obligations (Mendez 2010). Indeed, the EU legal system codifies the respect of international obligations and the pursuit of cooperation with third countries and IOs. The fact that these core elements are spelled out in Article 3(5) TFEU, which defines the objectives of the integration process, means that they are given constitutional relevance. Therefore, at the level of primary law, the Treaties impose a number of limits on the institutions in relation to the development of the AFSJ. In the case of asylum law and border controls, this means that the measures adopted for the attainment of AFSJ objectives must respect international commitments undertaken by the EU, notably the provisions of the Geneva Convention of 1951 as well as the provisions of the ECHR, independently from the accession of the EU to either the ECHR or the Geneva Convention.[8]

Yet, the relationship between the AFSJ and IOs is not limited to the sphere of EU asylum and migration law. While Title V of Part Three of the TFEU does not provide any other express rule or objective concerning the relationship between the AFSJ and IOs, Part Five of the TFEU on the Union's external action does provide for sufficient instruments to establish cooperative frameworks between the EU and IOs in the AFSJ fields. First, it must be borne in mind that the fields of the AFSJ are also covered by the 'implied powers' doctrine codified in Article 216(1) TFEU. According to this provision, the EU may conclude agreements with third countries *and* IOs when, in the absence of an express external competence, the conclusion of an agreement is provided for in a binding act, when an agreement is likely to affect or alter existing common rules, and when the conclusion of an agreement is necessary for the attainment of an objective of the Treaties. This is a broad mandate that actually confers a large competence to conclude agreements with IOs in the fields of the AFSJ; a mandate that is actually strengthened if one considers that other provisions on the external action of the EU foresee cooperation with IOs. A first instrument provided by the Treaties that strengthens the mandate of the EU to cooperate with IOs, is that of association agreements: while these are traditionally concluded by the EU with third countries with a view to establishing a special form of cooperation that involves reciprocal rights and obligations, Article 217 TFEU expressly allows for the EU to conclude these types of agreements with IOs as well. Second, Article 220 TFEU expressly provides a competence to establish 'appropriate forms of cooperation' with the organs of the United Nations and its agencies, the Council of Europe and other international organizations.

Overall, it may be inferred from this analysis that the EU's commitment to multilateralism is anchored to a number of provisions in the Treaties that allow the Union to cooperate with IOs in JHA-related matters. The role of most international organizations is conditioned to the conclusion of an agreement with the EU. Thus, IOs will play an active and significant role in the development of the AFSJ only if the EU has concluded an international agreement with a given organization on the basis of Articles 216 or 217 TFEU. Alternatively, if the EU and an IO agree to establish 'an appropriate form of cooperation' on the basis of Article 220 TFEU, an organization may equally play a role in the development of the AFSJ. However, while the first option refers to the formal conclusion of agreements following the procedure established in Article 218 TFEU, the latter is open to both formal and informal instruments of cooperation; thus conferring to the High Representative of the Union for Foreign Affairs and Security policy (HR) and the Commission the authority to establish partnerships and cooperation frameworks with IOs without having to go through the procedural requirements of Article 218 TFEU.

The relationship between the AFSJ and IOs from a policy perspective

The Tampere conclusions

In order to develop the EU as an AFSJ, the European Council has adopted a number of programmatic documents, or quinquennial plans, that have been integrated into general and sector-specific documents by the Commission. This is undoubtedly a peculiar trait of the AFSJ, because the European Council has preserved for itself a leading role in this field. The European Council began to shape the creation of the AFSJ through programmatic documents in 1999, a few months after the entry into force of the Amsterdam Treaty. On that occasion it considered that, in order to allow the EU to become a global actor in AFSJ matters, it was necessary for the EU to cooperate closely not only with third countries, but also with international organizations such as the Council of Europe, the OSCE, the OECD and the United Nations (European Council 1999, par. 8). Interestingly, this phrasing suggests an instrumental role of IOs for the AFSJ and its external dimension: in order for the EU to 'develop a capacity to act and be regarded as a significant partner on the international scene' (ibid.), the EU will (also) engage with IOs. This functional relationship, however, is not representative of the overarching strategy that the European Council was pursuing. For instance, when looking into the development of the Common European Asylum System (CEAS), paragraph 14 of the Tampere Conclusions called for the EU to *consult* with the UNHCR and other international organizations: in this case, the cooperation with an IO was not meant to assert the EU as a global actor; rather, it sought to develop an internal policy only. Furthermore, the Council of Europe was identified as the EU partner to fight against racism and xenophobia (par. 19) and to develop a communication toolkit related to judicial cooperation (par. 29).

In the aftermath of Tampere, the relationship between the EU and IOs in the AFSJ was further specified (Cremona 2008). The European Council meeting in Feira in 2000 identified three different dimensions through which EU–IOs cooperation could take place: (1) cooperation with IOs tasked with the production of norms and standards; (2) cooperation with organizations that undertake a practical function in their domain, and (3) cooperation with IOs in which not all member states participate (Council of the European Union 2000). As a matter of fact, the European Council sought to define the relationship between the AFSJ and IOs under two main categories: cooperation to affirm the actorness of the EU at the global level (the EU as a normative power), and cooperation to establish, strengthen and develop internal rules (the external dimension of JHA).

The Hague Programme and the strategy on the external AFSJ

In the fall of 2004, the European Council approved The Hague Programme on the AFSJ (European Council 2004). The only express reference to IOs is present in Section 3.5 of the program that deals with judicial cooperation and justice matters in which the Council and the Commission are asked to ensure coherence between EU and international standards. It also fosters cooperation with IOs such as The Hague Conference on Private International Law and the Council of Europe in order to coordinate activities and maximize the consistency between EU measures and those adopted by these IOs. In addition, the program also called for the accession of the then Community to The Hague Conference on Private International Law, which took place in 2007.

Soon after the adoption of The Hague Programme, the Commission issued a communication entitled 'Strategy on the External Dimension of the AFSJ' (COM (2005) 491 final). The relationship between IOs and the AFSJ presented in the strategy was marked by its historical context; that is, the fight against terrorism in the aftermath of the attacks in Madrid and London. What is particularly relevant here is the change in the EU's attitude towards the external dimension of the AFSJ: from acting as an instrument to foster integration into the AFSJ, it evolved into a sub-policy in which the EU should exercise its role as a global actor and finally became a tool in fighting security threats. As a result of this, the document called upon the institutions to promote the adoption of multilateral initiatives in relation to transnational organized crime, money laundering and corruption, and to support the works of international organizations and groups such as the Financial Action Task Force (FATF).

In reality, however, the document overall is rather fuzzy and does not clarify how the EU should make use of its different instruments to pursue such cooperation with IOs. For instance, while the document considers IOs as a good platform to promote EU values and priorities, it places more emphasis on the promotion of international conventions and fora rather than discussing cooperative mechanisms for the EU and member states with AFSJ–relevant IOs.

The Stockholm Programme and beyond

The most recent and comprehensive quinquennial program for the AFSJ was adopted during the Swedish presidency of the Council of the European Union in the fall of 2009.[9] Four main ideas emerged from the program with regard to the EU's cooperation with IOs. First, it confirmed the multilateral vocation of the EU and its external AFSJ project. Second, the document reaffirmed the prominent position of the UN and the Council of Europe as partners in the AFSJ. By referring to the EU–Council of Europe Memorandum of Understanding of 2007, the Stockholm Programme made clear that the EU considered the Council of Europe to be a key norm-setter and promoter of international conventions, for instance, on human trafficking. Finally, the Stockholm Programme also referred expressly to EU cooperation with Interpol and The Hague Conference on Private International Law.

A striking feature of the Stockholm Programme is the holistic way in which it promoted the activities of different IOs. In relation to the attainment of internal AFSJ objectives, it referred to a number of international conventions adopted within the framework of activities of numerous IOs. For instance, section 2.3.2 made allusion to the United Nations Convention on the Rights of the Child. At the same time, the program promoted the activities of the different IOs in relation to specific policies that may appear distant from the AFSJ project and resonate rather with broader foreign policy objectives such as the European Security Strategy of 2003 (European Council 2003) or the Global Strategy of the EU adopted in June 2016 (European External Action Service 2016). As a result, the holistic approach adopted in the Stockholm Programme towards AFSJ–IO relations reflected the wider internal–external security nexus adopted by the EU with the European Security Strategy of 2003 (Matera 2012). Under this broad understanding, AFSJ objectives were mixed with foreign policy ones, such as the promotion of the rule of law and the fight against international impunity for crimes that fall under the jurisdiction of the ICC.

Promotion of IOs by the EU

The last substantive aspect that must be considered in this chapter relates to the promotion of IOs by the EU when it concludes bilateral agreements with third countries. Especially in recent years, the EU has tried to promote certain international conventions and the works of IOs when dealing with external partners. Yet, despite its commitment to multilateralism and the internationalization of certain conventions, the EU has managed to achieve these objectives only with targeted, primarily neighboring, countries.

The recent agreements with Georgia, Moldova and Ukraine reveal a systematic reference to international conventions and standards in JHA fields. The European Neighbourhood Policy (ENP) agreements are structured around two cardinal points: the EU's support in the implementation of international conventions and standards related to the AFSJ in the targeted country as well as the establishment of a link between the bilateral agreement in question and international initiatives such as UN Resolution 1373(2001) to combat terrorism, the Geneva Convention Relating to the Status of Refugees of 1951, and other UN-related conventions (for example, the agreement with Ukraine: Council of the European Union 2014). The overall ambition to integrate in a consistent manner AFSJ elements into the external instruments and policies of the AFSJ seems partially attained. The agreements concluded under the Stabilization and Association Process (SAP) contain similar rules. For instance, Article 85 of the recent association agreement with Kosovo makes clear that the country should adopt and implement legislation to meet the standards of the Geneva Convention with special attention to the non-refoulement principle. It should also incorporate other IO-related rules on the fight against the financing of terrorism or the implementation of the recommendations of the FATF (Council of the European Union 2015). Indeed, the promotion of standards and norms adopted by IOs shows the attachment of the EU to multilateralism, the promotion of international law, and human rights. This becomes particularly evident when the EU inserts clauses in the framework of development and cooperation agreements. For instance, Articles 22 and 23 of the

Partnership and Cooperation Agreement with the Philippines make an express reference to the FATF and UNTOC as the legislative framework that the two parties should utilize in order to cooperate in the future (Council of the European Union 2011).

Conclusion: the role of IOs in the AFSJ

The purpose of this chapter was to analyze the main characteristics of the relationship between the EU and international organizations in JHA-related matters. While the AFSJ project has a strong vocation for internal operational cooperation, the ambitious policy programs established since 1999 have foreseen the establishment of cooperation mechanisms with third countries and international organizations. The amount of scholarly research on the relationship between the AFSJ and IOs is scarce and predominantly follows two lines of study: either the relationship is analyzed from a legal perspective, focusing on the evolution of internal and external EU competences, or it is analyzed from the perspective of the 'normative power Europe' approach.

The chapter has argued that the EU's strategy on AFSJ–IOs relations reflects three main goals: first, the development of the EU as an internal AFSJ; second, the participation of the EU in the decision-making process of international norms as promoted by IOs, and third, the promotion of norms and regulations stemming from IOs in order to consolidate relations with third countries. Conversely, this contribution has also shown that IOs may unilaterally try to influence the EU for the purpose of promoting their mission, as is particularly evident in the case of the UNHCR.

In the specific context of the relationship between the AFSJ and IOs, the EU privileges the creation of a system of network governance, whereby functional and technical cooperation is preferred to the establishment of more traditional formal relations (Lavenex 2011: 122). This becomes evident if one takes into account the analysis conducted in relation to the cooperation between AFSJ agencies and IOs. While this may be a direct consequence of the fact that the EU is mostly a coordinator and promoter of common rules and policies, the creation of specialized agencies by the EU bypasses the functional limitations that Brussels has at an operational level. In external relations, the use of these institutionalized forms of technical cooperation allows the EU to use more flexible instruments to seek partnerships with other external actors such as IOs (as well as third countries). However, it should be noted that the bypassing of formal approaches, such as the adoption of legislation, can only be tolerated if these new governance methods do not directly affect the rights of individuals. It is, however, not clear whether the existing agreements between EU agencies and IOs pose a problem in this respect.

Another element that emerges from the analysis is the way in which the EU promotes the works and standards adopted by IOs in the JHA field. The EU has become a keen promoter of international law and standards in the context of bilateral negotiations. While this is used to benefit its internal purposes (for instance, in the case of readmission clauses; see Cassarino, Chapter 7, this volume), the EU nonetheless systematically inserts clauses that call upon parties to guarantee that, in the context of their cooperation, certain conventions and measures adopted by IOs are respected.

This chapter suggests that the role of IOs in the AFSJ can be distinguished in three ways: self-determination, consolidation and expansion. With regard to self-determination, the unilateral reference to the measures of IOs and the conclusion of agreements with IOs reflect the need for the EU to clearly define its role and identity to member states with contrasting prerogatives. This is of special importance in the AFSJ because the EU does not have enforcement powers as strong as those it possesses; for instance, in the field of competition law. Second, the conclusion of hard and soft forms of cooperation with IOs allows the EU to consolidate its internal position as an actor in JHA (vis-à-vis particular member states). Third, EU–IOs relations allow the EU to foster the enforcement of AFSJ policies.

Conversely, IOs play different roles in the AFSJ. For instance, they seek the conclusion of 'soft agreements' with a view to influencing EU norms and governance in a specific AFSJ field – especially in the field of migration (Lavenex 2015). Second, IOs have emerged as agents of the EU; IOs active in the fields of migration such as UNHCR and IOM are called upon to implement EU policies such as resettlement or the management of the housing crisis linked to the refugee crisis in Greece (UNHCR 2017).

It is difficult to ascertain the extent to which these patterns are valid for all AFSJ sub-policies. It is equally difficult to ascertain the extent to which the influence of IOs on the EU in all its different forms actually has an impact upon the adoption of legislative acts and court decisions within the EU and within partner countries. Future research may build upon these findings and further investigate these aspects.

Notes

1 The author would like to thank the editors of this book for the assistance provided in the finalization of this chapter; any errors are solely those of the author.
2 OJ L 297, October 26, 2006, p. 1.
3 OJ L 262, September 22, 2006, p. 44.
4 OJ L 287, October 29, 2008, p. 1.
5 OJ L 260, August 30, 2014, p. 4.
6 OJ L 115, April 28, 2006, p. 50.
7 European Court of Human Rights, MSS vs. Belgium and Greece, Judgment of January 21, 2011, Application No. 30696/09.
8 While the accession to the ECHR is pending, albeit temporarily blocked by Opinion 2/13 of the Court of Justice (Opinion of the Court pursuant Article 218 (11) TFEU, December 18, 2014, ECLI:EU:C:2014:2454), the EU cannot accede the Geneva Convention of 1951 and its protocols because the Convention itself is open for accession only to states ex Article 39 thereof (www.unhcr.org/protect/PROTECTION/3b66c2aa10.pdf).
9 In the fall of 2014, during the Italian presidency of the Council, it was decided for the first time not to adopt a five-year plan and simply to adopt a number of strategic guidelines with no specific reference to international organizations (www.consilium.europa.eu/en/policies/strategic-guidelines-jha/).

Bibliography

Commission (2005). A Strategy on the External Dimension of the Area of Freedom, Security and Justice. COM (2005) 491 final.
Council of the European Union (2000). European Union Priorities and Policy Objectives for External Relations in the Field of Justice and Home Affairs, June 6, document, 7653/00.
Council of the European Union (2011). EU–Philippines Partnership and Cooperation Agreement of 2011. Available at: https://eeas.europa.eu/headquarters/headquarters-homepage_en/7707/EU-Philippines%20partnership%20cooperation%20agreement (accessed April 2017).
Council of the European Union (2014). EU–Ukraine Association Agreement. Available at: http://eeas.europa.eu/archives/delegations/ukraine/eu_ukraine/association_agreement/index_en.htm (accessed April 2017).
Council of the European Union (2015). Stabilisation and Association Agreement between the EU and Kosovo. Available at: http://data.consilium.europa.eu/doc/document/ST-10728-2015-REV-1/en/pdf (accessed April 2017).
Cremona, M. (2008). EU External Action in the JHA Domain: A Legal Perspective. EUI Working Papers, LAW 2008/24. Available at: http://cadmus.eui.eu/bitstream/handle/1814/9487/LAW_2008_24.pdf (accessed April 2017).

Eckes, C. (2014). External Relations Law: How the Outside Shapes the Inside. In C.C. Murphy and D.A. Arcarazo (eds), *EU Security and Justice Law: After Lisbon and Stockholm*. Oxford: Hart Publishing, pp. 186–206.

European Commission (2017). Report from the European Commission to the European Parliament, the European Council and the Council, Fifth Report on the Progress Made in the Implementation of the EU–Turkey Statement, COM 2.3.2017, COM(2017) 204 final.

European Council (1999). Tampere European Council, October 15 and 16, 1999. Presidency Conclusions. Available at: www.europarl.europa.eu/summits/tam_en.htm (accessed April 2017).

European Council (2003). A Secure Europe in a Better World. European Security Strategy, December 12. Available at: www.consilium.europa.eu/uedocs/cmsUpload/78367.pdf (accessed April 2017).

European Council (2004) The Hague Programme; Strengthening Freedom, Security and Justice in the European Union. Brussels, October 27.

European Council (2010). The Stockholm Programme – An Open and Secure Europe Serving and Protecting its Citizens, OJ C115 04.05.2010.

European Council (2014). Conclusions, June 26/27, 2014, EUCO 79/14. Available at: www.consilium. europa.eu/en/policies/strategic-guidelines-jha/ (accessed April 2017).

European External Action Service (2016). Shared Vision, Common Action: A Stronger Europe. A Global Strategy for the European Union's Foreign and Security Policy. Available at: http://eeas.europa.eu/archives/docs/top_stories/pdf/eugs_review_web.pdf (accessed April 2017).

European Union (2016). Treaty on European Union, OJ C 202, June 7.

European Union (2016). Treaty on the Functioning of the European Union, OJ C 202, June 7.

IOM (2016). IOM Begins Resettlement Syrians to Europe under EU–Turkey Deal, April 4. Available at: www.iom-nederland.nl/en/602-iom-begins-resettlement-syrians-to-europe-under-eu-turkey-deal (accessed April 2017).

Lavenex, S. (2011). Channels of Externalisation of EU Justice and Home Affairs. In M. Cremona, J. Monar and S. Poli (eds), *The External Dimension of the European Union's Area of Freedom, Security and Justice*, Brussels: Peter Lang, College of Europe Studies, pp. 119–138.

Lavenex, S. (2015). Multilevelling EU External Governance: The Role of International Organizations in the Diffusion of EU Migration Policies. *Journal of Ethnic and Migration Studies*, 42(4), pp. 554–570.

Mananashvili, S. (2015). The Diffusion of the EU Asylum Acquis in the Eastern Neighbourhood: A Test for the EU's Normative Power. *European Foreign Affairs Review*, 20(2), pp. 187–206.

Matera, C. (2012). The European Union Area of Freedom, Security and Justice and the Fight against New Security Threats. New Trends and Old Constitutional Challenges. In M. Arcari and L. Balmond (eds), *Global Governance and The Challenges of Collective Security*. Naples: Editoriale Scientifica, pp. 69–87.

Matera, C. (2013). The Influence of International Organisations on the EU's Area of Freedom, Security and Justice: A First Inquiry. In R.A. Wessel and S. Blockmans (eds), *Between Autonomy and Dependence. The EU Legal Order under the Influence of International Organisations*. New York: Springer Verlag, pp. 269–296.

Mendez, M. (2010). The Legal Effect of Community Agreements: Maximalist Treaty Enforcement and Judicial Avoidance Techniques. *European Journal of International Law*, 21(1), pp. 83–104.

Mitsilegas, V. (2011). The European Union and the Implementation of International Norms in Criminal Matters. In M. Cremona, J. Monar and S. Poli (eds), *The External Dimension of the European Union's Area of Freedom, Security and Justice*. Brussels: Peter Lang, College of Europe Studies, pp. 239–272.

Monar, J. (2014). The EU's Growing External Role in the AFSJ Domain: Factors, Framework and Forms of Action. *Cambridge Review of International Affairs*, 27(1), pp. 147–166.

Moreno-Lax, V. and Gragl, P. (2016). Introduction: Beyond Monism, Dualism, Pluralism: The Quest for a (Fully-fledged) Theoretical Framework: Co-implication, Embeddedness, and Interdependency between Public International Law and Eu Law. *Yearbook of European Law*, 35(1), pp. 455–470.

Peers, S. (2016). *EU Justice and Home Affairs Law. Volume II: EU Criminal Law, Policing and Civil Law*. Oxford: Oxford University Press.

Santos Vara, J. (2015). The External Activities of AFSJ Agencies: The Weakness of Democratic and Judicial Controls. *European Foreign Affairs Review*, 20(1), pp. 118–136.

Tampere Conclusions (1999). Available at: www.consilium.europa.eu/en/european-council/conclusions/1993-2003/ (accessed April 2017).

The Hague Programme (2004). Strengthening Freedom, Security and Justice in the European Union, Council Document 16054/04, December 13. Available at: http://eur-lex.europa.eu/legal-content/EN/ALL/?uri=CELEX:52005XG0303(01) (accessed April 2017).

Tuominen, H. (2013). The Changing Context of Global Governance and the Normative Power of the European Union. In A. Boening, A. Kremer and A. van Loon (eds), *Global Power Europe*. Vol. 1: *Global Power Shift*. Berlin/Heidelberg: Springer Verlag.

UNHCR (2017). UNHCR Accommodation Programme on Housing for Asylum Seekers in Greece. Available at: www.unhcr.org/news/latest/2017/4/58ef48504/home-home-under-unhcr-accommodation-programme.html (accessed April 2017).

Van Vooren, B. and Wessel, R.A. (2014). *EU External Relations Law: Text, Cases and Materials*. Cambridge: Cambridge University Press.

Wessel, R.A. and Blockmans, S. (eds.) (2013). *Between Autonomy and Dependence. The EU Legal Order under the Influence of International Organisations*. New York: Springer Verlag.

Wessel, R.A., Marin, L. and Matera, C. (2011). The External Dimension of the EU's Area of Freedom, Security and Justice. In C. Eckes and T. Konstadinides (eds), *Crime within the Area of Freedom, Security and Justice. A European Public Order*. Oxford: Oxford University Press, pp. 272–300.

Whitman, R. (ed.) (2011). *Normative Power Europe. Empirical and Theoretical Perspectives*. Basingstoke: Palgrave Macmillan.

INDEX

Page locators in **bold** and *italics* represents figures and tables, respectively.

9/11 attacks 150, 163, 165, 230, 336

Accession Partnership documents (2001) 288
Accession, Treaty of (2003) 254
Accession Treaty with Croatia (2013) 254
Accession with Romania and Bulgaria, Treaty of (2005) 254
Account Preservation Order 205
ACP (Africa, Caribbean and Pacific countries)–EU Partnership Process 323
Action Plan, EU: to combat organised crime 150; on combatting terrorism 158, 186; ECOWAS 330; on integration of third-country nationals 222; against migrant smuggling 72; Ouagadougou Action Plan 327; Valencia Action Plan 311
actor-based approaches, for policy-making: advocacy coalitions and 45; epistemic communities and 44–5; policy entrepreneurship 45–6; policy networks 43–4
actor-network theory (A-NT) 26, 43–6, 186
Advocacy Coalition Framework (ACF) 43, 45
Africa–EU relations, on organized crime: controversial aspects of 330–1; cooperation by regional action plans 327–8; Cotonou Agreement (2010) 323, 326; cross-border regional cooperation projects 324; drug trafficking *see* drug trafficking; ECOWAS Action Plan 330; on EU's external action on OC 325–6; external dimension of 323–5; on fighting international drug trafficking 329–31; fragmented agenda and 328–9; global fora and 326–7; Gulf of Guinea Action Plan (2015–2020) 327; Human Trafficking Initiative 327; Khartoum Process 101, 327, 332; Lisbon Summit (2007) on 326; Ouagadougou Action Plan 327; and overview on actions and programs 329–30; Plan of Action on Trafficking of Human Beings 327; Rabat Process (2006) 327; remote policing and securitization issues 324–5; Sahel Strategic Regional Action Plan (2015–2020) 327, 329, 331; strategic partnership 326–9; *see also* Joint Africa–EU Strategy (JAES)
African Peace Facility 363, 368
African Union Commission 327
Afripol 328
AFSJ agencies: on breach of fundamental rights 451–3; budget of 449; Budgets and Budgetary Control Committees 449; Civil Liberties, Justice and Home Affairs Committee (LIBE) 449, 450; democratic control over 448–51; development of 446–8; European Asylum Support Office (EASO) 448; Europol 447; Frontex 447–8; human rights challenges 451–2; judicial review over 453; Management Board of 449, 451
Agenda for Migration (2015) 453
agencification, of policing and judiciary work 283
Al-Qaeda 36, 399
AMERIPOL *see* Police Community of the Americas
Amity and Cooperation, Treaty of (2012) 374
Amnesty International 77, 350, 464
Amsterdam, Treaty of (1997) 4, 49, 60, 63, 71, 83–4, 86, 94, 111, 126, 138, 140, 193, 204, 215, 229, 231, 253–4, 256–8, 290, 298, 386, 396, 411, 417, 423, 438
anti-discrimination policies 235
anti-smuggling operations 70, 72–3

480

Index

Application of the Principles of Subsidiarity and Proportionality 434
Arab Spring 95, 310, 312, 313, 314, 318, 378
Arab uprising *see* Arab Spring
Area of Freedom, Security and Justice (AFSJ) 3, 25, 31, 36, 46, 86, 138, 150, 177, 180, 197, 205, 229, 298, 324, 396, 414, 429; academic communities dominating 4–5; academic research in the field of 4–6; agencies of *see* AFSJ agencies; and autonomy of core member states 230–3; court and mutual recognition in 400–2; Court of Justice and 397–400; cyber crime policies challenges and their impact upon 151–3; development of 236; establishment of 86–7; Europeanization of 439, 454, 464; external dimension of 9–10, 12–13; inter-parliamentary cooperation in 439–41; mercantilization of 319–20; normative *versus* non-normative approaches 5–6; objectives of 468; parliamentary scrutiny of 435–7; process of agencification 445; relationship between IOs and 469–70; role of national parliaments in *see* national parliaments; securitization, issue of 35–7; studying NGOs in 459–61
arms embargo, in high seas 73
ASEAN–EU relationship 371–2; Amity and Cooperation, Treaty of (2012) 374; Bandar Seri Begawan Plan of Action (2013–17) 374, 375; on capacity-building programs 376; Common Foreign and Security Policy (CFSP) 373; on counter-terrorism 376–7; on cross-border cooperation 378; Declaration to Combat Terrorism 376; on interregional agenda 375; Joint Declaration to Combat Terrorism 375; law enforcement agencies 378; on maritime security 379; on migration and border management 377–8; Ministerial Meeting 373; on non-traditional security (NTS) 371, 374–6; on regional 'soft security issues' 375; role of security in 372–4; Senior Official Meeting on Transnational Crime in Hanoi (2003) 378; Shangri-La Dialogue 372–4; 'Strengthening the Rule of Law and Security in Indonesia' program 376
ASEANPOL 10, 376, 377
Asian financial crisis (1997/1978) 373
Assemblée Nationale 440, 441
Assembly of the European Coal and Steel Community 386
Assisted Voluntary Returns Programme (UK) 78, 88
Association of Southeast Asian Nations (ASEAN): ASEAN Way, principles of 373, 376; Common Foreign and Security Policy (CFSP) 373; Regional Forum Intersession Meeting on Counterterrorism and Transnational Crime 377; relation with EU *see* ASEAN–EU relationship; security challenges 372; state-centric security concepts 373
asylum and refugee protection, EU policies on: Asylum Procedures Directive 2004/83/EC 60; burden-sharing, principle of 62, 244; Common European Asylum System (CEAS) 60; Dublin III Regulation (2016) 65, 237, 244; EU–Turkey statement on 66, 292–4; evolution of 59–61; external dimensions of migration and 64–5; extraterritorial processing of asylum claims 66; extra-territorialization of protection responsibilities 64–5; 'first-country-of-entry' principle 65; Geneva Refugee Convention (1951) 59; Global Approach for Migration (2005) 61, 64; Global Approach for Migration and Mobility (2011) 61, 64; institutional and procedural aspects of 63–4; Migration Management Support Teams 65; nature of European integration and 62; non-refoulement, principle of 66; normalization of 63; Qualification Directive 2003/9/EC 60; Reception Directive 2005/85/EC 60; refugee crisis of 2015 and 35, 61, 63, 65–6; Regional Protection Zones 66; on relocation of asylum-seekers 65; responsibility, principle of 62; rights-based approach to 63; 'safe country of asylum' policy 104; scholarly debates on 61–5; securitization of 62–3; in Southern Europe 243–5; Strategic Guidelines (2014) on 61; Transit Processing Centres 66; on use of safe third countries 65
asylum lottery 61
Asylum, Migration and Integration Fund (AMIF) 60, 218
asylum-hopping 60
asylum-processing facilities, establishment of 104
asylum-seekers: from Balkan countries 113; country of origin policies 235; fundamental rights of 79, 83; human rights of 350; relocation mechanism of 237
asylum-shopping 60
Australia–EU JHA cooperation: Agenda for Cooperation (2003) 353; on border management and immigration control 348–50; on counter-terrorism measures 353; current debates on 346–7; framework of 352–4; Joint Declaration of 1997 353; Partnership Agenda 353; PNR agreement 353; way forward to 354
Australian Customs and Border Protection Service 353

'balancing mechanisms' of state action, idea of 405
Bali Concord II 373, 376
Balkan asylum-seekers 113, 301
Bandar Seri Begawan Plan of Action (2013–2017) 374, 375, 376
Bangemann Report (1994) 149

Barcelona Process (1995) 310, 311, 319
benchmarking system 278
Benelux countries 229
Berlin Process 283
biometric technology 103; passports with 304
biopolitical governmentality 26
bio-politics 313
Blair, Tony 66; New Vision for Refugees (2003) 66
boat people, phenomenon of 103
Border Assistance Mission to Moldova and Ukraine (EUBAM) 101
border management 62, 248, 288; and border practices in Europe 99; cross-border mobility, issue of 73, 104; Entry/Exit System (EES) 180; European Border Surveillance System (EUROSUR) 103; in European Union 100–2; Europeanization of border policies 99; EU–Russia cooperation on 303; goal of creating 99; integrated see Integrated Border Management System; 'Jungle effect' 106; Khartoum Process 101, 327, 332; main pillars of 241; for managing migratory flows 101; National Action Plan on Integrated Border Management 289; policies on 102–5; policy-making process for 102; politics of building barriers 99; privileged border-crossers 104; Regional Protection Programs for 101; Schengen border regime on see Schengen Agreement (1985); 'smart borders' initiatives for 102–3; smart borders package 180; smart technologies for 103; social sorting of migrants 103; Southern European model of 242; Syrian refugee crisis, impact of 102, 105; teichopolitics of 99, 100–5; to track cross-border travelers 103; 'twinning programs' initiatives for 101
border security: cross-border mobility, criminalization of 73, 104; EU border crisis 105; European Border and Coast Guard Regulation 72; *Sistema Integrado de Vigilacia Exterior* (SIVE) 242; smart borders 26, 102–3; US–Mexico border 75
border surveillance system 231; European Border Surveillance System (EUROSUR) 103, 182, 377
border-free Europe 106
Bourdieu, Pierre 184
Braudel, Fernand 310
Brexit Referendum (2016) 37, 130, 131; Brexit Day 260–1; decision-making rules 259; 'emergency brake' rule 259; EU's negotiation guidelines on 260–1; general JHA rules on 256–8; legal framework of 253–9; Mixed Committee on 255; *passerelle clause* 258; 'pseudo-veto' rule 259; qualified majority voting (QMV) on 258–9; rules on enhanced cooperation and 258–9; Schengen acquis 253–5, 259

Brussels Convention (1968) 203
Brussels I Regulation 204, 206
Budgets and Budgetary Control Committees 449

Canada–Czech visa dispute 351
Canada–EU JHA cooperation: on border control and immigration 347–8; Canada–Czech visa dispute and 351; Canada–EU visa waiver programme 112; current debates on 346–7; framework of 351–2; Partnership Agenda 351, 352; people-to-people contacts and working relations 352; PNR agreement 352; on refugee policy 351; way forward to 354
Canada–US border politics 348
Canadian refugee policy, European influence on 351
Caritas Europa 416, 463, 464
Caviedes, Alex 128
Central and Eastern Europe: attempts to limit judicial power in 268–9; collapse of communism in 264; common values based on the rule of law 265–7; constitution of 264; controversies and challenges at the EU level 270–1; depoliticization of the judiciary in 268; empowerment of the Commission 267; establishment of judicial councils 267–8; framework to complement Article 7 TEU 270–1; horizontal policy instruments 266–7; judicial independence in 267–9; judicial institutions in 266; judicial reforms in 267; membership in EU 265; National Judicial Council (NCJ) 269
channel of communication 362
Charter for Peace and Stability (2001) 311
Charter of Fundamental Rights see EU Charter of Fundamental Rights (EUCFR)
child pornography 150, 341
Churches' Commission for Migrants in Europe (CCME) 463
citizenship: European 48, 217; freedom of movement 70
civil security governance 25
civil society organizations 26, 75, 294, 458
Cocaine Route Programme 327, 331, 367
cocaine trafficking 329–31, 367
Code of Conduct, on maritime security 328
COMCRIME 149
Committee of Permanent Representatives (COREPER) 421, 431
Common Agendas on Migration and Mobility (CAMMs) 91
Common Basic Principles on Migrant Integration 215, 218
Common European Asylum System (CEAS) 60, 65, 91, 233, 235, 413, 473; creation and development of 83

Common Foreign and Security Policy (CFSP) 373, 386, 400, 450
Common Framework for the Integration of Third-country Nationals 218
Common Security and Defence Policy (CSDP) 73, 138, 314, 327
common travel area 256, 260
Community Code on Visas 71
comparative politics (CP) 42, 49, 63, 230, 264
Comprehensive Crime Control Act (1984), US 149
Computer Emergency Response Teams (CERT) 361
Computer Fraud and Abuse Act (1986), US 149
Comunidad de Policías de América (AMERIPOL) see Police Community of the Americas
confidence-building measures 311
Convention on Mutual Assistance in Criminal Matters 258
Cooperation against cocaine trafficking from Latin America to West Africa (COLACAO) 367
Cooperation and Verification Mechanism 269, 278
Cooperation Programme on Drugs Policies with EU (COPOLAD) 360, 366
Copenhagen criteria (1993) 277–8
Copenhagen School 30–6, 313
corrupt business practices 141
Cotonou Agreement (2010) 323, 326
Council Conclusions on Security and Development 316
Council of Europe (CoE) 87, 195, 264, 271, 294, 341, 474; actors, institutions and interactions in 424; alternatives to venue-shopping 424; bureaucracy and presidency, role of 427–8; constituencies of 427; Council-specific informal rules 425; decision-making rules 423, 425–7; hierarchy in 427; intergovernmentalism in 428–30; lock-in and misfit 424; Luxembourg compromise 426; member state cooperation in 422–3; memorandum of understanding 469, 475; negotiations on Dublin II Regulation 425; Permanent Representatives of 427; reciprocity and appropriate behavior in 424–5; regulatory competition 424; 'shadow of the vote' 426; sharing of power with Commission and EP 430; Venice Commission of 271; venue-shopping hypothesis 424; voting or consensus in 425–7
Council of Europe Cybercrime Convention 341
Council of Ministers 131, 133, 427, 431, 460
counter-terrorism, EU policy on 35, 45; Action Plan on Combatting Terrorism 158; burden of proof 164; cooperation with ASEAN 376–7; against Daesh threat 158; effectiveness of 164; historical evolution and key actors of 157–9; intelligence exchange 164; literature review and theoretical explanations of 159–63; major debates on 163–5; objectives of 158; post 9/11 attacks 165; tradeoff between security and liberty 164–5
country of origin: designated 351–2; policies, for grant of asylum 235, 243, 317; safe 351
Court of Justice of the EU (CJEU) 46, 94, 396, 410, 472; empowerment of 7; jurisdiction in civil matters 204
Cox, Robert 21
crime–terror nexus, concept of 142
criminal law, in EU: *Caldararu and Aryanosi* case 197; competences among the member states 193; Court of Justice's jurisdiction over 193; European Criminal Law Academic Network 192, 196; evolution of 193–5; Framework Decision on 194, 197; importance of 196; institutional framework of 193–5; journals specializing in 192; mutual recognition, principle of 196–7; national territoriality of 195; similarities and/or divergences of 197; substance of 195–7
Critical Information Infrastructure protection (CIIP) 149
Critical Maritime Routes Programme 327
cross-border mobility, criminalization of 73
cross-border regional cooperation projects 324
cross-border travelers, proposals for: Entry–Exit System 103; Registered Traveller Program 103
cross-pillarization, idea of 64
cyber crime 146; Action Plan to Combat Organised Crime 150; challenges associated with 151–3; COMCRIME 149; concept of 147–8; copyright-related offenses 148; costs of 147; Council of Europe Cybercrime Convention 148, 341; criminalization of 152; Critical Information Infrastructure protection (CIIP) 149; Cyber Security Strategy 152, 341; defense against 149; definitions of 148–9; European Cyber Crime Centre (EC3) 152; EU–US cooperation on 336, 340, 341; evolution of 149–51; Framework Decision on Attacks Against Information Systems 150; General Policy on the Fight against Cyber Crime 151; identification of 147; impact upon AFSJ 151–3; legislations for combating 149, 152; off-the-shelf tools, use of 147; Safer Internet Action Plan 150; strategy for combating 147, 152; Working Group on Cybercrime and Cybersecurity (WGCC), EU–US 341

data privacy 337
Data Protection Authorities (DPAs) 170, 174–5
data protection, EU policies on 169–70; European Data Protection Supervisor (EDPS) 170, 173; EU–US Umbrella Agreement and 172;

data protection, EU policies on *continued*
  future research avenues on 175–8; General Data Protection Regulation (GDPR) 169, 171, 173, 174, 176; general regulatory instruments 170–2; impact on academics 174–5; Police and Criminal Justice Data Protection Directive 169, 172, 173, 174, 178; Regulation 45/2001 172–6, 178; Regulation 794/2016 174; regulatory state at the EU agency level 174; scholarly debates on 175–8; specific regulatory state on 172; as unexplored territory for legal research 178
de Bruycker, Philippe 5
death penalty: EU's campaign against 339; EU–US cooperation on 338–9
Deauville Partnership 318
decision-making: Community Method of 49; intergovernmental 48; logic of 48
DEMIG VISA database 111, 117, 119
designated country of origin, notion of 351–2
Development Cooperation Instrument (DCI) 362, 363
digital revolution 12, 146
drug trafficking 327; Cocaine Route Programme (2009) 330–1, 367; cocaine trafficking 329; Drug Strategy (2005–2012) 329–30; Drugs Action Plan (2013–2016) 330; ECOWAS Action Plan 330; fight against 364; Maritime Analysis and Operations Centre-Narcotics (MAOC-N) 330; Praia Plan of Action 330
Dublin Convention (1990) 59–60, 62, 104, 106, 132
Dublin II Regulation (2003) 425
Dublin III Regulation (2016) 65, 402, 413, 416
Dublin rules, for Syrian refugees 237, 244

early warning mechanism (EWM) 434–5, 439
Eastern Partnership (EaP) 10, 13, 113, 115, 300, 302, 306
East–West confrontation 236
Economic Monetary Union (EMU) 386
ECOWAS Action Plan 330, 331
electronic surveillance 188
Electronic System for Travel Authorization (ESTA), US 348, 416
Electronic Travel Authorization (ETA) 348, 353
electronic visas: biometric technology 103; processing of 103; Visa Information System (VIS) 103
'emergency brake' rule 259
enforced destitution, idea of 78
enhanced cooperation, rules on 258–9
epistemic communities 41–2, 44–5; concept of 43; defined 44
equality, principle of 299
ethnic profiling, for grant of visa 113

EU Agency for large-scale IT systems within the Area of Freedom, Security and Justice (EULISA) 446
EU agenda: on freedom of movement 11; on illegal immigration 87; on management of migration 314; on policy entrepreneurs 430
EU Border Assistance Mission to the Republic of Moldova and to Ukraine (EUBAM) 101, 303
EU Charter of Fundamental Rights (EUCFR) 74, 85–6, 207–9, 211, 352, 397, 399, 402, 429, 452
EU Directives: Asylum Procedures Directive 60, 289, 293, 411; Blue Card Directive 127, 128, 218; Carriers Sanctions 76; Data Retention Directive (DRD) 181, 183, 340; Employers Sanctions Directive 76; ePrivacy Directive 151; Facilitation Directive 78; Family Reunification Directive 215, 216, 217–18, 219, 233; Long-term Residence Directive 215, 216–17, 219; Network and Information Systems Directive 152; Passenger Name Record Directive 159; PNR Directive 172; Police and Criminal Justice Data Protection Directive 169, 172, 173, 174, 178; Qualification Directive 60; Recast Reception Conditions Directive 412; Reception Conditions Directive 411, 412; Recital 4 of 76; Returns Directive 76, 96n11; Single Permit Directive 129
EU Drug Strategy (2005–2012) 329–30
EU institutions, decision-making and the role of 6–8, 10–12
EU Integrated Border Management Assistance Mission (EUBAM) 318
EU law 253, 464; on citizenship 221; competences among the member states 193; criminal law *see* criminal law, in EU; and ECJ case law 260; effectiveness of 399; general principles of 84, 193; global approach of 340; *ne bis in idem* principle 194; 'Prüm' legislation 258
EU–Africa Plan of Action on Trafficking of Human Beings 327
EU–Horn of Africa Migration Route Initiative *see* Khartoum Process
EU–Jordan Compact 318
EU–Morocco readmission agreement 314
EUNAVFORMED *see* Operation Sophia (2015)
EURODAC (fingerprint database) 60, 103, 169, 174, 185, 231, 416
Eurojust 141, 159, 173, 174, 196, 234, 291, 428, 446
Euro–Mediterranean Partnership (EMP) 310, 311
European Agency for Operational Cooperation at the External Border 303
European Agenda on Migration (2015) 73, 328
European Agenda on Security (2015) 158
European Arrest Warrant (EAW) 159, 196, 236, 257, 400, 405, 412, 414, 436

Index

European Asylum Support Office (EASO) 61, 65, 446, 448
European Border and Coast Guard (EBCG) Agency *see* Frontex
European Border Guard Teams (EBGTs) 412, 414, 447
European Border Surveillance System (EUROSUR) 103, 231, 377
European Charter of Fundamental Rights 352
European Commission 5, 45–6, 91, 126, 180, 182, 233, 270, 282, 290, 409–16, 463; Action Plan on Return 73; Asylum Procedures Directive 293, 411; on coherent global approach to migration 64; communitarization of policies with the Lisbon Treaty 412; comparison to other EU institutions 416; competences with the Amsterdam Treaty 411; Directorate-General for Neighbourhood and Enlargement Negotiations (DG NEAR) 283; in early cooperation on JHA 410–11; impact of 410–14; influence of 412–14; negotiation on readmission agreements 83; positions of 414–16; as promoter of enhanced integration 414; as promoter of individual freedoms or security 414–15; qualified majority voting 410; Recast Reception Conditions Directive 412; Reception Conditions Directive 411, 412; on refugee quota system 413; sharing of power with Council 430; Tampere summit 411; on variance between policy areas 415–16
European Commission for the Efficiency of Justice (CEPEJ) 271
European Communities (EC) 157, 350–1
European Convention on Human Rights (ECHR) 86, 207, 402, 403, 472
European Council 60, 421, 428; Council Conclusions (2015) 73; *de novo* bodies 428; fight against terrorism 36; intergovernmentalism in 428; president of 428; role in defining JHA 429; role of 429; of Santa Maria de Feira 137
European Council of Tampere (1999) 86, 126, 216, 429
European Council on Refugees and Exiles (ECRE) 463
European Court of Human Rights (ECtHR) 64, 289, 312; *Hirsii Jamaa vs. Italy* 312
European Court of Justice (ECJ) 194, 233, 261, 314, 352, 396–406, 411, 422; and Area of Freedom, Security and Justice (AFSJ) 397–400; 'balancing mechanisms' of state action 405; *Caldararu and Aryanosi* case 197, 402; cooperation with other courts 402–3; EAW Framework Decision 400–1; *Kadi* cases 399–400; *Melloni* ruling 197, 401–2; *ne bis in idem* principle 194, 405; Schengen system 397; *Solange* doctrine 403; as trustee court 404–5

European Criminal Law Academic Network (ECLAN) 4, 192, 196
European Cyber Crime Centre (EC3) 152
European Data Protection Supervisor (EDPS) 170, 173–7
European Development Fund (EDF) 329–30
European Economic Community (EEC) 59, 149
European External Action Service (EEAS) 73, 91, 312, 315, 339, 360
European harmonization on immigration and asylum, fundamental pillar of 241
European integration: European Integration Forum 218; European Integration Fund 215, 218, 222; impact on mobility of non-EU nationals 70; nature of 62; project of 413; theories of 236
European Investigation Order (EIO) 196
European Judicial Atlas and Handbooks 205
European Judicial Network 205
European Migration Network 215, 219, 236
European Monitoring Centre for Drugs and Drug Addiction 446
European Neighbourhood Policy (ENP) 87, 95, 310, 311, 475; Strategy Papers of 298
European Ombudsman 341, 452
European Parliament (EP) 45, 49, 60, 84, 133, 159, 195, 233, 295, 316, 352, 366, 409, 416, 422, 435, 449–50, 463; Assembly of the European Coal and Steel Community 386; Committee on Civil Liberties and Justice and Home Affairs 164; decision-making 386, 393; empowerment of 6, 385; entrepreneurship qualities of 46; influence of 391–3; institutional changes in 385–7; integration theories 387–8; in justice and home affairs 385, 387–8; legislative and budgetary functions of 85; on legitimating norms and the role of actors 390–1; Maastricht, Treaty of (1992) 385, 386; new institutionalism and 388–91; Paris, Treaty of (1951) 386; sharing of power with Council 430; time horizons and shifting coalitions 388–90; 'venue-shopping' thesis 387–8; voting behavior, in area of migration 389
European Police Academy 234
European Police College (CEPOL) 446
European Police Office *see* Europol
European Public Prosecutor Office (EPPO) 169, 174, 195, 439, 441
European refugee crisis (2015) 35, 61, 63, 65–6, 77
European Refugee Fund (ERF) 60, 62
European Security Strategy (2003) 158, 374, 475
European Ship Owners Association 79
European Travel Information and Authorisation System (ETIAS) 231, 416
European Union (EU) 19, 66; *Accession Partnership* documents (2001) 288; Action Plan against

485

European Union (EU) *continued*
　Migrant Smuggling 72; Action Plan on Combatting Terrorism 186; Area of Freedom, Security and Justice (AFSJ) 25, 31; border governance in 100–2; border security 26; Charter of Fundamental Rights of 74, 85–6, 402, 404; civil security governance 25; Common Strategy on Russia 298; counter-terrorism cooperation 47; counter-terrorist policies 35; Global Strategy 276; Guidelines on its Foreign and Security Policy in East Asia 374; irregular immigration policies *see* irregular immigration, EU policies on; justice and home affairs, governance in 22–6; public policy approach *see* public policy approach; relation with Western Balkans 281; relations with the Schengen associates 260; rules on differentiated integration 260; securitizing role of 34; Stabilization and Association Agreements (SAA) 275–7, 279; Strategy for Security and Development 327
European Union Agency for Asylum 236, 448, 454
European Union Agency for Fundamental Rights 446
European Website on Integration 215, 218
Europeanization, process of 79, 161
European-scale intelligence networks 164
Europol 8, 23, 49, 73, 103, 140–1, 151, 158–9, 173, 234, 257, 291, 351, 360, 377, 391, 446, 447; European Migrant Smuggling Centre 72; Europol Malware Analysis Solution (EMAS) 361; internal referral unit (IRU) 319; joint investigation teams (JITs) 447; Joint Supervisory Body (JSB) 174; Organized Crime Threat Assessments (OCTAs) 141; Regulation (2016) 449, 452; Terrorist Financing Tracking Programme (TFTP) 164
Euroskepticism, notion of 51, 91
EUROsociAL program 364
Eurozone 260
EU–Ukraine Association Agreement 299–300
executive empowerment 23, 25–6
extradition assistance, EU–US cooperation on 336, 337–8

Facilitators Package 71, 78
family reunification 349; EU law on 220; European Commission proposal on 219; Family Reunification Directive 215, 216, 217–18, 220, 222, 233; right to 217, 221, 223
Financial Action Task Force (FATF) 22, 163, 474
'first-country-of-entry' principle 65
flexible solidarity, principle of 83
foreign direct investments (FDI) 88, 119, 372
Framework Decision: on Attacks Against Information Systems 150, 153; on Combatting Fraud and Counterfeiting 151, 154n10; on Combatting the Sexual Exploitation of Children and Child Pornography 150
freedom of movement, for EU citizens 26, 70–1, 163, 221, 413
Freedom, Security and Justice (FSJ) 84
French Independent Constitutional Authority for the Defense of Rights 94
Frontex 49, 50, 71–3, 159, 174, 236, 248, 255, 303, 313, 377, 391, 414–15, 446, 447–8, 450, 452–5; Consultative Forum on human rights 452; EBCG Regulation 452, 453; European Border Guard Teams (EBGTs) 447; fundamental rights obligations 452; Fundamental Rights Strategy 452; Mare Nostrum (military and humanitarian operation) 75, 248n2; Operation Triton (2015) 75, 100; powers of 451; Rapid Border Intervention Teams (RABITs) 447; regulations of 449, 451; Western Balkans Annual Risk Analysis 277

gap hypothesis 229, 236
Geddes, Andrew 127
General Data Protection Regulation (GDPR) 169, 171, 173, 174, 176
General Policy on the Fight against Cyber Crime 151
General Secretariat of the Council (GSC) 83
Geneva Refugee Convention (1951) 59, 288, 350, 472, 475
Global Approach for Migration (GAM, 2005) 61, 64, 88
Global Approach for Migration and Mobility (2011) 61, 64
Global Strategy, for EU's foreign and security policy 276, 316, 340, 475
good governance, in migration management 304–5
Great Recession (2008) 127
Greek asylum system 248n4
Group of Eight (G8) 149
Guidelines on its Foreign and Security Policy in East Asia (EU) 374
Guidelines on the Freedom of Religion or Belief 316
Gulf of Guinea Action Plan (2015–2020) 327
Gutierrez Zarza, A. 176

Haas, Ernst B. 409
habitus (system of dispositions), concept of 184
Hague Conference on Private International Law (2007) 468–9, 474
Hague Programme (2004) 61, 359
Hammar, Thomas 215
High Commissioner on Human Rights 350
home affairs and technology 180–2, 187
homeland security 4, 45
House of Lords (UK) 73, 127, 437

human rights 463; EBCG Regulation on 452, 453; Frontex Consultative Forum on 452; High Commissioner on Human Rights 350; infringements of 452; violations of 77, 451–2
Human Rights Watch 350
human trafficking 73, 87, 195, 327–8, 368, 375, 378, 392, 440, 475

ideas-based approaches, for policy-making 49–50
identity determination dilemma 75
Immigration Liaison Officers (ILOs) 103
information and data processing: controversies over 183; as disposition and practice 184–5; for electronic surveillance 188; EU 'meta-norms' on 182; home affairs and technology 180–2; as instrument and actant 185–7; internalization of 182; norms-focused 183; PNR data processing 186–7; proliferation of 182, 185; Schengen Information System (SIS) 180; securitizing effects of 186; as security norm 182–4; societal effects of 187–8; SWIFT data, EU–US agreement on 182; Visa Information System (VIS) 180
institutional-focused approaches, for policy-making 46–9; historical 47; rational choice 48–9; sociological 47–8
Instrument for Stability (IfS) 327
Integrated Border Management System 102, 378; EU standards of 303; migration-driven cooperation agenda on 306; progressing militarization of 12
intelligence and law enforcement services 319
intensive transgovernmentalism 23–4, 51, 422
intergovernmental organizations (IGOs) 458, 468; agreements concluded by agencies with 470; cooperation in JHA 470–3; Hague Programme 474; hard law, soft law and hybrid forms of cooperation 469–70; promotion of, by EU 475–6; relations with AFSJ 469–70; relations with EU 469, 474, 477; role of 476–7; soft agreements 477; Stockholm Programme 474–5; strategy on the external AFSJ 474; Tampere conclusions 473–4; treaty provisions relevant for relations with 470–3
internal security, governance of 19–26; Area of Freedom, Security and Justice 23; complexities of 21; definition of 21; EU justice and home affairs on 22–6; EU policy on 19; failure in 21; family resemblances of 20–1; fight against terrorism and 25; by government 21; with government 21; intensive transgovernmentalism for 23; nodal policing governance and 22; ordinary legislative procedure for 23; post-Cold War discourse on 22; problem-solving *versus* critical approaches for 21; spill-over effect of 21; supranational 23; and transformation of security provision 21–2; transgovernmental networks for 23; without government 21

International Civil Aviation Organization 163
International Criminal Court 352, 469
International Maritime Organization 163
International Monetary Fund 264
International Organization for Migration (IOM) 76, 101, 470
international relations (IR) 30–2, 41, 42, 50, 76, 137–8, 147–8, 162, 325, 353, 458, 464, 471
international security network, concept of 360–1
Internet Corporation for Assigned Names and Numbers (ICANNs) 341
Interpol 360, 378, 468, 470, 475
irregular immigration, EU policies on: Action Plan against Migrant Smuggling 72; anti-smuggling and expulsion policies 70, 72–3; background of 71–2; challenges facing 70; Common Security and Defense Policy (CSDP) 73; effectiveness of 70, 73–5; on expulsions of irregular immigrants 70, 74, 76–7; guarantees and frameworks of rights 72; humanitarian issues regarding 75; identity determination dilemma 75; management of arrivals 75–6; pre-return policies 77; Readmission Agreement 74–5; social trust and 78–9; system to return irregular migrants 73; third-country nationals ordered to leave and enforced returns 74; unintended consequences of 77–8; voluntary returns 74
Islamic terrorism 36, 236
Italy–Libya cooperation: on asylum system 243, 245; against illegal migration 312

Jakarta Center for Law Enforcement Cooperation 353, 376
job-creating activities 88
Joint Africa–EU Strategy (JAES) 326–8; Second Action Plan (2011–2013) 327
Joint Cybercrime Action Taskforce (J-CAT) 152, 361
Joint EC–US Task Force on Critical Infrastructure Protection 341
joint investigation teams (JITs) 195, 337, 447
Joint Migration Declarations (JMDs) 90
Joint Operational Team (JOT) MARE 72
Joint Parliamentary Scrutiny Group 450, 454
Joint Way Forward (JWF) 90, 91
judicial cooperation, in civil matters: Account Preservation Order 205; Brussels Convention (1968) on 203; Brussels I Regulation on 204; Brussels IIa Regulation on 204, 207; cross-border implications of 204, 208; enforcement of 205–9; European Court of Justice, jurisdiction of 204; Evidence Regulation on 204; harmonization of 208–9; historical evolution of 203–5; importance of 203; intergovernmental cooperation on 203; and judicial protection 205–9; key instruments of 203–5; Maintenance Regulation on 204;

judicial cooperation, in civil matters *continued*
  member states' civil justice systems and 208; mutual recognition and mutual trust, nature of 206–7; overarching measures on 205; Payment Order Procedure 204; Rome Convention (1980) on 203; Rome I Regulation on 204; Rome II Regulation on 204; Rome III Regulation on 204; scholarly debates on 209–10; Service Regulation on 204; Small Claims Procedure 204; Succession Regulation on 204
justice and home affairs (JHA) *see* Area of Freedom, Security and Justice (AFSJ)
juxtaposed controls 103

Khartoum Process 101, 327, 332
Kingdon, J.W. 33, 37, 51
knowledge-based experts *see* epistemic communities
Kofi Annan Foundation 330
Kosovo crisis (1997) 245

labor immigration policy: Blue Card Directive 127, 128; creation of 124; debates regarding 127–30; for freedom of labor mobility 125, 130; future policy and research challenges 130–3; genesis of 125–7; on intra-EU migration 130; politicization of 125; Single Permit Directive 129; and theories of European integration 128
labor market: dual 130; single 130, 149
labor migration 124–33, 235, 303, 313, 413, 460, 461
labor recruitment 125
Latin America–EU JHA cooperation: Cocaine Route Programme (2009) 367; components of 363; Cooperation Programme on Drugs Policies with EU (COPOLAD) 360; Coordination and Cooperation Mechanism on Drugs (1998) 366; Declaration of EU-CELAC (2013) 364; Development Cooperation Instrument (DCI) 362, 363; institutional approaches 359–60; institutionalization of 362–4; on international security network 360–1; in justice and home affairs 361–2; Justice and Security-Sector Reform (JSSR) 364; Multiannual Indicative Regional Programme for Latin America 362, 363; Plan Colombia 364, 366; regional cooperation *363*; under security–development nexus 358–9, 368; theoretical approaches to 359–61; on transnational organized crime 364–8
Law on Foreigners and International Protection 288, 294
Le Drian, Jean-Yves 372
Lisbon, Treaty of (2009) 23, 51, 60, 71, 84, 89, 159, 170, 193–5, 198, 204, 215, 254, 255, 258, 312, 324, 339, 393, 397, 398, 412, 416, 434, 435, 439, 449, 453; Declaration 21 of 171; expiration of 257; ratification of 171; Title V Protocol 256
logic of appropriateness 48
logic of consequentiality, 48
Luxembourg compromise 426

Maastricht, Treaty of (1992) 4, 60, 63, 140, 158, 193, 204, 253, 385, 386, 396, 410, 422, 434, 461
Macedonian crisis 276
Mare Nostrum (military and humanitarian operation) 75, 242, 248n2
Maritime Analysis and Operations Centre-Narcotics (MAOC-N) 330
maritime interdiction, of migration 103
maritime security, ASEAN–EU relationship on 379
maritime surveillance 73, 379
Marseille Summit 311
Mediterranean migration crisis of 2015 243
member states, of Europe 229–30; anti-discrimination policies 235; autonomy of 230–3; codification of terrorist offenses 234; Common European Asylum System (CEAS) 233, 235; convergence hypothesis 236; counter-terrorism policies 234; European crises 236–7; European justice and home affairs and 230–3; Family Reunification Directive 233; gap hypothesis 236; globalization, Europeanization and convergence in 233–6; hardening of control of 230–2; mechanisms of convergence 235–6; from national towards European models 233–4; new intergovernmentalism 232; and new limits of control 232–3; police cooperation 234; refugee crisis 236–7; 'religious subsistence level' doctrine 233; securitization of 230–2; supranational modes of cooperation 236; supranationalization of 232–3, 234; venue-shopping processes 230–2, 236
membership conditionality 281
Memorandum of Understanding 328, 469, 475
Mercosur (Common Market of the South) 360
Middle East and North Africa (MENA) region 310, 314; destabilization of 319; EU–Jordan Compact 318; Macro-Financial Assistance operations 318; relation with EU 316; state failure in 319; *see also* Southern Mediterranean countries, JHA policies on
migrant integration, policy for 215; Action Plan on the Integration of Third-Country Nationals 222; civic integration 221; Common Basic Principles 218, 222; Common Framework for the Integration of Third-country Nationals 218; as condition for rights 221–3; Europeanization of 221; Family Reunification Directive 217–18,

219; geopolitics of 314; Indicators for Migrant Integration 218; Long-term Residence Directive 216–17, 219; minimum safety net 220; National Contact Points on Integration 218; negotiating and implementing 219–21; non-binding 218–19; 'soft governance' initiatives 218–19

migrants' rights: EU agenda on 11; and European Parliament 388; safety net for 219–21; violation of 312

migration: from African countries 90; assisted voluntary return (AVR) programs 88; boat people, phenomenon of 103; Common Agendas on Migration and Mobility (CAMMs) 91; Common European Asylum System (CEAS) 233; countries of origin 87, 117, 231, 243; criminalization of 71; EU–Turkey deal 231; fight against illegal 83, 87; Joint Migration Declarations (JMDs) 90; management of 88, 90; maritime interdiction of 103; mass arrivals of migrants 87; 'safe country of asylum' policy 104; social sorting of 103; in Southern Europe 240; substitution effects 117; *see also* asylum and refugee protection, EU policies on

Migration, Asylum, Refugees Regional Initiative (MARRI) 283

Migration Management Support Teams 65

Migration Policy Group (MPG) 463

migration-driven cooperation agenda: Association Agreement with Ukraine 299–300; challenge of coherence in 304–5; with East European countries 298, 299–304; Eastern Partnership (EaP) 300, 302; EU's Common Strategy on Russia 298; evolution of 299–304; fight against corruption 302; good governance 305; Integrated Border Management 303, 306; labor migration regulation 303; legally binding instruments 299–302; on mobility of workers 299; Mobility Partnerships 302–3, 306; non-legally binding instruments 302–3; operational cooperation instruments 303–4; Partnership and Cooperation Agreements 298, 299; readmission–visa facilitation nexus 300; Strategic Partnership on 299; on treatment of workers 300; on use of soft law instruments 302; Visa Facilitation Agreements 300; Visa Liberalisation Action Plan 301; Visa Liberalisation Dialogues 301; Working Arrangements 303

migration–security nexus 243

mobility partnerships (MPs) 88, 90, 96n9, 232, 302–3, 306

money laundering 31, 138, 141, 163, 196, 277, 287, 290, 298, 326, 366, 375, 378, 398, 474

'more for more' principle 95

Multiannual Indicative Regional Programme for Latin America 362, 363

multi-level governance, concept of 24, 312, 424, 465

multilevel parliamentary field, concept of 440

Muslim Brotherhood 316

Mutual Legal Assistance (MLA) Agreement, EU–US cooperation on 336, 338

mutual recognition, principle of 7, 61, 72, 141, 159, 195, 196–7, 205, 206–7, 210, 400–2

National Action Plan on Asylum and Migration (2005) 289

National Action Plan on Integrated Border Management 289

National Contact Points on Integration 218

National Judicial Council (NCJ) 268–70

national parliaments: AFSJ policy process 435; empirical research on the role of 437–9; and European Parliament (EP) 435; and inter-parliamentary cooperation in the AFSJ 439–41; inter-parliamentary meetings 440; and parliamentary scrutiny of the AFSJ 435–7; role of 434; 'venue-shopping' thesis 436

national police data, cross-border exchange of 258

National Security Agency (NSA), US 336

ne bis in idem principle 194, 405

Neighborhood Policy *see* European Neighbourhood Policy (ENP)

New York Declaration on Migration and Refugees (2016) 79

Nice, Treaty of (2003) 204, 258, 425

non-governmental organizations (NGOs) 289, 458; Area of Freedom, Security and Justice (AFSJ) 459–61; bringing in 461–2; Brussels-based 460, 463–4; Church-affiliated 464; EU–NGO interactions 459, 464; Europeanizing of 463; goals and strategies of 463–4; political opportunity structures (POS) 459; preferences and priorities of 462

non-refoulement, principle of 66, 245, 288, 312, 451, 472

non-traditional security (NTS) 10, 25, 371

North Atlantic Treaty Organization (NATO) 314

Odysseus Network for Legal Studies on Immigration and Asylum in Europe 5

Operation 'Active Endeavour' (2002) 314

Operation Atalanta (2013) 328

Operation Sophia (2015) 73, 76, 313

Operation Sovereign Borders (OSB, 2013) 350

Operation Triton (2015) 75, 100

Organization for Economic Cooperation and Development (OECD) 149, 264

Organization of American States (OAS) 360

organized crime (OC): Action Plan to Combat 138; Africa–EU relations on *see* Africa–EU relations, on organized crime; analyses of 140;

organized crime (OC) *continued*
   corrupt business practices 141; crime–terror nexus 142; defined 139; detrimental effects on the state 137; EU policies on 136; EU–Latin America relations on 364–8; EU–Russia relations to combat 298; Instrument for Stability (IfS) 327; internationalization of 137; legislation dealing with the fight against 138; money laundering 141; operationalization of 137, 139; Organized Crime Threat Assessments (OCTAs) 141; origins and evolution of 136–8; policy debates on 140–2; research agenda on 142–3; Sahel Strategy (2011) to combat 327; terrorism *see* terrorism; theoretical debates on 138–40; understanding of 137; United Nations Convention Against Transnational Organized Crime 139, 326
Ouagadougou Action Plan 327

Pan-African program 363
Paris, Treaty of (1951) 386
Partnership on Peace and Security 326
Passenger Name Recognition (PNR) 45
Passenger Name Record (PNR) 180, 231; collection of 172; EU–Canada agreements on 352; EU–US agreements on 172, 182, 187, 336, 339, 340, 346; global approach to 340; 'Second Generation' Agreement 340
passerelle clause, of qualified majority voting 258
patrimony, of dispositions 184
Payment Order Procedure 204
Permanent Working Group on Drugs 410
Plan Colombia 364, 366
Police Community of the Americas 361
Police Working Group on Terrorism 164
policy communities 44
policy conditionality, importance of 113, 281
policy cycle, for fighting serious and organized crime 23
policy entrepreneurs 41, 43, 45–6, 100, 128, 149, 160, 223, 267, 391, 392, 430
policy networks, concept of 43–4
policy-making, in EU 43–4; in area of asylum *see* asylum and refugee protection, EU policies on; ideas-based approaches for 49–50; supranational 49
political opportunity structures (POS) 459
Praia Plan of Action 330
pre-emptive governance 181
Privacy Act (1974), US 342
privileged border-crossers 104
problem-solving 9, 19, 21, 42, 160, 229, 429
Proliferation Security Initiative 22
Prüm, Treaty of (2005) 49, 87, 96n7, 258, 260; 'Prüm' legislation 258
pseudo-veto 259–60
public policy approach: actor-based 43–6; advocacy coalitions 45; Community Method of decision-making 41; comparative politics (CP), emergence of 42; cross-cutting 50–2; decision-making 48; epistemic communities 44–5; in EU studies and JHA research 41, 42–3; historical institutionalism and 47; ideas-based 49–50; institutional-focused 46–9; overview of 42; and policy entrepreneurship 45–6; policy networks 43–4; 'principal–agent' dynamics on 49; process of policy-making 43; rational choice institutionalism 48–9; 'Rhodes Model' of network analysis 44; sociological 47–8; supranational legal framework 41
public–private partnerships 21, 25, 341
Putin, Vladimir 300

Quadro Group 87
qualified majority voting (QMV) 60, 258, 386, 410; 'emergency brake' rule 259; *passerelle clause* 258; 'pseudo-veto' rule 259
quota system, for refugees 348, 413

Rabat Process (2006) 95, 327
Radicalisation Awareness Network 26, 159
Radio Free Europe 277
Radio Liberty 277
Rapid Border Intervention Teams (RABITs) 447
rapprochement, period of 71
rational-choice institutionalism 388, 424
Readmission Agreement, EU (EURA) 74–5; and arrangements linked to readmission *92–3*; assisted voluntary return (AVR) programs 88; Common Agendas on Migration and Mobility (CAMMs) 91; common rules and procedures 83; contingency gap in 84, 85–6; drive for normative 86–7; EU drive for flexibility on 89–94; EU member states' bilateral arrangements on 91; EU member states' modus operandi and practices 84; EU's approach to cooperation on 84; and EU–Turkey statement on refugees 94, 277; on fight against illegal migration 83, 87; implementation of 87; Joint Readmission Committee (JRC) 84; Joint Way Forward (JWF) 91; mobility partnerships (MPs) 90; monitoring mechanisms of 85, 90; 'more for more' principle 95; negotiation of 83, 87; with non-EU countries 89; non-legally binding arrangements for 94; as non-legally binding framework 88; Partnership Framework (PF) for 90–1, 94; prelude to the EU drive for flexibility on 87–9; special representative on a common readmission policy 87; Standard Operating Procedures (SOPs) 90; with third countries on migration 91; Treaty on the Functioning of the European Union (TFEU) on 84; unmet preconditions of 84–5; visa policy of EU and 113

readmission–visa facilitation nexus 300
Reception Directive 2005/85/EC 60
refoulement, concept of 77, 294
refugees: Dublin rules for 237; EU policies on protection of *see* asylum and refugee protection, EU policies on; EU–Turkey agreement on 66, 94, 115, 232, 237, 277, 291, 292–4, 470; first countries of asylum 244; Mediterranean migration crisis of 2015 243; quota system 413; redistribution scheme 102; Refugee Convention (1951) 89; refugee crisis 236–7, 413; transit phenomenon 245; *see also* asylum-seekers; migration
Regional Protection Zones, for refugees and asylum seekers 66
'religious subsistence level' doctrine 233
remote policing 324
resilience, concept of 318
return migration, theory of 71, 76–7, 79
'Rhodes Model' of network analysis 44
Roe, P. 33
Rome Convention (1980) 203
Rome Declaration (1990) 362
Rome, Treaty of (1957) 124–5, 203, 386
Rules of Civil Procedure for Europe 210
Russia–EU relations: on border management 303; on combating organized crime 298; Common Spaces 300, 302; EU–Russia Summit (2003) 300; externalities of 304–5; on fight against corruption 302; on migration issues 304; objective of 300; readmission–visa facilitation nexus 300; on visa facilitation agreement 115, 300

Sabatier, P.A. 45
'safe country of asylum' policy 104
safe country of origin, notion of 235, 351
Safer Internet Action Plan 150
Sahel Strategic Regional Action Plan (2015–2020) 329, 331
SARS flu epidemic 373
Schengen Agreement (1985) 23, 59, 63, 70, 99, 138, 240, 241, 253, 386, 410; Borders Code 71, 102, 247; Schengen project 59; Schengen redux 105–6
Schengen Convention (1990) 23, 253, 438
Schengen Information System (SIS) 71, 174, 180, 231, 254, 377
science and technology studies (STS) 5, 181
securitization: of asylum and migration 35, 62–3; avenues for research on 35–7; concept of 30, 32; Copenhagen School approach for 30, 31–2, 34; core tenets of 32; from criticisms to improvements 32–4; defined 30; EU justice and home affairs and 35–7; EU legislation on 34–5; Kingdon's model of 33, 37; process and framework of 34–5, 37; psycho-cultural disposition of 30; Roe's model of 33; soft security issues 36; speech acts 32–3
security governance: open-ended 27; transformation of 21–2, 25
'shadow of the vote' 426
Shangri-La Dialogue 372–4
Single European Act (1986) 386
Sistema Integrado de Vigilacia Exterior (SIVE), Spain 103, 242
Small Claims Procedure 204
'smart borders' initiatives 102–3
social insecurity 78
social trust 70, 78–9
'soft governance' initiatives 218
Solange doctrine 403
Southeast Europe Police Chiefs Association 283
Southeast European Cooperation Initiative 283
Southeast European Prosecutors Advisory Group 283
Southern Europe: asylum and refugee protection in 243–5; asylum systems, heterogeneity of 245; border policing 241; as 'first countries of asylum' 244; lack of an asylum tradition in 244; management of external border 241–3; migration history of 240; non-refoulement, principle of 245; North–South divide 240, 241; role of internal controls in 246–7; struggle against irregular migration 243; welfare-magnet thesis 240
Southern Mediterranean countries, JHA policies on: Association Agreements 311; broadening and deepening of the policy area 317–18; building of state and societal resilience 315–17; capacity-building measures 315; counter-radicalization initiatives 316; Euromed Police, Justice and Migration programs 311; EU's relationship with 310; governance literature on 311–12; inter-civilizational dialogues 316; internal–external security nexus 315–16, 318; Macro-Financial Assistance operations 318; mercantilization of 318–19; militarization, issue of 318; Muslim Brotherhood 316; pitfalls of the first-wave approaches 314; post-Arab uprisings wave 315–17; pre-Arab uprisings wave 311–14; readmission agreements with EU 312; religious engagement 316; role for new technologies 319; securitization literature on 313–14; societal and state resilience 316–17; trends and the future of ED JHA research 317–19; Valencia Action Plan (2000) 311
Stabilization and Association Agreements (SAA) 275–7
Stabilization and Association Process (SAP) 275–7, 279, 475
Standard Operating Procedures (SOPs) 90
Ständige Arbeitsgemeinschaft Rauschgift (STAR) *see* Permanent Working Group on Drugs

Index

state capture, dynamics of 10, 276, 282, 283
Statewatch 198, 350
Stockholm Programme (2009) 61, 206, 324, 474–5
Storme Committee (1994) 210
subsidiarity, principle of 193, 387, 434–5, 439–41
sustainable development 316, 330, 471
Sustainable Fisheries Partnership Agreements 328
Swedish initiative 181
SWIFT data 184; EU–US agreement on 182, 339, 390, 416
Syrian refugee crisis 102, 105, 313; Dublin rules for 237; EU–Turkey agreement on 232, 237

Technical Assistance and Exchange of Information (TAIEX) 266
teichopolitics 99, 100–5
temporary protection visas (TPVs) 349
terrorism 35, 141; 9/11 terrorist attacks 36; Action Plan on Combatting Terrorism 158; attack on European countries 319; Bali bombings (2002) 353, 373, 375; bombing of the Australian Embassy in Jakarta 353; crime–terror nexus 142; EU policy on combating *see* counter-terrorism, EU policy on; European Security Strategy on 158; fight against 293, 298, 315; Framework Decision on the Definition of Terrorism 37; global fight against 36; 'home-grown' terrorists 319; Internal Security Strategy against 158; Islamic 36, 236; UN Resolution 1373(2001) to combat 475; use of new technologies in terrorist attacks 319; war against *see* war against terrorism
terrorism financing 46, 159, 277; Terrorist Financing Tracking Programme (TFTP) 164, 172, 180, 182
Terrorism, Radicalism, Extremism and political Violence (TREVI) group 138, 158, 410, 422
Terrorisme, Radicalisme et Violence Internationale see Terrorism, Radicalism, Extremism and political Violence (TREVI) group
Terrorist Financial Tracking Program (TFTP), EU–US 339
Third Pillar, on justice and home affairs 23, 126, 149, 151, 176, 198
third-country nationals (TCNs) 66, 72, 74, 76, 101, 120, 188, 215–19, 290, 402
Three Ms, concept of 318
total fertility rates (TFR) 127, 132
transgovernmental networks 6, 23, 26, 422
Transit Processing Centres, for refugees and asylum seekers 66
transnational security 25, 371
Treaty on European Union (TEU, 1993) 124, 272, 472
Treaty on the Functioning of the European Union (TFEU) 84, 95, 171, 176, 203, 204, 209, 342, 396, 397, 400, 450

Trump, Donald 12
Turkey–EU relations 314; on anti-terror laws 293; on asylum standards 294; on border management 294; on dealing with irregular migrants 94, 232, 237, 277, 317; on disproportionate repressive measures 293; in field of justice and home affairs 287–94; on fight against terrorism 293; on readmission agreement 290–2; on refugee statement 66, 292–4; on Turkey's EU accession process 287–90; on Turkey's migration policies 289; on visa liberalization process 115, 291, 295
'twinning programs' initiatives 101, 266–7

Ukrainian–Moldovan border 303
Unasur (Union of South American Nations) 360
United Nations (UN): Convention against Corruption (UNCAC) 469; Convention on Transnational Organised Crime (UNTOC) 139, 326, 469; General Assembly Special Session on Drugs (UNGASS) 326; High Commissioner for Refugees (UNHCR) 62, 288–90, 292, 294, 415, 469–70, 472, 476–7; Security Council 163
US–EU cooperation: on criminal law enforcement 337; on cyber crime and cyber security 336, 341; on data privacy 337; on death penalty 338–9; evolution of 343; on extradition assistance 336, 337–8; fundamental rights in 341–2; on 'global' approach to legal integration between legal orders 340–1; on human rights 337; joint awareness-raising activities 341; Joint EC–US Task Force on Critical Infrastructure Protection 341; Joint Reviews of agreements 339; on legal integration challenges 341–2; Mutual Legal Assistance (MLA) Agreement 336, 338; 'New Accountability' mechanisms 339; new era of 342; overview of 341–2; on Passenger Name Records (PNR) 172, 182, 187, 336, 339, 340, 346; during post 9/11 period 336, 339; on public–private partnerships 341; Snowden revelations, effects of 336; 'soft power' cooperation 338–9; SWIFT agreement 182, 339, 390, 416; Terrorist Financial Tracking Program 339; Umbrella Agreement (2016) 342; Working Group on Cybercrime and Cybersecurity (WGCC) 341
US–Mexico border 75

Valencia Action Plan (2000) 311
Valletta Summit (2015) 90
Venice Commission 269, 271, 272
venue-shopping hypothesis 48, 51, 63, 128, 230–2, 236, 424, 436
visa applications: auto-grant system 353; extra-territorial refusal of 118
visa incentive 113

Visa Information System (VIS) 71, 103, 174, 180, 231, 255
visa policy of EU: auto-grant system, for visa 353; Balkan asylum-seekers, issue of 113; on Canada–Czech visa dispute 351; Canada–EU visa waiver programme 112; conditionality of 113; Council Regulation 539/2001 on 113; deflection effects 118; DEMIG VISA database 111, 119; development of 111–13; and economic implications of visa restrictions 118–20; effects of 115–20; Electronic Travel Authorization (ETA) 353; electronic visas 103; on ethnic profiling for grant of visa 113; EU Visa-Free Dialogues for Eastern Partnership countries 113; and EU–Russian competition 115, 300; on EU–Turkey visa liberalization process 115, 291, 295; extra-territorial refusal, of visa applications 118; as first line of defence 110; impact on labor market 117; influence on migratory processes 117–18; internal *versus* external visa restrictions of EU member states **112**; migration crisis and 115; political dynamics and migratory effects of 110; and readmission agreement 113; Schengen visa regime 112; selective liberalization of 242; temporary protection visas (TPVs) 349; Visa Code 111; Visa Facilitation Agreements 9, 300, 306; visa facilitation and liberalization 113–15; visa facilitation–readmission nexus 300; Visa Information System (VIS) 71, 103, 174; Visa Liberalisation Action Plan 301; Visa Liberalisation Dialogues 301; and visa requirements for the Schengen area **116**; on visa suspension mechanism 113; on visa-free corridors 117; on visa-free travel opportunities 111, 115
visa restrictions: deterrence effects of 119; economic implications of 118–20; impact on international tourism 120; negative repercussions of 119; temporary protection visas (TPVs) 349
visa war 112

Visegrad Group (V4) 83

war against terrorism 36, 174
War on Drugs 331, 362, 364
Warsaw Pact 236
Weimar Triangle 83
West Africa Commission on Drugs (WACD) 330, 331
Western Balkans: anti-corruption policies 282; Berlin Process 283; border crossings by migrants 277; 'Brexit' issue 280; country- and policy-specific dialogues in *280*; EU's approach towards JHA in 277–9; EU's objectives in justice and home affairs in 275–7; EU's Stabilization and Association Process for 275–7; external governance and Europeanization 280–1; external incentives model 280; impact of the EU in the field of JHA 281–2; informal institutions in 282; law-related challenges 275; prevention of insecurity spill-overs from 276–7; radicalization of Balkan youth in 277; relation with EU 281; research dealing with JHA in 279–82; role in preventing jihadists from entering EU 277; rule of law and EU-driven institutionalization in 276; security and stability in 282; as target for EU action in justice and home affairs (JHA) 275; Western Balkans Annual Risk Analysis 277; wire-tapping scandal 276
Westphalian sovereignty 21
White Paper on Completing the Internal Market (1985) 149
White Paper on Growth, Competitiveness and Employment (1993) 149
wire-tapping scandal 276
Working Group on Cybercrime and Cybersecurity (WGCC), EU–US 341; 'global' rule-making objectives 341
World Bank 264, 282, 377
world risk society 371

zero-tolerance policy 350

Taylor & Francis eBooks

Helping you to choose the right eBooks for your Library

Add Routledge titles to your library's digital collection today. Taylor and Francis ebooks contains over 50,000 titles in the Humanities, Social Sciences, Behavioural Sciences, Built Environment and Law.

Choose from a range of subject packages or create your own!

Benefits for you
- Free MARC records
- COUNTER-compliant usage statistics
- Flexible purchase and pricing options
- All titles DRM-free.

Benefits for your user
- Off-site, anytime access via Athens or referring URL
- Print or copy pages or chapters
- Full content search
- Bookmark, highlight and annotate text
- Access to thousands of pages of quality research at the click of a button.

REQUEST YOUR FREE INSTITUTIONAL TRIAL TODAY

Free Trials Available
We offer free trials to qualifying academic, corporate and government customers.

eCollections – Choose from over 30 subject eCollections, including:

Archaeology	Language Learning
Architecture	Law
Asian Studies	Literature
Business & Management	Media & Communication
Classical Studies	Middle East Studies
Construction	Music
Creative & Media Arts	Philosophy
Criminology & Criminal Justice	Planning
Economics	Politics
Education	Psychology & Mental Health
Energy	Religion
Engineering	Security
English Language & Linguistics	Social Work
Environment & Sustainability	Sociology
Geography	Sport
Health Studies	Theatre & Performance
History	Tourism, Hospitality & Events

For more information, pricing enquiries or to order a free trial, please contact your local sales team:
www.tandfebooks.com/page/sales

The home of Routledge books

www.tandfebooks.com